Praise for *The Big Book of Women Saints:*

"*The Big Book of Women Saints* is a beautiful and concise guide to the luminous women who inspire us to deeper faith. It is a welcomed daily reminder that holy women show us the way every day."
— Edward L. Beck, author of *God Underneath: Spiritual Memoirs of a Catholic Priest* and *Soul Provider: Spiritual Steps to Limitless Love*

"This book is something we have been waiting for. The author has captured beautifully and meditatively the spirit of an army of women saints. Although saintly women have never been ignored, it's wonderful to meet so many whom we really did not know. If you are interested in saints, or if you are interested in the role of women in the Church, this is the book for you to read next. It is a joyful experience in getting to know saints."
— Father Benedict J. Groeschel, CFR, author of *The Journey Toward God*

"Heaven sent! In a world where we are frequently focused on the power of Hollywood this book is sent to remind us of the power of heaven. Throughout biblical history there are stories of people sent by God to achieve missions impossible. This book is truly a treasure of hope, containing stories about a collection of women sent closer to home and to our times to carry out the work entrusted to them. In writing this book Sarah Gallick provides us with comfort and hope in what could best be described as a diary of daily divine inspiration for everyone."
— Susan Crimp, author of *Touched by a Saint: Personal Encounters with Mother Teresa*

"The women called saints are first in line in the army of powerful people who changed the world for the better. They are often avoided because to acknowledge the grandeur of their accomplishments is to acknowledge the grandeur of God. None of us would be the same if these great women had not lived and altered the course of history."
— Father George W. Rutler, author of *A Crisis of Saints*

"Through historical scholarship, *The Big Book of Women Saints* retrieves long-forgotten women of great faith and introduces us to the some 160 more 'raised to the altar' over the past thirty years. On many fronts, it does great service."

> —Dr. Thomas H. Groome, director, Boston College's Institute of Religious Education and Personal Ministry and author of *What Makes Us Catholic*

"Sarah Gallick has introduced us to many remarkable women saints who demonstrate with their lives (contrary to popular opinion) how important women have always been in the Catholic Church."

> —Alicia Colon, columnist, *The New York Sun*

"From beginning to end *The Big Book of Women Saints* is a treasure. An informative, enlightening, enjoyable read. We owe a debt of gratitude to Sarah Gallick for bringing to light the lives of these holy, valiant women!"

> —Sister Nancy Richter, O.P., Dominican Sister of Sparkill, NY

THE BIG BOOK OF
Women Saints

THE BIG BOOK OF
Women Saints

Sarah Gallick

HarperSanFrancisco
A Division of HarperCollins*Publishers*

FIRST EDITION

Library of Congress Cataloging-in-Publication Data is available upon request.

ISBN 978–0–06–082512–6
ISBN 10: 0–06–082512-X

07 08 09 10 11 RRD (H) 10 9 8 7 6 5 4 3 2 1

In loving memory of Sister Jeanne Monica Mayer, O.P.,
and the Sisters of Saint Dominic of Amityville
who taught me for eight years at
Saint Kilian's School in Farmingdale, New York.

This is a small payment on a debt that can never be repaid.

INTRODUCTION

The single most important thing to know about the saints is that they were once people just like us. We are all called to be saints, but the saints answered that call fearlessly and completely. Those of us who make it into heaven will become part of their great company. We will never know the names of most of these men and women until we get there, but in the meantime the Church does single out some of them for special recognition and veneration by those of us who still struggle along in this world.

The more than five hundred notable women described in this book are among that illustrious company. Each is a canonized saint or blessed of the Catholic Church. Each lived her life to the fullest and triumphed over worldly challenges without sacrificing her soul. Each shared a unique quality that has been called the feminine genius. Pope John Paul II often saluted this "feminine genius." In a 1995 encyclical, *Evangelium Vitae* (The Gospel of Life), he appealed to women to promote a "new feminism," one that would reject the temptation to imitate the male model in order to affirm the true genius of women in every aspect of society.

The women saints include martyrs and mystics, rebellious daughters, loving wives and mothers, reformed prostitutes, restless visionaries and humble recluses, but all were blessed with a unique ability to influence the world for the better and an extraordinary capacity for love.

What Is a Saint?

The *Catechism of the Catholic Church* defines a saint as "the 'holy one' who leads a life in union with God through the grace of Christ and receives the reward of eternal life." The Church itself is called "the communion of saints." Everyone in heaven is a member of this communion of saints.

From the earliest days of the Church, some of these faithful have been singled out for special recognition, or "canonized," which means that the Church proposes them as models and intercessors to be venerated as saints.

How Saints Get That Way: The Canonization Process

The first Roman Catholic saints were mostly martyrs. They were first recognized by popular acclamation, which was later confirmed by the local bishops. The martyrs' graves were considered sacred sites and churches were built over them, which led to the tradition of naming churches for saints.

By the tenth century, the process had become formalized and the ultimate decision about canonization resided with the pope in Rome. The first saint formally recognized by the Vatican was Ulrich of Augsburg, a pious bishop who was canonized by Pope John XV in 993. Ulrich's spiritual mentor, Wiborada of Saint Gall (May 2), became the first woman formally canonized by the Vatican, in 1047. (A reclusive bookbinder in a monastery famed as a center of learning, Wiborada predicted an invasion by the Hungarians and urged the monks to save the library before they saved her. She was martyred in 925 but the library she loved still stands in what is now St. Gallen, Switzerland.)

Since the twelfth century the pope has been the Church's sole authority for canonizing saints. But not even a pope can "make" a saint. As Pope Paul VI explained at the canonization of Julie Billiart (April 8): "We do not create, we do not confer saintliness, we recognize it, we proclaim it."

This proclamation comes only after a rigorous investigation by the Congregation for the Causes of Saints. A committee of judges, a canon lawyer and other high-ranking religious, the Congregation studies the life and death of the candidate. They pore over her writings and scrutinize the miracles said to have been worked by God through her intercession. This process used to take many years, even centuries, but it has been reformed and updated several times since 1983. Gone is the Defender of the Faith, better known as the Devil's Advocate, who was dedicated to presenting all conceivable arguments against canonization.

The Congregation is still open to hearing negative information, however. One of Mother Teresa's harshest critics, journalist Christopher Hitchens, was invited to share his experiences and insights with them and did.

Mother Teresa (September 5) was beatified only six years after her death, but there have been other fast-trackers. Francis of Assisi was canonized just two years after his death, and Pope Innocent IV had to be talked out of canonizing Clare of Assisi (August 11) at her funeral. Both Bridget of Sweden (July 23) and Elizabeth of Hungary (November 17) were canonized twenty years after their deaths. Thérèse of Lisieux (October 1) had been dead only twenty-eight years when she was elevated to sainthood. Elzear was canonized in 1369 and his widow, Delphine de Signe (November 29), was still alive to attend the ceremony. It took almost fifty years for Maria Goretti (July 6) to be canonized, but she was so young when she died that both her mother and her repentant murderer attended her canonization in 1950.

The Three Steps to Sainthood

By far the best book about the process of saint-making today is Kenneth Woodward's *Making Saints*. What follows here is merely a summary of the three steps: recognition of heroic virtue, beatification, and canonization.

Recognition of Heroic Virtue.
An individual must be dead for five years before she can even be considered for recognition of her heroic virtue. This process is usually initiated by the

bishop of her local diocese and the individual is then called a Servant of God. Her life and writings are closely examined until the investigators conclude that she practiced the theological virtues of faith, hope, and charity as well as the cardinal virtues of prudence, justice, temperance, and fortitude to a heroic degree. At that point the individual is declared Venerable, and the cause for her canonization is officially launched. Among the women currently in this group are Pauline Jaricot, founder of the Society for the Propagation of the Faith; Rose Hawthorne Lathrop, daughter of the novelist Nathaniel Hawthorne and founder of a religious order devoted to victims of terminal cancer; and Dorothy Day, founder of the Catholic Worker movement.

Beatification and the First Miracle.
The campaign is now taken up by the Congregation for the Causes of Saints, which is based in the Vatican. The Congregation appoints a postulator who leads the investigation into miracles attributed to the candidate's intercession. Today these miracles are usually healings and cures. Such cures must be "instantaneous, not expected and complete."

The miracles are not reserved for Catholics, however. In 1963 a Protestant laborer, Carl Eric Kalen, was miraculously healed through the intercession of Elizabeth Ann Seton (January 4) at a hospital in Yonkers, New York. This was accepted as a canonization miracle, and twelve years later, he attended the ceremony in Rome.

The Congregation also recognizes miracles in cases where the candidate has influenced an extraordinary event that cannot be explained by the laws of science. The Peruvian naval officer who saved his submarine crew through the intercession of Marija Petkovic (July 2) is such an example.

When civil and ecclesiastic investigations are completed, the Congregation can choose to recommend that the candidate be beatified. The pope can then choose to declare her Blessed, which means that she can be venerated on a local level and by her religious order. In Marija Petkovic's case, for example, she is venerated in her homeland of Croatia, in Peru where she was a missionary, and by the Franciscan Daughters of Mercy, the order she founded.

Canonization.
Even after an individual is declared Blessed, investigation continues, while supporters await a second miracle. This miracle must occur after beatification. Once canonized, an individual is declared worthy of veneration by the Universal Church. A new saint is usually given a specific feast day in the Church's Universal Calendar. On that day the saint is remembered at Mass and in the Church's Divine Office.

John Paul II and the Saints

In his long reign as pope (1978–2005), John Paul II elevated more saints and blesseds than any other pope in history: 1,338 beatifications and 482 canonizations. These were hardly hasty investigations, however. The causes for Agnes of Prague (March 6), Magdalene of Nagasaki (October 20), and Ana de los Angeles (January 19) had been around for centuries, but revolutions, world wars, and natural disasters slowed their progress. The secret archives of Republican Spain, the Third Reich, and the Soviet Union only became available at the end of the twentieth century. Many of John Paul's canonizations and beatifications were collective events—for example, the 120 Martyrs of China and the 108 Polish Martyrs of World War II. Such group honors were not unique to John Paul, however. The Sixteen Carmelite Martyrs of Compiègne (July 17) were beatified by Pius X in 1906, and the Forty Martyrs of England and Wales were canonized by Paul VI in 1970. Among the earliest such groups were the Theban Legion, Christian soldiers in the Imperial Roman army who refused to sacrifice to pagan gods and were consequently martyred in 287.

Far from cheapening the canonization process, John Paul enriched it by giving many nations and ethnic groups saints and blesseds of their own. Among his "firsts," John Paul beatified the first Native American, Kateri Tekakwitha (April 17), the first Australian, Mary Ellen MacKillop (August 7), and the first citizen of Zaire, Anuarite Nengapeta (December 1).

John Paul's successor, Benedict XVI, continues to refine the process, most notably by waiving the five-year waiting period so that John Paul's own cause for sainthood could be launched immediately.

Relics and Mystical Phenomena

It is impossible to talk about many of these saints without referring to relics and mystical phenomena. The subject of relics is distinctly Catholic and difficult to summarize in a few sentences. I therefore recommend the books of Joan Carroll Cruz, especially *Relics* and *The Incorruptibles*. As for the visions and revelations of the saints, *A Still, Small Voice: A Practical Guide on Reported Revelations*, by Benedict J. Groeschel, C.F.R., is a sympathetic but pragmatic examination of these phenomena. Finally, anyone interested in learning more about the actual physical phenomena—ecstasies (trances), stigmata, multiplication of food, and the "odor of sanctity"—would do well to read *The Physical Phenomena of Mysticism* by Herbert Thurston, S.J.

I have included many of the most notable phenomena associated with these saints and blesseds. Among the most colorful are the stigmata and the phenomena of incorruption. Yes, they are fantastic, which is one reason the Church approaches them with great skepticism. In fact, no saint has ever been canonized solely because he or she manifested the stigmata or because his or her corpse remained incorrupt. Perhaps the most fantastic element in these fantastic stories is that the saints who exhibited the most exotic signs were often the most capable administrators. In the end, the best comment on the mystics may come from C. S. Lewis, who wrote that these saints are "caught up into that world where pain and pleasure take on transfinite values and where all our arithmetic is dismayed. Once more, the inexplicable meets us."

Patron Saints

Every Catholic child selects a patron saint when he or she receives the sacrament of Confirmation. Unfortunately, for most of us, the only time we think about this saint or any of the other patron saints is when we need their intercession. But saints are not vending machines, and it is worth getting to know at least a few so that you can identify your own particular patrons. For, while many saints have been officially declared patrons or long adopted as patrons by certain groups, there are many others who, although never officially recognized as patrons, seem to be open to particular causes. I think, for example, of Katharine Mary Drexel (March 3), who is best known for her work among Native and African Americans, but whose beatification and canonization miracles restored hearing to deaf children.

Saints as Goddesses

There are those who would dismiss saints as merely pagan gods and goddesses who were repackaged by the Church. Sigrid Undset, the Nobel-prize-winning author, addressed this very question and concluded, "The most ignorant and simple Catholics have always known that [the saints] are the very opposite of gods: they are human beings."

KEY TO ENTRIES

Dates:

Most of the saints and blesseds are listed on their feast days. Wherever possible I have tried to include the dates of birth and death. Dates for beatification and canonization are in the Annotated Sources and Web Sites section at the back of the book.

Names:

Many saints are known by several names. There is the name they were given at baptism, sometimes a married name, and a name they took in religion. I have listed the women according to their most familiar name, with alternates in parentheses. I usually relied on the saint's religious order for the last word on her name, but even here sources can differ. (Marie Madeleine Postel is known as Julie Postel in Germany, for example.) When in doubt, I have generally used the Library of Congress's listing for the primary name. I have also included modern versions of the names—for example, Geneviève has given us Jennifer.

Words of the Saints:

Quotes from the saints appear in italics.

ACKNOWLEDGMENTS

This book was blessed with early support and encouragement from Mother Agnes Donovan, S.V., and I am deeply grateful for the prayers of the Sisters of Life. Father Joseph Koterski, S.J., kindly arranged for me to have access to the Fordham University Library. Monsigner Thomas P. Leonard, pastor of Holy Trinity Church, encouraged me, answered my questions, and even lent me an 1846 twelve-volume edition of Butler's *Lives of the Saints*, which has been enlightening and helpful.

Many religious orders associated with Saints and Blesseds in this book have generously provided material and answered my questions. I have acknowledged them individually in Annotated Sources and Web Sites. Nona Aguilar, Anne Conlon, and Ellen Clark read and critiqued the manuscript in the early stages. I am also grateful for the generosity of the late Richard B. Consolas for whom I pray every day. Michael Clark, Maria Gallo, Maria del Carmen Ferrer, and Susan Sommers have always helped me just by being there. My nephew, Nicholas Gallick, gave me access to databases I didn't know existed and answered my computer questions. My brother, Brian Gallick, archived my manuscript in progress so that I always knew the work was safe on CDs miles away from my home. Denise Marcil and her associates Mary-Kay Przybycien and Maura Kye read endless early versions of the proposal and helped me focus on what I wanted to say and how best to say it. The staff of the New York Public Library Humanities Division and the Fordham University Library at Rose Hill were enormously helpful. I am also grateful to the Dominican Sisters of Sparkill for the serenity I found at their retreat house, Corazón, and to their neighbors, the Dominicans Sisters of Saint Joseph, who generously opened their library to me. Thanks are also due to Eric Brandt for his endless patience while he awaited the complete manuscript, to Carolyn Allison-Holland for shepherding this demanding project through production, and to Anne Collins for her diligent copyediting.

Finally, I thank all the wonderful women Saints and Blesseds whose example has encouraged me throughout this project.

MARY, MOTHER OF GOD

First century

Today marks the Solemnity of Mary,[1] when we honor the mother of God and celebrate the fact that she is also our mother and the mother of all the members of the communion of saints.

"God has disposed that, thanks to her, the Incarnation, Redemption, the Eucharist and Communion would reach us," writes one contemporary cardinal. "Mary was the first to receive in her womb the Body and the Blood of Christ. The Incarnation was history's first Communion. The first tabernacle was her immaculate heart.... Before any apostle or priest, it is Mary who gives Jesus to the world."

"Only a few words from the Virgin Mary have come down to us in the Gospels," writes Saint Edith Stein (August 9). "But these few words are like heavy grains of pure gold. When they melt in the ardor of loving meditation, they more than suffice to bathe our entire lives in a luminous golden glow."

Mary was with Jesus at Calvary, when he commended her to the care of John the Evangelist. Tradition holds that she spent the rest of her earthly life in prayer and supplication.[2]

The Genius of Mary, the Mother of God:

Just a few of the titles from the *Litany to the Blessed Virgin Mary* capture the Blessed Mother's genius. She is the Mother of Christ, Virgin most Prudent, Mirror of Justice, Help of Christians, Queen of Angels, Queen of Martyrs, Queen of All Saints, and Queen of Peace.

Reflection:

"My soul proclaims the greatness of the Lord; / my spirit rejoices in God my savior."

Luke 1:46–47

BLESSED STEPHANIE QUINZANI

b. February 5, 1457, Orzinuovo, Italy
d. January 2, 1530, Soncino, Italy

Every Friday night for forty years Stephanie went into an ecstasy or trance in which she reenacted the entire Passion of Christ, including the stigmata, while she remained oblivious to the world around her. Eyewitnesses saw only her agony. When, in her mind, Stephanie was nailed to the Cross, her arms became so rigid that not even the strongest men could move them. Her facial features reflected all the suffering of Christ. When the ecstasy ended, Stephanie returned to being a robust country girl and her face was once again plump and healthy. After one such event, twenty-one respected witnesses signed a testimony to what they had seen.

Stephanie was blessed with many spiritual gifts, including the ability to read souls. Among those who consulted her were Angela Merici (January 27) and Osanna of Mantua (June 20). Stephanie persuaded one woman to give up a plan to poison fourteen people. Even as her fame spread, she continued to perform humble works of mercy and to earn her living by manual labor. A community of more than thirty women grew up around her, and she built a monastery to house them. Many wealthy admirers offered to build grand monasteries for her in other cities, but Stephanie chose to remain in Soncino. (Perhaps out of gratitude, Soncino exempted her monastery from all taxes.)

The weekly visions and the acclaim that came with them did not bring Stephanie any peace, however. For forty years she suffered fears that God had abandoned her. These ended only when an angel told her, *"There are several means for a reasonable creature to rise to perfect love of God, but the principal one is a life of suffering,. . . Affliction is the road to perfect love and perfect transformation."*

The Genius of Stephanie Quinzani:

Blessed with a tenacious spirit, Stephanie continued her good works in spite of her spiritual torment and physical trials. Her life truly was an imitation of Christ.

Reflection:

"Trust in the LORD with all your heart, / on your own intelligence rely not; / In all your ways be mindful of him, / and he will make straight your paths."

Proverbs 3:5–6

SAINT GENEVIÈVE OF PARIS
(Jennifer, Geneva)

b. c. 422, Nanterre, France

d. 500, Paris, France

The patron saint of women soldiers was only seven years old when Germanus, bishop of Auxerre,[3] passed through her village. Everyone wanted his blessing, but he singled out Geneviève and declared that she was destined for a holy life.

Geneviève had to work out for herself what that holy life would be. The only holy women she knew were anchorites or pious hermits, and their reclusive life was not for her. Craving activity and service, she moved to Paris at the age of fifteen and became known for her good works and miracles.

Her great moment came in 451 as Attila the Hun, the most feared warrior in Europe, prepared to invade Paris. Geneviève pleaded with her neighbors not to abandon the city, and she gathered the women to pray, asking God to save the city. *"Forsake not your homes,"* Geneviève said, *"for God has heard my prayers. Attila shall retreat."* Many men denounced Geneviève as a madwoman, a false prophet, and a witch. They were ready to drown her in the Seine, but word of her troubles reached her old mentor, Germanus, who was on his deathbed in Ravenna. He sent his archdeacon with a gift of blessed bread to convince the people that Geneviève was a truly holy woman.

As she predicted, Attila did retreat. For reasons historians still cannot explain, the warrior known as the Scourge of God suddenly changed course and spared Paris. Two years later he was dead, having failed to conquer the world after all.

The Genius of Geneviève of Paris:
Geneviève later interceded with other kings and generals to free military prisoners. She even broke through a blockade to bring bread into Paris. Drawing courage from her complete trust in God, she insisted, *"God will protect us. We must rely on him."*

Reflection:
"For the Lord is God; he crushes warfare, / and sets his encampment among his people; / he snatched me from the hands of my persecutors. . . . the Lord Almighty thwarted them, / by a woman's hand he confounded them."

Judith 16:2, 5

Saint Elizabeth Ann Seton

b. August 28, 1774, New York, New York
d. January 4, 1821, Emmitsburg, Maryland

Elizabeth was a happily married New York socialite, the mother of five children, and an active member of the Protestant Daughters of Charity. She even danced with George Washington at his 1797 birthday ball. Things changed when her husband's business failed, along with his health. She sailed with him to Italy, hoping that he would recover there, but he died in Genoa on the day after Christmas, 1803.

By the time Elizabeth returned to New York she had begun a spiritual journey that would climax when she entered the Catholic Church in 1805. The Catholic faith had been legal in New York for less than a decade, and it was still controversial. Elizabeth intended to support her family by teaching, but after her conversion, worried parents pulled their children from her school, fearing that she would try to convert them.

She left New York and sailed with her children to a new life in Emmitsburg, Maryland, where she founded the American Sisters of Charity, the first religious congregation of women in the United States. She modeled them after the Sisters of Charity founded in France by Vincent de Paul and Louise de Marillac (March 15). Elizabeth established the first Catholic orphanage in the United States and the first free Catholic day school, which marked the beginning of the American parochial school system. Canonized in 1975, she became the United States's first native-born saint.

The Genius of Elizabeth Ann Seton:
A life-altering tragedy led Elizabeth Seton to make a profound spiritual decision that left a lasting impact on her Church and her country. She advises us: *"Faith lifts the staggering soul on one side, Hope supports it on the other. Experience says it must be, and Love says let it be."*

Reflection:
"Make known to me your ways, LORD, teach me your paths.
Guide me in your truth and teach me, / For you are God my savior.
For you I will wait all the long day / because of your goodness, LORD."
                                                                Psalm 25:4–5

SAINT GENOVEVA TORRES MORALES

b. January 3, 1870, Almenara, Spain
d. January 5, 1956, Madrid, Spain

At the age of thirteen, already an orphan, Genoveva lay on a kitchen table while a doctor amputated her left leg without anesthesia. For the rest of her life, she walked on crutches and lived with constant pain, yet she was able to look beyond her own suffering to help others.

After the operation, gangrene set in and Genoveva was expected to die. Her only relative, a brother, turned her over to an orphanage run by the Carmelite Sisters of Charity. Genoveva made a surprising recovery and spent the next nine years in the Mercy Home. She hoped to become a Carmelite herself but was rejected because of her disability. When she aged out of the orphanage, she set up house in Valencia with two other women. They supported themselves by needlework and still found time to assist their neighbors. With the help of her pastor, Genoveva opened a boardinghouse for working women. It was so successful that Genoveva expanded to six other cities, including Madrid and Barcelona.

In 1925 Genoveva and eighteen associates formed the religious order known as the Angelicas. During the Spanish Civil War (1936–39), the government closed down most of their boardinghouses, but Genoveva assured her Angelicas, *"Even if I must suffer greatly, thanks be to God's mercy, I will not lack courage."* When peace returned, Genoveva immediately began to rebuild. Today the Angelicas thrive in Spain, Italy, and South America.

The Genius of Genoveva Torres Morales:
Genoveva's physical disability never discouraged her. She understood that true happiness comes when we know, love, and serve God. Toward the end of her life, Genoveva could write, *"In the middle of my physical sufferings, the inner music of my soul will not stop praising God with acts of virtue offering him my love."*

Reflection:
"Beloved, do not be surprised that a trial by fire is occurring among you, as if something strange were happening to you. But rejoice to the extent that you share in the sufferings of Christ, so that when his glory is revealed you may also rejoice exultantly."

1 Peter 4:12–13

January 6

Saint Raphaela María Porras

b. March 1, 1850, Pedro Abad, Córdoba, Spain
d. January 6, 1925, Rome, Italy

In the prime of her life, Raphaela was removed from leadership of the religious order she had founded and barred from any future role. Rather than challenge this injustice and destroy the order's reputation, she accepted her exile to a small convent in Rome. False rumors that she had mental problems followed Raphaela to her new home, and the sisters there ignored her. She endured thirty years of this "purgatory of inactivity," making herself useful by sweeping the floor or collecting stockings to darn.

Raphaela's situation was especially painful because one of the leaders of the movement against her was own sister, Dolores. In 1873 Raphaela and Dolores had formed the congregation known as the Handmaids of the Sacred Heart. Although young and inexperienced, Raphaela showed a gift for working with people, and as the congregation expanded, her many letters to Handmaids were full of concern for their welfare. *"Take care of yourself,"* she wrote to one sister. *"God does not want his spouses to look as though he fed them on lizards."*

Meanwhile, Dolores accumulated resentments that made her a willing tool for another jealous Handmaid who coveted Raphaela's leadership role. Ironically, a few years after ousting Raphaela, Dolores herself was overthrown and banished. She wrote to Raphaela, asking forgiveness, and Raphaela continued to correspond with her, without a word of reproach, until Dolores's death.

Shortly before Raphaela's own death, she was recognized and honored as the founder of a great order. When she was canonized in 1977, her official portrait showed the new saint at prayer, with her ever-present sewing basket beside her.

The Genius of Raphaela María Porras:

Raphaela advises us to *"Keep a holy simplicity. Remain perfectly at peace, certain that God makes it his business to make you successful."*

Reflection:

"If you bring your gift to the altar, and there recall that your brother has anything against you, leave your gift there at the altar, go first and be reconciled with your brother, and then come and offer your gift."

Matthew 5:23–24

BLESSED MARIE-THÉRÈSE HAZE

b. February 27, 1782, Liège, Belgium
d. January 7, 1876, Liège, Belgium

By the time that Marie-Thérèse Haze was invited to manage Belgium's most notorious beggars' prison, she had established a reputation for rehabilitating outcasts. She did more than clean up prison inmates, however. She turned some of them into heroes.

This role was a far cry from her original plan. Marie-Thérèse had founded the Daughters of the Cross of Liège to educate poor children, but her free school and orphanage succeeded so well that in 1841 the Belgian government asked her to manage a women's prison. The prison housed prostitutes, beggars, and petty thieves in conditions so awful that it was said they left prison even worse off than when they entered. Marie-Thérèse arrived at the prison with some trepidation and immediately went to work. She began by improving the quality of the food, and then introduced periods of silence. Gradually, the women's feelings moved from distrust to respect to confidence. Acknowledging this success, the government asked Marie-Thérèse to manage the beggars' prison at Reckheim, a festering collection of Belgium's poorest men, women, and children. After turning that around, she founded the Refuge, a shelter for prostitutes and women of the streets. She began with sixty-five women, many of them ravaged by incurable venereal diseases. This was a time of terrible epidemics, and the Daughters were called all over Belgium to nurse victims of cholera, smallpox, and typhoid. When she did not have enough Daughters to meet the need, Marie-Thérèse appealed to the inmates of the Refuge. The women, scorned by society, gladly volunteered to accompany the Daughters and became indispensable to their work. Under Marie-Thérèse's guidance, they emerged as true heroes.

The Genius of Marie-Thérèse Haze:
Marie-Thérèse's calm, dignified bearing reflected an inner peace that was contagious. "Her whole demeanor was a silent sermon," wrote one contemporary. "Her actions were done noiselessly, her reprimands, even when most severe, were given with calmness and dignity."

Reflection:
"Then Jesus said to his disciples, 'Whoever wishes to come after me must deny himself, take up his cross, and follow me.'"

Matthew 16:24–26

SAINT ZDISLAVA OF LEMBERK

b. c. 1220 Kižanov, Žďár nad Sázavou, Vysoina kraj (Czech Republic)
d. January 1, 1252, Jablonné, eská Lípa, Libereckyá kraj
(Czech Republic)

The daughter of a warrior prince and an Italian noblewoman, Zdislava grew up safe inside a fortified castle at a time when eastern Europe was devastated by invading Tartar tribes. At fifteen she was married to Havel Lemberk and moved from her father's castle to her husband's.

Contemporaries described Count Lemberk as violent and arrogant, but he adored Zdislava and asked only that she dress beautifully and preside over his lavish victory banquets. Still, Zdislava could not ignore the beggars outside her castle gates. Many of their villages had been destroyed by warriors like her husband. At about this time, Zdislava met the Dominican missionaries Hyacinth and Ceslaus[4] and became a Dominican tertiary (lay associate). Besides rearing four children and keeping Havel happy, she fed the poor from her castle kitchen and treated them with medications that she mixed herself. Contemporaries claimed that Zdislava revived at least five corpses, healed lepers, and returned sight to a blind man.

She and Havel built many churches; the most famous, now known as the basilica of St Laurent and St Zdislava, is considered one of the great monuments of northern Bohemia. Zdislava would slip in at night and take care of some of the construction herself. She died soon after the basilica was completed, and legend has it that she later appeared to Havel, dressed in a red robe, leaving behind a small piece of the fabric to console him.

Zdislava was long regarded as a patron saint of Bohemia, but her cause for sainthood was delayed by two world wars and the descent of the Iron Curtain. She was formally canonized in 1995.

The Genius of Zdislava of Lemberk:
Zdislava sacrificed the quiet, contemplative life for the responsibilities of a wife and mother. Her marriage to a difficult and demanding man marked the beginning of her ministry to all those in need.

Reflection:
"Be on your guard, stand firm in the faith, be courageous, be strong. Your every act should be done with love."
1 Corinthians 16:13–14

BLESSED ALIX LE CLERC

b. February 2, 1576, Remiremont, Duchy of Lorraine, France
d. January 9, 1622, Nancy, Duchy of Lorraine, France

Tall and fair, with blue eyes and a charming manner, Alix came of age when the churches were empty and the taverns full. She loved music and dancing and all the "vanities" that her world had to offer until, one Sunday at Mass, she was disturbed by the sound of a drum. This happened three Sundays in a row, until she saw that the devil himself was playing the drum while he led a parade of revelers. This began a vision of hell so terrifying that afterward Alix resolved to change her ways.

She sought out her new pastor, Peter Fourier,[5] who encouraged her to enter the Poor Clares. Her father thought their life was too strict and urged her to consider the Tertiaries of St Elizabeth. While struggling with this decision, Alix dreamed that neither Clare of Assisi (August 11) nor Elizabeth of Hungary (November 17) wanted her for their orders! She concluded that she was being called to found a new order dedicated to educating young women.

Fourier doubted that Alix could ever recruit teachers from among the frivolous local belles, but within six weeks, three young women joined her and Fourier gave Alix his blessing. She and Fourier began a long struggle for official approval. In the post-Reformation climate, all women's religious orders were restricted or "enclosed" behind convent walls, but Alix and Fourier agreed that her group had to be free of such restrictions. It took twenty years before they were officially recognized as the Congregation of Notre Dame. When they were finally permitted to make their religious vows of poverty, chastity, and obedience, Alix added a fourth: never to abandon their commitment to the education of young women. Today her congregation is known in America as the Notre Dame Sisters and elsewhere as the Congregation of Our Lady and the Canonesses of Saint Augustine. They are active in thirteen countries from China to the Congo.

The Genius of Alix Le Clerc:
 Alix's guiding precept was always *"To do all the good possible."*

Reflection:
 "Vanity of vanities! . . . All things are vanity!"
 Ecclesiastes 1:2 (Doudy-Rheims Bible)

January 10

SAINT LÉONIE AVIAT

(Françoise de Sales Aviat)

b. September 16, 1844, Sezanne, France
d. January 10, 1914, Perugia, Italy

Francis de Sales[6] is known as the Saint Maker because of his great influence. More than two hundred years after his death, the Salesian legacy still loomed large, which is why his name appears so often in the story of Léonie Aviat.

Léonie came of age during the Industrial Revolution, when young women were leaving farms and villages to work in the textile mills at Troyes. A concerned young priest there, Louis Brisson,[7] established the Francis de Sales Project, a club where the girls could socialize in a safe environment. As the club expanded, Father Brisson desperately needed a manager. His mentor, Marie de Sales,[8] recommended her former student, Léonie Aviat.

Léonie threw herself into the project, vowing to be a *"worker among the workers."* This was easier said than done, but confident that this was the role God had given her, she prayed to Him for strength: *"Give me a new heart to love and serve you faithfully."*

At the age of twenty-two, with Father Brisson and Mother Chappuis, Léonie cofounded the Oblate Sisters of St Francis de Sales and dedicated herself to educating factory girls. In 1871 she took vows and a new name: Françoise de Sales, although she is still best known by her baptismal name. She and Brisson established worker hostels all over Europe and founded missions and schools in South Africa and South America. Today the Oblate Sisters are also at work in Maryland, Pennsylvania, and Virginia.

The Genius of Léonie Aviat:
Describing herself as *"God's little instrument,"* Léonie lived according to her own maxim that one must *"do everything with God and nothing without him."*

Reflection:
"If I have the gift of prophecy and comprehend all mysteries and all knowledge; if I have all faith so as to move mountains, but do not have love, I am nothing."

1 Corinthians 13:2

January 11

Blessed Angela of Foligno

b. c. 1248, Foligno, Italy
d. January 4, 1309, Foligno, Italy

Angela has been called the Swooning Saint and Teacher of Theologians, but until she reached her thirties she was frivolous, worldly, and self-absorbed. A spiritual crisis left her too ashamed to go to Confession, so she prayed to Francis of Assisi,[9] the former playboy who had preached about "holy poverty." He appeared to her in a dream, and Angela characteristically demanded to know what had taken him so long. Francis replied, *"Sister, if you had asked me sooner, I would have answered you sooner. Nonetheless, your request is granted."*

Angela returned to the sacraments. Within a year she lost her mother, her husband, and her sons, losses that she accepted as God's will. She gave away her inheritance and made a pilgrimage to Francis's shrine in nearby Assisi. During Mass at the basilica there she was overcome and cried out, *"Love still unknown, Why? Why? Why?"* At the elevation of the Host, she began rolling on the floor in ecstasy. This drew a great crowd, including her cousin, Arnaldo,[10] a Franciscan brother attached to the basilica. He ordered Angela to leave Assisi and warned her friends not to bring her back.

A year later, Arnaldo was assigned to Foligno and began to see more of Angela. He became convinced that she had experienced a true mystical encounter with Christ and transcribed her account of her spiritual journey. This became a classic of Western spirituality, and Angela is honored as a patron of scholars and theologians. Franciscans celebrate her feast on January 4.

The Genius of Angela of Foligno:

Angela found strength in the Lord's Prayer, advising: *"I have never found a better way for realizing His mercy than by saying that prayer which Jesus himself taught us."*

Reflection:

"Our Father, who art in heaven, hallowed be thy name; thy kingdom come; thy will be done on earth as it is in heaven. Give us this day our daily bread; and forgive us our trespasses as we forgive those who trespass against us; and lead us not into temptation; but deliver us from evil."

Matthew 6:9–15

January 12

SAINT MARGUERITE BOURGEOYS

b. April 17, 1620, Troyes, Champagne, France
d. January 12, 1700, Montreal, Quebec, Canada

A founder of Montreal and the first woman proclaimed a saint by John Paul II, Marguerite Bourgeoys spent years contending with bishops who wanted to enclose her community. She finally won her case by arguing that the Blessed Mother had never been restricted behind convent walls.

Growing up, Marguerite had a special relationship with Our Lady. Although certain that she had a religious vocation, she was rejected by the Carmelites and Poor Clares. When the original founder of Montreal, Paul de Maisonneuve, invited her to start a school in the colony, Marguerite feared that she was not up to the job. She prayed to the Blessed Mother, who told her, *"Go, I will not forsake you."* Marguerite sailed to New France with one hundred and eight men and six *filles du roi* or "daughters of the King," the seventeenth-century version of mail-order brides. By the time they landed, everyone was already calling her Sister. She opened her first school in an abandoned stable, welcoming native girls and colonists alike. She also set up workshops where women could learn crafts to support themselves, and she became their trusted friend and counselor. Marguerite recruited more teachers from France and formed the Congregation of Notre Dame of Montreal, one of the first uncloistered religious communities for women in the Catholic Church. When a skeptical bishop questioned her plans, Marguerite replied, *"The Blessed Virgin was never cloistered . . . she never excused herself from any journey on which there was good to be done or some work of charity to be performed."* With that, Marguerite won approval for her congregation. They are at work today in Japan, Africa, France, and the Americas.

The Genius of Marguerite Bourgeoys:
  Patricia Simpson, a Notre Dame Sister and historian, writes that Marguerite "can tell us something about meeting the challenge of the present, in which we are all pioneers, and about the need for understanding and compassion, which are no less important now than they were three centuries ago."

Reflection:
  "The LORD is my light and my salvation; / whom do I fear? / The LORD is my life's refuge; / of whom am I afraid?"
                                                                Psalm 27:1

January 13

BLESSED VERONICA OF BINASCO

(Veronica of Milan, Giovanna Negroni)

b. 1445, Binasco, Italy
d. January 14, 1497, Milan, Italy

Giovanna was turned away from several convents because she was illiterate. She struggled to learn to read and write until the Blessed Mother appeared to her in a dream and assured Giovanna that there were only three lessons she needed to learn: purity of heart, patience, and the Passion of Christ.

With purity of heart, Giovanna concerned herself only with pleasing God. With patience, she learned not to judge her neighbor but to pray for those who lacked virtue. And by meditating on the Passion, she learned to forget her own problems and remember the wrongs that Christ suffered for our sake. After three years of studying these lessons, Giovanna was received into an Augustinian convent, taking the name Veronica[11] because of her devotion to the Passion. Still unable to read Latin, she could not sing the Divine Office, the beautiful prayers that every educated religious recited daily, but she was blessed with wondrous revelations. Finally an angel appeared in her cell, holding a Psalter, and with the angel's help, Veronica learned to sing the Divine Office.

On another occasion, Veronica visited the decadent court of Pope Alexander VI. The sight of the humble nun amused his entourage, but he silenced them, saying, "You are in the presence of a holy woman."

The Genius of Veronica of Binasco:
Even in the last stages of a fatal illness, Veronica refused special treatment, insisting, *"I must work while I can, while I have time."*

Reflection:
"Do we need, as some do, letters of recommendation to you or from you? You are our letter, written on our hearts, known and read by all, shown to be a letter of Christ administered by us, written not in ink but by the Spirit of the living God, not on tablets of stone but on tablets that are hearts of flesh. Such confidence we have through Christ toward God."

2 Corinthians 3:1–4

Blessed Paula of Tuscany

b. 1318, Florence, Italy
d. January 6, 1357, Florence, Italy

Short, plump, and kindhearted, Paula had a vision of the Blessed Mother, who directed her to visit the local Camaldoli monastery. There she met Brother Sylvester,[12] the cook, and their spiritual lives became forever linked.

After a wild youth, Sylvester had experienced a miraculous conversion and entered the monastery two years before Paula was born. In *Camaldoli: A Journey into Its History and Spirituality*, Lino Vigilucci writes that Paula found in the forty-year-old Sylvester "the father of her soul." Her earthly father had other ideas and took Paula off to Genoa to forget about the monastery. On returning to Florence, however, Paula immediately returned to Sylvester. He encouraged her to establish a convent with two other young women. Paula spent most of her day in prayer, sometimes even forgetting to serve the meals Sylvester sent from his monastery kitchen. (History does not tell us how her two companions reacted.)

Paula revered Sylvester. "*God filled him with the spirit of wisdom and understanding,*" she said, "*and robed him with a stole of honesty and truth.*" One day, seized with the fire of the Holy Spirit, Sylvester ran through the street shouting, "*What is God? What is God?*" No one had an answer until he came to Paula, who responded, "*God is love. He is love!*" With her support, Sylvester became an adviser to half of Florence. He was illiterate, so Paula read him the Scripture that he would interpret. Shortly after his death during the great plague of 1348, Sylvester appeared to Paula and assured her, "*What was freed from the body had been assumed into heaven.*" Paula outlived him by nineteen years. When she died after a brief illness, the monks mourned her as one of their own. She was interred beside Sylvester, and they rest together in the mother church of the Camaldolese Order, which venerates her on January 5.

The Genius of Paula of Tuscany:
Paula understood the meaning of love, and recognized it in others, even the eccentric Sylvester.

Reflection:
"Blessed are the peacemakers, / for they will be called children of God."
Matthew 5:9

January 15

SAINT ITA OF LIMERICK
(Deirdre)

b. c. 475, Drum, County Waterford, Ireland
d. January 15, 570, Cill Ide (Killeedy), Ireland

Deirdre's father, a powerful chieftain, resisted her desire for monastic life until an angel assured him that she would become an advocate for many souls on Judgment Day. On making her religious vows, she took the name Ita, which means "thirsting for divine love." Angels then led Ita to the foot of a mountain on the Cork–Kerry border, where she founded her monastery. She called it Cluain Creadail ("Holy Meadow"), but it became known as Killeedy ("Church of Ita").

Ita's monastery drew men and women from all over Ireland. She also supervised a boys' school where she molded several future saints, most famously Brendan the Navigator,[13] who sailed to the New World long before Columbus. Young Brendan once asked Ita what three things God loved most. She replied, *"True faith in God, simplicity of spirit and a light heart."* And what, Brendan asked, was most hateful to God? Ita answered: *"Crudeness, love of evil and greed."*

On another occasion, a grieving mother sought Ita's help. Her son had murdered his own brother and the local chieftain had condemned him to death. Ita asked that the young man be spared so that he could do penance for his terrible sin. Moved by Ita's defense, the chieftain freed the youth but warned Ita that she would be held responsible. He recommended that she immediately get the murderer started on a rigorous program of penance. Here, too, Ita disagreed. She believed that penance could never be forced. It would take time, but her patience was rewarded by the killer's change of heart.

The Genius of Ita of Limerick:
Ita understood that no one could change overnight. True reform comes only with patience, time, and love.

Reflection:
"As the deer longs for streams of water, / so my soul longs for you, O God. / My being thirsts for God, the living God. / When can I go and see the face of God?"

Psalm 42:2–3

January 16

BLESSED GERTRUDE OF DELFT

(Gertrude van Oosten)

b. c. 1300, Voorburg, Holland
d. January 6, 1358, Delft, Holland

Gertrude was a poor country girl whose fiancé left her for another woman. Brokenhearted, she resolved to devote herself to God and begged to enter Delft's beguinage. In doing so, she became part of one of the most interesting women's movements in history.

The Beguines sprang up in Europe in the Middle Ages and flourished in the Netherlands and Belgium. They offered unattached women the chance to lead a spiritual life without taking permanent vows or enduring the rigors of a monastery. The women held on to their own property, and many operated successful businesses. Gertrude, one of the most famous Beguines, worked as a maid. In her leisure time, she would stand on the bridges of Delft, singing hymns with two companions. Her nickname, Gertrude van Oosten, which means "Gertrude from the east," came from her favorite hymn, *"Het daghet in den Oosten"* (Day breaks in the east).

On Holy Thursday, 1340, while meditating on the Passion, Gertrude experienced the stigmata on her hands, feet, and side. Witnesses saw blood flow from these wounds seven times a day. Curious crowds descended on her beguinage and Gertrude, fearing the sin of pride, prayed that the bleeding would stop. It did, but the scars of the stigmata remained, and Gertrude was left so weak that she could barely walk for the last eighteen years of her life. She was blessed with other mystic gifts and wrote forty-five meditations as well as a number of hymns.

When Gertrude learned that her former rival had lost several babies at birth, she visited her and assured her of her forgiveness. They prayed together and the woman later gave birth to healthy children. Gertrude herself died peacefully on January 6, the day on which she is venerated in Antwerp.

The Genius of Gertrude of Delft:
> As a girl, Gertrude waited on the crowds that flocked to Delft for festivals. She said that she experienced as much of God's goodness in those tumultuous days as in the solitude of her last years.

Reflection:
> *"The foolishness of God is wiser than human wisdom, and the weakness of God is stronger than human strength."*
>
> 1 Corinthians 1:25

SAINT ROSELINE VILLENEUVE

b. 1267, Villeneuve Castle, Provence, France
d. January 17, 1329, Celle-Roubaud, Provence, France

Roseline grew up in a pink stone castle that still towers over the village of des Arcs. She yearned to enter a convent, but her parents resisted, so she would slip through the castle gates to take bread to the poor. Her father once caught her and demanded to see what she was hiding in her apron. She opened it and out spilled not bread, but roses. After this miracle her parents allowed thirteen-year-old Roseline to enter the Carthusian abbey at Bertaud.

Carthusians spent most of their day alone in silence, gathering only for meals, also taken in silence. Roseline the novice was assigned to the kitchen. She once fell so deep in prayer that she forgot all about preparing dinner, until the bell summoned the nuns to the dining hall. Fortunately, angels appeared to set the table and prepare the dinner for Roseline. Similar miracles continued throughout her life. In 1300 her family built an abbey for her at Celle-Roubaud, near their castle, where she served as prioress until her death. A few years later, her brother Helion, a veteran of the Crusades, was captured by Saracens. He prayed to his deceased sister and the enemy panicked and fled, leaving him free to return to Provence.

Roseline's tomb at Celle-Roubaud became a popular pilgrimage site, but after the Revolution the monastery was deconsecrated and passed through a series of owners. Today it is at the center of a large vineyard called Château Sainte Roseline. The chapel has been restored and contemporary artists were commissioned to create works honoring Roseline. Pilgrims can venerate Roseline and see Marc Chagall's mosaic, *The Angels' Dinner,* and Diego Giacometti's bronze sculpture, *The Miracle of the Roses,* among other works.

The Genius of Roseline of Villeneuve:

By embracing the strict Carthusian Rule, Roseline did not turn away from the world so much as she sought to look at it in a fresh way, with total alertness to the Holy Spirit. When asked what was the best way to get to heaven, she replied, *"To know oneself."*

Reflection:

"We know that all things work for good for those who love God, who are called according to his purpose."

Romans 8:28

SAINT MARGARET OF HUNGARY
(Margit)

b. 1242, Buda, Hungary
d. January 18, 1271, St Mary's Isle (now Margaret Insel), Hungary

Mongol warriors had invaded Hungary and King Bela IV and Queen Mary were facing certain death at their hands. In desperation, they promised to consecrate their unborn child to God if he would spare their country. As they prayed, a storm broke. It lasted for three days and when it cleared, the Mongols had retreated.

A few months later, the queen gave birth to Margaret, and when she was three and a half years old, her parents honored their vow by delivering her to the Dominican convent at Veszprém. She thrived there, taking final vows at the age of twelve. Those vows became an issue a few years later. Margaret had matured into a beauty and Ottokar, the Iron King of Bohemia, wanted her as his bride to seal his alliance with Hungary. Pope Alexander IV agreed to annul Margaret's religious vows, and her parents assured her that they were still honoring their promise to God because she would still be sacrificing herself for their country.

Margaret disagreed. *"I will never give up the life to which I am vowed,"* she insisted. *"I prefer the Heavenly Kingdom to that which has been offered me by the King of Bohemia, so also do I prefer to die rather than obey commands that would bring death to my soul."*

Her parents gave up, and built a convent for Margaret on an island in the middle of the Danube. She was said to perform many miracles there and was known to make the river rise and fall at her will.

The Genius of Margaret of Hungary:
Margaret made every minute count, explaining: *"Many of the people who look forward to a long life put off doing good works, since they think that they will have plenty of time before they die. As for me, I prefer to be among those who consider that they have no time to lose if they wish to give God all the glory that they can before they die."*

Reflection:
"Whoever wishes to save his life will lose it, but whoever loses his life for my sake and that of the gospel will save it."

Mark 8:35

BLESSED ANA DE LOS ANGELES MONTEAGUDO

b. c. July 26, 1604, Arequipa, Peru
d. January 10, 1686, Arequipa, Peru

Arequipa is famous for its mild climate, but inside Ana's convent conditions were stormy. In fact, they had become a scandal, and everyone knew that something had to be done. The only question was what. When wild tales about the convent reached the new bishop of Arequipa, he paid them a visit and questioned the nuns closely. They freely acknowledged that the atmosphere there had become relaxed, but they were also proud to point to their devout novice-mistress, Sister Ana de los Angeles. Ana had spent more than thirty years in the convent and had been entrusted with mentoring the youngest nuns.

The bishop encouraged the nuns to elect Ana their new prioress. Poor Ana did not feel capable of fulfilling this honor, but when the voice of God commanded her to accept the new position, she obeyed. Everyone was happy, and the bishop went home, leaving Ana to carry out the actual task of reform. This would not be easy.

Taking her new job seriously, Ana insisted that the nuns observe every aspect of the Dominican Rule, especially the required hours of silence. She even made them give up their beloved gold jewelry. Not everyone accepted Ana's reforms. Hot coals were poured on her head, someone pushed her into an open grave, and she survived three poisoning attempts. Remaining serene, she blamed all these episodes on Satan, who was clearly unhappy with her progress.

At the end of her three-year term, with the convent back on track, Ana retired as prioress and returned to her life of contemplation. Thirty-six years later, she died peacefully in her sleep with her rosary in her hands. She is venerated in Peru and by the Dominican Order on January 10.

The Genius of Ana de los Angeles:
Ana recognized that God never gives us a task we cannot handle. Embracing her challenge, she was blessed with success and satisfaction.

Reflection:
"Come to me, all you who labor and are burdened, and I will give you rest. Take my yoke upon you and learn from me, for I am meek and humble of heart; and you will find rest for yourselves."

Matthew 11:28–29

SAINT EUSTOCHIA CALAFATO
(Eustochia of Messina, Smeralda Calafato)

b. March 25, 1434, Annunziata, Messina, Sicily
d. January 20, 1485, Montevergine, Messina, Sicily

From the beginning, Eustochia was special: she was born in a stable on Good Friday. Her parents had been on the way to their country villa when she arrived. Her devout mother, who had prayed for a daughter after three sons, named her precious jewel Smeralda (Emerald). At fourteen, Smeralda wanted to become a Poor Clare, but her father arranged her marriage to a wealthy widower. When he died before the wedding, her father negotiated another marriage, but that man also died, followed by her father. Smeralda finally overcame family resistance and entered the convent of Santa Maria di Basico, one of the richest in Sicily, taking the religious name Eustochia after Eustochium Julia.[14] Eustochia discovered that her new convent had drifted away from the "holy poverty" of Clare of Assisi (August 11). For more than a decade, Eustochia struggled to be an authentic Franciscan in this materialistic atmosphere. She finally received permission to found a new convent, Santa Maria Accomandata, but her next challenge was the male clergy that resisted her reforms. When the Little Friars of the Observance refused to consecrate her new monastery, Eustochia appealed directly to Rome. The friars were threatened with excommunication unless they assumed the spiritual care of her nuns. Although Eustochia clashed with many men throughout her life, women loved her. She drew so many vocations to her community that they soon outgrew the building and moved to Montevergine, near Messina, where their convent still stands, and where Eustochia is honored with an annual procession.

The Genius of Eustochia Calafato:
Eustochia often led her nuns in two-hour Scripture study sessions. When they gathered around her deathbed, she spoke about the Passion for an hour before passing to her final rest.

Reflection:
"I am the vine, you are the branches. Whoever remains in me and I in him will bear much fruit, because without me you can do nothing."
John 15:5, opening citation of her canonization homily

SAINT AGNES OF ROME

b. c. 292, Rome, Italy
d. c. 305, Rome, Italy

Agnes is the patron saint of the meek, but there was nothing meek about her. She was barely thirteen when she became one of Christianity's greatest heroes.

She grew up during Emperor Diocletian's last great effort to stamp out Christianity. Thousands of Christians went to the lions in the Coliseum rather than deny their faith. At the height of this persecution, Agnes was called before the magistrate and ordered to sacrifice to the Roman gods. She refused, saying: *"I belong to Him whom the angels serve."* For that she was stripped and exposed in the Piazza Navona, then condemned to death. Led to the chopping block, she stood still, prayed, and offered her neck while her executioner shook as if he were the one about to die. The great Ambrose of Milan[15] saluted her, writing: *"Girls her age can hardly bear the angry eyes of their parents and the prick of a needle makes them cry. . . . Agnes, on the contrary, remains dauntless in the hands of her executioners, stained with her blood."*

Her story spread throughout the Empire, and it is worth noting that the persecution ended shortly after her sacrifice. Less than a decade later, the emperor Constantine issued the Edict of Milan, giving full legal recognition to all Christians. His daughter, Constantia, erected over Agnes's tomb a basilica known as St Agnes Outside the Walls. Another church dedicated to Agnes was erected at the Piazza Navona. Both churches still stand as monuments to one of the first and greatest women saints.

The Genius of Agnes of Rome:
Flattery, promises, and threats could not distract Agnes from her commitment to Christ. We too belong to *"Him whom the angels serve,"* and we can draw the same strength and courage from Him.

Reflection:
"At that time, Jesus said in reply, 'I give praise to you, Father, Lord of heaven and earth, for although you have hidden these things from the wise and the learned you have revealed them to the childlike.'"

Matthew 11:25

BLESSED BOLESLAWA LAMENT

b. July 3, 1862, Lowicz, Lodzkie, Poland
d. January 29, 1946, Bialystok, Podlaskie, Poland

Boleslawa personally witnessed the terrible cost of ethnic and religious hatreds. Devoting her life to Christian unity, she founded the first congregation of women dedicated to ecumenism.

Boleslawa was a twenty-two-year-old novice at a convent in Poland when her spiritual director asked her to take on a delicate assignment: moving to Mohilev, the provincial capital of Belarus, to open a settlement house. In an area where Orthodox Christians far outnumbered Roman Catholics, Boleslawa offered educational and religious activities to both while supporting herself as a tailor.

As Boleslawa's mission progressed, she founded a new congregation dedicated to bringing Orthodox Christians into communion with the Catholic Church. Boleslawa received no financial support from the Church. Her only resources were her faith and her desire to live a full religious life, while reaching out to Orthodox Christians.

After two years, Boleslawa moved her growing congregation to St Petersburg, Russia, but she and her companions suffered great material deprivation there. At the worst moment, when their money, food, and fuel were exhausted, she called a meeting to discuss abandoning the mission. That very day, however, a letter arrived asking her to take charge of a parish orphanage. The Sisters took this as a sign of God's providence and an indication of divine approval. Soon they expanded their work to other parishes until the Russian Revolution and the rise of Soviet communism forced them to return to Poland.

Today Boleslawa's congregation, known as the Missionary Sisters of the Holy Family, is active in eastern Europe, Africa, and the United States, strengthening the faith of the faithful by promoting unity between Catholic and Orthodox churches. Her feast day is January 29.

The Genius of Boleslawa Lament:
Long before Vatican II, Boleslawa was an apostle for ecumenism in daily life. Totally consecrated to love, she sought to unite her will with God's, *"like two pieces of wax pressed into one."*

Reflection:
"Holy Father, keep them in your name that you have given me, so that they may be one just as we are."
John 17:11, often cited by Boleslawa as her inspiration

BLESSED MARIANNE OF MOLOKAI

(Barbara Cope)

b. January 23, 1838, Heppenheim, Hessen (Germany)
d. August 9, 1918, Molokai, Hawaii

The kingdom of Hawaii was battling an epidemic of leprosy in 1883 when Marianne Cope, a Franciscan nun from upstate New York, answered its desperate call for help.

Baptized Barbara, she was less than two years old when her immigrant family came to America, and she left school after the eighth grade to work in a mill. At twenty-four she entered the Sisters of the Third Order of St Francis in Syracuse, New York, taking the name Marianne, and soon demonstrated outstanding administrative ability coupled with great compassion. By 1883, she was Mother Provincial (chief executive officer) of the congregation and responsible for their remarkable and expanding hospital system. In secular terms, Marianne was at the peak of her career, but she gave it up to work with leprosy patients. In her first five years in Hawaii, she built a hospital and a children's home. The government banished confirmed cases of leprosy to the island of Molokai, and Marianne moved there herself in 1888, joining Father Damien,[16] who was dying of the disease. With a woman's genius, she turned a barren windswept island into a garden. Author Robert Louis Stevenson visited Molokai and was so impressed with Marianne's work that he dedicated a poem to her and sent the music-loving Sisters the gift of a piano.

The Genius of Marianne of Molokai:
After twenty years among the lepers, Marianne could write to her nephew, *"I do not think of reward. I am working for God, and do so cheerfully. How many graces did He not shower down on me, from my birth till now. Should I live a thousand years I could not in ever so small a degree thank Him for His gifts and blessings—I do not expect a high place in heaven—I shall be thankful for a little corner where I may love God for all eternity."*

Reflection:
"Then I heard the voice of the Lord saying, 'Whom shall I send? Who will go for us?' 'Here I am,' I said; 'send me!'"
Isaiah 6:8, cited during her beatification homily

BLESSED JOSEFA MARIA OF BENIGANIM

(Beata Inez, Inez de Beniganim)

b. February 9, 1625, Beniganim, Valencia (Spain)
d. January 21, 1696, Beniganim, Valencia (Spain)

From childhood, Josefa was surrounded by miracles. An orphan, she lived as a servant in her uncle's house. He once fired a gun at her but missed and hit a wall. The family repeatedly plastered over the bullet holes, but they always came through. Another time, a young man cornered Josefa in a hayloft and tried to force himself on her. She boxed his ears and escaped through a tiny window, landing without a scratch. Both of these miracles were mentioned at her beatification.

Overcoming more obstacles, Josefa entered an Augustinian convent and became Josefa Maria of Santa Inez. An earthquake struck in the middle of the ceremony while she was receiving her religious habit. People ran from the church, but Josefa assured the priest, *"Be not afraid, keep calm! The devil caused this, for he is full of wrath at his failure to keep me out of the convent."*

Once the Lord himself offered Josefa a choice: either suffer in bed for three years or remain silent for the same length of time, whichever she thought would do her the most good. She chose silence, in order not to neglect her duties. For the next three years, Josefa spoke only on principal feast days. Her guardian angel placed an hourglass beside her, and as long as the sand continued to run, she spoke eloquently about heavenly things. But as soon as the last grain of sand ran down, she went silent. That same guardian angel once took Josefa to a lake where a woman was planning to drown herself. Josefa led the woman away from the shore, freed her soul from despair, and brought her back to the sacraments.

Josefa is venerated in Valencia and by the Augustinian Order on January 23.

The Genius of Josefa Maria of Beniganim

When a priest asked the dying Josefa why she did not beg God to end her pain, she answered, *"God knows my sufferings; if it please Him that I shall be afflicted, it is all the same to me."*

Reflection:

"The fear of the LORD *is the beginning of knowledge; wisdom and instruction fools despise."*

Proverbs 1:7

SAINT DWYNWEN

b. ?, Brecknock, Wales
d. c. 460, Llanddwyn Island, Anglesey, Wales

Wales's patron saint of lovers has accumulated many colorful legends, but the facts are hard to come by. We know that her name means "Dwyn the blessed," and that she was one of twenty-four daughters of the Welsh king Brychan of Brecknock, but unlike her sisters, rowdy Gladys (March 29) and restless Keyne (October 9), Dwynwen decided to settle in one place to consecrate herself to God.

She said goodbye to her lover, Prince Maelon, and retired to the isolated southwest tip of the island of Anglesey. Maelon followed, refusing to accept rejection, and Dwynwen was torn because she still loved him. One night while Dwynwen was sleeping, an angel appeared and offered her a delicious liqueur. She sipped it and immediately woke up cured of her love for Maelon. He was still lurking around Anglesey, and hoping to cure him as well, Dwynwen shared the drink with him, but Maelon immediately turned into a block of ice, leaving Dwynwen feeling worse than ever. She no longer loved Maelon, but she did not want to hurt him. According to the legend, Dwynwen prayed to God for help. He took pity on her and granted her three requests.

Naturally, she thought of Maelon first and asked that he be freed from the ice. Once loose, Maelon disappeared from Dwynwen's life. Next, she asked to intercede for other lovers so that they could either obtain the object of their affection or mend their heartache. Finally, she asked that she would never again wish to be married. God granted Dwynwen all three requests. A miraculous spring appeared at the site of her dream, now called Llanddwyn, and she built an abbey there. She continued to perform many miracles, and it was said that no pilgrim ever left Llanddwyn with a lovesick heart or a troubled mind. Lovers still flock to the site of her spring at Anglesey, considered one of the most romantic places in Wales.

The Genius of Dwynwen:

Dwynwen is remembered for her advice, *"There is none so loveable as the cheerful."*

Reflection:

"Gladness of heart is the very life of man, / cheerfulness prolongs his days."
Sirach 30:22

BLESSED TERESA GRILLO MICHEL

b. September 25, 1855, Spinetta Marengo, Alessandria, Italy
d. January 25, 1944, Alessandria, Italy

"Holy Mary, let me die" had become Teresa's constant prayer. A childless widow at thirty-six, she was convinced that she had nothing to live for. A cousin encouraged her to read about Joseph Cottolengo,[17] a saintly priest who had worked among the urban poor in Turin. Cottolengo's total trust in Divine Providence had a profound effect on Teresa, inspiring her to open her own home to the poor.

After two years, Teresa sold her home and purchased an old building in the slums. She began expanding and the Little Refuge of Divine Providence was born. Teresa had to cope with skeptical authorities, and her own horrified friends and relatives, but in 1899, with eight associates, she founded the Congregation of the Little Sisters of Divine Providence. They wear a distinctive blue veil that signifies faith and a white habit, symbolizing their eternal hope. Teresa's vision spread in Italy and then to South America. She crossed the Atlantic six times to oversee numerous kindergartens, orphanages, schools, and hospitals in Brazil and Argentina, making her final voyage in 1928 at the age of seventy-three.

The Genius of Teresa Grillo Michel:

Teresa's many letters are full of wise advice. In one she reminds us: *"Divine Providence has never gone bankrupt . . . even though at times it makes us wait, it nevertheless always ends up sending what is necessary on time."* And in another: *"The Lord speaks more easily through those who are humble and uncomplicated. There is a knowledge which is not learned from books, but which He himself places in the heart."*

Reflection:

"Love is patient, love is kind. It is not jealous, [it] is not pompous, it is not inflated, it is not rude, it does not seek its own interests, it is not quick-tempered, it does not brood over injury, it does not rejoice over wrongdoing but rejoices with the truth. It bears all things, believes all things, hopes all things, endures all things."

1 Corinthians 13:4–6

SAINT ANGELA MERICI

b. c. 1470–75, Desenzano del Garda, Italy
d. January 27, 1540, Brescia, Italy

Angela was born into wealth in the Brescia region of northern Italy, but by the time she was twenty-six God had taken most of her family. She grieved most for the younger sister who had been her best friend, and resolved to live a life of prayer and good works until she discovered why God had spared her.

At about this time Angela had two remarkable visions. In the first, the skies opened and Ursula and her Companions (October 21) descended to earth. In the middle of the company was Angela's lost sister. Not long after that, Angela had the second vision: an infinite number of young women, all wearing crowns, being led by angels up a ladder to heaven. As Angela watched, a voice told her that she too would establish an army of virgins.

Angela devoted herself to good works. She was an expert horsewoman and rode wherever she was needed, whether to teach catechism or nurse plague victims. Angela's reputation spread and in 1525 Pope Clement VII asked her to take charge of all of Rome's charitable institutions. Afraid, Angela declined, explaining that God had another plan for her back in Brescia. Angela was nearly sixty when she had a vision in which Christ rebuked her for neglecting her vocation. She knew that she could delay no longer. She gathered twelve women from all of Brescia's social classes. This Society of St Ursula committed to a chaste life and serving their families and society in prisons, hospitals, and the poorest neighborhoods.

It is almost impossible to imagine how radical Angela's concept was. The Society needed no convent because they continued to live in their own homes. They wore no habit, but the simplest street clothes. The Ursulines are regarded as the Church's first female teaching order, and they played a major role in Catholic education in the United States.

The Genius of Angela Merici:

"Do not lose heart," Angela tells us, *"even if you should discover that you lack qualities necessary for the work to which you are called. He who called you will not desert you, but the moment you are in need he will stretch out his saving hand."*

Reflection:

"And suddenly this rivulet of mine became a river, / then this stream of mine, a sea. Thus do I send my teachings forth shining like the dawn, / to become known afar off."

Sirach 24:29b–30

January 28

BLESSED OLYMPIA BIDA

(Olga Bida)

b. 1903, Tsebliv, Lviv, Ukraine
d. January 28, 1952, Tomsk, Siberia, Russia

In the summer of 1951, Olympia Bida and Lavrentia Herasymiv[18] were arrested by the Soviet secret police and charged with leading prayers at a funeral. Convicted, sentenced to hard labor, and transported to Siberia, they would never see Ukraine again. Both women were Sisters of St Joseph (Josephian Sisters), members of an order founded by Father Zygmunt Gorazdowski[19] and dedicated to nursing the sick and bringing religious instruction to rural villages.

Such activity had been outlawed since 1946, when the Communist government dissolved Ukraine's Byzantine-rite Catholic Church and launched a persecution of priests and nuns who remained loyal to the pope. In spite of the danger, the Josephian Sisters continued to arrange underground services for the faithful, and at one such service Olympia and Lavrentia were arrested. They joined thousands of Ukrainians in exile in Siberia. In spite of her own failing health, Olympia managed to organize Sisters in other camps for prayers and mutual support, until she succumbed to illness. She and Lavrentia were among the martyrs beatified with Mykola Charnetsky[20] and Companions in 2001. Other women in that group were Tarsykia Matskiv (June 27) and Josaphata Hordashevska (November 21).

The Genius of Olympia Bida:

Olympia never lost her trust in God, writing from Siberia: *"He is with us here, in the midst of these forests and waters. He doesn't forget about us. . . . Because of our faith, because of a divine matter, we suffer, and what could be better than this? Let's follow him bravely."*

Reflection:

"For his sake I have accepted the loss of all things and I consider them so much rubbish, that I may gain Christ . . . to know him and the power of his resurrection and [the] sharing of his sufferings by being conformed to his death."
Philippians 3:8, 10

Saint Bathildis, Queen of France

b. at time and place unknown
d. January 30, 680, Chelles, France

The slave girl who became queen of France never even knew her real name. Norse pirates kidnapped her from a Saxon tribe, and by the time she was sold in a slave market she was known only as Bathildis, which in the Norse language means "maid of the women's quarters."

She was acquired by Archibald, a powerful adviser to King Clovis II. A widower, Archibald wanted to marry her, but Bathildis was not interested. He moved on to someone else, but put Bathildis in charge of his household. She fulfilled this position without ever arousing the jealousy of Archibald's new wife or the rest of the palace staff. Even King Clovis was impressed with how well the former slave handled her new status, and proposed to make her his wife and queen. Bathildis accepted.

Bathildis managed local affairs while Clovis was off uniting the Frankish tribes into one kingdom. After eight years of marriage, he fell ill and on his deathbed designated Bathildis as regent for Clotaire III, the oldest of their three sons. The new queen immediately abolished slavery throughout her kingdom and deftly balanced rival factions among landowners and clergy. She eliminated infanticide, a common practice in the Middle Ages, and repealed the heavy taxes that had forced many families to resort to it. She was also an outspoken critic of clerical corruption and outlawed the lucrative trade in ecclesiastic positions (simony).

Bathildis founded hospitals and monasteries, including the abbey at Chelles. When Clotaire III was old enough, she turned the throne over to him and retired to Chelles, where she lived as an ordinary nun. She gave wise advice when asked and always worked with great humility. Her feast day is January 30.

The Genius of Bathildis:

Bathildis used her power to rule with grace and generosity. When the time came, she was able to give it all up. In retirement she was known for never acting without consulting others.

Reflection:

"All bitterness, fury, anger, shouting, and reviling must be removed from you, along with all malice. [And] be kind to one another, compassionate, forgiving one another as God has forgiven you in Christ."

Ephesians 4:31–32

SAINT HYACINTHA MARISCOTTI
(Giacinta, Jacinta)

b. 1588, Vignanello, Viterbo, Italy
d. January 30, 1640, Viterbo, Italy

Vain, frivolous, and proud of her noble rank, Hyacintha was shattered when her lover married her younger sister. She proceeded to make life so unbearable for her family that they virtually forced her into a Franciscan convent. Arriving there with her own servants and personal chef, she demanded a suite of rooms and furnished them lavishly. She entertained male and female visitors while ignoring her superiors' reprimands. Her father tried to talk with Hyacintha about her scandalous life, but she brushed him off, saying, *"I am a nun but I intend to live according to my rank."*

One day, confined to bed with a mild illness, Hyacintha sent for the convent's new confessor. A true Franciscan, he took one look at her luxurious boudoir and refused to enter the room, warning her that heaven was no place for fools. His words pierced her heart. *"Is there no hope for me?"* Hyacintha called after him. *"Have I shut myself up in a cloister only to lose my soul? Do I give up all hope of salvation?"* She resolved to change her life, giving up her luxurious suite and moving into a small, barren cell. She gave away her silk and velvet gowns and donned habits discarded by the other nuns. She begged their forgiveness, leaving them stunned at this miraculous conversion. Of course it couldn't last. Hyacintha had a relapse, but eventually made a sincere and permanent recovery. The sisters she once scandalized elected her vice-superior and novice-mistress, and she founded and directed two benevolent societies. The papal bull announcing Hyacintha's canonization declared, "[T]hrough her apostolate of charity she won more souls to God than many preachers of her time."

The Genius of Hyacintha Mariscotti:

The frivolous girl became a wise woman and a compassionate mentor. To one overly serious young Sister, she wrote, *"Do not think that God is a tyrant. Drive away sadness, I implore and pray you."*

Reflection:

"No one experiencing temptation should say, 'I am being tempted by God'; for God is not subject to temptation to evil, and he himself tempts no one. Rather, each person is tempted when he is lured and enticed by his own desire."

James 1:13–14

SAINT MARCELLA OF ROME

b. 325, Rome, Italy
d. 410, Rome, Italy

Marcella shared a deep spiritual friendship with Saint Jerome[21] that continued long after he left for the Holy Land.

When Marcella was a child, her mother, Albina, welcomed Jerome into their home. He told her stories about the monasteries for women being founded in the Holy Land. When Marcella was widowed shortly after marriage, she gave up her luxurious robes and jewelry and became the first woman in Rome to assume the coarse brown monk's robe, turning her palace into a virtual monastery. It was here that Fabiola (December 31) was inspired to establish the first hospital in Rome.

Marcella, her sister Asella,[22] and their mother were joined by other future saints, including Marcellina,[23] Lea,[24] and Paula[25] and her daughters Blaesila and Eustochium. The women were not bound by any vows, and they came and went as they pleased. Jerome called Marcella's home the domestic church. She studied Hebrew to understand Scripture better, then questioned Jerome so closely on the fine points that he complained his disciple was becoming his judge.

When Jerome returned to the Holy Land with Paula and Eustochium, Marcella decided to remain in Rome with her adopted daughter, Principia.[26] They were there when the Goths swooped down and sacked Rome in 410. Some of the marauders invaded Marcella's palace and demanded her fortune. There was none because, as Jerome said, Marcella chose *"to store her money in the stomachs of the poor."* The barbarians flogged the eighty-five-year-old woman mercilessly. She endured their abuse, begging only that they spare Principia. This moved them to stop, and they took Marcella and Principia to the basilica of St Paul, which had been designated a sanctuary. Marcella never recovered from the beating and died in Principia's arms a few days later.

The Genius of Marcella of Rome:

Jerome wrote: *"How much virtue and ability, how much holiness and purity, I found in her. I am ashamed to say, both lest I might exceed the bounds of men's belief, and lest I might increase your sorrow by reminding you of what you have lost."*

Reflection:

"In my heart I treasure your promise, / that I may not sin against you."
Psalm 119:11, cited by Jerome in his eulogy for Marcella

Saint Brigid of Ireland

(Bridget, Bride, Brie, Britta)

b. c. 450, Faughart, County Louth, Ireland
d. c. 525, Kildare, Ireland

Teacher, miracle worker, and patron of the arts, Brigid inspired many legends that can obscure the real woman. Most historians agree that she was born out of wedlock and brought up in foster care—possibly on a dairy farm; she is often shown with a handsome cow. Her mother was a slave and her father a Druid chieftain. At some point, he claimed Brigid and raised her with his other children. When she resisted marriage he allowed her to take the veil, and she established a religious community near the Liffey River. Settling by a great oak tree, Brigid built the monastery later known as Kil-Dare (Gaelic, "Cell of the Oak"), ruling over a community of nuns and monks that became a center of scholarship. Aided by her faithful cook Flora,[27] Brigid welcomed pilgrims, saying: *"Christ is in the person of every faithful guest."* Many of her miracles concern hospitality. For example, she once changed water into ale, providing seventeen churches with enough libations to celebrate Easter for ten days. According to *The Book of Armagh*, an illuminated manuscript preserved at Trinity College, Dublin, Brigid shared a "friendship of charity" with Saint Patrick[28] and "they had but one heart and one mind." Another legend has Brigid praying at Patrick's deathbed and wrapping him in a shroud she wove herself.

For a thousand years, until her monastery was destroyed in the sixteenth century, a memorial fire burned at Brigid's tomb. The flame is now lit at Kildare's Anglican cathedral on her feast day. Brigid is a patron of children of unmarried parents, scholars, poets, healers, and dairy workers. With Patrick, she is co-patron of Ireland.

The Genius of Brigid of Ireland:
  Brigid drew strength from the eight Beatitudes, and she suggested that each of her nuns choose one for a personal devotion. Brigid herself chose Mercy.

Reflection:
  "Blessed are the merciful, / for they will be shown mercy."

Matthew 5:7

SAINT ANNA THE PROPHETESS
(Hannah)
AND THE FEAST OF THE PRESENTATION

First century, Jerusalem

The feast of the Presentation commemorates the ritual visit that Joseph and Mary made to the great Temple in Jerusalem.[29] There, as observant Jews, they presented the infant Jesus to God. Traditional paintings show Mary carrying the Infant and Joseph holding their offering of a pair of doves. They are usually flanked by two elders, Simeon[30] and Anna, who are considered the first of the New Testament saints.

Anna was an eighty-four-year-old widow who spent her days praying in the Temple. Many visitors sought her wisdom. Simeon was also old, but he had been assured by the Holy Spirit that he would not die before he had seen the Christ of the Lord. When the Holy Family entered the Temple, Simeon immediately recognized the Messiah. Taking the baby in his arms, he blessed God, saying: *"Now Master, you may let your servant go in peace, according to your word, for my eyes have seen your salvation, which you prepared in sight of all the peoples, a light for revelation to the Gentiles, and glory for your people Israel."* Simeon blessed Joseph and Mary but warned her: *"this child is destined for the fall and rise of many in Israel, and to be a sign that will be contradicted—and you yourself a sword will pierce."*

At that moment, Anna joined them, confirming the event, giving thanks to God, and speaking about the child to everyone in the Temple. Anna is venerated on September 1.

The Genius of Anna the Prophetess:
Pope John Paul II linked Anna's encounter in the Temple to the role women would play in Jesus' work of redemption. He wrote: "We can glimpse in the prophetess Anna all women who, with holiness of life and in prayerful expectation, are ready to accept Christ's presence and to praise God every day for the marvels wrought by his everlasting mercy."

Reflection:
"And coming forward at that very time, [Anna] gave thanks to God and spoke about the child to all who were awaiting the redemption of Jerusalem."

Luke 2:38

SAINT CLAUDINE THÉVENET

(Marie Saint-Ignatius Thévenet)

b. March 30, 1774, Lyons, France
d. February 3, 1837, Lyons, France

Revolution broke out in France when Claudine was fifteen years old. Three years later, the spirit of "liberty, equality, fraternity" had been eclipsed by the Reign of Terror. Citizens of Lyons rebelled and their city was under siege for two months. When it was lifted, thousands were arrested, including Claudine's two older brothers. For months she visited them daily in prison. One morning she encountered a line of men who were being marched toward the execution grounds. Spying her brothers among them, she moved closer. One brother whispered: "Forgive, Claudie, as we forgive." He and the other prisoners were executed that afternoon, but she would never forget her brother's words.

When peace returned, Claudine devoted herself to good works. She was more than forty years old when, at her pastor's request, she took in two destitute young women and taught them silk weaving so that they could support themselves. This marked the beginning of the Providence Homes, where a girl could learn a lucrative trade, keep her own savings account, and leave at the age of eighteen with a trousseau that she had made herself.

Other women joined Claudine in this work. She advised them *"to speak to God with joy and out of the fullness of their own hearts, and not for too long a time."* They were to avoid sour faces, she warned, because *"cheerful virtue is loved and easily gains others to God."* After four years, Claudine formed a religious community that became known as the Sisters of Jesus Mary. They remain dedicated to the education of poor girls and to Claudine's mission: *"to look at others in a way that enables us to discover in each one a promise, an expectation, an epiphany of the Divine Presence."*

The Genius of Claudine Thévenet:

For Claudine there was *"no greater misfortune than to live and die without knowing God."* She urged her associates *"to speak with zeal, with ardor and with charity, show affection and feeling for the sick, listen with patience and bear rebuffs without being discouraged."*

Reflection:

"What good is it, my brothers, if someone says he has faith but does not have works? . . . Faith without works is dead."

James 2:14, 26

February 4

SAINT MARIA DE MATTIAS

b. February 4, 1805, Vallecorsa, Frosinone, Italy
d. August 20, 1866, Rome, Italy

Maria grew up in a violent era. While Napoleon warred with the Papal States, bandits preyed on remote hill towns like hers. She was nine years old and leaving Holy Thursday services when she witnessed a massacre in the town square. Her own godfather was among the victims whose bodies were left mutilated and exposed as a warning to others.

In 1822 Maria heard Gaspar del Bufalo[31] preach against such banditry. She wrote that immediately *"I felt a great urge to imitate him—to tell others about Jesus and let them know that Jesus loved them so much that he shed his blood for them."* She was certain that she was being called to serve God, but unsure how. Was she called to a cloistered life of prayer? Could she preach like Gaspar? He encouraged her to pray and seek additional advice. A few years later, she founded the Adorers of the Blood of Christ, who engage in adoration of Christ crucified and risen. She designed their distinctive silver pendant: a heart engraved with three drops representing the Blood of Jesus, and a cross that symbolizes their commitment to promoting reconciliation. Blessed with a genius for public speaking, Maria became known as "the woman who preaches," drawing huge crowds as she traveled by mule in the Italian hills.

Today the Adorers are active in twenty-six countries, witnessing God's love and ministering that love to others. Because of Maria's devotion to the Precious Blood, there is a movement to have her declared the patron saint of blood donors.

The Genius of Maria de Mattias:
"Let us pray and place much confidence in prayer," Maria advised the Adorers. *"Beg our good Jesus fervently and with lively faith for the grace to know how to deal well with others. Be of good heart and have peace."*

Reflection:
"You were ransomed from your futile conduct, handed on by your ancestors, not with perishable things like silver or gold but with the precious blood of Christ as of a spotless unblemished lamb."

1 Peter 1:18–19

February 5

Saint Agatha of Catania

b. c. 235, Catania or Palermo, Sicily
d. c. 250, Catania, Sicily

Agatha was a wealthy heiress who spurned the Roman consul Quintianus because she had consecrated herself to God. The consul did not take rejection well. He had Agatha arrested and sent to Aphrodisia, a madam who had turned her own six daughters into prostitutes. Agatha spent a month in the brothel, but nobody could seduce her. Aphrodisia complained that Agatha's head was harder than the lava of Mount Etna and predicted that the rocks there would soften before Agatha abandoned her faith.

Quintianus had Agatha tortured, but she remained cheerful until he ordered her breasts removed with pincers. She reproached him: *"Cruel tyrant, do you not blush to torture my breast, you that sucked the breasts of a woman yourself?"* Far from blushing, he sent Agatha back to prison and banned all food and medication. She was comforted by a vision of Saint Peter,[32] who restored her breasts. The next morning, Quintianus furiously ordered Agatha stripped and rolled over live coals. At this point an earthquake shook Catania. The citizens blamed Quintianus and demanded that he release Agatha. He sent her back to prison, where she surrendered her soul to God and the earthquake stopped. Quintianus meanwhile fled the city, only to drown in the Simeto River. Tradition has it that on Agatha's feast day his cries can be heard on the water.

Agatha is a patron of nurses, nannies, and jewelers, and is invoked against breast diseases.

The Genius of Agatha:

In the thirteenth century, the emperor Frederick II was planning to destroy Catania when its citizens invited him to the last Mass in Agatha's cathedral. During the service, on every page of his missal, Frederick found the words "Do not harm Agatha's homeland, because she avenges injuries." He dropped his plan, and her warning still appears on the façade of her cathedral.

Reflection:

"This momentary light affliction is producing for us an eternal weight of glory beyond all comparison, as we look not to what is seen but to what is unseen; for what is seen is transitory, but what is unseen is eternal."

2 Corinthians 4:17–18

February 6

Saint Dorothy

d. February 6, 311, Caesarea, Cappadocia (Turkey)

Dorothy is usually represented as a young woman wearing a crown of flowers or carrying a basket of fruit and flowers. Legend has it that she lived during the Diocletian persecutions. Her sisters, Callista and Christa, became apostates, but Dorothy remained loyal to the Christian faith. She was denounced and dragged in front of Sapricus, the Roman prefect, but she would not budge. *"Oh, Sapricus,"* she cried, *"if you could only see the gardens of Paradise where the Bridegroom awaits the faithful Bride, you would not hope to shake me with threats of torture and death."* This enraged Sapricus, who offered Callista and Christa great rewards to change their sister's mind.

Instead, they begged Dorothy to pray that God would forgive them for ever denying Him. All three sisters were tried and condemned to death. Callista and Christa were plunged into a boiling cauldron, while Dorothy was sentenced to be beheaded. As she was led to her execution, Dorothy encountered Theophilus Scholasticus, a sardonic young lawyer who had opposed her in court. *"Bride of Christ,"* he yelled as Dorothy passed by, *"bring me some fruit and flowers from your Bridegroom's garden."* Dorothy promised to do so. Shortly after she was martyred, an angel brought Theophilus a basket containing three fragrant roses and three fresh apples. The lawyer tasted the fruit and smelled the roses, literally and spiritually. He became a Christian, and then a martyr himself.

Dorothy is a patron of gardeners, brewers, and newlyweds. Theophilus, Callista, and Christa are all venerated as saints with her on February 6.

The Genius of Dorothy:

Dorothy consoled her sisters: *"Say not, dear sisters, that your sin is past forgiveness, never doubt the Divine Mercy. In one moment the Heavenly Physician can heal the wounds of your souls. . . . Repent with all your hearts, and in God's name I promise you pardon."*

Reflection:

"I tell you, my friends, do not be afraid of those who kill the body but after that can do no more . . . I tell you, everyone who acknowledges me before others the Son of Man will acknowledge before the angels of God. But whoever denies me before others will be denied before the angels of God."

Luke 12:4, 8

SAINT COLETTE OF CORBIE
(Nicolette Boellet)

b. January 13, 1381, Corbie, Picardy, France
d. March 6, 1447, Ghent, Flanders

Colette was a miracle baby, born to a mother who was more than sixty years old. Baptized Nicolette, she was always known by her nickname. She grew into a tall, striking woman who entered and left several religious orders while struggling to find her vocation. She was especially disappointed in the Poor Clares, who had drifted from the rigorous Rule of Clare of Assisi (August 11). After that experience, Colette spent three years in seclusion as an anchorite or hermit, until her mission became clear: God was calling her to return the Franciscans to the strict holy poverty of their founders.

Seeking authority for this daring venture, Colette won an audience with Pope Benedict XIII in Provence. Although later discredited as a schismatic pope, Benedict recognized a saint when he saw one and put Colette in charge of all three Franciscan orders—the First Order (Friars Minor), the Second (Poor Clares), and the Third (Brothers and Sisters of Penance)—with the power to found new monasteries and choose their confessors. Colette met resistance immediately, but there were also signs that her work was blessed, such as when she saved the life of a woman dying in childbirth. This marked the beginning of her reputation as a patron of expectant mothers.

It is difficult to document Colette's meeting with Joan of Arc (May 30), but we know that Joan made a retreat at a Moulins convent while Colette was there. Some historians believe they met in secret because Colette needed to maintain neutrality in a time of war.

The Genius of Colette of Corbie:
It would have been easier for Colette to establish a new religious order, but that was not what she was called to do. She found the strength for her bold reforms through her rigorous spiritual life, devoting every Friday to fasting and contemplation of the Passion.

Reflection:
"As for me, I will look to the LORD, / I will put my trust in God my savior; / my God will hear me! Rejoice not over me, O my enemy! / Though I have fallen, I will arise; / though I sit in darkness, the LORD is my light."

Micah 7:7–8

SAINT JOSEPHINE BAKHITA

b. c. 1868, Darfur, Sudan
d. February 8, 1947, Vicenza, Italy

Josephine was about nine years old when she was seized by Arab slave traders, and she never saw her homeland again. Her captors, who called her Bakhita ("fortunate one"), sold her in a Khartoum slave market. Bakhita passed through five brutal owners, one of whom had her tattooed over her entire body, sparing only her face. In Istanbul she was acquired by the Italian consul, Calisto Legnani, the first person to show her any kindness. When he was called back to Genoa, she begged to go with him.

In Genoa, the Michieli family asked to keep Bakhita as a nurse for their infant daughter. They treated her generously, and when they left the country on business, they boarded Bakhita and the baby with the Canossian Daughters of Charity in Venice. The Michielis had embraced the anticlerical spirit of their time, and this was Bakhita's first exposure to Christianity. She recognized something she had been looking for all her life. *"Seeing the sun, the moon and the stars, I said to myself: who could be the Master of these beautiful things? And I felt a real desire to see him, to know him and to pay him homage."* She asked for religious instruction and was baptized Josephine. When the Michielis returned, Bakhita asserted her legal right to stay in the convent. The Michielis objected and the dispute went to the civil courts, with Bakhita emerging as a free woman who belonged only to God.

Three years later, Bakhita became a Canossian sister herself. For the next fifty years, until her death, she was the beloved gatekeeper for a compound that included a kindergarten, orphanage, recreational center, and school.

The Genius of Josephine Bakhita:

Bakhita never lost faith in Divine Providence. At the end of her life, she was asked if she was ready to go to heaven. She replied, *"I neither wish to go nor to stay. God knows where to find me when he wants me."*

Reflection:

"As proof that you are children, God sent the spirit of his Son into our hearts, crying out, 'Abba, Father!' So you are no longer a slave but a child, and if a child then also an heir, through God."

Galatians 4:6–7

SAINT APOLLONIA OF ALEXANDRIA

d. 249, Alexandria, Egypt

Unlike most of the early female martyrs, Apollonia was not a young girl but a middle-aged deaconess. Her ordeal was recorded by an eyewitness, Dionysius,[33] and circulated among the Christian community immediately.

According to Dionysius, "*A certain prophet and poet stirred up the heathen mob against the Christians.... They were convinced that the only way to show their piety was to kill us. This brave mob started by seizing an elderly man named Metranus. They called on him to utter impious expressions, and when he refused, they clubbed him, and pricked his face and eyes; after which ... they stoned him to death. Next, they led a Christian woman called Quinta[34] to the temple of an idol and attempted to force her to worship. When she turned away in disgust, they tied her by the feet, and dragged her through Alexandria, over the rough stones of the paved streets, dashing her against the millstones, and scourging her at the same time, until they brought her to the same place, where they stoned her to death.*"

The mob set fire to whatever they could not carry away. The whole city was in flames when they seized Apollonia, smashing her jaw and breaking all her teeth, then dragging her to the city gates where a bonfire was blazing. They threatened to burn her alive unless she denied her Christian faith, but when they loosened her restraints, she leaped into the flames and was burned to death.

She is a patron of dentists and is invoked against toothaches and gum disease.

The Genius of Apollonia:

Refusing to deny her faith, Apollonia faced death with the courage and strength that can only come from the Holy Spirit.

Reflection:

"*I called upon your name, O LORD, / from the bottom of the pit; / You heard me call, 'Let not your ear be deaf to my cry for help!' / You came to my aid when I called to you; / you said, 'Have no fear!' / You defended me in mortal danger, / you redeemed my life.*"

Lamentations 3:55–58

February 10

Saint Scholastica

b. c. 480, Nursia, Italy
d. 547, Monte Cassino, Italy

Like many of the great saints, Scholastica would not take no for an answer. Her twin brother, Benedict,[35] learned that the hard way when God overruled him and let Scholastica have her way.

Born into a wealthy Christian family, Scholastica was educated at home and consecrated to God at an early age. Meanwhile, her brother spent years on a spiritual journey that ended at Monte Cassino, where he established his monastery. Scholastica built a convent nearby, but Benedict's Rule allowed them to see each other only once a year. They would meet at a small cabin outside Monte Cassino. On one such occasion, as night approached and Benedict prepared to leave, Scholastica begged him to stay a little longer. He refused because he had to set an example to the other monks. Scholastica turned to God and prayed, flooding her table with tears. Suddenly there was a clap of thunder followed by rain, lightning, and thunder so intense that Benedict dared not step outside. He demanded to know what Scholastica had done. *"I prayed to you, and you wouldn't listen,"* she said. *"Then I prayed to God and he heard me. Go now, if you can, and send me away and return to your monastery."*

Of course, Benedict could not ignore the will of God and was forced to stay.

The Genius of Scholastica:
Scholastica had the power to do more because she loved more, and because she was not afraid to ask for God's help.

Reflection:
"If any of you lacks wisdom, he should ask God who gives to all generously and ungrudgingly, and he will be given it. But he should ask in faith, not doubting, for the one who doubts is like a wave of the sea that is driven and tossed about by the wind. For that person must not suppose that he will receive anything from the Lord, since he is a man of two minds, unstable in all his ways."
James 1:5–8

February 11

BLESSED JACINTA MARTO

b. March 5, 1910, Santarém, Portugal
d. February 20, 1920, Lisbon, Portugal

In 1917 Russia was wracked by revolution, while the United States and most of Europe were caught up in World War I. Far removed from this turmoil, near the village of Fatima, seven-year-old Jacinta tended sheep with her nine-year-old brother Francisco[36] and their ten-year-old cousin Lucia.[37] A year earlier, an angel had visited the children three times and taught them several prayers. *"Above all,"* the angel warned, *"accept and bear with submission the suffering which the Lord will send you."*

On May 13 Our Lady herself appeared to the children and asked them to return to the field on the thirteenth day of the month for the next six months. They were not to tell anyone, but Jacinta could not keep the secret. As the news of Our Lady's appearances spread, a negative reaction set in. The local mayor, an atheist, held the children captive and threatened to have them killed if they did not deny the visions. *"If they kill us,"* Jacinta said, *"it won't matter much, will it? Because we'll all go straight to heaven."* The children were finally freed and Our Lady made her last appearance at Fatima that October. A year later, Jacinta died of tuberculosis and influenza.

In 1981, on the same day and at the same hour that Our Lady first appeared at Fatima, Pope John Paul II was shot in St Peter's Square. He credited his miraculous recovery to the intercession of Our Lady of Fatima, who is celebrated on May 13, and to Jacinta, who is venerated in Portugal on February 20.

The Genius of Jacinta Marto:
In his beatification homily, John Paul praised the little girl who boasted: *"I love our Lord and our Lady so much that I never get tired of telling them that I love them."*

Reflection:
Have no anxiety at all, but in everything, by prayer and petition, with thanksgiving, make your requests known to God.

Philippians 4:6

BLESSED HUMBELINE

b. 1092, Fontaine-les-Dijon, Burgundy, France
d. 1141, Jully-les-Nonnains, Burgundy, France

Humbeline was the only daughter of Tescelin, lord of Fontaines, and Aleth of Montbard,[38] a formidable woman who defied convention by teaching her seven children herself. Aleth died suddenly when her son Bernard[39] was nineteen and Humbeline a year younger. Bernard took it very hard, and Humbeline consoled him.

Bernard soon entered a nearby monastery and convinced thirty companions to join him. Three years later, he established his own monastery at Clairvaux, where he was joined by his widowed father and five brothers. The wives of his followers formed a women's monastery at Jully-les-Nonnains, but Humbeline preferred the material world. She made a brilliant marriage and her adoring husband lavished her with fine clothes and jewels. She loved music, had a beautiful singing voice, and was known as a fearless horsewoman. Yet she missed her brother Bernard and decided to visit him at Clairvaux. She arrived at the monastery accompanied by her usual splendid entourage. The gatekeeper was shocked at such display, and Bernard refused to see her. Humbeline burst into tears, crying, *"I may indeed be a sinful woman, but it was for such as me that Christ died on the Cross."*

Her words touched Bernard and he relented. With his help, Humbeline rediscovered the spiritual lessons that their mother had taught them. A few years later, she entered the women's monastery herself and she is regarded as the founder of the Cistercian nuns.

The Genius of Humbeline:

Humbeline reminded her brother of what really matters: that Christ died for us all. Bernard could scorn her appearance, but *"as a servant of God he should not refuse to help my soul."*

Reflection:

"I rejoiced when they said to me, 'Let us go to the house of the Lord.'"
Psalm 122:1 (Humbeline's last words)

BLESSED EUSTOCHIA OF PADUA

(Lucrezia Bellini)

b. 1444, Padua, Italy
d. February 13, 1469, Padua, Italy

The "Cinderella of the Cloister" was born in scandal: her mother was a nun at the convent of San Prosdocimo. The mother disappears from her story, but the father had her baptized Lucrezia and when she was four years old, he took her into his home. Unfortunately, his wife beat, starved, and abused Lucrezia, who began to show symptoms of demonic possession.

When an exorcism performed by the bishop brought only temporary relief, Lucrezia's father returned her to the convent. Surrounded by louche nuns, she became isolated and withdrawn. The death of the abbess gave the bishop a chance to reform the convent. The nuns balked, disregarded their vows, and went home to their families, leaving sixteen-year-old Lucrezia alone in the deserted building. When a new abbess arrived with nuns of unquestioned virtue, Lucrezia asked to stay. The nuns resisted this living reminder of the convent's sordid past, but the abbess overruled them and allowed Lucrezia to be vested with the habit on January 15, 1461. She took the name Eustochia.[40]

At this point, the devil returned in full force. He tried to strangle Eustochia and beat her bloody. She vomited uncontrollably and attacked other nuns. The community was convinced that she was a witch, and the people of Padua clamored to burn her at the stake, but the abbess protected her. After four years of suffering, Eustochia was allowed to make final vows and died peacefully a few years later. In the end, the devil could not overcome her.

The Genius of Eustochia of Padua:

Eustochia never doubted God's plan, saying: *"In calling me to the life of the cloister, God did not call me to an existence of tranquility and ease. If I find my path strewn with thorns, it is a sign that that is the path by which He wishes to lead me to Him—for it is the same path that was trodden by Jesus Christ."*

Reflection:

"There is no fear in love, but perfect love drives out fear because fear has to do with punishment, and so one who fears is not yet perfect in love."

1 John 4:18

BLESSED CLARE OF RIMINI
(Clare Agolanti)

b. 1282, Rimini, Italy
d. February 10, 1346, Rimini, Italy

Clare Agolanti was frivolous, beautiful, and completely self-indulgent. Her life was an open scandal. These were violent and decadent times, and her own father and brother were executed together on the scaffold, while another brother was banished from Rimini. Clare inherited a fortune from her first husband, married again, and lost herself in worldly pleasures.

She attended Sunday Mass out of habit but with little faith until, at the age of thirty-four, she heard a voice say: *"Clare, try to say just one Our Father and one Hail Mary to the glory of God, without thinking of anything else."* As she recited the prayers, she began to feel a deep sense of remorse for her life. Shortly after this, Clare experienced a vision of the Blessed Mother that gave her the strength to turn her life around. She converted her second husband, and after his death, she devoted herself to charity. Her rigorous penances were considered extreme even by her contemporaries. (She once swallowed a live toad.) She slept on bare boards, survived on bread and water, and spent half the night in prayer. During the day, she nursed the sick and showed a gift for reconciling families. She converted many women from immoral lives, and endowed dowries for many poor girls.

Clare spent every Lent in a niche in one of Rimini's ancient city walls. Oblivious to the rain and cold, she became known as the Saint of the Watchtower. Clare was no recluse, however. When she learned that her exiled brother was ailing, she rushed to his bedside, nursed him back to health, and brought him home to Rimini. So many other women were drawn to Clare that she built a monastery to house them. She never became a nun herself, however. Her feast day is February 10.

The Genius of Clare of Rimini:
Clare recited the Lord's Prayer a hundred times a day. She was able to give herself completely to a life of self-denial yet was always available to perform acts of charity.

Reflection:
*"Turn away your face from my sins; / blot out all my guilt.
A clean heart create for me, God; / renew in me a steadfast spirit."*
Psalm 51:11–12

Blessed Anna Katharina Emmerich

b. September 8, 1774, Flamsche, Westphalia, Germany
d. February 9, 1824, Dülmen, Westphalia, Germany

There are two Anna Katharina stories. The first is the mystic's journey and the private revelations that inspired Mel Gibson's film *The Passion of the Christ*. The second is her cause for canonization, which was dropped in 1928 with an uncharacteristic public announcement by the Congregation for the Causes of Saints, only to be successfully reopened fifty years later.

Anna Katharina had a normal childhood, except for her religious visions. At fifteen she was apprenticed to a dressmaker who said her only fault was a fondness for smart clothes. At twenty-eight, after many rejections, Anna Katharina was accepted by an Augustinian convent. She had begun to experience the pain of invisible stigmata, and by the time the German government suppressed all convents in 1811, she was a virtual invalid. She began to bleed from her hands, feet, and forehead and was closely examined by a Church commission that included three medical doctors. In a time of great hostility to the Catholic faith, they were concerned about arousing ridicule, but they emerged convinced that Anna Katharina and her stigmata were authentic. The civil government followed with a second, harsher inquiry but failed to find any evidence of fraud.

A popular poet, Clemens Brentano, took up Anna Katharina's cause and transcribed her visions. Nine years after her death, he published *The Dolorous Passion of Our Lord Jesus Christ After the Meditations of Ann Catherine Emmerich*. Controversial material in this book led the Congregation to halt her cause for sainthood in 1928. It took years for her supporters to prove that Brentano had distorted his reports. In 1973 Pope Paul VI lifted the ban, and Anna Katharina was beatified in 2004. The Augustinian Order keeps her feast day on February 9.

The Genius of Anna Katharina Emmerich:

As a young woman, Anna Katharina prayed to God: *"I know not what to do; I cannot help myself; You have arranged it all, so You must manage it for me."*

Reflection:

"He himself bore our sins in his body upon the cross, so that, free from sin, we might live for righteousness. By his wounds you have been healed."

1 Peter 2:24, cited in her beatification homily

February 16

BLESSED FILIPPA MARERI

b. c. 1190, Cicolano, Rieti, Italy
d. February 16, 1236, Borgo San Pietro, Rieti, Italy

After hearing about the life that Clare of Assisi (August 11) was leading, Filippa decided that she, too, would embrace holy poverty. This upset her family, especially her brother Thomas, so Filippa ran away, taking shelter with some companions in a mountain cave. After several months, Thomas came to ask her forgiveness and agreed to endow her community with property near an abandoned monastery. Filippa drew up a contract for Thomas, which was later confirmed by the diocese of Rieti and the Roman Curia.

Filippa and her associates organized a convent on the new site. The women spent most of their day in prayer. They also mixed medications that they dispensed to the sick without charge. When Filippa prayed in the convent chapel, she always carried a small wooden cup to catch her tears so that they did not wet the floor. The water in the cup was said to have miraculous powers and could heal abscesses and throat disorders.

Legend has it that while Filippa was dying, a small white cloud rested like a snowball in the middle of her cloister. It remained there for three days, disappearing only after Filippa's soul was carried up to heaven. The next day a crowd gathered outside the convent, holding lighted candles and chanting, "Santa Filippa, Santa Filippa." To the people of the Rieti region, she was already a saint. Her tomb soon became a pilgrimage site known for many miracles. In 1706, after her body was excavated, her heart was found incorrupt and is today preserved in a silver reliquary. Filippa is considered the first female saint of the Franciscan Order.

In 1940 Filippa's monastery and most of the historic village around it were moved uphill to make way for an artificial lake. Today the Sisters of Filippa Mareri continue her work in a convent where her heart and cup are still venerated.

The Genius of Filippa Mareri:
It is said that Filippa tried to live the gospel in a world that had forgotten it.

Reflection:
"The peace of God that surpasses all understanding will guard your hearts and minds in Christ Jesus."

Philippians 4:7 (Filippa's last words to her Sisters)

Blessed Eusebia Palomino

b. December 15, 1899, Salamanca, Spain
d. February 10, 1935, Huelva, Spain

At the age of twelve, Eusebia was working as a nanny in Salamanca. In her free time she volunteered to help the Salesian Sisters, assisting in their kitchen, collecting firewood, and running errands. She would have liked to become a Salesian herself, but this seemed out of the question for an illiterate girl with no dowry. She confided as much to the Mother General when the latter visited Salamanca. The Mother General told Eusebia not to worry and soon accepted her into the order.

Eusebia was sent to a school in southwestern Spain and put in charge of the kitchen. She was an awkward little peasant with large coarse hands, and the children made fun of her until she won them over with her stories. She told them about the lives of the saints, adventures of the missionaries, and the Salesian founder, John Bosco.[41] The children spread the word about their gifted teacher, and parents, seminarians, and even priests came to hear her. Through her gift for storytelling, Eusebia worked to fulfill her yearning: *"to make every house resound in prayer."*

When an anti-Catholic persecution arose in Spain, Eusebia offered herself to God for the salvation of her country. Her offer was accepted, and in August 1932 she was struck by a mysterious illness. For the next three years, she lived with excruciating pain, tormented by premonitions of Spain's approaching civil war. Among other horrors, she saw visions of blood around her superior, Carmen Moreno Benítez (September 22), and warned her: *"You will suffer much."* This was confirmed when Carmen was martyred in 1936. The Salesians commemorate Eusebia on February 9.

The Genius of Eusebia Palomino:
Eusebia was convinced that *"The soul without prayer is like a garden without water, like a forge without a fire, like a ship without a rudder."*

Reflection:
"I came to you in weakness and fear and much trembling, and my message and my proclamation were not with persuasive [words of] wisdom, but with a demonstration of spirit and power, so that your faith might rest not on human wisdom but on the power of God."

1 Corinthians 2:3–5

February 18

SAINT ELFLEDA OF WHITBY

b. c. 654, Northumbria, England
d. 714, Whitby, Yorkshire, England

For thirty years, Penda, the pagan king of Mercia, battled to exterminate the Christians of Northumbria. Penda had slain five Anglo-Saxon kings by the time King Oswy offered his entire treasury to make peace, but Penda was not interested in peace.

King Oswy turned to heaven, vowing to consecrate his newborn daughter, Elfleda, to God if he could defeat Penda. The next morning, though greatly outnumbered, the Northumbrians triumphed, slew Penda, and firmly established Christianity in England. A grateful Oswy entrusted the infant Elfleda to the abbess Hilda of Whitby (November 4), who raised her in her monastery. At twenty-five, Elfleda succeeded Hilda as abbess, becoming one of the most influential women of her time. She even reconciled the feuding archbishop of Canterbury and the bishop of York.

Elfleda was devoted to Cuthbert of Lindesfarne,[42] often consulting him about affairs of state and her family. Once, when Cuthbert was living on the remote island of Lindesfarne, she asked to confer with him about an urgent matter. They sailed from different directions to rendezvous on the more accessible island of Coquet. There Elfleda revealed her concern about a successor for her childless brother Egfrid. Cuthbert told her that Egfrid had only a year to live, but he assured her that her half-brother Aldfrid was well qualified. Elfleda hardly knew Aldfrid, who had grown up in Ireland. A year later, Cuthbert's prophecy was fulfilled when Egfrid was killed in battle and Aldfrid inherited the throne, ruling with Elfleda's support. According to the historian Sabine Baring-Gould, "All the Northumbrians regarded her as the consoler and best counselor of the kingdom." Elfleda is venerated on February 8.

The Genius of Elfleda of Whitby:
Elfleda was not blind to the realities of life. She observed: *"Oh how divided in aim are the hearts of men! Some enjoy the wealth they have gained, others love riches but never have any to enjoy."*

Reflection:
"Undeniably great is the mystery of devotion, / Who was manifested in the flesh, / vindicated in the spirit, / seen by angels, / proclaimed by Gentiles, / believed in throughout the world, / taken up in glory."

1 Timothy 3:16

BLESSED ELIZABETH CANORI MORA

b. November 21, 1774, Rome, Italy
d. February 5, 1825, Rome, Italy

Elizabeth was unprepared when her dream marriage to Christopher Mora turned into a nightmare. Just months after their wedding, her husband took a mistress. While Elizabeth bore four daughters, two of whom died in infancy, Christopher caroused and let his law practice fall apart. She took in sewing to feed her children. Christopher's prominent family blamed her and claimed that he would have been a better husband with a different wife. Even her priest suggested an ecclesiastic separation, but she refused to consider it.

After seven miserable years, a humiliating move into the home of her in-laws, and a near-fatal illness, Elizabeth literally saw the light: she experienced a vision of a heart pierced by a heated dart. Feeling the presence of God's love, she concluded that He had called her to a particular mission and that she would abandon herself to it. She began to build a life for herself and her daughters, becoming an active member of the Trinitarian Third Order,[43] finding a modest apartment for her family, and making it a refuge for others who needed help. She developed a reputation for generosity, kindness, and miraculous powers. She always included Christopher in their daughters' lives, and he was at her bedside when she died.

The Trinitarians keep Elizabeth's feast day on February 4. Her relics at their church in Rome have been associated with many miracles.

The Genius of Elizabeth Canori Mora:
A well-known feminist has criticized Elizabeth's beatification for sending a message "that submissiveness is what counts." In truth, there was nothing submissive about Elizabeth unless you count her decision to submit to the will of God. Elizabeth believed that a vow she made before God could not be dissolved. She was determined to save her husband's soul and she succeeded. After her death, Christopher was ordained a Franciscan priest, and nine years later he died a holy death at the age of seventy-two.

Reflection:
"Then Peter approaching asked him, 'Lord, if my brother sins against me, how often must I forgive him? As many as seven times?'
"Jesus answered, 'I say to you, not seven times but seventy-seven times.'"
Matthew 18:21–22

SAINT JEANNE DE VALOIS, QUEEN
(Joan of France)

b. April 23, 1464, Nogent-le-Roi, France
d. February 4, 1505, Bourges, France

King Louis XI of France was desperate for a male heir but got Jeanne instead. She was born hunchbacked, lame, and so unattractive that he could not bear the sight of her. Jeanne was twenty-six days old when he arranged her betrothal to her two-year-old cousin Louis, son of the Duke of Orleans, then packed her off to be raised by the kindly Count and Countess of Linières.

When she was twelve, Jeanne returned to the royal court for her wedding. The Duchess of Orleans was shocked at her appearance, screamed, "Must my son marry this deformed girl?" and fainted. Louis later claimed that the king threatened to kill him and his mother if he did not go through with the wedding. Jeanne's marriage contract required Louis to visit her four times a year, but for the rest of the time he ignored her. When her father died, Louis lost a power struggle for the throne and was imprisoned for three years while Jeanne took care of everything and governed the Duchy of Orleans until she negotiated a pardon for him. In 1498 he finally inherited the crown of France, becoming King Louis XII. His first official act was to ask Rome to annul their marriage, citing his lack of consent and claiming that she was unable to consummate the marriage. Although Jeanne insisted that hers had been a valid marriage in every way, the Church granted the king his annulment.

Jeanne received a generous financial settlement, became the Duchess of Berry, and founded the Order of the Virgin Mary (Annunciades), which is still active today. When she died, Louis insisted on giving her a royal funeral. It is said that he knelt before her coffin, begged her pardon for the wrongs he had done her, and invoked her intercession. Her feast day is February 4.

The Genius of Jeanne de Valois:
Devoted to the Blessed Mother, Jeanne accepted her annulment ordeal in the spirit of the Annunciation, saying: *"Be it done to me and her own if so it is to be."*

Reflection:
"Your light must shine before others, that they may see your good deeds and glorify your heavenly Father."

Matthew 5:16

BLESSED MARIE RIVIER
(Marinette)

b. December 19, 1768, Montpezat-sous-Bauzon, Ardèche, France
d. February 3, 1838, Bourg-Saint-Andéol, Ardèche, France

Childhood illness left Marinette barely four feet tall and dependent on crutches, but she stood tall during the darkest days of the French Revolution. One priest who worked with her said that Marinette "acted like a pastor and preached as eloquently as a Jesuit." Pope Pius IX[44] called her the Woman Apostle.

Marinette felt called to serve God, and when her disability ruled out entering a religious order, she started a small parish school. Marinette might have lived out life as a simple country schoolteacher, but in 1789 France was swept up in a revolution that soon degenerated into the Reign of Terror. Convents were dissolved, churches were closed, and priests and nuns went to the guillotine. Marinette risked her life to lead the faithful at secret Sunday assemblies. When calm returned, she and five companions formed the Order of the Presentation of Mary, dedicated to educating young people and adults about their faith. In Marinette's words, they were *"bringing the fire of the knowledge and love of Jesus Christ everywhere."* None of them had much formal education, and they were often ridiculed for their presumption, but they attracted many vocations. By 1810 Marinette had opened forty-six schools. When asked how she managed to finance them, she smiled and pointed to a statue of the Blessed Mother, saying, *"I have never looked for money except in prayer, and it always came."*

Today the Sisters of the Presentation, also known as the White Ladies, are active in eighteen countries. They celebrate Marinette's feast on February 3.

The Genius of Maria Rivier:
Marinette urged her growing congregation: *"Learn to converse with God at the bottom of your heart."* And: *"Never do anything without consulting God first, and seek to do his will."*

Reflection:
"God chose the foolish of the world to shame the wise, and God chose the weak of the world to shame the strong, and God chose the lowly and despised of the world, those who count for nothing, to reduce to nothing those who are something, so that no human being might boast before God."
1 Corinthians 1:27–29

SAINT CATHERINE DEI RICCI

b. April 23, 1522, Florence, Italy
d. February 2, 1590, Prato, Italy

Catherine was born in a palace at the height of the Renaissance. She entered a Dominican convent but was considered so stupid and undisciplined that she barely made it to her final vows. As she matured, however, her dedication and humility won the respect of the entire community.

For twelve years, beginning in Lent, 1542, Catherine spent every Friday in a state of ecstasy (trance), as she relived Christ's journey to Calvary and manifested the stigmata. The head of the Dominican Order investigated and declared, "There is nothing to doubt about this soul, but everything to revere." Still dubious, Pope Paul III sent his own man, a cardinal, who also became convinced that Catherine's experience was authentic. She maintained an extensive correspondence with the spiritual leaders of her time, including Philip Neri,[45] a practical man not given to visions. Neri resided in Rome and Catherine was in Tuscany, but he claimed that she appeared to him and they conversed together at length. This meeting was sworn to by five witnesses and is mentioned in the bull of Philip Neri's canonization.

During the investigation that led to Catherine's own canonization, more than twenty nuns testified about the celestial fragrance that clung to her and lingered in the room where she died. Some compared this "odor of sanctity" to violets, but most could not liken it to anything on earth. Her incorrupt body is venerated at the basilica at Prato. The Dominican Order keeps her feast on February 4.

The Genius of Catherine dei Ricci:
Catherine ably governed her convent and warned her nuns against too much austerity: *"We are not to aim at dying, but at living to do good."*

Reflection:
"This, rather, is the fasting that I wish: / releasing those bound unjustly, / untying the thongs of the yoke; / Setting free the oppressed, / breaking every yoke; / Sharing your bread with the hungry, / sheltering the oppressed and the homeless; / Clothing the naked when you see them, / and not turning your back on your own."

Isaiah 58:6–7

SAINT VERDIANA

b. 1182, Castelfiorentino, Italy
d. February 1, 1242, Castelfiorentino, Italy

The saint who liked snakes was twelve when she went to work for an uncle. Impressed with her ability, he put her in charge of a warehouse where he stockpiled beans, a staple of Tuscan cuisine. When famine hit, he sold them at top price. Verdiana was unaware of this sale and distributed all the beans to the poor. Finding the warehouse empty, the buyer complained to her uncle, who complained to Verdiana. She prayed all night and the warehouse was refilled. Her delighted uncle bragged about his wonder-working niece and she was besieged with requests for more miracles. To escape such attention, Verdiana went on a pilgrimage. When she returned, the people begged her not to leave again. She agreed, if she could live as an anchorite (hermit). The town erected a small cell next to a church, and it became Verdiana's home for the next thirty-four years. Tradition has it that Francis of Assisi[46] visited Verdiana there. She advised another visitor, Cristiana of Santa Croce,[47] to return to her hometown and establish a convent there.

Verdiana shared her daily meal with two large snakes. If they didn't care for it, they would beat her unconscious, but when one was killed and the other ran away, Verdiana recognized that her own time was near. She received the last rites, then knelt before her window. Opening her Psalter to the Prayer of Repentance (Psalm 51), she fixed her eyes on heaven and gave up her spirit. It is said that Verdiana still works miracles and protects against fire and demonic possession. Her feast is kept on February 1.

The Genius of Verdiana

Verdiana saw every day as an opportunity to exercise Christian charity, and from her small anchorhold, her influence extended to an entire province.

Reflection:

"Have mercy on me, God, in your goodness; in your abundant compassion blot out my offense."

Psalm 51:1

BLESSED ELA FITZPATRICK

b. 1191, Amesbury, Wiltshire, England
d. August 24, 1261, Lacock, Wiltshire, England

Lacock Abbey is the site of Hogwarts Academy in the Harry Potter films, but few moviegoers know that the historic abbey was built by Ela, Countess of Salisbury and Sheriff of Wiltshire, or that she inherited her titles and vast estates from her father when she was seven years old.

Concerned about her safety, Ela's mother spirited her off to Normandy. At ten, Ela returned to England and King Richard arranged her marriage to his half-brother, William Longsword. William was called violent and unscrupulous, but he and Ela were happy together. While he was off on military adventures, she remained at the castle with their four sons and four daughters. Ela's only problem was her husband's casual approach to their faith, but that changed after a miraculous encounter at sea.

In 1219 William was returning from Egypt when his ship was caught in a three-day storm in the English Channel. Everyone aboard expected to die. In their darkest moment, a great shining light fell on the ship, as if the mainmast were in flames, and everyone aboard beheld a beautiful young woman. William was convinced that it was the Blessed Mother and that she had spared them. Meanwhile, he had been gone so long that even the king was sure he was dead and had pressured Ela to remarry. Ambitious noblemen courted her, but she turned them all away. Ela's loyalty was rewarded when William returned home with a strengthened faith. He told her about the vision at sea, and with her help he returned to the sacraments.

Together Ela and William helped build the cathedral at Salisbury and each laid a foundation stone. Widowed in 1226, she founded Hinton Priory for men and Lacock Abbey for women. She took the veil at Lacock and became abbess there in 1241. Ela is commemorated on February 1.

The Genius of Ela Fitzpatrick:

Like so many of the great Anglo-Saxon abbesses, Ela ruled an abbey the size of a small city, and she ruled it well. Her epitaph reminds us that she was "full of deeds of holy charity."

Reflection:

"If you desire wisdom, keep the commandments, / and the LORD *will bestow her upon you."*

Sirach 1:23

SAINT WALBURGA

b. 710, Dorsetshire, England
d. February 25, 779, Heidenheim, Germany

One of the most popular saints of the Middle Ages, Walburga still draws pilgrims to her shrine in Eichstätt, Germany, where a healing oil is said to flow from her bones.

Walburga was an Anglo-Saxon noblewoman who entered Wimborne Abbey at the age of eleven and eventually took the veil there as a Benedictine nun. She spent twenty-five years at Wimborne before joining her brothers Willibald and Wynnebald,[48] who were missionaries in Germany. By the time she died, Walburga was overseeing a double monastery at Heidenheim. One hundred years later, her grave was opened in order to transport her relics to a new shrine in Eichstätt. Her bones were found covered with an oil that has since been credited with miraculous powers.

Actually, Walburga had always been surrounded by miracles. She was once guided at night to the home of a dying girl. She stood in the darkness outside the house, not announcing her name or rank. When the girl's father saw Walburga, surrounded by his fierce guard dogs, he assumed that she was an intruder and warned her that she would be torn to pieces. Walburga answered that she was not afraid, that He who brought her there would take her safely home. The father realized that she was the holy abbess and welcomed her inside. Walburga spent the night praying beside the girl, and in the morning she was completely recovered. Walburga's miracles continued long after her death, and the miraculous oil still flows from her bones from October through February. The nuns at Eichstätt capture it in tiny flasks that they distribute to the faithful.

The Genius of Walburga:
According to the nuns at her shrine, Walburga's genius was in being "open to God, to his calling, to his guidance, to his demands so as to be ready in every situation to accept his plan."

Reflection:
"To do your will is my delight; / My God, your law is in my heart!"

Psalm 40:9

SAINT PAULA MONTAL FORNÉS

b. October 11, 1799, Arenys de Mar, Barcelona, Spain
d. February 26, 1889, Olesa de Montserrat, Barcelona, Spain

At the age of eleven, Paula went to work as a lace maker to help support her widowed mother and four younger siblings. She still found time to teach catechism in her parish, and through this work she discovered her gift for teaching.

Paula believed that a woman who was not well educated was not prepared for life. Women were the essential element in the transformation of society, especially through the family, yet there were few opportunities for poor women to obtain an education until Paula felt called to provide it. In 1829 she left her coastal village and opened a school for girls in the city of Figueras on the border between France and Spain. She was influenced by the work of Joseph Calasanz,[49] founder of the Order of the Pious Schools (Piarist Fathers). Working closely with the Piarist Fathers, Paula established a second school in her hometown of Arenys de Mar. By the time Paula established a third school, in Barcelona, she was ready to start a religious congregation. The Piarist Fathers helped her found the order now known as the Sisters of the Pious Schools (Escolapias). Like the Piarists, they take a fourth vow, to dedicate themselves to teaching.

When Paula took her final vows, she added the name of her patron saint, becoming Paula of Saint Joseph of Calasanz. Surprisingly, she was never elected to a leadership position in the order she founded but spent the next thirty years establishing more schools and mentoring the first 130 Escolapias. Today her congregation is active on four continents.

The Genius of Paula Montal Fornés:

> Calling for a *"civilization of love,"* Paula advised: *"We are bound to seek the tranquility and progress of society that are only possible with a transparent life, which is the life that God asks us to live."*

Reflection:

> *"Give alms from your possessions. Do not turn your face away from any of the poor, and God's face will not be turned away from you."*
>
> Tobit 4:7

Saint Anne Line

b. c. 1565, Dunmow, Essex, England
d. February 27, 1601, London, England

Many scholars believe that Shakespeare wrote his poem "The Phoenix and the Turtle" to commemorate the martyrdom of Anne Line. The phoenix and the turtle symbolize Anne and her husband, whose shared faith and love inspired everyone who knew them.

Born into a wealthy Calvinist family, Anne was disinherited when she converted to Catholicism. She married another convert, Roger Line, who had renounced an even greater fortune. Their queen, Elizabeth I, had barred Catholic priests from England under penalty of death, and faithful Catholics were risking their lives to hide priests in their homes and celebrate Mass in secret. Anne and Roger were attending a secret Mass when authorities arrived and arrested their young priest. Convicted of illegally entering England, he was disemboweled at Tyburn ten weeks later. Roger was exiled to Flanders, where he died of fever. Alone in London, her health failing, Anne took charge of a safe house for priests, managing their finances and fending off the curious. One grateful priest recalled that Anne was always "full of kindness, very discreet and possessed her soul in great peace." On February 2, 1601, she was arrested with two priests and sentenced to hang at Tyburn. Too weak to stand, she was carried to the scaffold in a chair. As she stepped up to the rope, she found strength to shout to the crowd: *"I am sentenced for harboring a Catholic priest and so far am I from repenting for having done so, that I wish, with all my soul, that where I have entertained one, I could have entertained thousands."*

Anne was canonized with the Forty Martyrs of England and Wales. She is a patron of childless women, converts, and widows.

The Genius of Anne Line:
Shakespeare saluted Anne and Roger as "hearts remote yet not asunder" because no distance could shake their commitment to their faith and each other.

Reflection:
"It does not concern me in the least that I be judged by you or any human tribunal; I do not even pass judgment on myself; I am not conscious of anything against me, but I do not thereby stand acquitted; the one who judges me is the Lord."

1 Corinthians 4:3–4

BLESSED VILLANA DE BOTTI

b. 1332, Florence, Italy
d. January 29, 1361, Florence, Italy

Villana was sixteen years old when the Black Plague swept Florence, killing more than 100,000 people. Most of those who survived abandoned themselves to the pleasures of the world. A few, like Villana, were drawn to religion, but when she began to talk about a religious vocation, her wealthy father quickly arranged her marriage.

Villana embraced married life, losing herself in a whirl of clothes, jewels, and parties. Then one night while seated before a mirror, preparing for yet another gala ball, Villana saw a horrifying face reflected back at her. She moved from room to room, but every mirror in her palace reflected the same terrible face. She knew that she was looking at her soul, which had been corrupted by her decadent lifestyle. Villana never made it to the ball that night. Instead, she exchanged her fine gown for her simplest cloak and hurried to the nearby church of Santa Maria Novella to make a sincere confession. In the days that followed, she began distributing food and clothing to the poor in the square in front of the church, and volunteered in the Franciscan hospital nearby.

Villana dedicated herself to studying Scripture and contemplating the Crucifixion. Her father disapproved, but when he lost his fortune and his health, Villana took him in and nursed him until his death. Villana did not have much time left herself, but she begged her confessor not to pray for her recovery. She was consoled by a vision of Catherine of Alexandria (November 25), who assured Villana that she was holding a crown for her in heaven.

Villana died at the age of twenty-nine. So many people wanted to pay their respects that her body remained on display for thirty-seven days. It is said that Villana promised to send one friend flowers from heaven, and when the woman bent over Villana's coffin, a shower of flowers fell from the sky.

The Genius of Villana de Botti:
    Daring to reject conspicuous consumption, Villana redeemed herself by caring for the material needs of those less fortunate.

Reflection:
    "They are your servants, your people, whom you freed by your great might and your strong hand."

Nehemiah 1:10

February 29

BLESSED ANTONIA OF FLORENCE
(Antoinette)

b. 1401, Florence, Italy
d. February 28, 1472, L'Aquila, Italy

Antonia, who came from a prominent family, had been widowed twice by the time she was twenty-seven years old. Concluding that marriage was not for her, she entered the Franciscan community that had recently been founded by Angelina of Montegiove (July 15). Angelina created one of the first Third Order communities for women, and for a time this was exactly what Antonia needed. She spent two years studying with Angelina in Florence. As Angelina's community expanded, Antonia took on more responsibility. She transferred first to their convent in Foligno, then became superior of the convent in L'Aquila, in central Italy, where she remained for thirteen years.

Something was lacking, however. Antonia was looking for a Rule that demanded more of her. In L'Aquila, the Franciscan John Capistrano[50] became her spiritual director and she confided her concerns to him. He encouraged Antonia to found a new convent following the austere Rule of the Poor Clares. Antonia served as abbess of the new convent for seven years. In spite of the rigorous life, the convent grew to include one hundred women.

Antonia was an invalid for the last fifteen years of her life, but she bore her trials bravely. Since her death, her body has remained incorrupt. For four hundred years it was venerated at the convent in L'Aquila, but the convent and the relic have since moved to nearby Paganica.

Antonia is honored by the Franciscan Order on February 28.

The Genius of Antonia of Florence:
She continually sought new challenges.

Reflection:
"Tell the rich in the present age not to be proud and not to rely on so uncertain a thing as wealth but rather on God, who richly provides us with all things for our enjoyment. Tell them to do good, to be rich in good works, to be generous, ready to share, thus accumulating as treasure a good foundation for the future, so as to win the life that is true life."

1 Timothy 6:17–19

69

BLESSED GIOVANNA MARIA BONOMO
(Jane)

b. August 15, 1606, Asiago, Vicenza, Italy
d. March 1, 1670, Bassano del Grappa, Italy

When Giovanna played the violin, people would stand outside her monastery just to listen. But she was also a controversial mystic who was severely punished by her local bishop.

Giovanna was only two years old when her father killed a man in a jealous rage. He went to prison for two years and emerged a better man. He became Giovanna's most generous supporter when she entered a Benedictine monastery.

Soon after making religious vows, Giovanna began experiencing visions and ecstasies, but what really disturbed the bishop was Giovanna's belief that salvation could come only through abandoning oneself completely to God. He ordered Giovanna to burn all her writings. For seven years she was not allowed to write to her father or speak to anyone outside the monastery. Nevertheless, her community elected her abbess in 1652 and, like many of the great mystics, she proved to be an outstanding manager. She received many gifts and contributions, and distributed the best of them to the needy, saying: *"Does it seem right to give the worst to the poor?"*

Soon after Giovanna died peacefully, the bishop's representative arrived, determined to break up the crowds that had come to venerate her. He was furious to hear people already talking about her as a saint. "What saint?" he demanded. "She is a nun like all the others." The crowd erupted, threatened to stone him, and forced him to flee. Today, Giovanna is venerated at the church of Blessed Maria Giovanna Bonomo in Asiago.

The Genius of Giovanna Maria Bonomo:
Refusing to brood about her problems, she prayed: *"Do, O my Lord, think about it for me, for I will not let my thoughts dwell on it, and if it be pleasing to You, I wish to think of nothing else but You."*

Reflection:
"There is nothing hidden except to be made visible; nothing is secret except to come to light. Anyone who has ears to hear ought to hear."

Mark 4:22

March 2

SAINT ANGELA DE LA CRUZ
(María de los Angeles Guerrero González, Angelita)

b. January 30, 1846, Seville, Spain
d. March 2, 1932, Seville, Spain

Like so many saints, Angelita found that her life unfolded in unexpected ways. She left school at the age of twelve to work in a shoe factory. She later tried life with two different religious orders, but neither experience worked out. She returned to the factory, declaring that if she could not become a nun in a convent, *"I will be a nun in the world."* Her sympathetic pastor advised her to keep a journal, which she did for the next two years, gradually discerning that she was called to build a congregation dedicated to serving the poor. At the age of twenty-nine, she left the factory for good to concentrate on building this congregation. Two months later, she moved into a small rented house with three like-minded women. They called themselves the Company of the Cross, spending their time at home in prayer and silent meditation, but always on call, day and night, to assist the poor and the dying. Angelita considered them angels who had been called to be *"poor with the poor in order to bring them to Christ."*

Many people doubted that her community could survive entirely on alms, but for Angelita that dependence on charity was a key element in their spirituality. She called it *"the charity of urgency . . . which brings help to the one who needs it at that moment."* By the time Angelita died peacefully at the age of eighty-six, the Company of the Cross had spread throughout Spain, Italy, and Argentina and they continue their work today.

The Genius of Madre Angelita:

Angelita knew that God had a plan for her, but it took patience to discern it. In life's difficult moments, it is important to remember that God has a plan for us, too.

Reflection:

"Whoever wishes to be great among you will be your servant; whoever wishes to be first among you will be the slave of all. For the Son of Man did not come to be served but to serve and to give his life as a ransom for many."

Mark 10:44–45
(words of Christ often cited by Madre Angelita)

72

Saint Katharine Mary Drexel

b. November 26, 1858, Philadelphia, Pennsylvania
d. March 3, 1955, Cornwell Heights, Pennsylvania

Katharine Drexel was a Philadelphia debutante from a wealthy family and her decision to become a nun made national news. Born shortly before the Civil War, she came of age during Reconstruction. Her mother died when she was an infant, but Katharine's father and her beloved stepmother brought up Katharine and her two sisters with a strong social conscience. The family often visited reservations and missions in the western states, where she saw firsthand the suffering of displaced Native Americans and former slaves.

In 1887, after the death of her parents, Katharine and her sisters traveled to Europe. They were granted a private audience with Pope Leo XIII,[51] who shared Katharine's interest in social issues. She told him about America's need for missionaries and he asked, "Why don't you become a missionary yourself?" That question haunted her when she returned to Philadelphia. Katharine came to consider it an invitation from God to devote herself to the Indians and African Americans. She founded the order now known as the Sisters of the Blessed Sacrament, and during the fifty years until her death Katharine established nearly sixty schools for Native Americans and African Americans. One of her greatest achievements was the founding of Xavier University in New Orleans, which today sends more African American graduates to medical schools than any other university in the country.

The Genius of Katharine Drexel:
She advises: *"Manifest yourself. You have no time to occupy your thoughts with that complacency or consideration of what others will think. Your business is simply, 'What will my Father in heaven think?'"*

Reflection:
"If anyone says 'I love God,' but hates his brother, he is a liar; for whoever does not love a brother whom he has seen cannot love God whom he has not seen. This is the commandment we have from Him: whoever loves God must also love his brother."

1 John 4:20–21

March 4

✧

Saint Teresa Eustochio Verzeri

b. July 31, 1801, Bergamo, Italy
d. March 3, 1852, Brescia, Italy

In the beginning, Teresa had great trouble committing to her vocation. She entered the local Benedictine convent three times but always left before taking final vows. The first time, everyone agreed that she was too young. The second time, she left to start a school in a small mountain village, but the school failed. Finally, Teresa left to devote herself to educating poor girls, and at last she had found her calling.

Teresa was ahead of her time, tolerant in her methods, and sensitive to individuality. She recommended that the young be allowed *"a holy freedom so that they may do so willingly, and with full agreement that which, oppressed by command, would only be accomplished as a burden and with violence."* She kept her schools open on weekends and holidays to provide a safe place for recreation.

The bishop of Bergamo supported Teresa at first but later opposed her innovations and assured her that he did not need a new order. Teresa persisted and founded the Daughters of the Sacred Heart of Jesus. Devotion to the Sacred Heart was new and still somewhat controversial, but Teresa saw the Sacred Heart as the source of all love.

During epidemics, Teresa turned her schools into temporary hospitals. As her mission expanded, she stayed in touch with her Daughters by letters, more than three thousand of which are in the convent archives in Brescia. In one she wrote: *"To you and to your institute, Jesus Christ has given the precious gift of his Heart, for from no one else can you learn holiness, he being the inexhaustible source of true holiness."* Her life had a great influence on Frances Cabrini (November 13), who was educated by the Daughters and grew up hearing stories about Teresa's work. Today the Daughters are active in Europe, Africa, and South America. Her feast day is celebrated on March 3.

The Genius of Teresa Verzeri:

Teresa reminds us: *"True charity grows in vigor and conquers through patience."*

Reflection:

"Not many of you should become teachers, my brothers, for you realize that we will be judged more strictly, for we all fall short in many respects."

James 3:1–2

THE BLESSED MARTYRS OF LAVAL

Françoise Mézière
d. February 5–June 25, 1794, Mayenne, France

Françoise Trehet
d. February 5–June 25, 1794, Mayenne, France

Jeanne Véron
d. February 5–June 25, 1794, Mayenne, France

Marie Monica Lhuilier
d. February 5–June 25, 1794, Mayenne, France

Among the Martyrs of Laval were four women who had little in common except a shared faith and commitment to public service. During the French Revolution, a court convicted them of resisting the new anti-Christian government and sentenced them to the guillotine.

The first one executed was **Françoise Mézière,** a laywoman who cofounded a free school and supervised it for nineteen years. She was followed to the guillotine by **Françoise Trehet** and **Jeanne Véron,** Sisters of Charity of Our Lady of Evron, who continued to teach and care for the sick even after their order was suppressed. Françoise and Jeanne were accused of nursing monarchists, and Françoise answered that they cared for the sick because they were all brothers in Christ. Jeanne, crippled by dropsy, was carried to the guillotine on a stretcher. The last martyr, **Marie Lhuilier,** was a member of the Hospital Canonesses of the Mercy of Jesus. She too had devoted her life to the sick, and according to her order, "her crime was her refusal to surrender her habit."

The Martyrs of Laval also included fourteen priests and one layman. They are commemorated together on June 19.

The Genius of the Martyrs of Laval:
They remained steadfastly loyal to their faith and their God.

Reflection:
"This wise virgin has chosen the better part for herself; it shall not be taken away from her."
Luke 10:42, Communion antiphon for Memorial Mass for Marie Lhuilier

SAINT AGNES OF PRAGUE
(Agnes of Bohemia)

b. June 20, 1211, Prague, Bohemia (Czech Republic)
d. March 6, 1282, Prague, Bohemia (Czech Republic)

Ottokar, king of Bohemia, arranged for his daughter Agnes to marry Frederick II, emperor of Germany. After Ottokar's death, his son, King Wenceslaus III, intended to go through with the arrangement, but Agnes had other ideas. She wanted to take a vow of holy poverty and enter the Poor Clare convent in Prague. She convinced Pope Gregory IX to intervene and he declared that the princess did not have to marry the emperor. Frederick acknowledged defeat, declaring that if Agnes had preferred an earthly king, he would have avenged himself with a sword, but since she had chosen the King of Kings he could not object.

Clare of Assisi (August 11) wrote to congratulate Agnes: *"What you hold, may you continue to hold, what you do, may you keep doing and not stop, but with swift pace, nimble step, and feet that do not stumble."* This launched a remarkable correspondence that lasted until Clare's death, although they never met face-to-face. Agnes continued to assert her strong will, even challenging the pope when he disagreed with her commitment to holy poverty. She embraced the Franciscan ideal and insisted that she and her convent must own nothing. The Holy See, however, was never comfortable with this position. After Agnes dispensed with her royal dowry by building a hospital in Prague, Gregory IX issued a bull forcing her convent to treat the hospital as its property. Agnes did not want any such endowment, and for three years she bombarded the pope with letters until he bowed to her request and withdrew his order, conferring the Privilege of Poverty on Agnes and her Poor Clares.

The Genius of Agnes of Prague:

Wars and the descent of the Iron Curtain delayed Agnes's canonization for seven hundred years, but she was finally proclaimed a saint on November 12, 1989. Celebrations in Czechoslovakia launched a six-week period known as the Velvet Revolution, which ended forty years of Communist rule there without firing a single shot.

Reflection:

"For freedom Christ set us free; so stand firm and do not submit again to the yoke of slavery."

Galatians 5:1

SAINT FELICITY AND SAINT PERPETUA

d. 203, Carthage (Tunis)

Perpetua was still nursing her infant son and Felicity was about to give birth when they were arrested with a small group of catechumens who had been preparing to become Christians. At first, they were guarded in a private house. Perpetua's pagan father visited her there and tried to change her mind. She pointed to a water jug and said: *"Can that vessel, change its name?"* He said no, and she replied: *"Nor can I call myself any other than I am, a Christian."* Later, Perpetua and Felicity and their companions took the final step and were baptized.

On the day of their trial, Perpetua's father brought her son and urged her to think about him. This broke Perpetua's heart, but she told her father that it was God's will and not her choice. The next day the pagan judge ordered her to offer a sacrifice for the prosperity of the Roman emperors. She still refused. "Are you then a Christian?" he asked. She answered, *"Yes, I am,"* and was condemned to face the wild animals in the arena.

Felicity gave birth in prison and her daughter was adopted by a Christian woman. Three days later, she and Perpetua and their companions were led to the arena. This spectacle was the main event in a great celebration honoring the emperor's son. The guards tried to force Perpetua and her companions to dress up as the gods of Carthage, but Perpetua, who had become the leader of the Christian prisoners, absolutely refused. They were willing to be martyred for their faith, she said, but they would do so dressed as Christians.

The Genius of Felicity and Perpetua:

Perpetua recorded the events leading up to their deaths in a journal that was carefully preserved. Her account is considered one of the first pieces of writing by a Christian woman. For centuries it was read aloud at Mass on the anniversary of their martyrdom. Pilgrims still pray in the ruins of the amphitheater in Carthage, as Pope John Paul II did in 1996.

Reflection:

"God so loved the world that he gave his only Son, so that everyone who believes in him might not perish but might have eternal life."

John 3:16

March 8

SAINT CUNEGUNDA THE EMPRESS

d. March 3, 1033, Karffungen, Germany

Cunegunda and her husband, Henry II,[52] also known as Henry the Good, were happy together, although he once made her walk barefoot and blindfolded over red-hot plowshares to prove that she was faithful. Her own power was so great that when Henry was elected king of the Germans, Cunegunda was crowned queen in a separate ceremony. Two years later she and Henry traveled together to Rome, where they were simultaneously crowned emperor and empress.

Their childless marriage puzzled outsiders, and Henry was not immune to gossip. When his enemies accused Cunegunda of adultery, she was forced into the plowshares ordeal. She emerged unscathed, shaming her accusers and proving that she was under divine protection. Henry made generous amends. For him, at least, having Cunegunda as his wife and trusted adviser was more important than having heirs. Cunegunda encouraged him to found the bishopric of Bamberg, and it was said that Cunegunda's silk threads defended the city around it better than walls or towers. After Henry's death in 1025, she oversaw his empire for a year until his successor could be elected, then she retired to a convent.

Eight years later, as Cunegunda lay dying, she was horrified to see that a cloth of gold had been prepared to cover her. She insisted that it be removed. Once assured that she would be buried in the traditional coarse brown cloth of an ordinary sister, Cunegunda passed away in peace. Her body was carried to the cathedral at Bamberg to rest beside that of her husband. Cunegunda's feast was formerly on March 3, but she and Henry now share July 13. They are considered patrons of childless couples.

The Genius of Cunegunda the Empress:
In bowing to the will of God, Cunegunda accepted her childless state. She and her husband grew in their love for each other and found fulfillment in caring for many orphaned children.

Reflection:
"Admire not how sinners live, / but trust in the LORD *and wait for his light."*
Sirach 11:21

SAINT FRANCES OF ROME

b. c. 1387, Rome, Italy
d. March 9, 1440, Rome, Italy

Frances was very young and devout when she married into one of the most prominent families in Rome. Her in-laws found her piety hilarious, but her husband, Lorenzo, defended her and they grew to love Frances as much as he did. She gave birth to two sons and a daughter, John Baptist, John Evangelist, and Agnes. After the death of her mother-in-law, Frances became mistress of a large household. These responsibilities forced her to cut back her religious activities and she acknowledged: "A *married woman must, when called upon, quit her devotions to God at the altar, to find him in her household affairs.*"

Frances's troubles began in 1409 when Rome was invaded, then wracked by a civil war. Her husband was banished. Enemies tried to take John Baptist hostage, but he escaped and joined his father in exile. Famine was followed by a plague that claimed John Evangelist. Their palace was destroyed, and Frances and her sister-in-law Vanozza built a hospital in the ruins, often bringing in victims in their arms. One morning after John Evangelist had been dead about a year, Frances suddenly saw him in front of her, accompanied by a beautiful angel. He told her how happy he was but warned her to prepare to surrender Agnes next. After promising Frances that the angel would remain as her companion, John the Evangelist disappeared. Agnes died of the plague, but Frances was consoled by the return of her husband and John Baptist and by the angel who remained visible to her until the day she died.

In 1425 Frances founded the Oblates of Mary of Tor de'Specchi, and when widowed she took the veil with them. Guided by the light of her guardian angel, she moved around her city at night, performing good works. For that reason, she was declared a patron of motorists in 1925.

The Genius of Frances of Rome:
In a time of terrible calamities, Frances balanced duty to her extended family with service to her community. Her motto was always: "*God's will is mine.*"

Reflection:
"*The* LORD *gave and the* LORD *has taken away; / blessed be the name of the* LORD!"

Job 1:21

BLESSED EUGÉNIE MILLERET DE BROU

b. August 25, 1817, Metz, Moselle, France
d. March 10, 1898, Auteuil, Hauts-de-Seine, France

Eugénie was born in the family castle. Her father was a prominent politician, but by the time she was thirteen he had lost his fortune and her parents had divorced. Her father and brother moved to Switzerland, while Eugénie accompanied her mother to Paris. Five years later, her mother was dead of cholera.

Until then Eugénie had been indifferent to religion. Her friends and family regarded the Catholic Church as part of the Old Regime. Eugénie shared these beliefs, but at the age of twenty, she was deeply moved by a Lenten sermon at Notre Dame cathedral. For the first time, she felt a profound desire to know God. She began studying theology with Father Marie-Theodore Combalot, who saw her potential before Eugénie saw it herself. With his support, she founded the Sisters of the Assumption of Mary (Assumption Sisters), dedicated to educating young women. Summarizing her philosophy, Eugénie wrote: *"How great it would be if characters were imbued with the power of the Gospel; if souls were set on fire with zeal for God's truth, and with the desire that his kingdom should come; if the wisdom revealed by the Son of God himself, and the knowledge of all united to him, became the philosophy, the principles, the end of all education!"* The motto of her Assumption Sisters became "Thy Kingdom Come."

Eugénie proved to be a brilliant teacher and she advised: *"To educate is to allow the good to break through the rock that imprisons it and bring it to the light where it can blossom and shed its radiance."* Her students mastered both science and culture and emerged as well-rounded women who were prepared to play a serious role in society. Today the Assumption Sisters are at work in twenty-nine countries on four continents.

The Genius of Eugénie Milleret de Brou:

Eugénie could write: *"I believe that each one of us has a mission on this earth. We must seek how God can use each of us for the spread and the realization of the Gospel."*

Reflection:

"As Christ's sufferings overflow to us, so through Christ does our encouragement also overflow."

2 Corinthians 1:5

March 11

Saint Teresa Margaret Redi
(Teresa Margaret of the Sacred Heart)

b. September 1, 1747, Arezzo, Tuscany, Italy
d. March 7, 1770, Florence, Tuscany, Italy

Is it possible that Teresa Margaret was "too good to live"? Her confessor wrote that souls like hers "seem unable to continue to live much longer naturally. So, in accord with the usual way of God's providence, they tend to be called early into the better world."

Born into a noble family, she entered a Discalced Carmelite monastery at the age of seventeen, taking her religious name in honor of Teresa of Avila (October 15) and Margaret Mary Alacoque (October 16). When not at work in the convent infirmary, she was at prayer, determined *"to love for all those who do not know how to love."* She abandoned herself completely to God's love, writing, *"Always receive with equal contentment from God's hand either consolations or sufferings, peace or distress, health or illness. Ask nothing, refuse nothing, but always be ready to do and to suffer anything that comes from His Providence."* She wanted only to be fully united with Christ and to love Him for all eternity. With that in mind, an elderly nun who was near death promised to ask Him to allow Teresa Margaret to join her quickly. Four months later, Teresa Margaret followed her to the grave. An agonizing eighteen-hour siege of peritonitis had left Teresa Margaret's body swollen and discolored, but hours after her death it returned to its former beauty and remains incorrupt at her monastery today. The Carmelites celebrate her feast on September 1.

The Genius of Teresa Margaret Redi:

One need not accomplish great things to become a saint. One biographer wrote that Teresa Margaret "saw fit to pray wherever she happened to be. She made a cell of her heart and whether she conversed with others, was on her way somewhere, or in the midst of the thousand inevitable distractions of everyday life, she had the art of retiring within herself and of hiding herself in God."

Reflection:

"God is greater than our hearts and knows everything. Beloved, if [our] hearts do not condemn us, we have confidence in God and receive from him whatever we ask, because we keep his commandments and do what pleases him."
1 John 3:20–22

March 12

SAINT FINA CIARDI

(Seraphina of San Gimignano)

b. 1238, San Gimignano, Italy
d. March 12, 1253, San Gimignano, Italy

The Saint of the Violets grew up in a city torn by gang wars. When a street fight broke out between the Guelphs and the Ghibellines, no one was safe. Her widowed mother was killed while watching a gang battle from her doorway, leaving Fina destitute.

From the age of ten, Fina had been paralyzed from the neck down, spending her days flat on her back on an oak plank, her world confined to a sparsely furnished upstairs room. If she was left alone, mice and rats gnawed at her sores. Yet Fina never complained and was always gentle, loving, and concerned about others. With the loss of her mother, she depended on a neighbor, Beldia, who nursed her in spite of her own withered hand. It was clear that the girl did not have long to live, and she drew comfort from a dream about Gregory the Great,[53] who told her that he would bring her rest. Fina died on his feast day and, according to local legend, she went directly to heaven, outraging the demons that had hoped to claim her. Furious at losing their prize, they rocked the town, filling the air with terrifying whirlwinds. This uproar was cut short by the bells of San Gimignano, rung by invisible angelic hands, testifying to Fina's holiness. When Beldia lifted Fina's body from the board where she had lain for so long, the wood was covered with white violets. Beldia touched them and her withered hand was healed. Soon more violets sprouted on the watchtowers and at her tomb. To this day, the people of San Gimignano call them Saint Fina's flowers.

The Genius of Fina Ciardi:

Resigning herself to the will of God, Fina patiently endured unspeakable pain while showing compassion for the poor and suffering.

Reflection:

"You nourished your people with food of angels / and furnished them bread from heaven, ready to hand, untoiled-for, / endowed with all delights and conforming to every taste."

Wisdom 16:20

March 13

SAINT AGNES KOU YING TSAO
(Agnes Cao Guiyang)

b. 1821, Wujiazhai, Guizhou, China
d. March 1, 1856, Su-Lik-Hien, Guanxi, China

The first Catholic woman martyred in China, Agnes was born into a devout family, but after the death of her parents she married a widower who was ten years older. He treated her badly, starved her, and forbade her to pray. Agnes left him but returned to nurse him in his final illness. When he died, her in-laws threw her out of the house.

Agnes was struggling to support herself when she met Auguste Chapdelaine,[54] a French missionary priest who was impressed with her knowledge of Scripture and the catechism. He asked her to move to Guanxi in southwest China to provide religious instruction for the thirty or so Catholic families residing there. Working closely with a layman, Laurence Bai Xiaoman, Agnes traveled to other villages to give religious instruction. She was arrested in Yaojiaguan with Chapdelaine and Laurence Bai. Chapdelaine was beaten and tortured, then beheaded, and his remains were fed to wild dogs. Next, Laurence was beheaded. Agnes still refused to deny her faith. Confined to a cage and forced to stand day and night for three days, she finally expired.

She was canonized in 2000 with the Martyrs of China.[55] Her feast day is March 1.

The Genius of Agnes Kou Ying Tsao:
Steadfast and courageous, Agnes remained faithful in spite of torture. When sent to the cage and certain death, she responded, *"Even at death's door I will not deny my God."*

Reflection:
"[Jesus said to his disciples] Love your enemies, do good to those who hate you, bless those who curse you, pray for those who mistreat you. To the person who strikes you on one cheek, offer the other one as well, and from the person who takes your cloak, do not withhold even your tunic."

Luke 6:27–30

SAINT MATILDA QUEEN OF SAXONY
(Maud)

b. c. 895, Engern, Westphalia, Saxony
d. March 14, 968, Quedlinburg, Saxony

The founder of the Saxon dynasty was called Henry the Fowler because he loved hunting with hawks, which is what he was doing when he first saw Matilda. Henry was so smitten with the young noblewoman that he had his marriage annulled and proceeded to marry her. Five years later he was elected duke, then crowned King Henry I of Germany, and Matilda became queen. In spite of the questionable beginning, their marriage was a happy one. For seventeen years, Matilda wielded a good influence over Henry and he helped her in all her charities. On his deathbed, Henry thanked Matilda for restraining his anger, leading him to govern with justice and mercy, and always admonishing him to take the part of the oppressed. He left her in charge of his vast estates and their five children.

Alas, Matilda tried to block her oldest son, Otto, who was in line to succeed his father. She had always favored Otto's younger brother, Henry, because, it is said, Henry closely resembled his father. Matilda claimed that since Henry was the first son born after their father became king, he was the rightful heir. Her ploy failed, and Otto was crowned king in 936. Three years later, the brothers were at war until Matilda intervened and got Otto to make Henry duke of Bavaria. The reconciled brothers then turned on their mother and accused her of bankrupting the kingdom with her charities. To keep peace, Matilda renounced her inherited estates and retired to a villa in Westphalia. A few years later, Otto's wife, Adelaide (December 16), insisted on a reconciliation. The sons made a public apology and Matilda returned to the royal court. Many of her descendants became saints, including her great-grandson, Emperor Henry II, and his wife, Cunegunda (March 8).

The Genius of Matilda of Saxony:
Matilda's marriage began under a cloud, and she was far from a perfect mother, but her generous, compassionate spirit enabled her to overcome her mistakes.

Reflection:
"Be angry but do not sin; do not let the sun set on your anger, and do not leave room for the devil."

Ephesians 4:26

March 15

SAINT LOUISE DE MARILLAC

b. August 12, 1591, Ferrieres-en-Brie, France
d. March 15, 1660, Paris, France

Louise was born out of wedlock and her mother died soon after. Her father provided generously for her material needs, but by the time she was twenty-two, he was also dead. Louise's prominent relatives arranged her marriage to a young court official. The marriage was happy and after the birth of her son, Louise balanced motherhood, an active social life, and a commitment to charity. In 1621 her husband's health began to fail, and Louise nursed him through a difficult four-year illness. His death left her emotionally drained.

By then she had met Vincent de Paul[56] and become his chief collaborator. Vincent had organized the Ladies of Charity, noblewomen who gave money and time, but he needed women willing to do hands-on care. Louise recruited unpretentious country girls, called them the Daughters of Charity, and trained them herself. She successfully navigated class differences between the Ladies and the Daughters and advised them all: *"May you never take the attitude of merely getting the task done. You must show [the poor] affection; serving them from the heart—inquiring of them what they need; speaking to them gently and compassionately; procuring necessary help for them without being too bothersome or too eager."*

Louise's congregation, known today as the Daughters of Charity of St Vincent de Paul, has become the largest religious order in the world. John XXIII declared her the patron saint of social workers.

The Genius of Louise de Marillac:
"Vincent's reputation made the work possible, but it was Louise's sheer competence in organization and training her young women that made the movement a success," writes Kathleen Jones, author of *Women Saints*. Louise advises: *"Prudence consists in speaking about important matters only."*

Reflection:
"Be merciful, just as [also] your Father is merciful. Stop judging and you will not be judged. Stop condemning and you will not be condemned. Forgive and you will be forgiven."

Luke 6:36–37

SAINT EUSEBIA OF HAMAY

b. c. 637, Flanders

d. 680, Hamay, Belgium

Eusebia was the third in a line of remarkably headstrong women. Her mother, Rictrude,[57] was the daughter of a Visigoth king who became a Christian when she married Adalbald, a Frankish prince who had defeated her tribe. After Adalbald was murdered by her relatives when Eusebia was about eight years old, Rictrude moved her children to the security of a monastery she built at Marchiennes on the Scarpe River.

Adalbald's mother, Gertrude the Elder,[58] had already founded a monastery on the opposite side of the river at Hamay. Rictrude allowed Eusebia to live with Gertrude, who groomed her to inherit Hamay. When Gertrude died, Eusebia succeeded her, and the nuns and monks at Hamay accepted their twelve-year-old abbess. Rictrude, however, thought that Eusebia was too young to be her own mistress, much less to govern others. She repeatedly ordered her to return to Marchiennes. Eusebia refused. Rictrude finally had to request a *lettre de cachet* from the king to compel her daughter to join her at Marchiennes.

Eusebia crossed the river, in a procession with the entire population of Hamay. She still missed her abbey and at night would slip away to sing prayers in her own chapel there. Rictrude ordered her to stop, and when Eusebia continued to visit Hamay, Rictrude had a young man beat her with a stick. It snapped and fell to the ground, immediately took root, and eventually grew into a stately tree. This miracle forced Rictrude to yield and Eusebia was allowed to return to Hamay.

The Genius of Eusebia of Hamay:

Eusebia defied her mother, but for a good cause. In spite of her youth, she became an excellent abbess who governed wisely. It was said that she lived "the life of an angel on earth."

Reflection:

"There is an appointed time for everything, / and a time for every affair under the heavens."

Ecclesiastes 3:1

SAINT GERTRUDE OF NIVELLES

b. 626, Landen, Belgium
d. March 17, 659, Nivelles, Belgium

Gertrude is a patron of cats and gardens and a guardian against mice and rats. In the Middle Ages, artists represented her with mice running up her cloak or staff. They symbolized the suffering souls in purgatory who were under her protection.

Gertrude's father, Pepin, had advised three generations of kings. After his death, her mother, Itta,[59] erected a double monastery at Nivelles and put Gertrude in charge. They welcomed many pilgrims, and Gertrude even gave the saintly Irish brothers Foillan and Ultan[60] land upon which to build their own monastery at Fosses. Foillan commuted to Nivelles to celebrate Mass and instruct the monks and nuns in chants and Scripture. Gertrude herself knew the Bible by heart. After the death of her mother, she delegated practical management of Nivelles to a small committee of nuns and monks while she concentrated on spiritual matters. Her health was failing, and at thirty-two she stepped down, allowing her twenty-year-old niece Wilfetrude[61] to succeed her as abbess. When a pilgrim at Fosse learned that Gertrude was dying, he sent word that she should fear nothing, for Saint Patrick[62] was already with God and waiting to welcome her in glory. Gertrude died on Patrick's feast day.

The Genius of Gertrude of Nivelles:

Gertrude lived with her mother in perfect harmony—something many contemporary mothers and daughters might pray for.

Reflection:

"Wisdom has built her house . . . she calls / from the heights out over the city: / 'Let whoever is simple turn in here; / to him who lacks understanding, I say, / Come, eat of my food, / and drink of the wine I have mixed! / Forsake foolishness that you might live; / advance in the ways of understanding. . . . / For by me your days will be multiplied / and the years of your life increased.'"

Proverbs 9:1, 3–6, 11

BLESSED MARTHE LE BOUTEILLER
(Aimée-Adèle Le Bouteiller)

b. December 2, 1816, Percy, Manche, France
d. March 18, 1883, Saint-Sauveur-le-Vicomte, Manche, France

Adèle grew up in a small rural village, helping her widowed mother run the family farm and later working as a housemaid. She still found time to volunteer in her parish school, and she always joined in the parish's annual pilgrimage to the ancient shrine of Our Lady of Chapelle-sur-Vire.

On the pilgrimage route in 1841, Adèle visited the abbey at Saint-Sauveur-le-Vicomte. Built by Benedictines in the tenth century, the abbey had been confiscated during the Revolution and allowed to go to ruin. It was scheduled for demolition when Julie Postel (July 16) purchased the property for her Sisters of the Christian Schools in 1832. When Adèle visited, the eighty-four-year-old foundress was still on the scene and actively supervising the massive restoration. Adèle was drawn to Julie's spirituality and asked to be admitted to the order. She was received by Julie Postel herself and took the name Marthe. Her novice-mistress was Placide Viel (March 26).

Marthe was assigned to the convent kitchen, then the fields, and finally the wine cellar where she spent the next forty years distilling wine and cider for the Sisters, servants, and laborers. In the tradition of monastic hospitality, the Sisters also offered their wine and cider to any visitors passing through. Marthe distributed wine to as many as 250 people a day. During the Franco-Prussian War, when the abbey's supplies were almost gone, Marthe hung a picture of the Blessed Mother in the distillery and prayed intensely. From that moment the cider and other supplies never ran out. She truly earned her nickname, "Sister Cider."

The Genius of Marthe Le Bouteiller:
Marthe's was a hidden life during which she lived Julie Postel's maxim: *"Let us do the most good possible while being as hidden as possible."*

Reflection:
"Be doers of the word and not hearers only, deluding yourself. For if anyone is a hearer of the word and not a doer, he is like a man who looks at his own face in a mirror. He sees himself, then goes off and promptly forgets what he looked like."

James 1:22–24

Blessed Annunciata Cocchetti

b. May 19, 1800, Rovato, Brescia, Italy
d. March 23, 1882, Cemmo di Capo di Ponte, Brescia, Italy

Annunciata was orphaned at the age of seven. Her two brothers went to live with an uncle in Milan while Annunciata was raised by her beloved grandmother. She grew up with *"a passion to educate"* and at twenty-two was running a school. Annunciata expected to join the order founded by Magdalene of Canossa (May 8), but after her grandmother died, her uncle insisted that she come to live in Milan before she made such a commitment.

The six years Annunciata spent in Milan only strengthened her vocation, and in 1831 she accepted an invitation to supervise a school in Cemmo. Father Luca Passi and a devout noblewoman, Erminia Panzerini, had founded the school under the patronage of Saint Dorothy (February 6), but they desperately needed a director with Annunciata's abilities. She knew nothing about their isolated region but welcomed the opportunity to supervise a school. She attracted many new students, sometimes teaching one hundred in a single class. Annunciata still expected to enter the Canossians, until their foundress informed her that *"the Lord has other plans for you."* Those other plans became clear after Erminia Panzerini died, leaving her entire estate to the school. With this legacy, Annunciata and Father Luca cofounded the Sisters of St Dorothy of Cemmo. The congregation rapidly expanded to other communities. Every Sunday, Annunciata would walk to these towns to confer with and encourage her Sisters. At work today in Europe, Africa, and Latin America, they commemorate Annunciata on March 23.

The Genius of Annunciata Cocchetti:

Annunciata needed great tact to manage Father Luca and Erminia, but she always assured her Sisters: *"Life is beautiful, even when it takes sacrifice and hard work."*

Reflection:

"People were bringing children to him that he might touch them, but the disciples rebuked them. When Jesus saw this he became indignant and said to them, 'Let the children come to me; do not prevent them, for the kingdom of God belongs to such as these. Amen, I say to you, whoever does not accept the kingdom of God like a child will not enter it.'"

Mark 10:13–15

SAINT MARÍA JOSEFA SANCHO DE GUERRA

(María Josefa of the Heart of Jesus)

b. September 7, 1842, Vitoria, Alava, Spain
d. March 20, 1912, Bilbao, Vizcaya, Spain

At the age of two, Josefa suffered a fall that left her legs paralyzed. Her parents took her to the shrine of Michael the Archangel in Aralar, where she was cured and began a lifetime devotion to him.

When she was fifteen, Josefa was sent to Madrid to complete her education. Her plans to enter a cloistered, contemplative convent were postponed when she came down with near-fatal typhus. During her long convalescence she recognized that she was called to an active life. On recovering, she entered the Congregation of the Servants of Mary, Ministers to the Sick, recently founded by Soledad Torres Acosta (October 12) and dedicated to attending the sick in their own homes. After a few years, encouraged by Madre Soledad, Josefa left the Servants of Mary with three companions and moved to Bilbao, where she founded the Institute of the Servants of Jesus of Charity to care for the sick in hospitals and in their homes.

During the Carlist wars, Josefa and the Servants of Jesus heroically attended patients suffering from highly contagious diseases such as cholera, typhus, and tuberculosis. Josefa led a very active life, founding more than forty convents before heart disease confined her to Bilbao. Today her spiritual daughters are present in Europe, Latin America, and Asia, where they also care for elderly women and abandoned children. Josefa's fame has grown because of the many graces and favors received through her intercession.

The Genius of María Josefa Sancho de Guerra:

Josefa encouraged her associates: *"Do not believe, sisters, that caring for the sick consists only in giving them medicine and food. There is another kind of care which you should never forget; that of the heart which seeks to adapt to the suffering person, going to meet his needs."*

Reflection:

"I am convinced that neither death, nor life, nor angels, nor principalities, nor present things, nor future things, nor powers, nor height, nor depth, nor any other creature will be able to separate us from the love of God in Christ Jesus our Lord."

Romans 8:38–39

Saint Benedetta Cambiagio Frassinello

b. October 2, 1791, Langasco, Italy
d. March 21, 1858, Ronca Scrivia, Italy

Benedetta and her husband, Giovanni Frassinello, struggled to balance a call to serve God with their deep love for each other. Each had considered a religious vocation, and two years after their wedding, while nursing Benedetta's sister Maria through a terminal illness, they agreed to live as brother and sister. After Maria's death, Giovanni entered a monastery and Benedetta entered an Ursuline convent. A year later, illness forced Benedetta to return to Pavia where she was miraculously cured after a vision of Jerome Emiliani.[63] From then on, she dedicated herself to teaching catechism and life skills to poor and homeless young women. Giovanni left the monastery to assist her, and they made a vow of perpetual chastity in front of the bishop, consecrating themselves to charitable work. Benedetta attracted many young volunteers; at one point, she was so popular that the local government designated her "Promoter of Public Instruction." But after the death of the bishop who had been her protector, Benedetta's unusual marriage drew gossip. She turned over control of her institute to the new bishop, and with Giovanni and five companions moved to her husband's hometown near Genoa and founded the Benedictine Sisters of Providence (Benedettine) there. The congregation grew quickly, bringing quality education to young women and promoting their right to that education. Today the Benedettine are active in Italy, Spain, Burundi, Ivory Coast, Peru, and Brazil. They honor Benedetta's motto: *"To lend myself gladly wherever there is an urgent need."*

The Genius of Benedetta Frassinello:
Guided by the Holy Spirit and an unwavering faith in Divine Providence, Benedetta could say with confidence: *"When God wants something, he does not fail to find the appropriate means."*

Reflection:
"The [Samaritan] woman said to Him, 'I know that the Messiah is coming, the one called the Anointed; when he comes, he will tell us everything.' Jesus said to her, 'I am he, the one who is speaking with you.'"

John 4:25–26

March 22

❦

BLESSED SYBILLINA BISCOSSI

b. 1287, Pavia, Italy
d. March 19, 1367, Pavia, Italy

Already orphaned and on her own, Sybillina went blind at the age of twelve. She found shelter in a Dominican convent and surprised the nuns by learning to make lace and by chanting their hymns and prayers with them.

Sybillina was devoted to Saint Dominic[64] and fully expected him to restore her sight. When he did not come through, she reproached him: *"Is this the way you cheat me, blessed Dominic, after I have prayed so long and so fervently for something so reasonable? Give me back the prayers and praises and everything else I have offered you in vain."* At that point, Dominic appeared to Sybillina in a dream and said: *"Here you must suffer darkness so that you may one day behold eternal light."* She understood that she must work her way to heaven through the darkness on earth.

Sybillina decided to become a recluse. She and a companion were sealed into a tiny cell attached to a church. Her companion soon gave up and left, but Sybillina endured, refusing to have a fire, sleeping on a board, and eating almost nothing. A steady stream of the sick and the sick at heart came to her window seeking help, and she was credited with many miracles. She was also blessed with great gifts of discernment. Legend has it that one a day a priest passed her window with Viaticum (Eucharist) for the sick. She warned him that the host he was carrying was not consecrated. He discovered that he had indeed taken a host from the wrong container.

Sybillina lived to the age of eighty, following all the Masses in the church and selling her lace to earn alms for the poor. Her feast day is March 23, and she is commemorated by the Dominican Order on April 19.

The Genius of Sybillina Biscossi:

Through prayer, Sybillina came to understand that her personal darkness could be a light to others.

Reflection:

"Look upon me, answer me, LORD, my God! / Give light to my eyes lest I sleep in death, Lest my enemy say, 'I have prevailed,' / lest my foes rejoice at my downfall."

Psalm 13:4–5

March 23

SAINT RAFQA OF LEBANON
(Rafqa Butrosyah Choboq ar-Rayes)

b. June 29, 1832, Himlaya, Metn Nord, Lebanon
d. March 23, 1914, Jrabta, Batrun, Ash Shamal, Lebanon

Most of us pray to God for blessings, but Rafqa asked Him to send her suffering. *"In union with your suffering, Jesus"* became her constant prayer.

Born in an ancient Christian community in northern Lebanon, Rafqa entered the Marian Order (Mariamettes) and trained as a teacher. Two months after she was assigned to Deir-el-Qamar, the Druz, a Muslim sect, massacred more than seven thousand Christians and destroyed 360 villages. Rafqa was deeply affected by this violence, and when her congregation merged with another ten years later, she chose instead to enter a new contemplative order. She embraced their ascetic life for the next fifteen years until, safe and secure at the age of fifty-three, she asked God to test her fidelity. For the next thirty years Rafqa was afflicted with a series of illnesses that left her blind and completely disabled. She was examined by numerous doctors, but there was no scientific explanation for her condition. Rafqa remained serene, assuring her superior: *"I am the one who asked for sickness with my full will and freedom. I do not have the right to complain or to be disturbed by it."* A few nights after Rafqa's funeral, a radiant light appeared around her tomb. The site still draws thousands of Christian and Muslim pilgrims, and the light is said to reappear whenever a cure occurs there.

The Genius of Rafqa:

Rafqa's union with Christ gave her the power to endure great pain and suffering. She said: *"Sickness accepted with patience and thanksgiving purifies the soul as the fire purifies God."*

Reflection:

"Cast all your worries upon him because He cares for you. Be sober and vigilant. Your opponent the devil is prowling around like a roaring lion looking for [someone] to devour. Resist him, steadfast in faith, knowing that your fellow believers throughout the world undergo the same sufferings. The God of grace who called you to his eternal glory through Christ [Jesus] will himself restore, confirm, strengthen and establish you after you have suffered a little. To him be dominion forever. Amen."

1 Peter 5:7–11 (Rafqa's favorite meditation)

SAINT CATHERINE OF SWEDEN
(Karen of Vadstena)

b. c. 1331, Uppland, Sweden
d. March 24, 1381, Vadstena, Sweden

Catherine was the favorite daughter of Bridget of Sweden (July 23), one of the most important women of the Middle Ages. The widowed Bridget left for Rome in 1350 to observe the Jubilee Year. Appalled at the corruption she found there, Bridget felt compelled to stay and work for Church reform. She begged Catherine to join her. Catherine left her ailing husband in Sweden and upon reaching Rome learned that he had passed away. Tall, fair, and very beautiful, she stood out in Rome and tried to avoid attention by attending Mass at a remote church in the vineyards. One determined admirer hid among the vines with his servants poised to seize her, but at the critical moment a handsome stag ran by, diverting their attention while Catherine passed unnoticed. For that reason, artists often represent Catherine beside a stag.

After twenty-five years in Rome, Catherine and her mother planned a pilgrimage to the Holy Land. Her brothers, roguish Karl and pious Birger, came from Sweden to join them. They paused in Naples at the court of the Queen Joanna, where Karl and Joanna launched a shameless affair although he had a wife in Sweden and Joanna's husband (her third) was on a military venture in Spain. The scandal was resolved only when Karl caught a fever and died in his mother's arms. Joanna gave him a funeral worthy of her consort, after which Catherine and the other pilgrims sailed to the Holy Land. Bridget died soon after their return to Rome and Catherine conducted her body back to Sweden on a two-thousand-mile procession marked by many miracles. She dedicated the rest of her life to completing Bridget's work.

The Genius of Catherine of Sweden:
Catherine was content to be an unsung collaborator who was indispensable to her mother's work. It was largely through her efforts that Bridget was canonized only eighteen years after her death.

Reflection:
"Consider it all joy, . . . when you encounter various trials, for you know that the testing of your faith produces perseverance. And let perseverance be perfect, so that you may be perfect and complete, lacking in nothing."

James 1:2–4

SAINT LUCY FILIPPINI

b. January 13, 1672, Corneto-Tarquinia, Tuscany, Italy
d. March 25, 1732, Montefiascone, Italy

"The Saintly Teacher" was blessed with two remarkable mentors: Cardinal Mark Anthony Barbarigo and Rosa Venerini (May 7). Barbarigo met Lucy when she was just sixteen and, recognizing her talent, invited Rosa Venerini to train her for teaching.

At twenty Lucy opened her first school in Montefiascone—and discovered that she hated teaching! Often, after a day with her students, she would go back to her room and cry. Tormented by doubts, she became physically ill and was confined to bed for more than a year, until her illness suddenly subsided. Lucy returned to health confident that God had called her to teaching because he had given her the talent to do it well. In years to come, whenever things got difficult, Lucy would repeat: *"When a work is from God, God himself feels obliged to protect it."*

Lucy formed the Maestre Pie, now known as the Religious Teachers Filippini. These women traveled in groups of two or three and established free schools for girls in remote small towns. After Lucy had trained her teachers, she continued to meet with them regularly to strengthen their faith, encourage them, and pray with them. She also led retreats for women all over Italy. During the eight to ten days that a retreat lasted, Lucy spoke with such fervor that the women were often reduced to tears. She always closed by urging them to practice certain virtues. Until the end of her life Lucy continued traveling to hold these retreats, declaring: *"I long to be present in every corner of the earth, to be present everywhere and plead with all peoples of every sex, age and condition: 'Love God! Love God!'"*

The Genius of Lucy Filippini:
Lucy recognized that teaching is a vocation, a calling from God, and she lived the advice of her mentor, Cardinal Barbarigo: "The Church of God is not a restful garden but a working vineyard."

Reflection:
"Tend the flock of God in your midst, [overseeing] not by constraint but willingly, as God would have it, not for shameful profit but eagerly. Do not lord it over those assigned to you, but be examples to the flock."

1 Peter 5:2–3

BLESSED PLACIDE VIEL
(Victoria Eulalia Jacqueline Viel)

b. September 26, 1815, Quettehou, Manche, France
d. March 4, 1877, Saint-Sauveur-le-Vicomte, Manche, France

Victoria was a timid eighteen-year-old farm girl when she visited a cousin at the convent of the Sisters of the Christian Schools. The foundress and superior general, Marie Madeleine Postel (July 16), had recently acquired the ruined Benedictine abbey at Saint-Sauveur-le-Vicomte, and the Sisters were enthusiastically restoring it. Marie Madeleine saw something special in this young woman, seemingly recognizing that Victoria would someday lead the order. Marie Madeleine welcomed Victoria into the order, giving her the name Placide.

Although Placide had little formal education, she was blessed with excellent management skills. Marie Madeleine gave her increasing responsibilities and named her Assistant General at the age of twenty-six. This appointment caused some resentment among the Sisters, but Placide soon confirmed Marie Madeleine's judgment. Sent all over Europe to raise money to rebuild the abbey, Placide explained her gift for fund-raising: *"I went without fear, having the greatest faith in my Superior and confident that I was doing the work of the Lord."* She also established the congregation in Germany.

When Marie Madeleine Postel died in 1846, Placide succeeded her as superior general, completing the restoration of the abbey that Marie Madeleine had begun. During the Franco-Prussian War, Placide organized heroic relief efforts at Saint-Sauveur-le-Vicomte and nursed many soldiers at the abbey. The order honors her on March 4.

The Genius of Placide Viel:
Sisters are only human, and Placide's quick rise to leadership of the order caused some resentment. She was able to overcome this with tact and sensitivity.

Reflection:
"If you forgive others their transgressions, your heavenly Father will forgive you. But if you do not forgive others, neither will your Father forgive your transgressions."

Matthew 6:14–15

March 27

Blessed Angela Salawa
(Aniela Salawa)

b. September 9, 1881, Siepraw, Malopolskie, Poland
d. March 12, 1922, Kraków, Malopolskie, Poland

At sixteen Angela left the family farm to join her older sister as a housemaid in Kraków. For two years her main interests were pretty clothes and a good time, but her sister's sudden death launched Angela on a spiritual journey.

She would often find herself alone in churches where she talked to God and confided how hard it was to avoid temptations. She offered herself completely to Him and began to keep a journal of her mystical experiences, writing: *"Whatever I do, I do because of God's love and because of His constant presence in my life. He is my loving and caring Father. One should always think that way and nothing would be hard or difficult."* She became a Franciscan tertiary, and during World War I she spent her free hours attending hospitalized soldiers who called her "the young saint." Such attention only embarrassed Angela, who wrote in her journal: *"If you do something special and good for others, make sure that no one knows about it—just be humble about it. Hide it from the eyes of the people, so your offering will be received by Jesus Christ as pure and good-hearted."*

Angela gradually discerned that her vocation was to suffer with Christ. She accepted this and prayed many hours before the Blessed Sacrament. By May 1917 she was too sick to work, and offered up her terminal illness for the liberation of Poland. She died serenely and was buried in the Franciscan church in Kraków. The site continues to draw many pilgrims. She is venerated by Franciscans on March 12.

The Genius of Angela Salawa:

John Paul II counted Angela among his protector saints. "How many times I prayed before her tomb," he said at her 1991 beatification, "so deeply were her words impressed in my mind and heart: *'Lord, I live by your will, I shall die when you so desire, save me because you can.'"*

Reflection:

"I am the good shepherd, and I know mine and mine know me, just as the Father knows me and I know the Father; and I will lay down my life for the sheep."

John 10:14–15

♈

BLESSED JEANNE-MARIE DE MAILLÉ

b. April 14, 1332, Roche Sainte Quentin, Touraine, France
d. March 28, 1414, Tours, France

As a child, Jeanne saved young Robert, Baron de Sille, from drowning in a pond. Years later, her grandfather arranged their marriage, but Jeanne convinced her husband to live celibately.

This was during the Hundred Years War between France and England. When Robert was badly wounded at Poitiers and captured by the British, Jeanne sold her jewels and horses to pay his ransom. Once he was freed, they ministered to other captives together. It was said that Jeanne could teach even a magpie to pray, and she once persuaded the king of France to free all the prisoners in Tours. When Robert died, his family blamed Jeanne for pauperizing his estate and evicted her from his lands. A former servant took her in, but like Jeanne's in-laws, the woman could not appreciate Jeanne's sacrifice and abused her.

Destitute, Jeanne went home to her mother, who taught her how to mix medicines to support herself. She pressured Jeanne to remarry while she was still beautiful. To avoid this, Jeanne retreated to a small house in Tours where she nursed lepers, prostitutes, and other outcasts. She entered the Third Order of St Francis and lived by begging. Jeanne was so highly regarded that the Duke of Anjou named her the godmother for his son. The little boy would clap his hands whenever Jeanne gave him a catechism lesson. All children loved her and would follow her in the street, calling out *"Blessed be God and our Lord Jesus Christ,"* the prayer she had taught them.

The Genius of Jeanne-Marie de Maillé:
Jeanne's desire for a celibate marriage was inspired by legends about Cecilia of Rome (November 22). Through such self-denial, Jeanne and her husband found a strength that helped them to help others.

Reflection:
"Come now, you who say, 'Today or tomorrow we shall go into such and such a town, spend a year there doing business, and make a profit.' —you have no idea what your life will be like tomorrow. You are a puff of smoke that appears briefly and then disappears. Instead you should say, 'If the Lord wills it, we shall live to do this or that.'"

James 4:13–15

SAINT GLADYS OF WALES

Fifth century, Wales

Gladys eloped with a robber bridegroom and had a brief flirtation with King Arthur before she gave birth to one of the great Welsh saints.

She was the daughter of Brychan, Druid chieftain of Brecknock, who also fathered Dwynwen (January 25) and Keyne (October 9). The warrior lord Gwynllyw sought Gladys's hand in marriage, and after Brychan refused him, he decided to take Gladys by force. Leading three hundred armed men across the mountains and down into Talgarth, where Brychan held court, he found Gladys, swept her up onto his horse, and fled with Brychan's men in hot pursuit. While on the run, the lovers encountered King Arthur, whose advisers had to talk him out of taking Gladys for himself. Instead, he negotiated peace between Brychan and Gwynllyw. The lovers were free to lead a riotous life, plundering South Wales. Time would prove that theirs was a match made in heaven. When Gladys's first son, Cadoc,[65] was born inside their camp, the new parents sent their robber band on a celebration raid. The band brought back a cow for the banquet, but the owner, an elderly Irish monk, stormed into the camp demanding restitution. Gladys and Gwynllyw were impressed with his courage, and although they were Druids, they asked him to baptize their newborn son. Cadoc grew up a devout Christian deeply distressed by his parents' freebooting lifestyle. He begged them to change their ways. Gladys advised her husband: *"Let us trust to our son, and he will be father to us in heaven."* Gwynllyw yielded, and they confessed their sins and were baptized together, devoting the rest of their lives to good works.

The Genius of Gladys:

Like all the great Celtic saints, Gladys is obscured by many legends, but it is clear that whether eloping with Gwynllyw, baptizing her firstborn in a new religion, or embracing Christianity herself, she was always open to God's will.

Reflection:

"Some rely on chariots, others on horses, / but we on the name of the LORD *our God.*

They collapse and fall, / but we stand strong and firm.

LORD, *grant victory to the king; / answer when we call upon you."*

Psalm 20:8–10

March 30

BLESSED MARIA KARLOWSKA
(Maria of Jesus Crucified)

b. September 4, 1865, Stupowka (now Karowo), Poland
d. March 23, 1935, Pniewite, Poland

A professional dressmaker, Maria was visiting the sick at night when she encountered prostitutes for the first time. Many of these women suffered from syphilis, which was potentially fatal and, if left untreated, progressed to paralysis and dementia. (There was no cure until the introduction of penicillin.) They were scorned by society when they were healthy and abandoned when they became ill, yet Maria understood that even the most hardened among them could be saved.

This work took her from the venereal disease wards of charity hospitals to secret brothels unknown even to the police. In 1884 she opened her first House of the Good Shepherd, a refuge for women who wanted to change their lives. Her zeal attracted disciples with whom she founded the Sisters of the Good Shepherd of Divine Providence (Good Shepherd Sisters) and a rehabilitation program based on charity, mercy, and prayer. No one was forced to participate in religious exercises because, Maria said, *"Every religious practice is a free act."* She urged her Sisters to discover each woman's abilities and help her to fulfill them. Many of the women went on to become wives and mothers. Others remained with the Sisters, assisting in their mission. In 1928 the Polish government recognized Maria Karlowska's service to her country with the Cross of Gold. She is venerated in Poland on March 23.

The Genius of Maria Karlowska:

At Maria's beatification, Pope John Paul II cited her Feminine Genius, "revealed in deep sensitivity to human suffering, in tact, openness and readiness to help, and in other qualities proper to the feminine heart. Often this is shown without drawing attention to itself and therefore is sometimes undervalued.... How much this 'feminine genius' is needed, that today's world may esteem the values of life, responsibility and faithfulness; that it may preserve respect for human dignity!"

Reflection:

"'Yet even now,' says the LORD, / 'return to me with your whole heart, / with fasting, and weeping, and mourning; / Rend your hearts, not your garments, / and return to the LORD, your God. / For gracious and merciful is he, / slow to anger, rich in kindness / and relenting in punishment.'"

Joel 2:12–13

Blessed Natalie Tulasiewicz

b. April 9, 1906, Rzeszow, Poland
d. March 31, 1945, Ravensbrück, Germany

At the beatification of the Polish Martyrs of World War II,[66] Pope John Paul II read out the names of all 108 martyrs. It was impossible for him to describe their individual heroism, but he singled out a few, including Natalie Tulasiewicz.

Her childhood tuberculosis had ruled out a religious vocation, so Natalie became a schoolteacher, earning an advanced degree in Polish literature. When Germany invaded Poland, she saw clearly that she was called to be a martyr. She volunteered to work among Polish prisoners of war and was assigned to a factory in Hanover where she secretly organized religious activities. On April 29, 1944, Natalie was arrested, beaten, and tortured. She was half-dead when she was transported to Ravensbrück, a camp created specifically to hold women who had worked in the resistance. By the time she arrived, it held more than forty thousand women under appalling conditions. They came from all over Europe and she communicated with them in French and German. She even started learning Italian.

Although frail from tuberculosis and torture, Natalie managed to organize religious life in the camp, and hoped to return someday to her factory in Hanover. On Good Friday, she summoned her remaining strength, climbed onto a stool in her barracks, and gave a talk on the Passion and Resurrection. Two days later, she was taken to the gas chamber and executed.

The Genius of Natalie Tulasiewicz:
Well read and sophisticated, Natalie insisted that a true Christian must know not only how to suffer but how to be joyful.

Reflection:
"I say this so that no one may deceive you by specious arguments. For even if I am absent in the flesh, yet I am with you in spirit, rejoicing as I observe your good order and the firmness of your faith in Christ. So, as you received Christ Jesus the Lord, walk in him, rooted in him and built upon him and established in the faith as you were taught, abounding in thanksgiving."
Colossians 2:4–7

April 1

SAINT CATALINA TOMÁS
(Catherine of Palma)

b. May 1, 1531, Valdemuzza, Majorca, Spain
d. April 5, 1574, Palma de Majorca, Spain

Majorcans regarded Catalina as a saint from the day she died, but the formal process took more than three hundred years. Even the papal bull of canonization noted that "the saint's cause dragged on too long."

At age three, Catalina could say the Rosary, and at four she knew her entire catechism, but at seven she became an orphan, left at the mercy of two uncles who put her to work herding sheep. Unable to attend daily Mass, she built small altars for herself wherever her flock paused in the fields. Catalina yearned to enter a convent, but she was illiterate and her uncles refused to give her a dowry. Finally, the Canonesses of St Augustine agreed to admit her as a lay nun, consigned to the most menial tasks. From the day she arrived at their convent, Catalina experienced ecstasies that lasted as long as three weeks. She was attacked by devils, talked with souls in purgatory, prophesied the future, and performed miracles. The novitiate traditionally lasts for one year, but Catalina's dragged on for two years and seven months, possibly for the same reasons that her canonization later took so long.

The devils that tormented Catalina terrified her convent, but she assured them: *"Fear not, sisters, Christ is with us."* They once watched in horror as an invisible devil lifted Catalina into the air and tossed her down a well. Majorcans commemorate that encounter with an annual parade in which they dress up as the devils. Catalina died peacefully, and forty years after her death, her body was exhumed and found incorrupt. It is venerated at her former convent.

The Genius of Catalina Tomás:
Many people sought Catalina's counsel, but she remained an example of faith and humility. It is said that her words were like arrows that pierced the hearts of her visitors with love.

Reflection:
"No trial has come to you but what is human. God is faithful and will not let you be tried beyond your strength; but with the trial he will also provide a way out, so that you may be able to bear it."

1 Corinthians 10:13

BLESSED LAURA EVANGELISTA
(María of Saint Joseph Alvarado Cardozo)

b. April 25, 1875, Choroni, Aragua, Venezuela
d. April 2, 1967, Maracay, Aragua, Venezuela

Laura was born out of wedlock. Her father disdained religion but did not object when her mother had her baptized. He later moved the family to Maracay, an industrial center, so that Laura would have a better education.

At eighteen, Laura wanted to enter a contemplative religious order but her pastor, Vicente López Aveledo, asked her to wait. Maracay was soon swept up in a smallpox epidemic. Father López Aveledo opened the city's first hospital and Laura joined the volunteers there, going home only when her parents insisted. She was twenty-four years old when López Aveledo named her director of the hospital. Days later, her father suffered a stroke and she rushed to his bedside. The lifelong agnostic consented to receive the last rites and to marry her mother, then died in peace. Laura fasted for the next ten years, living on nothing but the daily Eucharist, offering this penance for the sake of her father's soul.

Laura and López Aveledo founded a religious congregation dedicated to nursing the sick poor. She declared: *"Those rejected by everyone are ours. Those no one wants to take are ours."* Ecclesiastic approval stalled until Laura entrusted their cause to Rita of Cascia (May 22), patron of the impossible. Tuberculosis claimed López Aveledo in 1917, leaving Laura to lead the congregation on her own. She expanded their mission, building thirty-seven homes for orphaned children and the elderly. Today her congregation is known as the Augustinian Recollect Sisters of the Heart of Jesus. Laura died peacefully just short of her ninety-second birthday, and even before she was buried miraculous healings were being attributed to her. Almost thirty years later, her body was exhumed and found incorrupt.

The Genius of Laura Evangelista:
Faced with a harsh new superior at the hospital, many volunteers rebelled, but Laura endured her demands until the woman was asked to leave. Afterward Laura would only say, *"She was my great teacher."*

Reflection:
"Jesus spoke to them again, saying, 'I am the light of the world. Whoever follows me will not walk in darkness, but will have the light of life.'"

John 8:12

BLESSED KATHERINE CELESTYNA FARON

b. April 24, 1913, Zabrze, Malopolskie, Poland
d. April 9, 1944, Owcim (Auschwitz), Malopolskie, Poland

"I realize that life in the love of God is the happiest," Celestyna wrote as she awaited certain death in a Nazi concentration camp.

Celestyna had entered the convent of the Little Servant Sisters of the Immaculate Conception at the age of seventeen. She was called to work with children and the Servant Sisters say that she "poured hope into their souls." By the time the German army invaded Poland in 1939, Celestyna had become superior of her convent and was directing its preschool. The Nazis arrested her on February 19, 1942, and for a year they shuttled her among prisons where she was tortured and abused. On January 6, 1943, Celestyna was sent to the Auschwitz-Birkenau concentration camp. Although weakened by typhoid and tuberculosis, she never complained but devoted herself to the other prisoners. She shared her rations, words of encouragement, her exemplary confidence in God, and her sense of humor. Celestyna urged the other prisoners not to lose faith, assuring them that this too would pass, and that Jesus had sent them to atone for the sins of the world. She suffered the most because she was deprived of the Eucharist, but shortly before Easter, a priest arrived at the camp with consecrated wafers hidden in the hem of his clothes and was able to give Celestyna the Eucharist before her death.

In a final gift of love, Celestyna made a private vow to offer her life for the conversion of a troubled priest. She suffered heroically and died on Easter morning. Through her sacrifice, the priest recovered his faith and became instrumental in bringing back another priest. Celestyna was beatified with the 108 Polish Martyrs of World War II[67] and is commemorated in Poland on April 9.

The Genius of Celestyna Faron:
Celestyna vowed *"to become a holocaust for Jesus in the way of love and sacrifice and to follow the spotless lamb."*

Reflection:
"If, then, we have died with Christ, we believe that we shall also live with him. We know that Christ, raised from the dead, dies no more; death no longer has power over him."

Romans 6:8–9

BLESSED CLARE GAMBACORTA

(Theodora, Tora)

b. 1362, Florence or Venice, Italy
d. April 17, 1419, Pisa, Italy

Clare was the daughter of the powerful doge (governor) of Pisa, who arranged her marriage when she was thirteen. She and her young husband were still living with her mother-in-law when Catherine of Siena (April 29) visited Pisa and Clare became her devoted disciple. Catherine wrote many letters encouraging Clare to "*Strip yourself of self. Love God with a free and loyal love.*"

Widowed at fifteen, Clare resisted another marriage and entered a Franciscan convent, but her brothers threatened to burn it down unless she was released. Her father kept her at home under guard and asked Alphonsus Pecha, Bridget of Sweden's (July 23) last confessor, to counsel her. Pecha told her stories about Bridget, who had been dead for five years and was still one of the most admired women in Europe. Deeply impressed by Bridget's spirituality and achievements, Clare maintained a devotion to her for the rest of her life. Pecha convinced Clare's father that she had a genuine vocation and arranged for her to be admitted to a Dominican convent. Once inside, however, Clare was disappointed. The nuns were lax and not observing enclosure. She found seven women she called "*lilies among thorns*" who shared her desire for a strict Dominican Rule. Among them was Maria Mancini,[68] a widow with grown children, who became the first member of Clare's new community. After Clare's death, Maria Mancini succeeded her as abbess, and they share a common feast day, April 17.

The Genius of Clare Gambacorta:

Clare's influence spread far beyond convent walls. She directed a team of lay sisters (not bound by enclosure) who visited hospitals and prisons, and she created a system to receive and educate foundlings. She also commissioned a series of murals honoring Catherine and Bridget that can still be seen in Pisa.

Reflection:

"*As a lily among thorns, / so is my beloved among women.*"

Song of Songs 2:2

SAINT CRESCENTIA HÖSS
(Crescentia of Kaufbeuren)

b. October 20, 1682, Kaufbeuren, Germany
d. April 5, 1744, Kaufbeuren, Germany

Catholics made up less than a third of the population of Kaufbeuren, but many Protestants, including the mayor, would attend Mass just to hear Crescentia sing.

She yearned to enter a Franciscan convent, but the nuns would not admit her without a dowry. The nuns lived next to a rowdy tavern and needed to buy out the owner to gain some peace. At this point, the mayor stepped in and negotiated a deal for them. All he asked in return was that they admit the young girl with the beautiful voice.

Crescentia eventually became superior of the convent and both Catholics and Protestants sought her counsel. Those who could not visit wrote letters. In the first six months of 1737, Crescentia received more than eight hundred such letters. She answered them all, advising on matters of faith and worldly problems. One woman wrote about her mother, who fretted that she had made an invalid confession and was going to hell for it. Crescentia called such worrying *"a waste of time that could be used for good work"* and concluded, *"Entreat your mother to stop shedding tears and to be happy in God, who embraces us in his eternal love."* When a court pharmacist wrote that his work left no time to pray or even visit a church, Crescentia advised him to offer his work itself to God.

A few months after Crescentia's death, the local bishop assigned two priests to investigate her case, but they clashed with the nuns. To avoid controversy the bishop shelved the investigation completely, and Crescentia was not canonized until 2001. Today she is revered as a most approachable saint, and her tomb is visited by the faithful of all religions.

The Genius of Crescentia Höss:
Crescentia urged total acceptance of the Divine Will. She once wrote to a friend: *"We must allow God to fulfill his holy will in us. Through him everything becomes good and right."*

Reflection:
"I will sing to the LORD all my life; / I will sing to my God while I live. / May my theme be pleasing to God; I will rejoice in the LORD."

Psalm 104:33–34

BLESSED JULIANA OF MONT-CORNILLON

(Juliana of Liège)

b. 1192, Retinnes, Belgium
d. April 5, 1258, Fosses, Belgium

At the age of fourteen, Juliana began having dreams about a full moon marred by a dark stain. Neither she nor her guardian, Sister Sapientia, understood it. Years passed before Juliana recognized it as a call to introduce a new feast to the Church.

As an orphan, Juliana had been entrusted to a convent at Mont-Cornillon. By age eighteen, she had taken the veil there and turned over her entire fortune to the convent. Two years later, she succeeded Sapientia as prioress. Juliana now understood her dream: the moon was Christ's Church, and the dark stain signified the absence of a feast commemorating his gift of himself in the Eucharist. She was called to introduce that feast, which would become known as Corpus Christi. Her bishop agreed to arrange a festival for the diocese, but she met resistance from colleagues, who called her Juliana the Dreamer. A priest who coveted her convent's endowment spread stories that she had misused funds to promote her feast. Juliana had not kept good records, which left her vulnerable to his lies. He stirred up a mob that stormed the convent. Juliana escaped, taking refuge with Eve,[69] a recluse, and with sympathetic monasteries. At last, the powerful abbess of Salzinne took up Juliana's cause and negotiated an annuity from her convent. Juliana died peacefully two years later. Fifty years after her death, Pope Clement V authorized the feast of Corpus Christi for the entire Church. It is celebrated in the United States on the first Sunday after Trinity Sunday.

The Genius of Juliana of Mont-Cornillon:

In spite of her troubles, Juliana was consulted by many people who suffered from what we would call depression. She advised: *"Put these things out of your mind, and turn your whole heart to the Lord, and he will drive all your sufferings away."*

Reflection:

"Do not repay anyone evil for evil; be concerned for what is noble in the sight of all."

Romans 12:17

BLESSED BARBE ACARIE

(Marie of the Incarnation)

b. February 1, 1566, Paris, France
d. April 18, 1618, Pontoise, France

Barbe's mother arranged for her to marry Pierre Acarie, a prominent businessman from a powerful family. They had six children and Barbe lived the life of a society matron, so beautiful and charming that she was dubbed "la belle Acarie."

Pierre disapproved of her taste for romance novels and brought home some pious books instead. Barbe opened one to be polite and the words of Saint Augustine,[70] *"He is indeed a miser for whom God is not enough,"* captured her attention and deeply touched her. Soon Pierre went from worrying that Barbe was too frivolous to complaining that she spent too much time in church. He had her denounced from the pulpit and temporarily barred from the sacraments. In 1590 Pierre was caught up in a failed rebellion against the king and went into exile, leaving his financial affairs in chaos and Barbe and her children homeless. She held off their creditors and with no help from Pierre managed to return their family to solvency. She even convinced the king to allow Pierre to return to Paris.

All this time, Barbe was growing spiritually. After reading the autobiography of Teresa of Avila (October 15), she had a dream in which Teresa asked her to introduce the Discalced Carmelite Order into France. Barbe considered the idea ridiculous, but when Teresa visited again, she could not ignore her wishes. This was a delicate mission: Barbe had to win permission from the French king, who was not enthusiastic about importing nuns from Spain. Her Carmels (convents) proved so successful that they expanded to England and northern Europe. After Pierre's death in 1613, Barbe entered the Carmel at Amiens. She died on Easter, and her feast day is April 18. She is a patron of pregnant women and difficult births.

The Genius of Barbe Acarie:
Combining mystical experiences with the management skills of a born homemaker, Barbe nurtured a demanding husband and family while reaching out to society at large.

Reflection:
"Charm is deceptive and beauty fleeting; / the woman who fears the LORD is to be praised."

Proverbs 31:30

SAINT JULIE BILLIART

(Marie Rose Julia Billiart)

b. July 12, 1751, Cuvilly, France
d. April 8, 1816, Namur, Belgium

Julie's first home was above her father's dry goods shop. His business failed when Julie was sixteen, and for the next few years she traveled alone to larger towns, sometimes on foot, sometimes on horseback, as she tried to sell off the remaining inventory. One night, robbers invaded Julie's home and shot her father in front of her. He recovered, but the shock sent Julie into a traumatic paralysis that left her an invalid for the next twenty years.

The villagers, who called her the Saint of Cuvilly, continued to visit Julie for religious instruction and advice. When the French Revolution broke out in 1789, she was targeted by the anti-Christian government. Friends hid her in a cartload of straw and hustled her away to Compiègne. At about this time, Julie experienced a vision in which she was called to found a religious congregation marked by the Cross. After several years of exile in Compiègne, she met Françoise Blin de Bourdon, Viscountess of Gizaincourt. They were unlikely allies: the viscountess was elegant and sophisticated whereas Julie was a simple woman who, because of her paralysis, had difficulty speaking. Yet together they established the congregation now known as the Sisters of Notre Dame de Namur and dedicated themselves to educating young women.

Soon after the founding, Julie was cured of her paralysis, a miracle she credited to a novena to the Sacred Heart. She resumed traveling, and the former invalid made 120 trips on foot and horseback, founding fifteen convents. Julie recommended simplicity in all things: *"As the sunflower turns to the sun, so the mind and heart of a nun who possesses this virtue turn always to God, from whom she receives the light of his Wisdom to guide her, and the heart of his Love to sanctify her."*

The Genius of Julie Billiart:

Throughout her eventful life, Julie would say, *"Oh how good is the good God."* She assured her Sisters: *"Time is like loose change. It is given to us here below to buy the real things of eternity."*

Reflection:

"My spirit rejoices in God my savior."

Luke 1:47 (Magnificat; Julie Billiart's last words)

April 9

SAINT MARY CLOPAS
(Mary of Cleophas)

First century

One of three Marys[71] present with the Blessed Mother at the Crucifixion, Mary Clopas watched from a distance. She saw darkness descend at noon, and she heard Jesus cry out on the cross and surrender his spirit. At that moment, the earth quaked, rocks split, and tombs opened. She saw the terror in the faces of the soldiers keeping guard and heard them say, "Truly, this was the Son of God!"

That night, Mary Clopas and the other women prepared Jesus for burial. Joseph of Arimathea[72] had secured the body, wrapped it in clean linen, laid it in a fresh tomb, and rolled a huge stone across the entrance before he left. Mary Clopas and Mary Magdalene remained behind until Pilate, urged on by the Pharisees, sealed the tomb and posted a guard there. Following Jewish custom, Mary Clopas stayed away from the tomb on the Sabbath. She returned at dawn on Easter, prepared to anoint Jesus's body. But Mary Clopas and her companions were stunned to discover that the heavy stone had already been rolled back and the tomb was empty. An angel clad in white told them: *"He is risen."* Fearful but overjoyed, the women ran to tell the disciples. On the way, they met Jesus, who greeted them, saying: *"Do not be afraid. Go tell my brothers to go to Galilee, and there they will see me."*

The Genius of Mary Clopas:

Mary Clopas and her companions were united by their love for Christ and his message. As they prepared to perform a traditional work of mercy, they became the first to receive the Good News of the Resurrection.

Reflection:

"Do not be afraid! I know that you are seeking Jesus the crucified. / He is not here, for he has been raised just as he said. Come and see the place where he lay. / Then go quickly and tell his disciples, 'He has been raised from the dead, and he is going before you to Galilee; there you will see him.' Behold, I have told you."

Matthew 28:5–7

April 10

SAINT MARY OF EGYPT

b. c. 344, Egypt
d. c. 421, in the desert beyond the Jordan

Mary of Egypt, a singer, musician, and courtesan, was strolling the docks in Alexandria one morning when she met a crowd bound for the Holy Land to celebrate the feast of the True Cross.[73] Never one to miss a good time, Mary hopped aboard their ship and partied all the way to Jerusalem.

On arrival, she was eager to see the Cross, which was exposed in the basilica, but an invisible force barred her at the door. Mary fell to her knees, begging the Blessed Mother to let her look upon the Cross just once. With that, the barrier dissolved. As Mary prayed before the relic, she heard a voice say: *"Pass over Jordan and you will find rest."* Instead of returning home, she purchased three small loaves of bread and walked into the desert, where she remained, living on roots and wild dates and the three loaves that never ran out. After forty-seven years, Mary was found by an elderly priest on a Lenten retreat. She told him her story and they prayed together. He agreed to return in a year to bring her the sacraments, but when he did, he discovered that she had died peacefully shortly after their encounter. With the help of a lion, he buried her in the desert. Her feast day is April 2.

The Genius of Mary of Egypt:

The story of Mary's redemption became one of the most popular in Europe. Almost a thousand years after her death, an irascible and greedy businessman, John Colombini,[74] read her biography and was so moved that he gave away everything he owned and devoted the rest of his life to charity. With Mary of Egypt as his patron, Colombini achieved many conversions, reconciled estranged friends, and returned property to its rightful owners.

Reflection:

"A king's secret it is prudent to keep, but the works of God are to be declared and made known. Praise them with due honor. Do good, and evil will not find its way to you."

Tobit 12:7

April 11

Saint Gemma Galgani

b. *March 12, 1878, Camigliano, Italy*
d. *April 11, 1903, Lucca, Italy*

Gemma experienced extraordinary visions, ecstasies, and stigmata that have survived scrupulous twentieth-century investigation.

After the death of her pharmacist father, Gemma and her seven orphaned siblings were distributed among relatives. As a child, she began hearing voices that called her to suffer for the sinners of the world. On the eve of the feast of the Sacred Heart, June 8, 1899, the stigmata appeared on Gemma's hands for the first time. In the years that followed, the stigmata would regularly appear at 8:00 P.M. Thursday night and last until 3:00 P.M. Friday. Gemma would bleed profusely and observers could touch the actual wounds, but when the bleeding stopped, the raw flesh healed and left no trace of a wound or scar. A Passionist priest encouraged her to keep a journal describing her mystical experiences. In it she wrote: *"Praise to the unbounded love of Jesus, who, moved to pity by my misery, offers me every means of coming to His Love."* She died of tuberculosis at the age of twenty-five.

Were her wounds the product of hysteria or truly supernatural? Gemma acknowledged that she might be a hysteric, but investigators remain convinced that there was never any fakery involved, nor any diabolic deception. Her canonization decree pointedly avoids mentioning the stigmata, and only cites Gemma as a "living example of what Christian suffering ought to be: that is, to suffer in the spirit of faith, of penance, and of charity." She is a patron of pharmacists, orphans, and hospitals. More recently, she has been suggested as a patron of the lonely because of the isolation she endured.

The Genius of Gemma Galgani:

Throughout her suffering, Gemma's faith remained unshaken. She prayed: *"If I saw the gates of Hell open and I stood on the brink of the abyss, I should not despair, I should not lose hope of mercy, because I should trust in you, my God."*

Reflection:

"Behold, he is coming amid the clouds, / and every eye will see him, / even those who pierced him. / All the peoples of the earth will lament him. / Yes. Amen."
Revelation 1:7

April 12

BLESSED MARY ELISABETH HESSELBLAD

b. June 4, 1870, Foglavik, Västergötland, Sweden
d. April 24, 1957, Rome, Italy

A pioneer in ecumenism and Christian unity, Elisabeth was still a child when she first pondered Christ's words about one Shepherd and one fold. After asking Him to show her this one true fold, she recalled, "*I felt a wonderful peace coming into my soul and there seemed to be a voice that answered, 'Yes, my child, one day I will show you.*'"

Brought up in the National Church of Sweden (Lutheran), Elisabeth had never met a Catholic until she came to New York at the age of eighteen. As a student nurse at Roosevelt Hospital, she cared for injured construction workers, many of whom were Catholic immigrants. Their rosaries, devotion to Mary, and other practices were strange but intriguing. She began studying the Catholic faith and was received into the Church in 1902. She subsequently felt called to revive the Bridgettine Order, founded by Bridget of Sweden (July 23) but barred from her homeland since the Reformation. Elisabeth went to Rome and was received into the nearly moribund order. She was soon joined by three English postulants and the revival was launched. She acquired Bridget's former home in Rome, which became the Bridgettine motherhouse, and during World War II, she sheltered many Jews and antifascists there. She shared a friendship with Rome's chief rabbi, Eugenio Zolli, who later converted to Catholicism. In 2005 Elisabeth was honored as a Righteous Gentile[75] for her contribution during the Holocaust. Her feast day is April 24.

The Genius of Elisabeth Hesselblad:

Elisabeth explained how she accomplished what seemed impossible: "*God gave me the grace very early to understand that all difficulties are sent to be overcome. With the aid of God, anything can be surmounted, but without his help, all strength is useless.*"

Reflection:

"*I have other sheep who do not belong to this fold. These also I must lead, and they will hear my voice, and there will be one flock, one shepherd.*"

John 10:16

Blessed Margaret of Città di Castello
(Margaret of Metola)

b. 1287, Metola, Spoleto, Italy
d. 1320, Città di Castello, Umbria, Italy

Blind, hunchbacked, and barely four feet tall, Margaret was an embarrassment to her parents, who raised her in seclusion inside their castle. Hearing about miracles at a church in Castello, they took her there, prayed for a cure, and when none came, abandoned her there. All of Margaret's biographers agree on these facts, although they disagree about her age at the time. Some say that she was only five years old; others believe that she was almost sixteen. Whatever her age, she was completely unprepared to be on her own.

A pious couple took Margaret into their home and she gained a reputation as a miracle worker, preserving her benefactors' house from fire and restoring sight to a woman who was going blind. She once confided to her confessor that every time she attended Mass she saw Christ Incarnate on the altar. He suggested that she more likely sensed Christ's Presence, but Margaret insisted that she most definitely saw Christ. Well, then, the priest asked gently, could she explain what Christ looked like? *"Oh, Father,"* Margaret sighed, *"you are asking me to describe Infinite Beauty."*

In her final hours, a procession of Dominican friars arrived to give Margaret the last rites and she died contemplating the Eucharist. A crowd kept a vigil outside her home and insisted that she be entombed in their church like a saint. A few years later Margaret's body was moved, and when her coffin was opened her body was found incorrupt. Her heart contained three precious stones marked with images of her favorite meditations: the Virgin Mary, the birth of Christ, and the Holy Family's flight into Egypt. Today Margaret's incorrupt body is venerated on an altar at the church of St Dominic in Città di Castello. She is a patron of the unborn and those born with disabilities.

The Genius of Margaret of Città di Castello:
In spite of her afflictions and the rejection by her parents, Margaret could say: *"Oh, if you only knew what I have in my heart."*

Reflection:
"For my father and my mother have left me; but the Lord has taken me up."
Psalm 27:10, keynote to pamphlet about Margaret

April 14

SAINT LYDWINA OF SCHIEDAM

b. April 18, 1380, Schiedam, Netherlands
d. April 14, 1433, Schiedam, Netherlands

Lydwina was a typical teenager until a skating accident brought on years of suffering. Although she was treated by some famous doctors, her broken rib never healed and gangrene set in, followed by unspeakable complications. One biographer wrote: "She would have been dead twenty times over if these afflictions had been natural; one alone would have been enough to kill her." It was four years before Lydwina could accept her suffering as God's will. She ate almost nothing, her sight failed, and she began to experience visions. Her guardian angel took her to wonderful places, including the church she had attended as a young girl and a field full of tulips. At other times, the angel took her to Bethlehem and Calvary.

Visitors came from as far away as Germany and England to seek her counsel. Many troubled clergy consulted Lydwina, and her sickroom became "a hospital for souls." She surprised one visitor with an exact description of his monastery, explaining that she had been there frequently while in ecstasy and had met the monks' guardian angels there. Local officials remained skeptical, observing Lydwina closely for three months before concluding that no trickery was involved. When enemy soldiers occupied Schiedam, they guarded Lydwina's room for nine days, hoping to expose her as a fraud, but they reported that their hostage appeared to live on air alone. It was said that shortly after Lydwina's death her body became whole again and her face as beautiful as a young girl's. She is the patron saint of skaters.

The Genius of Lydwina:

Lydwina lived at the mercy of others, and some, like her sister-in-law, could be cruel. Once, the visiting Duke of Bavaria asked Lydwina, "How can you endure this harpy?" She replied: *"It is a good thing to suffer the impertinence and weaknesses of such people, if only to correct them by patience, and to teach oneself not to get irritated."*

Reflection:

"He has worn away my flesh and my skin, / he has broken my bones; / He has beset me round about / with poverty and weariness; / He has left me to dwell in the dark / like those long dead."

Lamentations 3:4–6

Blessed Hosanna of Kotor

(Katarina Kosic)

b. November 25, 1493, Kumano, Montenegro (Yugoslavia)
d. April 27, 1565, Kotor, Montenegro (Yugoslavia)

Born in the mountains overlooking the ancient city of Kotor, Katarina was baptized in her parents' schismatic church and spent her early childhood tending sheep. Her mother taught her that God made the world and everything in it, and that He was born of a virgin and was crucified. Katarina longed to see Christ and prayed that God would show himself to her, just once.

Her prayer was answered one evening while she was gathering the sheep in a meadow. She saw a beautiful child and ran to embrace him, but he rose into the air and vanished. Katarina was convinced that she had seen the Infant Jesus, but her mother told her not to tell silly stories. Soon after, alone at midday on a hill with her sheep, Katarina saw Christ on the Cross. Such visions continued throughout her life. After her father's death, her mother allowed Katarina to go to Kotor and receive religious instruction at the Roman Catholic cathedral. Impressed with the sermons there, she asked to be confined to a hermit's cell attached to the building, and at twenty-one she made religious vows, taking the name Hosanna.

When an earthquake destroyed Hosanna's first home, she moved to a tiny cell in another church. She spent the next forty-four years in prayer and penitence and experiencing a mystical union with Christ. The people of Kotor, who venerated Hosanna as a living saint, often asked for her intercession. She was also skilled at embroidery and sold her work to raise money for distribution to the poor. A sample of her needlework is preserved in Kotor's cathedral. Her feast day is April 27.

The Genius of Hosanna of Kotor:

Contemporaries called her their Angel of Peace because she reconciled so many feuding families. Today she is considered an apostle of Christian unity and a patron of the ecumenical movement.

Reflection:

"The crowds preceding him and those following kept crying and saying: / 'Hosanna to the Son of David; / blessed is he who comes in the name of the Lord; / hosanna in the highest.'"

Matthew 21:9

SAINT BERNADETTE SOUBIROUS
(Marie-Bernarde Soubirous)

b. January 7, 1844, Lourdes, Hautes-Pyrénées, France
d. April 16, 1879, Nevers, Nièvre, France

The extreme poverty of Bernadette's family kept her out of school, and at fourteen she still did not know the catechism well enough to make her First Communion. Yet Bernadette was chosen to be Our Lady's instrument at Lourdes.

On February 11, 1858, Bernadette was out collecting firewood with friends. She lagged behind and was alone near a grotto when she heard the sound of rushing wind and saw a beautiful young woman in a long white dress surrounded by a bright light and holding a rosary with large white beads. Awestruck, Bernadette took out her own rosary and began to pray. The woman smiled and joined her. By the time they had finished, Bernadette understood that this was Our Lady, who was calling her to become her confidant and collaborator in spreading the saving work of her Son. In months to come, Our Lady appeared in the grotto eighteen times, speaking to Bernadette about the need for people to do penance for their sins. Our Lady told her: *"I do not promise you happiness in this world, but in the next."* She also showed Bernadette where to find the underground spring that to this day supplies the healing waters at Lourdes.

That June, Bernadette was finally allowed to make her First Communion. A month later, the apparitions ended, but the miraculous waters continued to draw pilgrims to Lourdes. Bernadette refused to profit materially in any way and sought seclusion with the Sisters of Charity and Christian Instruction at Nevers. She embraced a humble and hidden life with them, until she died from tuberculosis of the bone. Bernadette's incorrupt body is now venerated in the altar at her convent. The feast of Our Lady of Lourdes is celebrated on February 11, and the shrine continues to yield miraculous healings.

The Genius of Bernadette:
Serenely confident about what she had seen and heard, Bernadette could say: *"I am not asked to make you believe; I am asked to tell you."*

Reflection:
"The Spirit and the bride say, 'Come.' Let the hearer say, 'Come.' Let the one who thirsts come forward, and the one who wants it receive the gift of life-giving water."

Revelation 22:17

April 17

Blessed Kateri Tekakwitha
(Catherine)

b. 1656, Ossernenon, Auriesville, New York
d. April 17, 1680, Sault St. Louis, Montreal, Canada

The Lily of the Mohawks was the daughter of an Algonquin mother and Iroquois father. Orphaned young and left nearly blind by smallpox, Tekakwitha (= "puts things in order") was a servant in her Mohawk uncle's home when she learned about Christianity from Jesuit missionaries who had lodged with him.

She astonished Father Claude Chauchetière with her saintly qualities. He was losing faith, but Tekakwitha's fervor renewed his own. He considered her chosen by God and on Easter, 1676, baptized her with the name Catherine, for Catherine of Siena (April 29). Today she is best known as Kateri, a name created in 1891 by a prominent historian, Ellen Hardin Walworth, who concluded that this was how the Iroquois would have pronounced Catherine. Kateri's devotion made her tribe's pagan majority uncomfortable. They ridiculed her and stoned her when she prayed. In 1677 Kateri ran away and joined the many Christian tribes that had gathered on the Prairie de la Madeleine in Quebec. There she made her First Communion and gave herself completely to God. Kateri also visited the Montreal convent founded by Marguerite Bourgeoys (January 12). This was Kateri's first encounter with women in religious orders, and it greatly influenced her spirituality.

Kateri's health had always been fragile. After a brief illness, she received the last rites on Wednesday during Holy Week and died that afternoon at the age of twenty-four. Moments later her smallpox scars disappeared and her face became radiant. Her tomb in Quebec still draws many pilgrims and reports of miracles. In 1980 Kateri became the first Native American to be beatified. She is the patron of Native Americans and refugees.

The Genius of Kateri Tekakwitha:
> Kateri's Jesuit confessor, Pierre Cholonec, wrote that she excelled in every virtue and "gave us the impression she had made each virtue her particular concern, as though it were the only one to be practiced."

Reflection:
> *"Having become perfect in a short while, / he reached the fullness of a long career; / for his soul was pleasing to the* LORD, / *therefore he sped him out of the midst of wickedness."*
> Wisdom 4:13–14, cited in Cholonec's tribute to Kateri

Blessed Marie Anne Blondin

(Esther Blondin)

b. April 18, 1809, Terrebone, Quebec, Canada
d. January 2, 1890, Lachine, Quebec, Canada

Esther grew up without formal schooling. At twenty-two she went to work as a domestic in a convent where the nuns taught her to read and write. She became a teacher herself and was concerned that so many French Canadians were growing up illiterate. The Church in Canada insisted on separate schools for girls and boys, and rural parishes too poor to finance two schools chose to have none.

In 1848 Esther approached the bishop of Montreal about founding a religious congregation devoted to coeducating rural boys and girls. He considered this "rather rash and contrary to established order" but allowed her to experiment. Two years later she founded the Sisters of St Anne. Taking the religious name Marie Anne, she became the first superior, and prayed daily to Saint Anne (July 26) *"to bestow on her spiritual daughters the necessary virtues to be educators of the Christian youth."* Success brought a power struggle with a new chaplain who forced Marie Anne to resign as superior and barred her from any administrative responsibilities. Assigned to the basement laundry, she took her move philosophically, saying, *"The deeper a tree sinks its roots, the greater its chances of growing and producing fruit."* She remained a spiritual mother, and generations of novices sought her encouragement. Although she was officially ignored even after death, the Sisters kept her story alive. By 1917 a new chaplain had heard so much about Marie Anne that he began a series of conferences to study her life and work. Interest continues to grow, and many favors have been attributed to her intercession. Her spiritual daughters continue her work in Canada, the United States, Haiti, Chile, and Cameroon.

The Genius of Marie Anne Blondin:

A pamphlet from the Sisters of St Anne explains: "Like any prophet invested with a mission of salvation, Mother Marie Anne lived persecution by forgiving without restriction, convinced that there is *'More happiness in forgiving than in revenge.'*"

Reflection:

"O God, more powerful than all, hear the voice of those in despair. Save us from the power of the wicked, and deliver me from my fear."

Esther C:30

SAINT CASILDA OF TOLEDO

birthdate unknown, Toledo, Spain
d. c. 1050, La Buraba, Castile, Spain

Casilda was the daughter of the Muslim emir of Toledo. She was known for her generosity and her kindness to Christian captives. She brought them food and other necessities, and they in turn answered her questions about their faith.

Casilda was about seventeen when she was hit by a mysterious illness. She apparently could not stop menstruating. None of the distinguished Arab doctors she consulted could cure her. Christian friends advised her to visit the lakes of San Vicente de Briviesca in the Catholic kingdom of Castile. Casilda's father reluctantly gave permission for her to make the trip north, and she traveled there in an enormous caravan, with an entourage befitting a Muslim princess.

At La Buraba, in the Burgos Mountains, Casilda drank from the medicinal springs and was healed. In gratitude, she asked to be baptized quietly and never returned to her palace in Toledo. Renouncing the pleasures of the world, she chose to live as a hermit in a cave. It is said that as long as Casilda dwelt in the mountains, no shepherd ever suffered a mishap there. Another legend says that she was one hundred years old when she died. Her body was found in her cave and moved to the nearby church of San Vicente.

In 1750 a great shrine was dedicated to Casilda on the site of her cave. Although she is not well known outside Spain, Casilda has always been greatly revered there and she inspired some of Spain's greatest artists. Tirso de Molina wrote a play about Casilda, and Francisco de Zurbarán's portrait of her hangs in the Prado in Madrid. Women continue to invoke her for fertility and menstrual problems. Her feast day is April 9.

The Genius of Casilda:
By practicing the Corporal Works of Mercy, especially those that call on us to feed the hungry and visit the captive, Casilda proved herself a true Christian long before she was baptized.

Reflection:
"How can I repay the LORD / for all the good done for me?"

Psalm 116:12

SAINT AGNES OF MONTEPULCIANO
(Agnes de Segni)

b. June 28, 1268, Gracciano Vecchio, Siena, Italy
d. April 20, 1317, Montepulciano, Siena, Italy

At the age of nine, Agnes convinced her parents to allow her to enter a Franciscan monastery at Montepulciano. A few years later she left to become the prioress of a new monastery near Orvieto. This required a papal dispensation because she was only fifteen, but Agnes governed wisely for twenty-two years. As her reputation grew, the people of Montepulciano invited her back. They demolished a brothel and built a monastery for her on the site. Once installed in her new home, Agnes adopted the relatively new and austere Dominican Rule.

Agnes lived on bread and water and is said to have received Communion regularly from an angel. She was blessed with many spiritual gifts: her prayers cast out demons, multiplied loaves of bread, and healed the sick. It was said that wherever she knelt to pray, flowers grew. During her ecstasies she was often showered with fine white grains of manna in the shape of a cross. Agnes had a hot temper, however, and if any nuns approached her while she was in prayer she might berate them for disturbing her unity with Christ.

Catherine of Siena (April 29), born thirty years after Agnes's death, was devoted to her and visited Agnes's shrine at Montepulciano several times. Catherine's visits were marked by supernatural events. Once, she brought her sister-in-law Lisa and two nieces, and Agnes's miraculous manna fell on them like dew, covering everyone in the chapel with such abundance that Lisa scooped up a handful.

The Genius of Agnes of Montepulciano:
Agnes once reported a visit from the Blessed Mother during which she was allowed to hold the baby Jesus for a few hours. When Mary wanted the child back, Agnes refused to let him go. The two of them engaged in a tug-of-love, which the real mother won. Agnes did manage to tear a cross from the baby's neck, a relic still venerated at Montepulciano. As historian Rudolph Bell puts it: "The young saint knew what she wanted, and she did not easily allow anyone to get in her way."

Reflection:
"Many signs and wonders were done among the people at the hands of the apostles."

Acts 5:12

SAINT FARA OF FAREMOUTIERS
(Burgundofara)

b. c. 603, Poincy, Burgundy, France
d. c. 645, Faremoutiers, Brie, France

Fara was the daughter of Agneric, a powerful nobleman. By age fourteen she had consecrated herself to God, and when Agneric insisted on arranging her marriage, Fara became seriously ill. She dreamed about a holy man and heard a voice that said: *"Whatsoever this man tells you to do, do it and you will be healed."*

Fara was near death when Eustace of Luxeuil[76] visited her castle and she immediately recognized him from her dream. He blamed Agneric for Fara's suffering, because he had not honored her vow to God. Agneric agreed to let Fara have her way. Eustace blessed her and she recovered, but as soon as he left, Agneric resumed negotiating her marriage. This was too much for Fara and she ran away. Agneric dispatched his vassals with orders to bring her back dead or alive. *"Do you believe that I fear death?"* said Fara when the men cornered her in a church. She dared them to kill her: *"Ah! How happy should I be to give my life in so just a cause to Him who has given His life for me!"* She held the men at bay until Eustace arrived. He took Fara back to her father, who repented for good and allowed her to take the veil.

Fara built a double monastery with separate quarters for men and women. They observed a strict Rule, drinking no wine, and no milk during Lent and Advent, and making a strict examination of conscience three times a day. Her community became famous as Faremoutier (=Fara's monastery) and attracted many future saints. Her feast day is April 3.

The Genius of Fara:

Fara was the first to see through a meddling monk who posed as a reformer and convinced several saintly abbots to relax their Rule. She denounced him as a liar and a fraud. Eventually the other abbots recognized that Fara was right and returned to their old rigor.

Reflection:

"A new hymn I will sing to my God. / O LORD, great are you and glorious, / wonderful in power and unsurpassable."

Judith 16:13

❦

BLESSED MARIA GABRIELLA SAGHEDDU
(Gabriella of Unity)

b. *March 17, 1914, Dorgali, Sardinia*
d. *April 23, 1939, Grottaferrata, Italy*

At age twenty-one, Gabriella left her rural village to enter a Trappist monastery near Rome. She embraced the rigorous life, writing to her family: *"I dig, I hoe, I do everything that comes along."* When the time came, she freely offered herself for the cause of Christian Unity.

Gabriella probably never met anyone who was not a Roman Catholic, yet she had a deep intuition about divisions among Christians. Through her abbess, Pia Gullini, she learned about Paul Couturier, the French priest who had introduced an annual week of prayer for Christian Unity. During the 1938 observations, Mother Pia read aloud Couturier's letter asking for prayers and spiritual sacrifices, and Gabriella was moved to offer her own life for the cause. *"I feel the Lord asks this of me"* was her only explanation. Soon after, Gabriella was stricken with tuberculosis, suffered for fifteen months, and died on the eve of Good Shepherd Sunday (second Sunday after Easter).

A year later, the first book about Gabriella appeared in print. The ecclesiastic establishment was skeptical and Mother Pia was exiled to Switzerland. Nevertheless, Gabriella's reputation as a patron of Unity spread among clergy of many faiths in England and France. In 1957, as her abbey prepared to move to Viterbo, Gabriella's grave was exhumed and her body found incorrupt. Her cause moved swiftly, and her 1983 beatification was attended by representatives of the Anglican, Lutheran, and Orthodox churches.

The Genius of Gabriella Sagheddu:
On the day of her religious vows, Gabriella wrote: *"In the simplicity of my heart, I offer you everything with joy, O Lord. I thank you with all my heart and, by pronouncing the holy vows, I abandon myself entirely to you."* She accepted her suffering as a sign of Christ's special love for her.

Reflection:
"I pray not only for them, but also for those who will believe in me through their word, so that they may all be one, as you, Father, are in me and I in you, that they also may be in us, that the world may believe that you sent me."

John 17:20–21

April 23

BLESSED TERESA MARIA
OF THE CROSS MANETTI

(Teresa Adelaida Cesina, Bettina)

b. March 2, 1846, Campi Bisenzio, Florence, Italy
d. April 23, 1910, Campi Bisenzio, Florence, Italy

A woman of action who also understood the importance of prayer, Bettina grew up in a small town near Florence and throughout her life was known for the lively, cheerful disposition that made her a natural leader.

At twenty-one, Bettina and two companions rented a small house on the bank of the Bisenzio River with the intention of dedicating themselves to prayer, penance, and charity. They nursed the sick and prepared children for their First Communion. More women joined them, and Bettina, inspired by Teresa of Avila (October 15), adopted the Carmelite spirituality.

The mission continued to expand. Bettina was forty-one when a dying woman asked her to take her orphaned children. Bettina saw this as a direction from God and set about building a large orphanage. The following year, she and twenty-six members of her institute officially took the veil as Third Order Carmelites. She took the religious name Teresa Maria of the Cross, but was always known as Mother Bettina. In 1904 Bettina sent sisters to establish their first community in Lebanon. That year the institute was formally approved as the Carmelite Sisters of St Teresa. Three years later they opened another house at Haifa, at the foot of Mount Carmel.

Bettina's particular cross was illness. Lifelong stomach ailments worsened after 1906, and at one point she was falsely diagnosed as delusional. The surgeon who finally confirmed that Bettina suffered from a malignant tumor was deeply impressed by her fortitude and her determination to offer her suffering for the good of her community. As Bettina lay dying, she was thinking of the gate of heaven. Her last words were: *"Oh, it is open! See, I am coming! I am coming!"*

The Genius of Teresa Manetti:

"God makes saints with a chisel, not a paintbrush," said Mother Bettina. Although her own life was often harsh and demanding, what everyone remembered about Bettina was her "quality of joy."

Reflection:

"When the Son of Man comes, will he find faith on earth?"
Luke 18:8, keynote for her beatification homily

SAINT MARY EUPHRASIA PELLETIER
(Rose-Virginie Pelletier)

b. July 21, 1796, Noirmoutier, Vendée, France
d. April 24, 1868, Angers, France

At age nineteen Rose entered the convent of Our Lady of Charity of the Refuge, taking the religious name Mary Euphrasia. The convent sheltered fallen women but had suffered during the French Revolution. The Sisters were struggling to rebuild, and at first they welcomed Euphrasia's energy and imagination.

Euphrasia was eager to establish refuges in other towns, but some Sisters feared that this would tax their meager resources. They called Euphrasia a spendthrift and accused her of personal ambition. Euphrasia herself was not sure that her motives were heaven-sent. She asked a dying Sister to send her a sign from heaven if she was truly inspired by God. A few days after the elderly Sister died, a bishop invited Euphrasia to open a refuge in Angers. Euphrasia had the sign she had asked for, but her challenges were just beginning. She was frustrated by the lack of sharing among convents of the same order and recognized that they would never grow unless they had a system for sharing resources and staff. When her Sisters resisted, she made the painful decision to leave the order in which she had spent more than twenty years. She founded the Congregation of Our Lady of Charity of the Good Shepherd (Good Shepherd Sisters) and became its first superior-general. In 1841 Euphrasia sent the first Good Shepherd Sisters to Louisville, Kentucky. Today her Sisters are serving in sixty-five countries all over the world.

The Genius of Mary Euphrasia Pelletier:

Euphrasia was blessed with managerial skills, but she credited her successes to something else, writing: *"It is well known that I had neither riches, nor talent nor external charm, but I have always loved, and I have loved with all the strength of my heart."*

Reflection:

"Where jealousy and selfish ambition exist, there is disorder and every foul practice. But the wisdom from above is first of all pure, then peaceable, gentle, compliant, full of mercy and good fruits, without inconstancy or insincerity."
James 3:16–17

April 25

Blessed Pauline von Mallinckrodt

b. June 3, 1817, Minden, Westphalia, Germany
d. April 30, 1881, Westphalia, Germany

Pauline was the beloved daughter of a Lutheran father and a Catholic mother. Besides her family, the greatest influence on her life was her headmistress, Louise Hensel,[77] who encouraged her to work for the good of society.

As a young woman, Pauline took in Margretchen, a blind girl who was considered hopelessly retarded. Pauline taught Margretchen to manage her own basic hygiene and to read a pre-Braille alphabet. She blossomed under Pauline's encouragement. Pauline then took in another blind student, and another. By 1842 her home had become Germany's first institute for the blind. She traveled around Europe to study other schools, and when she was unable to find suitable teachers, she founded the Sisters of Christian Charity. Pauline soon extended their mission to general education. Her greatest challenge came in 1871 when Chancellor Otto von Bismarck launched the Kulturkampf, a campaign to subordinate all religious institutions to the state. Convents were closed all over Germany and Pauline began looking to America. In 1873 she sent her first Sisters to New Orleans, where they established a school, followed by a motherhouse in Wilkes Barre, Pennsylvania. The Sisters of Christian Charity continue to serve in schools in North and South America. They commemorate Pauline on April 30.

The Genius of Pauline von Mallinckrodt:
> Pauline advised: *"Love for the children is the best teacher. . . . One can entrust children only to someone who loves them. Love in your heart, love in your tone of voice, love in your conduct toward the children—that attracts them with an irresistible force, and it also draws down God's blessing upon them and us."*

Reflection:
> *"When you come to serve the LORD, / prepare yourself for trials. / Be sincere of heart and steadfast, / undisturbed in time of adversity."*
>
> Sirach 2:1–2

BLESSED CATHERINE OF PALLANZA
(Catherine Morriggia)

b. 1437, Pallanza, Verbania, Italy
d. April 6, 1478, Sacro Monte, Varese, Italy

BLESSED JULIANA OF BUSTO-VERGHERA
(Juliana Puricelli)

b. 1427, Busto Arizio, Italy
d. August 15, 1501, Sacro Monte, Varese, Italy

At the height of the Renaissance, two very different women retreated to the Sacred Mountain that soars above Lake Lugano. The woman later known as Juliana was born in a poorhouse and toiled in the cotton fields. Her father beat her when she refused to marry. After years of suffering, she left home, making her way to the Sacred Mountain, already the home of Catherine, a pious hermit. Catherine had been born into wealth and privilege, but her entire family was wiped out by the plague. Alone in the world at fifteen, Catherine retreated to a cave on the mountain. She had been there for two years when she welcomed her new companion and named her Juliana,[78] after a saint who had also been abused by her father. More women joined them on the mountain and they built a monastery there, adopting the Rule of Saint Augustine. Juliana even introduced a new devotion, called the Robe of the Virgin, which consisted of saying 100,000 Hail Marys a year.

When the armies of Charles V invaded the region in 1544, his soldiers broke into Juliana's tomb, looking for treasure. They found her incorrupt body instead. According to legend, Juliana raised her hand to warn them back, and the earth trembled as the would-be looters made a quick escape. Later, the incorrupt bodies of both Juliana and Catherine were moved to the cathedral of St Ambrose in Milan. Their small community survives on the Sacred Mountain. The feast day for Catherine and Juliana is April 27.

The Genius of Juliana and Catherine:
In the serenity of the mountain, they supported each other and welcomed other pilgrims.

Reflection:
"When I cried out, you answered; / you strengthened my spirit."

Psalm 138:3

April 27

Saint Zita of Lucca

b. 1218, Bozzanello, Monsagrati, Italy
d. April 27, 1278, Lucca, Italy

Every spring the city of Lucca goes wild with daffodils and the air is filled with their fragrance. It is all to honor Zita, who spent her entire adult life as a servant in the home of the Fatinelli family.

She was twelve when her parents brought her to work for the Fatinellis. (This sort of position was so prized that Zita's parents brought along a basket of fruits from their farm to thank them.) Zita was delighted to be living next to Lucca's basilica, but the entire city was soon put under an interdict (churches closed). For the next three years, Zita walked fifteen miles to Pisa to attend Mass. Her employers found this piety ridiculous, but her sincerity and kindness won them over.

One cold Christmas Eve, after the interdict had been lifted, Zita was leaving for Mass when Signor Fatinelli insisted that she borrow his fur coat. At the steps of the basilica, Zita encountered a shivering beggar. She impulsively wrapped him in the coat while she went inside. After the Mass the beggar was gone, and so was Signor Fatinelli's fur coat. As expected, he was furious, and Zita felt terrible. The next day, however, a stranger appeared at the door and handed Zita the lost coat. She was convinced that the beggar had been an angel, and since then the site where she encountered him has been known as the Angel's Door.

Zita eventually managed the entire Fatinelli household, treating all the servants with great kindness. On the night she died, a star lit up the mansion as if it were midday. Everyone took this as a sign that Zita was already in heaven. She is a patron of domestic workers and is invoked to find lost objects, especially keys.

The Genius of Zita of Lucca:
Zita was guided by the two questions her mother taught her: *"Will this be pleasing to God? Will this be displeasing to God?"* That was all that Zita ever needed to know.

Reflection:
"She watches the conduct of her household, / and eats not her food in idleness."

Proverbs 31:27 (motto on old holy card for Saint Zita)

SAINT GIANNA BERETTA MOLLA

b. October 4, 1922, Magenta (Milan), Italy
d. April 28, 1962, Monza (Milan), Italy

A very modern saint, Gianna balanced children, a husband, and a busy medical practice and still found time for skiing, rock climbing, and playing the piano. She also did volunteer work with groups like Catholic Action. Gianna loved her life, but she willingly sacrificed it for the sake of her unborn child.

Gianna had grown up in a large, devout family. One sister became a nun and two brothers became priests, but Gianna's vocation was medicine, marriage, and motherhood. She shared a family practice with another brother, often making housecalls on her motorbike. She continued to practice after her marriage to Pietro Molla, an engineer, and the births of their children Pierluigi, Mariolina, and Laura. In 1961, after several miscarriages, Gianna was two months pregnant when she was diagnosed with a uterine tumor. Doctors offered three options. Only one could keep the pregnancy viable, but it could also have fatal complications at delivery. As a doctor, Gianna made an informed decision and chose the third option in spite of the risks. Throughout the next six months, Gianna reiterated to her doctors and family that if they had to decide whether to save her or the child, they must save the child.

Gianna entered the hospital on Good Friday. The following morning, after giving birth to a healthy daughter, Gianna Emanuela, she contracted peritonitis and died eight days later. Thirty-eight years later, another young woman, Elisabete Arcolino Camparini, resisted her doctors' urgings to terminate her pregnancy. They considered it hopeless because she had lost all her amniotic fluid in her third month. Elisabete prayed to Gianna, relying on her intercession, and confounded medical experts by giving birth to a healthy daughter she named Gianna Maria. This was recognized as Gianna's canonization miracle.

The Genius of Gianna Beretta Molla:
Gianna's postulator cautions that her story is about more than her sacrifice. Hers was "a life lived with great intensity and a profound love of God and her fellow man."

Reflection:
"When one finds a worthy wife, / her value is far beyond pearls. / Her husband, entrusting his heart to her, / has an unfailing prize."

Proverbs 31:10–11

Saint Catherine of Siena

(Catherine Benincasa)

b. March 25, 1347, Siena, Italy
d. April 29, 1380, Rome, Italy

One of the most brilliant and influential women who ever lived, Catherine came of age when the Church and society were in chaos. She was the youngest of twenty-five children of prosperous parents who tried to squelch her religious fervor. Despite their efforts, Catherine entered a Dominican convent, but after three years returned home to live as a nun in the world—a most unusual idea for her time.

When plague swept Siena, Catherine devoted herself to nursing. She was as concerned with the victims' souls as she was with their physical health. She proved so helpful that she was invited to Pisa, where she first experienced the stigmata. Soon the pope, exiled in Avignon, commissioned three Dominican friars, including Raymond de Capua,[79] to hear the confessions of Catherine's many converts.

Next, the people of Florence sent for her. Pope Gregory had put Florence under interdict and its people were unable to celebrate Mass or receive the sacraments. They appointed Catherine their ambassador to the pope and sent her to Avignon. The sheer luxury of his quarters there disgusted her. Catherine urged the pope to return to Rome for his own good and the good of the Church. She warned: *"Self love has poisoned the whole world and the mystic body of the Church."*

Catherine convinced Pope Gregory to return to Rome in 1377.

In 1970, in recognition of her great learning and sanctity, Catherine was proclaimed a Doctor of the Church.[80] She is, with Edith Stein (August 9) and Bridget of Sweden (July 23), a co-patron of Europe.

The Genius of Catherine of Siena:

Catherine said: *"There is no perfect virtue—none that bears fruit—unless it is exercised by means of our neighbor."* She exercised this virtue throughout her life, whether in nursing lepers, negotiating peace between feuding cities, or bringing the papacy back to Rome.

Reflection:

"Jesus answered, 'Whoever loves me will keep my word, and my Father will love him, and we will come to him and make our dwelling with him.'"

John 14:23, cited by Catherine in Letter 105

BLESSED MARIE OF THE INCARNATION
(Marie Guyart)

b. October 28, 1599, Tours, France
d. April 30, 1672, Quebec, Canada

As a young widow with an infant, Marie Guyart managed her family's commercial transport business, but when her son Claude was twelve, she made the difficult decision to leave him in the care of her married sister and enter an Ursuline convent. *"I felt more in leaving my son, whom I loved so much, than if I had given away all possessions imaginable,"* Marie later wrote. *"It seemed that I was being hacked in two!"*

In 1639 Marie left France for Quebec, where she founded a school for the daughters of colonists and natives. At the age of forty she learned the Algonquin and Montagnais languages, and by fifty she had mastered Huron. She composed catechisms and translation dictionaries for each language, and devoted herself to Quebec's natives and colonists for thirty-two years.

Marie maintained a lively correspondence with her son, advising him: *"God has wonderful treasures of goodness for simple souls who trust themselves to Him. You must believe that we have a God who cared for us in every minute of the past, and who will continue to do so in the future."* When Claude became a Benedictine priest and asked her forgiveness, she replied: *"Why do you ask of me pardon for what you call the follies of your youth? Don't you realize that everything had to happen just that way so that the consequences would give us real cause to bless God?"*

The Genius of Marie of the Incarnation:

Marie described the rewards of contemplation: *"When the soul has reached this state, it makes very little difference whether it is buried in business worries or enjoys restful solitude. It is all the same for the soul, for everything that touches it, everything that surrounds it, everything that strikes its senses does not prevent its enjoyment of love's presence."*

Reflection:

"When his parents saw him, they were astonished, and his mother said to him, 'Son, why have you done this to us? Your father and I have been looking for you with great anxiety.' And he said to them, 'Why were you looking for me? Did you not know that I must be in my Father's house?'"

Luke 2:48–49

Saint Panacea de Muzzi

b. 1368, Quarona, Novara, Italy
d. 1383, Quarona, Novara, Italy

Panacea was fifteen when she was martyred by her abusive stepmother. Her birth mother, Maria, had died when Panacea was only three, and her father Lorenzo's new wife, Margarita, disliked her and beat her often. Panacea was probably relieved when Margarita sent her into the hills with the sheep. On her way home, Panacea often stopped to pray at the church of John the Baptist.

One night, Panacea became so absorbed in prayer that her sheep got tired of waiting and wandered home on their own. With no sign of Panacea, her stepmother had to go out in the dark to look for her, arming herself with the distaff from her spinning wheel. When she found Panacea in the church, still lost in prayer, she was furious and began beating her with the distaff until she was dead. Lorenzo arrived and found his daughter's body, with the distaff on fire beside her. He could not put out the fire, and therefore could not move her. Word spread, and other villagers came to see this miracle. They finally carried her body to Ghemme, where she was buried beside her mother. Within twenty years of Panacea's death, two small chapels had been dedicated to her, one on the site of her martyrdom, the other near her grave. In time her body was moved to Agamio, where it is venerated today. She is honored on May 5 in Novara and on the first Friday of May in Valsesia. The church of John the Baptist in Quarona has two vivid frescoes that portray Panacea's martyrdom. Residents there make an annual pilgrimage to her tomb in Ghemme.

The Genius of Panacea:

Overcoming her stepmother's abuse, Panacea found strength in prayer. Her faithfulness in daily life, in spite of adversity and misunderstandings, make Panacea an example of holiness.

Reflection:

"Peace I leave with you; my peace I give to you. Not as the world gives do I give it to you. Do not let your hearts be troubled or afraid. . . . If you loved me, you will rejoice that I am going to the Father; for the Father is greater than I."

John 14:27–28

May 2

SAINT WIBORADA OF SAINT GALL

birthdate unknown, Klingnau, Aargau, Switzerland
d. 925, Saint Gall, Switzerland

The patron saint of librarians is usually represented holding a book in one hand and a battle-ax in the other. That is because Wiborada was hacked to death while protecting the great library at the Abbey of St Gall.[81]

Earlier in life, Wiborada's close relationship with her brother Hatto[82] stirred rumors of incest. She was called before the bishop and exonerated. So many people began coming from great distances to seek her prayers and counsel that Wiborada asked to retire to a cell beside the church of St Magnus. She continued to work as a bookbinder for the library at Saint Gall. She also nursed a dying girl, Rachild,[83] who miraculously recovered and remained with her.

Wiborada dreamed that the Magyars would invade Saint Gall. She warned the monks, who wanted her to join them in their fortress, but she insisted that they take the books first. The Magyars descended and burned the church of St Magnus to the ground. Only Wiborada's cell remained standing. They burst in, looking for a fabulous treasure, but found only Wiborada praying, so they hacked her to death with their battle-axes. Wiborada was venerated as a saint from that moment, and many miracles were reported at her tomb. In 1047 she became the first woman formally canonized by the Vatican. Pope Clement II observed that it had taken the clergy a hundred years to honor Wiborada whereas God had been manifesting her holiness all along. The library that she saved still draws scholars from all over the world.

The Genius of Wiborada:

Wiborada tutored Ulric,[84] a future bishop of Augsburg known for his high moral standards, and advised him to deal with temptation by praying: "O God, make speed to save me!"

Reflection:

"The LORD gives wisdom, / from his mouth come knowledge and understanding."

Proverbs 2:6

Saint Maura

b. c. 283, Perapis, Thebes
d. 298, Antioch, Egypt

Among the first of the black African saints, Maura was a young newlywed when she was martyred with her husband, Timothy. The Roman emperor had ordered that all Christian books be burned. Timothy was a deacon, responsible for protecting the sacred scriptures, and he refused to surrender the Gospels. He was brought before Arianus,[85] the governor of Thebes, who ordered him tortured and blinded. Timothy still refused to surrender them.

Maura had been married to Timothy for only three weeks and she was desperate to have her husband back. She accepted a bribe from Arianus to talk Timothy out of his madness. He reproached Maura for clinging to the material world and urged her to enter the kingdom of heaven through martyrdom. Maura was so impressed by Timothy's commitment that she returned Arianus's bribe. At first Arianus misunderstood her motives, and assured Maura that he would find her a new and better mate. But Maura had decided that Christ meant more to her than all earthly considerations. She was ready to suffer and die for Him.

Arianus condemned Maura and Timothy to be crucified near each other. Determined to make an example of them, he had them fastened to crosses so that they would die as slowly as possible. Maura and Timothy lingered for nine days, encouraging each other. On the tenth day, an angel came for their souls. Maura's name means "dark complexion," and in Macedonia the feast of Maura and Timothy is known as Black Day.

The Genius of Maura:

Maura's faith helped to start Arianus on his own path to martyrdom. He was deeply moved by her humility, her refusal to keep his bribe, and most of all, her unwavering love for God and her husband.

Reflection:

"Chastised a little, they shall be greatly blessed, / because God tried them / and found them worthy of himself. / As gold in a furnace, he proved them, / and as sacrificial offerings he took them to himself."

Wisdom 3:5–6

BLESSED CATHERINE OF PARC-AUX-DAMES

(Catherine of Louvain)

b. c. 1210, Cologne, Germany
d. Louvain, Belgium

Rachel was the daughter of a Jewish merchant who moved to Louvain when she was about five years old. Among his friends was a priest, Master Reiner, chaplain to the duke of Brabant. Rachel often eavesdropped when they discussed religion, and she began asking questions herself.

Rachel was about eight years old when she dreamed that the Blessed Mother told her to go to Reiner. He took her to a Cistercian monastery, Parc-aux-Dames, where she was baptized and took the name Catherine, which the Blessed Mother had called her in the dream. Her horrified parents immediately complained to the duke and to Pope Honorius III. They begged that she be returned to them until she was twelve, the legal age at which a girl could join a religious community without parental consent. The duke ordered her return, but the head of the Cistercian Order talked him out of it. Catherine's parents were supported by the bishop of Liège, who ordered Parc-aux-Dames to give her up.

In an unprecedented move, Catherine received permission to address the bishop's court herself. Her logic convinced the learned clergymen that Catherine's call was the work of the Holy Spirit. The bishop of Liège, however, continued to take her parents' side for the next two years. It took another five years before Catherine could make her final vows as a nun at Parc-aux-Dames. She spent the rest of her life there and was honored as a miracle worker even before her death.

The Genius of Catherine of Parc-aux-Dames:
Armed only with strength and intelligence, Catherine overcame the most powerful men in her world in order to fulfill a call to follow Christ.

Reflection:
"Jesus said, 'Amen, I say to you, there is no one who has given up house or brothers or sisters or mother or father or children or lands for my sake and for the sake of the gospel who will not receive a hundred times more now in this present age: houses and brothers and sisters and mothers and children and lands, with persecutions, and eternal life in the age to come.'"

Mark 10:29–30

BLESSED JUTTA OF PRUSSIA
(Judith of Sangerhausen)

b. c. 1200, Sangerhausen, Thuringia
d. May 5, 1260, Kulmsee, Prussia (now Chelmza, Poland)

Jutta was fifteen when her noble family arranged her marriage to a Polish baron, Johannes Konopacki of Bielcza. The marriage was a happy one and all four of their children entered religious orders. Jutta's husband died while on a Crusade in the Holy Land.

At this point, Tartars invaded Poland, torching whole villages and clogging the river Vistula with Christian corpses. When the Tartars moved on to northern Germany (Prussia), Jutta felt called to do something for the suffering Christians there. Encouraged by her friend, Mechthild of Magdeburg (October 31), Jutta left her comfortable life behind and arrived in Prussia in 1260. She moved into a rundown cottage in the forest not far from Kulm, near a great marsh called Bielcza. There she led a solitary, austere life, spending most of her time in prayer. She was seen to levitate and remain suspended in the air while she prayed. When Jutta went to the new church at Kulm, she usually walked through the woods, around the marsh, but legend has it that she sometimes took a shortcut and walked straight across the water.

After four years in the forest, Jutta died of fever. Her confessor, the bishop of Kulm, intended to honor her wishes for a quiet burial but changed his plans when people began pouring into Kulm to pay their respects. No one in Prussia had ever seen a peaceful crowd that size. Thirteen priests assisted at her funeral, a remarkable number since most of the missionaries had been massacred by the Tartars. Jutta was buried in the church of the Holy Trinity, in Kulmsee, now a cathedral, where a chapel is dedicated to her.

The Genius of Jutta of Prussia:

In a world in chaos, Jutta prayed for peace. She once said: *"Three things can lead us close to God. They are physical suffering, exile in a foreign land, and choosing poverty for God."* Jutta chose to embrace all three.

Reflection:

"Rejoice always. Pray without ceasing. In all circumstances give thanks, for this is the will of God for you in Christ Jesus."

1 Thessalonians 5:16–18

BLESSED ANNA ROSA GATTORNO

b. October 14, 1831, Genoa, Italy
d. May 6, 1900, Rome, Italy

Rosa married at twenty-one, and for six years she was a happy wife and mother. Then, after the birth of her third child, a sudden illness left her firstborn, Carlotta, deaf and mute; her husband died; and she lost her infant son. These tragedies only strengthened the widowed Rosa's conviction that God was calling her to make a total gift of self.

Rosa felt called to found a new and innovative congregation called the Daughters of St Anne, Mother of Mary Immaculate. Members would serve the sick of either sex and teach in a coed elementary school. This would mean separation from her surviving son and daughter, to whom she was devoted. She consulted with Pius IX,[86] who urged Rosa to begin immediately, adding: *"This Institute will spread in all parts of the world as swiftly as the flight of the dove. God will take care of your children; you must think of God and His work."* Rosa entrusted her children to relatives and officially founded the Daughters in 1866. In spite of Pius IX's encouragement, it took Rosa twenty-six years to get Church bureaucrats to recognize the Daughters as a religious order. Among other issues, they objected to her plan to admit widows, ignoring the fact that she herself was a widow. Long and heated negotiations did not keep Rosa from sending her Daughters to missions all over Italy and South America, until at one point the Sacred Congregation annulled the Daughters' charter and threatened to deprive them of the sacraments. Calmer heads finally prevailed, and in 1892 Rosa won approval of her Rule. Today thirty-five hundred Daughters continue her mission on three continents.

The Genius of Anna Rosa Gattorno:

Drawing her strength from almost constant prayer, Rosa advised: *"Prayer is the key to grace: it opens up the Lord's treasures."*

Reflection:

"LORD, who may abide in your tent? / Who may dwell on your holy mountain?
Whoever walks without blame, / doing what is right, / speaking truth from the heart."

Psalm 15:1–2

Saint Rosa Venerini

b. *February 9, 1656, Viterbo, Italy*
d. *May 7, 1728, Rome, Italy*

After the death of her fiancé, Rosa entered a contemplative convent, but that quiet life was not for her. She returned home and looked after a younger brother and sister until they were on their own. At twenty-four, finding herself living alone, she began to invite local women into her home to pray the Rosary.

Rosa discovered that many of her friends knew almost nothing about their faith, and most could not read or write. Her gift for teaching them led her to establish the first public school for girls in Italy and to train the Pious Teachers (Maestre Pie Venerini) who joined her. Rosa was determined to reach young women who had no access to quality education. As the Venerini Institute expanded, Cardinal Barbarigo of Montefiascone invited Rosa to open schools in his diocese, and to train Lucy Filippini (March 25) in her methods. Barbarigo would have gladly kept Rosa there, but she cherished her independence and refused to be tied to one diocese. Determined to go wherever her schools were needed, Rosa traveled through remote hill towns on a mule and lived on alms, even while sometimes being harassed by those who opposed her innovations. Priests worried that she was usurping their power and noblemen disapproved of her efforts to educate the lowly, but Rosa never abandoned her motto: *"Educate to set free."*

Her spiritual daughters, the Venerini Sisters, have been engaged in various ministries in the United States since 1909. Today they are also at work in India, Europe, Africa, and South America.

The Genius of Rosa Venerini:
As she lay dying, a priest asked if Rosa wanted to pray to God to restore her health so that she could serve Him a little longer. She replied: *"Father, I find myself so completely attached to his divine will that I desire neither to live nor to die. I wish to live so long as he desires and I wish to serve him for as long as he desires and no longer."*

Reflection:
"If I give away everything I own, and if I hand my body over so that I may boast, but do not have love, I gain nothing."

1 Corinthians 13:3

May 8

Saint Magdalene of Canossa
(Maddalena Gabriela di Canossa)

b. March 1, 1774, Verona, Italy
d. April 10, 1835, Verona, Italy

When Magdalene Canossa began working among the poor, her relatives worried that she would disgrace their noble name. In fact, she would become the most illustrious of them all.

Magdalene's father, the marquis, died suddenly when she was five. Her mother soon remarried, leaving the children to be raised by an uncle. The Canossa palace was at the center of a war between France and Austria, and Magdalene grew up familiar with the sounds of bombs and cannons. When Napoleon commandeered the palace for his headquarters, Magdalene's family continued to live there. One day she slipped and fell, and a gallant French officer moved to help her to her feet. Magdalene assured him she didn't need his help. At that moment, Napoleon himself stepped in. "Leave her alone. Don't touch her," he barked. "She is an angel."

A few years later, while Magdalene was at Mass, a passage from the Book of Tobit inspired her to dedicate herself to charity. She was working in Verona's most squalid neighborhood when she boldly wrote to Napoleon requesting the use of an abandoned monastery there. Perhaps remembering the angel, he gave Magdalene the building and she set up her first school for girls. Concerned with educating the whole woman, she forbade corporal punishment and trained her teachers to correct the girls gently and lovingly. Hardened street urchins blossomed under Magdalene's care. By 1828 she had received papal approval for her institute, known today as the Canossian Daughters of Charity. Imaginative and resourceful, she also founded an order of priests and a Third Order for laypeople. Today the Canossian Family is active all over the world, especially in Italy, Latin America, and the Philippines.

The Genius of Magdalene of Canossa:
Throughout her life, Magdalene drew strength from love, saying: *"Those who love are never tired, since love knows no burden."*

Reflection:
"Perform good works all the days of your life, and do not tread the paths of wrongdoing. For if you are steadfast in your service, your good works will bring success, not only to you, but also to all those who live uprightly."
Tobit 4:5–6 (the passage that influenced Magdalene)

May 9

Saint Catherine of Bologna

(Caterina Vigri)

b. September 8, 1413, Bologna, Italy
d. March 9, 1463, Bologna, Italy

Catherine grew up at the court of the prince of Ferrara as a lady in waiting for his young daughter. After the princess married, Catherine was free to enter a convent. Living the quiet, contemplative life of a Poor Clare in Ferrara, Catherine composed music, painted miniatures, and wrote an important treatise, *The Seven Spiritual Weapons*. Her life was also marked by supernatural events. For example, Catherine spent one Christmas Eve in the convent chapel reciting a thousand Hail Marys. Suddenly, a great light filled the chapel and Catherine saw the Blessed Mother smiling in front of her and holding her infant Son. Trembling between love and fear, Catherine bent to kiss the child and instantly all was dark; the vision was gone. She told no one but recorded the experience in the margin of her breviary (prayer book), where it was found after her death.

After twenty-four years at Ferrara, Catherine was invited to establish a convent in Bologna. Her fifteen companions elected her abbess, a position she held even after her death. She was buried a few hours after she expired, according to Poor Clare tradition, in the ground without a coffin. Almost immediately, visitors noticed a remarkable fragrance around her grave, and after reports of miraculous cures, the nuns had Catherine's body exhumed. Even after eighteen days in the ground, her face retained its original beauty. Her incorrupt body was kept in the chapel, and for two years the nuns continued to regard her as their abbess. The body was finally moved to the church of Corpus Christi, where it remains incorrupt and is venerated today. Catherine is a patron of artists, especially painters.

The Genius of Catherine of Bologna:

As abbess, Catherine asked her Clares to observe three rules: always speak well of everyone, practice constant humility, and never meddle in the business of others.

Reflection:

"[Jesus proclaimed] I came into the world as light, so that everyone who believes in me might not remain in darkness. And if anyone hears my words and does not observe them, I do not condemn him, for I did not come to condemn the world but to save the world."

John 12:46–47

BLESSED THERESA OF JESUS GERHARDINGER

(Carolina Gerhardinger)

b. June 20, 1797, Stadtamhof, Bavaria (Germany)
d. May 9, 1879, München, Bavaria (Germany)

Carolina was educated by the Canonesses of Notre Dame, the community cofounded by Alix Le Clerc (January 9). She was about to graduate when the government shut down all parochial schools and expelled all religious. Carolina's pastor encouraged her to take up their work. Certified by the state in 1812, she began teaching in the school where she had been a student. By 1820 the government had lifted the ban on convents, and in 1833 she founded the School Sisters of Notre Dame, taking the religious name Theresa of Jesus. She introduced a new model of religious life that allowed the Sisters to serve many small communities, mainly in rural areas: they lived in groups of two or three rather than gathered in a large central convent. Theresa also created a unifying central government designed to maintain a common spirit among the far-flung Sisters.

The new bishop did not appreciate Theresa's innovations. He threatened to excommunicate her and forbade her to travel, but Theresa persevered and moved the motherhouse to Munich. Answering a call from German emigrants in the United States, Theresa took five Sisters to Pennsylvania in 1847. They were informed on arrival that the local bishop preferred that they return to Germany. Unconvinced that this was God's will, Theresa took her Sisters to Baltimore, where she was encouraged by the saintly John Neumann.[87] In the next five weeks, she and Mother Caroline Freiss traveled more than two thousand miles by stagecoach and steamboat. After a year, Theresa returned to Germany, delegating Mother Caroline to lead the Sisters in North America. Today more than four thousand School Sisters of Notre Dame carry on their work in thirty countries on five continents. They celebrate their own Mother Theresa on May 9.

The Genius of Theresa Gerhardinger:
Theresa tells us: *"What matters is that you serve God not as much as you want, but as much as is possible for you."*

Reflection:
"His mother said to the servers, 'Do whatever he tells you.'"

John 2:5

BLESSED MARIA CATHERINE OF SAINT ROSE OF VITERBO

(Constance Domenica Troiani)

b. January 19, 1813, Giuliano di Roma, Italy
d. May 6, 1887, Cairo, Egypt

Constance was six years old when her widowed father entrusted her to the Sisters of Charity in Ferentino. Coming of age there, she took religious vows along with the religious name Maria Catherine of Saint Rose of Viterbo.

For twenty-four years, Catherine devoted herself to the Sisters of Charity, supervising their convent school. She was forty-six years old when her quiet life took a surprising turn. A visiting priest who had just returned from Egypt spoke to her convent about the urgent need for missionary sisters. Catherine and five other Sisters answered his call for volunteers. They sailed to Cairo in 1859, becoming the first missionary sisters in Egypt, and immediately opened an orphanage and a school for girls of every race and religious affiliation. The mission grew so quickly that Catherine requested more Sisters from Ferentino. But the Sisters had always considered Egypt a temporary mission and wanted Catherine to come home. In order to continue her work in Egypt, Catherine severed her community from their longtime home. She gained papal approval for a new order, known today as the Franciscan Missionary Sisters of the Immaculate Heart of Mary.

Catherine opened another foundation in Jerusalem and found several important patrons, including the sultan of Constantinople and Ferdinand de Lesseps, the engineer who built the Suez Canal. She also began a mission, "the Vine of St Joseph," to ransom young Sudanese women who had been sold into slavery by Arab traders. The grateful women called her *Mamma Bianca* ("white mother"), and she died beloved by Christians and Muslims alike. Today her order is active all over the world, "wherever the needs of God's people are." The Franciscans venerate her on May 6.

The Genius of Catherine of Saint Rose of Viterbo:
During a cholera epidemic in Cairo, a Sister asked, "Doesn't our misery frighten you?" Catherine replied, "*My dear, only a lack of faith frightens me.*"

Reflection:
"Amen, amen, I say to you, unless a grain of wheat falls to the ground and dies, it remains just a grain of wheat; but if it dies, it produces much fruit."
John 12:24, cited at her beatification

May 12

Blessed Imelda Lambertini

b. c. 1322, Bologna, Italy
d. May 12, 1333, Val di Pietra, Italy

The patron saint of first communicants was another one of those headstrong girls who became great saints. Imelda was not a martyr, however. She simply died of joy.

The daughter of a noble family, nine-year-old Imelda was placed in a Dominican convent outside the walls of Bologna. She was the youngest of several girls boarding there, and she became the Sisters' pet. They allowed Imelda to pray with them and even to wear a modified Dominican habit, but they drew the line at letting her receive Communion. Imelda cried when told that she must be fourteen to receive the Eucharist. She appealed to the convent chaplain, but he refused to make an exception.

On the eve of the feast of the Ascension, after the Sisters and older girls had received Communion, the priest left and as the Sisters began to follow him out of the convent chapel, Imelda remained behind, praying silently. Suddenly a heavenly fragrance filled the air and a radiant Host was seen hovering over Imelda's head. Some Sisters said that the Host had emerged from the tabernacle, while others said it descended from heaven. They called the priest back to see. He could not understand what it meant at first, and simply knelt in adoration. As he knelt, the Host descended onto the paten. Bowing to Divine Will, he understood that he had no choice but to give Imelda her first Communion. Tasting the Host, Imelda was so overcome that she collapsed and died in an ecstasy of joy. The Sisters said that she died in *osculo Domini* ("in the kiss of the Lord").

Imelda's body was placed in a marble tomb in the convent sacristy. Every year, on the anniversary of her death, the Sisters commemorated her with prayers and hymns. Two hundred years later, they moved to a new convent inside Bologna's city walls, and today Imelda's relics are venerated there at the church of Saint Sigismund.

The Genius of Imelda Lambertini:
Strong-willed, impatient, and eager for experience, Imelda was no perfect little girl, but she achieved perfect joy in the Eucharist.

Reflection:
"Ask and it will be given to you; seek and you will find; knock and the door will be opened to you."

Matthew 7:7

May 13

BLESSED JULIAN OF NORWICH

b. c. 1342, Unknown
d. c. 1423, Norwich, England

Julian has been called the first Englishwoman of letters, and her writings are considered the most beautiful mystical works in the English language. Yet we know almost nothing about her, except what we glean from her writings. Even her name probably comes from the church of St Julian, where she chose to live as an anchorite at the center of Norwich's busy commercial district. She kept a maidservant who took care of her shopping and errands, and she conversed with many visitors who came to her window, but most of her day was taken up with prayer, study, and meditation.

When Julian was about thirty years old, during a brief, near-fatal illness, she experienced a series of sixteen visions that opened her to the depths of God's unconditional love. She described the visions in *Showings*, then spent the next thirty years meditating on them. That process produced her longer book, *Revelations of Divine Love*. Julian's most famous pronouncement assures us: *"All shall be well, and all shall be well, and all manner of thing shall be well."*

Julian also tells us: *"The reason we are not fully at rest in heart and soul is because we seek rest in those things that are so small and have no rest within them, and pay no attention to our God, who is Almighty, All-wise, All-good, and the only real rest."*

The Genius of Julian of Norwich:

Near the end of the *Revelations* Julian summed up what she had learned: *"I saw very certainly in this and in everything that before God made us he loved us, which love was never abated and never will be. And in this love he has done all his works, and in this love he has made all things profitable to us, and in this love our life is everlasting."*

Reflection:

"I, too, hearing of your faith in the Lord Jesus and of your love for all the holy ones, do not cease giving thanks for you, remembering you in my prayers, that the God of our Lord Jesus Christ, the Father of glory, may give you a spirit of wisdom and revelation resulting in knowledge of him."

Ephesians 1:15–17

SAINT MARY MAZZARELLO

(Maria Domenica Mazzarello)

b. May 9, 1837, Mornese, Alessandria, Italy
d. May 14, 1881, Nizza Monferrato, Italy

Mary did not learn to read and write until she was thirty-five, but long before that she was speaking out about holy matters in a clear and persuasive way.

A robust young peasant, Mary could outwork any man in the fields until a serious bout of typhoid at the age of twenty-four left her in fragile health. Seeking a less demanding way to earn a living, she trained as a dressmaker. By 1861 Mary and her friend Petronilla had established their own shop. *"Let every stitch be an act for the love of God,"* she told Petronilla. When a widowed peddler asked them to take his two young daughters as apprentices, Mary and Petronilla began a vocational school. They took their students to church and on cultural outings. Such activities had to be discreet, as anything associated with religion was, if not outright illegal, discouraged by Italy's anticlerical government. In 1864 Mary's pastor introduced her to John Bosco,[88] who was already famous for his charity work. Mary and John Bosco cofounded the Daughters of Mary Help of Christians (Salesian Sisters), dedicated to educating young girls. Under her guidance, it would become the second largest congregation of women religious in the Church.

Mary's sense of humor never failed her. Once, Petronilla was worried that their success could spell problems—they were attracting all these smart, well-educated girls. *"Shh!"* whispered Mary. *"If they find out how much we don't know, they'll never let us stay."*

The Genius of Mary Mazzarello:

Mary told her students: *"God does not take into account if someone did more work than another, but whether all used the talents that he gave them."*

Reflection:

"I give you praise, Father, Lord of heaven and earth, for although you have hidden these things from the wise and the learned you have revealed them to the childlike. Yes, Father, such has been your gracious will."

Luke 10:21 (Gospel reading for the Mass on her feast)

May 15

SAINT DYMPHNA OF GHEEL

b. c. 620, Oriel, Ireland
d. c. 640, Gheel, Belgium

The patron saint of the mentally ill was the daughter of Damon, an Irish king. Dymphna and her mother were baptized by the elderly priest Gerebernus.[89] When the queen died, however, Damon went mad with grief. He became obsessed with Dymphna, who was the image of her mother, and tried to make her his bride.

Dymphna and Gerebernus fled to Belgium, finding sanctuary among a small community of hermits at Gheel. The king tracked them down and ordered his vassals to kill them. They beheaded Gerebernus but balked at hurting Dymphna, so the king unleashed his own sword and cut off her head. According to legend, certain lunatics who witnessed Dymphna's martyrdom were immediately cured. Others who prayed at her grave also found relief. As the stories spread, more families brought their mentally ill relatives to Gheel and prayed for a miracle. On leaving, they sometimes boarded their relatives in the homes of local families. A unique community gradually grew up around Dymphna's shrine, where the mentally ill found a supportive environment in private homes. A large and beautiful church was dedicated to Dymphna in 1340, and her relics are still venerated there. For centuries Gheel celebrated Dymphna's legacy every twenty-five years. Since 1975 the five-day festival occurs every five years. Devotion to her as a patron for the mentally ill spread to the United States, and in 1939 a chapel was dedicated to Dymphna on the grounds of Massillon State Hospital (now Heartland Behavioral Healthcare) in Ohio. The Franciscan Mission Association sponsors twelve masses a year at her shrine in Gheel, among other devotions. Dymphna is also considered a guardian of family harmony.

The Genius of Dymphna of Gheel:
There are those who dismiss Dymphna's story as a pious legend, but modern health-care providers are taking another look at Gheel's traditions. The World Health Organization describes Gheel as "one of the best examples of how communities can become carers of the mentally ill."

Reflection:
"Blessed are the poor in spirit, / for theirs is the kingdom of heaven."
                                                                    Matthew 5:3

SAINT MARGARET OF CORTONA
(Margherita di Laviano)

b. 1247, Laviano, Perugia, Italy
d. February 22, 1297, Cortona, Arezzo, Italy

Margaret was too beautiful for life on the farm. She gladly ran off with a nobleman, Arsenio del Monte, although marriage was out of the question. For nine years, she lived in his castle and bore him a son. She paraded around town on a fine horse, dressed in sumptuous gowns with gold chains in her hair. All that changed when Arsenio's dogs returned from a hunting trip without him and led Margaret to his body. The shocking sight of her murdered lover, heartlessly tossed into a ditch, brought on Margaret's profound conversion.

Margaret took her little boy and walked to Cortona, where a widow and her daughter-in-law sheltered them and introduced her to the Franciscans who became her spiritual directors. Margaret found work as a midwife and established a hospital. While praying, she heard God speak to her for the first time, saying: *"I have made you a mirror for sinners; from you shall the most hardened sinner learn how ready I am to be merciful."* She began a public ministry and brought many sinners back to the sacraments, ended feuds, and saved at least one would-be suicide by cutting down the rope he had used to hang himself. One priest complained that she was sending too many people to Confession, that he could only clean out so many stalls in one day. The Lord at once advised Margaret: *"Tell him from me that when he hears confessions he is not cleaning out stalls, but preparing in human hearts a home for me."*

Margaret is a patron of the homeless, single mothers, and midwives. Her feast day is on February 22, but Cortona and the Franciscan Order commemorate her on May 16.

The Genius of Margaret of Cortona:
Ever grateful, Margaret once asked God why he had forgiven her. *"I have destined you to be the net of sinners,"* the Lord replied. *"I wish that you should be a light to those who are seated in darkness; I wish that the example of your conversion should preach hopefulness to those who despair."*

Reflection:
"My sacrifice, God, is a broken spirit; / God, do not spurn a broken, humbled heart."

Psalm 51:19

May 17

BLESSED ULRIKA NISCH

(Franziska Nisch)

b. September 18, 1882, Mittelbiberach-Oberdorf, Germany
d. May 8, 1913, Hegne, Germany

Born out of wedlock, Ulrika Nisch spent her life in obscurity. Since her death she has interceded for thousands, and the number of pilgrims who visit her tomb in Hegne, Germany, has quietly grown to more than 100,000 a year.

Ulrika left school at the age of twelve, and at twenty-two she was working in Switzerland as the nanny to a schoolmaster's four children. That year she was hospitalized with a serious infection. The care she received from the Sisters of Mercy of the Holy Cross confirmed her desire to become a nun. She had begun to experience frequent visits from angels and saints, which she confided to her pastor. He arranged for her to be admitted to the Holy Cross convent in spite of her illegitimate birth and lack of a dowry. She took the religious name Ulrika. (She had been baptized Franziska.) When the novice-mistress asked Sister Ulrika what sort of work she was prepared to do, she answered, *"Give me a job where I can make many sacrifices."* She was assigned to work in the kitchen.

Ulrika was a mystic and visionary in an order in which mysticism is not particularly valued. Theirs is an active apostolate, established to perform works of mercy. Ulrika tried to hide her experiences, but they were observed by other Sisters. An associate explained that when questioned, "she quietly reported visions of Christ, including as an infant, but especially as Bridegroom. She had frequent special knowledge of the future, including World War I, and she had an 'odor of sanctity.'" Early in 1912 Ulrika's health began to fail. Diagnosed with tuberculosis, she died "unselfishly, just as she had lived," and was buried in the convent cemetery. It is likely that no one was more surprised than the Sisters of the Holy Cross when the grave of their sweet but obscure cook began to draw a steady stream of pilgrims, who have credited Ulrika with many miracles. She is venerated in Hegne on May 8.

The Genius of Ulrika Nisch:
Ulrika's motto was always: *"Love knows no measure."*

Reflection:
"Blessed are the clean of heart, / for they will see God."
Matthew 5:8, cited in her beatification homily

BLESSED BLANDINE MERTEN
(Maria Magdalena Merten)

b. July 10, 1883, Düppenweiler on the Saar, Germany
d. May 18, 1918, Trier, Germany

Blandine's official biographer calls her "a hidden bride of Christ," and even today she remains little known outside Germany. Although she lived in obscurity, Blandine was "a loving source of grace," and she continues to offer that grace to the many pilgrims who visit her grave.

Baptized Maria Merten, she trained as a teacher and taught in public schools for six years, until 1908, when she and her older sister, Elise, entered the convent of the Ursulines of Mount Calvary, near Ahrweiler. She took her religious name from the early Christian martyr Blandina of Lyons (June 2). In 1913, on the eve of World War I, she made the traditional vows of poverty, chastity, and obedience, to which she added a fourth: offering herself as a willing sacrifice to Christ.

Blandine soon developed tuberculosis, and in the fall of 1916 she entered a sanitarium at the Ursuline convent in Trier. Although seriously ill, she was always cheerful, writing: *"O holy will of God, I love you above all things, and I would like to live on earth as though nothing existed except God and me. I want to love God more than any creature has ever loved him."* In February 1918, as she entered the last stages of her illness, the city of Trier was strafed by the first round-the-clock air raid in history. She remained calm and resigned to God's will, dying peacefully three months later. She was buried in the convent cemetery, and since then, the number of people who pray at her grave has steadily increased. Pilgrims come to ask Blandine's intercession and to thank her for past favors. Still others write to the Ursulines of Mount Calvary about Blandine. Some have seen their petitions granted, while others have been given the strength to carry their cross. Many credit Blandine with restoring their faith and their ability to pray.

The Genius of Blandine Merten:
She did nothing out of the ordinary, but did the ordinary extremely well. As Blandine wrote: *"The loving Lord does not need extraordinary works: He desires only love."*

Reflection:
"Blessed are the meek, / for they will inherit the land."

Matthew 5:5

Blessed Umiliana de'Cerchi

b. 1220, Florence, Italy
d. May 19, 1246, Florence, Italy

In an age in which marriage was all about property and power, Umiliana's father negotiated her marriage to a moneylender with great attention to economics but little thought to compatibility. Her only consolations were the births of two daughters and the support of her sister-in-law, Ravenna. The older, more sophisticated Ravenna ran their extended family's household and provided cover for Umiliana's charities.

When Umiliana's much-older husband died, she settled his debts and returned to her father's house. Custom dictated that she leave her daughters with her in-laws. Fortunately, Ravenna saw that they remained close to their mother. Umiliana was still only twenty and her father was eager to arrange another marriage. When Umiliana refused, he banished her to an attic room. She resolved to live in abstinence, and eventually became a Franciscan tertiary, devoting her time to prayer and good works. Umiliana was blessed with a gift for miracles, but she was also beset by devils, one of whom appeared in the form of a serpent, wrapping his tail around her feet and leaning his head against her cheek.

As she lay dying, tormented by thirst and demons, one servant grew tired of her constant pleas for water and hit her on the head with a pitcher. Umiliana's friend Gisla brought her an image of the Blessed Mother with Christ on the cross and placed it where Umiliana could see it. She also burned incense and sprinkled Umiliana's body with holy water. The demons fled, leaving her to die in peace at age twenty-seven.

Immediately there was a call to make her a saint. Among those who went on the record about Umiliana's sanctity were three brothers-in-law, her grandmother, and three household servants (we do not know if the pitcher-tosser was one of them).

The Genius of Umiliana de'Cerchi:
Blessed with a gift for friendship, Umiliana found an important ally in her sister-in-law Ravenna, and she later overcame her father's oppression through her network of women friends.

Reflection:
"Every one of you who does not renounce all his possessions cannot be my disciple."

Luke 14:33

BLESSED COLOMBA OF RIETI

(Angiola Guardagnoli)

b. February 2, 1467, Rieti, Umbria, Italy
d. May 20, 1501, Perugia, Umbria, Italy

While the baby was being baptized Angiola ("little angel"), a white dove flew into the church and settled on her head. After that, she was always called Colomba ("dove").

Reluctantly accepting her refusal to marry, Colomba's parents allowed her to live at home as a Dominican tertiary. She began experiencing ecstasies, mystical phenomena, and a vision that led her to leave Rieti and head north on foot. A series of miraculous adventures brought Colomba to the city of Perugia, where she was welcomed with great fanfare and credited with saving them from a bloody civil war. The notorious Lucrezia Borgia tried to lure Colomba to Spoleto and, when that failed, launched a campaign of slander against her. After a year of Lucrezia's harassment, Colomba's health broke down. During her last illness, she was tormented by diabolical visions of food and naked bodies but consoled by a vision of Saint Dominic,[90] who brought her a garland of flowers and assured her that she would soon join him in heaven. While the people of Perugia wept at the loss of their saint, Colomba welcomed death. Her lavish funeral had barely begun when a white dove flew into the church, settled on her coffin, draped with purple and gold, and remained there until the Mass ended. Among those who later reported visions of Colomba was her contemporary Osanna of Mantua (June 20).

The Genius of Colomba of Rieti:

Soon after arriving in Perugia, Colomba encountered a woman carrying three loaves of fresh bread. She asked for a taste and the woman insisted that Colomba take a whole loaf. When the woman reached home and discovered that she still had three loaves, she searched out Colomba, who explained: *"Don't be surprised. That which is given for the love of God is never diminished but increases."*

Reflection:

"You who dwell in the shelter of the Most High, / who abide in the shadow of the Almighty, Say to the LORD, 'My refuge and fortress, / my God in whom I trust.'"

Psalm 91:1–2 (Colomba recited this psalm daily)

May 21

BLESSED MARIE LOUISE TRICHET

b. May 7, 1684, Poitiers, France
d. April 28, 1759, Saint-Laurent-sur-Sèvre, Vendee, France

When Louise Trichet was seventeen, she consulted a new priest, Louis de Montfort,[91] about her desire to enter a convent. Montfort asked her to work with him at the local hospital instead, marking the start of a collaboration in the tradition of Francis and Clare (August 11) and Francis de Sales and Jane de Chantal (August 5).

The hospital was really a sordid workhouse for destitute men, women, and children. Montfort's attempts at reform had caused the entire staff to walk out, and disabled inmates were keeping it going. They needed Louise's help, and when the bishop refused her permission to work there, she had herself admitted as a pauper. Her mother warned, "You will become as mad as this priest," but Louise gladly shared the life of the inmates: their work, their meals, and their sleeping quarters. After a year, Montfort asked her to wear a habit and she took the name Marie Louise of Jesus. This marked the beginning of the Daughters of Wisdom, whose name signifies that they are the daughters of Jesus Christ who is Incarnate Wisdom. For a long time, Louise was the only member, and when conflicts with the bishop forced Montfort to leave Poitiers, she struggled to run the hospital on her own. Montfort returned in 1713 but died suddenly three years later, leaving Louise with complete responsibility. At that point, her gift for management emerged in full force. She outlived Montfort by forty-three years, establishing more than thirty new foundations and admitting 174 new Daughters. Today, 2,000 Daughters work in twenty-five countries. They commemorate Louise on May 7.

The Genius of Marie Louise Trichet:
With no formal training, Louise found strength and inspiration in her faith. She advised one troubled novice: *"I suggest you make a half hour's meditation at the feet of Christ and listen to what he has to say to you."*

Reflection:
"Resplendent and unfading is Wisdom, / and she is readily perceived by those who love her, / and found by those who seek her."

Wisdom 6:12

❦

SAINT RITA OF CASCIA

b. 1381, Roccaporena, Italy
d. May 22, 1457, Cascia, Italy

The Saint of the Impossible was a miracle baby. Legend has it that an angel appeared to Amata Ferri and told her that after twelve years of childless marriage she would bear a daughter and name her Margherita. All her life she would be known as Rita.

When Rita was only a few months old, her parents left her in a basket under a shady tree while they cut wheat in nearby fields. A peasant who had cut his hand was looking for help when he saw bees swarming around the baby's mouth. He brushed them away and his wound was suddenly healed. This miracle of the bees was the first of many in Rita's life.

At sixteen, Rita wanted to enter a convent, but her elderly parents insisted that she marry the wealthy Paolo Mancini. They were together for eighteen years, and Rita bore two sons, but she suffered from Paolo's violent temper. He beat her and broke all her wedding china. Paolo's rages made many enemies and one night, while returning from nearby Cascia, he was murdered. When a neighbor brought Rita the news, she responded: *"May God pardon the murderers, as I have already forgiven them."* Her sons were not as generous. They had inherited their father's temper and joined his family in a vendetta. Rita lived in fear that her sons would die like their father. Instead, they were taken during an epidemic. Rita was consoled by the knowledge that they died in a state of grace.

She next sought to join the Augustinian Order, which appealed to her because members were not cloistered but moved around freely to help the sick and afflicted. They did not admit widows, however. Rita pleaded with the prioress to make an exception, but after two interviews the prioress still rejected her. (It is possible that the nuns did not want to antagonize Rita's violent in-laws.) Then one night, three great saints appeared to Rita in a dream: John the Baptist, Augustine of Hippo, and Nicholas of Tolentine. By the light of the moon they led Rita to the convent. She knocked at the gate but everyone was asleep. The next thing Rita knew, she was sitting in the convent chapel. When dawn arrived, the nuns marched in for morning prayers. They saw Rita but said nothing. Finally the prioress arrived, but she could tell that Rita was as surprised as everyone else. Bowing to the will of God, she allowed Rita to take her place among them.

The convent's novice-mistress tried to test Rita's vocation. She once ordered Rita to water a dry, dead stick every day until it blossomed. Rita obediently watered the branch until it miraculously sprouted green leaves. Six centuries later, the Vine of Saint Rita still blooms in the convent courtyard. The Sisters harvest the grapes, and the leaves are dried, powdered, and given away to the faithful.

Rita had been a nun for more than two decades when she was so moved by a homily on the Passion of Christ that she stood before a crucifix and begged Christ to allow her to share his pain. Suddenly, a piece of thorn fell from the crucifix and embedded itself in Rita's forehead. The wound brought her terrible suffering for fifteen years, and it is the reason that Rita is usually represented with a crown of thorns over her nun's veil.

Rita was bedridden during the last winter of her life. A visiting cousin asked if she wanted anything. Rita yearned to smell a rose from her parents' garden, but it was January and her cousin considered this impossible. She returned to their village and discovered that a single red rose was blooming exactly where Rita said it would be. She brought it to Rita, who gave thanks to God for this sign of his love. She died a few months later. Today the annual celebration at Rita's shrine in Cascia includes a blessing of motorbikes. The riders gather in front of her shrine to ask Rita's protection and to offer her red roses.

The Genius of Rita of Cascia:
From her miraculous birth to the fragrant rose at her deathbed, Rita proved that with faith nothing is impossible.

Reflection:
"Fear not, my children; call out to God! / He who brought this upon you will remember you. / As your hearts have been disposed to stray from God, / turn now ten times the more to seek him; / For he who has brought disaster upon you / will, in saving you, bring you back enduring joy."
Baruch 4:27–29

❧

BLESSED CATHERINE SIMON DE LONGPRÉ

(Marie-Catherine of Saint Augustine)

b. May 3, 1632, Saint-Sauveur-de-Vicomte, Normandy, France
d. March 8, 1668, Quebec, Canada

Young Catherine was used to getting her own way, and when her older sister entered a convent, she insisted on joining her. Catherine, who was twelve at the time, made such a fuss that her father and the abbess gave in. Four years later, Catherine begged to join a group of nuns destined for Quebec. Her father petitioned the courts to block her but finally had to let her go.

Catherine's community had established the first public hospital north of Mexico, and she devoted herself to caring for the sick. In spite of her youth, she was a gifted nurse and manager, and her superior wrote: "It was impossible to see her and not to love her." Catherine was devoted to the memory of Jean de Brébeuf,[92] a Jesuit missionary martyred by the Iroquois a year after her arrival. They never met, but Catherine regarded him as her spiritual director, assigned by God. Francis Laval,[93] the first bishop of Quebec, often asked Catherine to pray for special intentions, especially for the colony and the Indians. Shortly before she died at the age of thirty-six, she said: "My God, I *adore your divine perfections; I adore your divine justice; I abandon myself to it with my whole heart."*

Catherine is considered a founder of the Catholic Church in Canada, and her community, known today as the Augustines of the Mercy of Jesus, continues to serve in hospitals in North America. She is venerated by the Augustinian Order on May 8.

The Genius of Catherine Simon de Longpré:

Blessed with mystical gifts, Catherine also endured spiritual trials and temptations. In a series of visions, Catherine saw three stages of hell, each more awful than the next, but the worst, she reported, was reserved for those who abused the graces that God had given them.

Reflection:

"Draw your strength from the Lord and from his mighty power."

Ephesians 6:10

BLESSED MARGARET POLE

b. August 14, 1471, Castle Farley, England
d. May 28, 1541, East Smithfield Green, England

Henry VIII once called Margaret Pole "the most saintly woman in England," but all that goodwill vanished when he discarded his first wife to marry Anne Boleyn.

Margaret had forged a close friendship with Henry's first wife, Catherine of Aragon, and he named Margaret godmother for their daughter Mary Tudor. When Henry defied the Church and married Anne Boleyn in 1533, Margaret withdrew from his court. Three years later, Henry had Anne Boleyn beheaded and took a third wife, Jane Seymour, who died in childbirth. By then Henry had made his final break with Rome and declared himself head of the Church in England. He pressed Margaret's son, Reginald, a cardinal, to legitimize this claim, but Reginald insisted on the primacy of the pope. Reginald was on the Continent and out of reach, so Henry took out his disappointment on Margaret and her family. He had two of her other sons taken to the Tower of London and executed for treason. Ten days later, Margaret was arrested and held in the Tower under miserable conditions for the next two years.

Meanwhile, Henry took a fourth wife, Catherine Howard, who sent Margaret warm clothing and other comforts, leading some to believe that she would soon be freed. Instead, on May 27, 1541, Margaret was informed that, without a trial, she had been sentenced to be executed the following day.

When seventy-year-old Margaret was ordered to lay her head on the chopping block, she refused, saying, *"Thus should traitors die. I am none!"* She insisted on standing erect when she was beheaded. A year later, her son the cardinal was one of three legates who presided at the opening of the Council of Trent, launching the Catholic Counter-Reformation. Throughout his life Cardinal Pole declared himself proud to be the son of a martyr. Margaret is venerated on May 28.

The Genius of Margaret Pole:

When her faith was put to the test, Margaret refused to compromise.

Reflection:

"[Jesus told them] When you stand to pray, forgive anyone against whom you have a grievance, so that your heavenly Father may in turn forgive you your faults."

Mark 11:25

Saint Maria Maddalena de' Pazzi
(Catherine de' Pazzi)

b. April 2, 1566, Florence, Italy
d. May 25, 1607, Florence, Italy

The Ecstatic Saint was one of the most important mystics of the Renaissance. She entered the convent of Maria degli Angeli at the age of sixteen, taking the name Maria Maddalena. The convent had been founded by Carmelites, and although no longer under that Rule, the eighty nuns there maintained the austere Carmelite traditions.

During her novitiate, Maria Maddalena fell seriously ill. Because she was expected to die, she was allowed to make her vows early. She immediately went into an ecstasy that lasted forty days and concluded with her miraculous recovery. After this, Maria Maddalena had daily visions during which she spoke to the Father, Son, and Holy Spirit, but especially the Son, whom she referred to as the Word. When Maria Maddalena entered a rapture, the other nuns transcribed her utterances, but, like other mystics, she was never satisfied with the hard copy of her experiences. Devils tried to distract her by screaming in her ear, pushing her down stairs, and wrapping themselves around her body like snakes. She threw some out a window and ultimately overcame them all. Maria Maddalena held many important posts in her convent, and was elected superior three years before her death.

Intensely private, Maria Maddalena never wanted her raptures exposed to anyone outside her convent. The transcriptions were not widely circulated during her lifetime, but more than fifty nuns testified during her canonization inquiry. Her body remains incorrupt and is venerated at the Carmelite church in Florence.

The Genius of Maria Maddalena de' Pazzi:
Maria Maddalena was known for her common sense. She prayed: *"Come Holy Spirit. Spirit of truth. You are the reward of the saints, the comforter of souls, light in the darkness, riches to the poor, treasure to lovers, food for the hungry, comfort to those who are wandering, to sum up, you are the one in whom all treasures are contained."*

Reflection:
"In the beginning was the Word, / and the Word was with God, / and the Word was God."

John 1:1

SAINT MARIANA DE PAREDES

b. October 31, 1618, Quito, Ecuador
d. May 26, 1645, Quito, Ecuador

Mariana's was a "family of consequence" in one of the most beautiful and sophisticated cities of colonial South America. She was educated at home, and like Rose of Lima (August 23), she made her home her convent. Every day at noon, she welcomed the poor at her door with a large basket of fresh bread. Mystery surrounded this "angels' bread," which never seemed to run out.

In 1645 Quito was rocked by earthquakes that killed more than two thousand people, followed by epidemics of measles and diphtheria that claimed thousands more. At the beginning of Lent, a long-dormant volcano erupted. Many viewed these calamities as a judgment from God, and on the Fourth Sunday of Lent they filled the church of La Compañia. Father Alonso de Rojas, Mariana's confessor, celebrated the Mass and declared that these tragedies had been caused by sin. He called upon the people of Quito to repent and offered himself to God as a victim to save them from the punishment that they had brought on themselves. Mariana stood up in the crowded church and announced that she would ask God to take her life instead of the priest's. After Mass, she went home and was immediately hit with a serious illness. As her health declined, the earthquakes stopped, the plagues ceased, and the deadly volcano went silent. Mariana lingered for more than a month, cheerfully receiving many visitors. On Ascension Thursday, surrounded by her family and friends, she breathed her last. The entire city of Quito gathered for her funeral, and her coffin was covered with flowers. From that moment the people considered Mariana a saint, and they continue to credit their Lily of Quito with protecting Ecuador from invasion and epidemics.

The Genius of Mariana de Paredes:

> With little education or life experience, and without ever leaving home, Mariana managed to start a small school, the first free clinic in Quito, and a nursery for children, all supported only by the love of God.

Reflection:

> *"I command you: be firm and steadfast! Do not fear nor be dismayed, for the* LORD, *your God, is with you wherever you go."*
>
> Joshua 1:9 (theme of Father de Rojas's homily)

SAINT URSULA LEDÓCHOWSKA

(Julia Maria Ledóchowska, Maria Ursula of Jesus)

b. *April 17, 1865, Loosdorf, Austria*
d. *May 29, 1939, Rome, Italy*

Julia and her sister Maria Theresa (July 5) were born into an old and distinguished Polish family. At age twenty-one, Julia entered an Ursuline convent, taking the name Maria Ursula of Jesus, and spent the next twenty years teaching in a girls' school. The drama of her life began in 1907 when she was sent to Russia to supervise a new school in St Petersburg.

Ursula established a convent there and then a second convent in Sortavala, Finland, which was then part of Russia. She became an apostle of ecumenism, opening these convents for other faith services and Bible study. When asked her political affiliation, Ursula answered: *"My policy is love."* Not everyone approved, and she was under constant surveillance by the secret police. When World War I broke out, Ursula was expelled from Russia and stranded in neutral Sweden for the duration. She finally returned to Poland in 1920, but she had changed and could not return to her former convent. A Protestant friend helped her buy a small farm, and in 1923 she founded the Ursulines of the Agonizing Heart of Jesus, known as the Grey Ursulines because of their habits. They bred horses and trained as veterinarians and grooms. Their restaurant and catering operation supported four houses of charity in Warsaw.

"She had a genius for friendship," the London *Times* reported in her death notice, "and her weekly letters never failed in spite of her endless work." Today there are one hundred Grey Ursuline communities in twelve countries. They commemorate Ursula on May 29.

The Genius of Ursula Ledóchowska:

Ursula taught her Sisters: *"It is not enough to pray, 'Thy kingdom come,' but to work, so that the Kingdom of God will exist among us today."*

Reflection:

"I will bless the LORD at all times; / praise will always be in my mouth. / My soul will glory in the LORD / that the poor may hear and be glad. / Magnify the LORD with me; let us exalt his name together. / I sought the LORD, who answered me, / delivered me from all my fears."

Psalm 34:2–5

SAINT UBALDESCA TACCINI

b. 1136, Castello di Calcinaia, Italy
d. May 28, 1206, Pisa, Italy

One day when Ubaldesca was fifteen, her parents went to work in the fields, leaving her home alone to bake bread. No sooner had she put her loaves in the oven than an angel appeared and told her to go to Pisa and live a life of penitence with the Order of the Hospital of St John of Jerusalem (Hospitallers).

Ubaldesca was skeptical, since she had no dowry. The angel told her not to worry, assuring her that the Hospitallers were more concerned with virtue than money. She ran to tell her parents, who dropped their work and immediately took her to Pisa, twenty miles away. To their surprise, the abbess and her forty nuns were expecting them, because they had been visited by the same angel. The nuns led Ubaldesca to their chapel with great joy and solemnly invested her in the Hospitaller habit. Her parents returned home, and it was only the next day that they remembered the bread in their oven. They expected to find only ashes, but the loaves were golden brown as if just baked. They took some of the miracle bread to the convent as a gift of thanksgiving. Ubaldesca was surrounded by such miracles for the rest of her life. One of the most famous occurred at the church of San Sepolcro when two women saw her drawing water from a well and begged her to draw some for them and bless it. When she did so, it became wine, which is why Ubaldesca is usually shown with a bucket. Visitors to San Sepolcro can still see the miraculous well.

Ubaldesca died peacefully on Trinity Sunday, and her community was consoled by a vision of her soul mounting to heaven, accompanied by a multitude of singing angels. It is said that twenty-two invalids were healed during her funeral procession.

The Genius of Ubaldesca Taccini:

Although known as a nurse and miracle worker, Ubaldesca was equally admired for her humility. When her convent was in need, Ubaldesca was never too proud to go out herself and beg for alms.

Reflection:

"Do not rejoice because the spirits are subject to you, but rejoice because your names are written in heaven."

Luke 10:20

SAINT BONA OF PISA

b. c. 1156, Pisa, Italy
d. May 29, 1207, Pisa, Italy

The patron of flight attendants and tour guides was the daughter of a single mother. Bona grew up believing that her father had vanished on a pilgrimage to the Holy Land. When a vision assured her that he was alive, she traveled to Jerusalem, only to discover that her parents had never been married.

Her father's legal wife was a Levantine noblewoman, and none of their three sons, the Patriarch of Jerusalem, the Master of the Temple, and a Knight Hospitaller, wanted anything to do with Bona. In fact, they tried to intercept her ship before it landed. She escaped and visited the shrines of the Holy Land until she was captured by Saracen pirates and ransomed by the city of Pisa. Home again, she retreated to a small cell attached to her parish church until a vision of James the Great[94] called her to lead a pilgrimage to his shrine, Santiago de Compostella in Spain. This was the most important Christian shrine of the Middle Ages, and Bona ultimately led at least nine pilgrimages there. Each thousand-mile journey could take as long as nine months.

Bona is said to have prophesied the coming of the Dominican Order, and she was blessed with the ability to read hearts and minds. One day, for example, Bona and some friends requested a votive Mass from their pastor, but he demurred, pleading a sore throat. Bona saw that the real problem was a secret but minor fault that he believed kept him from a state of grace. She called him aside, revealed the fault, and chastised him for his scrupulosity. The women got their votive Mass.

The Genius of Bona of Pisa:
Whether it was discovering that she was born out of wedlock or traveling thousands of miles, Bona faced all of life's challenges bravely and with complete commitment.

Reflection:
"One never put to the proof knows little, / whereas with travel a man adds to his resourcefulness. / I have seen much in my travels, / learned more than ever I could say."

Sirach 34:10–11

May 30

SAINT JOAN OF ARC
(Jeanne d'Arc)

b. January 6, 1412, Domremy, France
d. May 30, 1431, Rouen, France

At age thirteen, Joan began hearing the voices of angels and saints. By the time she was sixteen, the voices were ordering her to save France, which was mired in a war with England. Joan pleaded, *"I am a poor girl; I do not know how to ride or fight,"* but Michael the Archangel insisted: *"It is God who commands it."*

In March of 1429, Joan managed an interview with the beleaguered French king, Charles VII. He had swapped his royal robes with a courtier, but she recognized him immediately. Joan's voices had also informed her of the king's private doubts about his own legitimacy, and she put those doubts to rest. Convinced that Joan's message was divinely inspired, Charles put her in charge of a small army, which she led into Orléans. In one week Joan freed a city that had been under siege for seven months. More battles followed, and after Joan drove the English out of France, she conducted Charles to Reims, standing by as he was crowned king on July 17, 1429. She left his court the following March in a dispute over tactics. Two months later, Joan was taken prisoner in Burgundy and sold to the English. The ungrateful Charles refused to ransom her, so the English turned Joan over to French ecclesiastics who put her through a disgraceful nine-month trial. Joan was convicted of heresy and witchcraft and burned at the stake in Rouen's market square. When her heart remained incorrupt, it was thrown into the Seine, along with her ashes.

Twenty years later, Joan's case was reopened. A new king, Charles VIII, ordered a new trial and she was declared innocent in 1451. To the shame of France and England, it took almost five hundred years before she was finally canonized in 1920. Today Joan is the patron saint of France, soldiers, and radio.

The Genius of Joan of Arc:
Fearless in battle, compassionate in victory, forgiving to those who betrayed her, Joan remains a shining example of a faithful Christian soldier.

Reflection:
"No one is disgraced who waits for you, / but only those who lightly break faith."

Psalm 25:3

BLESSED BATTISTA VARANO

(Camilla Varani)

b. April 9, 1458, Camerino, Macerata, Italy
d. May 31, 1524, Camerino, Macerata, Italy

"Reading devout books tired me or made me laugh," Battista admitted. *"I had such an aversion for religious that I could scarcely bear to look at them."* In spite of this attitude, Battista became one of the most brilliant and acclaimed religious scholars of her time.

Baptized Camilla, daughter of the longtime ruler of Camerino, she was mostly concerned with dancing and similar amusements. Her life took a turn during Good Friday services when a priest urged worshipers to take a few minutes every Friday to meditate on Christ's sufferings and his love. Camilla considered this meditation the beginning of her spiritual life. Her commitment grew, and she entered a Poor Clare convent at Urbino, taking the name Battista in honor of John the Baptist. She was blessed with mystic gifts and visions. Once, two angels carried Battista to the foot of the cross on Calvary and she remained there in spirit for two months. When she asked Christ how great was the sorrow in his heart, he replied from the cross: *"As great as the love which I bear toward my creatures."* Before Battista left, Christ decorated her soul with three lilies, and she believed that the fragrance stayed with her for the rest of her life.

Battista's father and two brothers were murdered by Cesare Borgia, whom she forgave and prayed for. At the age of thirty-three she began to write the story of her spiritual journey. Her confessor respected her wishes and shared the manuscript with no one until after her death. It was then published as *My Spiritual Life,* and it remains a classic description of the mystic life.

The Genius of Battista Varano:

Intensely devoted to the Passion of Christ, Battista remained grateful to God for the privilege of her visions. She wrote: *"The more He showered His benefits upon me, the more unworthy I believed myself to be; I therefore considered His graces, not so much as gifts, as deposits, which He confided to my care, or rather as funds with which I should traffic for His benefit."*

Reflection:

"The heavens declare the glory of God; / the sky proclaims its builder's craft."
Psalm 19:2

BLESSED MARGARET EBNER

b. c. 1291, Donauworth, Bavaria, Germany
d. June 20, 1351, Medingen, Bavaria, Germany

The first woman beatified by Pope John Paul II, Margaret Ebner was one of a loosely knit group of mystics who called themselves the Friends of God. She came from a wealthy family and received an excellent education before entering the Dominican convent of Maria Medingen. In 1312 a serious illness left Margaret paralyzed and in constant pain, but she was also blessed with profound spiritual gifts, including visions and revelations. Outside the convent, Louis of Bavaria was waging war over his right to the throne and Margaret offered her suffering for the victims of this war. She was suddenly healed in 1325, at about the time she met Henry of Nordlingen, a priest who was in contact with most of the notable mystics of the day. Henry and Margaret disagreed about politics (she supported Louis of Bavaria, while Henry, the Dominican Order, and the pope all opposed him), but these differences did not prevent Henry from becoming Margaret's spiritual director. Margaret wrote an account of her revelations that Henry circulated, making her well known in Switzerland, Germany, and northern Italy. Her writings are still regarded as classics of Western spirituality.

Margaret kept her silence from Thursday to Sunday and throughout Lent and Advent. The Dominican historian Mary Jean Dorcy suggests: "She was too busy listening to the things God had to say to be occupied with other conversation." Pilgrims continue to visit Margaret's tomb at Medingen, and she is commemorated by the Dominican Order on June 20.

The Genius of Margaret Ebner:

Before approaching dinner, Margaret always prayed: *"I ask you, my Lord, to feed me with your sweet grace, strengthen me with your pure love, surround me with your boundless mercy, and embrace me with your pure truth, which encompasses for us all your graces so that they may increase in us and never be taken from us until we enter into eternal life."*

Reflection:

"You are my friends if you do what I command you. I no longer call you slaves, because a slave does not know what his master is doing. I have called you friends, because I have told you everything I have heard from my Father."
John 15:14–15

Saint Blandina of Lyons

d. 177, Lyons, France

Of the forty-nine Christians arrested in Lyons in the summer of 177, the slave Blandina was considered the most fragile. Her mistress feared that she would die of exhaustion or be terrified into apostasy (abandoning her faith). In the end, however, Blandina set an example of courage that inspired Christians for generations.

Twenty-four of Blandina's companions were beheaded, the "dignified" execution reserved for Roman citizens. Eighteen others died in prison, and two men were roasted to death in iron chairs. The executioners then tortured Blandina, demanding that she make up fantastic stories as some of the other frightened slaves had done. She held fast, repeating: *"I am a Christian; and we commit no wrongdoing."*

During the gladiatorial games, they tied Blandina to a wooden cross in the arena. As she hung there, she encouraged her companions, and when none of the wild beasts would touch her, she was cut down and sent back to prison. By the last day of the games, Blandina and Ponticus, a boy of fifteen, were the only survivors from their original group. Once again, they were ordered to swear by the idols. Ponticus refused and was immediately put to death. Blandina was scourged and made to sit in a burning chair, after which she was wrapped in a net and thrown down before a wild cow that tore her limb from limb. The bodies of Blandina and the others were fed to dogs. What remained was burned and the ashes thrown into the Rhone River. Today a post at the center of the ruined Roman amphitheater commemorates Blandina and her companions.

The Genius of Blandina:

One admiring eyewitness wrote: "The child was filled with such strength that the torturers ... acknowledged that they were beaten and that there was nothing more that they *could* do to her."

Reflection:

"You have heard that it was said, 'You shall love your neighbor and hate your enemy.' But I say to you, love your enemies, and pray for those who persecute you, that you may be children of your heavenly Father, for he makes his sun rise on the bad and the good, and causes rain to fall on the just and the unjust."

Matthew 5:43–45

Saint Clotilda, Queen of France

b. c. 475, Lyons, France
d. June 3, 545, Tours, France

When the king of Burgundy was killed in battle, he left four sons who fought bitterly among themselves. One of them was Clotilda's father. During this power struggle, her uncle Gundebald cut her father's throat, murdered her two brothers, and threw her mother down a well, leaving only Clotilda and her sister, Sedelenda, alive. Sedelenda entered a convent, but Clotilda was brought to Gundebald's palace and prepared for a strategic marriage to Clovis, king of the Franks, when she was about seventeen.

In spite of her violent family, Clotilda was a gentle soul and devout Christian. Clovis, a pagan, agreed to have their first son baptized, but when the baby died he accused Clotilda of angering his gods. Clotilda still convinced him to allow their second son to be baptized. Little Clodomir also became ill, and Clovis was furious, but Clotilda's prayers brought the child's recovery.

Clovis still had not committed to Christianity, but as he prepared for a battle with the fierce Alemanni tribe, he prayed to Clotilda's God, vowing that if He would give him victory, he would be baptized. Tradition says that at the moment the Alemanni fled the battlefield, an angel brought Clotilda three white lilies. Clovis adopted this "fleur-de-lis" as his emblem and kept his vow to become a Christian. At the lavish ceremony, three thousand Franks followed his example and were baptized. Clovis went on to conquer southern Gaul and Burgundy. Encouraged by Clotilda, he governed humanely. After Clovis's death, his kingdom was divided among his four sons. In a tragic reprise of the wars between her father and uncles, Clotilda lived to see her sons turn against one another. She could not bear to remain in Paris and retired to Tours, where she died. Clotilda is a patron of adopted children.

The Genius of Clotilda:
Although her own children disappointed her, as biographer Godefroid Kurth writes, "Clotilda accomplished the mission assigned her by Providence: she was made the instrument in the conversion of a great people, who were to be for centuries the leaders of Catholic civilization."

Reflection:
"The unbelieving husband is made holy through his wife."
1 Corinthians 7:14

BLESSED MERCEDES DE JESÚS MOLINA

(María Mercedes Molina de Ayala)

b. September 24, 1828, Baba, Los Ríos, Ecuador
d. June 12, 1883, Riobamba, Ecuador

The Rose of the Guyas was a beautiful heiress who led a worldly life until she was twenty-one, when a fall from a horse and a broken arm gave her some quiet time to think and pray. Mercedes dreamed she saw a garden full of beautiful roses, with one enormous rose standing out among them. Mercedes understood that the roses represented the many souls that needed to be saved, and the largest rose was her own soul. She believed that God was calling her to minister *"to as many afflicted hearts as there are in the world."*

Mercedes lived in the sophisticated city of Guayaquil, and at first she followed the example of Mariana de Paredes (May 26), devoting herself to charity and founding a free school for poor children. One of her teachers was the mystic Narcissa Morán (August 31), who shared Mercedes's home with two other teachers. They attended daily Mass together and called themselves the "Eucharistic women." In 1870 Mercedes volunteered to assist Jesuit missionaries working among the Jíbaro tribes at the entrance to the Amazon rain forest. She spent three difficult and dangerous years there until the Jesuits had to leave. Mercedes was disappointed but accepted this as God's will. She went to the city of Riobamba and in 1873 founded the Sisters of Mariana of Jesus (Marianitas), with Mariana de Paredes as their patron saint. They devoted themselves to educating young people and women at risk. When Mercedes took her religious vows, she added "de Jesús" to her name to show her total surrender to Christ.

Today her Marianitas are at work on five continents, running orphanages and shelters for women parolees. They commemorate Mercedes on June 12.

The Genius of Mercedes de Jesús:

Mercedes was not discouraged by the failure of the mission to the Jíbaros. In fact, it only strengthened her commitment to offer *"as much love for as much suffering as there is in the world."*

Reflection:

"When I was young and innocent, / I sought wisdom. / She came to me in her beauty, / and until the end I will cultivate her."

Sirach 51:13–14, cited in her beatification homily

BLESSED MARIA DROSTE ZU VISCHERING

(Maria of the Divine Heart)

b. September 8, 1863, Münster, Germany
d. June 8, 1899, Oporto, Portugal

A hot temper and an iron will are hardly the qualifications for a saint, and Maria had to master both. She grew up in the family castle, but in spite of her early years of privilege, Maria was drawn to a religious order dedicated to troubled women. At twenty-five, she entered the Sisters of the Good Shepherd, taking the name Maria of the Divine Heart.

Just a few years later, Maria was sent to Portugal. Her new convent housed more than one hundred troubled girls, many with a history of theft or prostitution. The Sisters were deeply in debt and the convent was threatened with closing. Maria's first act was to dedicate the convent to the Sacred Heart and she credited His divine providence for her success in restoring order and financial stability.

Only her confessor was aware that Maria was also leading an intense mystical life. In 1897 she reluctantly confided that she had received a message from God who wanted the world consecrated to his Divine Heart and wanted her to relay this information in writing to Pope Leo XIII. In her letter, Maria explained that God was asking for the consecration of the world and not simply the Catholic Church because of his desire *"to embrace all hearts in his love and mercy,"* including those *"who have not received spiritual life through baptism."*

Long suffering from spinal disease, she confided to her confessor: *"My mission on earth will be completed as soon as the consecration is done."* Two weeks later, Leo XIII issued the encyclical "Annum Sacrum: on Consecration to the Sacred Heart." Maria was called to heaven at the age of thirty-six.

The Good Shepherd Sisters commemorate her on June 8.

The Genius of Maria Droste zu Vischering:

Maria believed in obedience, writing: *"Yes, obedience can impose sacrifices that are more painful than death. But God gives us strength and courage when we can count, not on ourselves, but on him alone."*

Reflection:

"From his fullness we have all received, grace in place of grace, because while the law was given through Moses, grace and truth came through Jesus Christ."

John 1:16–17

June 6

BLESSED MARIAM THRESIA
CHIRAMEL MANKIDIYAN

b. April 26, 1876, Puthenchira, Kerala, India
d. June 8, 1926, Thumpoor, Kerala, India

Thresia's mother died when she was twelve, after which Thresia devoted herself to abandoned victims of leprosy and smallpox and their orphaned children. With her own once-prominent family in decline, Thresia placed complete trust in the Holy Family (December 27). She saw them frequently in visions and relied on them for guidance. In 1904, after a vision of the Blessed Mother, she added the name Mariam (Mary). Blessed with mystical gifts, Thresia was often surrounded by an aura of light, and on Fridays people gathered to see her levitate while in ecstasy. Her skeptical bishop insisted that Thresia submit to repeated exorcisms. Nevertheless, in 1913 he allowed her to build a small retreat where she and her three companions shared a life of prayer and austerity. They left only to visit the sick, sometimes shocking their neighbors by taking to the streets without male protection. In 1914 the bishop recognized them as the Congregation of the Holy Family. Thresia nurtured the congregation with great care, and in spite of an ongoing world war, she managed to build convents, schools, hostels, and an orphanage. Today the congregation has more than fifteen hundred sisters serving in Kerala and in Germany, Italy, and Ghana.

After Thresia's death (from diabetes), she became known as a miracle worker. Her most notable healing was a fourteen-year-old boy who had been born with two club feet. His case was examined by nine doctors in India and Italy before it was approved as a miracle by the Congregation for the Causes of Saints, satisfying the requirement for her beatification. The boy, now a married father of two, attended her beatification ceremony. Thresia is commemorated by her congregation on June 8.

The Genius of Mariam Thresia:

> Thresia advised, *"Don't talk too much. What is the advantage of it? You talk as if you were honest and just. Only God knows the inside and outside."*

Reflection:

> *"I have been crucified with Christ; yet I live, no longer I, but Christ lives in me; insofar as I now live in the flesh; I live by faith in the Son of God who has loved me and given himself up for me."*

> Galatians 2:19–20

BLESSED ANNE OF SAINT BARTHOLOMEW

(Ana García Manzanas)

b. October 1, 1550, Almendral, Castile, Spain
d. June 7, 1626, Antwerp, Belgium

When Teresa of Avila (October 15) established her first reformed Carmelite convent, Ana García, an illiterate shepherd, eagerly asked to be admitted. She was turned away because she was too young, but a few years later she was accepted by the Discalced Carmelites and took the religious name Anne of Saint Bartholomew.

Anne's humility made her a favorite with Teresa, who called her *"a great servant of God,"* and she learned to read and write by copying Teresa's letters. She nursed Teresa during her last illness and the saint died in her arms. Six years later, Anne was sent to France with six other nuns to introduce the Carmelites there. In spite of her humble origins, Anne was not afraid to speak truth to power. When the widowed Jane de Chantal (August 5) tried to enter the Discalced Carmelites, Anne discouraged her, saying that Teresa would not accept Jane as a daughter because God had other plans for her. (Jane later founded the Visitation Order.) On the other hand, Anne worked closely with Barbe Acarie (April 7), who played a key role in bringing Anne and the Carmelites to France.

In 1611 Anne moved on to Belgium. It is said that her prayers saved the city of Antwerp when it was under siege by the prince of Orange. Anne remained at Antwerp until her death, four years after the canonization of her beloved mentor, Teresa.

The Genius of Anne of Saint Bartholomew:
Anne worried that she was just a weak straw, until she dreamed that the Lord told her: *"With straws I light my fire."* With His help, she navigated political and cultural challenges in three countries.

Reflection:
"Let the prophet who has a dream recount his dream; let him who has my word speak my word truthfully! / What has straw to do with the wheat? / says the LORD. */ Is not my word like fire, says the* LORD; */ like a hammer shattering rocks?"*

Jeremiah 23:28–29

June 8

SAINT MELANIA THE ELDER

b. Rome, Italy
d. c. 400, Jerusalem

Melania was one of the first Roman women to visit the Holy Land. Widowed at twenty-two, she joined a Christian study circle in the home of Marcella of Rome (January 31) and later sailed to North Africa. One of Melania's first stops was a desert monastery where she presented the abbot Pambo[95] with several chests. *"May God reward you,"* said Pambo, and without opening them, he directed his steward to distribute the contents among the neediest monasteries.

Melania could not contain herself. *"Father, I wish you to know that there are three hundred pounds of silver there,"* she said. Pambo replied: *"Daughter, He for whom you brought it has no need to be told the quantity. . . . If you made this present to me it might be well to tell me the weight and the value, but if you offer it to God, who did not disdain a gift of two mites, be silent."*

Lesson learned, Melania moved on, disguising herself as a slave in order to visit Christians in prison and building a monastery in Jerusalem where she presided over fifty nuns. After thirty-five years in the Holy Land, Melania returned to Rome to meet her granddaughter, Melania the Younger.[96] Forty days after returning to Jerusalem, she died in her sleep.

The Genius of Melania the Elder:

Melania's kinsman, Paulinus of Nola,[97] wrote: *"What a woman she is, if it is permissible to call such a manly Christian a woman! . . . she loftily cast herself down to a humble way of life, so that as a strong member of the weak sex she might censure indolent men."*

Reflection:

"The LORD makes poor and makes rich, / he humbles, he also exalts."
1 Samuel 2:7, cited by Paulinus in his memoir about Melania

THREE SPIRITUAL DAUGHTERS

Blessed Diana Andalò, *d. 1236, Bologna, Italy*

Blessed Cecilia Caesarini, *d. 1290, Bologna, Italy*

Blessed Amata of San Sisto, *d. 1270, Bologna, Italy*

The three women that Dominic de Guzmán[98] called his spiritual daughters played key roles in the early growth of the Dominican Order.

Diana Andalò came from one of Bologna's most important families and enjoyed all the privileges of her class. When Dominican preachers arrived in Bologna in 1218, she convinced her grandfather to give them land and a church under his patronage. But when Diana tried to enter the order, her family tracked her down, beat her, and dragged her home. In the year it took Diana to recover from her injuries, her father relented and allowed her to build a convent in Bologna. Diana began with four companions, and she asked for more nuns from the convent of San Sisto in Rome, who had learned the Rule from Dominic himself. In this group were Cecilia and Amata.

Cecilia Caesarini, a high-spirited noblewoman, had been a novice in the most scandalous convent in Rome. When Dominic came there to preach about reform, the nuns surprised their families and friends by accepting his strict Rule. Cecilia became the first woman to receive the veil from Dominic.

There is a legend that a week after Cecilia made her vows at San Sisto, Dominic was preaching to a crowd there when a possessed woman became disruptive. She (or rather the seven devils inside her) insulted Dominic throughout his sermon. Finally, Dominic raised his hand, made the sign of the cross, and commanded the devils to release her. She spit up hot coals and blood but was finally free. She soon took the veil from Dominic, who gave her the name Amata, which means "beloved."

The three Blesseds are buried together at their convent in Bologna.

The Genius of Diana, Cecilia, and Amata:

Neither family pressure, abuse, nor the devil himself could conquer these women. Their writings are priceless historical records. Diana's correspondence with Jordan of Saxony[99] chronicles the spread of Dominican missionaries. Cecilia's memoir is all we know of the human side of Saint Dominic.

Reflection:

"Oh, the depth of the riches and wisdom and knowledge of God! How inscrutable are his judgments and how unsearchable his ways!"

Romans 11:33

June 10

BLESSED ANNE MARIE TAIGI

b. May 29, 1769, Siena, Italy
d. June 9, 1837, Rome, Italy

"I lived for forty-eight years or so with this saintly soul and never did I hear from her a word of impatience or discord." So Dominic Taigi testified to investigators for the canonization of his wife, Anne Marie. "I used to go home often dead tired and a little distraught after my day's work and difficulties with my employers," he recalled, "and she would restore my serenity of mind." (When Dominic was "a little distraught," he was known to throw an armchair through their apartment window.)

Anne Marie was five years old when her parents came to Rome as servants for the noble Chiga family. Her mother hoped that her beautiful only child would make a good match and recoup the family fortune, but Anne Marie fell in love with Dominic, a porter in the Chiga household. Her mother never forgave her. Dominic was hot-tempered, but he adored his young wife. After the birth of her first child, in 1790, Anne Marie began to see a brilliant light, surrounded by thorns, and visible only to her. She believed that it represented Eternal Wisdom, in whose light she foresaw future events and read the secrets of hearts. She become a Trinitarian tertiary,[100] and would have liked to live with Dominic as brother and sister, but there he drew the line. While raising four children on Dominic's modest wages, Anne Marie became an adviser to popes and cardinals, a counselor to her neighbors, and a miracle worker before and after her death. Her incorrupt body is venerated at San Crisogono in Rome, and she is commemorated on June 9.

The Genius of Anne Marie Taigi:

Anne Marie refused to profit from her gifts, assuring her visitors: *"I serve God, and he is richer than you."*

Reflection:

"You husbands should live with your wives in understanding, showing honor to the weaker female sex, since we are joint heirs of the gift of life, so that your prayers may not be hindered."

1 Peter 3:7

❦

Saint Paula Frassinetti

b. March 3, 1809, Genoa, Italy
d. June 11, 1882, Rome, Italy

By the age of nine, Paula was running her widowed father's household and mothering her four brothers, all of whom became priests. Her oldest brother encouraged her to form the Sisters of St Dorothy (Dorotheans), who first distinguished themselves by nursing cholera victims. After months of work on a Rule, Paula and another Dorothean presented their first draft to two Jesuits for comments. The priests ridiculed them and their Rule. Paula accepted this with her usual humility, but her companion was indignant. Returning to the convent, she told everyone about the insult to their foundress. Paula remained serene, saying: *"It is a great mercy when Our Lord allows us to be humbled. Like trees battered by the storm, that strike their roots even deeper in the earth, and so grow stronger, we also shall grow spiritually, if God deigns to let us be battered by the winds of contradiction."*

In 1848 Pius IX's[101] prime minister was stabbed to death on the steps of Rome's Parliament. The pope himself was forced to flee the city with cardinals and other clergy. Rome descended into riots and anarchy, but Paula and her companions refused to abandon the community that depended on them. Gathering the Sisters together, Paula urged them to pray to Saint Joseph, Guardian of the Holy Family, and he protected them until order was restored.

By the time Paula died, her Dorotheans had expanded to Portugal and Brazil. Her incorrupt body has been moved to the chapel of the motherhouse where she is venerated today.

The Genius of Paula Frassinetti:
Paula advised one young Sister: *"You must be a visible guardian angel to your children but a quick-eyed angel, alive to all their needs. Watch over them with vigilance and prudence, but let them feel you trust them."* Paula was especially sensitive to disfigured children, whom she called *"pictures of God without a frame."*

Reflection:
"Beloved, let us love one another, because love is of God; everyone who loves is begotten by God and knows God. Whoever is without love does not know God, for God is love."

1 John 4:7–8

BLESSED FLORIDA CEVOLI

(Lucrezia Elena Cevoli)

b. November 11, 1685, Pisa, Italy
d. June 12, 1767, Città di Castello, Perugia, Italy

Lucrezia was determined to join the Poor Clare Capuchins in Città di Castello. Her family opposed it and so did the nuns there. No one believed that the pampered little countess could cope with the monastery's strict Rule. But at the age of eighteen Lucrezia got her way. Her family made a grand procession from Pisa to Città di Castello, where she took her vows in a lavish ceremony and the presiding bishop gave her a new name, Florida, in honor of the city's patron saint.[102]

Florida had chosen the monastery because of its saintly abbess, Veronica Giuliani (July 9). By the time Florida arrived, however, the bishop had removed Veronica from leadership and she was under a cloud because of her controversial stigmata. The nuns agreed that only Veronica was qualified to guide Florida, and they asked her to become the girl's novice-mistress. Veronica agreed only after a vision in which Jesus promised her, *"I will be your teacher and teach the novice."* Florida became an excellent nun: she worked in the kitchen, the dispensary, and the bakery and eventually became a novice-mistress herself. In 1716, when the Holy See lifted its ban on Veronica's leadership, she was immediately reelected abbess, and Florida was elected to serve as her vicar. When Veronica died in 1727, Florida succeeded her.

Florida was known for her devotion to Our Lady of Sorrows. She negotiated at least one peace treaty for Città di Castello, and she was a tireless letter writer, always closing with the phrase *"Shout joyfully to God, all you on earth."* For a time her fame actually eclipsed Veronica Giuliani's, but no doubt Florida would cite her greatest achievement as initiating the process of canonization for Veronica.

The Genius of Florida Cevoli:

Florida loved her teacher and venerated Veronica's superior gifts, but she also understood that she could not duplicate her. She always rejected any hint of favors or mystic phenomena that might draw comparisons with Veronica.

Reflection:

"Shout joyfully to God, all you on earth; / sing of his glorious name; / give him glorious praise."

Psalm 66:1–2

June 13

SAINT GERMAINE COUSIN
(Germaine of Pibrac)

b. 1579, Pibrac, France
d. 1601, Pibrac, France

In December 1644, two gravediggers opened a church crypt and discovered the perfectly preserved body of a young girl. Her crippled right hand held a candle. Around her head was a garland of wild carnations mixed with stalks of rye. The candle and the garland were traditions in Pibrac, and news of this discovery spread quickly. Two elderly residents recognized her as Germaine Cousin.

In some ways, Germaine's story is familiar. When her mother died, her father remarried, and her resentful stepmother insisted that Germaine be isolated from the other children. She was sent to watch the sheep. Germaine was happy in her solitude. Rain or shine, she never missed daily Mass, and took Communion every Sunday, while leaving her sheep in the care of her guardian angel.

She would be long forgotten, except that after the discovery of her tomb, miraculous cures were credited to her, and the process of her canonization was begun. This was interrupted by the French Revolution, and in 1793, the Revolutionary Commune decided that the corpse, still incorrupt, must be destroyed. Three men removed the body from its lead case and buried her in the sacristy with quicklime to speed decomposition. All three men were hit immediately by crippling illness; two of them implored Germaine to intercede for them and they were healed. In 1795, with peace restored, the canonization process was resumed.

During the terrible winter of 1845, Euphrasia Pelletier (April 24), the superior of a convent in Bourges, encouraged a novena to Germaine, and through her intercession, flour that was not expected to last three days yielded bread that fed the starving Sisters and their dependents for six months.

Germaine is a patron of abused children and the handicapped. She is commemorated in France on June 15.

The Genius of Germaine Cousin:
Pius IX[103] proclaiming Germaine's canonization in 1867, called her *"so remarkable for her transcendent virtues that she shone like a star."*

Reflection:
"Even if my father and mother forsake me, / the LORD will take me in."
Psalm 27:10

BLESSED MARIA THERESA SCHERER
(Catherine Scherer)

b. October 31, 1825, Meggen, Switzerland
d. June 16, 1888, Ingenbohl, Switzerland

"Of all the women we have ever seen, she was the most capable of assuming leadership," wrote Carl Hilty, a distinguished attorney who represented Theresa Scherer in a long drawn-out lawsuit. He added, "Though she came from simple surroundings, she was as much a queen by nature as the queen of Austria."

Baptized Catherine, she grew up during Switzerland's "storm against convents" (*klostersturm*). She shocked her family by turning down the chance to enter an established French convent, choosing instead the Sisters of the Holy Cross, a teaching order just founded by Theodosius Florentini and Bernarda Heimgartner.[104] Catherine took the religious name Maria Theresa and soon demonstrated a gift for teaching. Father Florentini, a Capuchin priest, was full of plans, while Mother Bernarda was more cautious. In the end, the community divided: some Sisters remained with Bernarda at Menzingen and fifty others joined Florentini and Theresa to form the Sisters of Mercy of the Holy Cross at Ingenbohl. Theresa was Superior when Florentini died suddenly in 1865, leaving a pile of debts from other projects. The Sisters were not legally responsible for those debts, and several bishops urged Theresa to walk away from them. She refused, unwilling to dishonor Florentini's memory. She struggled for four years, and just when she was free of debt, a powerful businessman presented a huge bill. Convinced that he was taking advantage, Theresa refused to pay. He sued, and she would not settle. Every time a court ruled in Theresa's favor, her nemesis appealed. In the end, with the help of Carl Hilty, a Protestant who donated his services, Theresa prevailed. Today, the Holy Cross Sisters are active all over the world. They commemorate Theresa on June 16.

The Genius of Maria Theresa Scherer:
She reminds us that one should always have *"one's hands at work and one's heart with God."*

Reflection:
"The judgment is merciless to one who has not shown mercy; mercy triumphs over judgment."

James 2:13

SAINT ALEYDIS OF LE CAMBRE

(Alice, Alix, Adelaide of Schaerbeek)

b. c. 1215, Schaerbeek, Belgium
d. June 11, 1250, Le Cambre, Belgium

Aleydis entered a Cistercian monastery at the age of seven as a boarder and stayed on to become a nun. Her days were serene until, when she was twenty-eight, she developed leprosy and had to be isolated from the community she loved.

In a dramatic ritual, the nuns sang funeral hymns as Aleydis exchanged her habit for the badges of a leper: a gray dress with a red belt, visor, and gloves. They led her to a small hut at the edge of the monastery grounds, where a priest scooped up some earth and sprinkled it over her head. "You are dead to the world," he said. "Thus live for God." Seeing her new home for the first time, Aleydis was overwhelmed and threw herself on the ground. As they lifted her, she had a vision of Christ crowned with thorns who assured her: *"My child, I will never leave you or forsake you."*

After three years, Aleydis was allowed to move to a small cell near the monastery chapel where she could see the altar and join in the prayers. A radiant light surrounded her, and she was said to heal other lepers with her touch. As the disease ravaged her face, Aleydis went blind. Another nun, Martha,[105] volunteered as her nurse and companion. Aleydis predicted that Martha would not catch leprosy but would die before her and go straight to heaven. Aleydis asked Martha to pray for her there, because, she admitted, *"I do not like pain."* Aleydis prayed constantly, and in spite of her blindness, she saw many encouraging visions and was consoled by her guardian angel.

The Genius of Aleydis of Le Cambre:

Aleydis accepted her cross from God, confident that she could offer her suffering to relieve the souls in purgatory.

Reflection:

"All of us, gazing with unveiled face on the glory of the Lord, are being transformed into the same image from glory to glory, as from the Lord who is the Spirit."

2 Corinthians 3:18

June 16

❦

SAINT LUTGARD OF AYWIÈRES

b. 1182, Tongres, Belgium
d. 1246, Couture-Saint-Germaine, Belgium

Lutgard's Benedictine convent was essentially a finishing school where girls of her class prepared for marriage. The tolerant nuns left Lutgard free to flirt with her many suitors until she experienced a vision of Christ in which he pointed to his bleeding heart and said: *"Behold here what you are to love, and how you are to love."*

A confused Lutgard consulted her confessor, but he too was unfamiliar with the Sacred Heart. This was four hundred years before the visions of Margaret Mary Alacoque (October 16), the saint most closely associated with the devotion. Besides, Lutgard's priest wondered why Christ would appear to such a frivolous girl. Nevertheless, Lutgard was allowed to become a Benedictine nun and threw herself into every aspect of prayer and work. Blessed with healing powers, she drew many visitors who disrupted convent life, so she asked God to take back his gift. He asked what she would take instead, and Lutgard requested a clearer understanding of the psalms. This insight proved more than she could handle, and she asked God to take back that gift too. *"What would you have me give you, Lutgard?"* he asked. Lutgard asked for his heart. God replied: *"It is I who want yours."* *"Take it,"* she said, and they exchanged hearts. Four years later, Lutgard was elected prioress of the convent, but she craved seclusion. Christina the Astonishing (July 25) recommended a move to the Cistercian convent at Aywières, and there Lutgard devoted the rest of her life to contemplation and prayer. She undertook three seven-year fasts in reparation for a spreading heresy, during which she lived on bread and beer (the standard drink of the Middle Ages). Blind in the last eleven years of her life, Lutgard regarded even that cross as a gift from God.

The Genius of Lutgard of Aywières:

Lutgard's spiritual heroism made her a favorite of Thomas Merton, the twentieth-century mystic, who wrote that she "is intended in the plans of God to inspire us all, each in his own manner, to follow her example of self-sacrifice as best we can."

Reflection:

"The eyes of the LORD *are upon those who love him; / he is their mighty shield and strong support."*

Sirach 34:16

THREE PORTUGUESE PRINCESSES

Saint Teresa, Queen of León (Tarasia of Portugal)
d. *June 17, 1250, Lorvão, Portugal*

Saint Sancha, Princess of Portugal (Sanctia)
d. *March 13, 1229, Alenquer, Portugal*

Saint Mafalda, Queen of Castile, d. *1252, Arouca, Portugal*

On their way to sainthood, the king of Portugal's daughters successfully fought their powerful brother for control of the lands their father left them.

Teresa, the oldest, married Alfonso IX, king of León, but after five years of marriage and three children, it was discovered that they were cousins. At first, Teresa and her husband resisted efforts to separate them. Teresa yielded only after Portugal was devastated by famine, pestilence, and war. Convinced that it was because of her sin, she agreed to have the marriage dissolved. She and her husband remained good friends. Teresa acquired a disgraced monastery at Lorvão, evicted the monks, restored the buildings, and installed nuns who followed the strict Cistercian Rule. She shared their life, although she did not take vows until just before her death.

Teresa's brother succeeded their father and became King Alfonso II in 1212. Better known as Alfonso the Fat, he refused to hand over property that their father had bequeathed to Teresa and her sister Sancha. To show that he meant business, Alfonso invaded Sancha's lands and killed some of her tenants. Teresa turned to her former husband, who sent a force commanded by their son Ferdinand. Alfonso the Fat was forced to turn over the properties and leave his sisters in peace.

Of the three sisters, Sancha was the most devout. She resisted Alfonso's plans to marry her to his nephew, the king of León and Castile. Like Teresa, Sancha assumed the Cistercian habit without taking final vows. (This allowed them to keep control of their property.) Sancha also helped the Dominicans and Franciscans make their first foundations in Portugal. At the end of her life, Sancha retired to her convent at Alenquer.

Teresa died in the chapel at Lorvão while listening to the nuns sing the Magnificat, and she was buried beside Sancha.

The youngest sister, Mafalda, was their brother's favorite, and he promoted her marriage to Henry I, king of Castile, until Pope Innocent III stepped in and annulled it on grounds of consanguinity. Mafalda then resolved to become a nun and built the monastery of Santa Maria de Arouca. She also built a hospice for pilgrims and a home for indigent widows, and she restored the cathedral at Porto that had been built by her grandmother. While return-ing from a visit to the cathedral, Mafalda was seized with a fever and knew she was dying. She ordered that her body be put on a mule and buried wherever it stopped. The mule carried Mafalda's body to the church in Arouca, knelt before the altar, laid down the precious burden, and died. Soon after, the nuns at Arouca reported seeing a vision of Mafalda in glory. Later, when their monastery was hit by fire, Mafalda appeared among the flames and saved the church and infirmary from destruction. The Cistercian Order cel-ebrates Teresa, Sancha, and Mafalda together on June 17.

The Genius of the Portuguese Princesses:

All three sisters were born to power and privilege. They knew how to use it and when to let it go.

Reflection:

"He has helped Israel his servant, / remembering his mercy."

Luke 1:54 (last verse heard by Teresa)

June 18

SAINT ELISABETH OF SCHÖNAU

b. c. 1129, Schönau, Germany
d. June 18, 1165, Schönau, Germany

Elisabeth was a protégé of Hildegard of Bingen (September 17), who called her *"my troubled daughter."* An outspoken critic of corrupt clergy, she joined Hildegard in a campaign against heresy.

Elisabeth came from a prominent family and was placed in the double monastery at Schönau at the age of eleven. At twenty-three she began experiencing revelations, usually while in an ecstatic trance. An angel ordered her to warn certain sinners about the woes that would befall them if they did not repent. When she was reluctant to do so, the angel took a whip and beat her so badly that her back ached for three days. Elisabeth enlisted her abbot, Hildelin, and was very distressed when the angel's prophecies were not fulfilled. She complained to the angel, who assured her that the sinners' contrition had postponed their doom. Other visions were fulfilled, however, and after three years, Hildelin asked Elisabeth's brother, Eckbert, to become her interlocutor. Eckbert, a priest in Cologne, moved permanently to Schönau, where he became a monk and succeeded Hildelin as abbot.

Elisabeth spent her entire life at Schönau, but as her fame spread, she corresponded with clergy and important figures all over Europe, and many of them visited her monastery. She had a strong practical side and at twenty-eight was elected abbess, ruling with great success. Her most controversial revelation concerns Ursula and her Companions (October 21), but modern scholars blame its fantastic content on her editor, Eckbert, who may have manipulated Elisabeth's original vision. He edited and published her complete works after her death.

The Genius of Elisabeth of Schönau:

Elisabeth, citing such Old Testament prophetesses as Deborah and Judith, wrote: *"People are scandalized that in these days the Lord deigns to magnify his great mercy in the frail sex. But why doesn't it cross their minds that a similar thing happened in the days of our fathers when, while men were given to indolence, holy women were filled with the spirit of God so that they could prophesy, energetically govern the people of God, and even win glorious victories over Israel's enemies?"*

Reflection:

"The angel of the LORD, who encamps with them, / delivers all who fear God."
Psalm 34:8

June 19

Saint Juliana Falconieri

b. 1270, Florence, Italy
d. June 12, 1341, Florence, Italy

Juliana's life began and ended with miracles. She was born to elderly parents who were long past hoping for a child, and in gratitude they built the church of the Annunciation in Florence. Her saintly uncle Alexis Falconieri[106] became her spiritual director.

Almost four decades earlier, Alexis and six other prominent citizens had experienced an Assumption Day (August 15) vision that inspired them to found the Servants of Mary (Servites). As they aged, leadership passed to Philip Benizi,[107] who began a cloistered Second Order for women. Juliana preferred an active apostolate and formed a Third Order dedicated to serving the sick. These women were called the Mantellate because they wore a short black cape (*mantella*) that freed their hands for work. Juliana governed the Mantellate for forty years, and her death was marked by a Eucharistic miracle.

In her last hours, Juliana was too weak to swallow and priests refused to give her Communion. One finally agreed to allow her to gaze on the Host. Her companions gathered around as the priest placed the Host on her breast. In that moment, Juliana breathed her last and the Host vanished, leaving witnesses convinced that she had miraculously absorbed it. After a few moments of stunned silence, they began preparing her body for burial. When they removed her habit, they discovered that the Host had left an imprint on Juliana's chest. Juliana's body was later placed in her family's chapel, where it is venerated today.

The Genius of Juliana Falconieri:
When Benizi was dying, he entrusted all three Servite Orders to Juliana's care, but she believed that God had other plans for her. As soon as the Servites elected a General to succeed Benizi, Juliana relinquished leadership and returned to her Mantellate.

Reflection:
"I tell you, do not worry about your life, what you will eat [or drink], or about your body, what you will wear. Is not life more than food and the body more than clothing?"

Matthew 6:25

June 20

BLESSED OSANNA OF MANTUA

(Osanna Andreasi)

b. January 17, 1449, Carbonarola, Mantua, Italy
d. June 18, 1505, Mantua, Italy

Osanna was a trusted adviser to two generations of Mantua's ruling Gonzaga family. This was no small achievement for someone whose own father did not believe in educating women. Fortunately, the Blessed Mother felt otherwise and taught Osanna to read and write.

Osanna had her first vision at the age of six when an angel told her to love God. Her father refused to let Osanna enter a convent, but he allowed her to become a Dominican tertiary at fourteen, living as a nun at home without taking final vows. Both her parents died the following year and Osanna took responsibility for her numerous younger brothers and sisters. She was greatly admired for the way she managed the family's worldly affairs.

Osanna experienced visions and ecstasies that sometimes lasted two or three days. She foretold future events, and wonderful benefits were obtained through her intercession. Local Dominican friars questioned her motives and refused to let her wear the Dominican habit. In time they acknowledged her humility, but Osanna remained a novice for thirty-seven years before she was allowed to take her final vows. Meanwhile, Osanna prayed to share in the sufferings of Christ. In 1476 she began to show the wounds of the Crown of Thorns and to bleed from her forehead, followed by the five wounds of the stigmata. Osanna kept most of these mystical graces to herself and only confided in one friend, a Benedictine monk, who published her letters after her death.

Colomba of Rieti (May 20) appeared to Osanna in two visions in which she promised that Osanna would soon join her in glory.

The Genius of Osanna of Mantua:
Throughout her life, Osanna followed the instructions she received from the angel early in life: *"Love God, all you who live on earth, for he has made all things for no other end than to be loved by you."*

Reflection:
"Get wisdom, get understanding! / Do not forget or turn aside from the words I utter. Forsake her not, and she will preserve you; / love her, and she will safeguard you."

Proverbs 4:5–6

BLESSED MARGARET BERMINGHAM BALL

b. c. 1515, Skryne, County Meath, Ireland
d. 1584, Dublin, Ireland

Margaret Ball may be the only martyr who was betrayed by her own son. Walter Ball denounced her in order to further his political ambitions.

Margaret's husband had been Lord Mayor of Dublin when it was still possible for Catholics like the Balls to hold public office in Ireland. When Elizabeth I ascended the English throne, she demanded that all those in public office swear an oath to her as head of the Church of Ireland. By that time, Margaret was a widow and out of public life. She might have been ignored by the authorities had not her son Walter, the oldest of her five children, made that impossible. He was determined to become Lord Mayor of Dublin even if it meant renouncing his Catholic faith. When Margaret learned of his plan, she assembled bishops, priests, and scholars in her home and attempted an intervention. They failed to persuade Walter that his faith was more important than political ambition. Walter took the oath and in return Elizabeth appointed him Commissioner for Ecclesiastical Causes.

Margaret continued to invite her son to dine with the bishops and priests she sheltered in her home, still hoping he would return to the faith. It is believed that Walter used information he gained there to betray clergymen and gain influence with the new government. He was appointed Lord Mayor of Dublin in 1580 and immediately had his mother and her chaplain arrested. Margaret was paraded through the streets of Dublin in a prisoner's cart to the taunts of the crowd. She was held at Dublin Castle for two years until she died. Margaret is commemorated on June 20.

The Genius of Margaret Ball:
Margaret would have been freed at any time if she had only taken the same oath as her son, but she refused to compromise her principles. Her four other children remained loyal to the faith she died for, and many of her descendants later held important positions in the Irish government.

Reflection:
"With your whole heart honor your father; / your mother's birthpangs forget not. Remember, of these parents you were born; / what can you give them for all they gave you?"

Sirach 7:27–28

BLESSED MICHELINA OF PESARO
(Michelina Metelli)

b. 1300, Pesaro, Urbino, Italy
d. June 19, 1356, Pesaro, Urbino, Italy

The women of Pesaro are famous for their beauty and Michelina was no exception. She married a duke of Rimini, and by the age of twenty she was a rich widow devoted to her only son.

Michelina sheltered a pious pilgrim called Syriana but scolded her for fasting, even on feast days. Syriana replied, "Oh, Michelina! If you could only taste the gifts of God, the things of the world would be bitter to you." Michelina showed Syriana her jewels, saying, *"Paradise lies in these things."* Syriana wore her down, however, and Michelina admitted that only love for her son kept her from renouncing the world. Syriana suggested that they pray to God to decide the boy's fate. They went to church together and prayed until Michelina heard a voice saying: *"Your son will be with Me in paradise, and thus I set you free from the love of him. Go in peace."*

Michelina raced home, arriving in time to see two angels carrying her son's soul to heaven. From that day on, she turned her palace into a hospital where she welcomed anyone in need. Her in-laws did not enjoy watching Michelina spend their inheritance and had her confined to a tower. The guards could not bear to keep such a beautiful young woman in chains and let her go, blaming her escape on an angel. After that, the family left Michelina alone. Syriana disappears from Michelina's story after her conversion, and some believe that she was an angel in disguise. Michelina is commemorated in Pesaro on June 20.

The Genius of Michelina:

In her terrible suffering, Michelina found grace and tasted the gifts of God.

Reflection:

"That I might not become too elated, a thorn in the flesh was given to me, an angel of Satan, to beat me, to keep me from being too elated. Three times I begged the Lord about this, that it might leave me, but he said to me, 'My grace is sufficient for you, for power is made perfect in weakness.' I will rather boast most gladly of my weaknesses, in order that the power of Christ may dwell with me."

2 Corinthians 12:7–9

Saint Audrey
(Etheldreda of Ely)

b. 636, Exning (or Erming), Suffolk, England
d. June 23, 679, Ely, England

One of the five daughters of King Anna, Audrey loved to wear gold necklaces studded with jewels. At sixteen she was forced to marry an elderly prince who gave her the Isle of Ely as a wedding gift and agreed to remain celibate.

Widowed after three years, Audrey retired to Ely until she was ordered to marry Egfrid, a prince of Northumbria. At fourteen, he was ten years younger than Audrey, but he adored her and honored her wish to live in celibacy. After twelve years of happiness, everything changed when Egfrid unexpectedly became king of Northumbria. Returning victorious from battling northern rebels, he demanded that Audrey consummate their marriage. Painful scenes followed and Audrey fled back to Ely, pursued by Egfrid, who was convinced that he could not live without her. After wandering for days on foot, Audrey finally reached Ely. The island was surrounded by impassable swamps, which finally convinced Egfrid that his wife was protected by a power greater than his own. Egfrid left Audrey in peace and later remarried. Audrey built a large double monastery at Ely. She died of a tumor on her neck, which she regarded as a punishment for her youthful passion for necklaces. Her sister Sexburga,[108] widow of the king of Kent, succeeded Audrey as abbess. Audrey was regarded as a protector of chastity and guardian against illnesses of the throat and neck. Her abbey became a cathedral, which still stands, but her incorrupt body was burned during the Reformation. Only her hand was saved and is venerated today at St Etheldreda's Roman Catholic church at Ely.

The Genius of Audrey:
Audrey's insistence on celibacy might strike some as unreasonable or quaint, but she was a woman who stood by her principles and clearly possessed great charm. In the end, Audrey always got what she wanted.

Reflection:
"Not everyone who says to me, 'Lord, Lord,' will enter the kingdom of heaven, but only the one who does the will of my Father in heaven."
Matthew 7:21 (from the Gospel reading for her Memorial Mass)

SAINT EMILIE DE VIALAR

b. September 12, 1797, Gaillac, Tarn, France
d. August 24, 1856, Marseilles, Bouches-du-Rhône, France

When Emilie was thirty-five, she inherited a fortune that freed her from her oppressive father and allowed her to found one of the first congregations of missionary women, the Sisters of St Joseph of the Apparition. Their name refers to the mystery of the Incarnation as revealed to Joseph in Matthew 1:18–25.

Emilie's congregation thrived, and in 1834 she and two companions sailed to Algeria to staff a new hospital. After she treated a sheik known as the Desert Serpent, he invited the Sisters to come to Biskra, an important trading center for his tribe, assuring them: "If an Arab showed the least disrespect to the cross you are wearing, I would have his head cut off that same instant." By 1839 Emilie's foundation in Algeria had grown to twenty Sisters, but their very success brought a power struggle with the local bishop. When he threatened to expel the Sisters, two hundred Algerian colonists signed a petition to the pope, pleading to keep them. A similar petition came from the Muslim community, praising the Sisters' friendship and sincere compassion. Emilie managed to get an audience with Pope Gregory XVI, who told her: "God must have great plans for your institute since he is making you endure such trials." Unfortunately, her nemesis was a master of Church bureaucracy. He put the Sisters under an interdict, banning them from the sacraments (in effect, excommunicating them). The ban was later lifted, but Emilie and her Sisters were finally forced to leave Algiers. She consoled them: *"This is only a trial. Take heart! Jesus Christ has suffered much more than we."* The bishop himself was soon forced to flee the country. Years later, he wrote to beg Emilie's forgiveness for the pain he had caused her. Today her Sisters serve in twenty-six countries on five continents and commemorate their foundress on June 23.

The Genius of Emilie de Vialar:
Like Joseph, Emilie trusted Divine Providence, advising, *"Quietly to trust in God is better than trying to safeguard material interests. I learned that from bitter experience."*

Reflection:
"When Joseph awoke, he did as the angel of the Lord had commanded him and took his wife into his home."

Matthew 1:24

June 25

꙳

BLESSED MARY OF OIGNIES

b. c. 1167, Nivelles, Brabant, Belgium
d. June 23, 1213, Oignies, Belgium

Mary's parents arranged her marriage to a young nobleman, but she soon convinced him to share a celibate life. They gave away all their property and turned their home into a hospice for lepers, shocking their families and stirring so much gossip that Mary left Nivelles and joined the Beguine[109] community at Oignies.

When contemplating the fate of sinners, herself included, Mary would sob like a woman in labor. A priest ordered her to be quiet, so she asked God to make him understand that her tears were beyond her control. That very day, while celebrating Mass, the priest was so wracked with sobs that he left the altar with his vestments soaked. Such wonders drew a young theology student, Jacques de Vitry,[110] to consult her. Following Mary's advice, de Vitry returned to Paris, finished his studies, and was ordained a priest. He went on to a brilliant career and credited his gift for preaching to Mary's prayers. She was devoted to the Eucharist, frequently experiencing the taste of honey in her mouth at Mass, and a sensation of sweetness when she received good spiritual advice. Mary sang continuously for three days before her death and asked to die in church. She was so revered by the local clergy that they prepared a bed for her in a side chapel, where she breathed her last. De Vitry assisted at her deathbed and wrote her biography, which had a great influence on Bridget of Sweden (July 23). Mary was considered a patron of women in childbirth and is commemorated on June 23.

The Genius of Mary of Oignies:
When de Vitry asked why she never suffered headaches with her tears, Mary explained: *"These tears are my feast; they are my bread day and night; they feed my mind. Rather than emptying and afflicting my head, they satisfy to my soul."*

Reflection:
"Stop judging, that you may not be judged. For as you judge, so will you be judged, and the measure with which you measure will be measured out to you."

Matthew 7:1–2

BLESSED MARGUERITE BAYS

b. September 8, 1815, La Pierraz, Fribourg, Switzerland
d. June 27, 1879, La Pierraz, Fribourg, Switzerland

A dressmaker who spent her entire life in the parish where she was born, Marguerite developed intestinal cancer at the age of thirty-five. She asked the Blessed Mother to intercede with her Son to exchange her suffering for a different pain that would enable her to share more directly in the Passion of Our Lord. Marguerite was miraculously cured of her cancer on December 8, 1854, at the very moment that Pius IX pronounced the dogma of the Immaculate Conception.

Marguerite had always been devout, but she chose not to enter a convent. Most of her life was "hidden in God." She remained at home, devoting herself to active charity and going wherever she was needed. It is said that Marguerite lived constantly in God's presence. The sight of weak faith in others caused her great suffering, and she prayed that their faith would be strengthened. She deplored human indifference to God, and only wanted to know: *"What can we do to love God more?"*

After her miraculous recovery from cancer, Marguerite was given a "mysterious affliction" that immobilized her in ecstasy every Friday. Physically and spiritually, she reenacted the phases of Jesus' Passion, from the Agony in the Garden to the Crucifixion and Death. Marguerite became a Third Order Franciscan, and at about that time she began to show signs of the stigmata. Like most authentic stigmatists, Marguerite went to great trouble to hide this great favor and avoided the world's attention until her death.

Pilgrims continue to visit Marguerite's former home in Pierraz, which is now a museum dedicated to her.

The Genius of Marguerite Bays:
In his beatification homily, John Paul II cited Marguerite among the women who from the beginning of Christian history have contributed "the language of the heart, of intuition and of dedication." He called her life "a long silent walk on the way of holiness."

Reflection:
"Enter through the narrow gate; for the gate is wide and the road broad that leads to destruction, and those who enter through it are many. How narrow the gate and constricted the road that leads to life. And those who find it are few."
Matthew 7:13–14

Blessed Tarsykia Olha Matskiv

b. *March 23, 1919, Chodoriv, Ukraine*
d. *July 18, 1944, Krystynopil, Ukraine*

At nineteen, Tarsykia defied her mother in order to enter the Sisters Servants of Mary Immaculate at Krystynopil. A year later the Soviet army invaded Ukraine and World War II began in earnest. Krystynopil was in the middle of battles between the Nazis and the Soviets, and that September, German planes bombed the convent. This was only the beginning of their wartime hardships, but nothing discouraged Tarsykia. In 1940 she professed her final vows and committed her life to the poor and displaced. On August 27, 1942, Tarsykia and the other Sisters quietly marked the fiftieth anniversary of their founding by Josaphata Hordashevska (November 21). By the summer of 1944, the Germans had begun to retreat as Soviet forces moved in. That July, Tarsykia made a private vow and offered to sacrifice her life to Christ. Such a vow is made without knowing when one might be called to honor it. Tarsykia was called the next day. She and fifty other Sisters had spent the night hiding in the convent cellar. At eight o'clock that morning, the bell rang at their front gate. Tarsykia went to answer it and found a Soviet soldier standing there. He shot her point blank and she died instantly.

The Sisters brought Tarsykia's body into the cellar. The next day Soviet soldiers returned to search the convent. When one soldier noticed her corpse, he bragged, "I killed her because she was a nun." The soldiers intended to kill them all, but neighbors intervened and forced the soldiers to withdraw. Tarsykia was buried in the convent garden, and in 1956 her remains were transferred to the cemetery in Lviv.

The Genius of Tarsykia Olha Matskiv:

"Our life is a continuous battle with many crosses," Tarsykia wrote her parents, *"but only with crosses are noble and heroic souls formed."* When her moment came, she took up her cross without hesitation.

Reflection:

"My eager expectation and hope is that I shall not be put to shame in any way, but that with all boldness, now as always, Christ will be magnified in my body, whether by life or by death. For to me life is Christ, and death is gain."

Philippians 1:20–21

THE FOUR MARTYRS OF WANGLA

Saint Lucy Wang Cheng
d. June 28, 1900, Wangla, Hebei, China

Saint Mary Fan Kun
d. June 28, 1900, Wangla, Hebei, China

Saint Mary Qi Yu
d. June 28, 1900, Wangla, Hebei, China

Saint Mary Zheng Xu
d. June 28, 1900, Wangla, Hebei, China

Lucy Wang Cheng and her companions came of age in a Catholic orphanage in Wangla just as antiforeign feeling was sweeping China.

The Boxers, a violent secret society, blamed China's woes on Europe and considered Christianity a European influence. In 1900, the Boxers slaughtered tens of thousands of Catholics and Protestants, most of them native Chinese whose families had been Christians for generations. On June 24 the Boxers invaded Wangla and murdered most of the Christians. They had other plans for Lucy Wang Cheng and her companions, however. They pressured the four girls to publicly abandon their faith. They refused. The Boxer leader, Ying Zheng, was infatuated with Lucy, and for four days he tried to convince her to marry him. She refused. Another Boxer tried the same approach with Mary Fan Kun and also failed. The four orphans remained united, while the Boxers humiliated and insulted them. When the youngest, eleven-year-old Mary Zheng Xu, began to sob, Lucy Wang Cheng told her: *"Don't cry, we are going to heaven soon. God has given us life and he will take it back. We should not be reluctant givers, but offer ourselves cheerfully."* They were given one last chance to reconsider and unanimously answered: *"No! We are daughters of God. We will not betray him."* With that they were executed.

The Genius of the Martyrs of Wangla:

When peace returned to China, Christians enjoyed religious tolerance until the Communist takeover in 1949. Since then, the bravery of these saints continues to sustain the faith of millions of Chinese.

Reflection:

"He came and preached peace to you who were far off and peace to those who were near, for through him we both have access in one Spirit to the Father."

Ephesians 2:17–18

SAINT VINCENZA GEROSA

(Caterina Gerosa)

b. October 29, 1784, Lovere, Bergamo, Italy
d. July 29, 1847, Lovere, Bergamo, Italy

Vincenza was twenty years older than Bartolomea Capitanio (July 11), but she recognized that her young friend was a creative genius. She gladly let Bartolomea take the lead when they cofounded the Sisters of Charity of Lovere. A year later, when Bartolomea died suddenly at the age of twenty-six, no one was more surprised than Vincenza that she kept their institute going on her own.

Baptized Caterina, she was raised in a large extended family that was financially comfortable but seething with conflicts. Her father was squeezed out of the family business, and after his death, her mother was forced out of their house, leaving seventeen-year-old Caterina behind. Caterina devoted herself to charity. She welcomed many needy people into her home and had a gift for sensing what someone needed without having to ask. Caterina and Bartolomea became close friends through their charitable activities. Bartolomea formed the plan for an institute to instruct the young and care for the sick, and on November 21, 1832, the feast of the Presentation of the Child Mary, Caterina and Bartolomea founded it. Caterina took the name Vincenza in honor of the great patron of charity Vincent de Paul.[111] Today their order is officially known as the Sisters of Charity of SS Bartolomea Capitanio and Vincenza Gerosa, and informally as the Sisters of the Child Mary. They are active in Europe, Asia, Africa, and the Americas. Vincenza Gerosa is commemorated on June 28.

The Genius of Vincenza Gerosa:

Three years after Bartolomea's death, an epidemic swept through the city of Lovere. Vincenza told her Sisters: *"The Lord presents himself to us in a variety of ways. Now he has come to visit us as a cholera victim."* She did not order the Sisters to nurse them, but she took the lead and they followed.

Reflection:

"Do nothing out of selfishness or out of vainglory; rather, humbly regard others as more important than yourselves, each looking out not for his own interests, but [also] everyone for those of others."

Philippians 2:3–4

BLESSED MARIA RAFFAELLA CIMATTI
(Santina Cimatti)

b. June 6, 1861, Celle di Faenza, Italy
d. June 23, 1945, Alatri, Italy

At the age of eighty-three, while nursing wounded soldiers, Raffaella Cimatti personally intervened to keep a German general from bombing the city of Alatri.

She was born into a poor but devout family and baptized Santina. Only two of her brothers survived and both became missionary priests. It was so obvious that Santina was destined for the religious life that her pastor allowed her to receive the sacrament of Confirmation when she was only seven, but Santina delayed entering a convent while she looked after her brothers and widowed mother. Finally, at the advanced age of twenty-eight, she was admitted to the Hospitaller Sisters of Mercy, taking the name Maria Raffaella and training as a nurse and pharmacist's assistant. In 1928 Raffaella became superior at Alatri, a post she held until she retired from leadership in 1940. She intended to devote her retirement years to prayer, but World War II intervened. As casualties mounted, Raffaella volunteered to attend the wounded soldiers. It is said that when Raffaella was not looking after a patient, she was in the chapel, and if her hands were not holding a patient, they were holding a rosary. Consoled by her care, the soldiers called her Mamma.

When Raffaella learned that the Nazi general Albert Kesserling intended to bomb Alatri to block the advance of the Allies, she confronted him at his headquarters and asked him to reconsider. Impressed by her courage and sincere concern, the general spared Alatri. Today her order has foundations all over the world, including assisted living homes in the United States. They commemorate Raffaella on June 23.

The Genius of Raffaella Cimatti:
Inspired by God's infinite mercy, Raffaella devoted her life to the suffering of others. She was always ready to listen and accept those who came to her seeking advice or comfort.

Reflection:
"Give and gifts will be given to you; a good measure, packed together, shaken down, and overflowing, will be poured into your lap. For the measure with which you measure will in return be measured out to you."

Luke 6:38

THE THIRTY-TWO BLESSED MARTYRS OF ORANGE

d. July 6–26, 1794, Orange, Vaucluse, France

In the spring of 1794, during the Reign of Terror, forty-two women belonging to four very different religious orders were arrested in southeastern France and charged with treason. Thousands of men and women were being executed as enemies of the Revolution, but what distinguished these women was that as prisoners they formed an impromptu religious community that set an example of faith and courage, even while thirty-two of them were martyred on the guillotine.

Their story began in the town of Bollène, where two convents thrived before the Revolution. The Ursulines of Bollène were teachers who operated schools for girls. The Sisters of the Blessed Sacrament (Sacramentines) were cloistered nuns who spent their days in prayer before the Eucharist. In 1792 the forces of the Revolutionary government closed all convents, regardless of their mission, and confiscated their property. The Sacramentine experience was typical: the nuns were given three days to leave their home. A similar scene was repeated in the Benedictine abbey at Caderousse, at the Cistercian monastery at Avignon, and at the Ursuline convent schools in Pont de Saint Esprit, Carpentras, Pernes, Sisteron, and Bollène. The displaced nuns struggled to support themselves until, eighteen months after the convent closings, the Revolutionary government began rounding up the nuns who still refused to take an oath to the state. Forty-two of them were transported to Orange to await trial for treason.

The day after they arrived in prison, the nuns met to collaborate on writing a single Rule that united them as a community. They began each day at 5:00 a.m. as if they were still in their convents, and their day was dominated by prayer. Every morning at nine, selected prisoners, including some from their group, were summoned before the judge. The accused were almost always convicted on the spot and taken to the old Roman amphitheater to await execution that night.

At six every evening the prison echoed with a drumroll and shouts of Vive la Nation! Vive la République! as the names of the condemned were announced. The remaining nuns would then say prayers for the dying, followed by a period of silence, on their knees, until they assumed that their companions had gone to the scaffold. They would then stand and sing the Te Deum, a traditional hymn of joy and thanksgiving, and Psalm 117. That summer, almost 600 men and women were brought before Orange's Revolutionary court and 332 of them died on the guillotine.

On July 6, Suzanne Agatha Deloye, a Benedictine, became the first nun called before the judge. Suzanne refused to swear the oath, saying, "I will not save my life at the cost of my faith." She was sent to the guillotine. By July 11, the pace had picked up. Eight nuns were executed in one day, among them forty-one-year-old Jeanne de Romillon. As she climbed the scaffold, the crowd shouted Vive la Nation. Jeanne responded: "Yes, Vive la Nation that brings me on this beautiful day the grace of martyrdom." Five nuns were executed on July 13, including the youngest Sacramentine, twenty-four-year-old Thérèse Marie Faurier. Some of the guards complained, "Look at these women—they die laughing." The last four nuns, including a seventy-five-year-old Sacramentine and a seventy-year-old Ursuline, died together on July 26. Two days later, the Reign of Terror collapsed and the ten surviving nuns were free to tell their story. The Thirty-two Martyrs of Orange are commemorated in France on July 9.

The Genius of the Martyrs of Orange:

Under the worst of circumstances, these women formed a new community and lived out the Sacramentine motto: "To love for those who do not love, to adore for those who do not adore; to praise for those who blaspheme."

Reflection:

"O LORD, do not relinquish your scepter to those that are naught. Let them not gloat over our ruin, but turn their own counsel against them and make an example of our chief enemy. Be mindful of us, O LORD. Manifest yourself in the time of our distress and give me courage. King of gods and Ruler of every power."

Esther C:22–23

July 2

BLESSED MARIJA PETKOVIC
(Maria of Jesus Crucified)

b. December 10, 1892, Blato, Croatia
d. July 9, 1966, Rome, Italy

Marija was born into a wealthy family, but a series of catastrophes changed her world completely. A vine disease ruined her region's winemaking economy and Croatia was further devastated by World War I and the Spanish influenza epidemic.

Recognizing that the need for active charity was greater than ever, Marija entered the convent of the Servants of Charity in 1919. Two months later the founders abandoned the enterprise, leaving Marija and two companions alone in a dilapidated convent. Undiscouraged, Marija founded a new order, the Daughters of Mercy. She took the name Maria of Jesus Crucified and was elected superior. During the next three decades, Marija established forty-six charitable communities in Yugoslavia, Latin America, and Italy. She made her first visit to Argentina in 1940, and the outbreak of World War II kept her there for the next twelve years.

Marija's work in Latin America led to her unusual beatification miracle. On August 26, 1988, a Peruvian naval submarine was near Lima when it struck a Japanese fishing boat and began to sink. Twenty-three sailors escaped, but three men in the engine room were killed and another twenty-two were trapped in the belly of the submarine. The ship's officer struggled to keep water from rushing in, but he was working with a broken hatch and pump. He had heard stories about Marija Petkovic from the nurses at his naval hospital and in desperation he prayed to her. Through Marija's intercession, he summoned the supernatural strength to operate the hatch and pump manually, thus saving himself and his crew. After investigations by the Peruvian military and the Congregation for the Causes of the Saints, this event was accepted as Marija's beatification miracle. She is venerated in Peru and Croatia on July 9.

The Genius of Marija Petkovic:
During her life Marija established forty-six communities with almost no visible means of support. She explained: *"If I had money, I would trust in money, but [without it] I trust only in God."*

Reflection:
"You were called for freedom. . . . But do not use this freedom as an opportunity for the flesh; rather, serve one another through love."

Galatians 5:13

BLESSED CATHERINE JARRIGE
(Catinon Menette)

b. October 4, 1754, Doumis, Chalvignac, France
d. July 4, 1836, Mauriac, Cantal, France

Resourceful and fearless, Catherine also had a sense of humor that averted many dangerous confrontations during the Reign of Terror. Known affectionately as Catinon or the Little Nun (although she was a laywoman), she sometimes dressed in rags to impersonate a drunken vagrant, heaping verbal abuse on the authorities and diverting their attention while a priest escaped.

Catherine had no formal education and went to work at the age of ten. By twenty she was a lacemaker in the city of Mauriac. She wore a leather apron with two large pockets, and in her free time she walked the streets, soliciting donations from the haves and dispensing them to the have-nots. She became a Dominican tertiary or "Menette," devoting herself to God while living in the world. Although Catherine loved to dance, as a Menette she made the great sacrifice of giving up dancing completely. When the Revolution began a war on Christianity, her life became more dangerous. Priests who refused to sign an oath to the Republic were forced into hiding. Catherine took them supplies so that they could celebrate Mass for the faithful. Catherine said that she was not afraid to die, that she would dance on the scaffold as gaily as she had danced in her youth. She was arrested twice, but the first time the case was dismissed for lack of evidence, and the second time, near the end of the Terror, her neighbors rebelled and forced the court to release her. She is credited with saving thousands of priests from the guillotine, but Catherine was probably prouder of the fact that for two years no one in her district went without the sacrament of Baptism or died without receiving the last rites. She is venerated in France on July 4.

The Genius of Catherine Jarrige:
Without education or worldly credentials, Catherine fearlessly protected the right of her neighbors to worship freely.

Reflection:
"Then the virgins shall make merry and dance, / and young men and old as well. / I will turn their mourning into joy, / I will console and gladden them after their sorrows."

Jeremiah 31:13, cited in her beatification homily

Saint Elizabeth, Queen of Portugal
(Isabel the Peacemaker, Isabella of Aragon)

b. 1271, Aljaferia, Zaragossa, Spain
d. July 4, 1336, Estremoz, Portugal

Elizabeth was the granddaughter of Jaime, king of Aragon, an aging lecher who had banned his entire family from the royal court. He attended Elizabeth's christening, however, and one look at her was enough for Jaime to reconcile with her father and declare Elizabeth "the rose of the house of Aragon." Elizabeth was six years old when her father succeeded Jaime and became King Pedro.

He arranged her marriage to Dinis, king of Portugal, when she was eleven, but Elizabeth did not actually meet her future husband until a year and a half later. She was twenty when her first child, Constance, was born, and her son, Afonso, was born the following year. Many of Elizabeth's peacemaking efforts involved her husband or her son. Portugal was at war with Castile when Elizabeth met with Castile's Queen María. Their three-day conference produced the Treaty of Alcanzas, which permanently defined the borders between Spain and Portugal. In 1302 Elizabeth convinced her feuding brother and son-in-law, the kings of Aragon and Castile respectively, to allow her husband to arbitrate their quarrel. This success led to a permanent alliance among them.

When her son Afonso went to war against his father, Elizabeth set out for the battlefield to reconcile them. Neither man would make the first move, so Elizabeth rode alone into their encampment and convinced the soldiers on both sides to lay down their arms. Afonso advanced to kiss his father's hand and peace was restored. Dinis had never been a model husband, but he made Elizabeth the executor of his estate and guardian of his numerous illegitimate children. When Dinis died in 1325, Elizabeth's son became King Afonso IV, and she retired to a convent in Coimbra. Every two years Coimbra holds a gala festival in her honor.

The Genius of Elizabeth of Portugal:
Elizabeth had a clear understanding of her role in life. She always dismissed praise for her generosity by saying: "*God made me queen so that I may serve others.*"

Reflection:
"*Much will be required of the person entrusted with much, and still more will be demanded of the person entrusted with more.*"

Luke 12:48

❦

BLESSED MARIA THERESA LEDÓCHOWSKA

b. April 29, 1863, Loosdorf, Austria
d. July 6, 1922, Rome, Italy

At the age of twenty-two, Maria Theresa read an antislavery pamphlet in which the author pleaded: "Christian women of Europe! It is up to you! If God has given you the talents for writing, use it in the service of this cause. You will find none holier." Maria Therese felt as if these words were addressed directly to her, and she took up the cause.

Maria Theresa came from a distinguished Polish family. Her older sister Ursula Ledóchowska (May 27) has been canonized. One brother, Vladimir, became superior general of the Jesuits, and another, Ignatius, died in a Nazi concentration camp. Maria Theresa was a lady in waiting to the elderly widow of Grand Duke Ferdinand IV when she began writing antislavery articles and pamphlets under the pseudonym Africanus. She corresponded with missionaries abroad and published their stories in her magazine, *Echo from Africa*. In 1891 Maria Theresa formally requested permission *"to resign from Austria's imperial court so as to transfer to the court of the Good Lord."* By 1894 she had founded the Missionary Sisters of St Peter Claver,[112] who seek to raise awareness about the missions and publish books in numerous African languages. During her lifetime Maria Theresa distributed 96,000 catechisms and other books in Africa. Today *Echo from Africa* is published in nine languages and distributed around the world. Maria Theresa is venerated on July 6.

The Genius of Maria Theresa Ledóchowska:

Maria Theresa made her motto *"The most divine of divine things is to cooperate in the saving of souls."*

Reflection:

"The Spirit of the Lord is upon me, / because he has anointed me / to bring glad tidings to the poor. / He has sent me to proclaim liberty to the captives / and recovery of sight to the blind, / to let the oppressed go free, / and to proclaim a year acceptable to the Lord."

Luke 4:18–19,
cited by John Paul II on the 25th anniversary of her beatification

July 6

Saint Maria Goretti

b. October 16, 1890, Corinaldo, Ancona, Italy
d. July 6, 1902, Nettuno, Rome, Italy

Maria was a poor peasant girl who was stabbed fourteen times while fighting off a rapist. She died forgiving her killer.

Maria was nine years old when her father succumbed to malaria. She looked after her younger brothers and sisters while her mother worked in the fields. As tenant farmers they shared a house with the wreckage of another family: the father was a drunk, the mother had died in a madhouse, and the oldest son, nineteen-year-old Alessandro Serenelli, home after five years at sea, spent his days staring at pornography.

Maria made her First Communion on May 29, 1902, and less than two months later, Alessandro made his first move. He propositioned her twice and was rejected. Tired of waiting, he tried to rape her. Maria fought him off and he stabbed her, over and over again. His younger brother came home to find Maria soaked in blood on the kitchen floor. She was taken to a hospital in a mule-drawn cart, where doctors worked on her to no avail. Maria received the last rites and showed compassion for her murderer, saying: *"Through love of Jesus, I forgive him with all my heart."* Alessandro refused to believe it. "That is not possible," he insisted. Not yet twenty-one, he avoided the death penalty and was sentenced to thirty years of hard labor. He remained unrepentant for six years, until he dreamed that Maria brought him an armful of lilies. This brought a change of heart and Alessandro became a model prisoner. Upon his release, he sought and received forgiveness from Maria's mother. He became a gardener at a Capuchin monastery, testified during the investigation into Maria's cause, and attended her canonization ceremony with her family. He died at the monastery in 1970.

The Genius of Maria Goretti:

A martyr for chastity and a model for youth, Maria Goretti also presents an enduring example of forgiveness.

Reflection:

"'I am completely trapped,' Susanna groaned. 'If I yield, it will be my death; if I refuse, I cannot escape your power. Yet it is better for me to fall into your power without guilt than to sin before the Lord.'"

Daniel 13:22–23

July 7

⁓

THE SEVEN BLESSED MARTYRS OF SHANXI (SHANSI)

d. July 9, 1900, Taiyuanfu, Shanxi Province, China

During the Boxer riots[113] fanatics massacred tens of thousands of Christians, including seven Franciscan Missionaries of Mary who had founded a hospital and orphanage in Shanxi's capital.

Natives of France, Italy, Belgium, and Holland, the sisters belonged to a new missionary order founded by Mary of the Passion (November 2). Their superior, Marie-Hermine de Jesus,[114] had become a missionary, she said, *"to save souls by caring for their bodies."* On arrival in May 1899, they were greeted by two hundred orphans, and more children were brought to them every day. The sisters treated them for scabies and typhoid and taught them to knit, to make lace, and to operate a sewing machine. As the Boxer violence escalated, the sisters prayed to God, not to spare them, but to give them strength. When their monsignor came to evacuate them, Sister Clelia Nanetti shook her head, *"Monsignor, flee? No. We came here to give our lives for God if needs be."* (Clelia did, however, get most of the orphans out of harm's way.)

The sisters were arrested with thirty-three other Christians, including a sixty-six-year-old widow and six orphaned children. Days later, three thousand Boxers watched them sing hymns as they filed in to face the viceroy. As the hearing began, the viceroy exchanged angry words with the bishop and then ordered his soldiers to kill them all. The Boxers immediately began hacking at heads and limbs. A Boxer witness said later: "What was most astonishing was to see these 'she-devil Christians' die singing." The Martyrs of Shanxi were canonized with the Martyrs of China.[115] They are venerated by the Franciscan Missionaries of Mary on July 10.

The Genius of the Martyrs of Shanxi:

Capturing the spirit of her sister martyrs, Anne Moreau wrote: *"I attach myself to the Will of God as the anchor of my salvation."*

Reflection:

"There is no greater love than to lay down one's life for those one loves."
John 15:13 (as it appears on the Franciscan Missionaries of Mary Web site)

SAINT SUNNIVA OF BERGEN

b. Ireland
d. c. 950, Selje, Norway

Norway's only female saint, Sunniva was a princess who fled Ireland to avoid marriage to a pagan.

Legend has it that a storm carried Sunniva and two of her ships north to the island of Selje. It appeared deserted, but farmers from the mainland used Selje as a pasture and feared that Sunniva and her companions intended to steal their cattle. They alerted their ruler, Haakon Jarl, a fierce defender of the old Norse gods, who immediately set sail to eliminate the Christian invaders. Sunniva and her companions retreated to a mountain cave. They were not afraid to die but prayed that God would spare them from the Norsemen's well-known atrocities. As they prayed, an avalanche of rocks sealed them inside the cave. By the time Haakon Jarl landed, he could not find a living soul on Selje. About forty years later, boatmen reported a strange and beautiful light in the mountains of Selje. The new king of Norway was a Christian convert, Olav Tryggveson, and he set out to investigate. Inside a mountain cave, Olav found the bones of many men, women, and children, the relics of Sunniva's companions. The most stunning discovery was the body of a young woman so perfectly preserved that she looked as if she had just fallen asleep. Olav, who was married to an Irish princess himself, recognized that this was the lost princess Sunniva and erected a church on the site. In 1170 Sunniva's incorrupt body was transferred to the cathedral in Bergen and later to Christ cathedral in Trondheim. The cathedral and Sunniva's relics were destroyed during the Reformation. Sigrid Undset, the Scandinavian novelist and Nobel Prize winner, noted that a feast day for Sunniva and her companions has been celebrated in Norway as long as there has been a calendar, giving her great historical credibility.

The Genius of Sunniva:
Sunniva willingly left her homeland and placed herself entirely in the hands of Divine Providence.

Reflection:
"We escaped with our lives / like a bird from the fowler's snare; / the snare was broken and we escaped. / Our help is the name of the Lord, / the maker of heaven and earth."
Psalm 124:7–8 (from an old liturgy for her feast day)

July 9

❧

SAINT VERONICA GIULIANI
(Ursula Giuliani)

b. December 27, 1660, Mercatello, Urbino, Italy
d. July 9, 1727, Città di Castello, Umbria, Italy

Ursula admitted to having been a feisty child: *"I was by nature passionate; every trifle excited me to irritation, and if it was a serious annoyance which befell me, I stamped on the ground like a horse."* At ten, Ursula heard God order her *"To war! To war!"* and asked a cousin to teach her fencing. When she accidentally wounded him, God rebuked her for misunderstanding: He had meant war on the world, the flesh, and the devil. Ursula gave up fencing and prepared to arm herself with prayer and meditation. At seventeen she became a Poor Clare Capuchin and took the name Veronica.

Her spiritual life deepened. Among her mystic gifts was the multiplication of food, so the convent never ran out of supplies. Maturing into a practical manager, Veronica was elected abbess. She negotiated with local landowners to divert some of their water and had plumbing installed to carry the water all over the monastery. When Veronica began manifesting the wounds of Christ's Crown of Thorns, the Sacred Tribunal of the Inquisition ordered an investigation. Florida Cevoli (June 12) later swore that she had seen *"purple marks like thorns"* on Veronica's forehead and that Veronica wept tears of blood. Doctors put her through humiliating examinations, she was confined for fifty days and deprived of the Eucharist, but no one could find a scientific explanation for Veronica's wounds. She was restored to leadership and remained abbess until her death. For thirty-three years, Veronica kept a daily diary of her mystical experiences. It was published in ten volumes during her canonization process, making her one of the best-documented examples of extraordinary mystic experiences.

The Genius of Veronica Giuliani:

Many people asked Veronica to pray for them, but the Lord warned her: *"Tell them that it is not enough to call upon me, they must come themselves and seek me."*

Reflection:

"[Wisdom] is an aura of the might of God / and a pure effusion of the glory of the Almighty; / therefore nought that is sullied enters into her. / For she is the refulgence of eternal light, / the spotless mirror of the power of God, / the image of his goodness."

Wisdom 7:25–26

Saint Amalberga of Ghent

(Amelia, Amalberga of Bilsen, Amalberga of Munsterbilzen)

birthdate unknown, Luxembourg
d. 772, Bilsen, Belgium

According to legend, Charles Martel, leader of the Franks, wanted Amalberga[116] to marry his son, Pippin. Amalberga assured Martel's representatives that she was not interested, so Martel, also known as "the Hammer," came to Luxembourg to talk to Amalberga himself. She fled to a chapel where one of the Hammer's men broke her arm, but she managed to escape to her aunt Landrada's[117] monastery at Bilsen.

Pippin and the Hammer pursued her, presenting Amalberga and her aunt with a bear that they had slain in the nearby forest. Not even this impressive offering could get Amalberga to change her mind, however. She remained at Bilsen and succeeded Landrada as abbess.

Amalberga was considered a mystic because her life was marked by miracles. Twice during famines, Amalberga caught a fish in the Scheldt River that fed everyone who was hungry. Another time, when Amalberga could not find a boat to take her across the Scheldt, a huge sturgeon offered to carry her on his back and brought her safely to the other side. In memory of this, fishermen used to make an annual offering of sturgeon at Amalberga's chapel in Mater. Her feast day is said to be the only time that sturgeon are seen in those waters. Amalberga is usually represented with a large fish. She died peacefully at Bilsen, and a school of sturgeon accompanied her body back to Temse for burial.

The Genius of Amalberga of Ghent:

Gifts, threats, and brute force could not get Amalberga to change her mind. Yet she could also forgive: she miraculously healed the man who broke her arm when he came down with a serious illness.

Reflection:

"By the grace of God I am what I am, and his grace to me has not been ineffective. Indeed, I have toiled harder than all of them; not I, however, but the grace of God [that is] with me."

1 Corinthians 15:10

SAINT BARTOLOMEA CAPITANIO

b. January 13, 1807, Lovere, Italy
d. July 26, 1833, Lovere, Italy

Bartolomea's father ran a successful grocery business until he took to drink and became known as Modesto the Madman. Her unwavering love for him gave Bartolomea early lessons in forgiveness.

Growing up in a large resort town in the Italian Alps, Bartolomea was only twelve when she confided to her friends, *"I want to be a saint. I want to be a saint soon. I want to be a great saint."* She felt called to active charity among her neighbors, and her pastor encouraged her to partner with Caterina Gerosa (June 29), an older woman who was experienced in such work. There was a twenty-year difference between them, but Bartolomea and Caterina discovered a shared vision for an institute dedicated to works of mercy. On November 21, 1832, they consecrated themselves to the project and the Sisters of Charity of Lovere was born.

Although both Bartolomea and Caterina were influenced by Louise de Marillac (March 15), they could not affiliate with her Daughters of Charity because it was regarded as a foreign organization. Even without the support of an established order, they managed to start a home for orphaned girls, a school, and a hospital. On the morning of April 1, 1833, Bartolomea suddenly developed a fever, was confined to bed, and began a six-month decline. As she lay dying, Bartolomea assured the Sisters: *"When I am in Heaven, I will be able to do a great deal more than I can here."* Eight months after founding the institute, Bartolomea "fell asleep in the Lord with the sweet names of Jesus and Mary on her lips." She is commemorated by her Sisters of Charity on July 26.

The Genius of Bartolomea Capitanio:
Bartolomea left hundreds of letters, spiritual notes, and instructions that reveal a heart full of charity, yet one that still struggled with doubts. At the age of twenty-two Bartolomea wrote in her journal that *"the love of Jesus should not be separated from a true love of one's neighbor."* This became the guiding principle of her life.

Reflection:
"Do not love the world or the things of the world. If anyone loves the world, the love of the Father is not in him."

1 John 2:15

July 12

Saint Clelia Barbieri

b. February 13, 1847, Le Budrie di San Giovanni di Persiceto, Bologna, Italy
d. July 13, 1870, Le Budrie di San Giovanni di Persiceto, Bologna, Italy

A year after Clelia died of tuberculosis at the age of twenty-three, her Sisters were praying in their chapel when a familiar voice joined theirs, fulfilling Clelia's promise: *"I die but I will never abandon you. I will always be with you."* Since then, Clelia's voice continues to be heard in all their convents.

At fourteen Clelia revitalized a parish group, attracting many new young members. Her pastor, Gaetano Guido, known as the *curatino* or "little priest," recognized Clelia's gifts and often sent young girls to her for catechism instruction. He tried to discourage Clelia from organizing a religious community because she was too young. Besides, the newly united Italian government was suppressing religious orders, confiscating church property, and banning religious vows. Those who defied these laws were subject to arrest. Clelia assured the *curatino* that her community was the will of God and their support would come from Him. Soon, an elderly schoolmaster donated his house, the first in a series of events that kept Clelia's little community growing. Clelia herself experienced mystical graces, but her physical health broke down. She promised her community that they would someday have a convent of their own, and soon after her death, when religious tolerance returned to Italy, they received a gift of land on which they built a proper convent. Known today as the Little Sisters of Our Lady of Sorrows, they are at work in Italy, Tanzania, and India, devoted to teaching Christian doctrine and assisting those in need. Clelia is venerated on July 13.

The Genius of Clelia Barbieri:
Clelia is considered the youngest founder of a religious community in the history of the Church. At her canonization, Pope John Paul II noted that Clelia was not the product of a particular spirituality, such as Dominican or Franciscan, but rather she was "the genuine product of that first and fundamental school of holiness, the parish church."

Reflection:
"Who is there like you, the God who removes guilt / and pardons sin for the remnant of his inheritance; / Who does not persist in anger forever, / but delights rather in clemency . . . ?"

Micah 7:18

July 13

SAINT TERESA OF THE ANDES
(Juanita Solar y Fernández)

b. July 13, 1900, Santiago, Chile
d. April 12, 1920, Los Andes, Valparaíso, Chile

Brilliant, vivacious, and hot-tempered, Juanita Solar shocked her wealthy family when she announced that she was becoming a Carmelite nun. This was a girl who rode horses high up into the Andes and who loved active sports, especially swimming and tennis.

At fourteen, Juanita read *The Story of a Soul* by Thérèse of Lisieux (October 1), and three years later she read the works of Elizabeth of the Trinity (November 8). While still a student, Juanita wrote a prize-winning essay describing the struggle between the forces of light and darkness. She concluded that although the struggle will never end, *"While the children of the shade demolish, the children of the light regenerate."* Soon Juanita received a revelation: that, like Thérèse and Elizabeth, she too would become a Carmelite. She gave herself over completely to prayer, and began to record her spiritual journey. On May 7, 1919, she was admitted as a novice and given the name Teresa of Jesus. Her abbess allowed her to maintain an extensive correspondence with the outside world. This was a highly unusual privilege for a novice, and it was fortunate, because Teresa did not have long to live. Felled by a sudden attack of typhus, she received the last rites. On April 7, 1920, she was allowed to make her religious profession although she had not yet completed her novitiate. (This is called *in articulo mortis*—"in the event of death"—and if the postulate recovers she must complete the novitiate.) After Teresa's death, the nuns and her family were surprised at how many strangers came to venerate the little saint. Soon miracles were reported at her tomb. Canonized in 1993, Teresa became Chile's first saint.

The Genius of Teresa of the Andes:

What could this mere girl accomplish in her brief lifetime? The answer: she lived, she loved, and she believed that *"Love is the fusion of two souls in one in order to bring about mutual perfection."*

Reflection:

"You were once darkness, but now you are light in the Lord. Live as children of light, for light produces every kind of goodness and righteousness and truth."
Ephesians 5:8–9

BLESSED ANNE-MARIE JAVOUHEY
(Nanette de Chamblanc)

b. November 10, 1779, Jallanges, France
d. July 15, 1851, Paris, France

Napoleon Bonaparte once said, "I know of only two good heads in France—my own and Mother Javouhey's. If she were a man I would make her a general." One of the first women to establish missions in Africa, Anne-Marie pioneered in the struggle for human rights for all races.

Shortly before she was to take the veil with the Sisters of Charity, Anne-Marie dreamed that Teresa of Avila (October 15) appeared to her, surrounded by children of many races, and urged her to found a new congregation to care for them. She confided this to her confessor, who immediately canceled the ceremony and sent Anne-Marie home. After several more false starts, she founded the Sisters of St Joseph and acquired the former monastery at Cluny that became their home. The French government asked her to organize schools and hospitals in France's African and Caribbean colonies, and Anne-Marie began this work with an arduous voyage to Madagascar. *"The perils of the sea do not frighten us,"* she wrote. *"Our aim is the hope of doing good, of winning a few souls for religion, of alleviating the poor sick and sustaining their courage in the midst of the greatest dangers."* Anne-Marie later took missionaries to Guadeloupe and Martinique, Senegal and Sierra Leone, but she fought with the bishop of Cayenne, who banned her from the sacraments for almost two years. Returning to France in 1830, she entered a long power struggle with the bishop of Autun. She won every battle, but by 1851 she was mortally ill and bedridden. Informed of the sudden death of her nemesis, Anne-Marie said only, *"So he's gone, that good bishop. God rest his soul,"* and asked that all papers concerning their dispute be destroyed. Today the Sisters of St Joseph of Cluny count more than three thousand members from Tanzania to Poland. They venerate Anne-Marie on July 14.

The Genius of Anne-Marie Javouhey:
Anne-Marie advised: *"God will give you the grace according to your needs; never doubt your strength when you count on him."*

Reflection:
"Your word is a lamp for my feet, / a light for my path."

Psalm 119:105

July 15

BLESSED ANGELINA OF MONTEGIOVE
(Angelina of Marsciano, Angelina of Corbara)

b. 1377, Montegiove, Orvieto, Terni, Italy
d. July 14, 1435, Foligno, Italy

Angelina's vow of chastity meant nothing to her father. He threatened to kill her if she did not marry the Count of Civitella del Tronto. On their wedding night, the count glimpsed Angelina with her guardian angel, and from that moment he considered it a privilege to share her celibacy and good works.

Widowed after two years, Angelina became a Franciscan tertiary, traveling the Abruzzi region with a growing band of women who shared her vow of celibacy. The young fortune hunters who had hoped to marry them complained to their overlord, Ladislas, king of Naples, calling Angelina a vagabond and a heretic. The king summoned Angelina. Although he had not announced his plans, Angelina knew that he intended to have her burned alive, and she prepared by filling the corner of her cloak with live coals. Facing him, she said: *"Allow me to speak in my own defense, and when I shall have done so, if you still consider me guilty, here is the fire to burn me and reduce me to ashes!"* Angelina held out the glowing coals, which miraculously damaged neither her habit nor her hands. The king was completely disarmed and soon let her go. Angelina and her companions made a pilgrimage to Assisi, then moved on to Foligno where she founded the first convent of the Franciscan Third Order. (Until then, all Franciscan tertiaries lived at home.) Among those she mentored were Margaret Dominici,[118] Antonia of Florence (February 29), and Paula of Foligno.[119]

The Genius of Angelina of Montegiove:
> Angelina made it clear that she did not condemn marriage and recommended the state of virginity only to those who had been given the grace to desire it.

Reflection:
> *"As the sparrow finds a home / and the swallow a nest to settle her young,*
> *My home is by your altars, LORD of hosts, my king and my God!"*
> Psalm 84:4

July 16

Saint Marie Madeleine Postel
(Julie Postel)

b. November 28, 1756, Barfleur, Normandy, France
d. July 16, 1846, Saint-Sauveur-le-Vicomte, Manche, France

Julie grew up in a seaside village where her father was a rope-maker, an important trade in the days of sailing ships. Her first schoolteacher recognized Julie's potential and arranged for her to board at a prestigious school for six years.

On finishing her studies, Julie returned to Barfleur and opened a free school. She was known for her gentle methods and for including the arts in her curriculum. After five years, however, the Revolution broke out and Julie's peaceful life as a small-town schoolteacher ended for good. The Revolutionary government suppressed Christianity in all forms and required all religious to take an oath to the state or face execution. Julie risked her life to shelter priests who celebrated Mass in her home, and they authorized her to carry the Eucharist on her person and administer it to the sick and dying. She continued to give religious instruction in secret, and when religious services were permitted again in 1801, Julie celebrated First Holy Communion with the children she had prepared. Unfortunately, the new pastor was jealous of her success, and in 1805 Julie left Barfleur for good. Two years later, taking the religious name Marie Madeleine, she founded a religious community dedicated to teaching the young and nursing the sick. Her community had to move many times until she acquired the ruins of an eleventh-century abbey at Saint-Sauveur-le-Vicomte. At the age of eighty-two Marie Madeleine embarked on restoring this property. Today it is the motherhouse for the Sisters of the Christian Schools of St Marie Madeleine Postel and draws visitors and students from all over the world. Her Sisters also continue her work in Germany, the Netherlands, Brazil, and Bolivia.

The Genius of Marie Madeleine Postel:
Observing the ruined abbey she planned to restore, Julie assured her dubious companions: *"God did not invite us to cry over the ruins of his temple, but to rebuild it in his first splendor. If we are faithful, all will be repaired."*

Reflection:
"By wisdom is a house built, / by understanding is it made firm; / And by knowledge are its rooms filled / with every precious and pleasing possession."
Proverbs 24:3–4

THE SIXTEEN BLESSED CARMELITE MARTYRS OF COMPIÈGNE

d. July 17, 1794, Paris, France

During the worst excesses of the Revolution, sixteen Carmelite nuns went to the guillotine together, deliberately offering their lives to God to end the Reign of Terror.

The Carmelites of Compiègne had been preparing for martyrdom since 1792 when the National Assembly evicted them from their convent. They refused to recognize Reason as France's official religion and were arrested on June 22, 1794. Hustled into a cart, seventy-five-year-old Anne Thouret could not move fast enough, so the forces of Reason threw her into the gutter. Anne stood up bleeding and thanked them for not killing her there, because she wanted to offer herself in martyrdom. The nuns were transported to Paris and on July 17 went before a prosecutor in the Hall of Freedom. Anne Pelras, thirty-four years old and said to have been very beautiful, asked the prosecutor to explain the charge of "persistent fanaticism." "By fanaticism, I mean your attachment to childish practices and your stupid beliefs," he said, then summarily sentenced all sixteen nuns to death on the guillotine. They went to the scaffold that night, beginning with the nineteen-year-old novice Marie-Geneviève Meunier. She started chanting Psalm 117 and the others took it up. A rowdy crowd usually gathered to watch such executions, but all eyewitnesses recorded that the crowd was uncharacteristically quiet that night. The sight of the Carmelites dampened the revelry. One of the last Carmelites to die, seventy-nine-year-old Marie Ann Piedcourt shouted to her executioner, *"I forgive you as heartily as I wish God to forgive me."*

The sixteen bodies were tossed into a new mass grave at the Picpus cemetery. In six weeks that summer, the Picpus sandpit received more than thirteen hundred enemies of the Revolution, ranging in age from fourteen to ninety. Similar scenes were being repeated all over France.

The Genius of the Carmelites of Compiègne:
One week after the sixteen Carmelites' sacrifice, Maximilien Robespierre, leader of the Committee of Public Safety, was arrested. He went to the guillotine on July 28 and the Reign of Terror died with him.

Reflection:
"Praise the LORD, all you nations! / Give glory, all you peoples! The LORD's love for us is strong; / The LORD is faithful forever. Hallelujah!"

Psalm 117

July 18

Saint Theneva of Glasgow
(Enoch, Thaney)

Seventh century, Scotland

Tradition has it that Theneva was the daughter of Lot, the half-pagan king of the Picts, a sister to Sir Gawain, and kin to King Arthur. Her father gave her a choice: she could marry Ewen, pagan prince of Cumbria, or be given as a slave to a swineherd. Theneva chose the swineherd because he was a Christian. Legends differ about which man was the father of her child, but it hardly matters, since neither was on the scene when Theneva, still unwed, was condemned to be stoned to death for the crime of fornication. No one dared to cast a stone at a royal princess, however, so she was taken to the top of the hill at Traprain Law, about twenty miles east of Edinburgh, and tossed over the edge in her chariot. She miraculously landed unharmed.

King Lot then ordered Theneva thrown into the sea, saying, "If she be worthy to live, her God will save her." They put Theneva into a small boat and set her adrift at Aberlady. That night, a strong wind carried the boat to the Isle of May, where she was surrounded by a school of fish that guided her to Culross. There Theneva collapsed with exhaustion and was found by Serf of Fife.[120] He delivered her baby and baptized him Kentigern.[121] Under their guidance, Kentigern became one of Scotland's greatest saints. Theneva ended her days in Glasgow where she and her son are honored as the patron saints of that city.

The Genius of Theneva of Glasgow:

Theneva's tormenters laughed when they cast her adrift, but she trusted that Christ would free her from the hand of death and the danger of the sea.

Reflection:

"When they continued asking him, he straightened up and said to them, 'Let the one among you who is without sin be the first to throw a stone at her.'"

John 8:7

THE THREE BLESSED CARMELITE MARTYRS OF GUADALAJARA

María Pilar of Saint Francis Borgia (Jacoba Martínez Gardia)
d. July 24, 1936, Guadalajara, Spain

Teresa of the Child Jesus and Saint John of the Cross
(Eusebia García y García)
d. July 24, 1936, Guadalajara, Spain

María Angela of Saint Joseph (Marciana Valtierra Tordesillas)
d. July 24, 1936, Guadalajara, Spain

Viva el Comunismo! (Long live Communism!) was the battle cry of Spain's anti-Christian Red militia. Catholics responded: *Viva Cristo Rey!* Long Live Christ the King! Because of that loyalty to Christ, Pilar, Teresa, and Angela became the first of thousands of religious who were martyred during the Spanish Civil War.[122]

All three were cloistered in a Carmel (monastery) in Guadalajara until July 21, 1936, when riots left the Red militia in control of the city. Members of the Carmel donned plain clothes and dispersed into small groups. Pilar, Angela, and Teresa spent two nights on the top floor of a nearby hotel, watching their city burn. Leaving the hotel they were spotted immediately. A woman shouted: "Shoot them! They're nuns." The militia fired. A bullet pierced Angela's heart, killing her instantly. Pilar, mortally wounded, was taken to the Red Cross hospital where she died forgiving her enemies. Teresa wandered away in a daze. The militia caught her and said if she would repeat *Viva el Comunismo!* they would let her go. She responded *Viva Cristo Rey!* and they shot her dead. The three martyrs are commemorated by the Carmelites on July 24.

The Genius of the Carmelite Martyrs of Guadalajara:
  Teresa spoke for all her sisters: *"If you ever write a death notice for me, please be sure to tell all my faults. I want God's mercy to be known."*

Reflection:
  "It is better to suffer for doing good, if that be the will of God, than for doing evil."

1 Peter 3:17

July 20

Saint Margaret of Antioch

(Marina, Marjorie, Pearl, Daisy)

b. c. 275, Antioch, Pisidia (Turkey)
d. c. July 20, 290, Antioch, Pisidia (Turkey)

At fifteen Margaret was brought before Olybrius, the Roman provost, who asked how she could worship a God who had been crucified. Margaret answered that he only knew about Christ's suffering and not the Resurrection. This infuriated Olybrius, who ordered her to be tortured. Even while she was being torn by hooks, Margaret berated him: *"You shameless hound and insatiable lion, you have power over my flesh, but Christ reserves my soul."* Olybrius covered his face because he could not bear the sight of so much blood, and ordered Margaret sent to prison. The devil appeared to her there in the form of a dragon and swallowed her. Margaret made the sign of the cross, his belly burst open, and she emerged. Next, the devil took her hand while she prayed, but Margaret caught him and threw him to the ground, setting her right foot on his neck. *"Lie still, fiend, under the feet of a woman,"* she ordered until the earth opened and swallowed him. After a few more such episodes, Olybrius sentenced Margaret to death. In her last moments, she asked God to pardon her tormenters and prayed that any pregnant woman might call on her for a safe delivery. A celestial voice announced that her prayers had been granted. Giving thanks, Margaret ordered the reluctant executioner to do his duty. He cut off her head, then collapsed dead at her feet. Margaret is one of the Fourteen Holy Helpers[123] and a patron of pregnant women and the terminally ill.

The Genius of Margaret of Antioch:

This is a saint with staying power. A fifth-century pope declared her legend apocryphal, but six hundred years later the Crusaders were still spreading Margaret's story all over Europe. Her cult was officially suppressed in 1969, because of a lack of historical evidence, but churches dedicated to Margaret remain and her legend lives on.

Reflection:

"Out of my distress I called to the LORD, / and he answered me; / From the midst of the nether world I cried for help, / and you heard my voice."

Jonah 2:3

BLESSED ALPHONSA OF INDIA

(Anna Muttathupandatu)

b. August 19, 1910, Kudamalloor, Kerala, India
d. July 28, 1946, Bharananganam, Kerala, India

The Passion Flower of Bharananganam lived and died in obscurity, yet today thousands of Christians make the pilgrimage to her shrine in Kerala.

Anna was eighteen when she entered a Franciscan Clarist convent. She made her vows there in 1936, taking the name Alphonsa of the Immaculate Conception. From then on, Alphonsa's life was marked by bouts of near-fatal illnesses and miraculous recoveries. All this drama tested the patience of her convent, but Alphonsa accepted misunderstandings with serenity. She wrote to her spiritual director: *"I sincerely desire to remain on this sick bed and suffer not only this, but anything else besides, even to the end of the world. I feel now that God has intended my life to be an oblation, a sacrifice of suffering."* Alphonsa began to demonstrate mystical gifts, including a gift of prophecy. She suffered violent convulsions that lasted for hours. To avoid disrupting the other sisters, she prayed that the convulsions would occur at regular times, and so they came every Friday. Her superiors suggested that she should pray for permanent relief, but Alphonsa rejected that idea, saying: *"Let the Lord do with me as he will, trampling over, wounding or piercing me, a humble sacrificial offering, for the sake of a world that is on its way to ruin, and for the priests and religious who are growing less fervent in their spiritual life."* Alphonsa died quietly, and it was the children at her convent school who began spreading her reputation as a powerful intercessor. She is venerated in India on July 28.

The Genius of Alphonsa:

Alphonsa prayed: *"Free me from my desire to be loved and esteemed. Guard me from my evil attempts to win fame and honor."*

Reflection:

"Now I rejoice in my sufferings for your sake, and in my flesh I am filling up what is lacking in the afflictions of Christ on behalf of his body, which is the church, of which I am a minister in accordance with God's stewardship given to me to bring to completion for you the word of God, the mystery hidden from ages and from generations past."

Colossians 1:24–26, cited in her beatification homily

SAINT MARY MAGDALENE
(Madeleine, Magdalen, Mary of Magdala)

First century

Tradition has always identified Mary Magdalene as the penitent who stalked Christ at the house of the Pharisee and insisted on washing His feet with her tears. She dried them with her hair, kissed them, and anointed them with oil from an alabaster jar. The Pharisee was appalled, but Christ said that she had shown the greater love and told her: *"Your sins are forgiven, your faith has saved you; go in peace."* She is believed to be the same Mary of Magdala who was possessed by seven demons until Jesus freed her. There is no evidence in Scripture for Mary Magdalene's reputation as a prostitute, but the label endures.

Whatever the truth about her life before the Crucifixion, Mary Magdalene was among the mourners at Calvary, and she became the first witness to the Resurrection. She arrived at Christ's tomb that morning shortly before dawn. Discovering that the stone had been moved, Mary Magdalene ran to the apostles Simon, Peter, and John and brought them back to see. They refused to stay because they did not yet understand the Resurrection, and it was left to Mary Magdalene to remain there and weep. Two angels in white asked her why she was weeping. She answered: *"They have taken my Lord, and I don't know where they laid him."* She did not recognize Jesus standing there until he said, *"Mary!"* She answered, *"Rabbouni"* (Teacher). Jesus told her to take a message to the disciples: *"I am going to my Father and your Father, to my God and your God."*

It is impossible to write about Mary Magdalene today without acknowledging *The Da Vinci Code*, which suggests that Mary Magdalene was a "holy vessel" that "bore the royal bloodline of Jesus Christ." Serious scholars find no reliable historical evidence that Jesus was married to her or anyone else.

The Genius of Mary Magdalene:
Philosophers from Thomas Aquinas to John Paul II have saluted Mary Magdalene as the Apostle to the Apostles because she was the first to see the resurrected Christ, and she was charged with bringing others the news.

Reflection:
"Mary of Magdala went and announced to the disciples, 'I have seen the Lord,' and what he told her."

John 20:18

Saint Bridget of Sweden
(Birgitta Birgersdotter)

b. 1303, Uppland, Sweden
d. July 23, 1373, Rome, Italy

Bridget was a brilliant visionary, devoted wife and mother, and fearless advocate for reform in the Church. Born into the nobility, she married a prince and bore eight children, including the saintly Catherine (March 24). After her husband's death, a revelation inspired Bridget to found the Order of the Most Holy Savior (Brigittines). In 1350 she made the two-thousand-mile journey from Sweden to Rome to celebrate a jubilee year and was deeply disappointed with the corruption she found there. While churches collapsed from neglect, the pope lived in luxurious exile in Avignon, France. Bridget insisted that only the pope's presence in Rome could restore moral force to the Church. She joined Catherine of Siena (April 29) in calling on him to return. (The pope did return, after Bridget's death.) At seventy, Bridget made a pilgrimage to the Holy Land and died soon after her return to Rome. Her *Revelations*, published posthumously, were studied by theologians all over Europe, and her visions influenced the work of such artists as Fra Angelico[124] and Michelangelo. Bridget's fame was eclipsed by the Reformation when most of her convents in Scandinavia were destroyed, but a twentieth-century convert, Mary Elisabeth Hesselblad (April 12), helped to revive interest. Today all of Sweden considers Bridget a national heroine. She has become a patron of the ecumenical movement and is commemorated by the Church of England and the Evangelical Lutheran Church in America. In 1999 John Paul II named Bridget a co-patron of Europe, with Catherine of Siena and Edith Stein (August 9).

The Genius of Bridget of Sweden:
In 1992 the future Pope Benedict XVI praised Bridget as Catholic, feminist, and politically engaged, and compared her to the Old Testament prophet Judith, who saved her people from a foreign tyrant as Bridget protected the Church from heresy and schism. Bridget prayed: *"Lord, show me the way and make me ready to follow it."*

Reflection:
"She was beautifully formed and lovely to behold. . . . No one had a bad word to say about her, for she was a very God-fearing woman."

Judith 8:7–8

Saint Kinga, Queen of Poland
(Cunegunda)

b. March 5, 1234, Eszergom, Hungary
d. July 24, 1292, Stary Sqcz, Sandeck, Poland

Named for her aunt Cunegunda (March 8) but always called Kinga, she was the sister of Margaret of Hungary (January 18). Kinga's parents, the king and queen of Hungary, arranged her marriage to Boleslaw, the future king of Poland. When her father raised the subject of her dowry, Kinga asked for the salt mine on the border between Hungary and Poland, which, she said, *"will be a blessing to my people and be of use to both rich and poor."* This mine provided Poland with salt for the first time and has continued to produce salt ever since.

After her wedding, great joyful crowds welcomed Kinga to Poland. She and her new husband made a public vow of perpetual chastity and governed together for forty years. Queen Kinga later confronted a knight who had moved his mistress into his castle, displacing his wife. Kinga arrived with her retinue, and the knight met them with sword drawn. This intimidated her courtiers but not Kinga, who just swept past him. She found the wronged wife confined to the servants' quarters and consoled her, then dragged the mistress across the courtyard and tossed her into a wagon. Hagiographers point out that surely God intervened, since Kinga was quite slender and the mistress was stout and strong. When Kinga was asked where she had sent the mistress, she said only that the woman had gone where she could serve God. As a widow, Kinga retired to a monastery.

Deep inside Kinga's salt mine at Wieliczka, workers in the seventeenth century carved a huge cathedral with a chapel dedicated to Kinga. The shrine continues to draw 600,000 visitors a year.

The Genius of Kinga:
Kinga's vow of celibacy might be baffling today, but as John Paul II noted in his canonization homily, her sacrifice brought her an inner freedom. He added: "She reminds us that the value of marriage, this indissoluble union of love between two persons, cannot be brought into question under any circumstances."

Reflection:
"As high as the heavens are above the earth, / so high are my ways above your ways / and my thoughts above your thoughts."

Isaiah 55:9

BLESSED CHRISTINA THE ASTONISHING

b. 1150, Brusthem, Belgium
d. 1224, Saint-Trond, Belgium

Christina lived quietly with two older sisters until her death at the age of thirty-two. The next day, her funeral service was interrupted when Christina arose from her coffin and soared like a bird up to the church rafters. Everyone fled in terror, but the priest continued saying Mass. When he finished, he ordered Christina to come down and go home.

Christina later explained that, while she was dead, angels had taken her to purgatory and hell, where she recognized the souls of many people she knew. Finally the angels brought her to paradise, where God offered her a choice: she could remain in heaven for all eternity or she could return to earth and suffer. Her sufferings would release the souls she had seen in purgatory, and by leading a life of penance, she could convert many others who were still living in the world. Without hesitation Christina chose to go back and suffer. From then on, she fled from human contact, preferring to stay in trees or on the tops of towers. She could walk steadily on the most dizzying precipice while reciting the psalms, but her self-inflicted mortifications could be horrifying. She immersed herself in cauldrons of boiling water and crept into hot ovens, always emerging unscathed. One day, extreme thirst brought her to the banquet table of a very wicked man. The sight of Christina moved him to uncharacteristic charity and he urged her to drink some wine. Christina then predicted that he would die penitent and pardoned. He did, much to the surprise of everyone who knew him. Toward the end of her life, Christina retired to a Benedictine convent where she encouraged Lutgard of Aywières (June 16). She is venerated in Belgium on July 24.

The Genius of Christina the Astonishing:

Clearly, Christina belongs among the saints who are to be admired rather than imitated, but even Herbert Thurston, the great Jesuit expert on mystic phenomena, conceded that Christina was blessed. It is the only way to account for the veneration in which she was held by the many sincere and intelligent people who knew her.

Reflection:

"Faith is the realization of what is hoped for and evidence of things not seen."
Hebrews 11:1

SAINT ANNE, MOTHER OF MARY
(Ann)

First century, Jerusalem

Sitting in her garden one day, Anne watched a bird bring food to its nestlings and said to herself: *"Every wife has children except me; the very birds in the trees have their children, but I have none."* Anne's husband, Joachim, also suffered. When he took an offering to the great Temple in Jerusalem, it was rejected because his childless marriage was regarded as a sign he had displeased God.

These and similar legends are all we know about the parents of Mary the Mother of God. Most of the stories arise from an apocryphal book called the Protevangelium of James the Lesser. According to this book, Anne and Joachim had been happily married for twenty years and still prayed that if God would make them parents, they would dedicate their child to his service.

While Joachim was in the fields, an angel appeared and told him that God had answered his prayers, that Anne would bear a daughter whom they were to name Mary. This child was to be raised in the Temple, and she would bear a great Lord through whom salvation would come to all people. Meanwhile, at home, Anne was worrying about her husband until the same angel visited her with the same message. Nine months later, Anne gave birth to their daughter, Mary.

Anne's color is emerald green and she protects pregnant women who wear green. Traditionally venerated on Tuesdays, she is especially pleased by those who attend Mass and Communion or give alms in her honor on that day. Others honor Anne by saying nine Hail Marys to commemorate the nine months she carried her daughter.

Anne is a powerful intercessor, especially for mothers and those who want to become mothers. She is a model for married women and a protector of widows. With Joachim she is a patron of married couples. She is also the patron of horsewomen, woodworkers, antique dealers, and those holding garage sales.

The Genius of Anne:
She is a model of faith, and as a mother, she prepared Mary to fulfill her destiny.

Reflection:
"The LORD sets a father in honor over his children; / a mother's authority he confirms over her sons. He who honors his father atones for sins; / he stores up riches who reveres his mother."

Sirach 3:2–4

Saint Lillian of Córdoba

(Liliosa)

Saint Natalie of Córdoba

d. July 27, 852, Córdoba, Spain

Once Lillian and Natalie and their husbands agreed to become martyrs, the two women simply went to Mass with their faces unveiled. That was all it took to bring on their sacrifice.

Lillian and Natalie came of age when southern Spain was controlled by the Moors, who tolerated Christians only as long as they observed Muslim laws. Both women had been secretly baptized Christians, but they married into an extended Muslim family. Natalie discovered that her new husband, Aurelius, was also a secret Christian. Lillian married Aurelius's cousin, Felix, and after she brought him back to the faith, the two couples began to yearn for a more openly Christian life. Their desire for martyrdom came gradually, especially after Aurelius saw a Christian beaten and dragged through the streets by a crowd demanding death for anyone who criticized Mohammed. Next, Natalie visited the future saints Flora and Mary (November 24) in prison. After Flora and Mary were executed, they appeared to Natalie in a dream and pledged to send a monk who would help her receive the crown of martyrdom. Natalie and Aurelius sold all their property and made a retreat at a monastery in the nearby mountains. A monk named George stopped there on his way to France after many years in Jerusalem, and Natalie became convinced that Flora and Mary had sent him. George and the two couples formed the plan for Natalie and Lillian to leave Mass with unveiled faces. As expected, they were recognized by a Muslim official. He denounced them to the magistrate, who ordered the five of them beheaded. Other Christians managed to retrieve their bodies and bury them. Six years later their relics were taken to Paris, but they were lost during the Revolution.

The Genius of Lillian and Natalie:

Christians like Lillian and Natalie were skilled at practicing their faith in secret, but they discovered that the more they honored it in private, the more they yearned to go public and share it with others.

Reflection:

"*I do not sit with deceivers, / nor with hypocrites do I mingle.*
I hate the company of evildoers; / with the wicked I do not sit."

Psalm 26:4–5

BLESSED MARIA TERESA KOWALSKA
(Mieczyslawa Kowalska)

b. 1902, Warsaw, Poland
d. July 25,1941, Dzialdowo, Warminsko-Mazurskie, Poland

At age twenty-one, Mieczyslawa entered the convent of the Capuchin Poor Clares and took the name Maria Teresa. Since the Russian Revolution of 1917, her father and other relatives had embraced atheistic Communism and enthusiastically supported the new Soviet Union. Maria Teresa did not share those beliefs and had entered the convent to make reparations for her family's choices.

For seventeen years, Maria Teresa lived an austere and hidden life devoted to prayer and Eucharistic contemplation, trusting completely in the providence of God. She was suffering from tuberculosis when German soldiers invaded her cloister at Przasnysz on April 2, 1941. The Nazis arrested all thirty-six nuns and transported them to a concentration camp at Dzialdowo. With little food or fresh water, disease was rampant and Maria Teresa's tuberculosis worsened. Too weak to leave her bunk, she abandoned herself to prayer, saying: *"I will not leave here alive; I offer my life in sacrifice so that the Sisters might return to the convent."* That night, she died of a pulmonary hemorrhage. Maria Teresa's body was removed and no one knows what became of her remains, but her holy death strengthened the surviving nuns. Confident that she had been welcomed into heaven, they held her in special veneration. They believed that Maria Teresa interceded for their liberation on August 7, just two weeks after her death. When they finally returned to their convent at Przasnysz in 1945, they continued to keep her memory alive privately. After the collapse of the Soviet Union, they were free to go public about her devotion and martyrdom. Maria Teresa is also commemorated on June 12 with the Capuchin Martyrs of the Concentration Camps (the only woman in that group) and with the Polish Martyrs of World War II.[125]

The Genius of Maria Teresa Kowalska:
Even when she lay helpless in her bed, Maria Teresa continued to serve others through the power of her prayers.

Reflection:
"Jesus told her, 'I am the resurrection and the life; whoever believes in me, even if he dies, will live, and everyone who lives and believes in me will never die.'"
John 11:25–26

SAINT MARTHA OF BETHANY

b. First century, Bethany, Jerusalem
d. c. 80, France

Martha and her sister Mary[126] welcomed Christ into their home, but Martha was stuck with the chores while Mary sat at his feet. Martha complained: *"Lord, do you not care that my sister has left me by myself to do the serving? Tell her to help me."* Christ answered that only one thing mattered and Mary had chosen that better part. He moved on and was several towns away when Martha and Mary sent word that their brother Lazarus was dying. By the time Christ returned to Bethany, Lazarus had been in his tomb for four days and the house was filled with mourners. Martha made it clear that she accepted Christ as the Messiah, and he then raised Lazarus from the dead.

According to legend, after the Resurrection, Martha and her siblings were crowded into a boat with seventy other Christians and pushed out to sea. They miraculously reached Marseilles, where Lazarus became the first bishop. Martha wandered around Provence, converting many people with her preaching and miracles. At Tarascon, villagers begged her to save them from a terrible dragon. Bigger than an ox, with a tail like a serpent, and stronger than twelve bears, he was gnawing on a fresh victim when Martha tracked him down in the woods. She threw holy water on him, showed him the cross, and he froze, so that the villagers could kill him with their spears. At their invitation, Martha remained in Tarascon until she died. Martha is the patron of cooks, homemakers, and the hospitality industry.

The Genius of Martha of Bethany:
Like Martha, we can become so consumed by the details of daily life that we forget the real reason we are here. Christ reminded Martha that only one thing matters and no one can take it from us.

Reflection:
"The Lord said to her, 'Martha, Martha, you are anxious and worried about many things. There is need of only one thing. Mary has chosen the better part and it will not be taken from her.'"

Luke 10:41–42

July 30

BLESSED ZDENKA SCHELINGOVA
(Cecilia)

b. December 24, 1916, Krivá, Northern Slovakia
d. July 31, 1955, Trnava, Trnavskya Kraj (Slovak Republic)

Baptized Cecilia, she became a Sister of Mercy of the Holy Cross at the age of nineteen, taking the name Zdenka. She studied nursing, later trained as an X-ray technician, and was working in a government hospital when her country became part of the People's Republic of Czechoslovakia, a satellite of the Soviet Union.

The new government began dissolving religious orders and shipping priests to Siberia. Church officials asked priests and nuns to cooperate with the government to avoid bloodshed. Zdenka's provincial superior also asked the Sisters to offer no resistance. Zdenka did not resist openly, but by 1952 she had secretly helped at least five priests to escape. That February, when she drugged a guard's tea so that another priest could get away, she was caught and arrested by the secret police. Interrogated in the Palace of Justice, repeatedly kicked in the breasts, Zdenka refused to name her accomplices. She was convicted of treason and sentenced to twelve years in prison. Her health deteriorated, especially after she underwent a brutal mastectomy without anesthesia, and by the following spring she was dying. Reluctant to have a martyr on their hands, prison officials discharged her. Zdenka tried to return to her congregation, but they would not admit her, citing fear of government reprisal. Not only had Zdenka defied civil authority, she had also broken her vow of obedience, and other convents turned her away as well. Finally, a friend took her in and she died a few days later. Zdenka showed heroic patience, and during her last ordeal she whispered, *"Forgiveness is the greatest thing in life."*

The Genius of Zdenka:

Zdenka wrote about her vocation as a nurse: *"From the altar of my Lord I go to my work. I take up my duties in the ward. I am not afraid of anything, I seek to begin everything with joy. I can proclaim the Lord's example better by my example than my words, just as we have to recognize Christ himself in the way he lived his life."*

Reflection:

"To you has been granted, for the sake of Christ, not only to believe in him but also to suffer for him."

Philippians 1:29

July 31

❦

Saint María de Jesús Sacramentado

(María Natividad Venegas de la Torre)

b. September 8, 1868, Zapotlanejo, Jalisco, Mexico
d. July 30, 1959, Guadalajara, Jalisco, Mexico

The woman that everyone calls Madre Nati became Mexico's first female saint by consistently delivering hospital care in spite of a revolution raging around her.

Nati was the youngest of twelve children and her mother died when she was quite young. Her father, an attorney, gave up his career to work for charity. The family suffered financial hardships but they were bolstered by his faith. He died when Nati was nineteen, and a few years later she moved to the city of Guadalajara and went to work in a charity hospital staffed by a lay group called the Daughters of the Sacred Heart of Jesus. Nati joined the Daughters and served as a nurse, then as a pharmacist and bookkeeper. At the age of thirty-one, she felt called to take religious vows, and under her leadership the Daughters became a religious order. She was elected superior and took the name María de Jesús Sacramentado.

Madre Nati carried on in spite of revolution, rebellion, and guerrilla war. In 1925 the Mexican government confiscated the property of church schools and hospitals, the seminary in Guadalajara, and the Knights of Columbus, among others, and drove the Church underground. Violence spread, leading to the bitter Cristero Rebellion, which filled the streets of Guadalajara with blood. Priests who refused to abandon their parishioners were arrested and executed by firing squad. Others were stabbed to death with bayonets or hanged. Churches were reopened in 1929, but violent conflicts continued sporadically for years. Throughout these difficulties, Madre Nati kept the Sacred Heart Hospital going. She died at peace, and since her death she has been credited with many miracles. She was canonized in 2000, along with twenty-five Mexican priests who were martyred during the Cristero Rebellion. She is commemorated in Mexico on July 30.

The Genius of Madre Nati:

By binding herself to God's will, Madre Nati lived in serenity and achievement in spite of the terrible times.

Reflection:

"Happy those concerned for the lowly and poor; / when misfortune strikes, the LORD *delivers them."*

Psalm 41:2 (Madre Nati's favorite psalm)

SAINT JEANNE ELISABETH BICHIER DES AGES

b. July 5, 1773, Le Blanc, Indre, France
d. August 26, 1838, La Puye, Vienne, France

Elisabeth was born in a grand chateau, but she came of age at the height of the French Revolution. Just a few weeks after her father died, the National Assembly moved to confiscate his estate. Nineteen-year-old Elisabeth had to fight the government for the right to her inheritance.

Elisabeth asked an uncle to instruct her in law and accounting so that she could defend her interests. The case dragged on for years, but she finally won and in 1796 Elisabeth and her mother moved to a small rural village. With no priest available, Elisabeth gathered local families for prayers and Scripture readings. She soon began collaborating with Andrew Fournet,[127] a priest who had reopened his church in a barn twenty-five miles away. The Revolution had taken a toll on established religious orders, and Father Fournet believed that Elisabeth was the perfect person to start a new women's congregation. He arranged for her to make retreats at two convents to learn more about religious life. When she returned, they cofounded the Daughters of the Cross, Sisters of St Andrew, who are dedicated to instructing poor girls, providing refuge for young women at risk, nursing the terminally ill, and caring for churches. By 1811 they had twenty-five members and continued to grow rapidly. Elisabeth used her legal training as she built more than sixty convents and schools. Her greatest acquisition was the ancient priory at La Puye, which became the motherhouse. Today her Daughters are at work in France, Ivory Coast, South America, and Canada. They celebrate her feast on August 26.

The Genius of Jeanne Elisabeth Bichier:
Elisabeth understood the need to educate herself for whatever lay ahead, whether it was a battle with the French government or expanding the work of her order.

Reflection:
"Everything that becomes visible is light. Therefore, it says: / 'Awake, O sleeper, / and arise from the dead, / and Christ will give you light.' / Watch carefully then how you live, not as foolish persons but as wise."

Ephesians 5:14–15

BLESSED MARÍA ENCARNACIÓN ROSAL

(Vincenta Rosal Vásquez)

b. October 27, 1815, Quezaltenango, Guatemala
d. August 24, 1886, Tulcán, Carchi, Ecuador

At seventeen, Vincenta Rosal was admitted to the House of Bethlehem in Guatemala City. Within a year she made her first religious vows there and took a new name: María Encarnación of the Sacred Heart. She also became concerned that the Bethlemites had drifted from their founder's original vision.[128] Encarnación moved to another convent that was better managed. This offered her plenty of time for quiet contemplation, but she missed the Bethlemites. They agreed to take her back and Encarnación made her final vows there in 1840.

Encarnación believed that she was called to reform the Bethlemites, but she kept this to herself for fifteen years while she served the poor of Guatemala City. When she was elected prioress, she was finally in a position to restore the Bethlemites' original Franciscan spirit of "holy poverty." The older sisters refused to accept her changes, however, and Encarnación bowed to reality. She left Guatemala City with several of the younger sisters and founded a new House of Bethlehem in Quezaltenango. The reformed foundation thrived, but in 1875 a revolutionary government suppressed all religious congregations and expelled the Bethlemites from Guatemala. Encarnación found a new home for them in Costa Rica, where they started a school. Today the Bethlemite Sisters manage schools and orphanages in thirteen countries. Encarnación's death was brought on by a fall from a horse at the age of sixty-six. She is venerated by the Franciscans on October 27 and in Guatemala on August 24.

The Genius of María Encarnación Rosal:
Among her reforms, Encarnación required the Bethlemite Sisters to dedicate the twenty-fifth day of each month to prayers of reparation for the sins of humankind.

Reflection:
"If you bestow your bread on the hungry / and satisfy the afflicted; / then light shall rise for you in the darkness, / and the gloom shall become for you like midday."

Isaiah 58:10

SAINT LYDIA PURPURARIA

First century, Philippi, Macedonia

The first Christian convert in Europe was a Macedonian businesswoman who dealt in luxury goods. Lydia Purpuraria's surname means "purple seller" and she plied her trade in a city that was famous for its dye works.

Lydia met Paul the Apostle[129] at Philippi. He had already traveled widely through Asia Minor, but the Holy Spirit prevented him from preaching in those regions. One night Paul had a vision in which a Macedonian begged, "Come over to Macedonia and help us." Convinced that God had called him there, Paul immediately sought passage to the Roman province of Macedonia. On arrival, Paul and his companions made their way to Philippi, the most important city in the province. On the Sabbath they went outside the city gate looking for a place to pray. They found a gathering of women and among them was Lydia, who dealt in purple cloth. Paul began to preach to the women.

Lydia listened and the Lord opened her heart to what Paul was saying. Soon, Lydia and her entire household were baptized into the Christian faith. She offered Paul and his companions an open invitation: *"If you consider me a believer in the Lord, come and stay at my home."* They accepted Lydia's offer and remained with her for as long as they were in Philippi.

The Genius of Lydia Purpuraria:

Lydia opened her heart to Paul's message, and her faith and hospitality enabled him to establish the first Christian community in Europe. She is believed to be part of the group that Paul had in mind when he later wrote: *"[T]hey have struggled at my side in promoting the gospel."*

Reflection:

"He made from one the whole human race to dwell on the entire surface of the earth, and he fixed the ordered seasons and the boundaries of their regions, so that people might seek God, even perhaps grope for him and find him, though indeed he is not far from any one of us."

Acts 17:26–27

BLESSED SANCJA JANINA SZYMKOWIAK
(Maria Santia)

b. July 10, 1910, Modanów, Wielkopolskie, Poland
d. August 29, 1942, Pozna, Wielkopolskie, Poland

A brilliant student with a gift for languages, Santia was in college when she made up her mind to become a saint. She found her path to heaven in a military barracks and prison hospital.

She grew up with every advantage, but what her school friends most remembered was her joyful personality. Her brother, a priest, introduced her to the Sisters of Our Lady of Sorrows (Seraphic Sisters), who served the sick poor. The more Santia learned about their work, the more she wanted to be one of them. In 1936 she entered their motherhouse in Poznan, taking the name Maria Santia. For the next two years, Santia taught in a nursery school and pursued a graduate degree in pharmacology. Her studies were cut short by Germany's invasion of Poland in 1939. The Nazi army occupied the city of Poznan, and the Seraphic Sisters were put under house arrest. Their convent became a barracks for German soldiers and a military prison. The captives were mainly French and English soldiers, and Santia became their nurse and interpreter. They called her Saint Santia, their Angel of Goodness. As the war dragged on, conditions deteriorated along with Santia's health. She developed tuberculosis of the pharynx but declined permission to return to her parents' home. Santia believed it was God's will that she attend the soldiers and prisoners. As she lay dying, the Sisters gathered around her bed and the superior asked Santia to remember them to God. Santia responded that she still wished to honor her vow of obedience, so the superior must order her to do so. She added: *"Because I die of love, and Love can refuse nothing with Love."* Since then, Santia has become well known for her intercessions. She is commemorated in Poland and by the Seraphic Sisters on August 18.

The Genius of Santia Szymkowiak:

Santia could say confidently: *"God's will is my will. Whatever he wants, I want."*

Reflection:

"Many say, 'May we see better times! / LORD, show us the light of your face!' But you have given my heart more joy / than they have when grain and wine abound."

Psalm 4:7–8

Saint Jane Frances de Chantal
(Jeanne Françoise Frémyot, Baroness de Chantal)

b. January 28, 1572, Dijon, France
d. December 13, 1641, Moulins, France

When Jane married the Baron de Chantal, she became the chatelaine of his rich but chaotic estates. She soon set his household in order and their marriage was a happy one. Jane had just given birth to their fourth child when her husband was mortally wounded in a hunting accident. He lingered for nine days in horrible pain. It took Jane years to forgive the cousin who shot him.

She fell into a three-year depression. She could not understand why God had taken a man as good as her husband and in such a terrible way. When Jane sought help from a well-meaning priest, he gave her a harsh regimen that was unrealistic for the mother of four young children. Fortunately, Jane met Francis de Sales[130] who guided her to look within for answers. When Jane felt called to found a new religious order, neither as austere as the Carmelites nor as lax as some of the older congregations had become, Francis encouraged her. In 1614 Jane formed the Congregation of the Visitation of Holy Mary (Visitation Sisters). Their name commemorates the Blessed Mother's visit to her cousin Elizabeth,[131] and they lived simply, dedicated to contemplation and prayer. They were enclosed, but not rigorously so, and they welcomed visits from those seeking advice and counsel. Francis had expected Jane to establish an activist community, serving the sick and the poor, but Jane held fast to her own idea. By the time Jane died, there were sixty-five Visitation convents in France, and she had visited them all. Her feast day is August 18.

The Genius of Jane Frances de Chantal:
Jane advises us: *"Hold your eyes on God and leave the doing to him. That is all the doing you have to worry about."* She also recommended: *"Be content to remain an empty vessel, simply receiving whatever the holy charity of the Savior may wish to pour in."*

Reflection:
"Blessed are you who believed that what was spoken to you by the Lord would be fulfilled."

Luke 1:45

August 6

❦

Blessed Francesca Rubatto
(Anna Maria Rubatto)

b. February 14, 1844, Carmagnola, Turin, Italy
d. August 6, 1904, Montevideo, Uruguay

At thirty-nine, following the death of her longtime employer, Anna Maria visited the seaside resort of Loano to contemplate her next step. One morning, while passing a construction site there, she heard an injured laborer moaning in pain. Anna Maria went to his aid, treated his injuries, and sent him home with two days' wages to ensure that he took time to rest.

All this was observed by the Capuchin Sisters of Loano who had commissioned the building. They invited her to share their life of Franciscan poverty. She accepted, taking the religious name Maria Francesca of Jesus and soon demonstrating her organizational abilities. Under Francesca's leadership, the Capuchin Sisters expanded to other cities in Italy, then to Uruguay and Argentina. The Capuchin friars asked Francesca to start a mission in the Brazilian rain forest. More experienced communities had turned the friars down, but Francesca agreed to honor the request. She brought six Capuchin Sisters to the mission and stayed with them in the rain forest for six months. A year after Francesca left, on March 13, 1901, the entire community, consisting of four friars, seven sisters, and almost three hundred native Christians, was slaughtered. Undiscouraged by this tragedy, she continued her work in South America and Italy, ultimately crossing the Atlantic seven times. Francesca died suddenly in Uruguay and at her request was buried at her convent in Montevideo, her first foundation in the New World. She is commemorated on August 9.

The Genius of Francesca Rubatto:
Francesca advised her novices: "*Serve the Lord joyfully, lovingly fulfil the duties entrusted to you, work tirelessly because you know how precious your work is in the sight of the Lord. And having worked hard for the glory of God whom you love so deeply, call yourself a useless servant of the Lord and be convinced of being one, because you know that you are not capable of anything without his divine help.*"

Reflection:
"*And the king will say to them in reply, 'Amen, I say to you, whatever you did for one of these least brothers of mine, you did for me.'*"
Matthew 25:40 (inspiration for her order's missionary work)

BLESSED MARY ELLEN MACKILLOP
(Mary of the Cross)

b. January 15, 1842, Fitzroy, Melbourne, Australia
d. August 8, 1909, North Sydney, Australia

One bishop dismissed Mary MacKillop as "an obstinate and ambitious woman" and another excommunicated her, but no one could ever discourage her.

While employed as a governess in a small town in Australia, Mary met Julian Tenison Woods.[132] Father Woods was responsible for the spiritual needs of residents in a vast 22,000-square-mile territory. The population of Australia had tripled between 1850 and 1860, yet there were still no public schools and few charitable institutions.

Mary and Father Woods founded the Sisters of St Joseph of the Sacred Heart (Josephites), Australia's first religious order, and she took the name Mary of the Cross. They started their school in a former stable and soon spread to other parts of Australia and New Zealand. Mary expanded the Josephites' mission to care for anyone in need: orphans, the aged, girls at risk, and the friendless.

When Father Woods ran up huge debts, the diocese started an investigation. Woods left Mary to deal with the bishop and never returned. Bishop Shiel accused her of taking control of the Josephites and ordered Mary to leave town. She sent word that she would not leave until she had presented her case. In response, the bishop arrived at her convent in full ceremonial garb, accompanied by four priests, and excommunicated Mary. Some of the sisters were distraught, but Mary remained calm. She responded: *"My only prayer is that His will may be done in the matter."* Five months later, on his deathbed, Bishop Shiel revoked Mary's excommunication. When she died, seventy-three priests attended her funeral Mass. Today Australia considers Mary MacKillop a national heroine. She is commemorated there on August 8.

The Genius of Mary Ellen MacKillop:
Mary's public achievements were great, but those who knew her personally all mentioned her unfailing kindness. In everything she said or did she showed respect and unconditional love.

Reflection:
"[Love] bears all things, believes all things, hopes all things, endures all things."

1 Corinthians 13:7

BLESSED JANE OF AZA
(Joan, Juana de Aza Ruíz de Guzmán)

b. c. 1140, Old Castile, Spain
d. 1203, Caleruega, Old Castile, Spain

While pregnant with her third child, Jane of Aza dreamed that she gave birth to a small black-and-white dog that immediately ran off with a torch in its teeth. A priest assured her that the dog symbolized fidelity and the torch stood for the warmth of charity. He predicted that Jane's child would set the world on fire. A few months later, she gave birth to Dominic,[133] who did indeed change the course of history by founding the Order of Preachers, better known as the Dominicans.

Jane was a Castilian noblewoman whose husband commanded a fort on the border of Christian Spain. Their first son, Anthony, became a priest and when their second son, Manez,[134] also began studying for Holy Orders, Jane prayed for a third son who would carry on the family name. She visited the shrine of Dominic of Silos,[135] who was known as a protector of women in labor. As she prayed there, the saint appeared in a vision and assured Jane that God would give her another son. She named him after Dominic of Silos, and in time, his fame would eclipse that of his patron saint. Jane sent Dominic off to university when he was fifteen, and he was studying theology there when a famine broke out. He sold his clothes to feed the hungry, inspiring other students and the schoolmasters to open their own pockets. This was the first demonstration of Dominic's gift for teaching by example. Jane herself is associated with only one miracle: it is said that from a single barrel she provided unlimited wine for the poor.

The Genius of Jane of Aza:
Jane taught Dominic his first prayers, but otherwise her story remains in the shadows. It is her son's achievements that speak for her.

Reflection:
"Train a boy in the way he should go; / even when he is old, he will not swerve from it."

Proverbs 22:6

SAINT EDITH STEIN

(Teresa Benedicta of the Cross)

b. October 12, 1891, Breslau, Germany (now Wroclaw, Poland)
d. August 9, 1942, Auschwitz, Germany

Born on Yom Kippur, the Jewish Day of Atonement, Edith Stein grew up in a large, loving orthodox Jewish family and went on to a brilliant academic career. She concentrated on phenomenology, a branch of philosophy that asks us to strip ourselves of preconceptions and belief systems in order to examine objectively all areas of human life. The quest to see things as they really are, to uncover the truth behind ordinary perceptions, motivated Edith throughout her life and ultimately led to her conversion.

Edith abandoned Judaism in college and had been an atheist for years when, in November 1917, she attended the funeral of a colleague. His widow showed surprising strength, which she credited to her Christian faith. This stirred Edith's intellectual curiosity, and she spent the next three years studying Christianity. She also prayed, asking God to show her the truth. In 1921 she read the autobiography of Teresa of Avila (October 15) and was deeply moved. Edith later wrote: *"This was my first encounter with the Cross and with the supernatural strength it gives. For the first time I saw the redemptive sufferings of Christ overcoming death. This was the moment when my unbelief broke down and Christ appeared to me in the mystery of the Cross."* The next day, Edith bought a Catholic catechism and began studying in earnest. A year later she was baptized.

Meanwhile, the Nazi government had begun implementing its anti-Semitic agenda. In spite of Edith's brilliant academic record, she was barred from Germany's state universities because she was regarded as Jewish by race. She supported herself by teaching at a Dominican college for women. Even with a heavy schedule, Edith always found time to pray. *"Heaven has a special kind of economy,"* she explained. *"I do not lengthen my working hours by any tricks. All I need is a quiet corner where I can talk to God each day as if there were nothing else to do. I try to make myself a tool for God. Not for myself, but only for him."*

Edith's spiritual journey continued, and at forty-two she entered the Carmelite convent in Cologne. She took the name Teresa Benedicta of the Cross and chose as her motto *"Ave Crux, Spes Unica"* ("Behold the Cross, Our Only Hope"). Soon Edith's sister Rosa was also baptized and joined her at the convent, although Rosa did not take religious vows. In November 1938, after Cologne was rocked by two nights of anti-Semitic riots, Edith feared that her presence was endangering the other nuns. A friend drove her to the Dutch border and she entered a Carmelite convent in Holland. Rosa joined her and lived outside the enclosure as she had in Cologne.

The German army soon marched into Holland, however, and in 1941 Catholic bishops issued a pastoral letter condemning Nazi persecution of Jews. In retaliation, the Nazis rounded up all priests and religious of Jewish ancestry. On August 2, 1942, they came for Edith and Rosa Stein. The sisters were given ten minutes to pack, then taken to a holding camp along with members of fifteen other religious orders. On August 7 they were put on trains for Auschwitz. A week later, Edith Stein was martyred in the gas chamber there.

In October 1999, Pope John Paul II proclaimed Edith Stein, Bridget of Sweden, and Catherine of Siena co-patrons of Europe.

The Genius of Edith Stein:

Shortly before her death, Edith wrote: *"I have an ever deeper and firmer belief that nothing is merely an accident when seen in the light of God, that my whole life down to the smallest details has been marked out for me in the plan of Divine Providence, and has a completely coherent meaning in God's all-seeing eyes. And so I am beginning to rejoice in the light of glory wherein this meaning will be unveiled to me."*

Reflection:

"May I never boast except in the cross of our Lord Jesus Christ, through which the world has been crucified to me, and I to the world."

Galatians 6:14, keynote for the homily at her canonization Mass

SAINT PHILOMENA OF MUGNANO

b. c. Third century, Greece
d. c. Third century, Rome, Italy

Many question whether Philomena even existed, but her supporters have included Pauline Jaricot,[136] at least five popes, and millions of the faithful who are convinced that she has interceded for them.

Excavators in Rome's catacombs unearthed a tombstone in 1802 bearing the inscription "Philomena, Peace be with you." When the stone was moved, they found a small skeleton and a broken vial covered with dried blood. This confirmed that it was a martyr's grave, because early Christians were known to collect the martyrs' blood and bury it with them. Philomena's relics were moved to a church near Naples, where they immediately became associated with favors, graces, and miracles. Soon, a priest, a nun, and an artist, all strangers to one another, reported that Philomena had appeared to them.

The best-known vision is that of Luisa de Jesus,[137] who reported that Philomena was the daughter of pagan nobility, who named her Philomena or "Daughter of Light." She was thirteen when they took her to Rome, where the emperor Diocletian asked for her hand but Philomena refused because she had consecrated herself to God, so Diocletian resolved to make an example of her. His guards tied Philomena to a column and scourged her until she was bathed in blood, then dragged her back to her dungeon. They left her to die in a dungeon, but two angels nursed her wounds and restored her strength. Diocletian then ordered Philomena tossed into the Tiber River with an anchor around her neck. An angel unfastened the anchor, which sank while Philomena was lifted to the riverbank, amid cries of joy from the crowd on shore. Next, Diocletian had Philomena dragged through the streets of Rome and shot with a shower of heated arrows. Each assault only brought more converts to Christ. Finally Philomena was beheaded, buried, and forgotten for more than a thousand years until her relics were discovered. She is commemorated on August 11.

The Genius of Philomena:

Though Philomena was removed from the liturgical calendar in 1961 for lack of historical evidence, private devotions are still permitted, and today Philomena is more popular than ever.

Reflection:

"If we are children, we are heirs as well: heirs of God, heirs with Christ, if only we suffer with him so as to be glorified with him."

Romans 8:17

August 11

SAINT CLARE OF ASSISI

(Chiara di Favarone)

b. c. 1193, Assisi, Italy
d. August 11, 1253, Assisi, Italy

A pregnant young countess was praying for a safe delivery when a voice assured her: "Do not be afraid, for you will joyfully bring forth a clear light, which will illuminate the world." She gave birth to a healthy girl and named her Chiara, or Clare, which means "clear light."

Clare was eighteen when she gave up her world of privilege to follow Francis of Assisi.[138] On the night of Palm Sunday, Clare went to the small church that Francis made his headquarters and traded her fine clothes for the coarse woolen robe that marked her as a follower of Il Poverello (the poor one). Clare's family considered Franciscan poverty degrading to her and a disgrace to their good name. They tracked her down in a chapel and begged her to come home, but Clare held fast to the altar until they gave up.

Clare was soon joined by her sister Agnes (November 19). Francis found them a small house near the church of San Damiano. This became their convent and Clare became the superior. In time, they were joined by their mother and sixteen other companions who were called the Poor Ladies of San Damiano. (Only after Clare's death did they become known as the Poor Clares.) They owned nothing, went barefoot even in winter, and slept on a bare floor. When Clare inherited a fortune from her father, she distributed everything to hospitals and the poor and kept nothing for the Poor Ladies.

Clare obtained approval from Pope Innocent III for her convent to live in "holy poverty." His successor, Gregory IX, tried to relax the harsh Rule that Clare had created for the Poor Ladies, but she resisted. The Poor Ladies survived entirely on whatever the Franciscan friars brought them from their own daily begging. Possibly this led to gossip, because Gregory ordered the friars not to enter the convent, not even to bring the Poor Ladies the Eucharist. "*Very well,*" said Clare, "*if the holy friars may not feed us with the bread of life, they shall not minister to us the bread that perishes.*" The Poor Ladies began what amounted to a hunger strike. Gregory, who had defeated the powerful emperor Frederic Barbarossa, was forced to yield to Clare of Assisi.

Clare ruled her convent for forty-two years, and although she never left Assisi, her influence spread all over Europe. One of her correspondents, Agnes of Prague (March 6), turned down marriage to an emperor to become a Poor Lady.

Clare's strength failed in old age, and she was confined to bed. One Christmas, she was too weak to attend Mass at the basilica, more than a mile away, but she saw and heard it all in a miraculous vision. This event led to Clare being named the patron of television.

In one of Clare's most famous miracles, she saved her nuns from a band of Saracens (Muslims) that descended on their convent. Clare rose from her sickbed, took the monstrance containing the Eucharist from the altar, and brandished it at the marauders while singing Psalm 9, which begins, *"I will praise you, Lord, with all my heart."* The terrified Saracens threw down their arms and fled.

Pope Innocent IV broke with tradition to attend Clare's funeral, and only the pressure of the cardinals restrained him from canonizing her on the spot. Two years later, his successor, Alexander IV, had that honor.

The Genius of Clare of Assisi:

In spite of her own austerities, Clare advised moderation, *"so that living and hoping in the Lord you may offer him a reasonable service and a sacrifice seasoned with the salt of prudence."*

Reflection:

"My enemies turn back; / they stumble and perish before you.
You upheld my right and my cause, / seated on your throne, judging justly."

Psalm 9:4–5

BLESSED ELVIRA MORAGAS CANTARERO
(María Sagrario of Saint Aloysius Gonzaga)

b. January 8, 1881, Lillo, Toledo, Spain
d. August 15, 1936, Madrid, Spain

Elvira's father, a prominent pharmacist, encouraged her to enter his profession, and she became one of the first women in Spain to obtain a degree in pharmacology. She planned to enter a Carmelite convent, but by 1911 both parents had died and she put off her plans until her younger brother had completed his studies.

Elvira was thirty-four years old when she was finally free to enter the Carmel in Madrid. Taking the name María Sagrario of Saint Aloysius Gonzaga,[139] she spent the next two decades progressing in spiritual perfection. By July 1, 1936, she had been elected prioress for the second time. That very day, rioters shattered all the convent windows, marking the start of Spain's bloody civil war. On July 20, looters invaded the building. Concerned about the mounting violence, Elvira arranged for her nuns to return to their families. They were dispersed throughout Spain, but she managed to stay in touch with them all, sending spiritual and material help. She urged them to accept the will of God, who, she reminded them, *"suffered so much for our love."* On August 14, Elvira was arrested and interrogated by the secret police. She refused to betray the members of her community or their supporters. The following day, on the feast of the Assumption, Elvira was taken to Madrid's most famous park, the Pradera of San Isidro, where she was executed by a firing squad. She is commemorated in Spain and by the Carmelite Order on August 16.

The Genius of Elvira Moragas:

As a pharmacist, Elvira did not merely dispense prescriptions. She was concerned about every individual she encountered. To the end, facing martyrdom, her concern was only for the safety of others.

Reflection:

"We who live are constantly being given up to death for the sake of Jesus, so that the life of Jesus may be manifested in our mortal flesh."
2 Corinthians 4:11 (from the Carmelite Mass for Blessed Elvira Moragas)

Saint Radegund, Queen of France

b. c. 520, Erfurt, Thuringia
d. August 13, 587, Poitiers, France

A daughter of the king of Thuringia, Radegund was eight years old when most of her family was murdered and she was carried off to France as part of the spoils of war. Clothaire, a wayward son of Clotilda (June 3), had Radegund groomed to become the fifth of his seven wives.

Radegund tried to do her duty, but she never loved her husband. He would insult her, then apologize and try to make up for it with lavish gifts. Radegund had been married to Clothaire for six years when he had her brother murdered. Her indifference became pure loathing. She began a pilgrimage, donating her jewels and most of her possessions to shrines along the way. At Noyon she asked the bishop to consecrate her as a nun. He was afraid to defy the king, until a disgusted Radegund went into the sacristy, put on a discarded robe, and presented herself before him, demanding to know whom she feared more, man or God. The bishop saw the light and consecrated Radegund as a deaconess, thus officially removing her from her husband's control. Considering her next step, she wrote: *"I asked myself, with all the ardor of which I am capable, how I could best forward the cause of other women, and how, if our Lord willed, my own personal desires might be of advantage to my sisters."* Radegund decided to found a monastery at Poitiers, which ultimately housed more than two hundred women. They shared all household tasks and spent their days in prayer and Scripture study.

The Genius of Radegund:

One day while still queen, Radegund was walking in the gardens of her palace when the cries of prisoners on the other side of the wall reminded her of her own captivity. There was nothing she could do for the prisoners but pray, and when she prayed, their shackles broke open and they were free. For this reason, Radegund is a patron of the wrongfully imprisoned.

Reflection:

"Put no trust in princes, / in mere mortals powerless to save.
When they breathe their last, they return to the earth; / that day all their planning comes to nothing."

Psalm 146:3–4

August 14

BLESSED ELISABETTA RENZI

b. November 19, 1786, Saludecio, Forli, Italy
d. August 14, 1859, Coriano, Rimini, Italy

Elisabetta's wealthy family encouraged her decision to become an Augustinian nun, but her novitiate was cut short when Napoleon closed down Italy's religious schools and convents. Elisabetta went home and devoted herself to good works for the next two years, until she was invited to teach in a school near Rimini.

Elisabetta welcomed this opportunity, but she soon had serious doubts about her qualifications. She was a great admirer of Magdalene of Canossa (May 8), who was educating poor girls in Verona, and wrote to Magdalene asking her to take over the school's management. Magdalene turned her down. She was nearing the end of her life and suggested that Elisabetta herself should take on the responsibility. Left with no choice, Elisabetta began to gather companions for this mission. She studied the religious constitutions of the Canossians and Rosa Venerini (May 7), and in 1839 she founded the Pious Teachers of Our Lady of Sorrows. She dedicated them to *"witnessing the preferential love of Christ for the poor, the weak, and the needy."*

Today the order is established from Brazil to Bangladesh. Known in the United States as the Sisters of Our Lady of Sorrows, and based in New Orleans, they live out Elisabetta's charism by working to form the whole individual, "so that our students will be able to make conscious and responsible decisions during their Christian adult years." In addition to teaching young children, the Sisters also participate actively in parish life as Eucharistic ministers, youth and music ministers, and assisting wherever else they are needed.

The Genius of Elisabetta Renzi:
Elisabetta said that she was drawn to serve God and his children *"with the affection of a thousand hearts, with the action of a thousand hands."* Her motto was always: *"Ardere et Lucere"* (to burn and to shine).

Reflection:
"Blessed be the God and Father of our Lord Jesus Christ, the Father of compassion and God of all encouragement, who encourages us in our every affliction, so that we may be able to encourage those who are in any affliction with the encouragement with which we ourselves are encouraged by God."
2 Corinthians 1:3–4

THE FEAST OF THE ASSUMPTION OF MARY

The Catholic catechism teaches that when the Blessed Mother's earthly life was completed, she was raised body and soul into heaven. There, spared the corruption of the grave, she is crowned with glory and enthroned above all the angels and saints. The feast of the Assumption commemorates this great event.

Yet Mary herself remains elusive. She is never quoted in Scripture after the wedding at Cana, and although she was present at Calvary we do not know what she might have said. Most of what we know about her life after the Resurrection comes from pious tradition and the revelations of the mystics. (These are private revelations and are not considered official Catholic dogma.) It was Elisabeth of Schönau (June 18), for example, who saw Mary soaring to heaven surrounded by angels, a vision that has become our most familiar image of the Assumption.

Tradition tells us that the Blessed Mother lived on for many years after the Resurrection, but historians argue about whether she remained at Jerusalem or took refuge in the city of Ephesus, in what is now Turkey. In a recent book, *Mary's House*, Donald Carroll makes the case that she spent her last years in Ephesus, with John and other apostles entrusted with her care. This is based on a French priest's discovery of a building believed to have been her home. Guided by the visions of Anna Katharina Emmerich (February 15), Father Julien Gouyet went to Ephesus in 1881 and found the ruins near the summit of Bulbul Dagi (Nightingale Mountain). Although the Church has reacted with typical caution, it has declared the restored building a shrine and at least two popes have visited the chapel there.

The Genius of the Assumption of Mary:
"She was the first and most faithful disciple of Jesus Christ," writes one Jesuit theologian, who calls the Assumption "a sign of hope for us that we too will rise to new life with Jesus Christ." To gain that new life, however, we must follow Mary's instruction at Cana: *"Do whatever He tells you."*

Reflection:
"A great sign appeared in the sky, a woman clothed with the sun, with the moon under her feet, and on her head a crown of twelve stars."

Revelation 12:1

Saint Jeanne Delanoue

(Jeanne de la Croix)

b. June 18, 1666, Saumur, France
d. August 17, 1735, Saumur, France

Jeanne had no use for religion. She was too busy getting rich. Her dry goods store was near Notre Dame des Ardilliers, a popular shrine, and she was always open for business, even on Sundays and feast days, which scandalized her pious neighbors. A casual conversation with an elderly pilgrim changed her life. *"She said so many beautiful things to me, about helping the poor,"* Jeanne recalled.

Jeanne began by giving away a dress. Soon she was feeding a parade of strangers, making no distinction between pilgrims and mere vagrants. Once she had taken in some homeless orphans, there was no turning back. With her attention diverted, her shop failed, but Jeanne gladly begged for alms when she had to. People who had known her all her life could only shake their heads. Jeanne was sheltering twelve people in her home when the roof fell in and she realized that she could no longer carry on alone. Other women were happy to join her work, and in 1704 they formed a community "to contemplate the face of Christ in the face of the poor." She became Jeanne de la Croix. Two years later, Louis de Montfort[140] visited her community and told Jeanne: *"Yes, it is the Spirit of God, which inspires you in this penitential life. Don't be afraid, therefore, in the future, but follow your inspirations."* Today the Sisters of Jeanne Delanoue maintain fifty-two institutions in France, Mali, Indonesia, and Madagascar.

The Genius of Jeanne Delanoue:

Not everyone was comfortable with Jeanne's dramatic transformation. Neighbors and priests criticized her excessive piety and "disordered charities," but she can be a great inspiration to recovering workaholics.

Reflection:

"If you hold back your foot on the sabbath / from following your own pursuits on my holy day; / If you call the sabbath a delight, / and the LORD's holy day honorable; / If you honor it by not following your ways, / seeking your own interests, or speaking with malice— / Then you shall delight in the LORD / and I will make you ride on the heights of the earth."

Isaiah 58:13–14

SAINT CLARE OF MONTEFALCO

b. 1268, Montefalco, Perugia, Italy
d. August 17, 1308, Montefalco, Perugia, Italy

Clare was six years old when she insisted on following her older sister Jane into a monastery. She thrived there, but Jane's death brought on her first spiritual crisis. At twenty-seven, Clare was elected to succeed her sister as abbess. *"I want to be a nun, not an abbess,"* Clare pleaded, but she governed wisely and even negotiated a treaty between the cities of Trevi and Montefalco. During a famine, her prayers brought angels with baskets of bread that sustained the monastery.

Clare was blessed with visions and revelations until the onset of her second crisis. For eleven years she was tormented by scruples, fatigue, and demonic temptations and feared that God had abandoned her. The prayers of her community were answered when Clare's visions and revelations returned. Her third and final crisis came when the Lord informed her, *"I have sought a place in the world where I might plant my cross, and have found no better site than your heart."* From then on, Clare suffered great pain, and during her final illness, she repeatedly told her nuns that they would find the cross of Christ engraved on her heart. Five days after Clare's death, nuns preparing to embalm her discovered a crucifix imprinted on her heart. Her canonization inquiry began in 1318 but dragged on for more than five hundred years. Scholar Katharine Park writes that the process was "the first in the Church's history to attempt to authenticate systematically the visions and revelations of a holy person, and her advocates [promoted her cause] in the face of an unprecedented level of skepticism and suspicion."

The Genius of Clare of Montefalco:

A certain Brother Bentivenga boasted that his faith was stronger than Clare's and only fear kept him from converting the world. Clare responded: *"As for me, I have no fear; and I would not dread to preach mine to the entire world, so great is the faith God has given me; and consequently my faith is better than yours."*

Reflection:

"Do not throw away your confidence; it will have great recompense. You need endurance to do the will of God and receive what he has promised."
Hebrews 10:35–36

SAINT HELEN, EMPRESS OF ROME

b. c. 250, Drepanum
d. c. 330, Helenopolis, formerly Drepanum, today Trapani, Sicily

A barmaid at an inn on the Black Sea, Helen became the mistress of an ambitious army officer. After they had been together more than thirteen years, Helen's lover made a political marriage and banished her, keeping custody of their son, Constantine. The boy grew up to be emperor of Rome, and one of his first acts as supreme ruler was to declare his mother empress. Constantine had converted to Christianity, and with his encouragement, Helen embraced the faith. A few years later, at the age of eighty, she led an expedition to the Holy Land, where she found the True Cross.

One of Helen's greatest admirers was the English author and Catholic convert Evelyn Waugh. He reminds us that Helen's discovery was about more than archaeology. She produced the True Cross at a time when the Church was threatened by new heresies and resurgent paganism. "Everything about Christianity was open to discussion, debate, interpretation," Waugh writes, "everything except the unreasonable assertion that God became man and died on the Cross; not a myth nor an allegory; true God, truly incarnate, tortured to death at a particular moment in time, at a particular geographical place, as a matter of plain historical fact." By recovering the True Cross, Helen managed "to turn the eyes of the world back to the planks of wood on which their salvation hung."

Soon after her discovery, Helen went home to Drepanum, which her son had restored and renamed in her honor. He was with her when she died there. The Cross itself was broken up and distributed as relics throughout the Christian world.

The Genius of Helen:
"What we can learn from Helen is something about the workings of God," writes Evelyn Waugh, "that He wants a different thing from each of us, laborious or easy, conspicuous or quite private, but something which only we can do and for which we were created."

Reflection:
"For many, as I have often told you and now tell you even in tears, conduct themselves as enemies of the cross of Christ. Their end is destruction. Their God is their stomach; their glory is in their 'shame.' Their minds are occupied with earthly things."

Philippians 3:18

August 19

BLESSED EMILY BICCHIERI

b. May 3, 1238, Vercelli, Italy
d. May 3, 1314, Vercelli, Italy

While pregnant, the countess Adalasia dreamed about a beautiful young woman in white robes who was crowned with a wreath of white roses. Other young women gathered around her, all dressed the same way, and they marched into a church that the countess had never seen before. Her priest assured her that the dream meant her child would become a saint. Soon after this, she gave birth to a daughter she named Emily.

In about 1256, Emily and her two sisters inherited their father's fortune. Emily used her share to found a Dominican monastery where she was joined by thirty companions. On the day of the dedication of their new church, Emily and the other young nuns entered the building in white gowns, veils, and wreaths of white roses. Emily's mother immediately recognized the scene from her long-ago dream. Emily's monastery was not cloistered, so the nuns could move about town freely, assisting wherever they were needed. Emily also eliminated the traditional two-tier system that divided the women into educated choir nuns who sang the Latin hymns and prayers and illiterate lay nuns who did the heavy labor. At Emily's convent, everyone shared the work. She is considered the spiritual mother of all active Dominican sisters working in schools, hospitals, and other institutions.

Emily had a special devotion to Christ's Crown of Thorns. She asked the Lord to let her share Christ's pain, and he granted her the stigmata in the form of a crown of thorns. This event lasted only three days, but Emily retained her great devotion for the rest of her life. The Dominican Order keeps Emily's feast on May 4.

The Genius of Emily Bicchieri:
Her motto was: *"To make all for God alone."*

Reflection:
"They stripped off his clothes and threw a scarlet military cloak about him. Weaving a crown out of thorns, they placed it on his head, and a reed in his right hand. And kneeling before him, they mocked him, saying, 'Hail, King of the Jews!'"

Matthew 27:28–29

August 20

BLESSED VICTORIA DIEZ
(Victoria Diez y Bustos de Molina)

b. November 11, 1903, Seville, Spain
d. August 12, 1936, Hornachuelos, Córdoba, Spain

What does a saint look like? Or a martyr? The official photograph of Victoria Diez shows a smiling young woman, stylishly dressed, with huge chandelier earrings. It is hard to imagine that this vivacious art teacher would end up dying for Christ at the bottom of a mineshaft.

Victoria had been teaching only a year when she was sent to Hornachuelos, a coal-mining town. She was responsible for seventy students and also taught catechism, organized evening classes for adults, and created a free library. She often went without necessities to provide her impoverished students with supplies. Two years after her arrival, Victoria was elected president of the local education council. She managed to obtain a new and bigger school building, which she furnished. But when civil war broke out in Spain in the summer of 1936, the village was taken over by anarchists. Victoria was arrested on August 11 and held overnight in a temporary jail. Witnesses remember that she remained calm and prayerful. At dawn, Victoria and seventeen men, including the parish priest, were led in chains on a seven-mile march. As they scaled a mountain to certain death, she comforted her companions, saying: "Come on, our reward is waiting for us." Their climb ended at an abandoned mineshaft where they were executed by a firing squad. Victoria's last words were: "Long live Christ the King!" Forty-four years after Victoria's martyrdom, the residents of Hornachuelos defeated a government effort to remove her name from the local school, saying: "Exemplary lives must not be forgotten." To this day they commemorate her as "a complete teacher in body and soul."

The Genius of Victoria Diez:

Victoria wrote: "Praying before the Blessed Sacrament I find strength, courage, light and all the love I need to help those entrusted to me on the way to salvation."

Reflection:

"If the world hates you, realize that it hated me first. If you belonged to the world, the world would love its own; but because you do not belong to the world, and I have chosen you out of the world, the world hates you."

John 15:18–19

BLESSED MARIAM BAOUARDY
(Mary of Jesus Crucified)

b. January 5, 1846, Abellin, Galilee, Palestine
d. August 26, 1878, Bethlehem

Mariam, the Little Arab, was orphaned at three and raised by relatives in Alexandria, Egypt. At thirteen she ran away to avoid an arranged marriage. She poured out her story to a sympathetic Muslim, but when she refused to convert to Islam he flew into a rage, cut her throat, and left her for dead. Mariam believed that she was brought back to life by the Blessed Virgin. Her story was fantastic, but doctors could not otherwise explain the livid scar on her neck and the damage to her vocal chords.

Mariam drifted to Marseilles, where she spent two years as a postulant in a convent. She began having mystical experiences, including the stigmata, that so disturbed the other nuns that they asked her to leave. The novice-mistress left with her and they entered the Carmelite convent at Pau. During her novitiate there, Mariam was beset by spiritual trials, including a diabolic possession that lasted forty days. Nevertheless, she was allowed to join the delegation sent to found a Carmel in Mangalore, India. Mariam took her final vows there, but when doubts arose about her authenticity she was sent back to Pau. In the summer of 1875, Mariam was part of a contingent sent to found a new Carmel in Bethlehem. By the time they moved into the half-finished monastery, she was already planning a second foundation at Nazareth. Unfortunately, while carrying water to the workers, Mariam slipped, fell, and broke her arm. Complications set in and she died from gangrene at the age of thirty-three. Mariam is considered a patron of peace for the Holy Land and is commemorated by the Carmelites on August 26.

The Genius of Mariam Baouardy:
Mariam combined her supernatural experiences with practical achievements, and advised: *"Always remember to love your neighbor; always prefer the one who tries your patience, who tests your virtue, because with her you can always merit: suffering is Love; the Law is Love."*

Reflection:
"In hope we were saved. Now hope that sees for itself is not hope. For who hopes for what one sees? But if we hope for what we do not see, we wait with endurance."

Romans 8:24–25

Blessed María Pilar
Izquierdo Albero

b. July 27, 1906, Zaragoza, Spain
d. August 29, 1945, San Sebastián, Spain

Pilar worked in a shoe factory from childhood until the age of twenty, when she was hit by a series of catastrophes. A fall from a streetcar fractured her pelvis and led to complications of blindness and paralysis. Confined to bed for the next decade, Pilar led a life that revolved around hospitals and her attic room. She used this time to pray, however, and began to discern a religious calling.

It was important to Pilar that Christ had come to humankind as a worker who combined his trade as a carpenter with his mission of evangelization. She began looking for a way to *"reproduce the active life of the Lord on earth through works of mercy."* In 1939, on the feast of the Immaculate Conception (December 8), Pilar attended Mass, and while receiving Communion, she experienced a miraculous and instantaneous recovery. Her vision returned and she was able to walk for the first time in years. She immediately moved to the capital city of Madrid to begin her missionary work. In spite of her good intentions, however, Pilar met resistance. The bishop of Madrid asked her to stop, and she was banned from exercising any form of apostolate for several years. In 1942 the bishop finally approved her community, but after two years, Pilar was beset by "calumny, intrigue and misunderstandings" that forced her to withdraw from the congregation she had founded. Accompanied by nine of her loyal nuns, Pilar moved to the city of San Sebastián, where she died a year later. After Pilar's death, her nuns were able to fulfill her plan for the community now known as the Missionary Work of Jesus and Mary. They are active in six countries from Spain to Mozambique and commemorate Pilar on August 27.

The Genius of María Pilar:
  Pilar's brief life was filled with emotional turmoil and pain, but even at her worst moments, she could say: *"In suffering I find so great a love for our Jesus that I could die."*

Reflection:
  "I will extol you, my God and king;
  I will bless your name forever."
            Psalm 145:1 (responsorial psalm at her beatification Mass)

SAINT ROSE OF LIMA
(Isabella Flores de Oliva)

b. April 20, 1586, Lima, Peru
d. August 24, 1617, Lima, Peru

The first canonized saint of the New World, Rose always insisted on following her own spiritual path.

She was baptized Isabella, but her nanny said that she was as beautiful as a rose, and the name stuck. At the age of five, Rose began to imitate Catherine of Siena (April 29), building a small chapel for herself in her family's garden. Like Catherine, Rose had a mother who did not always understand her. Rose sabotaged her mother's plans to arrange a marriage by cutting her beautiful hair and ruining her complexion. This hurt the family financially, and Rose helped support them by sewing. It was her idea to sell flowers from their garden, which is why Rose is the patron of florists and gardeners. Rose also resisted her confessor's efforts to seclude her inside a convent. Rose was convinced that she could follow a prayerful life in the world. She worked for ten hours a day, prayed for twelve, and slept for two—and still found time to advise Jesuit priests and Dominican friars. Rose also played guitar, wrote poems, and created collages to represent her mystical encounters with Christ. She was examined by several members of the Inquisition, who concluded that she was no heretic. A year later, the Dutch pirate Jorge Spitberg entered Lima's harbor, sending the city into a panic. People gathered in the cathedral, where Rose assured them: "*God provides, we trust to his providence.*" When the pirates reached the altar, they found Rose guarding the Eucharist. At the sight of a woman prepared to offer her life to save the sacrament, the hardened pirates retreated and left Lima immediately. Rose saved the city, but she died two years later, worn out by her many austerities.

The Genius of Rose of Lima:
Rose wrote: "*If only mortals would learn how great it is to possess divine grace, how beautiful, how noble, how precious. How many riches it hides within itself, how many joys and delights!*"

Reflection:
"*Only goodness and love will pursue me / all the days of my life;
I will dwell in the house of the LORD / for years to come.*"

Psalm 23:6

Saint María Micaela Desmaisières

b. January 1, 1809, Madrid, Spain
d. August 24, 1865, Valencia, Spain

Micaela was born into the Spanish aristocracy and grew up devoted to charity. At thirty-five, while volunteering in a hospital, she met prostitutes for the first time. As she learned about the abuse and shame they suffered, she resolved to devote herself to their rescue and rehabilitation.

Micaela established a refuge to shelter fallen women. The next step was to find volunteers to support this work. In 1856, with seven companions, Micaela formed the congregation known as the Sisters Adorers, Servants of the Most Blessed Sacrament and Charity (Adoratrices). They balanced adoration of the Blessed Sacrament with their work of redeeming prostitutes and girls at risk. In a few years, the Adoratrices had ten houses in Barcelona, Valencia, and Burgos. Micaela moved out of her family's mansion and into one of her refuges. Her socialite friends began to avoid her and the clergy insisted that her mission was hopeless. She was slandered, defamed, and threatened. Undiscouraged, Micaela enlisted laypeople in her work. She also helped the reformer priest Jerónimo Usera[141] to found the Sisters of the Love of God who are dedicated to agricultural and migrant workers. Micaela drafted their constitution and selected and trained the first postulants. She had taken the traditional vows of poverty, chastity, and obedience, but in about 1861 she added a fourth: she would always choose any opportunity for the most perfect exercise of those vows. With this in mind, Micaela postponed a business trip in order to nurse victims of an epidemic. She contracted cholera and died a victim of charity. The Adoratrices continue her work in South America and Asia.

The Genius of María Micaela:

Micaela's devotion to the Blessed Sacrament brought the nickname "madwoman of the Eucharist," but it also brought her enormous courage. In one typical episode, Micaela entered a brothel to rescue a girl held against her will. She was insulted and stoned, but Micaela got the girl and left smiling.

Reflection:

"Do not be conquered by evil but conquer evil with good."

Romans 12:21

Blessed María del Tránsito Cabanillas de Jesús Sacramentado

b. August 15, 1821, Carlos Paz, Córdoba, Argentina
d. August 25, 1885, San Vicente, Córdoba, Argentina

Tránsito Cabanillas, Argentina's first native-born blessed, did not discover her true purpose until she was past fifty.

Reared in a wealthy and devout family, Tránsito became an active catechist and regularly visited the poor and the sick. For years, she was drawn in two directions: she thought about establishing a school for poor and abandoned children, but at the same time she yearned to leave the world and enter a contemplative order where she could spend her days in prayer. In March 1873, at the age of fifty-two, Tránsito thought she had realized one dream when she was admitted to a new Carmelite monastery in Buenos Aires. Unfortunately, her health was not up to the austere Carmelite life and she left after thirteen months. By September 1874 Tránsito had recovered enough to enter a Visitation convent, but a few months later she left there too. Tránsito accepted the will of Divine Providence in all these disappointments and turned her attention back to the idea of her own foundation. Her Franciscan associates encouraged her, and she took a great step forward when a priest offered her a building.

On December 8, 1878, at the age of fifty-seven, Tránsito and two companions formed the Franciscan Third Order Missionaries of Argentina. They were soon joined by other women who shared their dedication to the care and education of orphans and poor children. Tránsito's last words were: "*I no longer need anything, because I can do nothing. But when I die, I will do much for you in heaven.*"

The Genius of Tránsito Cabanillas:

Making the most of her late-life vocation, Tránsito gave thanks for "*the very precious time that God has granted us to love him and sanctify ourselves.*" She advised: "*Let divine love be the motive for all our actions.*"

Reflection:

"*Were not our hearts burning [within us] while he spoke to us on the way and opened the scriptures to us?*"

Luke 24:32, keynote for her beatification homily

SAINT TERESA JORNET Y IBARS

(Teresa of Jesus)

b. May 9, 1843, Aytona, Catalonia, Spain
d. August 26, 1897, Liria, Valencia, Spain

The patron saint of senior citizens and retired people was twenty-five years old when she decided to devote herself to the destitute elderly. This was not Teresa Jornet's original plan for her life.

She had been preparing to take final vows as a Poor Clare when the Spanish government suppressed all convents and Teresa was forced to return home, feeling that God had rejected her. For several years, all Teresa could do was pray: *"Lord, what do you want me to do?"* She got her answer when she met Saturnino López Novoa, a priest who was working with destitute old people. Teresa knew immediately that this was why God had called her away from the Poor Clares. She opened a shelter with Saturnino and formed the community known today as the Little Sisters of the Abandoned Poor. There was never a shortage of elderly poor, and so Teresa expanded into other cities. In Valencia the first person the sisters welcomed was a ninety-nine-year-old quadriplegic. Teresa continued this work even while Spain was torn by revolution. When Valencia was bombed, almost everyone fled the city, but Teresa and the Little Sisters remained with their old ones. By the time Teresa died at the age of fifty-four, she had established more than one hundred shelters in Spain. Today the Little Sisters have more than two hundred houses in Europe, Africa, and the Americas.

Teresa's canonization process was begun in 1945 and she was declared a saint twenty-six years later. This unusually quick process testifies to the widespread reverence in which she was held. In 2004 Pope John Paul II blessed a statue of Teresa that has been placed in a niche at St Peter's Basilica.

The Genius of Teresa Jornet y Ibars:
Teresa is remembered for her commitment to the destitute elderly and for her acceptance of the will of Providence.

Reflection:
"Stand up in the presence of the aged, and show respect for the old: thus shall you fear your God."

Leviticus 19:32

August 27

❦

SAINT MONICA OF CARTHAGE

b. c. 331, Tagaste, Algeria
d. May 4, 387, Ostia, Italy

As a child in Roman North Africa, Monica was always the one sent to fetch wine from the cellar. She started sneaking sips herself, hiding her drunkenness from her family, but the servants noticed and made fun of her. Monica stopped immediately, and years later, with the same determined nature, she converted her pagan husband to Christianity before he died. Turning her son Augustine[142] around took more time.

A brilliant student, Augustine cared only about wine, women, and his academic career, but a priest assured Monica: "It is impossible that the son of so many tears should perish." At twenty-nine, Augustine accepted an academic post in Rome. Monica had begged him not to go, but he slipped away in the night. She pursued him to Rome, and then to Milan where he had been appointed a professor of rhetoric. She befriended his mentor, Ambrose,[143] bishop of Milan, who told Augustine that he was blessed to have such a wonderful mother. Monica's prayers were finally answered on Easter when she watched Ambrose baptize Augustine. A few months later, as they sailed home to Carthage, she died peacefully. Monica is the patron saint of long-suffering wives and mothers, lapsed Catholics, and alcoholics.

The Genius of Monica of Carthage:

When her son seemed lost for good, Monica had a dream in which an angel assured her: *"Where you are, there will your son be."* She told Augustine, who said scornfully that the angel meant she would come to see things his way. Monica answered: *"No, he did not say, 'where he is, there thou also,' but 'where thou art, there he also.'"* Augustine, the great debater, was more impressed by his mother's swift retort than by the dream itself. But when he was baptized, Monica's interpretation was confirmed.

Reflection:

"It is the hour now for you to awake from sleep. For our salvation is nearer now than when we first believed."

Romans 13:11
(the passage said to have moved Augustine to embrace Christianity)

BLESSED BRONISLAVA OF POLAND

b. c. 1203, Kamień, Lubelskie, Poland
d. August 29, 1259, Zwierzyniec, Lubelskie, Poland

When she was fifteen, Bronislava entered the Norbertine[144] abbey built by her great-grandfather and spent the next two decades in strict silence, prayer, and contemplation. This serenity ended shortly after she was elected prioress, when the Tartars invaded Poland. As they closed in on the abbey, Bronislava took up a crucifix, pressed it to her heart, and told her nuns: *"Do not fear anything—the cross will save us."* The Tartars set fire to the building, but Bronislava hit a stone wall three times with her crucifix and a passage opened, allowing the nuns to escape.

Bronislava later died peacefully and was entombed in the abbey. In 1604, while the building underwent renovations, her relics were translated to a nearby church. They were carried in during an exorcism and the priest impulsively added Bronislava to the list of saints he invoked. At the mention of her name, the Evil One immediately left his victim, confirming the power of Bronislava's intercession. Her decree of beatification notes: "She is to be feared by all Hell." Bronislava is commemorated on August 30.

The Genius of Bronislava of Poland:

A Polish officer serving in the French army was falsely accused of spying. Confined to a dungeon, he prayed to the saints of his youth. One night, a nun appeared to him in a dream and said she was Bronislava, which means "defender of a good name." She chided the officer for not coming to her but assured him that she would intercede anyway. The next morning the charges against him were dropped. He returned to Poland and built a chapel to honor Bronislava. She has become the patron of a good name, and her special mission is to restore damaged reputations.

Reflection:

"My lover speaks; he says to me, / 'Arise, my beloved, my beautiful one, / and come!'"

Song of Songs 2:10 (last words of Bronislava)

BLESSED JEANNE JUGAN

b. October 25, 1792, Cancale, Brittany, France
d. August 29, 1879, La Tour Saint-Joseph, France

As a young woman, Jeanne resisted pressure to marry, saying: "*God wants me for himself, he is keeping me for a work which is not yet known, for a work which is not yet founded.*"

Jeanne discovered that work when she and a friend rented a small house where they sheltered the elderly and disabled. She went out every day carrying a market basket and begged for food and supplies. The basket became the emblem of Jeanne's growing community. By 1842 they had formally organized as the Little Sisters of the Poor and elected Jeanne their superior. Unfortunately, a troubled priest, Augustin Le Pailleur, became obsessed with taking credit for her work. He annulled Jeanne's election, barred her from any leadership role, and claimed the titles superior general and founder for himself. Two years later, Jeanne was honored by the French Academy and a jealous Le Pailleur ordered that she was never to be allowed to go collecting again. She responded: "*You have stolen my work, but I give it to you gladly.*" To a young Sister she confided: "*She who holds her tongue keeps her soul.*" Jeanne spent the last twenty-seven years of her life in forced retirement, but she became a heroine to the young novices. As she lay blind and dying, she could say: "*I no longer see anything but God . . . He sees me, that is enough.*" A year after her death, Le Pailleur was summoned to Rome, where Pope Leo XIII stripped him of the titles he had stolen from Jeanne Jugan. He died in obscurity five years later.

The Genius of Jeanne Jugan:

Jeanne advised one troubled novice: "*When your patience and strength run out and you feel alone and helpless, Jesus is waiting for you in the chapel. Say to him, 'Jesus, you know exactly what is going on. You are all I have, and you know all things. Come to my help.' And then go, and don't worry about how you are going to manage. That you have told God about it is enough. He has a good memory.*"

Reflection:

"*Man's pride causes his humiliation, / but he who is humble of spirit obtains honor.*"

Proverbs 29:23

SAINT MARGARET CLITHEROW

b. 1556, York, England
d. March 25, 1586, York, England

The Pearl of York and patron of businesswomen and altar girls, Margaret Clitherow was so beloved that even her Protestant neighbors protected her.

Margaret married a prosperous widower, and they lived above his butcher shop on a narrow street called The Shambles. Both were Protestants when they married, but later Margaret returned to the old Roman Catholic faith. Catholic priests were at that time barred from England under penalty of death. Anyone who sheltered them could also be executed, but Margaret believed that if the priests were willing to risk their lives to celebrate Mass, she should be willing to risk hers to help them do so. For the next decade, Margaret was repeatedly jailed. She protected her husband by keeping him in the dark about her activities; meanwhile, she made their home the Catholic center of York.

In 1586 the house was raided and Margaret was imprisoned in York Castle. She stunned the court by refusing to enter a plea. Without a plea, they could not go forward with a trial. She said: *"Having made no offense, I need no trial."* For the next few days, court officials tried to get Margaret to submit to a jury trial. She told the court: *"If you say I have offended and must be tried, I will be tried by none but God and your own consciences."* The furious judge called Margaret a "naughty, willful woman" and sentenced her to be pressed to death. She accepted the sentence stoically, saying: *"Flesh is frail, but I trust in my Lord Jesus, that he will give me strength to bear all troubles and torments which shall be laid upon me for his sake."* When Margaret's husband learned her fate, he wept and said, "Let them take all I have and save my wife, for she is the best wife in all England."

Margaret was canonized with the Forty Martyrs of England and Wales. The only other women in the group were Margaret Ward[145] and Anne Line (February 27). Her house still stands in The Shambles and a weekly Mass is celebrated there.

The Genius of Margaret Clitherow:

Margaret's faith never wavered. Sentenced to be crushed to death, she said: *"I will accept willingly everything that God wills."*

Reflection:

"Do not be afraid of anything that you are going to suffer. Indeed, the devil will throw some of you into prison, that you may be tested, and you will face an ordeal for ten days. Remain faithful until death, and I will give you the crown of life."

Revelation 2:10

BLESSED NARCISA DE JESÚS
MARTILLO MORÁN

b. October 29, 1832, Nobol, Guyas, Ecuador
d. December 8, 1869, Lima, Peru

Narcisa's parents lived together for years without marriage, which was not unusual in their rural community. They married at some point but died by the time Narcisa was eighteen. She moved to the city of Guayaquil to dedicate herself to prayer and charity. Narcisa worked closely with Mercedes Molina (June 4) in providing a home and education for young women on the streets. Both blesseds were deeply affected by the story of Mariana de Paredes (May 26), who was beatified the year that Narcisa turned twenty-one. It is said that to know the story of Narcisa one only needs to know about Mariana.

Early in 1868 Narcisa traveled to Peru, where she lived as a guest in a Dominican convent in Lima and worked to support herself. It was becoming obvious that Narcisa was blessed with mystical gifts, among them the gifts of healing and prophecy. Her last spiritual director, Manuel Medina, was so confident that he was dealing with a saint that he began to collect Narcisa's writings and had them notarized while she was still alive. During her final illness, Narcisa heroically endured intense pain, offering herself as a victim for the conversion of sinners. After her death, the Sisters who entered her cell reported that a brilliant light radiated from her body and the room was filled with an exquisite perfume. (This is not uncommon with saints and is known as the "odor of sanctity.") Her body has remained incorrupt for more than one hundred years. In 1955, after lengthy negotiations, the government of Ecuador succeeded in having Narcisa's body returned to her homeland. In 1972 it was finally brought back to Nobol, where she is honored as a powerful intercessor.

The Genius of Narcisa de Jesús:

Because she made a successful journey from rural to urban life, Narcisa is regarded as a model for young women who leave small towns to work in large cities.

Reflection:

"Let the word of Christ dwell in you richly, as in all wisdom you teach and admonish one another, singing psalms, hymns, and spiritual songs with gratitude in your hearts to God."

Colossians 3:16

September 1

❦

SAINT DOUCELINE OF MARSEILLES
(Dulcinea)

b. 1214, Digne, France
d. September 1, 1274, Marseilles, France

At an early age, Douceline made a vow to observe the holy poverty preached by Francis of Assisi.[146] She formed a community of Beguines[147] at Hyères and, later, another one at Marseilles.

Virgins, widows, and even married women left their families to follow Douceline. Her brother Hugo of Digne, an important figure among early Franciscans, helped her organize her beguinage. She would travel through Provence, accompanied by as many as eighty Beguines, encouraging the people to penitence. She was credited with the gift of healing and rumored to have raised the dead. Douceline always stopped at any Franciscan church she passed. She would remain there in ecstasy, her arms in the air, from the first Mass to the last Angelus at sundown. Many people were dubious, and once, in church, a woman pierced her foot with a bodkin (a thick blunt needle) to test her. Douceline did not move and apparently felt nothing, until she emerged from her trance and suffered great pain from the wound. Other skeptics pricked Douceline with awls, jabbed her with needles, and even stabbed her with a chisel. She passed these tests, but suffered the terrible effects later.

Charles Anjou,[148] count of Provence and later king of Sicily and Naples, consulted Douceline on every important occasion and was said to be afraid of her. Charles was known for a terrible temper that not even the Franciscans could tame, but Douceline was always able to calm him. She was buried beside her brother at Marseilles, and her tomb became the site of many miracles.

The Genius of Douceline of Marseilles:
Douceline prized humility, and when a young Beguine complained that "Everyone despises us and people scorn our state," she replied: *"Tell them, 'It is my honor and my glory, my joy and my crown to be despised by your world.'"*

Reflection:
"One thing God has said; / two things I have heard:
Power belongs to God; / so too, Lord, does kindness."

Psalm 62:12–13

SAINT BEATRICE DE SILVA MENESES

b. 1424, Campo Mayor, Portugal
d. September 1, 1490, Toledo, Spain

While visiting a convent in Toledo, Queen Isabella[149] learned about a recluse who had resided there for decades. No one had ever seen her face, which she kept covered with a white veil. The mystery woman was summoned, and as the queen's servant lifted her veil, Isabella immediately recognized a cousin, Beatrice de Silva. She had not seen Beatrice in forty years, not since Isabella's mother, the queen of Castile, had thrown her into a dungeon in a jealous rage.

Beatrice shared the rest of her story: A beautiful, flirtatious young woman, she had come to Castile as a lady-in-waiting to Isabella's mother. There she found herself in a court rife with intrigue where men fought duels over her. When she caught the attention of the king, the jealous queen had ordered her tossed into a dungeon without food or water. Just when Beatrice thought she would die, the Blessed Mother appeared to her, promised to protect her, and told her that she would found a religious order dedicated to her Immaculate Conception (December 8). Beatrice miraculously escaped to Toledo, where she had remained until her reunion with Isabella. Determined to make up for her mother's cruelty, Isabella helped Beatrice write a Rule for her new order. This was four centuries before the Immaculate Conception was accepted as a dogma of the Church, but Beatrice and Isabella managed to get the Rule approved shortly before Beatrice's death. Her order is known today as the Franciscans of the Immaculate Conception of Our Lady (Conceptionists). Beatrice is usually represented with a six-pointed star on her forehead. This refers to a miraculous event at her deathbed when a brilliant light radiating from her face filled the room. Her feast day is August 17.

The Genius of Beatrice de Silva:
Out of her suffering, Beatrice created something great and lasting.

Reflection:
"I heard another voice from heaven say: / 'Depart from her, my people, / so as not to take part in her sins / and receive a share in her plagues, / for her sins are piled up to the sky, / and God remembers her crimes.'"

Revelation 18:4–5

September 3

Saint Rose of Viterbo

b. c. 1234, Viterbo, Italy
d. March 6, 1252, Viterbo, Italy

As a child, Rose had a vision in which Our Lord told her to fight without ceasing for God and the Church. At the time, German emperor Frederick II (1194–1250) was at war with the pope and had conquered northern Italy. When Frederick marched into Viterbo and was welcomed by local princes, seven-year-old Rose could not accept this. She began preaching in the streets, urging her neighbors to remain loyal to the Holy Father. Rose rallied so much opposition that the governor of Viterbo banished her and her parents.

Rose assured her mother and father that Christ would reward those who were persecuted for justice's sake. While preaching in Soriano, she prophesied that the emperor was dying and peace would soon be restored. A few weeks later, a messenger arrived and confirmed that Frederick was dead. Rose moved on to Vitorchiano, which was under the influence of a witch. She stood on a flaming pyre and preached for three hours, then led the witch and her followers back to the sacraments. Rose returned to Viterbo in triumph. She hoped to join the local Poor Clares, but the abbess was reluctant to admit such a celebrity. Ever humble, Rose said: *"Perhaps she will be more willing when I am dead—when I can be no danger to the humility of the convent. Then she will know that I only did what God told me."* Rose died at seventeen and was buried in her parish graveyard. Seven years later, she appeared to Pope Alexander IV three times in dreams, telling him that it was God's will that she be placed with the Poor Clares. Alexander ordered her body moved to the convent that had rejected her. In 1984 John Paul II visited Viterbo to celebrate the 750th anniversary of Rose's birth. Her feast day is September 4.

The Genius of Rose of Viterbo:

Rose advised: *"Live so as not to fear death. For those who live well in the world, death is not frightening but sweet and precious."*

Reflection:

"Blessed are those who are persecuted for the sake of righteousness, / for theirs is the kingdom of heaven."

Matthew 5:10

SAINT ROSALIE OF PALERMO

b. c. 1125, Palermo, Sicily
d. c. September 4, 1160, Palermo, Sicily

Tradition has it that Rosalie was the daughter of Sinibald, lord of Quisquina, a knight attached to the court of King William of Sicily. At age fourteen, though, she turned her back on the glamour of court life and followed two angels, one armed as a knight, the other dressed as a pilgrim, who took her to a cave high on Mount Quisquina. After a few years, Rosalie sought more privacy and the angels led her to the summit of Mount Pellegrino. There she spent the rest of her life in a small grotto, praying and weaving garlands of wildflowers that she strung around a large wooden crucifix. Rosalie passed away quietly in her cave and in time the dripping water encased her body in lime. Within sixty years, the people of Palermo had recognized Rosalie as a saint and dedicated a church to her, but in the centuries that followed they lost track of her cave. Rosalie reemerged in 1624 while a plague raged in Palermo. She appeared to a stricken soldier and ordered him to make a pilgrimage to the top of Mount Pellegrino. He did so, and returned with his health restored. People began to wonder whether Rosalie could save the entire city and searched for her cave. Entering the grotto, probably for the first time in centuries, they found her skeleton encased in a stalagmite. Rosalie's relics were translated to the cathedral in a great procession, and the plague that had ravaged Palermo for a year suddenly ceased. The grateful populace built a shrine dedicated to Rosalie on the mountainside near her cave. Palermo still honors her with two great feasts, on September 4 and on July 15, and she is venerated by Sicilians all over the world.

The Genius of Saint Rosalie:

> We might ask, how did this young woman manage? How did she survive winter in that cold, damp cave? But Rosalie was not concerned with such mundane matters. She was called to praise God, and that was what she did, until she entered his kingdom forever.

Reflection:

> "*All things came to be through him, / and without him nothing came to be. / What came to be through him was life, / and this life was the light of the human race; / the light shines in the darkness, / and the darkness has not overcome it.*"
>
> John 1:3–5

BLESSED TERESA OF CALCUTTA

(Agnes Gonxha Bojaxhiu)

b. August 26, 1910, Skopje, Macedonia
d. September 5, 1997, Calcutta, India

At age eighteen, Agnes Bojaxhiu left her homeland in the Balkans to join the Sisters of the Blessed Virgin Mary (Loreto Sisters) in Dublin. She learned English there and took the religious name Teresa. Assigned to India, she spent fifteen years teaching the daughters of Calcutta's wealthiest families. In 1942, during a retreat, she vowed *"to give God anything that he may ask . . . not to refuse him anything."* Four years later, Teresa experienced the first of a series of visions in which Jesus called on her to serve Him among the poorest of his poor, and to found an order of Indian nuns to spread the fire of his love. She shared these visions with no one but her spiritual director, who revealed them after her death. In 1948 Teresa left the school where she had taught and began assisting in the poorest neighborhoods of Calcutta. Soon she was able to rent a small building for a school, and in 1953 she opened her first home for abandoned children. Meanwhile, however, Teresa's visions had ceased and she feared that God had abandoned her. This spiritual darkness lasted until her death, but in spite of her private suffering, Teresa presented a face of unfailing faith to the world.

As her mission grew, Teresa founded the Missionaries of Charity, two orders of priests, and a secular congregation. Now known to the world as Mother Teresa, she was honored with the Nobel Peace Prize in 1979. By the time she died, nearly four thousand Missionaries of Charity were at work in 123 countries. India honored her with a state funeral, and her tomb in Calcutta has become a pilgrimage site. Pope John Paul II asked that Teresa's cause be accelerated and he was able to declare her Blessed just eight years after her death.

The Genius of Mother Teresa:
> Mother Teresa advised: *"Keep the joy of loving God in your heart, and share this joy with all you meet, especially your family."*

Reflection:
> *"Store up treasures in heaven, where neither moth nor decay destroy, nor thieves break in and steal. For where your treasure is, there also will your heart be."*
> Matthew 6:20–21

September 6

BLESSED MARTYRS OF NOWOGRÓDEK
(Maria Stella and Ten Companions)

d. August 1, 1943, Nowogródek, Poland (now Belarus)

At twenty-seven, Sister Maria Boromea was the youngest of the eleven Sisters of the Holy Family of Nazareth who were martyred by the Nazis at Nowogródek. Boromea had arrived at the convent in August 1939, but her final vows were delayed by the outbreak of World War II. During the war, Nowogródek was alternately controlled by the Nazi and Soviet armies. In the summer of 1943, Boromea had just returned from a brief visit to her family. The visit only confirmed her commitment to her vocation. "*Something pushed me to return to the nuns,*" she wrote to her novice-mistress. When Boromea returned, she found the Nazis in control of Nowogródek.

The superior of Boromea's convent was Mother Maria Stella of the Most Blessed Sacrament, a woman distinguished by "goodness, generosity and love of neighbor." Under Mother Stella's leadership, the convent at Nowogródek had grown from two sisters to twelve. The Holy Family Sisters looked after the local church, set up a school, and moved among the community performing works of charity without regard to religion. Catholics were a minority in Nowogródek, but their Protestant and Jewish neighbors regarded the Holy Family Sisters with respect and affection.

The arrival of a special Gestapo unit in the neighboring town of Baranowicz marked an increase in brutality and mass executions. On July 18, 1943, one hundred and twenty men from Nowogródek were arrested. While they waited for their fate to be decided, there was hardly a household in town that was not affected. The nuns felt called to offer themselves in place of the men. Mother Stella led their prayers, in which the nuns asked God: "*If sacrifice is needed, accept it from us and spare those who have families.*"

On July 31, the Holy Family Sisters were summoned by the Gestapo commandant. They left Sister Malgorzata[150] behind to watch the convent. Malgorzata would never see any of them alive again. The sisters met with the commandant and offered to be deported in the place of the men. He had another plan and ordered the eleven nuns loaded into a truck and taken to a field. He intended to execute them, but there were too many peasants at work and he did not want witnesses. The nuns were brought back to the Nazi headquarters and locked up in a wine cellar overnight. They were so cramped that they took turns lying down on the floor.

The next morning, Sunday, August 1, the eleven nuns, including Mother Maria Stella and Sister Boromea, were taken to a large pine forest where an open pit had been prepared for them. They were shot to death and immediately dumped into the mass grave. That night, a drunken Nazi officer confided some of the details to his landlady. "How they went," he said, "how those sisters went to their death!" A small boy, watching in the woods, had also seen the executions. The story began to spread.

Malgorzata, the only survivor, combed the area and finally found the fresh grave in the forest. She guarded it until the war ended in 1945 and the bodies could be exhumed. The eleven Holy Family Sisters now rest in the church of the Transfiguration in Nowogródek. They are commemorated in Poland and by their order on September 4.

The Genius of the Martyrs of Nowogródek:
The Sisters of the Holy Family of Nazareth fearlessly fulfilled their commitment to the moral and spiritual renewal of family life. None of the 120 men the nuns sought to save was executed. A few men were released at the time, and although most of the others were deported to slave labor camps, they all miraculously survived that ordeal and returned to their homes after the war.

Reflection:
"Do not be yoked with those who are different, with unbelievers. For what partnership do righteousness and lawlessness have? Or what fellowship does light have with darkness?"

2 Corinthians 6:14

BLESSED ANNA EUGENIA PICCO

b. November 8, 1867, Crescenzago, Milan, Italy
d. September 7, 1921, Parma, Italy

Eugenia's father was an internationally acclaimed musician, and at her baptism in Milan she was serenaded by violinists from La Scala. After that, she was left with her grandparents while her parents traveled the world, and she only saw them on short visits between tours. When Eugenia was seven, her mother, Adelaide, returned home alone and informed Eugenia that her father was dead. The truth was that Adelaide had left him for another man, and Eugenia never saw her father again. Adelaide took Eugenia to live with her new lover, with whom she had two more children. Eugenia spent the difficult years from seven to eighteen deprived of religious education or much moral training of any kind. There are hints that Adelaide's lover may have molested her.

In spite of the moral chaos in her home, Eugenia felt that she had a religious vocation. She hoped to join the Little Daughters of the Sacred Hearts of Jesus and Mary, who worked among young women in Parma, but her mother strongly objected. Adelaide intended Eugenia to have a singing career. On August 31, 1887, after many arguments, Eugenia ran away to Parma and was welcomed into the Little Daughters. Their founder, Agostino Chieppi,[151] became Eugenia's surrogate father, but he died before she made her final vows in 1894. Eugenia taught music, singing, and French, and in 1911 she was elected superior general, a post she would hold until her death. She became one of the most beloved religious figures in twentieth-century Italy. Today the order she nurtured is active in Europe, Africa, Asia, and the Americas.

The Genius of Eugenia Picco:

Eugenia wrote in her journal: *"[A]s Jesus chose bread, which is so ordinary, so must my life be ordinary, approachable to all and at the same time as humble and hidden as the yeast."*

Reflection:

"Sing to God, praise the divine name; exalt the rider of the clouds. Rejoice before this God whose name is the LORD."

Psalm 68:5

BLESSED DINA BÉLANGER
(Marie of Saint Cecilia of Rome)

b. April 30, 1897, Quebec, Canada
d. September 4, 1929, Sillery, Quebec, Canada

Dina was a pampered only child and even as a toddler was determined to become a saint. As a teenager she felt the stirrings of a religious vocation, but she was also a gifted pianist and she trained for a career in music.

Dina spent two years in New York City studying at a conservatory that is now part of the Juilliard School. Like any tourist, Dina rode the new subway trains and went shopping in fashionable stores. She wrote home enthusiastically about a little plum-colored fall suit she had bought and assured her parents that *"an excursion to New York might be taken for a jaunt through Paradise."* Yet, ultimately, all this pleasure could not distract her. *"The glitter of gold, the glamour of wealth had served but to detach me from earthly things,"* Dina wrote in her autobiography. *"The excitement, the agitation of the crowds had enlightened me to the price of time, the folly and the error of those who do not know how to appreciate it, much less employ it for the all-important matter of their salvation."*

Returning to Canada, Dina briefly pursued a career as a concert pianist, but this only confirmed her belief in her vocation. Convinced that *"the religious life is the preparation for the eternal life,"* she entered the convent of Jesus Maria in Quebec in 1923 and took her final vows five years later. Dina's choice of her religious name, Marie of Saint Cecilia of Rome, reflects her ongoing love for music.[152] In the convent Dina was known for her devotion to the Eucharist and her abundant joy. As she grew in spiritual perfection she was blessed with many mystical gifts, but soon after taking her final vows she was diagnosed with tuberculosis, and she died at the age of thirty-two. Dina described her spiritual journey in an autobiography, *Canticle of Love*, which was published after her death.

The Genius of Dina Bélanger:
Her motto was always, *"Love, and let Jesus and Mary have their way."*

Reflection:
"Sing praise to the LORD with the harp, / with the harp and melodious song."
Psalm 98:5

Blessed Seraphina Sforza

(Sueva of Montefeltro)

b. 1434, Montefeltro, Urbino, Italy
d. September 8, 1478, Pesaro, Italy

Sueva's powerful relatives, the Colonnas, arranged her marriage to Alexander Sforza (1409–1473), the duke of Pesaro, when she was fourteen and he was a widower of thirty-nine. The marriage worked until Alexander went off to war against Milan, leaving Sueva to manage his estates and rear his two young sons. When he returned six years later, he became convinced that Sueva had been unfaithful and accused her of trying to kill him.

Even Sueva's beloved stepsons insisted that their father was at fault. Servants later testified that Alexander abused her, tried to poison her, and dragged her by the hair through his castle before he locked her out and she found shelter with the Poor Clares. He moved his mistress, Pacifica, into his castle. He even ordered Sueva to return her wedding ring, but she responded that she would not give up her jewelry for whores to wear or encourage men to put away their wives. When Sueva's relatives demanded to know why she was living with the Poor Clares, Alexander took them to the convent with his personal scribe. He expected to record Sueva's admission that she had been unfaithful, but she refused to answer any questions. The Colonnas took her silence as guilt, but in fact it was the evil scribe who had been spreading lies about her. As the Colonnas were leaving, a young donkey bit the scribe's hand and would not let go until he proclaimed Sueva's innocence. Her reputation was restored, but Sueva chose to remain in the convent, where she took a new name: Seraphina. In time, Alexander turned on Pacifica, who left him, repented, and died a Christian death. Alexander also repented and visited Seraphina before he died. After fifteen years among the Poor Clares, she was unanimously elected abbess and died at peace three years later.

The Genius of Seraphina Sforza:
Was Seraphina a scheming adulteress or a lonely, flirtatious young woman? Only God and her confessor know the truth, but with His grace, Seraphina was willing to confess her sins, do penance, and amend her life.

Reflection:
"Wisdom builds her house, / but Folly tears hers down with her own hands."
Proverbs 14:1

SAINT PULCHERIA AUGUSTA, EMPRESS
(Cherie)

b. January 19, 399, Constantinople
d. July 453, Constantinople

At the age of fifteen, Pulcheria was declared empress of the Eastern empire and became regent for her brother Theodosius II, who was two years younger. Pulcheria and two younger sisters took public vows of chastity, inscribing their promises on a jeweled tablet in the church of Holy Wisdom (Saint Sophie)[153] at Constantinople and turning their palace into a virtual monastery. She devoted herself to affairs of state and preparing her brother to govern. When he was ready, Pulcheria officially stepped aside. His new wife resented her continued influence, however, so Pulcheria discreetly retired to her country villa. Affairs of state deteriorated until Theodosius exiled his wife and recalled his sister. Resuming control, Pulcheria arranged for the return of the body of John Chrysostom,[154] a distinguished Father of the Church who had been banished by her parents and died in exile. Chrysostom's relics were received with the highest honors, and Pulcheria and Theodosius publicly asked God's pardon for the sin their parents had committed by persecuting this holy man. When Theodosius took a fatal fall from a horse, Pulcheria was officially recognized as the sole ruler of the Eastern empire. To solidify her position, she married Marcian (392–457), a distinguished former general and senator. He agreed to a celibate marriage and Pulcheria crowned him emperor. The historian Edward Gibbon praised Pulcheria as a ruler who balanced piety with practicality, writing that "she alone, among all the descendants of the great Theodosius I, appears to have inherited any share of his manly spirit and abilities."

The Genius of Pulcheria Augusta:

While governing the Eastern empire for more than forty years, Pulcheria left her mark on early Christianity. She was devoted to the Blessed Mother in a time when this was not widespread, and she successfully fought emerging heresies that questioned the divine nature of Christ.

Reflection:

"See to it that no one captivate you with an empty, seductive philosophy according to human tradition, according to the elemental powers of the world and not according to Christ."

Colossians 2:8

September 11

BLESSED CATHERINE OF RACCONIGI
(Catherine Mattei)

b. 1480, Racconigi, Piemonte, Italy
d. September 4, 1547, Caramagna, Piemonte, Italy

The peasants in Italy's Piedmont region called Catherine *La Masca di Dio* (God's Sorceress) because her life was so full of miracles and wonders.

She was five years old when the Blessed Mother advised her that Christ wanted her heart. Catherine, a simple peasant girl, had no idea where her heart was, but Mary put her hand on her and said: *"There is your heart and you will give it to my Son every time you obey his commands and suffer something for his love."* Catherine believed that Christ appeared to her four times over twenty years, telling her: *"I come to live in you in order to purify, to illuminate, to set ablaze your heart and to give you life."* On each visit, he took her heart and once kept it for forty-five days before returning it. At other times, Catherine was persecuted by devils disguised as men, beasts, birds, and corpses, but she was defended by saints and angels who took her to heaven, hell, and purgatory. She recognized friends in all three places. Angels carried Catherine over great distances, and Lucy of Narni (November 14) was among those who reported her miraculous visits. All this time, Catherine led a normal life in the world and supported herself as a skilled silk weaver.

Catherine's greatest test came when she was thirty-two. For seven days she suffered terrible temptations. She considered suicide but could not go through with it because her heart now belonged to Jesus. She begged Him to send her any affliction He chose, but not to leave her exposed to more temptation. Jesus assured her, *"Fear nothing, since I am with you. Call me your hope."* He had been in her heart all the time. Later that year, jealous prelates who resented Catherine's influence brought her before the Inquisition on charges of heresy and witchcraft, but she was completely exonerated. The Dominican Order commemorates her on September 4.

The Genius of Catherine of Racconigi:
Catherine wrote her motto on her heart: *"Jesus, my hope."*

Reflection:
"You, LORD, are near to all who call upon you, / to all who call upon you in truth."

Psalm 145:18

BLESSED BRIGIDA MORELLO
(Brigida of Jesus)

b. June 17, 1610, San Michele di Pagana, Genoa, Italy
d. September 3, 1679, Piacenza, Italy

Brigida was born into an ancient and noble family, but life in a castle did not insulate her from the tragedies of the world. In 1633 she married Matteo Zancari and moved with him to a village near Piacenza. The region was still recovering from a plague epidemic, and Brigida devoted herself to nursing the victims until both she and Matteo fell ill. Matteo did not survive.

As a widow, Brigida made a vow of perpetual chastity and moved to Piacenza, hoping to enter a Capuchin monastery. She was turned away, and for the next few years she made her home her convent. She fasted, went barefoot even in winter, slept on a board, and spent most of her time praying in solitude. Elsewhere in Piacenza, another widow, the duchess Margarita de Farnese Medici, dreamed that Jesus showed her a scroll and said, *"This is your decree for the foundation of the Ursulines; your permission is marked in the sky."* Armed with that authorization, the duchess began looking for a woman to found a religious congregation that would staff her school for young women. Brigida's spiritual director recommended her to the duchess. On Ash Wednesday, 1649, Brigida and the duchess founded the Ursuline Sisters of Immaculate Mary with five other women. She took the name Brigida of Jesus and was elected prioress. Eighteen of the letters in which Brigida lays out her ideas about education have been preserved in the library of the University of Genoa. Brigida had many mystical experiences, and after her death the duke of Parma and Piacenza sponsored her cause for sainthood. It still took more than three hundred years until she was beatified in 1998. Today the Ursulines of Immaculate Mary are active in Italy, India, and Brazil. They commemorate Brigida on September 4.

The Genius of Brigida Morello:

Brigida loved to repeat: *"Trust, trust great heart! God is our Father and will never abandon us."*

Reflection:

"Whoever is in Christ is a new creation: the old things have passed away; behold, new things have come."

2 Corinthians 5:17

BLESSED MARIA EUTHYMIA ÜFFING
(Emma Üffing)

b. April 8, 1914, Halverde, Westphalia, Germany
d. September 9, 1955, Münster, Westphalia, Germany

"The life of Sister Maria Euthymia was a canticle to hope in the midst of war," wrote Emile Eche, a soldier priest who was imprisoned at Dinkslaken while Euthymia was a nurse there.

After she entered the Sisters of Mercy of Münster at age twenty, she wrote to her mother: *"I have found Him who my heart loves. I want to seize him and never leave him."* As a student nurse, Euthymia was assigned to a contagious disease ward in Dinkslaken. She received her nursing diploma just before the onset of World War II, and her ward became a barracks for eighty prisoners of war: English, French, and Russian soldiers, and Polish and Ukrainian slave laborers. Euthymia treated them all with unfailing respect. She even secretly prepared meals and hid them where the men could find them. She prayed with the sick and saw that those who requested the sacraments received them. After the war, Euthymia accepted a transfer to the laundry at the motherhouse in Münster, saying only: *"It is all for God almighty."* On July 8, 1955, she collapsed at work and was found to be suffering from a cancer of the intestine that had spread to other organs. She died two months later.

The documentation for Euthymia's cause for canonization contains more than 150,000 letters in which people from all over the world express gratitude for her intercession. She is commemorated in Germany and by the Sisters of Mercy of Münster on September 9.

The Genius of Maria Euthymia Üffing:
Euthymia lived her ordinary life in an extraordinary way, convinced that *"The Lord can use me like a ray of sunshine to brighten the day."*

Reflection:
"I had hardly left them / when I found him whom my heart loves.
I took hold of him and would not let him go / till I should bring him to the home of my mother, / to the room of my parent."

Song of Songs 3:4

SAINT NOTBURGA OF EBEN

b. c 1265, Rattenberg, Tyrol, Austria
d. September 14, 1313, Rattenberg, Tyrol, Austria

Notburga was a cook for the noble Rattenberg family. After the death of the old count and countess, she continued to serve their son Henry and his wife, Odilia. Henry's parents had encouraged Notburga to give their table scraps to the poor, but Odilia and Henry turned the poor away with nothing and ordered Notburga to feed all leftovers to Odilia's pampered pigs.

When Henry caught Notburga taking her own food to the poor, he ordered her out of the castle. She went to work for a farmer who promised that she could leave for services whenever the church bell rang. Late one Sunday during harvest season, however, Notburga was still in the field when the last bell rang. The farmer insisted that she continue cutting wheat. Notburga raised her sickle high, saying, *"God be the Judge, this sickle will be the witness of the agreement that I was to go."* It stayed suspended in the air for all the other reapers to see. The farmer reconsidered and let Notburga go say her prayers. Meanwhile, back in Rattenberg, everything had gone wrong and Henry was sure that he was being punished for dismissing Notburga. He begged her to return, promising that she could give away all the food she wanted. Notburga gave in and returned to Rattenberg. Henry soon recovered his fortune, and Notburga served as the Rattenbergs' housekeeper for another nineteen years. When she died, her coffin was placed in a cart pulled by two oxen. Without any guidance, they took Notburga's body to the chapel where she had always prayed. It is said that angels lifted her coffin and placed it in her grave there.

The Genius of Notburga of Eben:

An unusual saint for the Middle Ages, Notburga was neither a noble-woman nor a nun, neither a martyr nor a miracle worker, but she proved that even a humble servant could become a saint.

Reflection:

"None of us lives for oneself, and no one dies for oneself. For if we live, we live for the Lord, and if we die, we die for the Lord; so then, whether we live or die, we are the Lord's."

Romans 14:7–8

September 15

❦

SAINT CATHERINE OF GENOA
(Catterinetta Fieschi Adorno)

b. c. 1447, Genoa, Italy
d. September 15, 1510, Genoa, Italy

Sixteen-year-old Catherine's powerful family forced her to marry against her will in order to seal the peace between two feuding clans. She spent her first ten years of marriage in a state of depression while her husband, Giuliano Adorno, wasted his fortune, caroused with a mistress, and fathered a child out of wedlock.

On March 22, 1473, Catherine experienced such a sudden and overwhelming love of God and such an intense awareness of her sins that she almost collapsed. Afterward she spent several days in contemplation, during which she had a vision of Christ carrying the Cross. She stopped worrying about her husband's behavior, the opinions of others, or even her own frustrated dreams. From then on, Catherine devoted herself to prayer and attending to the poor in the slums of Genoa. Giuliano repented, became a Franciscan tertiary, and joined her work. They shared a modest house near the Pammatone Hospital, the largest charity hospital in Europe, and served there for the rest of their lives. Catherine gradually moved up the management ranks from a simple volunteer to hospital director. Giuliano became Pammatone's religious director and died in 1479, during a plague epidemic. He left his remaining fortune to Catherine to distribute to the poor. Catherine forgave his former mistress, took on responsibility for the support of his daughter, and even provided for the young woman in her will. Catherine had no children of her own, but she was blessed with a spiritual son, Ettore Vernazza, a wealthy young businessman who founded the Oratory of Divine Love under her influence. Father Benedict Groeschel considers this organization of laymen and clergy "Catherine's greatest single historical contribution," because it marked the beginning of serious reform in the Church.

The Genius of Catherine of Genoa:

After her change of heart, Catherine wrote: "*Since I began to love, love has never forsaken me. It has ever grown to its own fullness within my innermost heart.*"

Reflection:

"*[Jesus said] it was not you who chose me, but I who chose you and appointed you to go and bear fruit that will remain, so that whatever you ask the Father in my name he may give you.*"

John 15:16

September 16

Saint Edith of Wilton
(Edith the Younger)

b. 960, Kemsing, England
d. September 15, 984, Winchester, England

King Edgar the Peaceful[155] was riding through Kent one afternoon when he noticed a beautiful young woman, Wulfrida.[156] He carried her off to Kemsing where she gave birth to their daughter, Edith. Unfortunately, the king already had a queen, so Wulfrida took the infant Edith and retired to Wilton Abbey. As a penance for Edgar's adultery, the archbishop of Canterbury barred him from wearing his crown for seven years.

King Edgar was widowed a few years later and wanted to marry Wulfrida, but she preferred to remain at Wilton, where she ruled as abbess for more than thirty years and raised Edith to be "a wonder of beauty, learning and piety." At fifteen, Edith took the veil herself. King Edgar offered her an abbey of her own, but she chose to remain with her mother at Wilton. King Edgar died in 975 and was succeeded by Edith's thirteen-year-old half-brother, Edward.[157] He had not ruled long when she dreamed that her right eye fell out. Edith knew it was a warning that Edward was going to die. Soon after her dream, he was murdered. His supporters offered Edith the crown, but she refused. She died peacefully at the age of twenty-four. At that very moment, a nun looked inside the abbey church and saw hosts of angels singing sweetly. "Go away," one said. "The angels await the good maiden."

The Genius of Edith of Wilton:
Edith always dressed magnificently. When the bishop of Winchester chided her about this, she responded: *"The mind may be as modest and God-fearing under fine clothes as under a serge habit. The God I love looks to the heart and not to the dress."*

Reflection:
"Why are you anxious about clothes? Learn from the way the wild flowers grow. They do not work or spin. But I tell you that not even Solomon in all his splendor was clothed like one of them."

Matthew 6:28–29

BLESSED HILDEGARD OF BINGEN

b. 1098, Bermersheim, Germany
d. September 17, 1179, Bingen, Germany

"Heaven was opened and a fiery light of exceeding brilliance came and permeated my whole brain, and inflamed my whole heart and my whole breast not like a burning, but like a warming flame, as the sun warms anything its rays touch." Suddenly, God commanded Hildegard at the age of forty-two: *"Write what you see and hear!"* She could no longer put off going public with the visions she had experienced since childhood.

Hildegard was about seven years old when her parents placed her in the care of Jutta of Spanheim[158] to be educated and consecrated to God. For a long time, only Jutta and the monk Volmar[159] knew about Hildegard's visions. When Jutta died, Hildegard succeeded her as abbess, and Volmar became Hildegard's teacher and confidant. He encouraged her to record the visions in what became the book *Scivias* (The way of wisdom).

Hildegard was actively engaged with the world, denouncing the vices of society. She wrote to the loathsome archbishop of Mainz: *"You have a sort of zeal, trampling down all that oppose thee. But I warn you, cleanse the iniquity from the eye of your soul. . . . Turn to the Lord, for your time is at hand."* The archbishop replied that the people of Mainz "are dogs that bark but bite not." Hildegard warned: *"The dogs are slipped, and will tear you to pieces."* Her prophecy was confirmed when a butcher hacked the archbishop to death with a cleaver.

Hildegard's fame as the Sybil of the Rhine spread and visitors came from afar seeking spiritual comfort, instruction, help, and intercession. She was said to have the gift of healing, and she certainly had a talent for mixing herbal remedies and composing sacred music. Today, there are many editions of her writings, her musical compositions have been recorded, and pilgrims venerate her relics at the parish church in Bingen.

The Genius of Hildegard of Bingen:

Hildegard could write, in the voice of God: *"I am the breeze that nurtures all things green. I encourage blossoms to flourish with ripening fruits. I am the rain coming from the dew that causes the grasses to laugh with the joy of life."*

Reflection:

"Let us praise him the more, since we cannot fathom him, / for greater is he than all his works; / Awful indeed is the LORD*'s majesty, / and wonderful is his power."*

Sirach 43:29–30

September 18

Saint Richardis, Empress

b. c. 840, Alsace, France
d. September 18, 894, Andlau, Alsace, France

Richardis, daughter of the powerful count of Alsace, married Charles the Fat (c. 832–888), who unfortunately inherited very few of the leadership qualities of his great-grandfather Charlemagne. Charles was timid and frail, and only the unexpected deaths of his father, uncle, and two brothers left him king of Italy and emperor of France and Germany.

Charles and Richardis went to Rome in 880 to be crowned emperor and empress by the pope. Soon, though, it became clear that Charles was not up to the task. He failed to beat back the Saracens, or to protect France from the Normans, and he had to pay off the Norsemen to keep them away from Germany. Unable to maintain peace in the empire, Charles began suffering from terrible headaches, which he blamed on demonic possession. He had himself exorcised and even had incisions made in his skull to get rid of the devil. Nothing brought relief. Becoming delusional, he accused Richardis of having an affair with his former friend, a bishop. Richardis demanded to prove her innocence. She was wrapped in linen cloth that had been soaked with flammable liquid, then lit. It burned away, leaving Richardis unharmed, thus exonerating her from the false charge of adultery. Richardis received an ecclesiastic annulment in 887 and returned to Alsace. It was still a wild region where bears outnumbered people. Legend has it that a black she-bear led Richardis to the site where she built her monastery. Traces of the bear's scratches are still visible in the crypt there, and a statue of Richardis with her bear stands in Andlau's town square.

Although childless herself, Richardis is a patron of infertile women. Women visit her crypt at Andlau and sit astride a statue of the black bear while asking Richardis's intercession to become pregnant.

The Genius of Richardis:
Richardis kept her dignity in the face of her husband's false charges. She emerged from her humiliating trial with a strengthened faith.

Reflection:
"Whatever is true, whatever is honorable, whatever is just, whatever is pure, whatever is lovely, whatever is gracious, if there is any excellence and if there is anything worthy of praise, think about these things."

Philippians 4:8

Saint Emilie de Rodat

(Marie Emilie Guillemet de Rodat)

b. September 6, 1787, Château Druelle, Rodez, France
d. September 19, 1852, Villefranche de Rouergue, Aveyron, France

Emilie's pastor called her "a saint, but a headstrong saint." She was only eighteen months old when revolution rocked France and her parents sent her to her grandmother in the village of Villefranche de Rouergue. Emilie's first teacher was an aunt who had been a nun until the Revolutionary government shut down all convents and religious schools. At twelve, Emilie made her First Communion in secret because the sacraments were outlawed. A year later, when religious freedom was restored, Emilie was sent to the Maison Saint-Cyr, where she was taught by the Ursuline nuns.

At sixteen, Emilie reunited with her parents, but she was used to having her own way and soon returned to her grandmother. She began teaching at the Maison Saint-Cyr and hoped to enter their convent, but the sisters did not welcome her innovative ideas. Emilie's pastor helped her enter another convent, and then another, and another. Emilie never lasted anywhere very long, but she remained convinced that she had a vocation. One day, Emilie overheard a mother bemoaning the lack of free schools, and in that moment she recognized that she was called to teach poor children. She started a free school at Maison Saint-Cyr and was soon teaching forty children. Two women joined Emilie, marking the beginning of the Sisters of the Holy Family of Villefranche. By the time that Emilie made her religious vows in 1820, the Saint-Cyr Ursuline community had dissolved and she had acquired its property. She took responsibility for the remaining elderly sisters, initiating her community's commitment to the aged. Emilie expanded this mission to include caring for prisoners, prostitutes, and orphans. Emilie never actively recruited new sisters, saying, *"Religious vocations are brought about by the grace of God, not by any words of ours."* Her congregation, known today as the Sisters of the Holy Family of France, is active in Europe, South America, and Africa.

The Genius of Emilie de Rodat:

Emilie once said: *"I was bored only once in my life and that was when I turned away from God."*

Reflection:

"Where there is no knowledge, there is no wisdom."

Sirach 3:24

September 20

SAINT AGNES KIM HYO-JU

b. 1816, Bamseom, Seoul, South Korea
d. September 3, 1839, Small West Gate, Seoul, South Korea

SAINT COLUMBA KIM HYO-IM

b. 1814, Bamseom, Seoul, South Korea
d. September 26, 1839, Small West Gate, South Korea

Agnes and Columba were beautiful teenagers when they embraced Christianity. They were baptized into Korea's unique Catholic community, which had been founded by laypeople and managed to survive for centuries without priests.

In 1839 the Kim sisters were arrested for the crime of being Christians. The judge ordered them tortured, but guards went too far when they stripped Agnes and Columba and tossed them into the men's prison for two days. The hardened convicts were free to do whatever they wanted with the girls, but they were so in awe that they never touched them. The guards finally took Agnes and Columba back to the women's prison, but their ordeal was not over. The Kim sisters were put to the rack five times and beaten with sticks, yet they remained serene. The judge blamed their calm on witchcraft and had some symbols cut into their backs to dispel the charm. He then ordered each girl stabbed thirteen times with a red-hot awl. More terrible torture followed. From time to time the judge would interrupt and try a little tenderness, but threats, torture, and flattery left the Kim sisters equally unmoved. Agnes was finally taken outside the Small West Gate and beheaded. Korean law forbade the simultaneous execution of close relations, so Columba was not beheaded until three weeks later. The sisters are commemorated with the 103 Korean Martyrs.[160]

The Genius of Agnes and Columba Kim:

While awaiting execution, Columba vigorously protested the men's prison incident, saying: *"You can kill us, but you have no legal right to do that kind of thing to us."* The chief judge was forced to punish the guards involved. More important, Columba and Agnes helped to bring religious freedom to Korea through their sacrifice. Today there are more than four million Catholics in South Korea, making up almost 10 percent of the population.

Reflection:

"Even if you should suffer because of righteousness, blessed are you. Do not be afraid or terrified with fear of them, but sanctify Christ as Lord in your hearts."
1 Peter 3:14–15

September 21

BLESSED LUCY DE FREITAS

b. c. 1542, Japan
d. September 10, 1622, Nagasaki, Japan

A native Japanese and the widow of a Portuguese sailor, Lucy grew up in an era in which there were 200,000 Christians in Japan. This tolerance ended in 1588 when the emperor declared himself divine and expelled Catholic priests from Japan under penalty of death. Many of them stayed on anyway, protected by people like Lucy. Mass martyrdoms began in 1597 and continued on and off throughout Lucy's life, yet she and thousands of other Japanese remained faithful Christians.

Lucy became a fierce defender of the faith. She was called the Mother of the Friars because she sheltered so many Franciscan priests. She nursed the ailing Richard of Saint Anne[161] and was arrested with him and condemned to death. Most lay Christians were beheaded, but incorrigible offenders like Lucy were sentenced to die with the priests, tied to a stake on a slow fire. On the day of her execution, eighty-year-old Lucy held her crucifix high and led thirty-three priests, including Charles Spinola and Richard of Saint Anne, in a triumphal march, singing hymns and psalms. She spoke like a great preacher, irritating their guards so much that they snatched her crucifix and broke it into pieces. Lucy died praying for her persecutors and shouting, *"Let women show a courage that will confound the pagans!"* Lucy de Freitas is commemorated by the Franciscans on September 10, with the Blessed Martyrs of Japan on February 5, and with the 205 heroes of the Great Martyrdom of Nagasaki (1617–32) on September 12.

The Genius of Lucy de Freitas:

Lucy urged the other women to remember such early martyrs as Agatha (February 5), Cecilia (November 22), and Agnes (January 21) and said: *"God, who strengthened them, will support us also. We women will be as strong as men."*

Reflection:

"The Lamb who is in the center of the throne will shepherd them / and lead them to springs of life-giving water, / and God will wipe away every tear from their eyes."

Revelation 7:17

BLESSED AMPARO CARBONELL
(María de los Desamparados Carbonell Muñoz)

b. *November 9, 1893, Alboraya, Valencia, Spain*
d. *September 6, 1936, Barcelona, Spain*

BLESSED CARMEN MORENO
(María del Carmen Moreno Benítez)

b. *August 24, 1885, Villamartín, Cádiz, Spain*
d. *September 6, 1936, Barcelona, Spain*

In the summer of 1936, thousands of Spanish priests and religious were murdered, but many others were successfully evacuated. By August, among those waiting to leave were sixty-seven Daughters of Mary (Salesian Sisters) from Barcelona.

Their leader, Sister Felisa, asked for a volunteer to stay with Sister Carmela, who had just undergone cancer surgery. She got two: Amparo Carbonell, the community gardener, and Carmen Morena, the recently appointed vicar of their boarding school in nearby Sarrià. It would be difficult to imagine a less likely pair.

On August 7, the stolid Amparo and the urbane Carmen watched the evacuation ship leave Barcelona. True to their word, they took Sister Carmela to a safe house to lie low until the evacuation ship returned. They were well aware they would be closely monitored by the anti-Christian Red militia.

The evacuation ship arrived on September 1, but before Carmen and Amparo could arrange the proper documents, the militia arrested all three Sisters and hauled them before the Committee for Security. Sister Carmela was obviously dying and was released.

Carmen and Amparo were not heard from until September 6, when their battered corpses were brought to a hospital morgue. Both Carmen and Amparo had been beaten, then shot to death. They were beatified in 2001 with the Martyrs of the Spanish Civil War.[162]

The Genius of Amparo Carbonell and Carmen Moreno:
The sophisticated educator and the illiterate gardener were united by a spirit of charity and heroic sacrifice.

Reflection:
*"*LORD*, protect us always; / preserve us from this generation.*
On every side the wicked strut; / the shameless are extolled by all."
Psalm 12:8–9

BLESSED HELEN OF BOLOGNA

(Elena Duglioli dall'Oglio)

b. 1472, Bologna, Italy
d. September 23, 1520, Bologna, Italy

There is a legend that Helen was the daughter of a Turkish pasha, born in Constantinople and carried off to Bologna by angels on the day she was born. This fantastic tale has been traced to Peter de Lucca, a priest who knew and admired Helen. De Lucca worked hard for Helen's canonization, but the *Life* he wrote was so full of fantastic claims that it helped delay her beatification for more than three hundred years. This was unfortunate, because Helen was a truly noble woman whose good works live on in Bologna.

There is no doubt that Helen was the daughter of prominent local parents. They arranged her marriage at seventeen to forty-year-old Benedict dall'Oglio. She remained childless, and Peter de Lucca claimed that the marriage was celibate. Others are doubtful. What stands out is that in spite of the age difference, Helen's thirty-year marriage was "uncommonly harmonious, peaceful and happy." Among her gifts to the city of Bologna, Helen commissioned Raphael's *Saint Cecilia in Ecstasy* and worked closely with the artist on the concept and execution. For many years, the painting, depicting Cecilia of Rome (November 22), served as an altarpiece in Helen's chapel in the church of San Giovanni in Monte. It can now be seen in Bologna's art museum. Helen also founded an organization to discreetly help the "shamefaced poor," those too proud, or ashamed, to admit that they were in need. It is still active today. Helen outlived her husband by only a few years. She was entombed in her chapel, which is always brilliantly lit by votive candles and draped with mementos left by grateful pilgrims.

The Genius of Helen of Bologna:

Peter de Lucca concluded that Helen was born elsewhere because he misunderstood her frequent remark: *"I'm not an inhabitant but a pilgrim. This is not my country. These are not my family."* Surely Helen was referring to her home and family in heaven.

Reflection:

"When one finds a worthy wife, / her value is far beyond pearls. . . . / Give her a reward of her labors, / and let her works praise her at the city gates."
Proverbs 31:10, 31

BLESSED EMILIE TAVERNIER GAMELIN

b. February 19, 1800, Montreal, Quebec, Canada
d. September 23, 1851, Montreal, Quebec, Canada

Emilie sought solace for the loss of her husband and three infant sons in a devotion to Our Lady of Sorrows and in active charity. In 1830 she turned her home into a refuge for the destitute elderly, new immigrants, and children. Other women joined Emilie's work and she opened a second refuge. A benefactor donated a large building known as the Yellow House and Emilie dedicated the ground floor for use as a school. The value of Emilie's many accomplishments eluded the bishop of Montreal. He chose to invite the Daughters of Charity to take over the work that she had begun. They did not remain very long, however, and so, again ignoring Emilie, the bishop founded a new religious congregation. He set up their novitiate in Emilie's Yellow House but refused to admit her as a novice. The decree recognizing Emilie's heroic virtue praised her behavior during this difficult time when, a "stranger under her own roof, she was divested of all authority and even treated as an inferior." When one of the novices left, the bishop finally acknowledged that Emilie was called by God. She made her religious vows with the other six women, and the next day they elected her the first superior of the congregation known today as the Sisters of Providence.

Emilie's charity was all embracing. She invited some of her Sisters to learn sign language from Father Trépanier, a priest who taught catechism to the deaf. This led to cofounding the Institute for Deaf Mute Girls of Montreal (now part of the Raymond-Dewar Institute) and the Sisters of Our Lady of Seven Dolors, who are dedicated to the deaf. Today both orders are at work on five continents. They commemorate Emilie Gamelin on September 23.

The Genius of Emilie Gamelin:
    Rather than dwell on her tragic losses, Emilie applied her phenomenal management ability to helping others. Her last words were *"Humility, simplicity, charity. Above all, charity."*

Reflection:
    "She picks out a field to purchase; / out of her earnings she plants a vineyard."
    Proverbs 31:16 (featured on the Sisters of Providence website)

BLESSED BERNARDINA
MARIA JABLONSKA

b. June 13, 1878, Pizuny, Poland
d. September 23, 1940, Kraków, Poland

It is impossible to tell Bernardina's story without including her spiritual director, Albert Chmielowski,[163] a charismatic figure with a total commitment to the poor.

After the death of her mother when she was fifteen, Bernardina began considering a religious vocation. Three years later, she met Brother Albert and felt called to follow him. A man of nobility, character, and courage, Albert had lost a leg at eighteen while fighting in a Polish insurrection against the Russians. At thirty-five he abandoned a successful career as a painter to dedicate himself to the poor and homeless of Kraków. He organized his many followers into the Franciscan communities known as the Albertine Brothers and Albertine Sisters and encouraged them all to *"Be like the nourishing bread that's ready on the table for all who may be hungry."* Bernardina defied her overly protective father to run away and join the Albertines. She had never confronted true urban poverty before, however, and faced with reality, she suffered many doubts. Brother Albert enabled her to overcome them. He recognized her great gifts and in 1902 named twenty-four-year-old Bernardina the superior general of the Albertine Sisters. She remained superior until her death, thirty-eight years later. During World War II, the Albertine Sisters were among the Polish convents that sheltered Jewish women and children at great risk to themselves. Bernardina insisted: *"My neighbor's suffering is my suffering."* She is commemorated in Kraków and by the Albertines on September 23.

The Genius of Bernardina Maria Jablonska:
> In his beatification homily, John Paul II praised Bernardina as an example of the feminine genius that showed itself in her sensitivity to human suffering, her willingness to help others, and the nurturing qualities that are sometimes undervalued.

Reflection:
> *"Above all, let your love for one another be intense, because love covers a multitude of sins. Be hospitable to one another without complaining."*
>
> 1 Peter 4:8–9

September 26

SAINT THÉRÈSE COUDERC
(Marie Victoire Couderc)

b. February 1, 1805, Sablières, Ardeche, France
d. September 26, 1885, Fourvières, Lyon, France

Marie Victoire was twenty years old when she attended a mission (revival meeting) preached by a zealous young priest, Stephen Terme. At his invitation, she joined a new congregation dedicated to education. She took the religious name Thérèse, but instead of teaching, she was sent with two other sisters to the mountain village of La Louvesc where Father Terme oversaw the shrine of John Francis Regis.[164] Thérèse and her companions were supposed to manage a hostel for women pilgrims, but under her leadership, it developed into a retreat house where women could stay a few days and work on their spiritual life. In time, her congregation was divided into a teaching ministry (the Sisters of St Regis) and the retreat congregation known as the Sisters of Our Lady of the Cenacle.[165] At twenty-three Thérèse became the superior general of the retreat congregation.

Before Father Terme died in 1834, he confided care of the Cenacle community to the Jesuits. In their wisdom, the Jesuits demoted Thérèse and replaced her with a series of wealthy, well-connected women, each one more disastrous than the last. The Cenacle survived, however, and Thérèse continued to play an important if unacknowledged role behind the scenes. During the last twenty-five years of her life, she was granted many mystical graces and a revelation on the meaning of complete self-surrender to God. This became the keynote to her spirituality, and she wrote: *"The surrendered soul has found Paradise on earth."*

Today the Sisters of the Cenacle continue to lead retreats all over the world.

The Genius of Thérèse Couderc:
Removed from leadership, Thérèse said only: *"Great trials make great souls and fit them for the great things that God wishes to do through them."*

Reflection:
"Have among yourselves the same attitude that is also yours in Christ Jesus, / . . . he humbled himself, / becoming obedient to death, / even death on a cross."

Philippians 2:5, 8

BLESSED MARÍA DE LA CABEZA

(María Toribia)

b. c. 1080, Carraquiz, Spain
d. c. 1175, Madrid, Spain

María spent most of her life working beside her husband, Isidro,[166] as a tenant farmer on the vast estates of Juan de Vargas in Torrelaguna. Almost every morning before dawn, María crossed the Jamara River to pray in the chapel of Our Lady of Mercy near Carraquiz. María kept votive candles lit in front of a painting of Nuestra Señora de la Cabeza Coranado, which portrays the Blessed Mother and Christ's Crown of Thorns. Her devotion to the painting earned her the name María de la Cabeza.

María and Isidro lost their only son in childhood. As a childless couple working together, they were extremely close. This aroused jealousy and suspicion in the other laborers, who assured Isidro that his wife was slipping off to meet a shepherd. Isidro never questioned María's virtue, but the endless teasing finally forced him to provide his friends with proof. They hid themselves by the river. As dawn approached, the river swelled, and by the time María arrived at the bank, the water looked impassable. Unaware that she was being watched, María made the sign of the cross, removed her shawl, spread it on the water, and stepped on it. The men watched as María was miraculously carried across the river and then proceeded to the chapel. Clearly, the only Shepherd she was meeting was Christ.

Some legends claim that María got her name because her head (Spanish, *cabeza*) was conserved in a reliquary at the chapel while the rest of her relics were held in Torrelaguna. They were later reunited and moved to the cathedral in Madrid, where they rest near Isidro's tomb. María is celebrated in Spain on September 9.

The Genius of María de la Cabeza:

María and Isidro set an example of fidelity, affection, and support for each other in good times and bad.

Reflection:

"Raising his eyes toward his disciples he said: / 'Blessed are you who are poor, / for the kingdom of God is yours.'"

Luke 6:20

September 28

SAINT LIOBA OF BISCHOFFSHEIM

b. 710, Wessex, England
d. September 28, 782, Schornsheim, Germany

Lioba's parents had been childless for years when her mother dreamed she gave birth to a church bell that rang when she held it. A nurse told her that it meant she would bear a daughter, whom she must give to God just as Hannah had consecrated the infant Samuel to serve God in the temple.

When Lioba was born, her parents entrusted her to Tetta,[167] abbess of Wimborne, and Lioba later took the veil there. One night, Lioba dreamed that she pulled a purple thread from her mouth, but the more she pulled the more there was, until thread filled her hand. She wound it into a ball, but more thread kept coming until she woke up. An elderly nun explained that the purple thread signified the wise counsels Lioba would speak from her heart. It filled her hand because Lioba's words would become actions. And it formed a ball because her words and actions would affect far-off lands. This prophecy was fulfilled when Boniface,[168] the great missionary, asked Tetta to send nuns to the northern frontier of Europe. Tetta dispatched a group that included Lioba and Walburga (February 25). Boniface assigned Lioba to a large monastery at Bischoffsheim where she instructed new nuns in the Benedictine Rule, then dispatched them to convents throughout Germany. After Boniface was martyred, Lioba often prayed at his tomb in the abbey at Fulda. She was the only woman the monks allowed to enter their church, and they later buried her on the high altar.

The Genius of Lioba:

A contemporary wrote: "Lioba was always careful not to try to teach others anything she did not follow herself. Her speech was pleasing, her spirit bright, and her energy great. Her faith was all-powerful, her hope was full of great patience and her love was directed to her neighbor."

Reflection:

"He will guard the footsteps of his faithful ones, / but the wicked shall perish in the darkness. / For not by strength does man prevail."

1 Samuel 2:9

SAINT ANNA WANG

b. 1886, Majiazhuang, Weixian, Hebei Province, China
d. July 23, 1900, Majiazhuang, Weixian, Hebei Province, China

In the summer of 1900, the Boxers rampaged through China destroying anything they deemed "European." They slaughtered more than twenty-five thousand Christians: Catholics and Protestants, foreign missionaries and native Chinese. At the height of the riots, the governor of Hebei Province proclaimed, "Christians, hear and tremble! Give up this perverse religion!... The Boxers will not hurt persons. It is this religion they hate."

Anna Wang, a fourteen-year-old catechism teacher, heard his message, but her family had been Catholics for three generations and she was prepared to die as one. On July 21, Anna was arrested with a small group that included her widowed stepmother and locked up in the village hall overnight. In the morning, they were informed that they could walk down the hall, formally renounce Christianity, and be released. Anna's stepmother rose to leave, but Anna refused to go. Her stepmother tried to drag Anna out, but the girl clung to the door. Finally, the stepmother left without her. That night, Anna led her companions in prayers while the Boxers lit a few of the candles they had taken from a church. *"Look how beautiful these flames are,"* said Anna. *"But the glory of heaven is a million times more glorious than these beautiful flames."* The next morning, the Boxers marched them to their execution. Anna was the last, and they repeatedly hit her with their rifles. Song, the Boxer leader, begged Anna to renounce her faith, but she refused. The executioner raised his sword and hacked at her shoulder. She still refused and he severed her arm. Anna cried out, *"The door of heaven is open to all,"* repeated the name of Jesus three times, and laid her head on the block.

She is commemorated on September 28 with the 120 Martyrs of China.

The Genius of Anna Wang:

In the great tradition of girl martyrs from Agnes (January 21) to Maria Goretti (July 6), Anna Wang presents a model of spiritual courage.

Reflection:

"So Jesus said again, 'Amen, amen, I say to you, I am the gate for the sheep. . . . I am the gate. Whoever enters through me will be saved.'"

John 10:7, 9

SAINT MARINA OF OMURA

b. c. 1609, Japan
d. November 11, 1634, Nagasaki, Japan

When the Japanese government resumed persecuting Christians, Marina and her father turned their home into a refuge for the missionaries. She became a Dominican tertiary, consecrating herself to Christ.

When Marina was arrested, her jailers did not understand how a such a beautiful young girl could have made a vow of chastity. They shaved Marina's head and marched her barefoot through the province as if she were a whore or adulteress. This humiliation and loss of face could not break her. Marina's courage strengthened her companions and impressed even those who despised Christianity. Her walk of shame was marked by at least one miracle. According to the Dominican historian Mary Jean Dorcy, Marina was very thirsty and asked one of her guards to look for a stream nearby. He refused because it was obvious that there was no water for miles. Marina insisted that he should look, and he found a spring exactly where she told him. Christians believed that the stream had been placed there to comfort her. By the time Marina completed her procession, she had become a local heroine. Anxious to get rid of her, the magistrate ordered her execution. Marina and two priests were tied to stakes and surrounded with wood that slowly burned them to death. Debris from the fire filled the air of Nagasaki, and many of her admirers captured bits of ash to treasure as relics. To prevent just this sort of thing, the government had the rest of Marina's ashes thrown into the sea.

Marina is commemorated on September 28 with the sixteen other martyrs of Nagasaki.

The Genius of Marina of Omura:

> When missionaries were allowed to return to Japan in 1858, they were surprised to find twenty thousand Christians who had been practicing their faith in secret for more than two hundred years. These "secret Christians" had been strengthened by the example of Marina and her companions. She is still venerated by Christian women of Japan as an example of spiritual courage.

Reflection:

> *"These are the ones who have survived the time of great distress; they have washed their robes and made them white in the blood of the Lamb."*
> Revelation 7:14

SAINT THÉRÈSE OF LISIEUX

(Thérèse of the Child Jesus, Marie Thérèse, Thérèse Martin)

b. January 2, 1873, Alençon, France
d. September 30, 1897, Lisieux, France

"She flings herself into the most dreadful rages when things don't go as she wants them," wrote Zelie Martin[169] about her daughter Thérèse. When this little handful declared, *"I want to be a saint,"* nothing on earth could stop her.

Zelie died when Thérèse was five years old, after which she was coddled by her father and four older sisters. She yearned to follow two of her sisters into the Carmelite Order and at fourteen she managed to get her father's consent, but the Carmelite superior general insisted that she wait until she was twenty-one. He agreed to yield if the bishop overruled him, so on October 31, 1887, Thérèse and her father traveled to Bayeaux to present her case. She put her hair up for the first time, in an effort to look more mature. The bishop tried to dissuade Thérèse and seemed surprised when her father took her side, but Louis Martin knew his daughter better than anyone else. He respectfully informed the bishop that they were planning to join a diocesan pilgrimage to Rome and that Thérèse would not hesitate to ask the pope himself for permission. The bishop promised to consult with the superior general and to give Thérèse his decision while she was in Italy. Three days later, Thérèse and her sister Celine left for Rome with their father, visiting many shrines along the way.

On November 20, 1887, the pilgrims had an audience with Pope Leo XIII. Papal etiquette forbade anyone to address him unless first spoken to. One by one, the pilgrims were led to the Holy Father and allowed to kneel, kiss his ring, his feet, and then respectfully move on. Thérèse could not contain herself. She seized her moment to ask the pope for permission to enter Carmel. He made no commitment, and Thérèse continued her pilgrimage, returning to France in time for Christmas. The good news arrived on the eve of her fifteenth birthday: she would be admitted to Carmel at Easter.

On entering she took the name Thérèse of the Child Jesus and the Holy Face. She showed little promise as a novice. She knew nothing about even the simplest housekeeping chores and fell asleep during the hour-long meditations. The prioress called her "a disgrace" in front of the entire community. The novice-mistress was equally unsympathetic, even after Thérèse contracted tuberculosis and her health began to fail. Thérèse trusted everything to God, saying: *"Once I understood how impossible it was for me to do anything by myself, my task no longer seemed difficult."* By the time Thérèse turned twenty-two, her spirituality had matured so richly that she became the novice-mistress herself.

When her sister Pauline was elected prioress, she asked Thérèse to write an account of her childhood. Neither of them knew that Thérèse had less than three years to live. She spent that time completing her account, in the evenings when she had finished her work and prayers. After Thérèse's death, her writings were collected under the title *The Story of a Soul*. The book was published in September 1898 in an edition of two thousand copies and has sold steadily ever since. Today there are millions of copies in print and it has been translated into thirty-eight languages.

Thérèse was canonized less than thirty years after her death. In 1997 she became the third woman honored as a Doctor of the Church.[170] She is a patron of aviators and foreign missions.

Thérèse is usually shown holding a bouquet of red roses that recalls her promise: "*After my death, I will let fall a shower of roses. I will spend my heaven doing good upon earth. I will raise up a mighty host of little saints. My mission is to make God loved.*" Her roses appear in the countless favors that she continues to bestow on those who pray for her intercession.

The Genius of Thérèse of Lisieux:

Thérèse wrote: "*Perfection consists in doing His will, in being what He wills us to be.*" She called this the Little Way, through which any of us can become holy by doing the most ordinary tasks out of love for God and neighbor. Thérèse prayed: "*Jesus, help me to simplify my life by learning what you want me to be and becoming that person.*"

Reflection:

"*He called a child over, placed it in their midst, and said, 'Amen, I say to you, unless you turn and become like children, you will not enter the kingdom of heaven. Whoever humbles himself like this child is the greatest in the kingdom of heaven.'*"

Matthew 18:2–4

October 2

❦

SAINT FLORA OF BEAULIEU
(Fleur)

b. c. 1300, Maurs, Saint-Flour, France
d. c. October 5, 1347, Beaulieu, Quercy, France

Flora's confessor believed that she never in her life committed a mortal sin, yet she suffered from endless sexual temptations. The daughter of the Lord of Pons, she was fourteen when she joined the Hospitallers of St John of Jerusalem. As a contemplative nun, she spent her days praying, especially for the patients and staff of the order's large hospital at Beaulieu.

The devil tried to seduce Flora and when flattery failed, he used satanic logic: If she did not "agree to delight in the flesh and lose your chastity," he would make her life so miserable that she would give up all hope of salvation. Despair was the greatest sin, and since there was no forgiveness for it in this world or the next, the devil reasoned, it would be far better for Flora to get the carnal sin over with, then confess and do penance. Of course, Flora rejected this argument, and the more the devil taunted her, the more she prayed. The other nuns regarded her as insane or foolish, but Flora reminded herself that her misery was nothing compared to what Jesus suffered for sinners like her. In time, Flora was blessed with many mystical gifts. An angel gave her a symbolic sword to drive the devil away from her heart. This sword also gave Flora the power to help others, and it was said that no one approached her without receiving relief. Flora died in the odor of sanctity, surrounded by the fragrance of roses and lilies. It was also noted around her tomb, which became the site of many miracles. Her convent and hospital were destroyed during the Revolution, but her relics were saved and are venerated at Issendolus. Flora is a patron of abandoned women and victims of betrayal. Her traditional feast day is October 5.

The Genius of Flora of Beaulieu:
Flora fought off the devil by telling him, "*God without whom you can do nothing, orders you to stop testing me.*"

Reflection:
"*Everything created by God is good, and nothing is to be rejected when received with thanksgiving, for it is made holy by the invocation of God in prayer.*"
1 Timothy 4:4–5

SAINT THEODORE GUÉRIN

(Anne-Thérèse Guérin)

b. October 2, 1798, Etables-sur-Mer, Brittany, France
d. March 14, 1856, St Mary-of-the-Woods, Indiana

Mother Theodore always advised, "*Put yourself gently into the hands of Providence*," and she practiced this advice throughout her life.

Baptized Anne-Thérèse, she was twenty-five when she entered a new congregation, the Sisters of Providence of Ruille, becoming Sister Theodore and working to rebuild an educational system that had been destroyed by the French Revolution. Honored by the Académie Française for her work, Theodore might have gone on to a brilliant career in education, but she was called instead to the American frontier.

In 1840 Theodore led five Sisters of Providence to the Indiana Territory, to start a school and convent. After a stormy two-month voyage, they arrived in New York expecting to be met by the bishop of Vincennes. But he was not there, nor was anyone else. Fortunately, providence provided strangers and local clergy who enabled Theodore and her Sisters to make their way to Indiana by train, steamboat, and wagon. On arriving, they had expected to settle in Vincennes. Instead, they were taken by wagon to a forest near Terre Haute where four eager American postulants were waiting in a small frame farmhouse that became the Sisters' first motherhouse. Theodore and her Sisters soon built a log chapel, and a year later they opened St Mary-of-the-Woods Academy, which is now the oldest Roman Catholic college for women in the United States.

Theodore survived terrible winters and a fire that destroyed an entire harvest. At the same time, she struggled to master a new language and culture, and in 1843 she negotiated independence from the French congregation to form the Sisters of Providence of St Mary-of-the-Woods. This required her to return to France for almost a year. Theodore remained in touch with Indiana by letters, and she was well aware that the bishop was meddling in convent business without consulting with the Sisters.

The struggle continued after her return, coming to a head at the sixth Provincial Council in Baltimore in May 1846. In front of an archbishop and twenty-one fellow bishops, her antagonist denounced Theodore and called for her expulsion and excommunication. He also offered his resignation. He returned to Vincennes and informed Theodore that he was removing her as superior. He released her from her vows, dismissed her from her congregation, and ordered her to leave his diocese. Fortunately, word arrived that the Vatican had accepted the bishop's resignation and that his replacement was on his way. Her nemesis returned to France for good, and Theodore never had any problems with the new bishop or with his successor.

Today the Sisters of Providence of St Mary-of-the-Woods are active in more than twenty states as well as in Taiwan and the Philippines.

The Genius of Theodore Guérin:

As a leader and educator, Theodore recommended: *"We must possess all the virtues before we attempt to teach them to others."*

Reflection:

"Remain faithful to what you have learned and believed, because you know from whom you learned it, and that from infancy you have known [the] sacred scriptures, which are capable of giving you wisdom for salvation through faith in Christ Jesus."

2 Timothy 3:14–15

BLESSED ANNA SCHÄFFER

b. February 18, 1882, Mindelstetten, Bavaria, Germany
d. October 5, 1925, Mindelstetten, Bavaria, Germany

Anna dreamed of becoming a missionary in far-off lands. She went to work in the city to earn money for a dowry, but after the death of her father she returned to the family farm to help with her five younger siblings. She fully expected to become a missionary once they were on their own. She took a job in a local laundry, and then everything changed.

In 1901, while at work, Anna fell into a vat of boiling lye, badly scalding both legs. After a year in the hospital and more than thirty operations, she was sent home as an invalid. Her missionary dream was now out of the question. She rarely left her small upstairs room. In agony at first, Anna came to accept her suffering as God's will. She became a daily communicant and prayed to God to accept her as *"a little victim of reparation."* Soon she and her mother moved to a small house in a nearby village, where Anna supported herself and her mother by sewing, welcomed visitors, wrote her thoughts in twelve notebooks, and maintained an extensive correspondence. She wrote, *"I have three keys to Heaven. The biggest is made out of iron and is heavy—it is my suffering. The second is the sewing needle and the third is the penholder. With these different keys, I strive each day to open the door to Heaven."*

Children loved Anna, and the local brass band would play outside her window for her pleasure. On October 4, 1910, the feast of Francis of Assisi, she first manifested the stigmata. In order to avoid any sensationalism, she asked the Lord to remove the visible signs. After that, Anna only experienced the pain of the wounds. She is commemorated by the Franciscans on October 5.

The Genius of Anna Schäffer:
Anna struggled with chronic pain, but finally found many occasions for grace.

Reflection:
"We even boast of our afflictions, knowing that affliction produces endurance, and endurance, proven character, and proven character, hope, and hope does not disappoint, because the love of God has been poured out into our hearts through the holy Spirit that has been given to us."

Romans 5:3–5

Saint Faustina Kowalska

(Elena Kowalska)

b. August 25, 1905, Glogowiec, Poland
d. October 5, 1938, Cracovia, Poland

"Humanity will not find peace until it turns trustfully to Divine Mercy." This was the message that Jesus gave Faustina Kowalska, the obscure young nun He chose to introduce Divine Mercy.

The daughter of a working-class family, baptized Elena, she entered the Sisters of Our Lady of Mercy in 1925, taking the name Maria Faustina. On February 22, 1931, Faustina experienced a vision of Jesus in which He instructed her to produce his image as she saw Him. Working with a painter, Faustina produced the now-familiar portrait of the Merciful Jesus, with two beams of light radiating from his heart.

He further charged Faustina with three tasks: First, remind the world of God's merciful love for every human being. Second, spread devotion to the Divine Mercy through veneration of the image; instituting a feast of the Divine Mercy; reciting the chaplet[171] of the Divine Mercy; and praying at the Hour of Mercy (3:00 P.M.). And third, proclaim and entreat God's mercy for the world and an attitude of mercy toward one's neighbor.

In the summer of 1934, at the request of her confessor, Faustina began keeping a diary. This was a daunting prospect for a girl with less than three years of schooling, but she had no choice. *"It is my will,"* Jesus told her, *"that you should write. You do not live for yourself but for others' souls. Write so that they might learn to love me. Write of my mercy."*

Faustina recorded all the Lord's instructions and described the encounters between her soul and God.

Today Faustina's diary, published under the title *Divine Mercy in My Soul*, is ranked as a spiritual classic alongside the works of Teresa of Avila (October 15) and Thérèse of Lisieux (October 1).

The Genius of Faustina Kowalska:
Faustina wrote in her diary: *"Neither graces, nor revelations, nor raptures, nor gifts granted to a soul make it perfect. . . . My sanctity and perfection consist in the close union of my will with the will of God."*

Reflection:
"You won renown for your wondrous deeds; / gracious and merciful is the LORD.*"*

Psalm 111:4

October 6

SAINT MARY FRANCES OF THE FIVE WOUNDS

(Anna Maria Rosa Gallo)

b. March 25, 1715, Naples, Italy
d. October 6, 1791, Naples, Italy

Barbara Gallo was a nervous expectant mother when she consulted two priests, a Franciscan and a Jesuit. Each assured her that she would have a daughter who would become a saint. Her baby was born on the feast of the Annunciation and christened Anna Maria Rosa. She grew up to be one of the most thoroughly documented stigmatists in history.

Anna Maria's father, Francesco, manufactured gold lace and forced everyone in the household to produce it. From Anna Maria's early childhood, her guardian angel did her share of the work so that she could pray and still produce more lace than anyone else in the shop. Francesco's volcanic temper erupted when Anna Maria refused the marriage he had arranged. He beat her and locked her in her room, but finally allowed her to become a Franciscan tertiary. She took the name Mary Frances of the Five Wounds and consecrated herself to God.

On Fridays, especially during Lent, Mary Frances began to experience all the pains of Christ's Passion. At times her hands were completely perforated with the stigmata. Doctors and clergy could find no scientific explanation for the wounds. One priest testified: "I have seen them, I have touched them, and to tell the truth, I, as the apostle Saint Thomas did, have put my finger into the wounds of her hands and I have seen that the hole extended right through." He performed this test many times over the years, and the result was always the same.

In 1867 Mary Frances became Naples's first canonized saint. During World War II, when Naples was bombed more than one hundred times, the residents of her old neighborhood, the Spanish Quarter, credited her with sparing them from destruction.

The Genius of Mary Frances of the Five Wounds:
Strengthened by a lifelong devotion to the Blessed Mother, Mary Frances advised: *"Pray to her constantly, and you will have every grace you desire."*

Reflection:
"To each individual the manifestation of the Spirit is given for some benefit."
1 Corinthians 12:7

October 7

OUR LADY OF THE ROSARY
(Our Lady of Victory)

October 7 commemorates the Blessed Mother's intercession in one of the most decisive battles in Christian history, when the Rosary saved the Christian world.

When Mary revealed the Rosary to Saint Dominic,[172] she promised her protection to those who prayed it regularly. The Rosary was not truly appreciated as a spiritual weapon, however, until 1571, when Suleiman the Magnificent controlled the Mediterranean, the Red Sea, and the Persian Gulf and was well on his way to making Europe an Islamic state. As author and theologian Michael Novak has written, "Muslim fleets were raiding Christian cities with ever more daring, carrying off men as prisoners for their galley slaves and boys and girls for their harems, burning churches and looting treasuries. There was no unified Christian fleet to oppose them. All Italy was in danger of occupation."

Pope Pius V[173] urged Catholics to pray the Rosary and entreat Mary to protect Catholic lands. He managed to get Spain, Venice, and various Italian states to stop squabbling long enough to unite against the Ottoman menace, and he placed this Holy League under Mary's protection. Led by Don John of Austria (1547–1578), League ships met in the Bay of Lepanto off the west coast of Greece. On the morning of October 7, 1571, the Christian soldiers knelt before a crucifix and prayed the Rosary. Although they were vastly outnumbered—30,000 Christians to 75,000 Turks—the Holy League emerged victorious and credited Mary, Queen of the Rosary. Pius V declared the anniversary of the battle the feast of Our Lady of Victory. Since 1960 it has been known as the feast of Our Lady of the Rosary.

The Genius of Our Lady of the Rosary:
Michael Novak considers Lepanto " a story of wit and courage and victory against all odds." As always, Mary heard the prayers of the faithful and interceded to assure success.

Reflection:
"Rejoice always. Pray without ceasing. In all circumstances give thanks, for this is the will of God for you in Christ Jesus."

1 Thessalonians 5:16–18

October 8

SAINT PELAGIA THE PENITENT

d. c. 457, Mount Olivet, Jerusalem

Pelagia was an actress and dancer living in splendor at Antioch. She was at the height of her career when she encountered Nonnus, bishop of Heliopolis.[174] The elderly bishop was relaxing on the steps of a church when Pelagia passed by, wrapped in cloth of gold, draped in pearls, surrounded by slaves dressed as fabulously as she, and filling the street with the sound of bells and the scent of perfume. The priests with Nonnus looked away, but he reminded them: *"God will receive even such a one as this. At the last day he will set that woman before his face and compare her with us, his servants, and the comparison will turn to our condemnation. She dresses and paints herself again and again, she leaves no part of her task undone, she forgets no jewel, no pin; she spares no labor that she may serve her masters. But we—do we take half as much trouble to serve our Master?"*

The next day Pelagia wrote a note begging Nonnus to see her. When finally admitted, she asked to be baptized. Wary of an instant conversion, he sent Pelagia to the deaconess Romana for instruction. Pelagia soon freed all her slaves, allowing them to keep their gold collars. She was baptized with Romana as her godmother. After a pilgrimage to Jerusalem she retired to a cave on Mount Olivet, where she spent the rest of her life in prayer and penitence.

The Genius of Pelagia the Penitent:

Pelagia wrote to Nonnus: *"I have heard that your God has bowed the heavens and come down to earth, not to save the righteous but sinners. Such was his humility that he ate with publicans, lived among sinners and spoke with harlots. Therefore, my lord, since you are a true servant of Christ, do not spurn me who seeks to draw near the savior of the world and to behold his most holy countenance."*

Reflection:

"Remember your compassion and love, O LORD; / for they are ages old. Remember no more the sins of my youth; / remember me only in light of your love."

Psalm 25:6–7

SAINT KEYNE OF WALES
(Cain, Ceinwen)
d. October 8, 505, Wales

Cornwall has many historic wells, but none more famous than Keyne's well near Liskeard. According to legend, the water there has a unique effect on newlyweds: whoever drinks from it first will always have the upper hand in the marriage.

Keyne herself never married. One of at least twenty-four children of Brychan of Brecknock, she was a sister to Dwynwen (January 25) and Gladys (March 29). Legend has it that when her mother was expecting Keyne, rays of light shot from her breasts and she dreamed that she was nursing a dove. As a child Keyne sometimes shone like the sun. As a young woman she rejected many suitors and left Wales seeking a quiet retreat. On reaching Somerset, England, she wanted to settle in the forest, but the woods swarmed with snakes. She prayed to God who changed the snakes into stones. The town of Keynsham grew up around her retreat, and unique stones shaped like coiled serpents are still found there. After many years at Keynsham, she made a pilgrimage to Cornwall and stopped at Liskeard, where she found the source for her now-famous well. Keyne was visiting a shrine at St Michael's Mount when she ran into her nephew Cadoc,[175] who convinced her to return to Wales. Settling at Abergavenny, Keyne brought forth another miraculous spring. As she neared the end of her life, a pillar of fire appeared over her cell and two angels arrived to assist her. They removed Keyne's coarse shift and dressed her in a cloak of scarlet shot with gold, saying, *"Come with us, and we will introduce you to the kingdom of your Father."* Cadoc administered the last rites and buried her. Keyne's feast day is October 8.

The Genius of Keyne of Wales:
Keyne balanced a need for solitude with a craving for companionship. In her wanderings, she established churches in southwest Wales, Cornwall, and Somerset.

Reflection:
"Be not hasty in your utterance and let not your heart be quick to make a promise in God's presence. God is in heaven and you are on earth; therefore let your words be few."

Ecclesiastes 5:1

BLESSED MARIA ANGELA TRUSZKOWSKA

(Sophia Camilla Truszkowska)

b. May 16, 1825, Kalisz, Poland
d. October 10, 1899, Kraków, Malopolskie, Poland

Sophia was born into Poland's landed gentry and received an excellent education from parents who encouraged her spiritual side. As a young woman she became a Franciscan tertiary, taking the name Maria Angela and devoting herself to prayer and social work. With her father's financial support, she rented an apartment where she sheltered orphaned girls and aged women.

As her mission grew, Angela was often seen leading the orphans to pray at the nearby shrine of Felix of Cantalice.[176] People began calling Angela and her companions the Sisters of St Felix (Felician Sisters) even before they had formally organized as a congregation. Angela soon expanded their activities beyond the poor and disabled to include prisoners and the sick (notably wounded soldiers on both sides during several wars), and the Felician Sisters continue to accept any assignment for God's great glory.

Angela led with a compassionate heart. When some of the Sisters asked to dismiss a postulant who seemed unfit for anything, Angela responded: *"Leave the child in peace. She knows how to pray."* Angela kept the congregation together in spite of years of harassment during the Russian occupation, but her increasing deafness hindered her work and in 1869, at forty-four, she retired from active leadership. For the rest of her life she devoted herself to editing the Constitutions of the Congregation and to the convent garden and greenhouse.

Outside events, including two world wars, delayed the opening of Angela's cause for canonization until 1949. Cardinal Karol Wojtyla completed the first investigative process and forwarded it to the Holy See in 1969. Twenty-four years later, as Pope John Paul II, he presided over Angela's solemn beatification.

The Genius of Angela Truszkowska:

In spite of oppression and civil war, Angela urged her sisters: *"Help all without discrimination, friend and foe alike. . . . Everyone is our neighbor."*

Reflection:

"Religion that is pure and undefiled before God and the Father is this: to care for orphans and widows in their affliction and to keep oneself unstained by the world."

James 1:27

October 11

SAINT ETHELBURGA OF BARKING

birthdate unknown, Stallington, Lindsey, England
d. October 11, 676, Barking, England

Ethelburga was one of the five saintly daughters[177] of King Anna of East Anglia. When their brother Erconwald[178] founded an abbey at Barking, he put Ethelburga in charge. With no monastic experience, Ethelburga floundered, so Erconwald brought Hildelitha[179] from a monastery in France to train her in the Benedictine Rule. Ethelburga was an excellent student and Hildelitha soon stepped aside, demonstrating her confidence in Ethelburga's leadership by remaining at Barking as a nun. Barking was the first women's monastery in England (although it was actually a double monastery, housing men and women in separate quarters), and the nuns there were celebrated for their faith and their scholarship.

Many miracles have been attributed to Ethelburga, but one of the most interesting occurred several hundred years after her death. The monks at Barking convinced Queen Alftrude to remove the nuns, leaving the monks in complete control of the abbey. A few years after the nuns were evicted, the queen fell ill and dreamed that Ethelburga visited her, dressed in rags and complaining that the queen had abused her and her community. She warned Alftrude to prepare for death unless she returned the monastery to the nuns. Alftrude immediately recalled the community from exile and her health returned with them.

The Genius of Ethelburga of Barking:

The Venerable Bede[180] wrote that Ethelburga was *"upright in life and constantly planning for the needs of her community. . . . None who knew her holy life can doubt that when she departed this life the gates of our heavenly home opened at her coming."*

Reflection:

"Put on the armor of God, that you may be able to resist on the evil day and, having done everything, to hold your ground."

Ephesians 6:13

Saint María Soledad Torres Acosta
(Manuela Torres Acosta)

b. December 2, 1826, Madrid, Spain
d. October 11, 1887, Madrid, Spain

Manuela was on the waiting list for a contemplative order in which she planned to spend her time in prayer and meditation when she was called to a very different vocation: home nursing.

Father Michael Martínez y Sanz, a Servite priest, had become concerned about the lack of such care in Madrid. All nursing was done by religious orders inside their own institutions. Manuela agreed that there was a need for nurses who would visit the sick in their homes. She overcame Father Michael's reservations about her stamina and became one of the founding members of the Servants of Mary, Ministers to the Sick. On August 15, 1851, with six companions, she made her religious vows and took the name María Soledad. She did not come to nursing easily, but Soledad's struggles with fear and disgust helped her later counsel novices about their own doubts. The congregation grew rapidly in a time of civil unrest and epidemics, but turnover was high. In 1856 Soledad faced her greatest challenge when Father Michael left to found a mission in West Africa, taking half of the congregation with him. He insisted that Soledad must stay behind in Madrid as superior general or the community would fall apart. Soledad remained superior for thirty-five years in spite of slander, poverty, and the opposition of the Madrid government. One of her novices observed, "Mother Soledad is like an anvil: she is constantly taking a beating." Today there are more than two thousand Servants of Mary, Ministers to the Sick in twenty-one countries, providing care for the sick in their own homes at no charge. Her feast day is October 11.

The Genius of María Soledad Torres Acosta:
Marking the 175th anniversary of Soledad's birth, Pope John Paul II praised her unique genius: she saw that illness need not be an unbearable burden and that it must never deprive patients of their dignity. On the contrary, Soledad understood that illness could become an enriching experience for the patient's whole family.

Reflection:
"I was sick and you came to visit me."
Matthew 25:36 (motto of her Congregation)

BLESSED MADDALENA PANATTIERI

b. 1443, Trino, Vercelli, Italy
d. October 13, 1503, Trino, Vercelli, Italy

Women preachers are rare in Catholic history, but in her day Maddalena Panattieri was one of the most famous preachers in Italy.

A beautiful and well-educated noblewoman, Maddalena became a Dominican tertiary at the age of twenty. This was most unusual, as Third Order Dominicans were traditionally older women and widows. Maddalena continued to live at home while pursuing an active apostolate. She came to preaching indirectly because she loved to give children catechism lessons and she was so good that their mothers came to listen. They were joined by the fathers and then by the clergy. Her teaching became preaching. Maddalena often criticized usury, which was one of the great controversies of her day. The practice of collecting interest on loans had long been condemned by the Church (and in the Old and New Testaments), but as the merchant class expanded, many were beginning to question any restriction on their access to capital.

Maddalena's preaching drew crowds from all over northern Italy. Even the Dominican prior general came from Milan to hear her. Maddalena was also blessed with many mystical gifts, and like her contemporary Osanna of Mantua (June 20), she had a vision in which she received the Infant Jesus in her arms. She was often transported in spirit to the Holy Land and could describe in great and accurate detail the shrines she visited there. After her death, Maddalena was buried at her convent church. She was venerated there until the seventeenth century, when her relics were hidden in another church. In 1970 her relics were returned to Trino with appropriate ceremony.

The Genius of Maddalena Panattieri:

Maddalena always practiced what she preached. One day when an angry man, offended by her preaching, slapped her, she fell to her knees and said: *"Brother, here is the other cheek. I give it to you in the love of Christ."*

Reflection:

"You have heard it was said, 'An eye for an eye and a tooth for a tooth.' But I say to you, offer no resistance to one who is evil. When someone strikes you on [your] right cheek, turn the other one to him as well."

Matthew 5:38–39

BLESSED ALEXANDRINA MARIA DA COSTA

b. March 3, 1904, Balasar, Portugal
d. October 13, 1955, Balasar, Portugal

On the eve of Easter, fourteen-year-old Alexandrina was at home with her sister and an apprentice. They were sewing together in an upstairs room when three men invaded the house intent on rape. Alexandrina escaped through a window and fell thirteen feet to the ground. She grabbed a wooden board and staggered back into the house to defend the other girls. The startled men ran off, leaving them unharmed. Unfortunately, Alexandrina had injured her spine in the fall and began to have trouble walking. By nineteen she was completely paralyzed and remained bedridden until her death. Alexandrina came to understand that suffering was her vocation, that she had been called to be a victim soul. As a living witness to Christ's Passion, she would contribute to the redemption of humanity by enduring her suffering and offering it to God. In 1931 Alexandrina experienced a vision in which Jesus ordered her to *"Love, suffer, and make reparation."* Beginning in October 1938, for three hours every Friday, Alexandrina relived the Stations of the Cross to the accompaniment of excruciating pain. Word spread, drawing the reverent, the curious, and skeptical clergy, while Alexandrina remained serene. The reenactments ceased in March 1942, and for the last thirteen years of her life she consumed no food but the Eucharist. She baffled the medical experts who conducted many painful and humiliating tests on her. Honoring Jesus' instruction *"I want that while your heart is filled with suffering, on your lips there is a smile,"* Alexandrina obediently smiled at the thousands of pilgrims who sought her prayers and intercession. Today she is considered one of the most important mystics of the twentieth century. Alexandrina is commemorated by the Salesian Order on October 13.

The Genius of Alexandrina:

By accepting her call to become a victim soul, Alexandrina transcended her own suffering and became a witness to Christ's love. She died in peace saying, *"I am happy, because I am going to Heaven."*

Reflection:

"Keep yourselves in the love of God and wait for the mercy of our Lord Jesus Christ that leads to eternal life."

Jude 21

October 15

SAINT TERESA OF AVILA

(Teresa of Jesus, Teresa Sánchez Cepeda Dávila y Ahumada)

b. March 28, 1515, Avila, Old Castile, Spain
d. October 4, 1582, Alba de Tormes, Spain

Few who knew the young Teresa could have imagined that she would leave her mark on the world and her Church. Teresa was a typical upper-class girl who loved reading romances, dancing, and good food. At the age of twenty she entered the Carmelite convent of the Incarnation, where she continued to maintain an active social life for the next twenty years.

Life inside the convent was comfortable, to say the least. The nuns were not bound by any rule of enclosure, and Teresa's secular friends were never bored when they visited. Yet Teresa began to sense that Christ disapproved of her. *"When I was in the midst of the pleasures of the world,"* she wrote, *"remembrance of what I owed to God made me sad, and when I was praying to God my worldly affections disturbed me."*

The year 1555 marked Teresa's turning point. A painting of the Passion of Christ was displayed in the convent for an upcoming feast, and as Teresa stared at it, she felt that she truly understood Christ's suffering for the first time. This terrible understanding shook her to the depths of her soul. Teresa threw herself on the floor in front of the painting and felt all worldly ambition die within her. After that, she made more time for prayer, and began losing herself in ecstasy. Her superiors and her confessor worried that she might be deluded by the devil.

Teresa turned to the Jesuits for some spiritual direction. They prescribed more rigorous penances, but her visions only grew more vivid. The most famous is the transverberation of her heart, during which Teresa saw an angel with a golden spear tipped with fire, which he thrust again and again into her heart. She described it as *"an imaginary vision seen by the eyes of the soul."* The pain was very real, however, and lasted several days.

That summer, on the feast of Our Lady of Mount Carmel, patron of the Carmelite Order, Teresa and some of her closest friends gathered in her cell. They joked about their comfortable life and admitted that they longed for something closer to the original austere Carmelite Rule. Teresa's niece María de Ocampo even offered to buy a house where they could follow a life of true solitude. Teresa soon set up a small house where thirteen nuns could follow the primitive (original) Carmelite Rule: sleeping on straw, fasting eight months a year, abstaining from meat, and living in complete seclusion. At first they went barefoot, hence the name Discalced (Barefoot) Carmelites.[181]

The prioress and the other nuns at the Incarnation convent regarded Teresa's move as an implied criticism of their way of life. The provincial of the Carmelites sided with them and refused to recognize Teresa's new foundation. The bishop of Avila, however, believed that Teresa's reform could reinvigorate the Church. He encouraged her to travel all over Spain, establishing new foundations and reforming existing ones.

Each foundation had its own struggle. Once, down to her last five ducats, Teresa arrived in Toledo and was met with a chilly reception. *"Teresa and this money are indeed nothing,"* she admitted. *"But God, Teresa and these ducats suffice for the accomplishment of the undertaking."* The foundation was made.

During her last six years on earth, long-simmering conflicts with the old Order boiled over. Teresa was placed under house arrest in Toledo for two years while her writings were reviewed by the Inquisition. The papal nuncio denounced her as "a restless, disobedient and stubborn gadabout."

Even during this difficult time, Teresa guided her sisters through letters. She described her spiritual journey in her books, most notably *Autobiography, The Interior Castle,* and *The Way of Perfection.* She died in the arms of Anne of Saint Bartholomew (June 7). Her incorrupt body is venerated at Alba de Tormes, where pilgrims can also see her heart, still bearing the mark where it was pierced by the angel's golden arrow.

The Genius of Teresa of Avila:

In spite of her many achievements, Teresa remained humble. When dealing with a difficult person, she advised, *"Strive yourself to practice with great perfection the virtue opposite the fault that appears in her."*

Reflection:

"When they take you before synagogues and before rulers and authorities, do not worry about how or what your defense will be or about what you are to say. For the holy Spirit will teach you at that moment what you should say."

Luke 12:11–12

Saint Margaret Mary Alacoque

b. July 22, 1647, L'Hautecour, Burgundy, France
d. October 17, 1690, Paray-le-Monial, Burgundy, France

Margaret Mary left an indelible mark on the Church by introducing one of our most familiar devotions: the Sacred Heart of Jesus.

At age twenty-three, Margaret Mary entered a Visitation convent at Paray-le-Monial, near Lyon. She soon began having visions in which Christ showed her his heart in flames—a sign of his burning love for the souls that He had ransomed with his sacrifice on the Cross. Christ informed Margaret Mary that He had chosen her to institute a devotion to his Sacred Heart. When she tried to speak to her prioress about these visions, the prioress dismissed her as an overenthusiastic novice or worse. Fortunately, Margaret Mary was sent to the saintly Claude de la Colombière,[182] a Jesuit priest who questioned her closely and concluded that her revelations were divinely inspired.

According to Margaret Mary, Jesus made twelve specific promises to those who honor his Sacred Heart with acts of reparation and frequent Communion. Most notably, Christ said that those who receive Communion on the first Friday for nine consecutive months will find that *"My heart shall be their assured refuge at that last hour."* With the support of Father de la Colombière, confidence in Margaret Mary grew. She became a novice-mistress and introduced other Sisters to the devotion to the Sacred Heart. This devotion was officially recognized by Pope Clement XIII in 1765, seventy-five years after Margaret Mary's death. The feast of the Sacred Heart is observed on the first Friday following the second Sunday after Pentecost.

The Genius of Margaret Mary:

Even before entering the convent, Margaret Mary made a private vow: *"Wholly in God, and nothing in myself. All, all for God, and nothing for myself."* She lived this completely.

Reflection:

"With joy you will draw water / at the fountain of salvation, and say on that day: / Give thanks to the LORD, *acclaim his name; / among the nations make known his deeds, / proclaim how exalted is his name."*

Isaiah 12:3–4

October 17

SAINT MARGUERITE D'YOUVILLE
(Marie Marguerite Dufrost de Lajemmerais d'Youville)

b. October 15, 1701, Varennes, Quebec, Canada
d. December 23, 1771, Montreal, Quebec, Canada

Three days after her wedding, Marguerite learned that her new husband was trading liquor with the Indians for their furs. He continued this despised and illegal practice until he died in 1730, leaving her with two young sons and a mountain of debts. Marguerite opened a general store, and in a few years she had made herself financially secure and turned her attention to charity.

Montreal had only one badly mismanaged hospital, so Marguerite began to nurse destitute women in her home. Three companions joined her, and on December 31, 1737, they officially founded of the Sisters of Charity of Montreal. Rumors spread that Marguerite was continuing her husband's liquor trade, and when she and her Sisters arrived at Mass on All Saints' Day, 1738, they were met by an angry mob hurling stones and shouting, "Down with the Grey [Tipsy] Nuns."[183] The pastor refused to give the Grey Nuns Communion, but Marguerite reminded them that Christ had also been despised by a crowd. The Grey Nuns gradually won the respect of the community, and during the French and Indian Wars they nursed the wounded without regard to nationality. When a British soldier burst into Marguerite's sewing room pursued by an Indian waving a tomahawk, she hid the soldier, named Southworth, and sent the Indian in the opposite direction. Later, an English general was preparing to destroy the hospital until Southworth told him how Marguerite had saved his life. The general sent officers to question Marguerite, and they emerged convinced that her hospital was truly an "oasis of charity" and must be spared. Canonized in 1999, Marguerite is Canada's first native-born saint. Her feast day is October 16.

The Genius of Marguerite d'Youville:
Marguerite always told the Grey Nuns: *"The people must know that we never refuse to serve."*

Reflection:
"Lead me out of my prison, / that I may give thanks to your name.
Then the just shall gather around me / because you have been good to me."
Psalm 142:8

BLESSED MARIE-ROSE DUROCHER
(Eulalie Melanie Durocher)

b. *October 6, 1811, Saint-Antoine-sur-Richelieu, Quebec, Canada*
d. *October 6, 1849, Longueuil, Quebec, Canada*

The youngest of ten children and possibly a little spoiled, Eulalie attended at least two boarding schools but was always sent home because of vague health problems. Her concerned parents gave her a horse called Caesar for her eighteenth birthday. They hoped that riding would be good for her health and that caring for the horse would teach her responsibility. Their plan worked. Eulalie became a skilled horsewoman and even rode Caesar to Mass.

Sadly, not long after that, Eulalie's mother died. Her brother Theophile, a priest in nearby Beloeil, invited Eulalie to manage his household and the parish rectory. For the next thirteen years she learned a great deal about the spiritual and social needs of a parish, especially the need for schools. In 1843 the new bishop suggested that Eulalie form a religious congregation dedicated to education. Her brother strongly objected to losing his trusted right hand, but Eulalie overcame his resistance and with two companions founded the Sisters of the Holy Names of Jesus and Mary. She took the name Marie-Rose, writing to her sister: *"I wish to be a rose for Jesus Christ."* Within a year Marie-Rose had admitted nine novices and established her first school at Longueuil. The Sisters of the Holy Names expanded rapidly and by 1849 were teaching almost five hundred young women in five neighboring towns. In addition to fidelity to the gospel and devotion to the Blessed Sacrament and the Blessed Mother, Marie-Rose's students learned music, drawing, and homemaking skills. Although she died of tuberculosis at the age of thirty-eight, she left a tremendous legacy to the world of education.

Today the Sisters of the Holy Names are at work in Canada, the United States, Africa, Haiti, and South America. They commemorate Marie-Rose on October 6.

The Genius of Marie-Rose Durocher:
Marie-Rose assured her Sisters: *"If I thought I was renouncing the world to embrace religious life in peace and tranquility, I would have been mistaken; but such was not my intention."*

Reflection:
"I have come to set the earth on fire, and how I wish it were already blazing!"
Luke 12:49 (passage that inspired Marie-Rose)

BLESSED AGNES DE JESUS GALAND
(Agnes de Langeac)

b. November 17, 1602, Le Puy-in-Velay, Haute-Loire, France
d. October 19, 1634, Langeac, Haute-Loire, France

At age twenty-nine, Agnes was deposed as the prioress of her small Dominican convent. The community that had once honored Agnes as a miracle worker had turned on her. She accepted her demotion with serenity, recognizing that God had another plan for her. Agnes soon experienced a vision in which the Blessed Mother instructed her to pray for a troubled priest. She had never met the priest and knew nothing about him, yet she diligently followed Mary's direction for the next three years.

This is not surprising in a young woman who had considered herself a "slave of Mary" since she was eight years old. Agnes entered the convent at twenty-one and the community immediately recognized her spiritual qualities. Four years later, they elected her prioress, until false charges and jealousy led to her removal.

After her vision of Mary, Agnes's health began to fail. She was bedridden when she was informed that a priest had come to see her. She recognized immediately that this was the priest she had been praying for. He was Jean Jacques Olier[184] and his own story was equally miraculous. While on a spiritual retreat, he had dreamed about a Dominican nun praying for him, and he had traced her to this convent. Agnes informed Olier that she had been praying for his cause for years. With the help of Agnes's prayers, he overcame his spiritual crisis and went on to play a major role in religious reform in France. Agnes died in the odor of sanctity a few months later.

The Genius of Agnes de Jesus Galand:
Agnes's genius was that, like Mary, she accepted God's plan for her without reservation.

Reflection:
"Whatever you do, do from the heart, as for the Lord and not for others, knowing that you will receive from the Lord the due payment of the inheritance; be slaves of the Lord Christ."

Colossians 3:23–24

October 20

SAINT MAGDALENE OF NAGASAKI
(Mary Magdalene Kiota)

b. 1611, Nagasaki, Japan
d. October 15, 1634, Nagasaki, Japan

Jesuits brought Christianity to Japan in 1549, and by the time Magdalene was born there were 500,000 Japanese Christians, mostly concentrated in Nagasaki. Magdalene was still an infant when that era of tolerance ended and the shogun expelled all missionaries. In the next seven years, 30,000 Japanese Christians were martyred, including Magdalene's entire family.

When two Augustinian missionaries slipped into Nagasaki in 1625, Magdalene became their indispensable guide, liaison, and catechist. In 1629 a new shogun arrived with five hundred soldiers, determined to wipe out the Christian plague. Magdalene's missionaries were captured and burned alive, but she continued to baptize converts and sustain the faith of her fellow Christians. Visiting the missionary Jordan of Saint Stephen[185] in prison, she announced to his guards, *"I am a Christian, let me in."* Magdalene was finally arrested and sentenced to "the hole," where she was suspended from a gibbet and buried up to her waist in a pit of excrement. For thirteen days Magdalene sang hymns to her guards, until a sudden rainstorm filled the pit with water and she drowned. To prevent collection of any relics, the shogun ordered Magdalene's body burned and her ashes tossed into the sea.

By 1644 not a single missionary was left in Japan, but Japanese Christians continued to practice their faith as best they could for the next two centuries. When Japan finally reopened to the West, missionaries were met by thousands of "secret Christians," the spiritual descendants of Magdalene of Nagasaki. She is commemorated on August 20 by the Augustinian Order and on September 28 by the Dominicans.

The Genius of Magdalene of Nagasaki:
A model of faithfulness, Magdalene offered her life in imitation of Christ's sacrifice on the Cross.

Reflection:
"Thus says the LORD of hosts: Lo, I will rescue my people from the land of the rising sun, and from the land of the setting sun. I will bring them back to dwell within Jerusalem. They shall be my people, and I will be their God, with faithfulness and justice."

Zechariah 8:7–8

SAINT URSULA AND COMPANIONS

birthdate unknown
d. c. 453, Cologne, Germany

There are many versions of Ursula's story but most agree that she was a British princess, famous for her beauty, virtue, and learning, who resisted her many suitors because she had consecrated herself to Christ. Ursula finally agreed to marry Prince Conon on three conditions: First, he and his court must become Christians. Second, they would have a three-year engagement, during which she would travel to the shrines of the saints. Third, she wanted as companions ten noble virgins, each attended by a thousand handmaids, as well as another thousand handmaids attending Ursula herself. Prince Conon and his father the king agreed to everything, and on a May morning, Ursula and eleven thousand companions set sail from London. A strong wind swept them up the Rhine to Basel, where they disembarked and continued on foot across the Alps. On reaching Rome they were welcomed by Pope Cyriacus and Prince Conon, who had arrived there via another route. Conon joined Ursula in a vow of celibacy and the entire company sailed to Cologne, where they were captured and beheaded by the Huns. Ursula begged to die with her companions, but the barbarians were so awed by her beauty that they brought her to their leader Attila. He offered to make her his queen. She rejected him, so Attila drew his bow and pierced her breast with three arrows. Ursula fell dead, and her soul ascended to heaven with her companions. The people of Cologne buried the martyrs and built churches on the gravesites, the most famous being the church of the Holy Virgins.

The Genius of Ursula:

This is, of course, a fantastic tale. Some scholars suggest that the eleven thousand figure arose from a transcription error and that Ursula was martyred with only eleven companions. Although the historical facts may never be known, Ursula and her army of women inspired generations of Christians and she has long been a patron of girls and educators. Among her admirers was Angela Merici (January 27), who founded the Ursuline Order after a vision of the saint.

Reflection:

"Happy those whose way is blameless, / who walk by the teaching of the LORD. Happy those who observe God's decrees, / who seek the LORD with all their heart."

Psalm 119:1–2

October 22

SAINT BERTILLA BOSCARDIN

(Anna Francesca Boscardin)

b. October 6, 1888, Gioia di Brendola, Vicenza, Italy
d. October 20, 1922, Treviso, Italy

"*I am a goose, but teach me to be a saint,*" said the sixteen-year-old girl that everyone called the silly goose. She begged the Sisters of St Dorothy to admit her to their convent, and they finally gave in reluctantly, assigning her the religious name Bertilla and sending her to peel potatoes at their large charity hospital in Treviso.

The mother superior considered Bertilla incompetent and tried to get rid of her, but Bertilla hung on, taking a brief leave only to complete her vows at the motherhouse in Vicenza, then returning to Treviso. "My God, she is here again!" said the mother superior. Her hospital needed trained nurses, not what she called "this half-creature." She banished Bertilla to the kitchen where she could do the least damage. Soon after this, Bertilla was operated on for the removal of a cancerous tumor. By the time she recovered, the superior was short of nurses and desperately needed someone to cover the children's isolation ward. Bertilla was out of the question, of course, but as the superior combed the list of forty-five available sisters she was forced to rule out each one. She asked God to forgive her and put twenty-year-old Bertilla, the "silly goose," to work with the children. Most of them were suffering from diphtheria, had undergone tracheotomies, and needed constant attention. This serious responsibility seemed to free Bertilla of her awkwardness and she matured into competence.

One of the doctors at Treviso later testified that many of the children, separated from their families for the first time, arrived at the hospital in such a state that it took two or three days to calm them down. Meanwhile, he said, they were "like little beasts, beating, boxing, rolling under the bed, refusing food." Sister Bertilla, he recalled, "succeeded in rapidly becoming a mother to them all; after two or three hours the child, who was desperate, clung to her, calmly, as to his mother and followed her wherever she went. The ward, under her action, presented a moving spectacle: groups of children clinging to her. The ward was really exemplary." (In the spirit of the times, the doctor was a freethinking agnostic. He credited his late-life conversion to Bertilla's example.)

Many of the children would not recover, and Bertilla seemed to be the only one able to comfort their parents. Bertilla also supported the doctors, especially the young ones who were terrified at performing their first tracheotomies.

319

"They would always find her by their sides, without a sign of nervousness or fatigue, in the most critical and agitated moments," the doctor testified.

After two years, Bertilla was rotated to a series of other wards, always leaving behind her similar memories. During World War I, bombs hit Treviso but Bertilla remained with the patients who could not be moved, praying and providing marsala wine for those who needed it. In 1918 she was sent to a sanatorium for soldiers with tuberculosis. Ironically, the praise of the soldiers convinced a superior that Bertilla was too attached to them. She sent Bertilla back to the motherhouse, complaining that she was useless. The mother general felt differently and assigned Bertilla to a seminary where she nursed survivors of a devastating epidemic. Bertilla was grateful to be able to care for future priests. After five months she returned to the hospital at Treviso, where it soon became obvious that her cancer had returned. Doctors operated to remove a tumor in her abdomen, but she died a few days later at the age of thirty-four. She has become a beloved intercessor in heaven and was canonized less than forty years after her death. A plaque at the Treviso hospital commemorates Bertilla as "a soul of heroic goodness ... an angelic alleviator of human suffering in this place." She is venerated on October 20.

The Genius of Bertilla Boscardin:

When the war broke out in 1915, Bertilla wrote in her diary: *"Here I am, Lord, to do according to your will, under whatever aspect it presents itself, let it be life, death or terror."*

Reflection:

"I, then, a prisoner for the Lord, urge you to live in a manner worthy of the call you have received, with all humility and gentleness, with patience, bearing with one another through love, striving to preserve the unity of the spirit through the bond of peace."

Ephesians 4:1–3

BLESSED CATHERINE, QUEEN OF BOSNIA
(Katarina Vukcic-Kosaca)

b. 1424, Herzegovina
d. October 25, 1478, Rome, Italy

The daughter of the duke of Herzegovina, Catherine married Stephen Tomas, king of Bosnia, in 1446. He was already the father of an adult son, Stephen Tomasevic. Catherine and Stephen Tomas had a son and daughter. Widowed in 1459, Catherine became queen mother and her stepson became king. Unfortunately, Stephen Tomasevic was no match for the Turkish onslaught that had been expanding into eastern Europe since the fall of Constantinople. In 1463 Sultan Mehmed the Conqueror marched into Bosnia. While Catherine was in Dubrovnik, trying to enlist support for Bosnia, Stephen Tomasevic signed an agreement to embrace Islam, but the sultan drew his sword and beheaded Stephen anyway. Catherine's children,[186] Sigismund, seven, and Katharina, three, had remained with the king. They were taken captive and Catherine would never see them again. She escaped to Rome and spent her remaining years praying for her lost country and children. Catherine left her entire estate, including the sword and spurs that symbolized the royal reign, to the Holy See with instructions that if either of her children returned to the faith, he or she would inherit the crown. This never happened and Bosnia remained part of the Ottoman Empire for the next four hundred years.

The Genius of Catherine, Queen of Bosnia:
Catherine's strength and loyalty have inspired her countrymen for centuries. She remains one of the most beloved characters in Bosnian history and a patron of Croatians in exile.

Reflection:
"When I turned to all the works that my hands had wrought, and to the toil at which I had taken such pains, behold! all was vanity and a chase after wind, with nothing gained under the sun."

Ecclesiastes 2:11

SAINT ANGADRESIMA DE RENTY
(Angadreme, Angadrisma)

b. 615, Thérouanne, France
d. October 14, 695, Oroër, France

Two ambitious courtiers arranged the marriage of their children, Ansbert[187] and Angadresima, but the young people preferred a religious life and asked God to protect them from any attraction to each other. Angadresima was soon disfigured by smallpox and used her illness to convince her father to dissolve the engagement. He allowed her to enter a monastery, and at the moment she received the veil her beauty was restored. He built an abbey for her at Oroër, near Beauvais, in northern France, where she governed wisely for sixty years and was known as a miracle worker.

For centuries, the people of Beauvais revered Angadresima as a protector, and never more so than in 1472, when Charles the Bold and eighty thousand Burgundian soldiers held the city under siege. The people prayed to Angadresima and paraded her relics through the city. This revived their courage, and strengthened the women who fought beside the men. Young Jeanne Lainé attacked a soldier who was about to plant the Burgundian standard atop the city wall. Aided by Angadresima's intercession, Jeanne pushed him into a ditch, chopped down his standard pole with her ax, and waved the broken standard for the crowd to see and take heart. The Burgundians were forced to withdraw, leaving three thousand casualties, while the city of Beauvais lost only eighty men, confirming their faith in Angadresima. The young heroine became known as Jeanne Hachette. Louis XI established a holiday in June to commemorate Angadresima's protection of Beauvais, and women have always taken precedence over men in that day's procession. For centuries it honored both Angadresima and Jeanne Hachette, but increasing secularity has nearly eclipsed Angadresima's role. Her feast day is October 14.

The Genius of Angadresima:
It was said that in the monastery Angadresima was always the first at prayers and the last to rest.

Reflection:
"I thank you for you answered me; / you have been my savior.
The stone the builders rejected / has become the cornerstone."
Psalm 118:21–22

October 25

SAINT TABITHA OF JOPPA

(Dorcas)

First century, Joppa, Israel

Tabitha[188] is described in the Acts of the Apostles as "full of good works and almsdeeds," and she inspired the apostle Peter[189] to perform one of his first and most famous miracles.

Tabitha was financially independent and devoted herself to practical charity, such as making clothes for poor women. The women treasured these clothes because they were so well made. Tabitha was not just their benefactor but their friend, and when she died after a brief illness she was widely mourned. They laid Tabitha out in the upper room of her home and gathered there to pray. Hearing that the apostle Peter was in nearby Lydda, they sent messengers begging him to come to the upper room. When he arrived, they showed him the beautiful cloaks and tunics that Tabitha had made for them. He could see what kind of woman she was and how much they loved her. Peter sent them all outside, so that he would not be disturbed by their weeping. He knelt and prayed, then turned to the body and said, *"Tabitha, rise up."* She opened her eyes, saw Peter, and sat up. He gave Tabitha his hand and lifted her. Peter then called the women back to see their friend restored to life. News of this miracle spread all over Joppa, and because of it many came to believe in the Lord.

The Genius of Tabitha:

The great John Chrysostom[190] preached at least two sermons about Tabitha and urged Christians to follow her example: *"Transfer all the splendor of your house into your soul, and stow away all your fortune in your mind, and instead of a chest and a house, let heaven keep your gold."*

Reflection:

"Peter proceeded to speak and said, 'In truth, I see that God shows no partiality. Rather, in every nation whoever fears him and acts uprightly is acceptable to him.'"

Acts 10:34–35

BLESSED MARIE-THÉRÈSE SOUBIRAN
(Sophie de Soubiran)

b. May 16, 1834, Castelnaudary, Aude, France
d. June 7, 1889, Paris, France

Her beatification decree states that Marie-Thérèse was expelled from the religious order she founded "as a result of the secret and crafty intrigues of one of her Sisters." That hardly begins to capture the drama behind her ouster.

Born in her family's castle in southern Francei n 1861, she moved to Toulouse, taking the religious name Marie-Thérèse and forming the Sisters of Marie Auxiliatrice, dedicated to providing meals, shelter, and instruction to female factory workers.

In 1867 a new postulant joined the Sisters referred by a Jesuit priest. Julie was brilliant, forceful, and everything that Marie-Thérèse felt she could never be. Julie was also a complete fraud, although it would take years for the truth to emerge. Meanwhile, Julie was full of great plans. When the Franco-Prussian War forced them into temporary exile, they settled in Kent, England, where they welcomed shop girls and governesses.

Marie-Thérèse was increasingly uncomfortable with Julie's grand plans, which departed from the original simple spirit of Marie Auxiliatrice. When Julie revealed that the congregation was deeply in debt, she blamed Marie-Thérèse, accusing her of pride, ambition, and incompetence. Even Marie-Thérèse's longtime spiritual director fell under Julie's spell, recommending that Marie-Thérèse resign and stay away until the new mother general—Julie—had time to settle in. Marie-Thérèse found refuge with the Sisters of Charity in Paris. Weakened by tuberculosis, she remained in contact with some of the Sisters of Marie Auxiliatrice and assured them that within a year of her death, their situation would improve.

With Marie-Thérèse out of the way, Julie became even more erratic, but the Sisters had begun to see through her. In 1890 Julie went to Rome and from there she sent a letter of resignation. They never saw her again. But the story does not end there. The sisters soon discovered that their financial affairs had never been as dire as Julie claimed. Even more shocking, however, was the discovery that Julie was married and that her husband was still alive when she entered Marie Auxiliatrice. Julie's entire life had been a lie, and a great wrong had been done to Marie-Thérèse.

In September 1891 Marie-Thérèse's body was moved to the cemetery of the Sisters of Mary Auxiliatrice and she finally received the honors befitting a foundress. Today her congregation is active in Europe, Asia, and Africa.

The Genius of Marie-Thérèse Soubiran:

Marie-Thérèse never lost faith. Barred from the order she founded, she wrote: *"Those who put their trust in God are strong with God's own strength, which becomes theirs. They are carried along by it, they make their home in it, they are rich with all that infinite power, raised above all created things. Therefore, nothing disturbs or troubles them, for they are victorious in everything; victorious at all times in him whom the winds and the sea obey."*

Reflection:

"Though an army encamp against me, / my heart does not fear;
Though war be waged against me, / even then do I trust."

Psalm 27:3

SAINT FRIDESWIDE OF OXFORD
(Fréwisse)

b. c. 650, Eynsham, Kingdom of Mercia (England)
d. 735, Oxford, Kingdom of Mercia (England)

Frideswide was the daughter of Dida, prince of Eynsham in the Thames Valley. After her mother, Saerith, died, her father built a church and monastery for Frideswide, where she took the veil with twelve other young women.

Unfortunately, Algar, the earl of Leicester, became obsessed with Frideswide and planned to kidnap her and make her his wife. Frideswide fled to the Thames, found a boat, and floated downstream. Exactly where she landed is much debated. Several localities claim to have sheltered her during the three years she was away from Oxford. The townspeople of Binsey, not far from Oxford, claimed that she hid in a pigsty there. She prayed to Margaret of Antioch (July 20) and discovered a spring, which became a famous healing well. In gratitude, Frideswide established a chapel dedicated to Margaret, and pilgrims still visit Saint Margaret's well there. Across the English Channel, Frideswide is known as Fréwisse, and the French villagers of Bomy erected a shrine commemorating the three years they believed she spent with them.

When Frideswide returned to Oxford, Algar prepared to take her by force, but as he entered the city gates, he was struck blind. Once plunged into darkness, Algar saw the light and admitted that he had been wrong. Frideswide, moved by compassion, restored his sight, but for centuries no English king would enter Oxford for fear of being struck blind. For the rest of her life, Frideswide presided over her monastery in great holiness. Many miracles surrounded her before and after death. Frideswide's monastery is now Christ Church, the chief college at Oxford University, and her church, rebuilt in the twelfth century and now called Christ Church Cathedral, contains a shrine dedicated to her. She is the patron of both the city and the university of Oxford. Her feast is kept on October 19.

The Genius of Frideswide:

From childhood Frideswide took for her maxim, *"Whatsoever is not God is nothing."*

Reflection:

"I am content with weaknesses, insults, hardships, persecutions, and constraints, for the sake of Christ; for when I am weak, then I am strong."

2 Corinthians 12:10

October 28

BLESSED MARIE POUSSEPIN

b. October 14, 1653, Dourdan, France
d. January 24, 1744, Sainville, France

Marie's family's fortune was built on producing hand-knit silk stockings, but tastes changed and her father was unable to move with the times. When he died, thirty-year-old Marie inherited a pile of debts and a business on the verge of bankruptcy.

Marie was not discouraged, however. She had heard about a new English invention, the mechanical loom, and bought four on credit. She learned to use them herself, then trained her employees. Well ahead of her time, Marie established an apprentice program and generous performance bonuses. In four years she had paid off her father's debts and stabilized the business. She then handed over control to her younger brother and began teaching children in her home. Marie soon attracted like-minded women who called themselves the Dominican Sisters of the Presentation of Mary. She believed that they would be most effective by remaining in the world, supporting themselves, and sharing the lives of ordinary people, but in the post-Reformation climate, the bishop of Chartres was unwilling to recognize a women's community without enclosure. Dominican historians make it clear that the bishop also disliked the Dominican Order and did not want it in his diocese. Forbidden to have any public connection with Dominicans, Marie focused her attention on the work of her institute, establishing twenty houses in France before her death. It took two hundred years for her community to be allowed to use its formal title, "Dominican Sisters of Charity of the Presentation of the Most Blessed Virgin Mary." Today there are more than four thousand Sisters of the Presentation in thirty-seven countries, including the United States and Iraq. They celebrate Marie's feast day on October 14.

The Genius of Marie Poussepin:
Struggling to keep her congregation free from enclosure, Marie insisted: *"The community will not confine itself to closing in upon itself the abundance it has received from heaven. It will take the means to spread it abroad generously and abundantly."*

Reflection:
"There are different kinds of spiritual gifts but the same Spirit; there are different forms of service but the same Lord; there are different workings but the same God who produces all of them in everyone."
1 Corinthians 12:4–6

BLESSED RESTITUTA KAFKA
(Helene Kafka)

b. May 1, 1894, Brno-Hussowitz, Czech Republic
d. March 30, 1943, Vienna, Austria

Helene Kafka was a gifted pianist and her parents hoped she would pursue a musical career. When World War I broke out, however, she volunteered to attend wounded soldiers and discovered a different vocation. At nineteen she entered the Franciscan Sisters of Christian Charity, taking the name Restituta. She was assigned to the hospital at Mödling, not far from Vienna, and rose to become head surgical nurse, a position she held for twenty years.

Soon after Germany annexed Austria in March 1938, Restituta clashed with the Nazis over her hospital's new surgical wing. She refused to remove the crucifixes that hung in every room. They were removed anyway, and Restituta replaced them. *"I am a Viennese woman and I will not be silent,"* said Restituta. The Nazis failed to have her reassigned, but they did not give up. When a wounded soldier showed Restituta a satiric poem about the Führer, she found it so amusing that she circulated it to others. A doctor reported her to the Gestapo. She was arrested, charged with treason, and sentenced to death. Restituta was held in prison for more than a year while Austria's Cardinal and the Reich Minister of Justice sought to have her sentence commuted to ten years in prison. Finally word came from Martin Bormann, Adolf Hitler's closest aide, that the death sentence must be imposed to make an example of her.

Restituta was beheaded and buried in an unmarked grave. In 1988 her Sisters published a pamphlet about her, which renewed interest in her martyrdom and opened the investigation into her cause.

The Genius of Restituta Kafka:

To the end, Restituta insisted: *"I have lived for Christ, I want to die for Christ."*

Reflection:

"When [court officers] had brought in [the apostles] and made them stand before the Sanhedrin [the full senate of the Israelites], the high priest questioned them, 'We gave you strict orders [did we not?] to stop teaching in that name. Yet you have filled Jerusalem with your teaching and want to bring this man's blood upon us.' But Peter and the apostles said in reply, 'We must obey God rather than men.'"

Acts 5:27–29, cited in her beatification homily

BLESSED BENVENUTA BOJANI

b. May 14, 1255, Cividale del Friuli, Udine, Italy
d. 1292, Cividale del Friuli, Udine, Italy

Like many other mystics, Benvenuta Bojani struggled with the devil. He appeared as a handsome young man who taunted her and urged her to explore the pleasures of the world with him. When Benvenuta refused, he lifted her into the air and threw her on the floor. Benvenuta fought back, and once she even knocked the devil to the floor and put her foot on his neck while she gave him a piece of her mind.

Benvenuta ("welcome") was given that name because when she was born, the seventh daughter, her father surprised everyone by saying, "She too is welcome." Her companions remembered her as "the sweetest and most spiritual of contemplatives, so lovable in her holiness that her touch and presence inspired gladness and drove away temptations."

Benvenuta suffered so much from numbness, tremors, and shortness of breath that she could not lie down and for years had to sleep sitting in a chair. She could not walk and was carried to church once a week. She was finally cured after praying to Saint Dominic.[191] In gratitude she made a pilgrimage to his shrine at Bologna and afterward lived in perfect health for many years. The Dominican nuns in her town were impressed with Benvenuta's piety and invited her to stay with them in their convent whenever she chose. She cured one elderly nun of blindness and another of a mysterious and painful disorder that she suffered every winter. Benvenuta had the gifts of prophecy and bilocation, and had frequent raptures and ecstasies. She was buried in her family's tomb, but some time afterward when the tomb was opened, her body had disappeared. It was suspected that rival Dominican friars had carried her relics off to Bologna or Ravenna.

The Genius of Benvenuta Bojani:
To the Dominican Sisters, and to the people of Cividale, Benvenuta's short life was a miracle of light and example.

Reflection:
"When I say, 'My foot is slipping,' / your love, LORD, holds me up.
When cares increase within me, / your comfort gives me joy."

Psalm 94:18–19

BLESSED MECHTHILD OF MAGDEBURG

b. c. 1210, Lower Saxony, Germany
d. c. 1297, Helfta, Lower Saxony, Germany

During the forty-year reign of the abbess Gertrude of Hackeborn (c. 1240–1298), her monastery at Helfta was home to three notable mystics: Gertrude the Great (November 15), Mechthild of Hackeborn,[192] and, most influential of all, Mechthild of Magdeburg, author of *The Flowing Light of the Godhead*.

Mechthild had spent more than thirty years as a Beguine[193] in the city of Magdeburg, leading an ascetic, prayerful life. She was about forty when she began to write down the revelations she had been receiving from the Holy Spirit since childhood. This manuscript in progress was circulated all over Europe under the title *The Flowing Light of the Godhead*. When outraged clergymen threatened to burn her writings, Mechthild responded: *"No one could burn Truth."* No longer welcome in Magdeburg, but confident that *"God who had called me would take good care of me,"* Mechthild found a new home at Helfta where the abbess Gertrude, although neither a writer nor a mystic herself, encouraged these gifts in others. At first Mechthild was intimidated by the other nuns, but she soon discovered that they were familiar with her work and respected her wisdom and insights. She spent the rest of her life at Helfta and completed her book there.

Helfta was abandoned during the Reformation, but a community of Cistercian nuns returned there in 1999 and is restoring the monastery as a spiritual center and memorial to Mechthild and her companions.

The Genius of Mechthild of Magdeburg:
Mechthild experienced God with a ravishing passion, writing: *"O Lord, love me excessively and love often and long; the oftener you love me, so much the purer do I become; the more excessively you love me, the more beautiful I become; the longer you love me, the more holy will I become upon earth."*

Reflection:
"Probe me, God, know my heart; / try me, know my concerns.
See if my way is crooked, / then lead me in the ancient paths."
Psalm 139:23–24

THE FEAST OF ALL SAINTS

Today brings a reminder that we are all called to be saints. "Many of us, put off by the legends and halos of the saints, refuse to regard those faithful souls as of the same race as ourselves," wrote Marie des Douleurs,[194] a Benedictine nun. "Surely, humility is a wonderful thing, but we must not confuse humility with cowardice! It's a fine thing to confess that you don't amount to much; but to make up your mind to keep yourself down in this category is depressing and an insult to your Creator and Savior."

Marie des Douleurs assures us: "There are no boundary lines between sanctity and us. For all of us, including the greatest saints, as long as we are on earth, there are stretches of land that are extremely difficult to cross. Let us not regard the saints as of another race, but rather as older brothers and sisters who have gone on ahead of us; let us regard them as brave explorers and pioneers; let's not lose sight of their tracks and let's remember that what one human being has been able to do can also be done by another—and this isn't only true of evil!"

The Genius of All Saints:

Marie des Douleurs writes that by honoring those in heaven on the feast of All Saints and those still suffering in purgatory on the feast of All Souls tomorrow, we draw on mutual joy and strength. Realizing this, "we are seized by a great audacity; and with great spiritual strength we become aware of our role: to help and to be helped."

Reflection:

"See what love the Father has bestowed on us that we may be called the children of God. Yet so we are. The reason the world does not know us is that it did not know him. Beloved, we are God's children now; what we shall be has not yet been revealed."

1 John 3.1–3

BLESSED MARY OF THE PASSION
(Hélène de Chappotin de Neuville)

b. May 21, 1839, Nantes, France
d. November 15, 1904, San Remo, Italy

Baptized Hélène, she entered the Society of Marie Reparatrix[195] in 1864, taking the name Mary of the Passion. She was usually called simply Passion, which suited her, not only because of her devotion to the Passion of Christ, but because she herself was a most passionate woman.

Passion was sent to southern India, where she trained new Indian Sisters, worked with the British colonial government and its Protestant clergy, and sheltered destitute Hindu widows. She was appointed provincial for the entire Madura mission, but her conflicts with local Jesuits were mounting. In addition, Passion found her order's Rule unsuitable for the tropical climate, but when she wrote to her superior general in Paris suggesting adjustments, a new provincial was sent to replace her. Told to accept certain conditions or leave, Passion chose to leave, followed by nineteen other Sisters. She met with Pope Pius IX[196] in Rome and he approved her proposal for a new institute, known today as the Franciscan Missionaries of Mary. Passion's strong will brought her into fresh conflicts and the pope deposed her from office, only to restore her the following year. Today there are nine thousand Franciscan Missionaries of Mary at work in seventy-seven countries. They venerate Passion on November 15.

The Genius of Mary of the Passion:
So headstrong that she was twice removed from leadership posts, Passion mellowed in later life. When associates marveled at her patience, she would say with a smile: *"This ardent soul has not changed, she has just learned to let herself simmer."*

Reflection:
"We ourselves were once foolish, disobedient, deluded, slaves to various desires and pleasures, living in malice and envy, hateful ourselves and hating one another. / But when the kindness and generous love / of God our savior appeared, / [he saved us,] not because of any righteous deeds we had done, / but because of his mercy . . ."

Titus 3:3–5

BLESSED ALPAÏS OF CUDOT
(Alpaïs of Sens)

b. c. 1156, Triguéres, France
d. November 3, 1211, Cudot, France

Alpaïs was about twelve when she moved with her widowed mother and brothers to the town of Cudot. She suffered from a hideous, disfiguring disease that was probably leprosy, and when she became covered with festering sores and nearly paralyzed, her disgusted family abandoned her.

Alpaïs was almost dead of starvation and thirst when she had a vision in which the Blessed Mother appeared to her and healed her sores. Although Alpaïs remained paralyzed and confined to bed, she continued to have visions, especially of heaven, hell, and purgatory, which she described so vividly that royalty, clergy, and ordinary people came to seek her counsel. Alpaïs refused to make any claims about her visions; she would only report what she saw: *"However the truth of this thing may be, this one thing I know, that I am not deceived or deceiving; for what I say, I see as I say it, and I say it as I see it. . . . He alone knows it who knows everything."* The Blessed Mother had assured Alpaïs that because she bore her suffering with humility and patience she would thrive on celestial food alone, and until her death Alpaïs appeared to live solely on the Eucharist. Some skeptics suspected demonic possession, but the Cistercian priests became her strong supporters and built a church to accommodate the thousands of pilgrims who came to see her. They designed it so that Alpaïs could follow the Mass from a small window near her bed. In recent years, the annual procession honoring Alpaïs has been revived. Pilgrims fast and march almost thirteen miles from her birthplace at Triguéres to her tomb in the church at Cudot.

The Genius of Alpaïs of Cudot:

Alpaïs never lost faith and advised: *"As God is everywhere . . . so the soul is everywhere in the body, more powerfully in the heart and brain, as one says that God is in a special way in heaven."*

Reflection:

"I shall sing of your strength, / extol your love at dawn,
For you are my fortress, / my refuge in time of trouble.
My strength, your praise I sing; / you, God, are my fortress, my loving God."
Psalm 59:17–18

SAINT HILDA OF WHITBY
(Hilda of Hartlepool)

b. 614, West Saxony, England
d. November 17, 680, Whitby, Northumbria, England

When Edwin,[197] king of Northumbria, was baptized a Christian on Easter, 627, he was joined by his extended family, including his thirteen-year-old niece Hilda, who grew up to be one of the most important Englishwomen of all time.

At thirty-three Hilda became abbess of the monastery at Hartlepool, where kings and princes consulted her. She had been at Hartlepool nine years when King Oswy entrusted his infant daughter, Elfleda (February 18), to her care. At the same time, he gave Hilda a grant of land, where she built the monastery later known as Whitby. It was a double monastery, housing both monks and nuns, with the nuns superior to the monks, and all ruled by the abbess Hilda. Whitby became the first great seat of learning in the north of England, and Hilda trained many scholars and five future bishops. The most famous of her monks was Caedmon,[198] who is considered the father of English poetry.

At that time, all the religious houses in the north of England, including Whitby, followed the Celtic traditions, while houses in the south followed the Roman system. This led to bitter debates among rival factions, and in 664 a historic synod convened at Whitby to discuss the division. Hilda had a great influence on its conclusion when all sides agreed to acknowledge the supremacy of Rome.

Hilda is a patron of education and she is venerated on November 17.

The Genius of Hilda of Whitby:

Although Hilda had favored the Celtic Rule, unity and peace were more important to her than ethnic identity and tradition. Her influence was a decisive factor in uniting the English church.

Reflection:

"Happy the man who meditates on wisdom, / and reflects on knowledge. . . . / He will lean on her and not fall, he will trust in her and not be put to shame."
Sirach 14:20; 15:4

Saint Elizabeth
(Isabel)

First century

At the Annunciation,[199] the angel Gabriel informed Mary that she had been chosen to bear the Son of God. He added that her cousin Elizabeth was already pregnant and would also bear a son, *"for nothing will be impossible for God."* This was another miracle, because Elizabeth and her husband, Zechariah, had endured years of infertility.

Zechariah was praying in the temple when an angel announced that he and Elizabeth would have a son whom they were to call John, and who would bring joy to many. Zechariah reminded the angel that he and Elizabeth were both rather old for parenthood. He was immediately struck dumb and remained speechless throughout Elizabeth's pregnancy. Mary visited in Elizabeth's sixth month, an event commemorated as the Visitation,[200] and Elizabeth later gave birth to a son. Jubilant guests who gathered in her home for the traditional Jewish circumcision ritual had expected the baby to be named for his father, but Elizabeth insisted: *"No. He will be called John."* They looked to Zechariah to overrule her, but he motioned for a tablet and wrote on it: *"John is his name."* In that moment his speech returned.

Elizabeth's son would become known as John the Baptist.[201] She herself is a patron of pregnant women and those struggling with infertility.

The Genius of Saint Elizabeth:

Unlike her husband, Elizabeth immediately recognized the power of the Lord working within herself and Mary. Peter Ketter, author of *Christ and Womankind*, suggests that this was because "[h]er womanly soul dwelt more in that realm of mystery, where nature meets the supernatural, than did the priestly soul of her husband."

Reflection:

"Mary set out and traveled to the hill country in haste to a town of Judah, where she entered the house of Zechariah and greeted Elizabeth. When Elizabeth heard Mary's greeting, the infant leaped in her womb, and Elizabeth, filled with the holy Spirit, cried out in a loud voice and said, 'Most blessed are you among women, and blessed is the fruit of your womb.'"

Luke 1:39–42

November 6

SAINT BERTILLA OF CHELLES

birthdate unknown, Soissons, France
d. c. 705, Chelles, France

After Queen Bathildis (January 29) restored the enormous double abbey at Chelles in 657, she needed someone to run it. Theodechild,[202] abbess of Jouarre, recommended her prioress, Bertilla, who had already shown the tact and self-discipline needed to oversee the hundreds of monks and nuns at Jouarre. Bertilla's responsibilities at Chelles were even more delicate, because she eventually supervised two former queens, Bathildis and Hereswitha,[203] who retired there. Bertilla led Chelles for forty-six years, and under her leadership it became one of the most famous religious centers in Europe. Many Englishwomen came there to be trained in the monastic life and the Benedictine Rule. Some stayed at Chelles; others returned to England to pass on what they had learned.

Bertilla's contemporary biographer praised her for governing "like a man, with great sanctity and piety." He wrote that many of the recently converted Saxon kings asked Bertilla to send them nuns, monks, and books so that they could build monasteries and educate their own people. Bertilla was always willing to fill these requests, he said, "to speed the salvation of souls."

Her feast day is kept on November 5.

The Genius of Bertilla of Chelles:

Alban Butler, chronicler of saints, wrote that Bertilla, "showed by her conduct that no one commands well or with safety who has not first learned, and is not always ready, to obey well."

Meditation:

"This is my prayer: that your love may increase ever more and more in knowledge and every kind of perception, to discern what is of value, so that you may be pure and blameless for the day of Christ, filled with the fruit of righteousness that comes through Jesus Christ for the glory and praise of God."

Philippians 1:9–11

Blessed Lucy of Settefonti

b. c. 1100, Bologna, Italy
d. 1149, Settefonti, Italy

A handsome young knight named Rolando used to arrive on horseback to attend daily Mass at an isolated chapel on a rocky hill near Bologna. He was not there for the prayers, however, but to stare at the beautiful abbess Lucy who had built the chapel and the monastery attached to it.

The pious Lucy watched Mass from a window in her cell, and Rolando watched Lucy. When she realized what was happening, she closed her window. Rolando tried to talk to her, but she finally convinced him that she belonged to God alone. Heartbroken, he joined a crusade to the Holy Land and was unaware that on the day he left, Lucy died of a fever. Rolando was captured in Jerusalem and ordered to accept Islam or die. He thought of Lucy and prayed: "O Lucy, if you still live on earth, pray for the one who has loved you so much. If you are in heaven, ask the Lord that I may be delivered from my cruel enemies or at least have courage to die like a Christian soldier." The next morning Rolando awoke to the sound of church bells. He was still in chains, but he was standing outside the monastery of Settefonti. Lucy, more beautiful than ever, was standing before him. "Lucy, do you still live?" he exclaimed. She answered: *"I live the life eternal; go, lay your fetters on my tomb and thank God that your prayer was heard. Be assured that I love you with perfect charity. If your love is perfect, you shall share with me the joys of heaven."* Rolando later laid his chains at Lucy's tomb, and no one has been able to remove them since. Lucy's community relocated to Bologna in 1245 and her tomb, chains and all, was moved there in 1572. The Camaldolese Order honors Lucy as the founder of its female branch.

The Genius of Lucy of Settefonti:
Lucy had great compassion for the lovelorn Rolando. When he truly needed her help, she miraculously interceded to bring him home.

Reflection:
"Enter through the narrow gate; for the gate is wide and the road broad that leads to destruction, and those who enter through it are many."
Matthew 7:13

BLESSED ELIZABETH OF THE TRINITY
(Elizabeth Catez)

b. July 18, 1880, Camp d'Avor, Bourges, France
d. November 9, 1906, Dijon, France

A few hours before Elizabeth died, she wrote to a friend: *"I confide to you the secret which has made my life an anticipated heaven: the belief that a Being whose name is Love is dwelling within us at every moment of the day and night, and that he asks us to live in his company."*

Elizabeth's father, a French army officer, died when she was seven. She was very close to her mother and younger sister although they strongly opposed her desire to become a Carmelite. Beautiful, charming, and an accomplished pianist, she was courted by several beaux, but at twenty-one Elizabeth finally gained her mother's permission and entered the Carmel at Dijon, where she became Elizabeth of the Trinity.

Elizabeth considered herself a "Praise of Glory," as described in Paul's Letter to the Ephesians. She explained: *"A 'Praise of Glory' is a silent soul, a lyre beneath the mysterious touch of the Holy Spirit, from which He can draw divine harmonies. . . . A 'Praise of Glory' is a soul that contemplates God in faith and in simplicity. . . . Finally, a 'Praise of Glory' is one who is always giving thanks; whose acts, movements, thoughts, aspirations, while more deeply establishing her in love, are like an echo of the eternal Sanctus."*

After only a few years in the Carmel, Elizabeth's health began to fail. She died of Addison's disease at the age of twenty-six, leaving an enormous spiritual legacy, including a prayer to the Trinity that is now part of the Catholic catechism.

The Genius of Elizabeth of the Trinity:
Elizabeth regarded even her fatal illness as an opportunity for grace. She wrote: *"During painful times, when you feel a terrible void, think how the capacity of your soul is being enlarged so that it can receive God—becoming, as it were, infinite as God is infinite."*

Reflection:
"In [Christ] you also, who have heard the word of truth, the gospel of your salvation, and have believed in him, were sealed with the promised holy Spirit, which is the first installment of our inheritance toward redemption as God's possession, to the praise of his glory."

Ephesians 1:13–14

November 9

BLESSED ILONA OF HUNGARY
(Helen, Olympiade)

d. c. 1270, Veszprém, Hungary

Little is known about Countess Olympiade's early years, but by the time three-year-old Margaret of Hungary (January 18) was placed in her care, she was a widow with a daughter Margaret's age. The three of them entered the Dominican convent at Veszprém, and the countess took the religious name Ilona (Helen). It was said that Ilona was always surrounded by a heavenly light and that flowers sprang up from the ground wherever she stepped. She had only to touch a withered houseplant and it would revive and bloom again.

Life in the convent was demanding: the nuns chopped their own firewood, and to conserve candles, they lit them only during Mass. Once Ilona was so busy chopping wood that she was late for evening prayers. The other nuns started without her, sitting in darkness. When Ilona entered, two altar candles suddenly began to burn and kept burning until the nuns finished their prayers. This miracle was often repeated: candles on the altar would suddenly light themselves whenever Ilona appeared, but they would never burn out.

Ilona had a great devotion to the Passion of Christ and was blessed with the stigmata. The nuns later testified that they saw and even touched the wounds. Ilona had been dead for seventeen years when reports of miracles at her tomb led the nuns to exhume her body. It was found incorrupt and gave out a celestial fragrance. The wounds of the stigmata, which closed near the end of her life, had reopened in the tomb. A priest placed two fingers into the wound at her side. When he withdrew them they were covered in blood.

The Genius of Ilona of Hungary:

As the spiritual mother to Margaret of Hungary, Ilona formed the character of a saint who became the instrument for her country's spiritual rebirth.

Reflection:

"Take care, then, that the light in you not become darkness. If your whole body is full of light, and no part of it is in darkness, then it will be as full of light as a lamp illuminating you with its brightness."

Luke 11:35–36

BLESSED JANE OF SIGNA

(Joan, Giovanna da Signa)

b. c. 1245, Signa, Tuscany, Italy
d. November 9, 1307, Signa, Tuscany, Italy

Jane liked to pray under a great oak. Once, during a hailstorm, she sheltered her sheep beneath its branches. The other young shepherds soon joined her. The tree could never have provided cover for all of them, but Jane made the sign of the cross over their sheep and not one of the shepherds or their animals was touched by the storm. In the morning, they returned to their families, convinced that Jane's prayers had protected them.

Jane built a small retreat for herself near the bank of the Arno and lived there for the next four decades while she cured the sick, consoled the troubled, and helped the needy. It is said that she raised a child from the dead, restored sight to the blind, and multiplied loaves of bread for a woman who had been kind to her. At the moment Jane died, all three of Signa's churches began ringing their bells. A visitor found Jane in her cell, looking as if she had simply fallen asleep.

Long after her death, no one dared to plow the ground around Jane's great oak, but one farmer dismissed all the warnings, saying, "Blessed or no Blessed—I'm taking it down." He climbed the tree with an ax, but as he raised his arm to hack at a branch, he was thrown to the ground with such force that he was seriously injured and his ax blade was ruined. The oak itself was destroyed by lightning in 1761. Today there is a small chapel on the site and another on the site of Jane's hermitage. She is venerated throughout Tuscany three times a year: November 10, during Easter week, and August 10.

The Genius of Jane of Signa:

Jane seemed to have the power to control the rivers, the rain, and even livestock. Her biographer wrote: "Not only in the elements, but also in the animals does God demonstrate the power of the blessed Jane."

Reflection:

"Jesus said to them in reply, 'Have faith in God. . . . All that you ask for in prayer, believe that you will receive it and it shall be yours.'"

Mark 11:22, 24

Blessed Alice Kotowska

(Maria Jadwiga)

b. November 20, 1899, Warsaw, Poland
d. November 11, 1939, Piaśnica, Pomorskie, Poland

At the age of seventeen, Maria left medical school to join the Polish army and spent a year attending wounded soldiers. She was later recognized for her heroism with Poland's highest honor, the Polonia Restituta Service Cross.

Joining the Sisters of the Resurrection, Maria took the religious name Alice. In 1934 Alice and six Sisters traveled to northern Poland to establish a mission in Wejherowo. Alice had become superior of their convent and director of an education program when Germans invaded in September 1939. As a nun, a war hero, and a member of the intelligentsia, Alice was marked for death, but she refused to abandon the convent. On October 24, 1939, she was arrested by the Gestapo, then held in prison until November 11, when she was taken with a group to the forest in Piaśnica, shot to death, and tossed with the others into a mass grave. Alice's remaining Sisters were transported to a Nazi work camp in Bojanowo where more than four hundred nuns were already assigned to manual labor and deprived of the sacraments.

In 1991 when a Canonical Process of Beatification for Polish martyrs of World War II was begun, eighty-six-year-old Maria Adela Mankiewicz, one of the last remaining witnesses to Alice's life, personally traveled to Wloclawek to present her cause. Alice Kotowska was beatified in 1999 with the 108 Martyrs of Poland.[204]

Alice is considered a patron of families. Sister Teresa Matea Florczak, her official biographer, writes, "It seems that her specialty is interceding for graces for spiritual benefits, particularly those in which she herself excelled: recollection, silence, humility, self-control or a cheerful disposition."

The Genius of Alice Kotowska:

Alice considered only one thing truly important. She told her Sisters: *"What matters is to be united with God, to be immersed like a drop of water in the Ocean of His Mercy."*

Meditation:

"Put on the armor of God so that you may be able to stand firm against the tactics of the devil. For our struggle is not with flesh and blood but with the principalities, with the powers, with the world rulers of this present darkness, with the evil spirits in the heavens."

Ephesians 6:11–12

SAINT AGOSTINA PIETRANTONI

(Livia Pietrantoni)

b. March 27, 1864, Pozzaglia Sabina, Italy
d. November 13, 1884, Rome, Italy

At seven, Livia was lugging sacks of gravel for the men paving a new road. At twelve, she was traveling north with other migrant workers to harvest the olive crop. Hers was a hard life, but Livia was no victim. She never hesitated to stand up to the foreman if he treated her companions unfairly.

She was drawn to a religious life, but her family accused her of running away from hard work. Livia responded, *"I want a congregation where there is work day and night."* She certainly found that when, at twenty, she was admitted to the order founded by Jeanne Antide Thouret.[205] She was given the name Agostina, trained as a nurse, and assigned to the tuberculosis ward at Rome's enormous Santo Spirito charity hospital. Her patients included Giuseppe Romanelli, a ne'er-do-well who terrorized the hospital staff until he was expelled. He blamed Agostina, stalking her and stabbing her to death. She died praying for his soul. Romanelli was convicted of her murder and sentenced to life in prison. He survived only a year, but during that time he reconciled to Christ and received the last rites before he died.

The Genius of Agostina:

Agostina used to tell her co-workers: *"We will lie down for such a long time after death that it is worthwhile to keep standing while we are alive. Let us work now; one day we will rest."*

Reflection:

"Be on your guard! If your brother sins, rebuke him; and if he repents, forgive him. And if he wrongs you seven times in one day and returns to you seven times saying, 'I am sorry,' you should forgive him."

Luke 17:3–4

SAINT FRANCES XAVIER CABRINI
(Francesca Saverio Cabrini)

b. July 15, 1850, Sant'Angelo Lodigiano, Italy
d. December 22, 1917, Chicago, Illinois

Born in a small village in northern Italy, Frances Cabrini dreamed of becoming a missionary in China. By the time she arrived in America in 1889 she had founded numerous schools and orphanages in Italy and a religious order, the Missionary Sisters of the Sacred Heart of Jesus. She had also mastered the art of negotiating with Italy's anticlerical government and a Church hierarchy opposed to the idea of women missionaries.

Cabrini arrived in New York with six Missionary Sisters to found an orphanage at the invitation of Archbishop Michael Corrigan. She learned that he had disagreed with an American-born countess, who then withdrew financing. Cabrini reconciled all sides, and the orphanage was opened a few weeks later.

Cabrini next assumed management of a hospital in Piscataway, New Jersey. This was the first of hospitals across the country she named for Christopher Columbus. Cabrini also established foundations in South and Central America. In all, she founded sixty-seven institutions with almost no financial support from her Church. Blessed with a gift for bringing out generosity in others, she also shrewdly negotiated with landowners and contractors. Cabrini's heart finally gave out in Chicago—she collapsed while wrapping Christmas presents at an orphanage. She died the following day and is buried in New York.

Mother Cabrini was the first United States citizen canonized. She is the Universal Patron of Immigrants. Her feast is observed on November 13 in the United States and on December 22 in the rest of the world. Members of her order, also known as the Cabrini Sisters, continue her work on six continents.

The Genius of Frances Cabrini:
Cabrini described the source of her strength: *"The Holy Spirit is a sun whose light is reflected in just souls, a bottomless, shoreless ocean whose waters are beautiful, transparent, crystalline and life-giving, and flow continually and abundantly over souls who place no obstacle and do not oppose the Paraclete. Oh, the just souls who live in these saving waters are always happy, joyous, secure, peaceful, and full of trust and great confidence in God. They fear nothing and undertake all tasks with great courage."*

Reflection:
"I have the strength for everything through Him who strengthens me."
Philippians 4:13 (motto of Frances Cabrini)

Blessed Lucy of Narni
(Lucia Brocadelli)

b. December 13, 1476, Narni, Umbria, Italy
d. November 15, 1544, Ferrara, Italy

When Lucy was fifteen, her family arranged her marriage to Count Peter di Alessio of Milan. He indulged her for three years but when the marriage had still not been consummated, he lost patience and demanded his marital rights. Lucy ran off to a Dominican convent in Rome. Peter burned it down. Lucy then accepted an invitation to become prioress of a small convent at Viterbo, where she showed the first signs of the stigmata. During Holy Week of 1496, the wounds began to bleed profusely. Three successive papal commissions composed of doctors and theologians examined Lucy closely and declared the wounds authentic and unexplainable. Count Peter, however, still wanted his runaway wife back. He lurked around Viterbo until Lucy agreed to a meeting. At the sight of Lucy, aglow in spite of her wounds, Peter fell to his knees. By the end of the visit she had won his soul to God. Peter entered a Franciscan monastery and spent the rest of his life there.

By 1499 Lucy had attracted the attention of the duke of Ferrara, a devout Catholic and a great patron of the arts who had made Ferrara a center of the Renaissance. The duke fought with Viterbo for two years to bring Lucy to his city, then filled her new monastery with seventy-two nuns from Viterbo, Narni, and Ferrara, many of whom were there against their will and blamed Lucy. Her troubles mounted when the duke, her great protector and promoter, died in 1505, at the same time that her stigmata disappeared. The nuns' long-simmering resentment erupted, Lucy was removed as prioress, and she spent the next forty years confined to the convent. She died forgotten by the outside world but left behind a written account of her spiritual journey that was later widely circulated as *Seven Revelations*.

The Genius of Lucy of Narni:

At the height of her influence, Lucy softened hardened hearts, reconciled feuding factions, and resolved many misunderstandings. Her *Seven Revelations* is regarded as an important document in the study of women's religious expression.

Reflection:

"In our prosperity we cannot know our friends; / in adversity an enemy will not remain concealed."

Sirach 12:8

SAINT GERTRUDE THE GREAT
(Gertrude of Helfta)

b. January 6, 1256, Eisleben, Thuringia, Germany
d. November 17, 1302, Helfta, Saxony, Germany

"Ah! Wake up, O soul! How long will you sleep? Hear the word that I announce to you," wrote Gertrude in her great work, *The Herald of Divine Love.* *"Above the heavens there is a King who is held by desire for you. He loves you with his whole heart, and he loves beyond measure. He himself loves you so dulcetly and he himself cherishes you so faithfully that, for your sake, he humbly gave up his kingdom."*

Entrusted at the age of five to Mechthild,[206] the novice-mistress at Helfta, Gertrude was a precocious student, but by twenty-six she concluded that she had deprived herself of *"the sweet taste of true wisdom."* She abandoned all secular studies to concentrate exclusively on sacred texts. In the introduction to a new edition of *The Herald of Divine Love,* Sister Maximilian Marnau explains that Gertrude's conversion was not a conversion from sin to virtue: "It was simply a conversion from a life lived in a monastery and following a monastic rule, and so having God for its object but permitting other interests and motivations, to a life totally centered upon and given up wholly to God." Gertrude compiled books of wisdom of the saints and wrote prayers and spiritual exercises. According to her contemporary biographer, "She labored tirelessly at collecting and writing down everything that might be of use to others, without expecting any thanks, desiring only the good of souls. She imparted her writings to those most likely to profit by them."

The Genius of Gertrude the Great:

Of all the notable women who gathered at Helfta, Gertrude was considered the most brilliant. Her biographer wrote that "The Lord chose her as a special instrument to show forth the secrets of his love."

Reflection:

"Although you have not seen him you love him; even though you do not see him now yet believe in him, you rejoice with an indescribable and glorious joy, as you attain the goal of [your] faith, the salvation of your souls."

1 Peter 1:8–9

SAINT MARGARET OF SCOTLAND

b. c. 1045, Mecseknadas, Hungary
d. November 16, 1093, Edinburgh, Scotland

The Pearl of Scotland was the granddaughter of an English king, Edmund Ironside. Her father, Edward the Exile, was reared in the royal court of Hungary and her mother, Agatha, was a Hungarian princess. In 1057 the family returned to England, but Margaret's father soon died and in 1068 her mother made plans to return to Hungary. A storm forced their ship to land at Dunfermline, where Malcolm Canmore, king of Scotland, welcomed them to his fortified castle. The forty-year-old widower was smitten with Margaret. She became his second wife and was crowned queen of Scotland at the age of twenty-four.

Margaret was well educated and loved to discuss the Scriptures with scholars and theologians. Malcolm was an unpolished warrior, but he had a good heart and he adored Margaret. According to one contemporary, "Whatever pleased her, he loved for love of her." He could not read but loved to handle Margaret's books, some of which he had bound in gold and jewels for her.

Margaret raised their six sons and two daughters while Malcolm was often at war. He was killed in battle while fighting beside their eldest son, Edward. Four days later, Margaret died while reciting the Fifty-first Psalm. Many believe that she died of grief. Three of her surviving sons, Edgar, Alexander, and David,[207] successively inherited the crown of Scotland and all governed in a manner that did credit to their mother.

The Genius of Margaret of Scotland:
> In 1660 an anonymous monk praised Margaret as "the Idea of a Perfect Queen, one of those wise ones who by the sweetness of her conversation, the innocence of her deportment and force of her spirit reformed the disorders that had crept into her kingdom."

Reflection:
> *"Have mercy on me, God, in your goodness; / in your abundant compassion blot out my offense. . . . / Let me hear sounds of joy and gladness; / let the bones you have crushed rejoice."*

> Psalm 51: 3, 10

❦

Saint Elizabeth of Hungary

b. 1207, Pressburg, Hungary
d. November 19, 1231, Marburg, Hesse, Germany

A rarity among saints, Elizabeth experienced a truly passionate married life. When news reached Elizabeth that her husband of six years had died while on a crusade, she cried, *"If I could have him alive again, even though it costs the entire world, I would take him and then go begging with him forever."*

Betrothed to Louis in infancy, Elizabeth was carried to his family's castle in a silver cradle, escorted by Walter von Vargila, her lifelong guardian. Elizabeth and Louis were brought up together, until he unexpectedly succeeded his brother as landgrave (count) of Thuringia.

Elizabeth's concerned guardian asked Louis about his intentions. Louis pointed to a mountain and said, "If it were gold from top to bottom, I would cast it away before I would surrender my claim to Elizabeth. Let them say what they will, Elizabeth will be mine."

Whenever possible, Elizabeth laid aside her royal robes to help the poor. One winter day, carrying bread to her poor, Elizabeth ran into Louis, who asked what she was carrying in her apron, then playfully pulled it open. Instead of bread, he saw a mass of red and white roses, and a large luminous crucifix appeared over her head. He begged Elizabeth to continue on her way and carried one of the roses with him for the rest of his life. Later, when Elizabeth distributed her roses to the poor, the flowers turned to bread in their hands.

When news of Louis's death arrived, Elizabeth sobbed, *"Lord God! Lord God! He is dead and all the world is dead to me."* Brokenhearted, Elizabeth moved into a small hut and spent her remaining years in good works until she died.

A great Gothic church was built on the site of Elizabeth's tomb at Marburg. Elizabeth of Hungary is a patron saint of bakers, young brides, widows, and the falsely accused.

The Genius of Elizabeth of Hungary:
Elizabeth became a symbol of Christian charity because she shared the life of the people she served.

Reflection:
"I know indeed how to live in humble circumstances; I know also how to live with abundance. In every circumstance and in all things I have learned the secret of being well fed and of going hungry, of living in abundance and of being in need."
Philippians 4:12

SAINT ROSE PHILIPPINE DUCHESNE

b. August 29, 1769, Grenoble, France
d. November 18, 1852, St Charles, Missouri

When her parents refused to allow Philippine to enter a convent, she simply went there on her own and refused to leave. They let her stay until the French Revolution's religious suppression forced her return home to Grenoble, where she worked among the poor.

When calm returned, Philippine spent three years trying to revive her former convent before recognizing that she could not recapture the past. At that point she met Sophie Barat,[208] foundress of the Society of the Sacred Heart of Jesus, who agreed to receive her and four companions as novices. Though Philippine was elected secretary general of the society, she begged to be sent to a mission in America.

In 1818, Philippine was sent to the Louisiana Territory. She and her companions sailed for ten weeks to New Orleans, then took a steamboat to St Louis and settled at St Charles on the Missouri River. Philippine and her Sisters chopped their own firewood, cleaned their stables, milked their own cows, and grew their own vegetables.

Yet she could write: *"I never have the least doubt as to the will of God and his watchful care for the extension of his work in this country. My consolations exceed my trials ... my prayer is one continuous thanksgiving for the knowledge of that much-desired will of God."*

In 1820 Philippine opened the first free school for girls west of the Mississippi. She went on to play a significant role in the development of the territory, founding schools and convents in Louisiana and Missouri.

At the age of seventy-two, Philippine was invited to join a mission to the Potawatomi tribe in Kansas. She remained with the Potawatomi for a year. They dubbed her Woman-who-prays-always. Her health failing, Philippine returned to St Charles, but she never lost her love for them and wrote: *"I feel the same longing for the Rocky Mountain missions and any others like them that I experienced in France when I first begged to come to America."*

The Genius of Philippine Duchesne:

From the age of twelve, Philippine could not remember *"letting one day go by without praying for light to know God's Will and strength to do it."*

Reflection:

"In my Father's house there are many dwelling places. If there were not, would I have told you that I am going to prepare a place for you?"

John 14:2

SAINT AGNES OF ASSISI
(Catarina di Favarone)

b. 1197, Assisi, Italy
d. November 16, 1253, Assisi, Italy

Sixteen days after her older sister Clare (August 11) ran away to follow Francis of Assisi, Catarina joined her in the monastery where Clare had taken refuge. Their father was not about to let another daughter go and sent a squadron of armed kinsmen to bring Catarina home.

The men could not drag her away and her uncle Monaldo, beside himself with rage and frustration, drew his sword to strike her. His arm suddenly dropped at his side, withered and useless. Acknowledging that they were dealing with a supernatural power, the men withdrew and as they did so, Monaldo's arm was miraculously healed.

Francis gave her a new name, Agnes, after Agnes of Rome (January 21), and established Agnes and Clare at San Damiano. Other noblewomen soon joined them to form the Poor Ladies of San Damiano (Poor Clares). In 1219 Francis appointed Agnes abbess of a convent in Florence. The separation from her sister was almost too painful to bear. Agnes would not see her sister again for twenty years, returning to Assisi only when Clare was dying. Agnes followed her three months later, and she is now interred under the altar at Clare's basilica in Assisi.

The Genius of Agnes of Assisi:
Clare once asked her sister about her process of contemplation. Agnes explained: *"First, I seriously considered the goodness and patience of God and how each day he allows himself to be offended by sinners. Secondly, I meditated on the ineffable love that he brings to sinners and how for their salvation he underwent death and his most bitter passion. Thirdly, I pondered on the souls in purgatory and on their sufferings, and how of themselves they are not able in any way to obtain relief."* Characteristically, Agnes's thoughts and prayers were always about God's goodness and the needs of others, not herself.

Reflection:
"I know, O my God, that you put hearts to the test and that you take pleasure in uprightness. With a sincere heart I have willingly given all these things, and now with joy I have seen your people here present also giving to you generously."

1 Chronicles 29:17

BLESSED MARIA FORTUNATA VITI
(Anna Felicia Viti)

b. February 10, 1827, Veroli, Italy
d. November 20, 1922, Veroli, Italy

Fortunata spent more than seventy years inside a Benedictine monastery, always faithful to the Rule of "Prayer and Work" and to her personal motto: *"Oh, the power and the love of God."* The outside world barely noticed her death at age ninety-five or her entombment at a small burial vault on the outskirts of town. Yet less than fifteen years later, Fortunata's body was returned to Veroli in a triumphant procession and laid to rest inside her monastery church. By then she had become known as the Merciful Helper of Veroli.

Born Felicia Viti, she entered the monastery at the age of twenty-four, taking the religious name Fortunata. Few besides her confessor knew that from the beginning, Fortunata was taunted by devils who disturbed her prayers, sabotaged her sewing, and made it impossible for her to look at her food without seeing it as rotten and crawling with maggots. Fortunata was beloved by the other nuns, and even the birds would sing while they perched on her shoulders or her sewing machine. Fortunata's prayers seemed to have special power, and she was blessed with a unique insight into the needs of others. She urged those who came to her not to lose faith, reminding them, *"Short is the suffering, eternal the joy!"* After her death, the monastery began receiving testimony to favors granted from as far away as Austria and Kansas. The list grew to thousands of names, and in 1934 the abbess at Veroli proposed that Fortunata be considered for sainthood. As part of the process, Fortunata's relics were exhumed and returned to the abbey in a grand procession. Her beatification ceremony in 1967 was attended by two young mothers whose complete and instantaneous cures in childhood had been accepted as her beatification miracles. Pilgrims continue to pray at Fortunata's shrine in Veroli.

The Genius of Fortunata Viti:
Fortunata often told the nuns: *"When I am in heaven I will continue to do good to my neighbor,"* and that appears to be exactly what she has done.

Reflection:
"Everyone who exalts himself will be humbled, and the one who humbles himself will be exalted."

Luke 18:14

November 21

Blessed Josaphata Michaelina Hordashevska

(Yosafata Mykhailyna)

b. November 20, 1869, Lviv, Ukraine
d. April 7, 1919, Chervonograd (a.k.a. Krystonopol), Ukraine

Until Josaphata, the only option for a Ukrainian Catholic woman who wanted to lead a consecrated life was a contemplative order. Michaelina, as she was baptized, was about to enter such a contemplative order when she was invited to assist two priests who were forming a new apostolic congregation. In 1892 she became the first member of the Sisters Servants of Mary Immaculate and took the religious name Josaphata in honor of the Ukrainian martyr Josaphat Kuntsevych.[209] With no tradition to guide her, Josaphata simply looked for what her community needed and came up with solutions. The Sisters Servants cared for the sick, founded daycare centers for children, taught adults the basics of Christian living, cared for neglected village churches, and sewed church vestments. Living in a village without a doctor or a pharmacy, Josaphata even learned to mix medicinal herbs and medications.

Josaphata's contributions were not always appreciated. Some priests and even some Sisters did not believe that a woman could govern a congregation. She was forced to resign from the office of superior general and was twice denied permission to make her final vows. In 1909 she was barred from her own General Chapter meeting because only Sisters with perpetual vows were permitted. On May 10, 1909 the Sisters elected Josaphata vice-general in absentia, and she finally pronounced her perpetual vows the following day, seventeen years after she had cofounded the congregation.

She died, leaving more than fifty foundations, some as far as Canada and Brazil. Josaphata has become known as a powerful intercessor. She is venerated on November 20.

The Genius of Josaphata:
> Throughout her many trials, Josaphata never lost confidence in the mercy of God and the power of his Blessed Mother. She always advised her Sisters: *"I entrust everything to our Mary Immaculate."*

Reflection:
> *"It is idle to say God does not hear / or that the Almighty does not take notice. / Even though you say that you see him not, / the case is before him; with trembling should you wait upon him."*

Job 35:13–14

November 22

SAINT CECILIA OF ROME
(Aziliz, Cecily)

d. 177, Rome, Italy

Cecilia is the patron saint of musicians, singers, and poets, because she sang
in her heart to God alone. She was a young noblewoman who converted to
Christianity and made a vow of chastity, which her family ignored when
they arranged her marriage to Valerian, a pagan. Cecilia warned him that an
angel guarded her but that he would not see this angel unless he was baptized.
She sent him to the catacombs, where he was baptized. Returning home,
Valerian found an angel standing by Cecilia, holding two crowns of roses
and lilies, which he placed on their heads before vanishing. On hearing this
story, Valerian's brother Tibertius also agreed to be baptized. The brothers
devoted themselves to burying the Christian martyrs until they were thrown
into prison. There they converted their jailer, Maximus, and were executed
with him. Cecilia was caught burying them and condemned to death. The
executioner came to her home, an act of courtesy because of her high rank.
She was supposed to be suffocated in her steam room, but after twenty-four
hours, when the room was unsealed, Cecilia was unharmed. The prefect sent
another executioner to cut off her head. He struck three times but bungled the
job, and since Roman law did not allow a fourth try, he left Cecilia bleeding
to death. It took her three days to die, and during that time a steady stream of
the faithful visited her. She was buried with Valerian and his comartyrs, and
in 821 their relics were translated to the basilica built on the site of Cecilia's
former home.

The Genius of Cecilia of Rome:
> One of the most beloved of saints, Cecilia was a favorite of Thérèse of
> Lisieux (October 1), who admired her *"abandonment to God and her bound-*
> *less confidence in him."*

Reflection:
> *"Do not get drunk on wine, in which lies debauchery, but be filled with the*
> *Spirit, addressing one another [in] psalms and hymns and spiritual songs, sing-*
> *ing and playing to the Lord in your hearts, giving thanks always and for every-*
> *thing in the name of our Lord Jesus Christ to God the Father."*
> Ephesians 5:18–20

BLESSED ELIZABETH THE GOOD
(Elizabeth Achler, Elsbeth)

b. November 25, 1386, Waldsee, Swabia
d. November 25, 1420, Reute, Germany

From childhood Elizabeth was known as "the good Beth" because of her pious nature. She was the daughter of a prosperous weaver who operated his business in their home. All that commercial hubbub disturbed her prayer life, and seeking quiet, Elizabeth moved in with another Franciscan tertiary. Her disapproving father cut Elizabeth off without a penny. She struggled to get by, but after a particularly stressful day, she recognized that she had chosen the right path. *"The devil did this,"* she said, *" he wanted to make the work more difficult so that I would give up the service of God and return to the world."*

In 1407 Elizabeth entered a new Franciscan convent at Reute and began to experience mystical gifts, including the stigmata. This caused some resentment among the other nuns when her blood-soaked laundry aroused the curiosity of the village. Elizabeth's dying wish was that nothing be revealed about her, but her spiritual director compiled her biography immediately, recounting all the favors that she had received from God. Although more than 112 witnesses testified to miracles, Elizabeth's case stalled for three hundred years. In about 1757, a cardinal on his way to Vienna learned about the local devotion to Elizabeth and was moved to reopen her cause. She was finally beatified in 1766. Today thousands of pilgrims continue to visit her shrine in Germany.

The Genius of Elizabeth the Good:
Elizabeth's life paralleled the Great Schism (1378–1417), a dispute over papal succession that lasted through the reigns of three popes. Many of her supporters regarded her as a symbol of the suffering Church, and her official biography notes: "She carried not only the wounds of the Lord in her body, she carried also the wounds of humanity, the wounds of the Church."

Reflection:
"We have not received the spirit of the world but the Spirit that is from God, so that we may understand the things freely given us by God. And we speak about them not with words taught by human wisdom, but with words taught by the Spirit, describing spiritual realities in spiritual terms."
1 Corinthians 2:12–13

SAINT FLORA AND SAINT MARY OF CÓRDOBA

b. Ausianos, Spain
d. November 24, 851, Córdoba, Spain

Between 850 and 859, the Muslim government in Spain executed forty-eight Christians known as the Martyrs of Córdoba.[210] Flora and Mary were the first of nine women in the group.

Flora's Muslim father died when she was a child. Her mother raised her as a secret Christian, but as Flora matured, she wanted to go public with her faith. She fled to a convent, but her brother, a devout Muslim, threatened to kill all the Christians in Córdoba, forcing Flora to surrender to protect them. The *cadi* (judge) had her beaten until part of her skull was exposed, but as soon as she recovered, Flora scaled an extremely high wall and escaped from her brother's house again. While in hiding, she met Eulogius,[211] leader of the Christian rebels, and Mary, who was mourning her recently martyred brother, Walabonsus.[212] Flora and Mary agreed to make a courageous profession of their faith. They presented themselves to the *cadi*, who sentenced them to death. Eulogius was already in prison, but he managed to visit Flora and Mary shortly before their execution and wrote: "*[Flora] seemed to me an angel. A heavenly light surrounded her; her face lightened with happiness; she seemed already to be tasting the joys of the heavenly home . . . strengthened by her speech, I returned less sad to my somber cell.*" Five days after Flora and Mary were beheaded, Eulogius was freed, a miracle he attributed to their intercession.

The Genius of Flora and Mary:
Flora and Mary's martyrdom encouraged more Christians to publicly bear witness to their faith and helped turn the tide against Islam in occupied Spain.

Reflection:
"*Everyone who acknowledges me before others I will acknowledge before my heavenly Father. But whoever denies me before others, I will deny before my heavenly Father.*"
Matthew 10:32–33 (passage that influenced Flora's decision to go public)

Saint Catherine of Alexandria

b. c. 292, Famagosta, Cyprus
d. c. 310, Alexandria, Egypt

Catherine was eighteen years old, beautiful, brilliant, and immensely rich when the Roman emperor Maxentius came to town demanding sacrifices to his pagan gods. Catherine protested, and Maxentius recognized that he was not equipped to argue with her. He ordered fifty of his most learned philosophers to debate Catherine, promising them great rewards if they could get her to abandon her faith. At first the scholars were indignant at being asked to debate a young woman, but Catherine's arguments won them over. When all fifty embraced Christianity, the emperor ordered them burned alive.

Maxentius had Catherine thrown into a dungeon without food or water, then went off on a trip. During his absence his wife Faustina and her attendant Porphyrius visited Catherine in prison. She converted them both, and Porphyrius then converted two hundred soldiers. When the emperor returned and Faustina tried to defend Catherine, he ordered them all executed, then offered to make Catherine his new empress. When she refused, he designed a spiked wheel that was supposed to tear her to pieces, but when Catherine was bound to the wheel, a fire fell from heaven and destroyed it. (Hence the firework known as the Catherine wheel.) Maxentius then ordered Catherine beheaded. It is said that when the ax fell, milk poured from her body instead of blood. Angels carried her body to Mount Sinai, where the emperor Justinian later built a monastery to contain her relics. It still stands as the oldest continuously occupied monastery in the world. Catherine is always represented with a wheel. She is a patron of scholars, notaries, and students and a protector of nursing infants and those suffering from migraine headaches, and she was one of the Fourteen Holy Helpers.[213]

The Genius of Catherine of Alexandria:
   Although most of her story is now dismissed as legend, Catherine's wisdom, self-control, and bravery made her one of the most venerated saints of the Middle Ages.

Reflection:
   "Anyone who is so 'progressive' as not to remain in the teaching of Christ does not have God; whoever remains in the teaching has the Father and the Son."
   2 John 9

BLESSED GAETANA STERNI

b. June 26, 1827, Cassola, Vicenza, Italy
d. November 26, 1889, Bassano del Grappa, Vicenza, Italy

Gaetana fell in love at fifteen. Disregarding the advice of her widowed mother, she married a young widower and became the stepmother to his three children. They were extremely happy, even more so when Gaetana became pregnant. But after eight months of marriage her husband died suddenly. Five months later, Gaetana gave birth to a son who lived only two days.

Gaetana forced herself to go on for the sake of her three orphaned stepchildren. They adored Gaetana, but her in-laws regarded her with suspicion, took custody of the children, and insisted that she leave the house. She moved back with her mother but continued to console her stepchildren and was eventually able to reconcile with their family.

Gaetana came to believe that she had a religious calling, but after the death of her mother she was needed at home to care for her three younger brothers. She was twenty-six years old before she was free of her family obligations. By then Gaetana had discerned God's plan for her, but it was so appalling that she had trouble accepting it. God was calling her to serve in Bassano's homeless shelter, which housed more than one hundred unruly and degenerate beggars. Overcoming her distaste, Gaetana went to work at the shelter, saying it was *"only to do the wish of God."* After seven years there, Gaetana founded the Sisters of Divine Will, whom she consecrated *"in complete uniformity to the Divine Will through a total abandonment in God and a strong zeal for the well-being of one's neighbor, ready to sacrifice anything in order to make them well."* Gaetana remained at the shelter for thirty-six years, devoting herself to the residents with unceasing charity until the day she died. Today her congregation is at work in Europe, South America, and Africa.

The Genius of Gaetana Sterni:
Besides the traditional vows, Gaetana made a fourth vow to always choose the spiritually "more perfect" way in all her actions.

Reflection:
"Whatever you do, in word or in deed, do everything in the name of the Lord Jesus, giving thanks to God the Father through him."

Colossians 3:17

BLESSED MARIA CORSINI
(Maria Beltrame Quattrocchi)

b. June 24, 1884, Florence, Italy
d. August 26, 1965, Serravalle, Arezzo, Italy

In 2001 Maria and her husband, Luigi Beltrame Quattrocchi,[214] became the first married couple in Church history to be beatified together.

They met when Maria was a music student in Rome and Luigi was a young attorney. They married in 1905, and a year later their first child, Filippo,[215] was born, followed by Stefania and Cesare. At the end of 1913, Maria was pregnant again, but her doctors recommended an abortion. She and Luigi refused and placed their trust in God. Their daughter Enrichetta was born healthy and lived to celebrate her parents' beatification. Maria and Luigi attended daily Mass together, and prayed the Rosary with their children every night. During World War II, they sheltered many refugees in their home. Maria outlived Luigi by fourteen years and was buried beside him in Rome's Shrine of Our Lady of Divine Love. When their cause for sainthood was opened in 1994, young Gilbert Grossi sought their intercession. Virtually paralyzed by a severe form of arthritis, he prayed to be able to return to school and to marry. A few months after he began praying to Maria and Luigi, he experienced a miraculous and complete recovery, and today he is married and a practicing neurosurgeon in Milan. His recovery was accepted as the beatification miracle for Maria and Luigi. Their ceremony was attended by their three surviving children, and their wedding anniversary, November 25, was designated their feast day.

The Genius of Maria Corsini:
Maria summarized her philosophy of marriage: *"The joy of love is not in receiving it, but in giving love without pretense, giving it spontaneously and happily, without ever demanding it."*

Reflection:
"Husbands, love your wives, even as Christ loved the church and handed himself over for her. . . . So [also] husbands should love their wives as their own bodies. He who loves his wife loves himself."

Ephesians 5:25, 28

November 28

SAINT CATHERINE ZOE LABOURÉ

b. May 2, 1806, Fain-les-Moutiers, Dijon, France
d. December 31, 1876, Paris, France

The Miraculous Medal devotion is one of the most popular traditions in the Catholic Church. The oval medal portrays Mary standing on Earth, her foot crushing the head of a serpent and her hands outstretched to all who ask her assistance. She reminds us that no one who seeks her intercession will be left unaided. Yet few are aware that the medal came to us through a modest French nun who was visited by the Blessed Mother three times.

Catherine was twenty-four when she entered the novitiate of the Daughters of Charity in Paris. A few months later, while praying in the chapel, she experienced a vision of the Blessed Mother. She instructed Catherine to create a medal showing her as she appeared in the chapel, and she promised that all those who wore this medal would receive special graces. Catherine told her spiritual director, Father Jean Marie Aladel, but he remained skeptical. Mary appeared to Catherine twice more.

Catherine kept after Father Aladel until he consulted the archbishop of Paris who ordered the medal struck. The first two thousand were distributed in June 1832. Soon millions of people were wearing the medal and attributing so many favors to it that it became known as the Miraculous Medal.

Catherine spent the next forty-six years working in obscurity in a hospice for the aged. Her connection with the Miraculous Medal was revealed to the public only after her death. She now rests under the altar in the chapel where she experienced her three visions. A million and a half people visit the chapel every year. Millions more around the world wear the Miraculous Medal, and its feast day is on November 27. Catherine Labouré's feast is observed on the following day.

The Genius of Catherine Labouré:

"Whenever I go to the chapel, I put myself in the presence of our good Lord, and I say to him, 'Lord I am here. Tell me what you would have me to do.' If he gives me some task, I am content and I thank him. If he gives me nothing, I still thank him. . . . And then, I tell God everything that is in my heart. I tell him about my pains and my joys, and then I listen. If you listen, God will also speak to you. . . . God always speaks to you when you approach him plainly and simply."

Reflection:

"Give thanks to the LORD, who is good, / whose love endures forever."

Psalm 118:1

November 29

BLESSED DELPHINE DE SIGNE
(Delphine de Glandèves)

b. c. 1283, Château Puy-Michel, Languedoc, Provence, France
d. c. November 26, 1358, Apt, Provence, France

Delphine's parents died when she was very young, leaving her a fortune and a castle in Provence. Her cousin Charles II, king of Naples and Sicily, insisted on arranging her marriage to another cousin, Elzéar de Sabran.[216] She was fifteen and Elzéar was two years younger. Immediately after the wedding, Delphine confided that she had made a vow of chastity and Elzéar agreed to honor it. For the next twenty-five years, they lived quite happily as brother and sister.

They resided at Delphine's castle at Puy-Michel, devoting themselves to good works, until Elzéar's father died in 1310 and he went to Italy to settle the estate. He soon became a trusted aide to King Robert the Wise and Delphine joined him at the court of Naples. She was now over thirty, but still very beautiful, and beloved for her charming manner. While Elzéar was on the king's business in Paris, he came down with a fatal fever and as he lay dying, he declared that he owed any good in himself to Delphine. He was buried in the Franciscan church at Apt in Provence. Delphine moved nearby and set about giving away all of her lands and possessions. She owned so much that the process took many years. She outlived her husband by thirty-seven years and was buried beside him at Apt. The Franciscans traditionally honored Delphine on November 27, but today she is honored with Elzéar on September 26.

The Genius of Delphine de Signe:

In her last years, Delphine endured a painful illness with great patience. Her friends tried to console her, but she assured them: *"if people only knew the real value of suffering, they would send to buy it at the market as a thing of great price."*

Reflection:

"Jesus said to him, 'If you wish to be perfect, go, sell what you have and give to [the] poor, and you will have treasure in heaven. Then come, follow me.'"
Matthew 19:21

SAINT MAXELLENDIS
(Maxellende)

d. 670, Caudry, Cambrai, France

Maxellendis shocked her parents when she rejected their plans for her to marry Harduin d'Amerval. Maxellendis had made a vow of virginity and considered herself a bride of Christ, so marriage was out of the question. Outraged and insulted, Harduin decided to take her by force.

He gathered his friends and raided the house, threatening to kill Maxellendis if she would not marry him. She responded: *"I am not afraid, for my bridegroom Christ has said, 'do not fear those who kill the body but cannot kill the soul.'"* This made Harduin so angry that he stabbed her to death. At the sight of her blood, he was struck blind.

A large crowd gathered and carried Maxellendis to the basilica in Pomeriolas where they buried her the next day. Three years later, a devout widow, Amaltrude, dreamed that the Lord gave her a message for the bishop of Cambrai: he must move Maxellendis back to the site where she had been martyred. The bishop agreed to this and translated Maxellendis in a great procession from Pomeriolas back to Caudry. Harduin went to meet the procession, intending to throw himself on her bier, finally admit his guilt, and beg her forgiveness, but before he could speak, he was jostled by the crowd and knocked to the ground. When he stood up, his sight had been restored. Harduin ran to the bishop, who declared this a miracle and officially recognized Maxellendis as a saint. He had her relics placed in the basilica at Caudry, where they are venerated today. Her feast is kept on November 13. Maxellendis is invoked as a protector from diseases of the eye.

The Genius of Maxellendis:

Maxellendis assured her father that she did not condemn marriage and that it was perfectly fine when both parties entered into it freely.

Reflection:

"To the penitent He provides a way back, He encourages those who are losing hope. Return to the LORD and give up sin, pray to him and make your offenses few. Turn again to the Most High and away from sin, hate intensely what he loathes. . . . How great the mercy of the LORD, his forgiveness of those who return to him!"

Sirach 17:19–21, 24

December 1

BLESSED ANUARITE NENGAPETA
(Marie Clementine Nengapeta)

b. December 29, 1939, Wamba, Belgian Congo
d. December 1, 1964, Isiro, Republic of Zaire (Democratic Republic of Congo)

Anuarite was martyred by twentieth-century lions: a guerrilla force that terrorized the Congo after it won independence in 1960. They called themselves Simba (Swahili for lion), and they intended to erase every trace of European culture, including religious orders and vows of chastity.

Anuarite had made such a vow even before entering the local convent known as Jamaa Takatifu (Holy Family). She was teaching school when Simbas stormed the Holy Family compound. Claiming that marauders were in the area, they insisted on escorting the Sisters to the safety of their headquarters. The forty-six Sisters, including Anuarite, were packed into a truck with the armed soldiers. During the two-day journey, the men got drunker and more aggressive and taunted the Sisters about their vow of chastity. When they reached the Simba camp, Anuarite told the commander that he should just kill her, because she would not break her vow. He tried to force Anuarite and another Sister, Bokuma, into his car and when they resisted, he beat them with his gun, breaking Bokuma's arm. He knocked Anuarite to the ground, claiming that she had attacked him. Two more Simbas rushed up and stabbed her at least five times. Her last words were *"I forgive you, because you do not know what you are doing."* At that point, another officer fired a fatal shot through her heart. The sight of Anuarite, her white habit soaked with blood, calmed the Simba. They allowed the nuns to take Bokuma to a hospital, and later, to retrieve Anuarite's body for burial. Since 1980 she has been entombed in Isiro cathedral.

The Genius of Anuarite:
> Archbishop Mbogha Kambale Charles of Bukavu marked the fortieth anniversary of Anuarite's martyrdom by urging war-weary Congolese to imitate her courage, fidelity, and charity. "To meet the challenge to make our society more humane," he said, "we must follow the example of Anuarite."

Reflection:
> *"The LORD said, 'I have witnessed the affliction of my people in Egypt and have heard their cry of complaint against their slave drivers, so I know well what they are suffering.'"*
>
> Exodus 3:7

SAINT BIBIANA OF ROME
(Vivian)

d. 362, Rome, Italy

Bibiana was born into a powerful Christian family, but her life changed when the new emperor, Julian the Apostate, rejected his own baptism. He launched a campaign against all Christians, whom he referred to contemptuously as Galileans. When the new pagan governor, Apronianus, was in an accident and lost an eye, he blamed it on Christian magic and resolved to exterminate the Galileans once and for all. Bibiana's father, Flavian,[217] was one of the first arrested. A former governor himself, he refused to deny his faith and was branded on the face with a hot iron, then banished to Acquapendente to die. Three days later, Bibiana's mother, Dafrosa, was beheaded. Finally, Bibiana and her sister Demetria were brought before Apronianus, who ordered them scourged. Demetria collapsed and died on the spot. Apronianus briefly lodged Bibiana with a brothel keeper called Rufina, but she failed to corrupt her, and so Apronianus had Bibiana scourged with lead-tipped whips until she died. The church built over Bibiana's home still stands today. It contains the relics of her family as well as a statue of her by Bernini that is considered one of the finest in Rome.

The Genius of Bibiana:

Bibiana's story is considered mainly legend, but it is worth noting that about six months after her martyrdom, Julian the Apostate was mortally wounded in a minor battle with the Persians. Christians and pagans agreed that his dying words were "Thou has conquered, O Galilean." With Julian's demise, religious tolerance returned to the Roman Empire.

Reflection:

"For the grace of God has appeared, saving all and training us to reject godless ways and worldly desires and to live temperately, justly, and devoutly in this age, as we await the blessed hope, the appearance of the glory of the great God and of our savior Jesus Christ who gave himself for us to deliver us from all lawlessness and to cleanse for himself a people as his own, eager to do what is good."

Titus 2:11–14

December 3

BLESSED LIDUINA MENEGUZZI

(Elisa Angela Meneguzzi)

b. September 12, 1901, Giarre, Padua, Italy
d. December 2, 1941, Dire-Dawa, Ethiopia

Angela Meneguzzi was twenty-four when she entered a Salesian convent. Taking the religious name Liduina, she was assigned to a girls' boarding school where she embraced all her tasks: caring for the linens, attending to the altar, nursing the sick. Finally, in 1937 Liduina realized a lifetime dream when she was sent to Africa as a missionary nurse.

Liduina was stationed at a public hospital in Dire-Dawa, the second largest city in Ethiopia. This was her first exposure to a cosmopolitan population that included Muslims and pagans. During World War II, the hospital was taken over by the Italian military. Liduina tended the soldiers as she had tended the civilians, without regard to race or religion, but she never hesitated to speak about the goodness of God. The Muslims dubbed her "Sorella Gudda" or "Great Sister" and the soldiers called her their angel.

Soon Liduina's own health began to fail. Doctors discovered a stomach tumor and scheduled routine surgery. The night before her operation, Liduina made her rounds, assuring her patients that they were suffering far more than she was. Her operation was considered a success, but complications set in and she died a few days later. The sudden loss of their favorite nurse left the staff and the patients in shock. The soldiers insisted that Liduina be buried in their military cemetery. Twenty years later, her body was brought back to Padua where she is venerated at the Salesian motherhouse.

The Genius of Liduina:

> The decree of Liduina's heroic virtue reads: "The message that the Blessed Liduina brings to the Church and to the world is one of hope and love.... A love that is an urge to solidarity, to sharing and service, to following the example of Christ, who came not to be served, but to serve."

Reflection:

> *"Be patient, therefore, until the coming of the Lord. See how the farmer waits for the precious fruit of the earth, being patient with it until it receives the early and the late rains. You too must be patient. Make your hearts firm, because the coming of the Lord is at hand."*

> James 5:7–8

SAINT BARBARA OF NICOMEDIA

d. c. 238, Nicomedia, Turkey

According to legend, Barbara was the beautiful daughter of a wealthy merchant named Dioscorus who shut her up in a tower to keep her away from Christian influences. The only visitors he allowed were a series of brilliant philosophers and tutors who were supposed to educate Barbara about the pagan gods. All his efforts were undone at night, however, when Barbara stared at the stars and understood that they could not have been made by her father's gods. She managed to contact the Christians, received instruction, and was baptized.

When Barbara revealed her conversion to her father, he denounced her to the governor. The governor tried to persuade Barbara to honor his gods, and when she refused, he had her whipped. The whip turned into peacock feathers, and her wounds were miraculously healed. The governor then commanded that Barbara be beheaded. The executioner moved slowly, so Dioscorus seized the ax himself and cut off his daughter's head, then boasted that the emperor should honor him for this service. At that point, a thunderbolt fell from heaven and reduced him to a pile of ashes.

There is a legend that when Barbara was on her way to prison, a cherry branch clung to her robe. She kept it in her jail cell and watered it from her drinking cup until it blossomed on the day of her execution. This has given rise to the Advent tradition of the Barbarazweig, when branches are cut from a fruit tree, brought into the house, kept in water, and, if all goes well, blossom in time for Christmas.

Barbara is a patron of architects and engineers, firefighters, the artillery, and ballplayers, as well as a protector against lightning and explosions.

The Genius of Barbara:
Even shut away from the world, Barbara could see the truth as plainly as the stars in the sky.

Reflection:
"For I know well the plans I have in mind for you, says the LORD, *plans for your welfare, not for woe! plans to give you a future full of hope. When you call me, when you go to pray to me, I will listen to you. When you look for me, you will find me."*

Jeremiah 29:11–13

December 5

SAINT CRISPINA OF THAGURA

birthdate unknown, Thagura, Numidia (Tunisia)
d. December 5, 304, Theveste, Numidia (Tunisia)

Crispina was a proud African matriarch martyred during the Diocletian persecutions. Her story is unique because a vivid transcript of her argument with the Roman magistrate has survived. It reveals a courageous, articulate woman who was not afraid to die for her faith.

A wealthy Christian and the mother of several sons, Crispina was brought before the magistrate Anulinus and ordered to sacrifice to the Roman gods. She replied, *"I will never sacrifice, except to the One God and to our Lord Jesus Christ, His Son, who was born and suffered."* Crispina and the magistrate continued sparring until he exploded and called Crispina "hard and audacious." All of Africa had already submitted, he claimed, and she too would do so, or suffer the fate of her young friends Maxima, Donatilla, and Secunda.[218] Crispina was unmoved. *"Come what may, I will suffer for my faith,"* she said. Anulinus ended up pleading with Crispina to just bend her head and burn a little incense. Crispina answered: *"God is great and omnipotent, He made the sea and the green herbs, and the dry earth. How can I prefer His creatures to Himself?"*

Anulinus ordered her head shaved and warned, "I will cut off your head if you persist in mocking our venerable deities." Crispina replied, *"I should indeed lose my head if I took to worshipping them."* That was the last straw. "We can endure this impious Crispina no longer," he said and ordered her beheaded. Crispina responded, *"I give praise to Christ, I bless the Lord, who has thus deigned to deliver me out of your hands."*

The Genius of Crispina:
Crispina's faith and wit drew the admiration of her contemporaries. Her warning, *"True worship does not need force,"* continues to inspire us.

Reflection:
"Reflect on the precepts of the LORD, / let his commandments be your constant meditation; / Then he will enlighten your mind, / and the wisdom you desire he will grant."

Sirach 6:37

December 6

Blessed María Angela Astorch
(Jerónima María Astorch)

b. September 1, 1592, Barcelona, Spain
d. December 2, 1665, Murcia, Spain

The 1982 beatification of María Angela Astorch took even her Capuchin community by surprise, but María Angela had been doing the unexpected since she was seven years old. That year, while staying with her nanny in a village outside Barcelona, the little girl called Jerónima gorged herself on green almonds, collapsed, and died. Burial was delayed so that her older sister, a Poor Clare Capuchin, could make the trip from the city, accompanied by her superior, a well-known mystic. The superior was so moved by the sight of Jerónima's body that she begged the Blessed Virgin to restore the child to life. Miraculously, Jerónima began to breathe again.

Jerónima became a brilliant student who mastered Latin at the age of nine. She arrived at her convent school with all six volumes of the Breviary, the Church's official collection of daily prayers, Scripture, and ecclesiastical texts. This was required daily reading for all priests and religious, and Jerónima would make it the basis of her religious devotions. She wrote in her journal, "*My soul was like a butterfly, burning day and night with an insatiable thirst for my God.*"

She soon followed her sister into the Poor Clare Capuchins, taking the name María Angela. Her reputation spread, and in 1614 the archbishop of Zaragoza convened a special commission to test her knowledge of Latin and Scripture. Five interrogators gave María Angela a series of biblical citations to identify, which she did flawlessly, and then told her to create a sermon based on three verses from the Bible. She amazed them with her eloquence.

In 1645 María Angela founded a new monastery at Murcia that remains an important spiritual center. The Poor Clare Capuchins commemorate her on December 2.

The Genius of María Angela:
María Angela said that studying the prayers and readings in her Breviary helped her "*to keep in step with God.*"

Reflection:
"*Blessed be the* LORD / *Who has shown me wondrous love,* / *and been for me a city most secure.*"

Psalm 31:22

SAINT MARIA JOSEPHA ROSSELLO
(Geronima Benedetta Rossello)

b. May 27, 1811, Albissola Marina, Savona, Italy
d. December 7, 1880, Savona, Italy

The daughter of humble potters, Geronima Rossello was sixteen when she went to work as a housemaid. After nine years, her widowed employer offered to make Geronima her heir if she would give up her dream of entering a convent. Geronima could not do this and so they parted on affectionate terms.

Ironically, Geronima was rejected by the convent, but she continued to devote herself to charity and often prayed at the shrine of Our Lady of Mercy at Savona. While there one day, she was approached by a priest who needed help rescuing abandoned girls on the city's streets. Geronima was soon joined by two other women and they formed a religious community called the Daughters of Our Lady of Mercy. Geronima took the religious name Maria Josepha, and in 1859 opened her first House of Providence in Savona to shelter and educate girls at risk.

Her bishop allowed Josepha to form a group that encouraged vocations for the priesthood. This gives some sense of the reverence in which Josepha was held, because a woman mentoring future priests was unheard of. Meanwhile, she was also establishing new Houses of Providence in Italy and sending fifteen Daughters to Buenos Aires to begin their first mission there. Her last great work was a refuge for prostitutes who wished to reform their lives. By the time she died, Josepha had founded sixty-five benevolent institutions. Today her Daughters have 176 such homes in Italy and the Americas.

The Genius of Maria Josepha Rossello:
Josepha tells us: *"The hands should be at work, the heart with God."*

Reflection:
*"I went down to the potter's house and there he was, working at the wheel.
Whenever the object of clay which he was making turned out badly in his hand,
he tried again, making of the clay another object of whatever sort he pleased.
Then the word of the Lord came to me: Can I not do to you, house of Israel, as
this potter has done? says the LORD. Indeed, like clay in the hand of the potter,
so are you in my hand, house of Israel."*

Jeremiah 18:3–6

THE IMMACULATE CONCEPTION
(Immaculata, Concepción, Concetta)

The belief that Mary was the only human being ever born free of original sin was discussed for centuries before Pope Pius IX proclaimed the Immaculate Conception a dogma of the Church in 1854. Pius declared that Mary, from the instant of her conception, "by a singular privilege and grace of the omnipotent God, in consideration of the merits of Jesus Christ, the Savior of mankind, was preserved free from all stain of original sin."

Because Mary was born without sin, she was a stranger to sin. She never knew pride, jealousy, envy, or greed. She was blessed instead with an abundance of faith, patience, and love.

The Immaculate Conception is the patron of the United States.

The Genius of the Immaculate Conception:

The Immaculate Conception is about more than an absence of sin: she represents the fullness of grace. Frances Xavier Cabrini (November 13) described her genius: *"Until Mary Immaculate, the Woman par excellence, foretold by the prophets, Dawn of the Son of Justice, has appeared on earth, what was woman? But Mary appeared, the new Eve, the true Mother of the Living, and a new era arose for woman. She was no longer a slave but equal to man, no longer a servant, but mistress within her own walls, no longer the subject of disdain and contempt, but raised to the dignity of mother and educator, on whose knees generations are built up."*

Reflection:

"Then the angel [Gabriel] said to her, 'Do not be afraid, Mary, for you have found favor with God. Behold you will conceive in your womb and bear a son, and you shall name him Jesus. He will be great and will be called Son of the Most High, and the Lord God will give him the throne of David his father, and he will rule over the house of Jacob forever, and of his kingdom there will be no end.'"

Luke 1:30–33

December 9

SAINT ODILIA OF ALSACE
(Ottilie of Hohenburg)

b. c. 660, Alsace, France
d. c. 720, Alsace, France

Odilia was born blind and her father, Aldaric, duke of Alsace, ordered her left to die. Her mother, Bereswinda, was more compassionate and put her in the care of a peasant family that tended her basic needs but little else. Odilia was not even baptized until she was twelve years old. At that point, a bishop passing through insisted on giving her the sacrament. As he sprinkled her with holy water, she miraculously received the gift of sight. Odilia's baptismal name means "daughter of light."

News of this miracle rekindled her family's interest. Her brother Hugh impulsively retrieved Odilia, and the duke began planning a marriage for her. She objected, he ignored her, and she fled across the Rhine, taking refuge in a cave that closed up as he approached. Forced to acknowledge that Odilia was under God's protection, the duke asked God's forgiveness and the rock opened, releasing Odilia. The duke then gave Odilia a castle at Hohenburg, where she established a monastery that housed 130 nuns. Such monasteries traditionally provided hospitality for pilgrims, but Hohenburg was so high in the mountains that few pilgrims were willing to make the climb. Odilia built a second house at the foot of the mountain, where she welcomed so many pilgrims that her community outgrew its chapel and the duke built a huge church for them. He and his wife died soon after, and the daughter they had once abandoned mourned them so much that one of her chapels became known as the Chapel of Tears.

The monastery now known as Odilienberg is still a place of pilgrimage and was visited by Pope John Paul II in 1988. Odilia's feast day is December 13.

The Genius of Odilia of Alsace:
When the pilgrims would not come to her monastery, Odilia brought her monastery to them. In the same generous spirit, she forgave her parents for abandoning her.

Reflection:
"I will lead the blind on their journey; / by paths unknown I will guide them. / I will turn darkness into light before them, / and make crooked ways straight. / These things I do for them, / and I will not forsake them."

Isaiah 42:16

December 10

SAINT EULALIA OF MÉRIDA

b. c. 292, Mérida, Spain
d. 304, Mérida, Spain

Young girls who slip out at night when they are supposed to be asleep might have a patron saint in Eulalia. She was twelve years old during the Diocletian persecution, and when she began expressing a desire to become a martyr, her concerned Christian parents took her far away from the city. One night, Eulalia slipped out anyway and made her way back to Mérida on foot. Angels guided her so that she reached the city at dawn. She immediately presented herself to Dacian, the Roman judge, and berated him for abusing her fellow Christians. Unwilling to argue with a child, Dacian showed Eulalia an altar where she could offer some cake and burn a little frankincense in front of an idol. Eulalia responded by throwing down the idol, trampling the sacrificial cake, and spitting in Dacian's face. Not surprisingly, Dacian had her seized and carried off to be tortured.

On Dacian's orders, Eulalia was stripped and two guards tore at her sides with iron hooks. More tortures followed. She was close to death when the guards removed her from the rack and laid her on the ground, where snow covered her nakedness. As Eulalia breathed her last, a white dove was seen to leave her mouth and fly upward, frightening her tormenters so much that they fled. A great basilica was later built over Eulalia's tomb in Mérida. Her relics are venerated in the cathedral at Oviedo and another shrine is dedicated to her in Totana.

Legend has it that Eulalia protects those who sing hymns to her. She is the patron of Spain, and in 2004 the entire country celebrated a year-long jubilee marking the seventeenth century of her martyrdom.

The Genius of Eulalia of Mérida:
Eulalia fearlessly confronted the enemy, announcing: *"If you are looking for a Christian, here I am."*

Reflection:
"Jesus said to them, 'The light will be among you only a little while. Walk while you have the light, so that darkness may not overcome you. Whoever walks in the dark does not know where he is going. While you have the light, believe in the light, so that you may become children of the light.'"

John 12:35–36

Saint María Maravillas de Jesús
(Maravillas Pidal y Chico de Guzmán)

b. November 4, 1891, Madrid, Spain
d. December 11, 1974, La Alehuela, Madrid, Spain

Maravillas was named for Our Lady of Marvels, patron of her family's ancestral village, and she believed that she was born with a religious vocation. Influenced by the writings of Teresa of Avila (October 15), she entered a Carmelite monastery in 1920. Four years later, Maravillas felt called to found a new Carmel in Cerro de los Angeles, the site of a once-famous shrine to the Sacred Heart.

It took persistence, but in 1926 Maravillas and three companions moved into their new convent. They dedicated themselves to looking after the neglected shrine and praying for the salvation of souls. Her community grew quickly, but by 1931 Spain was experiencing the first tremors of approaching civil war. Although convents and churches were being destroyed, Maravillas could write: *"When they ask me if we are concerned, if we are afraid, it seems to me terribly strange! I think that anything that can happen to us is of so little importance, and that only the Glory of God is important. . . . Seeing so many offenses against God penetrates me to the deepest part of my soul; then lights up in the depths of myself like a silent love, in the darkness, but so strong that it sometimes seems irresistible."* By 1936, though, Maravillas could no longer ignore the danger. That July, the armed Red militia ordered her community to leave the shrine. It was two years before Maravillas could return, and by then the monastery and shrine were in ruins. She restored them and resumed convent life. Peace brought a growth in vocations and Maravillas made nine more foundations. In 1972 she united those monasteries with others sympathetic to them, and they were recognized by the Holy See as the Association of St Teresa.

The Genius of María Maravillas de Jesús:
Throughout her life, Maravillas repeated: *"I feel loved by the Lord."* As she lay dying, she could say with confidence, *"Death is no more than falling blindly into the arms of God."*

Reflection:
"Do not quench the Spirit. Do not despise prophetic utterances. Test everything; retain what is good. Refrain from every kind of evil."
1 Thessalonians 5:19–22

December 12

OUR LADY OF GUADALUPE

In 1999 Pope John Paul II declared Our Lady of Guadalupe patron of all the Americas. Since then, her image can be seen in Catholic churches from Alaska to Uruguay. She is represented exactly as she appears in the miraculous image she left for Juan Diego[219] almost five hundred years ago.

Juan Diego, a member of Mexico's Chichimeca tribe who had converted to Christianity, first encountered the Virgin at the top of Tepeyac Hill. She instructed him to have a temple built where she could *"show and make known and give all my love, my compassion, my help, and my protection to the people."* Juan Diego tried to bring this message to his bishop, but the latter demanded a sign from Mary herself. She told Juan Diego to gather wildflowers on the hill, then wrapped them in his *tilma* (apron) and instructed him to take it to the bishop for his sign. When the bishop opened it, roses spilled out, leaving a miraculous image of the Lady on the inside of the *tilma*. The bishop acknowledged that Juan had truly seen the mother of God.

Today a great basilica stands at Tepeyac Hill, where millions of pilgrims venerate the image of Our Lady of Guadalupe on the *tilma*. Coarsely woven of vegetable fiber, it should have decomposed centuries ago, but it remains intact, with colors as vivid as when they first appeared.

The Genius of Our Lady of Guadalupe:
Virgilio Elizondo, author of *Guadalupe: Mother of the New Creation*, believes that no other event since Pentecost has had such a "revolutionary, profound, lasting, far-reaching, healing and liberating impact on Christianity" as Mary's appearance at Tepeyac Hill. Father Elizondo writes: "She invited both the native people and the Church to a profound conversion to something new, and as such gave birth to both the new Church and the new humanity of the continent."

Reflection:
"I saw a new heaven and a new earth. The former heaven and the former earth had passed away, and the sea was no more. I also saw the holy city, a new Jerusalem, coming down out of heaven from God, prepared as a bride adorned for her husband."

Revelation 21:1–2

December 13

SAINT LUCY OF SYRACUSE

b. 284, Syracuse, Sicily
d. 304, Syracuse, Sicily

Lucy was a young noblewoman who lived in the time of the Diocletian persecution. Her father died when she was a child and she was very close to her mother, Eutychia.

Although Eutychia had raised Lucy as a Christian, she was negotiating Lucy's marriage to a prominent young pagan when she came down with a serious illness. At Lucy's suggestion, mother and daughter made a pilgrimage to the shrine of Agatha of Catania (February 5), who had been martyred fifty years earlier. At the shrine, Lucy had a dream in which Agatha assured her that her mother would recover. Eutychia was miraculously healed and agreed to give up her plans for Lucy's marriage. Lucy's suitor was not as agreeable, especially when he saw Lucy and Eutychia giving away their fortune to the poor. He denounced Lucy to the pagan governor. She was brought before the governor and ordered to sacrifice to the Roman gods. Of course, she refused. After much verbal sparring, he sent Lucy to a brothel, but although the attendants pulled and pushed, they could not move her. They even tied Lucy to a team of oxen, but nothing could make her budge. The governor then ordered a fire built around her, but it would not light. At this point, her eyes were torn out but the Holy Spirit replaced them. Finally, her throat was cut and she bled to death.

In the old Julian calendar, Lucy's feast day fell on the shortest day of the year. She is still associated with the coming of longer days and sunlight, especially in Scandinavia. Her feast day marks the beginning of Christmas celebrations in Sweden and some parts of Norway and Finland. Lucy is a patron of electricians and ophthalmologists, and a protector from blindness and diseases of the eye.

The Genius of Lucy of Syracuse:
According to her legend, Lucy promised: *"I shall cause believers in Christ to see the power of martyrdom, and from nonbelievers I shall remove the blindness caused by their pride."*

Reflection:
"What eye has not seen, and ear has not heard, / and what has not entered the human heart, / what God has prepared for those who love him."

1 Corinthians 2:9

December 14

Blessed Frances Schervier

b. January 3, 1819, Aachen, Germany
d. December 14, 1876, Aachen, Germany

Frances grew up in a mansion within sight of her father's factory, and early in life she decided to devote herself to others. Yet even she was startled when her friend Gertrud Frank[220] claimed she had a message from God: "The Lord wishes you to leave your home and family and to join with other people he will send you in order to save souls for him and heal his wounds."

Frances responded, *"If he chooses the senseless and the unworthy, then he himself must be responsible for the outcome."* She went forward, forming a religious community with Gertrud and three other women, all of them determined to live in pure Franciscan poverty. Ecclesiastic authorities were skeptical, but Frances had more confidence in Divine Providence than they did. She began by visiting the homes of the needy, and her community was soon sheltering former prostitutes. They created a sensation when thirty former prostitutes and eleven Sisters attended Mass together—after that episode, the pastor celebrated Mass for them at their rented house. Frances's Sisters nursed victims of cholera and smallpox epidemics, and in 1838 Frances sent Sisters to work with German immigrants in America. She visited them herself in Cincinnati in 1863, in the middle of the Civil War. Today her community is known as the Franciscan Sisters of the Poor. Hospitals and health-care institutions all over the United States bear the name Schervier, honoring Frances and her faith in Divine Providence.

The Genius of Frances Schervier:

Like most of her early adversaries, Bishop Johann Theodor Laurent came to admire Frances, writing: "She was right and acted according to a higher light ... she got further with her evangelical poverty and her trust in God than many another with all human means and the cleverest of administrations."

Reflection:

"The crowds asked [John the Baptist], 'What then should we do?' He said to them in reply, 'Whoever has two cloaks should share with the person who has none. And whoever has food should do likewise.'"

Luke 3:10–11

December 15

SAINT NINO OF GEORGIA
(Christiana, Ninon)

birthdate unknown, Colastri, Cappadocia (Turkey)
d. c. 320, Mtskheta, Iberia (Georgia)

Nino has been called the Woman Apostle, the Christian (Christiana), and the most successful missionary of the ancient Church because she brought Christianity to the pagan kingdom of Iberia.

Nino arrived in Iberia as a captive slave and soon became known for her devotion to prayer. According to local tradition, a woman with a sick child would carry it from house to house until she found a cure. One woman had carried her child everywhere and almost given up hope when she approached Nino. The slave said she did not know any human treatment, but she promised to pray to her God. She placed the infant on her cloak and prayed over it, asking Christ to deliver the child. This became the first of many infants that Nino cured.

News of this miracle reached Queen Nana, who was herself desperately ill. She sent for Nino, who cured her and taught her that Christ had made her recovery possible. Nana became a Christian, and urged her husband, King Mirian, to join her. He put her off, until one night he and his companions were lost in the forest. Mirian vowed that if Christ would deliver him from this darkness, he would forsake all other gods to worship Him. No sooner had Mirian made this vow than light appeared in the forest, and he returned to his palace unharmed. He became a Christian and the rest of his kingdom followed his example.

With Nino's help, the king and queen built a church that still stands in Mtskheta, the former capital of Georgia. They also sent envoys to the emperor Constantine requesting clergy to continue the work that Nino had begun. In the centuries that followed, the people of the region now known as the republic of Georgia have remained strong Christians.

The Genius of Nino of Georgia:
Nino dismissed the idea that she was a miracle worker, always insisting that her only power was the power of prayer.

Reflection:
"May all who seek you / rejoice and be glad in you.
May those who long for your help / always say, 'The LORD *be glorified.'"*

Psalm 40:17

SAINT ADELAIDE, EMPRESS

b. 931, Burgundy, France
d. December 16, 999, Seltz, Germany

Born a princess, married to a king, the beautiful Adelaide was imprisoned by the same couple that murdered her husband, then rescued by the emperor who became her second husband.

The daughter of the king of Burgundy, Adelaide was sixteen when she married Prince Lothaire. They were happy together and Adelaide gave birth to a daughter. Lothaire succeeded his father as king of Italy but then died suddenly. Everyone, including Adelaide, believed that he had been poisoned by Berengar III, his longtime rival, who immediately proclaimed himself the new king. Adelaide withdrew from court, but Berengar and his wife, Villa (said to be the meanest woman in Italy), would not leave her in peace. They wanted Adelaide to marry their son, but the twenty-year-old widow answered that if she married again it would be to a man who could avenge her husband's murder. Berengar and Villa then confined Adelaide to a castle on Lake Garda and allowed visits only from her priest and her maid. The priest managed to dig an escape tunnel for her, and disguised in men's clothes, she hid among fishermen on the Po River until she reached the fortress of her uncle, the duke of Canossa. From there, she appealed to Otto, emperor of Germany, for help. Otto dispatched a knight bearing his promise of help and a marriage proposal. The knight was unable to enter Canossa, which was under siege, so he fastened the emperor's letter to an arrow and shot it over the wall. Adelaide read it and accepted Otto's offer. He vanquished evil Berengar, had himself crowned king of the Franks and the Lombards, and married Adelaide on Christmas Day, 951. Otto was considered the ablest ruler since Charlemagne, and throughout Germany Adelaide was hailed as an angel of peace.

The Genius of Empress Adelaide:
Adelaide believed that the four months she suffered in prison made her a better woman. They gave her time to reflect, and she resolved never to stoop to revenge. It is said that she never forgot a kindness or remembered an injury.

Reflection:
"[The ideal wife] reaches out her hands to the poor, / and extends her arms to the needy."

Proverbs 31:20

376

December 17

SAINT OLYMPIAS OF CONSTANTINOPLE

b. c. 368, Constantinople (Istanbul), Turkey
d. c. 410, Nicomedia, Turkey

Olympias was a fabulously wealthy heiress married to the newly appointed prefect of Constantinople. When he died suddenly, the emperor Theodosius the Great wanted Olympias to marry his kinsman, but she insisted on remaining single. Theodosius tried to pressure her by seizing control of her properties, and when that failed, he barred Olympias from attending church or associating with the clergy. After a year, he gave up and she regained full control of her estates.

Olympias was so revered that Nectarius, patriarch of Constantinople, consecrated her a deaconess before she was thirty. (A deaconess was usually more than sixty.) Nectarius died in 397 and was succeeded by John Chrysostom.[221] He and Olympias collaborated in many works of charity and reform. She also formed a convent with fifty women near the great basilica of St Sophia.[222] Chrysostom's stormy primacy ended in his banishment in 404, but Olympias remained loyal to him and suffered for it. The new bishop dissolved her convent, which had grown to 250 women, the governor confiscated her household furnishings and sold them at public auction, and her own servants rebelled at her ascetic lifestyle, which they considered inappropriate for a woman of her rank. Olympias was finally exiled to Nicomedia, where she continued to encourage Chrysostom until his death.

The Genius of Olympias:

> Seventeen surviving letters from Chrysostom to Olympias give a portrait of the growing pains of the fourth-century Church. Chrysostom also wrote a treatise for her on the theme, *"No one is really injured except by himself."*

Reflection:

> *"Sing out, O heavens, and rejoice, O earth, / break forth into song, you mountains. / For the* LORD *comforts his people / and shows mercy to his afflicted."*
> Isaiah 49:13

BLESSED AGNES PHILA AND THE MARTYRS OF THAILAND

b. 1909, Ban Nahi, Nong Khai, Thailand
d. December 26, 1940, Ban Song Khon, Mukdahan, Thailand

On Christmas Day, 1940, police raided a village convent, interrupting two nuns, Agnes Phila and Lucy Khambang,[223] as they were teaching catechism. The chief ordered them to stop or be killed. Agnes responded, *"Be sure you have enough bullets."* He assured her that he had more than enough to kill them all.

Time was running out for Agnes and her companions. Their pastor had been deported, and ten days before Christmas, the leading parish layman had been shot to death. After the police chief's visit, Agnes and her companions prayed together, and she wrote to him saying: *"We are ready to give back our lives to God who has given them to us. . . . Please open the door of heaven to us."* The next day the police arrived to march Agnes and her companions to the Mekong River. Agnes insisted that they be taken to the cemetery instead, because it was a holy place. In addition to Lucy Khambang, the group included Agatha Phutta, the convent's fifty-nine-year-old housekeeper, and three young women: Bibiana Khamphai, fifteen, Cecilia Butsi, fourteen, and Maria Phon, sixteen. They marched together, singing hymns and gathering a crowd of admirers. At the cemetery, they prayed and Agnes assured them: *"My dear friends, we will soon be in heaven."* The police fired their rifles and left them for dead, but witnesses discovered that Agnes was still breathing. She insisted that they call the police back to finish the job, then thanked them for sending her to heaven and promised that she would pray for them there. Agnes and her companions are venerated at the Shrine of Our Lady of the Martyrs of Thailand in Song Khon. Their feast day in Thailand is December 16.

The Genius of Agnes Phila:
  Agnes assured her murderers: *"You may kill us, but you cannot kill the Church. You cannot kill God."*

Reflection:
  "Blessed are those who have been called to the wedding feast of the Lamb."
  Revelation 19:9

December 19

BLESSED MARY OF THE ANGELS
(Marianna Fontanella, Maria of Turin)

b. January 7, 1661, Turin, Italy
d. December 16, 1717, Turin, Italy

As a young woman, Marianna often contemplated the Passion of Christ, especially the moment when He was struck in the face while being held at the house of a high priest. She prayed to share Christ's suffering, and she remembered this when she attended a Holy Week service and a disturbed homeless man knelt next to her. After benediction, he suddenly slapped Marianna across the face, so hard that the sound echoed through the church. An uproar followed: men drew their swords and chased after him, while women gathered around Marianna, relieved that she was not seriously hurt. Marianna remained serene, convinced that God had sent the poor lunatic and allowed him to escape.

A few years later, she entered a Carmelite convent, taking the name Mary of the Angels. Her first years there were difficult and she struggled with spiritual desolation. The devil appeared to her, often in the form of a cat, and tempted her to destroy herself, but she finally emerged from this darkness with great mystical gifts. She was elected superior of the convent and became a valued counselor to the Italian royal family.

Mary of the Angels was surrounded by a sweet, indefinable fragrance called the odor of sanctity. During the process of her beatification, many witnesses testified about this fragrance. "When we wanted reverend mother," said one nun, "and could not find her in her cell, we tried to track her by the fragrance she had left behind." A royal princess testified: "The sweetness of this perfume resembled nothing earthly. The more one breathed it the more delicious it became." Long after her death the fragrance lingered in her empty cell. Mary of the Angels is commemorated by the Carmelites on December 16.

The Genius of Mary of the Angels:
> She tells us: *"The voice of God is soft and cannot be heard over the roar of the crowd. That is why one must free the heart of everything else so that it can welcome the Lord."*

Reflection:
> *"They spat in His face and struck him, while some slapped him, saying, 'Prophesy for us, Messiah: who is it that struck you?'"*
>
> Matthew 26:67–68

December 20

SAINT VIRGINIA CENTURIONE BRACELLI

b. April 2, 1587, Genoa, Italy
d. December 15, 1651, Genoa, Italy

A widow at twenty, with two daughters to rear, Virginia resisted her father's pressure to marry again. She preferred to stay with her mother-in-law, a noblewoman who encouraged her philanthropy.

Virginia had inherited a talent for politics from her father, the doge of Genoa, and she had a gift for enlisting officials and benefactors to support her work. Her first cause was the *madonette*, small shrines to the Blessed Mother that adorn the outer walls of buildings throughout Italy. Virginia organized a group to restore and maintain the more than nine hundred *madonette* in Genoa.

Virginia next joined with Genoa's Eighty Gentlemen of Mercy to create a female counterpart: the One Hundred Merciful Protectresses of the Poor. These laywomen reached out to people who were often too proud to ask for help. When war brought a wave of abandoned children, Virginia opened her home to them. Virginia was ahead of her time in recognizing that it was not enough to feed the hungry; they needed the tools and education to be able to feed themselves.

After her own daughters were married, Virginia and her associates formed a religious community called the Daughters of Our Lady of Mount Calvary and opened more shelters throughout northern Italy. Before her death, the order divided in two, with the Daughters remaining based in Genoa and the Sisters of Our Lady of Mount Calvary based in Rome. Their missions remain similar and sympathetic, and they continue her work in Italy, Poland, Latin America, the Philippines, Bangladesh, and Cameroon. Virginia is commemorated in Italy on December 15.

The Genius of Virginia Centurione Bracelli:
Virginia's motto was always *"to serve God through the poor,"* and she proved that it was not necessary to take the veil in order to make a difference in her city or her Church. A gifted peacemaker, she believed that when God is the goal, *"all disagreements are smoothed out, all difficulties overcome."*

Reflection:
"Taking a child, he placed it in their midst, and putting his arms around it, he said to them, 'Whoever receives one child such as this in my name, receives me; and whoever receives me, receives not me but the One who sent me.'"
Mark 9:36–37

December 21

SAINT MARIA CROCIFISSA DI ROSA
(Paola di Rosa)

b. November 6, 1813, Brescia, Italy
d. December 15, 1855, Brescia, Italy

Wealth and privilege were no protection from the epidemics that swept Europe in the nineteenth century. Paola was one of nine children of a wealthy manufacturer, but by the time she reached her teens, only she and her father, Clement di Rosa,[224] survived. He supported her activities, helped her navigate the bureaucracy, and became an active partner in her pioneering social work.

At seventeen, Paola was improving conditions for the women who worked in her father's mill. When a cholera epidemic hit Brescia in 1836, she threw herself into nursing the victims. Two years later, she founded two schools for the deaf and mute. She next gathered thirty-two like-minded women and trained them to staff the Civil Hospital in Brescia. The women were all volunteers, and they worked without any civil or ecclesiastical approval. Long before Florence Nightingale, Paola was training battlefield nurses to work on the front lines. When she made religious vows with the other Sisters in her new congregation, she took the name Maria Crocifissa, in honor of a beloved sister who died in 1839. The congregation became known as the Handmaids of Charity of Brescia, and today they are active in northern Italy and Croatia. Maria virtually worked herself to death and died a martyr to charity. She is commemorated by the Handmaids of Charity on December 15.

The Genius of Maria Crocifissa di Rosa:
> Maria's motto was always: *"I suffer from seeing suffering."* She told her Sisters: *"I can't go to bed with a quiet conscience if during the day I've missed any chance, however slight, of preventing wrongdoing or of helping to bring about some good."*

Reflection:
> *"Listen, my faithful children: open up your petals, / like roses planted near running waters; / Send up the sweet odor of incense, / break forth in blossoms like the lily. / Send up the sweet odor of your hymn of praise; / bless the LORD for all he has done!"*

> Sirach 39:13–14

BLESSED MATILDE TÉLLEZ ROBLES
(Matilde of the Sacred Heart)

b. May 30, 1841, Robledillo de la Vera, Cáceres, Spain
d. December 17, 1902, Don Benito, Badajoz, Spain

Matilde's family moved to Béjar in Salamanca when she was ten years old and she grew up active in her local parish. She was president of the Daughters of Mary for many years, but there came a time when she and like-minded friends wanted something more. After much discussion, they decided to form a religious association.

Eight friends agreed to become members of this new religious community, and Matilde lined up all the necessary permissions. This was no easy task in an anticlerical era, but Matilde even found a house for them to share. When the big day came, however, on March 19, 1875, only one woman, María Briz, showed up. Yet she and Matilda went forward, starting a free school for small children and a Sunday school for the older ones. In just a few years they were joined by six more women. Having outgrown their first house in Béjar, they moved to Don Benito, Badajoz. Matilde was a natural leader who drew her strength from adoration of the Blessed Sacrament.

When an epidemic claimed María Briz in 1885, Matilde and the surviving community dedicated themselves to caring for the sick. Matilde herself died seventeen years later, while visiting yet another home of the poor. By that time her community had grown to eight houses that supported schools, orphanages, and hospitals. Since 1962 the community has been known as the Daughters of Mary Mother of the Church. They administer to forty-seven communities in Europe and South America. Matilde is commemorated by the Daughters on December 15.

The Genius of Matilde Téllez Robles:
Matilde's lifelong motto was *"Prayer, action, sacrifice."* With that in mind, she vowed: *"I will bring you, Lord, all the hearts I can, so that they will love and adore you."*

Reflection:
"Be kind to your servant that I may live, / that I may keep your word.
Open my eyes to see clearly / the wonders of your teachings."
Psalm 119:17–18

December 23

BLESSED ELENA GUERRA

b. June 23, 1835, Lucca, Italy
d. April 11, 1914, Lucca, Italy

At nineteen, Elena was nursing victims of a cholera epidemic when she contracted the disease herself. She remained an invalid for eight years, using the time to read Scripture and study the history of the early Church. She was especially influenced by the story of Pentecost, when the Holy Spirit descended on the apostles in the form of tongues of fire. On recovering her health, Elena resumed an active life. She started a school in which her most famous student was Gemma Galgani (April 11) and she founded the Sisters of St Zita (April 27), who were dedicated to teaching.

In 1895 Elena wrote to Pope Leo XIII, urging him to renew the Church by fostering a greater devotion to the Holy Spirit. Leo is considered the first modern pope because he was dedicated to reconciling the Church with the modern age. Impressed by Elena's letter, he granted her a private audience, and at her recommendation, he called for every Catholic in the world to say an annual novena (nine days of prayer) to the Holy Spirit between the feast of the Ascension and Pentecost. At his suggestion, Elena changed the name of her congregation to the Oblate Sisters of the Holy Spirit. Today they are active in Italy, the Philippines, Canada, Rwanda, and Cameroon.

The Genius of Elena Guerra:

Pope John XXIII called Elena an Apostle of the Holy Spirit, and many consider her a pioneer of the modern Catholic charismatic movement. Elena assures us: *"We do not have to envy the Apostles and the first believers. We only have to dispose ourselves like them to receive Him well. He will come to us as He did to them."*

Reflection:

"We possess the prophetic message that is altogether reliable. You will do well to be attentive to it, as to a lamp shining in a dark place, until day dawns and the morning star rises in your hearts. Know this first of all, that there is no prophecy of scripture that is a matter of personal interpretation, for no prophecy ever came through human will; but rather human beings moved by the Holy Spirit spoke under the influence of God."

2 Peter 1:19–21

December 24

SAINT PAOLA ELISABETTA CERIOLI

(Costanza Onorata Cerioli)

b. January 28, 1816, Soncino, Cremona, Italy
d. December 24, 1865, Comonte di Seriate, Bergamo, Italy

Costanza was a beautiful aristocrat whose parents arranged her marriage to a wealthy nobleman. She was nineteen and Count Gaetano Busecchi-Tassis was fifty-nine. Costanza tried to be a good wife, but she lost three children at birth, and the aging count, demanding and possessive, resented the attention that she gave their frail only son, Carlo. The boy tried to comfort her by saying, "Don't be afraid, mother. God will give you other children." The year 1854 was her worst: Carlo died in January at the age of sixteen, and the count passed away on Christmas Day. These losses plunged Costanza into despair.

It took her months of prayer and contemplation of the Sorrowful Mother before she was able to discern God's plan for her. Recalling her son's words, Costanza decided to devote herself to other children. She began by opening her palace to homeless girls. With six companions, she founded the Sisters of the Holy Family, an order devoted to strengthening families in rural areas. She took the name Paola Elisabetta in honor of two saintly widows, Paula of Rome[225] and Elizabeth of Hungary (November 17). A few years later, with Brother Giovanni Capponi, she cofounded an order of priests called the Religious of the Holy Family. Inspired by the Holy Family of Nazareth (December 27), Paola strove to make her religious houses truly Christian families, united in dynamic love, harmonious fellowship, and strong faith.

The Genius of Paola Elisabetta Cerioli:
Paola's own family called her a fool for wasting her fortune on charity. She responded: *"If someone does good, he is considered foolish. In reality, though, people who have the spirit of the world are the fools, for they make themselves slaves to the world. Unfortunately, I, too, was once like that."*

Reflection:
"Put on then, as God's chosen ones, holy and beloved, heartfelt compassion, kindness, humility, gentleness, and patience, bearing with one another and forgiving one another, if one has a grievance against another; as the Lord has forgiven you, so must you also do."

Colossians 3:12–13

384

December 25

SAINTS AT THE NATIVITY

Many saints have described visions of the Nativity as if they had personally witnessed the event. Two of the most influential visionaries were Bridget of Sweden (July 23) and Veronica of Binasco (January 13).

Bridget believed that the Blessed Mother took her on a pilgrimage to Bethlehem, allowing her to witness the birth of Christ. Influenced by Bridget's report of her vision, artists began portraying the Christ Child lying naked on the ground as his mother knelt beside Him, before wrapping Him in swaddling clothes.

Veronica of Binasco influenced Renaissance portrayals of the Three Kings. The Gospels tell us that they came from the east bearing gifts of gold, frankincense, and myrrh, but they do not specify the exact number of kings. By Veronica's time, it was accepted that there were three. According to one of Veronica's visions, as the kings approached the Christ Child, they began to argue about who would adore him first. The youngest, most impulsive king approached first and kissed the Infant's feet, then aged before the eyes of the other two kings, until he was as old as them. The sight of the Child had matured the young king.

The Genius of the Saints at the Nativity:

The testaments of saints like Bridget and Veronica are considered "private revelations" and not Church dogma, but they have had a great influence on how we picture the Nativity today.

Reflection:

"And there were in the same country shepherds watching, and keeping the night watches over their flock. And behold an angel of the Lord stood by them, and the brightness of God shone round about them; and they feared with a great fear. And the angel said to them: fear not, for behold, I bring you good tidings of great joy, that shall be to all the people. For this day is born to you a Saviour, who is Christ the Lord, in the city of David. And this shall be a sign unto you. You shall find the infant wrapped in swaddling clothes and laid in a manger. And suddenly there was with the angel a multitude of the heavenly army, praising God, saying: 'Glory to God in the highest, and on earth peace to men of good will.'"

Luke 2:8–14 (Douay-Rheims ed.)

December 26

Saint Anastasia of Sirmium

d. c. 304, Sirmium (now Mitrowitz, Yugoslavia)

Anastasia was the daughter of Protasius, a pagan nobleman, and Fausta,[226] a secret Christian. Mother and daughter would disguise themselves in order to visit other Christians in prison, and Anastasia continued the visits even after her mother died and her father forced her to marry the pagan Publius. When Publius discovered that Anastasia was still a Christian, he was furious and confined her to their home. He died while on a diplomatic mission in Persia, and Anastasia immediately went public as a Christian. She was arrested and brought before Florus, the prefect of Illyria. Knowing that Anastasia had inherited a fortune, he said: "Give me all your riches, then you will be a true Christian; I will let you go and worship whom you please, and your poverty will please your God."

Anastasia replied: "*My master would have me sell what I have, and give to the poor; but you are not poor, and would spend it all in sinful luxury.*" Florus then condemned Anastasia to death by starvation, but she was fed by angels, so he set her adrift in a leaky ship crammed with 270 other Christians. They washed up on the island of Palmaria, where Anastasia consoled them until they were discovered and she was roasted alive. Anastasia said that she did not fear pain because she had Christ in her heart, so the governor had her heart brought to him after her death. He found the name of Jesus written on it.

The Genius of Anastasia of Sirmium:

Many legends obscure the real woman, yet this much is fact: Anastasia has been continuously honored as a martyr since the year 304, and her feast was fixed at December 25 long before the day was dedicated to the Nativity. To this day, Anastasia is commemorated in the Canon of the second Mass on Christmas Day.

Reflection:

"*Listen, O house of David! Is it not enough for you to weary men, must you also weary my God!? Therefore the Lord himself will give you this sign: the virgin shall be with child, and bear a son, and shall name him Immanuel.*"

Isaiah 7:13–14

December 27

THE FEAST OF THE HOLY
FAMILY OF NAZARETH

Our first view of Jesus, Mary, and Joseph as the Holy Family is in the Gospel of Luke: "The shepherds hastened to Bethlehem, where they found Mary and Joseph, and the baby lying in a manger" (2:16). After the departure of the Magi, an angel warned Joseph to flee Bethlehem with the infant Jesus and his mother. The Holy Family left for Egypt that night and remained there for several years. They returned to Nazareth only after King Herod was dead (Matthew 2:19–22).

Biblical scholars and historians still debate the details of the Holy Family. Did Mary have other children? What was the age difference between Joseph and his bride? Had he been married before? Did Jesus have brothers and sisters? These discussions miss the real significance of the Holy Family, which is that a man and a woman came together under less than ideal circumstances and welcomed a child into their world because it was God's plan for them. In following this plan, they became a vital part of salvation history.

The feast of the Holy Family was traditionally celebrated in January, but since the reforms of the Second Vatican Council it has been celebrated on the first Sunday after Christmas. In years when there is no Sunday between Christmas and New Year's Day, it is celebrated on December 30.

The Genius of the Holy Family:
All the members of the Holy Family chose to accept difficult tasks offered to them. Their love, born of free will, gave them the strength to respond to their duty to God, and provide a model for all families. John Paul II wrote that "The family, more than any other human reality, is the place in which the person is loved for himself and in which he learns to live 'the sincere gift of self.'... Thus the family is a school of love."

Reflection:
"Wives, be subordinate to your husbands, as is proper in the Lord. Husbands, love your wives, and avoid any bitterness toward them. Children, obey your parents in everything, for this is pleasing to the Lord. Fathers, do not provoke your children, so they may not become discouraged."

Colossians 3:18–21

THE FEAST OF THE HOLY INNOCENTS

First century

On their way to Bethlehem, the three kings known as the Magi stopped in Jerusalem where they visited Herod,[227] the new king of Israel. Herod was not happy to learn that a king had been born in the east, but he directed the Magi to Bethlehem, saying: "Go and search diligently for the child. When you have found him, bring me word, that I too may go and do him homage." Of course, he intended no such thing. He was terrified that the birth of this new King threatened his own right to rule.

The Magi reached Bethlehem and presented their gifts of gold, frankincense, and myrrh to the Infant King, but having been warned in a dream not to return to Herod, they went back to their homeland by another route. When Herod realized that the Magi had outwitted him, he wanted to protect himself, and ordered the massacre of all boys two years old and under in Bethlehem and the surrounding area.

This Massacre of the Innocents, which put hardened soldiers, innocent babies, and grieving mothers at the mercy of a power-mad egomaniac, has long fascinated artists, who have painted it in all its brutality. Art historian Stefano Zuffi writes that "there is no subject more atrocious in the entire history of sacred art.... And yet, the extreme tragedies of today's current events, in the very places cited in the Gospel, demonstrate that the Massacre of the Innocents is a recurring situation." The Holy Innocents were the first to die for Christ, and they are patrons of foundlings, orphans, and the unborn.

The Genius of the Holy Innocents:

The Holy Innocents were all boys, of course, but when we remember them, let us also remember the anguish of their mothers and the suffering of all women who have lost children, born and unborn.

Reflection:

". . . They have been ransomed as the first fruits of the human race for God and the Lamb. On their lips no deceit has been found; they are unblemished."

Revelation 14:4

December 29

Saint Christina of Markyate

b. c. 1096, Huntingdon, East Anglia, England
d. c. 1160, Markyate, Hertfordshire, England

Christina spent years on the run from her ambitious parents, two corrupt bishops, and a husband she never wanted. She eventually became the twelfth century's most famous recluse.

Christina made a vow of chastity when she was very young, but her beauty attracted the lecherous Ranulf Flambard, a powerful chief justice and corrupt priest. When Christina rejected him, Flambard conspired with her parents to arrange her marriage to a young nobleman. Her new husband was patient at first but finally left when he realized that the marriage would never be consummated.

Christina's father, however, was determined to make the marriage work and hauled her before an ecclesiastical committee. The priests explained that many married women had entered heaven, but Christina insisted that she had to honor the vow she had made to God, and cited Scripture to support her argument. The committee gave up, but Christina's parents did not. They bribed the bishop of Lincoln, who ordered her to return to her husband. Christina escaped and lived on the run for the next two years, finally taking refuge with an elderly monk who lived as a hermit in the village of Markyate. After his death, she inherited his little hut. She drew the attention of the saintly Geoffrey of Gorham, master of the school at St Albans, who created a Psalter, or prayer book, especially for her. He trusted Christina's advice, and in turn protected and supported her. In time, the Church authorities who had once persecuted Christina sought her counsel, while a community of women gathered around her. Geoffrey of Gorham established a Benedictine convent for them at Markyate.

Christina is venerated on December 5.

The Genius of Christina of Markyate:
Christina's commitment to her vow, her purity of intention, her fearless flight, and her ability to enlist support for her cause are all examples of the feminine genius in action.

Reflection:
"Deliver me, LORD, from the wicked; / preserve me from the violent,
From those who plan evil in their hearts, / who stir up conflicts every day,
Who sharpen their tongues like serpents, / venom of asps upon their lips."
Psalm 140:2–4

BLESSED MATTIA DEI NAZAREI
(Mattia de Matelica)

b. March 1, 1252, Matelica, Macerata, Italy
d. December 28, 1320, Matelica, Macerata, Italy

The only child of a nobleman, Mattia resisted his marriage plans for her and took refuge in a Poor Clare monastery. The abbess did not want to get involved in a family quarrel, so Mattia took matters into her own hands, put aside her sumptuous clothes, donned a brown Franciscan habit, and cut off her hair herself. Her outraged father arrived at the monastery and found Mattia in the chapel. He was so moved at the sight of her kneeling in prayer, however, that he relented and consented to her vocation.

Mattia served as abbess for forty years, always distinguished by her piety and strong will. When she was dying, it is said that she was wrapped in a beam of white light that illuminated the entire convent. She was buried in an ordinary grave, but the nuns soon bowed to community pressure and prepared to move her body to a more impressive tomb. When exhumed, the body was found incorrupt and gave off a sweet fragrance of jasmine. It was placed inside a reliquary on the high altar in the convent church. It still produces an oil, which the nuns collect in small vials and distribute to the faithful.

Mattia's most recent miracle occurred in 1987. A Franciscan tertiary dreamed that Mattia appeared to her and described a certain cancer patient at a Naples hospital. The tertiary was told to give this complete stranger one of Mattia's relics and some of her holy oil. She located the patient, a pharmacist who was receiving radiation treatment, and with his cooperation carried out Mattia's instructions. He was subsequently declared cured and returned to his profession. His periodic checkups are said to be preceded by the strong scent of jasmine.

Mattia is commemorated by Franciscans on November 7 and by Capuchins on December 30.

The Genius of Mattia dei Nazarei:
As she lay dying, Mattia gave her nuns a final blessing and urged them to love each other, because: *"God is love."*

Reflection:
"No one has ever seen God. Yet, if we love one another, God remains in us, and his love is brought to perfection in us."

1 John 4:12

SAINT FABIOLA OF ROME

d. December 27, 400, Rome, Italy

Fabiola came from one of the most illustrious families in Rome, but her first husband was an abusive degenerate. She left him, got a divorce, and married again, which was legal under Roman civil law but caused a great scandal among her fellow Christians.

After the death of her second husband, Fabiola made a public penance. On the day before Easter, she appeared before the gates of the basilica of St John Lateran, the center of Christian life in Rome, dressed in sackcloth, and acknowledged her sin. She asked all the angels and saints, and the gathered brothers and sisters, to pray for her. This act of humility made a great impression on Saint Jerome,[228] who wrote: *"As Fabiola was not ashamed of the Lord on earth, so he will not be ashamed of her in heaven."*

From then on, Fabiola devoted her huge fortune to the poor. She founded the first public hospital in Rome, and would walk the streets herself, gathering the most helpless cases. Soon she expanded beyond the city, to outer islands and remote settlements. *"Rome was not large enough for her compassionate kindness,"* wrote Jerome. In her zeal for charity, Fabiola found herself competing with Pammachius, a former senator. He and Fabiola vied to build a hospice for the thousands of pilgrims pouring into Rome. Finally, Jerome wrote, *"They united their resources and combined their plans so that harmony might forward what rivalry would have brought to naught."*

Her feast day is December 27.

The Genius of Fabiola:

As we prepare for a new year, Fabiola presents an example of a woman who could reinvent herself several times, fortified by her feminine genius. As Jerome wrote in her eulogy: *"To change one's disposition is a greater achievement than to change one's dress."*

Reflection:

"Rejoice in the Lord always. I shall say it again: rejoice! Your kindness should be known to all. The Lord is near."

Philippians 4:4–5

NOTES

January

1. **Mary.** See also Feast of the Presentation (February 2); Feast of the Immaculate Conception (December 8); Feast of Our Lady of Guadalupe (December 12); Feast of Our Lady of the Rosary (October 7). Also: Our Lady of Fatima, see Jacinta Marto (February 11); Our Lady of the Miraculous Medal, see Catherine Labouré (November 28); Our Lady of Lourdes, see Bernadette Soubirous (April 16).

2. For more information about Mary's last days, see Feast of the Assumption of Mary (August 15).

3. **St Germanus of Auxerre** (c. 378–448). The most famous clergyman of his day, he is venerated on July 31.

4. **St Hyacinth Odrowaz** (1185–1257), "the Apostle of Poland," and **St Ceslaus** (c. 1184–1242).

5. **St Peter Fourier** (1565–1640). Canonized in 1897.

6. **St Francis de Sales** (1567–1622). Canonized in 1665; declared a Doctor of the Church in 1877 and patron saint of journalists in 1923.

7. **Ven. Louis Brisson** (1817–1908) wrote: *"I need God. It's a hunger that devours me."*

8. **Ven. Marie-Thérèse Chappuis** (1793–1875), religious name Marie-Françoise de Sales, was blessed with great managerial gifts.

9. **St Francis of Assisi** (1181–1226). Mystic, reformer, and founder of the Franciscan Order.

10. **Bl Arnaldo of Foligno** (d. 1313).

11. **St Veronica** (first century). Pious legends assigned the name (from the Greek for "true image") to the woman who wiped Christ's face on his way to the Crucifixion and discovered that He had left an image of his face on her cloth. Her feast is July 12.

12. **Bl Sylvester** (d. 1348). Venerated June 9.

13. **St Brendan the Navigator** (c. 484–577). On Ita's advice, he searched for the Isles of the Blessed and discovered Madeira and the Canary Islands. She also advised him to give up wickerwork boats and start building his ships with oak planks.

14. **St Eustochium Julia** (c. 370–419). A daughter of **St Paula of Rome** (January 31, note), she helped St Jerome translate the Bible and is venerated on September 28.

15. **St Ambrose of Milan** (c. 339–397). One of the first Doctors of the Church, he received his religious instruction from his older sister, **St Marcellina** (January 31, note).

16. **Bl Damien de Veuster** (1840–1889), "apostle to the lepers," voluntarily joined the first victims deported to Molokai in 1864 and later contracted the disease himself.

17. **St Joseph Benedict Cottolengo** (1786–1842). Refusing all government support and relying solely on volunteers, he built the Little House of Divine Providence into a great medical institution. Canonized in 1934.

18. **Bl Lavrentia Herasymiv** (1911–1952). Subjected to harrowing conditions until her death, she is venerated on August 26.

19. **St Zygmunt Gorazdowski** (1845–1920). Founder of a refuge for single mothers and abandoned children, he was one of the first five saints canonized by Pope Benedict XVI on October 23, 2005.

20. **Bl Mykola Charnetsky** (1884–1959). Bishop and martyr, he spent six years in a Siberian labor camp.

21. **St Jerome** (c. 341 420) was a brilliant theologian who translated the New Testament from Hebrew and Greek into Latin, but his abrasive personality made him many enemies. In 386 he left Rome with SS Paula and Eustochium to found a monastery at Bethlehem.

22. **St Asella** (c. 334–c. 406). Jerome wrote of her: "Let widows and virgins imitate her. Let wives make much of her, let sinful women fear her, and let bishops look up to her." Venerated December 6.

23. **St Marcellina** (c. 330–398). Older sister of **St Ambrose** (note 15). Marcellina was a great influence on her brother and the subject of many of his writings. Venerated July 17.

24. **St Lea** (d. 384) joined Marcella's community after the death of her husband. Venerated March 22.

25. **St Paula of Rome** (347–404) was a wealthy young widow and mother of five. After the death of a daughter, **St Blaesila** (363–383), Paula followed Jerome to the Holy Land with another daughter, **St Eustochium Julia** (c. 370–419). Blaesila is venerated on January 22, Paula on January 26. For more about Eustochium, see note 14.

26. **St Principia** (d. c. 420). A consecrated virgin, she is venerated on May 11.

February

27. **St Flora** (Gaelic = Blath) (d. 523). Venerated January 29.
28. **St Patrick** (c. 390–c. 461) brought Christianity to Ireland and is venerated on March 17. Some scholars insist that his dates make a friendship with Brigid doubtful.
29. **The Temple** had been erected by King Solomon, and appears in significant events throughout Jesus's life.
30. **St Simeon Senex (The Elder).** Venerated October 8.
31. **St Gaspar del Bufalo** (1786–1837). Famed preacher who inspired many bandits to abandon their lives of crime. Canonized in 1954.
32. **St Peter the Apostle.** See **St Tabitha of Joppa** (October 25).
33. **St Dionysius of Alexandria** (d. 265), bishop and theologian. Venerated on November 17.
34. **St Quinta** (d. 249). Venerated February 8. **St Metranus** is venerated on January 31.
35. **St Benedict of Nursia** (480–550) created a simple Rule for his monastery that has been called "the epitome of Christianity."
36. **Bl Francisco Marto** (1908–1919). Beatified with Jacinta in 2000.
37. **Lucia Abobora** (1907–2005) spent most of her life in a Carmelite monastery. She attended the beatification ceremony and is interred beside Jacinta in the basilica at Fatima.
38. **Bl Aleth of Montbard** (d. c. 1105). All biographers of Bernard of Clairvaux credit his mother with forming his character. She is venerated on April 4.
39. **St Bernard of Clairvaux** (1090–1153) reformed the monastic movement and preached against heresy. Canonized just twenty years after his death.
40. **St Eustochium Julia.** See **St Eustochia Calafato** (January 20).
41. **St John Bosco.** See **St Mary Mazzarello** (May 14).

42. **St Cuthbert of Lindesfarne** (d. 687). Celtic missionary turned hermit.

43. **Trinitarians.** See **Bl Anne Marie Taigi** (June 10).

44. **Bl Pius IX.** See **Bl Anna Rosa Gattorno** (May 6).

45. **St Philip Neri** (1545–1595) rejected the family business to enter the priesthood; he reformed and revitalized the Church.

46. **St Francis of Assisi.** See **Bl Angela of Foligno** (January 11).

47. **Bl Cristiana of Santa Croce** (c. 1237–1310) learned to read after she was inspired by a vision of the Blessed Mother. Venerated on January 10.

48. **St Willibald** (d. 787) cofounded the abbey at Heidenheim with his brother **St Wynnebald** (d. 761). Their father, **St Richard** (d. 720), died in Italy while on a pilgrimage and is still venerated in Lucca as "King of the English."

49. **St Joseph de Calasanz** (1556–1648), a Spanish nobleman, established the first free public school in Europe and was canonized in 1767.

50. **St John Capistrano** (1386–1456), a lawyer and former governor of Perugia, was widowed at thirty. He became a Franciscan, a force for reform, and a papal legate to Palestine and Bohemia. Canonized in 1724.

March

51. **Leo XIII** (1810–1903). Elected pope in 1878, he was also significant in the lives of **Bl Maria Droste** (June 5), **St Thérèse of Lisieux** (October 1), **St Frances Cabrini** (November 13), and **Bl Elena Guerra** (December 23).

52. **St Henry II, Emperor** (973–1024). Crowned Holy Roman Emperor in 1014, he and Cunegunda were dedicated to maintaining peace. He was canonized in 1146.

53. **St Gregory the Great** (540–604). Pope, Doctor of the Church, and patron of musicians, he accomplished much in spite of chronic illness and constant pain.

54. **St Auguste Chapdelaine** (1814–1856) and **St Laurence Bai Xiaoman** (1821–1856) were canonized with the Martyrs of China.

55. **120 Martyrs of China.** See also **St Anna Wang** (September 29), the **Seven Blessed Martyrs of Shanxi** (July 7), and the **Four Martyrs of Wangla** (June 28).

56. **St Vincent de Paul** (1576–1660). Kidnapped by pirates as a youth and taken to Tunis, he escaped to Paris where he organized relief for orphans, fallen women, the poor, the blind, and the insane. Canonized in 1737 and later declared patron saint of all organizations devoted to works of charity.

57. **St Rictrude** (614–688) and her husband, **St Adalbald of Ostrevant** (d. 625), are patrons of large families. Her feast day is May 12.

58. **St Gertrude the Elder** (d. 649) was also the mother of Archibald, an important adviser to **St Bathildis** (January 29). Gertrude is venerated on December 6.

59. **St Itta** (d. 652), widow of **Bl Pepin of Landin** (d. c. 648), is venerated on May 8.

60. **St Foillan** (d. 655) was martyred while returning to Fosses; he was succeeded as abbot by **St Ultan of Fosses** (d. 686).

61. **St Wilfetrude** (d. c. 670) is venerated on November 23.

62. **St Patrick of Ireland.** See **St Brigid of Ireland** (February 1).

63. **St Jerome Emiliani** (1481–1537). Imprisoned as a young soldier, he miraculously escaped, was ordained a priest, devoted himself to charity, and founded the monastery where Giovanni Frassinello spent several years. Patron of orphans and abandoned children.

64. **St Dominic.** See **BB Diana, Cecilia, and Amata** (June 9).

65. **St Cadoc** (497–580), bishop and missionary who founded a famous monastery near Cardiff.

66. **Polish Martyrs of World War II.** Among the other women beatified were: **Alice Kotowska** (November 11), **Katherine Celestyna Faron** (April 3), and **Maria Teresa Kowalska** (July 28).

April

67. See **Bl Natalie Tulasiewicz** (March 31).
68. **Bl Maria Mancini** (1355–1431). For more information about this remarkable woman, see Annotated Sources and Web Sites under Clare Gambacorta.
69. **Bl Eve of Liège** (d. c. 1266). An anchorite at the church of St Martin, she remained Juliana's friend and after her death campaigned for her cause. Beatified 1904. Venerated March 14.
70. For more about **St Augustine,** see **Monica of Carthage** (August 27).
71. **Three Marys** (first century). The others were **St Mary Magdalene** (July 22) and **St Mary Salome.**
72. **St Joseph of Arimathea** (first century). His generosity inspired many legends.
73. **True Cross.** See **St Helen** (August 18).
74. **Bl John Colombini** (c. 1300–1367). **Bl Giovanna Bonomo** (March 1) recommended his conversion story to her father, a repentant murderer.
75. **Righteous Gentile.** An honor awarded by the Holocaust Martyrs' and Heroes' Remembrance Authority of Jerusalem to those who risked their lives to save Jews during the Holocaust. Other recipients include Oskar Schindler and Raoul Wallenberg.
76. **St Eustace of Luxeuil** (d. 629) governed six hundred monks and mentored many bishops and saints.
77. **Louise Hensel** (1798–1876). Daughter of a Lutheran pastor, she converted in 1818. As headmistress of St Leonard's Academy at Aix-la-Chapelle she mentored **Bl Frances Schervier** (December 14) and Ven. Clara Fey (1815–1894), founder of the Sisters of the Poor Child Jesus. Louise also introduced her friend **Bl Anna Katharina Emmerich** (February 15) to Clemens Brentano. Although never a nun herself, Louise retired to Pauline's convent in Padeborn.
78. **St Juliana** (d. 305). When she refused to marry a pagan, her father had her beaten and beheaded. One hundred and thirty people were converted by the spectacle of her suffering. She is venerated on February 16.
79. **Bl Raymond de Capua** (1330–1399) was Catherine's spiritual director for the last six years of her life. Although skeptical at first, he became convinced that she was a truly holy woman. When he was near death from the plague, Catherine stayed at his bedside, and he believed that her prayers saved his life. He later led a reform of the Dominican Order.
80. **Doctors of the Church.** Only thirty men and three women have been named as Doctors of the Church in recognition of their intellectual achievements and writings. By tradition, the first four were SS Gregory the Great, Ambrose, Augustine, and Jerome. In 1970 **Teresa of Avila** (October 15) became the first woman so honored, and Catherine was named a week later.

May

81. **St Gall** (d. c. 640). The abbey was named for an Irish missionary venerated as an apostle of Switzerland.
82. **St Hatto** (d. 985). Benedictine monk and hermit.
83. **St Rachild of St Gall** (d. 946). Buried beside Wiborada and venerated November 23.

84. **St Ulric of Augsburg** (890–973). In 993 he became the first saint formally canonized in Rome.

85. **St Arianus** (d. c. 311). After his own conversion, Arianus and four companions were condemned to drown at sea. Some legends say their bodies were carried ashore by dolphins.

86. **Bl Pius IX** (1792–1878). During the longest pontificate in history, he attempted to modernize papal bureaucracy, defined the dogma of the **Immaculate Conception** (December 8), and convened the First Vatican Council.

87. **St John Nepomucene Neumann** (1811–1860). Born in Bohemia and ordained in New York, he became the beloved bishop of Philadelphia. Canonized in 1977.

88. **St John Bosco** (1815–1888). Priest who founded the Order of Our Lady, Help of Christians and St Francis de Sales (Salesians), dedicated to the education of young boys. Canonized 1934.

89. **St Gerebernus** (seventh century) is venerated on the same day as Dymphna.

90. **St Dominic.** See **BB Diana, Cecilia, and Amata** (June 9).

91. **St Louis-Marie Grignion de Montfort** (1673–1716). Charismatic preacher and author of *True Devotion to Mary.*

92. **St Jean de Brébeuf** (1593–1649) converted seven thousand Hurons and created a dictionary and catechism in the Huron language. Canonized with the North American Martyrs.

93. **Bl Francis de Montmorency Laval** (1623–1708) also worked closely with **Marguerite Bourgeoys** (January 12).

94. **St James the Great** (d. 44). A brother of St John the Evangelist, he was martyred soon after the Resurrection (Acts 12:2).

June

95. **St Pambo** (c. 340–390), Egyptian-born pioneer of monasticism.

96. **St Melania the Younger** (383–439). She and her husband, **St Pinian,** were immensely rich, but after the deaths of their two children they devoted themselves to charity, and died in the Holy Land. Venerated December 31.

97. **St Paulinus of Nola** (354–431). Roman patrician who became a priest after the death of his only son. By the time of Melania's return he was bishop of Nola.

98. **St Dominic de Guzmán** (1170–1221). Founder of the Order of Preachers (Dominicans), he was canonized in 1234. For more information, see his mother, **Bl Jane of Aza** (August 8).

99. **Bl Jordan of Saxony** (1190–1237). On the death of Dominic, he succeeded him as Master General of the order.

100. **Order of the Most Holy Trinity,** founded to redeem Christians captured by Muslims, was the first order dedicated to rescuing captives. **Bl Elizabeth Canori Mora** (February 19) was also a Trinitarian tertiary.

101. **Bl Pius IX.** See **Bl Anna Rosa Gattorno** (May 6).

102. **St Florido** (520–599) had saved the city from Attila the Hun.

103. **Bl Pius IX, Pope.** For more information see **Bl Anna Rosa Gattorno** (May 6).

104. **Ven. Maria Bernarda Heimgartner** (1822–1863). The Sisters of the Holy Cross of Menzingen continue her work in Africa, South America, and Europe. Her cause for sainthood is active.

105. **Bl Martha of Le Cambre** (thirteenth century) predeceased Aleydis and is honored for her great charity and patience. Venerated July 5.

106. **St Alexis Falconieri** (1200–1310). Canonized with the Seven Founders of the Servite Order in 1887.

107. **St Philip Benizi** (1233–1285). Considered the "Eighth Founder." Canonized in 1671.

108. **St Sexburga** (c. 635–c. 699). Venerated July 6. For information about the other sisters, see Annotated Sources and Web Sites under Etheldreda.

109. **Beguines.** For more about this movement, see **Bl Gertrude of Delft** (January 16).

110. **de Vitry** (c. 1160–1240), scholar, historian, and cardinal.

111. **St Vincent de Paul.** For more information, see **St Louise de Marillac** (March 15).

July

112. **St Peter Claver** (1581–1654) spent forty-four years in Cartagena, Colombia, evangelizing and caring for African-born slaves in spite of abuse, humiliation, and censure.

113. **Boxer Rebellion.** See the **Four Martyrs of Wangla** (June 28) and **St Anna Wang** (September 29).

114. Details about all seven Martyrs of Shanxi are in the Annotated Sources and Web Sites section.

115. **120 Martyrs of China.** See **St Agnes Kou Ying Tsao** (March 13).

116. Two Amalbergas share this feast day and are sometimes confused. **St Amalberga of Maubeuge** (d. 690) and her husband, **St Witger,** count of Lorraine, were the parents of many saints.

117. **St Landrada** (d. c. 690) founded the monastery at Bilsen and is venerated July 8.

118. **Bl Margaret of Foligno** (1378–1440). Dunbar writes: "Angelina was like the sun among planets and Margaret was like the moon among stars." Venerated June 13.

119. **Bl Paula of Foligno** (d. 1470) and Antonia of Florence founded separate monasteries in Aquila. Paula is venerated on January 26.

120. **St Serf of Fife** (c. seventh century). A missionary bishop in Scotland who, like all the Celtic saints, is the subject of many contradictory legends.

121. **St Kentigern** (c. 518–603). Often called Mungo ("dearly beloved"), he became a missionary in Iona and Wales. He returned to Glasgow to die, and his grave became the site of the cathedral.

122. **Spanish Civil War.** See **Bl Amparo Carbonell** (September 22).

123. **Fourteen Holy Helpers,** a once-popular devotion that included men and women saints, notably **Barbara** (December 4) and **Catherine of Alexandria** (November 25).

124. **Bl John of Fiesole** (c. 1395–1455), better known as Fra Angelico, was declared the patron of all artists in 1984.

125. **108 Polish Martyrs of World War II.** See **Bl Natalie Tulasiewicz** (March 31).

126. **St Mary of Bethany** (first century). Modern scholars dismiss the tradition that she and **Mary Magdalen** (July 22) were the same woman. Mary and **St Lazarus** share this feast day.

August

127. **St Andrew Fournet** (1752–1834) risked his life to serve his parish during the Revolution.

128. **Bl Peter de Betancur** (c. 1619–1667). "The Saint Francis of the New World" came to Guatemala hoping to be ordained a priest but could not master literacy. He became a Franciscan tertiary devoted to the poor, forming the Con-

gregations of Our Lady of Bethlehem, known as the Bethlemite Brothers and Bethlemite Sisters.

129. **St Paul the Apostle** (d. 65). After his dramatic conversion, he evangelized throughout Greece and Asia Minor until he was martyred at Rome.

130. **St Francis de Sales.** See **St Léonie Aviat** (January 10).

131. **Visitation.** See **St Elizabeth** (November 5).

132. **Julian Tenison Woods** (1832–1889). After leaving Adelaide, he continued working as a scientist and missionary priest in Australia and Tasmania. He is honored by the Josephites as their cofounder.

133. **St Dominic de Guzmán.** See **Bl Diana Andalò** (June 9).

134. **Bl Manez de Guzmán** (d. 1238) became one of Dominic's first followers.

135. **St Dominic of Silos** (c. 1000–1073), a Benedictine monk who was famous for ransoming prisoners from the Muslims.

136. **Ven. Pauline-Marie Jaricot** (1799–1862), founder of the Society for the Propagation of the Faith, spent her substantial fortune on good works. Her miraculous cure was accepted as Philomena's canonization miracle.

137. **Ven. Luisa de Jesus** (1799–1875). A Dominican tertiary in Naples at the time of her vision, she later founded the Sisters of the Sorrowful Mother.

138. **St Francis of Assisi.** See **Bl Angela of Foligno** (January 11).

139. **St Aloysius Gonzaga** (1568–1591). He joined the Jesuits at seventeen and died in Rome while nursing plague victims. He is a protector of young students and patron of Christian youth.

140. **St Louis de Montfort.** See **Bl Louise Trichet** (May 21).

141. **Ven. Jerónimo Mariano Usera y Alarcón** (1810–1891) labored in Spain, Puerto Rico, and Cuba. Some sources claim that he was beatified in 2000, but this is incorrect.

142. **St Augustine of Hippo** (354–430), one of the greatest thinkers in Church history.

143. **St Ambrose.** See **St Agnes of Rome** (January 21).

144. **Norbertine.** Religious order founded by **St Norbert** (c. 1080–1134) and also known as the Canons Regular of Prémontré, or Premonstratensians. They consider themselves "the first, and perhaps the only Catholic Order where absolute equality was observed between the spiritual life of the Canons and that of the Canonesses."

145. **St Margaret Ward** (d. 1588), a native of Cheshire, was a servant in London when she orchestrated a priest's daring escape from prison. Captured, tried, and condemned to death, she was hanged, drawn, and quartered at Tyburn. She is venerated on August 30.

September

146. **St Francis of Assisi.** See **Bl Angela of Foligno** (January 11) and **St Clare of Assisi** (August 11).

147. **Beguines.** See **Bl Gertrude of Delft** (January 16).

148. **Charles Anjou** (1227–1285). See **Bl Delphine de Signe** (November 29).

149. **Ven. Isabella the Catholic, Queen of Spain** (1451–1504), also financed Christopher Columbus's journey to the New World.

150. **Sister Maria Malgorzata** (1896–1966) faithfully attended to the graves of the martyrs until her death. Her cause for sainthood was opened in 2002.

151. **Ven. Monsignor Agostino Chieppi** (1830–1891) cofounded the Little Daughters with philanthropist Anna Micheli (1828–1871).

152. **St Cecilia of Rome** (November 22) is a patron of musicians.

153. **St Sophie.** See **St Olympias of Constantinople** (December 17).

154. **St John Chrysostom.** See **St Olympias of Constantinople** (December 17) and **St Tabitha of Joppa** (October 25).

155. **St Edgar the Peaceful** (943–975), overcame youthful indiscretions to rule wisely and well.

156. **St Wulfrida of Wilton** (d. c. 998). Venerated on September 9.

157. **St Edward the Martyr** (c. 962–979). His stepmother conspired to have him murdered so that her ten-year-old son, Ethelred the Unready, could become king.

158. **Bl Jutta of Spanheim** (d. 1136), a noblewoman who retreated to a cell in Disibodenberg, where she received Hildegard. Other women joined Jutta and she formed a Benedictine community that she ruled for twenty years. After Jutta's death, a property dispute with the monks led Hildegard to move the women's monastery to Rupertsberg, near Bingen. Jutta is venerated December 22.

159. **Brother Volmar** (d. 1173), a monk at nearby Disibodenberg. As Jutta's community grew into a women's monastery, it remained under the governance of the abbot of Disibodenberg until her death.

160. The **103 Martyrs of Korea** canonized in 1984 include 93 native Koreans, of whom 47 were women. Historian Adrian Launay writes, "It says much for the importance accorded to women in Choison [Korea] that they were thought worth executing in such numbers." Venerated on September 20.

161. **Bl Richard of St Anne** (1585–1622), a Franciscan, and **Bl Charles Spinola** (c. 1564–1622), a Jesuit, were beatified with Lucy.

162. **130 Martyrs of the Spanish Civil War.** See also **Bl Elvira Moragas** (August 12), **Bl Victoria Diez** (August 20), and the **Bl Carmelite Martyrs of Guadalajara** (July 19).

163. **St Albert Chmielowski** (1845–1916) was the subject of a play by Pope John Paul II that was filmed as *Our God's Brother*. Canonized in 1989.

164. **John Francis Regis** (1597–1640), tireless Jesuit preacher canonized in 1737.

165. **The Cenacle.** After the Ascension, Mary and the apostles withdrew to pray in the upper room or cenacle, creating the first Christian community in Jerusalem (Acts 1:13–24).

166. **St Isidro the Laborer** (1080–1130), also known as Isidro the Farmer, was canonized March 12, 1622, and is the patron of Madrid.

167. **St Tetta of Wimborne** (d. c. 772) governed five hundred nuns "with consummate prudence and discretion." Venerated September 28.

168. **St Boniface** (c. 675–754), Apostle to the Germans, was martyred at Dokkum with fifty-two companions.

October

169. **Ven. Marie-Azélie Guérin Martin** (1831–1877) and her husband, **Ven. Louis Martin** (1823–1894), had considered religious vocations before marrying. Of their six surviving daughters, five entered religious life: one became a Visitation nun and the other four were Carmelites.

170. **Doctor of the Church.** See **St Catherine of Siena** (April 29).

171. **Chaplet of the Divine Mercy** is based on a prayer Faustina received in a vision: *"Eternal Father, I offer you the Body and Blood, Soul and Divinity of your dearly beloved Son, our Lord Jesus Christ, in atonement for my sins and for those of the entire world. For the sake of his sorrowful passion, have mercy on us and on the whole world."*

172. **St Dominic de Guzmán.** See **Bl Jane of Aza** (August 8) and **BB Diana, Cecilia, and Amata** (June 9).

173. **St Pius V** (1504–1572), the austere Dominican reformer who launched the Counter-Reformation.
174. **St Nonnus** (d. c. 458).
175. **St Cadoc.** See **St Gladys of Wales** (March 29).
176. **St Felix of Cantalice** (1515–1587), self-educated but eloquent preacher who was beloved by children.
177. **Five saintly daughters.** See **Audrey** (June 23).
178. **St Erconwald** (d. 693), bishop of London, blessed with the gift of miracles.
179. **St Hildelitha of Barking** (d. c. 717), an Anglo-Saxon princess who took the veil at either Chelles or Faremoutiers, and succeeded Ethelburga as abbess. Venerated on March 24.
180. **St Bede** (673–735), one of the most brilliant men in English history and author of *Ecclesiastical History of the English People*, declared a Doctor of the Church in 1899.
181. **Carmelites and Discalced Carmelites.** The subsequent dispute over reform was settled only when the Discalced Carmelites were recognized as a separate congregation in 1580.
182. **St Claude de la Colombière** (1641–1682), superior of the Jesuit house at Paray-le-Monial, became Margaret Mary's spiritual director in 1674.
183. **Grey Nuns.** *Gris*, meaning "gray," was also French slang for "tipsy." They were called the Grey (Tipsy) Nuns for eighteen years before they adopted a grey habit in 1753.
184. **Jean Jacques Olier** (1608–1657), ordained in 1633, founded the Society of Saint-Sulpice (Sulpicians), an international organization dedicated to educating future priests. His cause for sainthood was opened recently and is being investigated.
185. **St Jordan of St Stephen,** a Dominican priest, was martyred and canonized with **Marina of Omura** (September 30).
186. **Catherine's children** were taken to the sultan's court in Istanbul and raised in Islam. According to historian Frederick Babinger: "Under the name Ishak Bey, Sigismund became the sultan's companion at table and in his games and often entertained him with crude jests. Later, he became governor of Bolu in Asia Minor where he presumably ended his days." Katharina's fate is less certain. She is believed buried in Macedonia. Babinger writes: "What sufferings she had previously undergone lie shrouded in darkness."
187. **St Ansbert of Chaussy** (d. 693). Overcoming his father's objections, he became a monk, later bishop of Rouen, and wrote the *Life* of Angadresima.
188. **Tabitha** means "gazelle" in Aramaic, as does Dorcas in Greek.
189. **St Peter the Apostle** (d. c. 64) was born Simon and baptized Peter, the "rock" on which Christ would build His church. After the Ascension, Peter presided at Jerusalem, preached in Samaria, and was martyred in Rome.
190. **St John Chrysostom.** See **St Pulcheria** (September 10) and **St Olympias** (December 17).
191. **St Dominic de Guzmán.** See **Bl Jane of Aza** (August 8) and **BB Diana, Cecilia, and Amata** (June 9).
192. **St Mechthild of Hackeborn** (c. 1240–1298) sang so sweetly that she was called the Nightingale of the Lord. She is venerated on November 19.
193. **Beguines.** See **Bl Gertrude of Delft** (January 16).

194. **Mother Marie des Douleurs** (d. 1983), baptized Suzanne Wrotnowska, cofounded the Benedictine Sisters of Jesus Crucified in order to make the contemplative life accessible to women with physical disabilities. Their monasteries are in France, Japan, and the United States. Her collected writings have been published as *Joy Out of Sorrow*.

195. **Society of Marie Reparatrix,** founded by **Bl Emilie d'Oultremont d'Hooghvorst** (1818–1878), a widowed mother of four. She worked closely with the Jesuits, who asked her to send Sisters to India. Beatified in 1997, she is venerated on October 11.

196. **Bl Pius IX.** See **Bl Anna Rosa Gattorno** (May 6).

197. **St Edwin, King of Northumbria** (d. 633), was martyred while battling the pagan king Penda. His widow, **St Ethelburga of Lyminge** (d. c. 647), founded a monastery and is venerated on April 5.

198. **St Caedmon** (d. c. 680) was an elderly cowherd whose sudden gift of song was encouraged by Hilda.

199. **Feast of the Annunciation** is celebrated on March 25.

200. **Feast of the Visitation** is celebrated on May 31.

201. **St John the Baptist** (first century) left his parents at an early age to live in the desert, preaching and baptizing.

202. **St Theodechild** (d. c. 660), brilliant educator and first abbess of the double monastery at Jouarre near Meaux, France, is venerated on June 28.

203. **St Hereswitha** (d. c. 690), sister of **St Hilda of Whitby** (November 4) and mother of **SS Sexburga, Withburga, Ethelburga,** and **Etheldreda** (June 23), entered Chelles in 655 after the death of her husband. She is venerated on September 3.

204. **108 Martyrs of Poland.** See **Bl Natalie Tulasiewicz** (March 31).

205. **St Jeanne Antide Thouret** (1765–1828) was a Sister of Charity when the French Revolution shut down her convent. She opened a soup kitchen and founded the Daughters of Charity, risking her life to defy the Revolutionary government. She established convents in Switzerland and Italy, but fell victim to meddling clergy and a jealous associate who replaced her as superior. Canonized in 1934, she is venerated on August 24. Her order is known in the United States as the Sisters of Charity of St Joan Antida.

206. **St Mechthild of Hackeborn.** See **Bl Mechthild of Magdeburg** (October 31).

207. **St David, King of Scotland** (c. 1085–1153), her youngest son, reigned for almost thirty years and is considered Scotland's greatest king. His shrine at Dunfermline Abbey drew pilgrims until the Reformation.

208. **St Madeleine Sophie Barat** (1779–1865), founder of the Religious of the Sacred Heart, was a mentor to many. She was canonized in 1925, and her feast day is May 25.

209. **St Josaphat Kuntsevych** (1584–1623), archbishop of Polotsk, Lithuania and the first Catholic of the Eastern Rite to be formally canonized by Rome (1867).

210. **Martyrs of Córdoba.** See also **SS Lillian and Natalie of Córdoba** (July 27).

211. **St Eulogius** (d. 859) clashed with Church authorities because he encouraged resistance to Islam. Watkins explains: "The Church does not approve martyrdom resulting from gratuitously offensive behavior towards non-Christians."

212. **St Walabonsus** (d. 851), a deacon martyred with five companions for blasphemy and preaching against Islam.

213. **Fourteen Holy Helpers.** See **St Margaret of Antioch** (July 20).

214. **Bl Luigi Beltrame Quattrocchi** (1880–1951) held positions in the Italian government, retiring as an honorary deputy attorney general.

215. **Children:** Filippo (Father Tarcisio); Cesare (Father Paolino); Stefania (Sister Maria Cecilia), who died in 1993. Enrichetta, who had no religious vocation, devoted herself to the care of her parents and siblings.

216. **St Elzéar de Sabran** (1285–1323) was canonized in 1369.

December

217. **St Flavian of Acquapendente** (d. 362). His humiliating punishment was usually reserved for slaves. **St Dafrosa,** his widow, is venerated on January 4, and **St Demetria** is venerated on June 21.

218. **SS Maxima, Donatilla, and Secunda** (d. 304). Maxima and Donatilla were broiled on a gridiron; then, with twelve-year-old Secunda, they were thrown to wild beasts. When the animals refused to touch them, they were beheaded. They are venerated on July 30.

219. **St Juan Diego Cuauhtlatoatzin** (1474–1548), canonized in 2002, is a patron of indigenous peoples.

220. **Gertrud Frank** also predicted that she herself would die at the age of thirty-three, which she did.

221. **St John Chrysostom** (c. 347–407), whose surname means "golden mouth," was a brilliant orator and early Doctor of the Church. For more about his banishment, see **St Pulcheria Augusta** (September 10).

222. **St Sophia.** There is no such saint. The basilica built by Constantine in the fourth century was dedicated to Hagia Sophia (Holy Wisdom) and was replaced by the current magnificent building in 532. When Constantinople fell to the Ottoman Turks in 1453, it was converted to a mosque.

223. **Bl Lucy Khambang** (1917–1940) and Agnes Phila belonged to the Sisters of the Lovers of the Cross, a religious order limited to their diocese.

224. **Clement di Rosa** (1767–1850). Paola's mother, Countess Camilla Albani of Bergamo (1786–1824), died when Paola was eleven years old. Of the nine Di Rosa children, only Paola outlived her father, and by only five years.

225. **St Paula of Rome.** See **St Marcella of Rome** (January 31).

226. **St Fausta of Sirmium** (third century) is venerated on December 19.

227. **King Herod of Ascalon** (first century), also known as Herod the Great, should not to be confused with Herod of Antipon, who ordered the beheading of **St John the Baptist.**

228. **St Jerome.** See **St Marcella of Rome** (January 31).

ANNOTATED SOURCES AND WEB SITES

Other sources are cited in the Bibliography. Some of these Web sites are not in English, but they are well worth visiting because (1) online translation services are available and (2) they have many wonderful photographs and illustrations.

Introduction

Catechism of the Catholic Church, 2d ed., Libreria Editrice Vaticana, 1997 (Latin text), Washington, DC: U.S. Catholic Conference, 1997 (English trans.), 898.

Woodward, Kenneth L., *Making Saints: How the Catholic Church Determines Who Becomes a Saint, Who Doesn't, and Why*, New York: Simon & Schuster, 1990.

Annotated Sources and Web Sites for January

Agnes of Rome. Sources: Jones, Kathleen, *Women Saints: Lives of Faith and Courage*, New York: Orbis Books, 1999, 41, 43–47; Visser, Margaret, *The Geometry of Love: Space, Time, Mystery and Meaning in an Ordinary Church*, Canada: Harper Flamingo, 2000. **Web sites:** Basilica of the National Shrine of the Immaculate Conception, Washington, DC, offers a virtual tour that includes a shrine of St Agnes, set in the Crypt Church: *http://www.nationalshrineinteractive.com*; Guide to the Christian Catacombs of Rome: *http://www.catacombe.roma.it/*.

Alix Le Clerc. Beatified 1943, but because of the war, the actual ceremony was delayed until 1947. Alix took the religious name Marie Thérèse of Jesus, but it is never used by her order. **Sources:** Material supplied by Sister Geraldine M. Hall of the Congregation of Our Lady, East Yorkshire, and Sister Josita Hanus, N.D., of the Notre Dame Sisters, in Omaha, NE; West, Margaret St L., *Blessed Alix Le Clerc (Co-foundress with St Peter Fourier of the Canonesses of St Augustine of the Congregation of Our Lady)*, London: Douglas Organ, 1947. **Web sites:** American Province of Notre Dame Sisters: *http://www.notredamesisters.org/index.htm*; Order in France: *http://www.aeal.org/*; Congregation of Our Lady, Canonesses of St Augustine: *http://congregation-notredame.cef.fr/*.

Ana de los Angeles. Beatified 1985. **Source:** Gomez Cano, Sor Blanca, O.P., *Sor Ana de los Angeles Monteagudo*, Lima: Monasterio de Santa Catalina de Sena, 1983. **Web sites:** Official site of the city of Arequipa: *http://www.arequipalinda. com/santac/soranai.html*; Official site of the Santa Catalina Monastery: *http:// www.santacatalina.org.pe/vida_i.htm*; Official site of the Dominicans of Peru: *http://www.op.org/peru/santos/Beata-Ana/default.htm*.

Angela of Foligno. The Lord's Prayer reprinted here is the traditional version as it is recited at Mass, based on Matthew 6:9–152. It differs slightly from the version in the New American Bible. According to La Chance: "She was first given the title of 'Blessed' by public acclaim, and later recognized as such by a decree of Clement XI on July 11, 1701." **Sources:** Angela of Foligno, *Complete Works*, trans. with an introduction by Paul LaChance, O.F.M., Mahwah, NJ: Paulist Press, 1993; Obbard, Elizabeth Ruth, ed., *Medieval Women Mystics*, New Hyde Park, NY: New City Press, 2002. **Web sites:** The Cenacle of Blessed Angela was officially revived in 1989 and holds an annual meeting in Foligno to study the message of the woman Pope Pius XII called "the greatest Franciscan mystic":

http://www.beataangeladafoligno.it/; A virtual shrine created and maintained by Don Sergio Andrioli: *http://beataangela.altervista.org/*.

Angela Merici. Not even the order she founded is sure about Angela's exact birth date, and the name of her younger sister has also been lost. Beatified 1768; canonized 1807. **Sources:** O'Reilly, Bernard, L.D., *St Angela Merici and the Ursulines*, New York: D. & J. Sadlier, 1880; Undset, Sigrid, *Stages on the Road*, trans. from Norwegian by Arthur G. Chater, New York: Knopf, 1934, 69–134. **Web sites:** Daughters of Angela Merici, based in Brescia, have a detailed site with a tour of the Merici Museum: *http://www.angelamerici.it/*; Ursulines of the Chatham Union in Ontario, Canada: *http://www.ursulines.org/*; Ursulines of Brown Co., OH, have posted photos of their pilgrimage to Brescia in 2001: *http://www .ursulinesofbc.org/pilgrimage.htm*.

Bathildis. Source: Madigan, Shawn, *Mystics, Visionaries and Prophets: A Historical Anthology of Women's Spiritual Writings*, Minneapolis: Fortress, 1998, 59–73. **Web sites:** Institute Gasnier-Guy-Sainte-Bathilde, in Chelles, France, has a page dedicated to Bathildis: *http://www.gasnierguy-stebathilde.com/*; Parish of Sainte Andre at Chelles also has information: *http://perso.wanadoo.fr/cathochelles/#*.

Boleslawa Lament. Beatified 1991. **Sources:** Material supplied by Sister Danuta Zofia Kujalowicz; Gronkiewicz, Sr. Adriana Teresa, *Blessed Boleslawa Lament*, trans. Jan Kielbasa, S.J., Warsaw, 1991 (pamphlet). **Web site:** Missionary Sisters of the Holy Family, Chicago: *http://www.cmswr.org/member_communities/MSHF.htm*.

Dwynwen. Sources: Baring-Gould, Sabine, and John Fisher, *The Lives of the British Saints: The Saints of Wales and Cornwall and Such Irish Saints as Have Dedications in Britain*, London: C. J. Clark, 1907, 1:65–67; Blackburn, Bonnie, ed., *Oxford Companion to the Year*, Oxford: Oxford Univ. Press, 1999; Tregarneth, Anita, *Founders of the Faith in Wales*, Liverpool: Brythen Press, 1947. **Web sites:** Historic UK.com, a British tourist site, maintains a page dedicated to Dwynwen that includes a painting and a photograph of her island: *http://www.historic-uk.com/HistoryUK/Wales-History/StDwynwen.htm*; The BBC offers a virtual tour of Llanddwyn Island, which has not changed much since Dwynwen resided there: *http://www.bbc.co.uk/wales/northwest/sites/inpictures/pages/llanddwyn. shtml?1*.

Elizabeth Ann Seton. Beatified 1963; canonized 1975. **Sources:** Anonymous, *Mother Seton's Way to God*, New York: Sisters of Charity, n.d.; Barthel, Joan, "A Saint for All Reasons: The Making of the First American Saint Culminates in Rome Today," *New York Times Magazine*, Sept. 14, 1975, 13, 81 90; Dirvin, Joseph I., C.M., *Mrs Seton: Foundress of the American Sisters of Charity, New Canonization Edition*, New York: Farrar, Straus & Giroux, 1975; Kelly, Ellin, and Annabelle Melville, *Elizabeth Seton: Selected Writings*, New York: Paulist Press, 1987. **Web sites:** National Shrine of St Elizabeth Ann Seton, Emmitsburg, MD: *http://emmitsburg.net/setonshrine/*; Sisters of Charity of New York maintain a virtual shrine: *www.setonmuseum.org.mus*

Eustochia Calafato. Beatified 1782; canonized 1988. **Sources:** Bell, Rudolph M., *Holy Anorexia*, Chicago: Univ. of Chicago Press, 1985, 141–45; Calafato, Eustochium, *La Leggenda della Beata Eustochia da Messina*, ed. Michele Catalano, Messina: G. d'Anna, 1950. **Web site:** City of Messina site includes a page with information about Eustochia and stunning photographs of the church of Montevergine where her incorrupt body is venerated: *http://www.torrese.it/index.htm*.

Geneviève of Paris. Sources: Heinzelmann, Martin, *Les Vies Anciennes de Sainte Genevieve de Paris: Etudes Critiques*, Paris: H. Champion, 1986; Dubois, Jacques, O.S.B., *Sainte Genevieve de Paris: La Vie, la Culte, l'Art*, Paris: Beauchesne, 1982. **Web site:** St Genevieve Church in Las Cruces, NM, has pages dedicated to their patron, including a photograph of a beautiful statue imported from France: *http://www.saintgenevievechurch.org/*.

Genoveva Torres Morales. Beatified 1995; canonized 2003. **Sources:** Morales, Genoveva Torres, *Escritos Personales de la Reverandina Madre Genoveva Torres Morales*, Barcelona: Hermanas del Sagrado Corazón de Jesús, 1973; Vives, Bernadino Llorda, S.J., *Angel de la Soledad: La Madre Genoveva Torres Morales*, Zaragoza: Religiosas Angelicas, 1970. **Web site:** Angelicas maintain a detailed site: *http://www.angelicas.org/*.

Gertrude of Delft. Watkins says "cult not confirmed," but Geybels refers to her as "the beatified Gertrude of Oosten." She is in *The Catholic Encyclopedia* (1911) as a Venerable, but Robert F. McNamara refers to her as Blessed. **Sources:** Geybels, Hans, *Vulgariter Beghinae: Eight Centuries of Beguine History in the Low Countries*, Turnhout, Belgium: Brepols, 2004, 82, 126; McNamara, Father Robert F., "Bl Gertrude of Delft," *Saints Alive*, read online at *http://www.stthomasirondequoit.com/SaintsAlive/id250.htm*. **Web site:** A private site devoted to the tiles of Delft includes a virtual walking tour of the city and a photo of a statue of Gertrude. Created by Margo Allingham, "Dutch Tiles: Notes from a Neophyte": *http://www.tiles.org/pages/tilesite/mallingham/new_delft_p5.html*.

Hyacintha Mariscotti. Watkins assures us: "She is liturgically celebrated as a virgin, which she was not." Beatified 1726; canonized 1807. **Sources:** Blunt, Hugh Francis, *The Great Magdalens*, New York: Macmillan, 1928, 157–69; Monro, Margaret, *A Book of Unlikely Saints*, New York: Longmans, Green, 1943, 1–8. **Web sites:** Vignanello, Viterbo, has details about her illustrious family and photos of the castles: *http://www.latuscia.com/en_comune_vignanello.php*; Another Vignanello site has many photos and monuments: *http://www.comunevignanello.it/default.asp*.

Ita of Limerick. Source: Sellner, Edward C., *Wisdom of the Celtic Saints*, Notre Dame, IN: Ave Maria Press, 1993, 149–54. **Web site:** Monastic Ireland, part of the web portal of the Catholic Church in Ireland, has a detailed page dedicated to Ita: *http://www.catholicireland.net/monasticireland/index.htm*.

Josefa of Beniganim: Beatified 1888. **Sources:** Haliczer, Stephen, *Between Exaltation and Infamy: Female Mystics in the Golden Age of Spain*, New York: Oxford Univ. Press, 2002, throughout; Koneberg, Hermann, O.S.B., *Blessed Ones of 1888*, trans. from German by Eliza A. Donnelly, New York: Benziger Bros., 1888, 149–88.

Léonie Aviat. Beatified 1992; canonized 2001. **Sources:** Sister Anne Elizabeth of the Oblate Sisters of St Francis de Sales in Childs, MD, supplied material and confirmed her feast day; Poinsot, Sister Genevieve-Agnes, *A Beacon of Hope: Saint Leonie Frances de Sales Aviat*, Childs, MD: Oblate Sisters of St Francis de Sales, n.d. **Web sites:** Oblate Sisters of St Francis de Sales in Childs, MD: *http://www.oblatesisters.org/*; Oblates of St Francis de Sales, Toledo-Detroit Province: *http://www.oblates.us/saints.htm*.

Marcella of Rome. Sources: Baring-Gould, Rev. Sabine, *The Lives of the Saints: With Introduction and Additional Lives of English Martyrs, Cornish, Scottish, and Welsh Saints, and a Full Index to the Entire Work*, Edinburgh: John Grant, 1914, 2:470–71; Agnes B. C. Dunbar, *A Dictionary of Saintly Women*, London: George Bell & Sons, 1905, 2:8–10.

Margaret of Hungary. Beatified 1804; canonized 1943. **Source:** Catherine, Sister Mary, O.P., *Margaret, Princess of Hungary: A Newly Canonized Saint*, Oxford: Blackfriars, 1945.

Marguerite Bourgeoys. Beatified 1950; canonized 1982. **Sources:** Butler, Elizabeth F., *The Life of Venerable Marguerite Bourgeoys*, New York: P. J. Kenedy, 1932;

Poissant, Sister Simone, C.N.D., "In His Image: Saint Marguerite Bourgeoys (1630–1700)," *Canadian Catholic Review*, April 1984, 14–16; Simpson, Patricia, C.N.D., *Marguerite Bourgeoys and Montreal*, Montreal: McGill-Queen's Univ. Press, 1997. **Web sites:** Marguerite Bourgeoys Museum and Chapel, Montreal, Quebec, Canada: *http://www.marguerite-bourgeoys.com/*; Congregation of Notre Dame: *http://www.cnd-m.com/English2/HomeMain.htm*.

Marianne of Molokai. Beatified 2005. **Sources:** Material provided by Sister Mary Laurence Hanley of the Sisters of St Francis; Hanley, Mary Laurence, O.S.F., *A Brief Biographical Sketch and Spiritual Profile of Mother Marianne of Molokai*, Syracuse: Sisters of St Francis of Syracuse, 1977; Kelly, Joe, columns in the *Booneville Herald*, Booneville, NY. **Web sites:** Kalaupapa is now a national park. Its website has a page dedicated to Marianne: *http://www.nps.gov/kala/docs/story. htm*; Franciscan Sisters of Syracuse have details about her life: *http://www.osfsyr .org/default.htm*; Blake Pitcher of the *Syracuse and Utica Observer-Dispatch* has created a site with numerous photos of Marianne's life: *http://www.uticaod.com/ news/specialreports/2005_cope/flashpop.htm*.

Marie-Thérèse Haze. Beatified 1991. **Sources:** Daughter of the Cross, A, *Life of Mere Marie-Therese*, London: Burns & Oates, 1893; J.d.M., *La Venerable Mere Marie-Therese Haze: Fondatrice de la Congregation des Filles de la Croix de Liege, sa Vie et son Oeuvre*, Bruxelles: Librairie Albert Dewit, 1921. **Web site:** St. Peter's Church in Bombay has details about the work of the Daughters in India, under St. Joseph's Convent: *http://www.stpetersbandra.com*.

Mary, the Mother of God. Sources: Adels, *Wisdom of the Saints*, 91 (Cabrini quote); Moussa I Daoud, Cardinal Ignace, "Trinity, Mary, Church," speech given at the 11th Ordinary General Assembly of the Synod of Bishops, *L'Osservatore Romano* (weekly English ed.), Oct. 19, 2005, 19. **Web sites:** Marian Library/ International Marian Research Institute at the University of Dayton in Ohio: *http://www.udayton.edu/mary/*; The Mary Queen of the Universe Shrine, Orlando, FL: *http://www.maryqueenoftheuniverse.org*.

Olympia Bida. Beatified 2001. **Sources:** Glover, Janice, and Jaroslawa Kisyk, "Ukraine Welcomes Pope: Ukraine Welcomes a Pilgrim of Peace and Brotherhood," read online at www.Catholicinsight.com, July/Aug. 2001; Turii, Oleh, "The Papal Visit to Ukraine, June 23–27, 2001," *Ukrainian Weekly*, July 8, 2001, read online at: *www.ukrweekly.com/Archive/2001/270123.shtml*.

Paula of Tuscany. *The Book of Saints* (1947) gives Paula's dates and feast day (January 5) and says "she was instrumental in bringing the feuds between Pisa and Florence to a peaceful settlement." She is gone from the 2002 edition. **Source:** Vigilucci, Lino, *Camaldoli: A Journey into Its History and Spirituality*, trans. Peter-Damian Belisle, Trabuco Canyon, CA: Source Books, 1995.

Raphaela María Porras. Beatified 1952; canonized 1977. **Sources:** Material provided by Sister Joy Payton of the St Raphaela Center, Haverford, PA; Lawson, Wiliam, S.J., *Blessed Rafaela Maria Porras: 1850–1925, Foundress of the Handmaids of the Sacred Heart*, Dublin: Clonmore & Reynolds, 1963; Porras, Raphaela, *Letters of Saint Raphaela Mary of the Sacred Heart of Jesus*, Norfolk, England: Carmelite Monastery, 1975; Yanez, Inmaculada [sic], *Foundations for a Building: Saint Raphaela Mary of the Sacred Heart*, trans. from Spanish by Norah Birch, ACI, n.d.; Yanez, Inmaculada [sic], *Saint Raphaela Mary*, trans. from Spanish by Amar Siempre, London: Ludo Press, 1985. **Web sites:** Handmaids of the Sacred Heart of Jesus: *http://www.acjusa.org/*.

Roseline Villeneuve. Beatified 1831. Never formally canonized, but reference books, including the *New Catholic Encyclopedia*, refer to her as Saint Roseline. **Source:** Sabatier, Pierre, *Sainte Roseline: Moniale-Chartreuse, 1263–1329*,

Marseille: Lafitte Reprints, 1974. **Web sites:** Chateau Sainte-Roseline is a commercial vineyard, but their website includes wonderful photographs of the interior of the chapel and of Roseline's incorrupt body: *http://www.sainte-roseline. com;* The Carthusian Order maintains a site that has interesting information about a way of life that has not changed much since the days of St Roseline: *http://www.chartreux.org.*

Stephanie Quinzani. Beatified 1740. **Sources:** Dorcy, Sister Mary Jean, O.P., *Saint Dominic's Family: The Lives of Over 300 Famous Dominicans,* Rockford, IL: Tan Books, 1983 (orig. published 1964 by Priory Press), 252–53; Lehmijoki-Gardner, Maiju, ed. and trans., *Dominican Penitent Women,* New York: Paulist Press, 2005 (Classics of Western Spirituality Series), throughout; Thurston, Herbert, S.J., *The Physical Phenomena of Mysticism,* ed. J. H. Crehan, S.J., Chicago: Henry Regnery, 1952, 201–2. **Web site:** Soncino's official website has a page dedicated to its churches, many of them associated with Stephanie: *http://www.prolocosoncino.it/index.php.*

Teresa Grillo Michel. Beatified 1998. **Source:** Material provided by Sister Maria Tamburro of the Little Sisters of Divine Providence.

Veronica of Binasco. Cult confirmed in 1517, when her name was entered into the Roman Martyrology. **Sources:** Rotelle, John E., O.S.A., ed., *Book of Augustinian Saints,* Villanova, PA: Augustinian Press, 2000, 150–51; Zarri, Gabriella, "Living Saints: A Typology of Female Sanctity in the Early Sixteenth Century," in *Women and Religion in Medieval and Renaissance Italy,* trans. Margery J. Schneider, ed. Daniel Bornstein and Roberto Rusconi, Chicago: Univ. of Chicago Press, 1996, 219–304. **Web sites:** Province of St Augustine (West Coast): *http://www.osa-west.org/;* Province of Our Mother of Good Counsel (Midwest): *http://www.midwestaugustinians.org/index.html.* Vincenzo Maddolino maintains a quirky site with much more information about her, in Italian only: *http://www .geocities.com/Paris/LeftBank/4494/bv1.htm.*

Zdislava of Lemberk. Beatified 1907; canonized 1995. When she was canonized, her feast day was fixed at January 4, but in the United States that date conflicts with the feast of Elizabeth Ann Seton. It is therefore kept by the Dominicans as a vigil on January 7 or 8, and in the Czech Republic on May 30. Watkins gives January 1, but this is incorrect. **Source:** Dorcy, *Saint Dominic's Family,* 47–48. **Web site:** The Diocese of Lemberk has many photographs: *http://zdislava.signaly .cz/index.php.*

Annotated Sources and Web Sites for February

Agatha of Catania. Source: Lanzi, Fernando, and Gioia Lanzi, *Saints and Their Symbols: Recognizing Saints in Art and in Popular Images,* trans. Matthew J. O'Connell, Collegeville, MN: Liturgical Press, 2004, 88–89. **Web site:** Archdiocese of Catania includes streaming video of the annual three-day festival in her honor. *http://www.circolosantagata.com/index.php.*

Anna Katharina Emmerich. Beatified 2004. **Sources:** O'Malley, John, S.J., "A Movie, a Mystic, and a Spiritual Tradition," *America,* March 15, 2004; Schmoger, Karl E., C.S.S.R., *The Life of Anne Catherine Emmerich,* Rockford, IL: Tan Books, 1976 ("reprinted from the 1968 edition of Maria Regina Guild, Los Angeles, California, itself reprinted from the English edition of 1885"); Woodward, *Making Saints,* 178–84. **Web sites:** Diocese of Munster, Germany: *http://www. kirchensite.de/index.php?cat_id=9366;* Augustinians of the Midwest (Province of Our Mother of Good Counsel), in Olympic Fields, IL: *http://www.midwestaugus-tinians.org/saints_annemmerich.html;* City of Dulmen has information created by

Dr. Clemens Engling, with links to other sites: *http://www.duelmen.de/kultur_bildung/emmerick/anna_katharina_emmerick_eng.htm.*

Anna the Prophetess. Source: John Paul II, "Christ Calls Women to Share His Mission," *L'Osservatore Romano*, weekly English ed., Jan. 15, 1997. **Web site:** University of Dayton, OH, Mary page: *http://www.udayton.edu/mary/.*

Anne Line. Beatified 1929 among the 136 English Martyrs; canonized 1970 among the Forty Martyrs of England and Wales. Their feast was formerly celebrated on October 25, but since 2001 they have been commemorated with the Martyrs of England on May 4. **Sources:** Finnis, John, and Patrick Martin, "Another Turn for the Turtle: Shakespeare's Intercession for Love's Martyr," *Times Literary Supplement,* April 18, 2003, 12–14; Walsh, James, S.J., *Forty Martyrs of England and Wales: Canonized by His Holiness Pope Paul VI on 25 October 1970* (pamphlet).

Antonia of Florence. Beatified 1847. **Sources:** Dunbar, *Saintly Women,* 1:77; Holböck, Ferdinand, *Married Saints and Blesseds Through the Centuries,* trans. Michael J. Miller, San Francisco: Ignatius Press, 2001, 285.

Apollonia. Sources: Baring-Gould, *Lives of the Saints,* 2:231–33; Dunbar, *Saintly Women,* 1:80–81.

Brigid of Ireland. Sources: Knowles, J. A., *Saint Brigid: Patroness of Ireland,* Cork: Brown and Nolan, 1907; Meehan, Bridget Mary, and Regina Madonna Oliver, *Praying with Celtic Holy Women,* Liguori, MO: Liguori, 2003; O'Hanlon, John, *Lives of the Irish Saints,* Dublin: James Duffy & Sons, 1875; Pennick, Nigel, *The Celtic Saints: An Illustrated and Authoritative Guide to These Extraordinary Men and Women,* New York: Sterling, 1997.

Catherine dei Ricci. Beatified 1732; canonized 1746. **Sources:** Butler, Alban, *The Lives of the Fathers, Martyrs and Other Principal Saints: Compiled from Original Monuments and Authentic Records,* Dublin: James Duffy, 1845, 2:123–37; Dorcy, *Saint Dominic's Family,* 325–26; Dunbar, *Saintly Women,* 1:164–65; Thurston, *Physical Phenomena of Mysticism,* 65, 66, 135–39, 168, 192, 228, 246; "Who Is the Most Important?" *Magnificat,* Feb. 2003, 354–56. **Web sites:** Photograph of the basilica of San Vincenzo and Santa Caterina dei Ricci, built in Prato at time of her beatification: *http://www.po-net.prato.it/artestoria/citta/eng/caterin.htm;* Dominican Sisters of St Catherine d'Ricci, in Elkins Park, PA, a religious community founded by two American sisters: *http://www.elkinsparkop.org/index.htm.*

Clare of Rimini. Beatified 1784. **Sources:** Baring-Gould, *Lives of the Saints,* 2:256–59; Blunt, *Great Magdalens,* 145–56; Caffiero, Marina, "From the Late Baroque Mystical Explosion to the Social Apostolate, 1650–1850," in *Women and Faith: Catholic Religious Life in Italy from Late Antiquity to the Present,* ed. Lucetta Scaraffia and Gabriella Zarri, Cambridge: Harvard Univ. Press, 1999, 189–91; Dunbar, *Saintly Women,* 1:187. **Web site:** Parish of Rimini: *http://www.cattolica.info/turismo/itinerari_sacri/index.html.*

Claudine Thévenet. Beatified 1981; canonized 1993. **Sources:** *L'Osservatore Romano;* Religious of Jesus and Mary, A., *Life and Works of Mother Mary St Ignatius (Claudine Thévenet),* Dublin: Clonmore & Reynolds, 1953. **Web site:** Religious of Jesus and Mary, U.S. Province: *http://www.rjm-us.org/.*

Colette. Beatified 1604; canonized 1807. **Sources:** Anonymous, *St. Clare and Her Order: A Story of Seven Centuries,* London: Mills & Boon, 1912, 171–95; Francis, Mother Mary, P.C.C., *Walled in Light: Saint Colette,* Chicago: Franciscan Herald Press, 1985 (orig. pub. New York: Sheed & Ward, 1959). **Web sites:** Monastery of the Poor Clares, Kokomo, IN: *http://www.thepoorclares.org/;* Poor Clares of Spokane, WA: *http://poorclare.com/;* Somme Tourist Board maintains a site with some information and a photograph of a statue: *http://www.somme-tourisme.com/*

uk/decouvrir/amienois/Corbie/corbie.asp; Her convent in Poligny, France: *http://www.ville-poligny.fr/article.php3?id–article=49.*

Dorothy. Sources: Butler, *Lives of the Fathers* (1845), 2:64–68; Dunbar, *Saintly Women,* 1:242–43. **Web site:** Sisters of St Dorothy, with pictures: *http://www.smsd.it.*

Ela Fitzpatrick. Listed as Blessed in Watkins, Dunbar, and the *Bibliotheca Sanctorum,* but none gives a date for beatification. **Sources:** Bowles, William Lisle, *Annals and Antiquities of Lacock Abbey, in the County of Wilts, with Memorials of the Foundress Ela Countess of Salisbury,* London: J. B. Nichols & Son, 1835; Dunbar, *Saintly Women,* 1:253–4; Ward, Bernard, *St Edmund: Archbishop of Canterbury, His Life, as Told by Old English Writers,* London: Sands & Co., 1903. **Web site:** Lacock Abbey is now part of England's National Trust: *http://www.nationaltrust.org.uk/places/lacock/.*

Elfleda of Whitby. Sources: Baring-Gould, *Lives of the Saints,* 2:214–20; Dunbar, *Saintly Women,* 1:254–5. **Web site:** Whitby Abbey, history and photos of the ruins: *http://www.whitby-yorkshire.co.uk/index.htm.*

Elizabeth Canori Mora. Beatified 1994. **Sources:** Canori Mora, Elisabetta, *La Mia Vita nel Cuore della Trinita: Diaro della Beata Elisabetta Canori Mora, Sposa e Madre,* Vatican City: Libreria Editrice Vaticana, 1996; Redi, Paolo, *Elisabetta Canori Mora: Un Amore Fedele tra le Mura de Casa,* Rome: Citta Nueva, 1995; Kissling, Frances, president of Catholics for a Free Choice, op-ed that first appeared in the *Los Angeles Times,* May 9, 1994, and is reprinted on the CFFC website: *www.catholicsforchoice.org.* **Web site:** Rome's Church of San Carlo Borromeo (Church of San Carlo alle Quattro Fontane), her parish church, has a great deal of information and many pictures: *http://www.sancarlino-borromini.it/.*

Eusebia Palomino. Beatified 2004. **Source:** Treece, Patricia, *Apparitions of Modern Saints: Appearances of Therese of Lisieux, Padre Pio, Don Bosco, and Others, Messages from God to His People on Earth* [abridged and updated version of book entitled *Messengers*], Ann Arbor: Servant Publications, 2001, 171–76. **Web sites:** Salesians of Don Bosco, the Eastern Province, Beatifications: *http://www.salesians.org/;* Salesians of Don Bosco, in Rome: *http://www.sdb.org/.*

Eustochia of Padua. Beatified 1760. **Sources:** Dunbar, *Saintly Women,* 1:299; Fraser, Mrs. Hugh, *Italian Yesterdays: Volume 1,* New York: Dodd, Mead, 1913; Thurston, Herbert, S.J., *Surprising Mystics,* ed. J. H. Crehan, S.J., Chicago: Henry Regnery, 1955, 133–47. Thurston calls her "a Cinderella of the cloister."

Filippa Mareri. Beatified 1806. **Source:** Brentano, Robert, *A New World in a Small Place: Church and Religion in the Diocese of Rieti, 1188–1378,* Berkeley: Univ. of California Press, 1994, 233–74. **Web site:** Sisters of Santa Filippa (Italian): *http://www.suoresantafilippa.it/.*

Humbeline. Beatified 1763. Watkins lists her as Saint but gives no canonization date. **Sources:** Luddy, Ailbe J., O.C., *Life and Teaching of St. Bernard,* Dublin: M. H. Gill & Son, 1927; Raymond, Father M., O.C.S.O., *The Family That Overtook Christ,* Boston: St Paul Editions, 1986 (prev. pub. 1942 as *The Sage of Citeaux: The Family That Overtook Christ*); Webb, Geoffrey, and Adrian Walker, *St. Bernard of Clairvaux: The Story of His Life as Recorded in the Vita Prima Bernardi by Certain of His Contemporaries, William of St. Thierry, Arnold of Bonnevaux, Geoffrey and Philip of Clairvaux, and Odo of Deuil,* Westminster, MD: Newman Press, 1960.

Jacinta Marto. Beatified 2000. Her birthdate is often given as March 11, 1910, but this is an error. According to Madigan: "The law at the time required that an infant be baptized—registered—eight days after birth. In fact, the custom was to baptize when convenient to the priest and the parents and let the birthday be registered as eight days beforehand." **Sources:** De Marchi, John, J.M.C., *The*

True Story of Fatima, ed. William Fay, St Paul, MN: Catechetical Guild Educational Society, 1952; Madigan, Leo, *The Children of Fatima*, Huntington, IN: Our Sunday Visitor, 2000. **Web sites:** Shrine of Our Lady of Fatima Official Site: *http://www.santuario-fatima.pt/portal/*; Virtual tour includes a video: *http://www.fatimavirtual.com/*; Blue Army of Our Lady of Fatima, in Asbury, NJ: *http://www.bluearmy.com/index.html*; Eternal Word Television Network has extensive Fatima information: *http://www.ewtn.com/fatima/*.

Jeanne de Valois. Beatified 1742; canonized 1950. **Sources:** Forester, Ann M. C., *The Good Duchess: Joan of France, 1464–1505*, London: Burns Oates & Washbourne, 1950; Levis-Mirepoix, Duc de, *Jeanne of France: Princess and Saint*, trans. Charlotte T. Muret, New York: Longmans, Green, 1940. **Web sites:** The Annunciade in Belgium: *http://www.annonciade.org/*; The Annunciade in France: *http://users.skynet.be/fa422258/index.htm*.

Josephine Bakhita. Beatified 1992; canonized 2000. **Sources:** Jones, *Women Saints*, 188–92; Knowles, Leo, *Modern Heroes of the Church*, Huntington, IN: Our Sunday Visitor, 2003, 127–36; Zanini, Roberto Italo, *Bakhita: Inchiesta su una Santa per il 2000*, Milan: San Paolo, 2000; Zanolini, Ida, *Tale of Wonder: Saint Giuseppina Bakhita, Revised and Enlarged Edition*, Rome: Editions du Signe, 2000 (orig. pub. 1931). **Web sites:** Canossian Daughters of Charity in the Philippines have produced *Bakhita the Musical*. Their website for the musical includes a photograph of the chapel in Vicenza where Bakhita is interred: *http://www.bakhitamusical.freeservers.com/home.htm*; Canossian Order maintains an official site with a page dedicated to Bakhita: *http://www.fdcc.org/*; National Black Catholic Congress also has a webpage dedicated to Bakhita: *http://www.nbccongress.org*.

Maria de Mattias. Beatified 1950; canonized 2003. **Sources:** Material provided by David Braun, Director of Communications, Adorers of the Blood of Christ, United States Region, St Louis, MO; Gegen, Loretta, A.S.C., *What Love Can Do: "A Vocation That Encircled the Globe,"* Belleville, IL: Record Printing & Advertising, n.d. **Web sites:** Adorers of the Blood of Christ, U.S. Province Office, St Louis, MO: *http://adorers.org/*; Adorers International: *http://www.asc.pcn.net/*; ASC Florence Province, based in central Italy and India, has its own site: *http://www.ascdirfi.it/inghomepage.htm*.

Maria Rivier. Beatified 1982. **Source:** Couriaud, P.M. Genevieve, "In His Image: Blessed Marie Rivier," *Canadian Catholic Review*, Nov. 1989, 379–83. **Web sites:** Sisters of the Presentation of Mary, Prince Albert, Saskatchewan: *http://www.presentationofmary.ca/*; Sisters of the Presentation of Mary, Methuen, MA: *http://www.presmarymethuen.org*; Sisters of the Presentation of Mary, International site: *http://cpminternational.org/cpmhomepageEng.htm*.

Paula Montal Fornés. Beatified 1993; canonized 2001. **Source:** Marín, Mª Dolores Pérez, Sch.P., "Paula Montal y Fornés," read online at *www.escolapias.org*. **Web sites:** Institute of Daughters of Mary, Religious of the Pious Schools (Escolapias): *http://www.escolapias.org/*; Escolapias in Aragón, Spain, also have an extensive site, with charmingly illustrated biography of St Paula Montal: *http://www.escolapiasaragon.org/*.

Scholastica. Sources: De Vogue, Adalbert, "The Meeting of Benedict and Scholastica: An Interpretation," *Cistercian Studies*, 1983, 167–83; Engs, Ruth Clifford, *Saint Scholastica: Finding Meaning in Her Story*, St Meinrad, IN: Abbey Press, 2003; Gregory the Great, *Life and Miracles of St. Benedict*, trans. Odo J. Zimmerman and Benedict R. Avery, Collegeville, MN: Liturgical Press, n.d.; Weigel, George, *The Courage to Be Catholic: Crisis, Reform and the Future of the Church*, New York: Basic Books, 2002, 4. **Web sites:** Order of St Benedict has much more about Scholastica and reproduces the entire text of St Gregory's story about her afternoon with her brother: *http://www.osb.org/gen/scholast.html*; Abbey of Montecassino, where the graves of Benedict and Scholastica are still venerated, also includes complete text of St Gregory's *Dialogues*, bk. II, which describes Scholastica's miracle: *http://www.officine.it/montecassino/main_e.htm*; This Umbria tourist site has extensive information under "religious itineraries": *http://www.itinerari.umbria2000.it/*.

Verdiana. Her name also appears as Virdiana and Viridiana. She was never formally canonized, but Pope Clement VII approved devotion to her 1533. She is referred to as Saint in most Franciscan histories. **Sources:** Bell, *Holy Anorexia*, 122–23; Hallack, Cecily, and Peter F. Anson, *These Made Peace: Studies in the Lives of the Beatified and Canonized Members of the Third Order of St Francis of Assisi*, rev. and ed. Marin A. Habig, O.F.M., Paterson, NJ: St Anthony Guild Press, 1957, 12–16; Thompson, Augustine, O.P., *Cities of God: The Religions of the Italian Communes, 1125–1325*, University Park, PA: Pennsylvania State Univ. Press, 2005, 188, 393, 395. **Web site:** Commune of Castelfiorentino includes pages for the Church of St Virdiana and the St Virdiana Museum: *http://www.comune.castelfiorentino.fi.it/*.

Villana de Botti. Beatified 1824. **Sources:** Dorcy, *Saint Dominic's Family*, 160–62; Jansen, Katherine Ludwig, *The Making of the Magdalen: Preaching and Popular Devotion in the Later Middle Ages*, Princeton: Princeton Univ. Press, 2000, 251–59, 289–90; Petroff, Elizabeth Alvida, *Body and Soul: Essays on Medieval Women and Mysticism*, New York: Oxford Univ. Press, 1994, 176. **Web site:** Tomb of Villa de'Botti at the church of Santa Maria Novella: *http://www.smn.it/arte/ch14.htm*.

Walburga. Sources: Material provided by Sister M. Pauline Laplante, O.S.B. and Sister Maria-Columba O'Larey, O.S.B., Benedictine Nuns of the Abbey of St Walburga, Virginia Dale, CO; Birgitta, Maria Anna, O.S.B., and Andreas Bauch, *Saint Walburga: Her Life and Heritage*, trans. Gerard Ellspermann, O.S.B., Eichstatt: Abbey St Walburga, 1985. **Web site:** Abbey of St Walburga: *http://www.walburga.org/*.

Annotated Sources and Web Sites for March

Agnes Kou Ying Tsao. Beatified 1900 with the Martyrs of the Society for the Foreign Missions of Paris (the only woman in the group); canonized 2000 with the Martyrs of China. **Sources:** Clark, Francis X., S.J., *Asian Saints: The 486 Catholic Canonized Saints and Blessed of Asia*, 2d ed., Quezon City, Philippines: Claretian Publications, 2000, 48; Haapala, Christine, and Matthew Carr, "Augustine Chao and the Chinese Martyrs," in *Saints of the Jubilee*, ed. Tim Drake, Bloomington, IN: 1st Books, 2002, 73–83; Neligan, Rev. William H., *Saintly Characters Recently Presented for Canonization*, New York: Edward Dunigan & Bro., 1859, 346–52. **Web sites:** St Agnes Kou Ying Tsao parish, Ontario, Canada: *http://www.saintagnestsao.org*; Chinese Martyrs Catholic Church, Ontario, Canada (click on First Introduction): *http://chinesemartyrs.org/*.

Agnes of Prague. Beatified 1874; canonized 1989. **Sources:** Dunbar, *Saintly Women*, 1:88–89; Mueller, Joan, *Clare of Assisi: The Letters to Agnes*, Collegeville, MN: Liturgical Press, 2003. **Web sites:** St Agnes of Bohemia Church in Chicago, IL: *http://www.stagnesofbohemia.org/*; Franciscan Archive, in Mansfield, MA, has a detailed history of Agnes: *http://www.franciscan-archive.org/*.

Angela de la Cruz. Beatified 1982; canonized 2003. **Source:** *L'Osservatore Romano*. **Web sites:** Franciscan Order in Valencia, Spain: *http://www.franciscanos.org/santoral/agatangela2.htm*; A lay admirer has created a devotional site: *http://www.antonioburgos.com/enlaces/varios/sorangela.html*.

Angela Salawa. Beatified 1991. **Source:** *L'Osservatore Romano.* **Web sites:** City of Krakow site offers a Saints Tour of the city: *http://www.krakow.pl/en/;* Devotional site with a photo of Angela: *http://www.katolicka.alleluja.pl/tekst .php?numer=17200.*

Annunciata Cocchetti. Beatified 1991. **Source:** *L'Osservatore Romano.* **Web sites:** Sisters of St Dorothy of Cemmo: *http://www.doroteedicemmo.it/;* Child's version of her life: *http://www.cocchetti.it/.*

Benedetta Cambiagio Frassinello. Beatified 1987; canonized 2002. **Sources:** Holböck, *Married Saints and Blesseds,* 258–59; Holböck, Ferdinand, *New Saints and Blesseds of the Catholic Church, Volume 2,* trans. Michael J. Miller, San Francisco: Ignatius Press, 2003, 221–23. **Web sites:** Benedictine Sisters of Providence Retreat House: *http://www.casacambiagio.it/template.php?pag=923;*

Catherine of Sweden. Beatified 1474. Never formally canonized, but in 1484 Pope Innocent VIII gave permission to venerate her as a saint. At least two Roman Catholic churches in the United States are dedicated to St Catherine of Sweden, in Wildwood, NJ, and Worcester, MA. **Sources:** Dunbar, *Saintly Women,* 1:156–58; Tjader Harris, Marguerite, ed., *Birgitta of Sweden: Life and Selected Revelations,* New York: Paulist Press, 1990 (Classics of Western Spirituality Series), 2–3; Holböck, *Married Saints and Blesseds,* 258–59. **Web sites:** Dedicated to St Bridget of Sweden, with information about Catherine: *http://birgitta .vadstena.se/;* Convent church in Rome where Lutheran services are held in the Chapel of St Catherine on Sundays and Thursdays: *http://roma.katolsk.no/ brigida.htm.*

Cunegunda the Empress. Canonized 1200. **Sources:** Baring-Gould, *Lives of the Saints,* 3:52–54; Dunbar, *Saintly Women,* 1:210–11; Holböck, *Married Saints and Blesseds,* 133–38.

Eugénie Milleret de Brou. Beatified 1975. **Source:** Lovat, Lady Alice, *The Life of Mère Marie Eugénie Milleret de Brou,* London: Sands & Co., 1925. **Web sites:** Sisters of the Assumption: *http://www.assumpta.fr/;* Assumption Sisters in the United States: *http://www.assumption.edu/;*

Eusebia of Hamay. Sources: Baring-Gould, *Lives of the Saints,* 3:279–80; Dunbar, *Saintly Women,* 1:2–3, 207–8.

Felicity and Perpetua. Sources: Baring-Gould, *Lives of the Saints,* 3:102–13; Salisbury, Joyce E., *Perpetua's Passion: The Death and Memory of a Young Roman Woman,* New York: Routledge, 1997.

Fina Ciardi. According to biographer Giovanni di Coppo, she was "canonized by acclamation" after saving San Gimignano from the plague in 1476. **Sources:** Baring-Gould, *Lives of the Saints,* 3:239–40; Santo Geminiano, Joannes de, *The Legend of Holy Fina, Virgin of Santo Gimignano: Now First Translated from the Trecento Italian of Fra Giovanni di Coppo, with Introduction and Notes by M. Mansfield,* New York: Duffield & Co., 1908. **Web sites:** Memorialized in a series of frescos by Domenico Ghirlandaio at the duomo of Gimignano, one of which can be seen on this Italian tourist site: *http://www.storiadellarte.com/ biografie/ghirlandaio/immghirlandaio/santa%20fina.htm;* Official site of San Gimignano (with information about the June festival): *http://www.sangimignano.net/.*

Frances of Rome. Canonized 1608. **Sources:** Fraser, Mrs. Hugh, *Storied Italy,* New York: Dodd, Mead, 1915, 96–182; Fullerton, Lady Georgiana, *The Life of St. Frances of Rome, of Blessed Lucy of Narni, of Dominica of Paradiso and of Anne de Montmorency,* New York: D. & J. Sadlier, 1885; Keyes, Frances Parkinson, *Three Ways of Love,* New York: Hawthorn Books, 1963, 41–126.

Gertrude of Nivelles. Sources: Baring-Gould, *Lives of the Saints,* 3:306–9; Dunbar, *Saintly Women,* 2:305; McNamara, Jo Ann, and John E. Halborg, eds. and trans., with E. Gordon Whatley, *Sainted Women of the Dark Ages*, Durham, NC: Duke Univ. Press, 1992, 220–34.

Giovanna Maria Bonomo. Beatified 1783. **Sources:** Material from Postulator, O.S.B., Cassinense, Italy; Anonymous, *The Life of Blessed Joanna Mary Bonomo, Benedictine Nun in the Monastery of St. Jerome, Bassano*, Rome: St Benedict's, 1896. **Web sites:** Commune of Asiago with many photos. See page devoted to Giovanna under "Cosa Visitare," including the statue in the town square erected on the 300th anniversary of her birth: *http://www.asiago.to/listaLuoghi.php.*

Gladys. Sources: Baring-Gould and Fisher, *Lives of the British Saints*, 3:202–4; Tregarneth, *Founders of the Faith in Wales*, 84–85.

Jeanne-Marie de Maillé. Beatified 1871. **Sources:** Habig, Marion A., O.F.M., *The Franciscan Book of Saints*, Chicago: Franciscan Herald Press, 1959, 788–90; Hallack and Anson, *These Made Peace*, 152–57.

Katharine Drexel. Beatified 1988; canonized 2000. **Sources:** Holt, Mary van Balen, *Meet Katharine Drexel: Heiress and God's Servant of the Oppressed*, Ann Arbor, MI: Charis, 2002; McSheffery, Daniel F., *Saint Katharine Drexel: Pioneer for Human Rights*, Totowa, NJ: Catholic Book Co., 2002; Tarry, Ellen, *Saint Katharine Drexel: Friend of the Oppressed*, Boston: Pauline Books & Media, 2000. **Web site:** Sisters of the Blessed Sacrament: *http://www.katharinedrexel.org/.*

Louise de Marillac. Beatified 1920; canonized 1934. **Sources:** Jones, *Women Saints*, 72–73, 97–103; Regnault, Sister Vincent, D.C., *Saint Louise de Marillac*, trans. from French by Sister Louise Sullivan, D.C., Rockford, IL: Tan Books, 1983 (reprint; orig. pub. 1974 in French by Editions S.O.S., Paris); Ryan, Frances, and John E. Rybolt, eds., *Vincent de Paul and Louise de Marillac: Rules, Conferences and Writings*, New York: Paulist Press, 1995 (Classics of Western Spirituality Series). **Web sites:** Sisters of Providence, Holyoke, MA: *http://www.sisofprov.org/;* International Site of the Vincentian Family: *http://www.famvin.org/.*

Lucy Filippini. Beatified 1926; canonized 1930. **Sources:** Bergamaschi, Pietro, *From the Land of the Etruscans*, trans. and adapted by Margherita Marchione, Rome: Edizioni di Storia de Letteratura, 1986; Parente, Pascal P., *Schoolteacher and Saint: A Biography of Saint Lucy Filippini*, St Meinrad, IN: Grail, 1953. **Web site:** Institute of the Religious Teachers Filippini: *http://www.filippiniusa.org/index.cfm.*

María Josefa Sancho de Guerra. Beatified 1992; canonized 2000. **Source:** *L'Osservatore Romano.* **Web site:** Servants of Jesus of Charity: *http://www.siervasdejesus.com/home_nueva.htm.*

Maria Karlowska. Beatified 1997. **Source:** *L'Osservatore Romano.*

Marthe Le Bouteiller. Beatified 1990. **Sources:** *L'Osservatore Romano;* Borrelli, Antonio, "Blessed Marta (Amata Adele) Le Bouteiller," read online at *www.Santibeati.it.* **Web sites:** Home site of the Sisters of Marie-Madeleine Postel has many photographs: *http://www.mmpostel.com/Page_1x.htm;* Site devoted to the shrine of Our Lady of Chapelle-sur-Vire: *http://perso.wanadoo.fr/normandies/cv.htm.*

Martyrs of Laval. Beatified 1955. **Source:** *L'Osservatore Romano.* **Web sites:** Sisters of Charity of Our Lady of Evron: *http://www.soeurs-charite-evron.com/;* Detailed site dedicated to Françoise Mézière (French text): *http://perso.wanadoo.fr/saintleger1/region1/53.francoisemeziere.htm.*

Matilda of Saxony. Sources: Baring-Gould, *Lives of the Saints*, 3:260–65; Dunbar, *Saintly Women*, 2:67–70. **Web site:** Quedlinburg is a UNESCO World Heritage site: *http://www.quedlinburg.de/neu/englisch/Tourismus/unesco_e.shtml.*

Natalie Tulasiewicz. Beatified 1999. Space does not permit including the stories of all the women among the 108 Martyrs: **Maria Ewa of Providence** (1885–1942) and **Maria Marta of Jesus** (1878–1942), Sisters of the Immaculate Conception of the Blessed Virgin Mary, caught hiding Jews in their convent and executed at Lublin; **Marianna Biernacka** (1888–1943), who traded places with a pregnant woman and was executed at Naumovichi, Belarus; **Maria Klemensa Staszewska** (1890–1943), Ursuline of the Roman Union, martyred at Auschwitz; **Julia Stanislawa Rodzinska** (1899–1945), Dominican who died of typhus at Stutthof; and **Maria Anna Kratochwil,** School Sister of Notre Dame, executed at Stanislawow, Ukraine. **Sources:** *L'Osservatore Romano;* Sokolowska, Katarzyna, "Bl. Natalia Tulasiewicz," read online at *www.hamburgpol.w.interia.pl/tulasiewicz .htm* and trans. from Polish by Marek Kruszon. **Web site:** Site dedicated to her: *http://hamburgpol.w.interia.pl/tulasiewicz.htm.*

Placide Viel. Beatified 1951. **Source:** *L'Osservatore Romano.* **Web site:** Sisters of St Marie-Madeleine Postel: *http://www.mmpostel.com/.*

Rafqa of Lebanon. Beatified 1985; canonized 2001. The Druze are considered a Muslim sect although their beliefs contain elements of Christianity. Her Baladita Order is now known as the Lebanese Maronite Order of St Anthony. **Sources:** *L'Osservatore Romano;* Zayek, Francis M., *Rafka, the Blind Mystic of Lebanon,* Still River, MA: St Bede's, 1980. **Web sites:** Official site of St Rafqa at the convent of St Joseph, Lebanon: *http://www.strafqa.org/index1.htm;* The blind mystic of Lebanon: *http://www.rafca.org/* [sic]; Our Lady of Lebanon, a Maronite Catholic church in Australia: *http://www.maronite.org.au/saints/rafqa.htm;* Abdallah maintains a devotional site: *http://www.lebanon.8m.com/.*

Sybillina Biscossi. Beatified 1854. **Sources:** Dorcy, *Saint Dominic's Family,* 172–74; Dunbar, *Saintly Women,* 2:223; Lehmijoki-Gardner, *Dominican Penitent Women,* 246.

Teresa Eustochio Verzeri. Beatified 1946; canonized 2001. **Source**: *L'Osservatore Romano.* **Web site**: Daughters of the Sacred Heart of Jesus include a biography of Teresa and photos of the church where her relics are venerated: *http://www .provitsacrocuore.org/index.php.*

Teresa Margaret Redi. Beatified 1929; canonized 1934. **Sources:** Bardi, Joseph, *St. Theresa Margaret,* trans. Margaret Mary Repton, Derby, NY: Daughters of St Paul, 1939; Rowe, Margaret, *God Is Love: St Teresa Margaret, Her Life,* Washington, DC: ICS Publications, 2003. **Web sites:** A Carmelite Sister's devotional site: *http://www.stteresamargaret.org/;* Main Carmelite site includes her among Great Carmelite Figures: *http://www.ocarm.org/eng/index.htm;* Carmelite province in Oklahoma: *http://www.oksister.com/Saints/teresa_margaret_redi.htm.*

Annotated Sources and Web Sites for April

Agnes of Montepulciano. Beatified 1534; canonized 1726. **Sources:** Bell, *Holy Anorexia,* 132; Cruz, Joan Carroll, *The Incorruptibles: A Study of the Incorruption of the Bodies of Various Catholic Saints and Beati,* Rockford, IL: Tan Books, 1977, 106–8; Da Capua, Raimondo, *Legenda Beate Agnetis de Monte Policiano,* ed. Silvia Nocentini, Rome: Edizioni del Galluzzo, 2001; Drane, Augusta Theodosia, *History of St. Catherine of Siena and Her Companions,* London: Burns & Oates, 1887, 239–40; Dunbar, *Saintly Women,* 1:36–37. **Web site:** Montepulciano home page includes photos of church where her body is venerated: *http://www .montepulciano.net/about-montepulciano.htm.*

Barbe Acarie. Beatified 1791. **Sources:** Dunbar, *Saintly Women,* 100; Jones, *Women Saints,* 128–36; Sheppard, Lancelot C., *Barbe Acarie: Wife and Mystic,* New York: David McKay Co., 1953. **Web site:** Friends of Madame Acarie: *http://www .madame-acarie.org/.*

Bernadette Soubirous. Beatified 1925; canonized 1933. **Sources:** Ball, Ann, *Modern Saints: Their Lives and Faces, Book One*, Rockford, IL: Tan Books, 1983, 71–79; Kempf, Rev. Constantine, S.J., *The Holiness of the Church in the Nineteenth Century: Saintly Men and Women of Our Own Times*, from the German by Rev. Francis Breymann, S.J., New York: Benziger Bros., 1916, 211–13; Trochu, François, *Saint Bernadette Soubirous, 1844–1879*, trans. and adapted by John Joyce, S.J., Rockford, IL: Tan Books (reprint of English ed. first pub. 1957). **Web sites:** Official site of the shrine at Lourdes: *http://www.lourdes-france.com/*; Convent where Bernadette spent her later years: *http://www.lourdes-fr.com/autres_sanctuaires/Anevers.htm*; Official site for Bernadette of Nevers: *http://www.sainte-bernadette-nevers.com/anglais/index.htm*.

Casilda of Toledo. Canonized 1750. **Source:** Espina, Concha, *Casilda de Toledo: Vida de Santa Casilda*. Madrid: Biblioteca Nueva, 1940. **Web site:** Shrine in Burgos: *http://personal.telefonica.terra.es/web/santuariostcasilda/*.

Catalina Tomás. Beatified 1792; canonized 1930. **Sources:** Dunbar, *Saintly Women*, 163; Haliczer, *Between Exaltation and Infamy*, throughout; Pettinati, Guido, S.S.P., *I Santi Canonizzati del Giorno*, Udine: Edizioni Segno, 1991, 78–83, as posted on *Totus Tuus Pagine Cattolico* (*http://paginecattoliche.it/*).

Catherine of Pallanza and Juliana of Busto-Verghera. Beatified 1769. **Source:** Material provided by Rev. Madre Abbadessa Rosella Pedroletti, Monastero Romite Ambrosiane. **Web site:** This private site reproduces much of the art celebrating Juliana: *http://www.itctosi.va.it/speciali/storia2/beatagiuliana.htm*.

Catherine of Siena. Canonized 1461. **Sources:** Baring-Gould, *Lives of the Saints*, 4:377–81; Catherine of Siena, *The Dialogue*, trans. and Introduction by Suzanne Noffke, O.P., New York: Paulist Press, 1980; Drane, *St. Catherine of Siena*, throughout; Dunbar, *Saintly Women*, 1:151–56. **Web sites:** Society of St Catherine of Siena, London, England: *http://www.caterinati.org.uk/index.html*; International Association of Caterinati: *http://www.caterinati.org/*; Basilica of Santa Maria Sopra Minerva, Rome: *http://www.basilicaminerva.it/*.

Celestyna Faron. Beatified 1999, among the 108 Polish Martyrs. **Sources:** Material supplied by Sister Malgorzata and Sister Philomena Nowicka of the Little Servant Sisters of the Immaculate Conception; Royal, Robert, *The Catholic Martyrs of the Twentieth Century: A Comprehensive World History*, New York: Crossroad, 2000, 192–215. **Web sites:** Little Servant Sisters of the Immaculate Conception, Cherry Hill, NJ, maintain a website, with some information about Celestyna under "History": *http://geocities.com/lsic2006/*; Home page of the order: *http://www.sluzebniczkinmp.pl/ds_cf.htm*.

Clare Gambacorta. Beatified 1830. Her associate **Bl Maria Mancini**, also known as Mary of Pisa, shared an unusual bond with Clare. When Maria was five, her guardian angel conducted her to where Peter Gambacorta, Clare's father, was being held as a political prisoner. She saw him suspended from a rope, and as she prayed for him, the rope broke. His jailers considered this a mark of providential favor and freed him, demanding only a heavy fine. The Blessed Mother appeared to Maria, ordered her to continue to pray every day for Peter, and foretold that one day Maria would owe her daily bread to the generosity of the man she had saved. Maria was beatified in 1855. **Sources:** Drane, *St. Catherine of Siena*, 302–4; Drane, Augusta Theodosia, *The Spirit of the Dominican Order: Illustrated from the Lives of Its Saints*, New York: Benziger Bros., 1896, throughout; Murphy, Sister Mary Evelyn, O.P., *Blessed Clara Gambacorta: A Thesis Presented to the Faculty of Philosophy of the University of Fribourg, Switzerland*, Fribourg: Imprimerie de L'Oeuvre de Saint-Paul, 1928.

Crescentia Höss. Beatified 1900; canonized 2001. **Sources:** Dunbar, *Saintly Women*, 1:208–9; Poernbacher, Karl, *Crescentia Hoess: A Saint for Our Time*, trans. Sister Clara Brill, F.S.P.A., and Ursula-Blank Chiu, La Crosse, WI: Franciscan Sisters of Perpetual Adoration, 2003; Thurston, *Physical Phenomena of Mysticism*, 192–93. **Web sites:** Tourist Board of Kaufbeuren maintains an extensive site under "Tourism"bless: *http://www.kaufbeuren.de*; Franciscan Sisters of Perpetual Adoration in La Crosse, WI, consider Crescentia their patron: *http://www.fspa .org/spirituality/crescentia.asp.*

Fara of Faremoutiers. Sources: Baring-Gould, *Lives of the Saints*, 12:105–7; Dunbar, *Saintly Women*, 1:307–8; McNamara and Halborg, *Sainted Women*, 155–75. **Web sites:** Official site of Faremoutiers, France, has detailed history of the monastery: *http://www.faremoutiers.org/*; church dedicated to St Fara in Palermo, Italy, includes information about its annual festival in her honor: *http://www.santafara.it/*.

Gemma Galgani. Beatified 1933; canonized 1940. First twentieth-century woman to be canonized and the first person canonized by Pius XII. **Sources:** Bell, Rudolph M., and Christina Mazzoni, *The Voices of Gemma Galgani: The Life and Afterlife of a Modern Saint*, Chicago: Univ. of Chicago Press, 2003; Monro, *Unlikely Saints*, 181; Thurston, *Physical Phenomena of Mysticism*, throughout; Walsh, Richard, "The Power Behind the Tiara," *Catholic World*, March 1944, 554–59. **Web sites:** A personal devotional site: *http://www.stgemma.com/*; Official site of her shrine in Lucca: *http://www.santagemma.it*; Devotional site: *http://www .corazones.org/lugares/italia/lucca/a_lucca.htm*; Another devotional site: *http:// www.santagemma.org/menu.html*.

Gianna Beretta Molla. Beatified 1994; canonized 2004 (marking the first time that a saint's husband and children were present at such a ceremony). **Sources:** Ball, Ann, *Faces of Holiness: Modern Saints in Photos and Words*, Huntington, IN: Our Sunday Visitor, 1998, 107–14; Pelucchi, Giuliana, *Blessed Gianna Beretta Molla: A Woman's Life, 1922–1962*, Boston: Pauline Books & Media, 2002. **Web sites:** Society of Blessed Gianna Beretta Molla: *http://www.saintgianna.org/*; Santa Gianna: *http://www.giannaberettamolla.org/principal.htm*.

Hosanna of Kotor. Beatified 1927. **Sources:** Dorcy, *Saint Dominic's Family*, 295–96; Dunbar, *Saintly Women*, 2:126–27. **Web site:** Croatian Conference of Bishops includes information about Croatian saints: *http://www.pope.hr/katolicka_crkva_ u_hrvatskoj.html*.

Juliana of Mont-Cornillon. Beatified 1869. **Sources:** Anonymous, *The Life of Juliana of Mont-Cornillon*, trans. from Latin, with Introduction and notes, by Barbara Newman, Toronto: Peregrina Translations Series, 1999; Baring-Gould, *Lives of the Saints*, 4:76–87; Bradbury, George Ambrose, O.C., *The Life of St Juliana of Cornillon*, New York: Henry H. Richardson & Co., 1922; Dunbar, *Saintly Women*, 1:441; Jones, *Women Saints*, 11–14. **Web site:** Canons Regular of St Augustine include her among their Blesseds: *http://www.augustiniancanons.org/*.

Julie Billiart. Beatified 1906; canonized 1969. **Sources:** Anonymous, *The Inner Life of the Sisters of Notre Dame*, New York: Benziger Bros., 1929; Charmot, Francois, S.J., *In the Light of the Trinity: The Spirituality of Blessed Julie Billiart, Foundress of the Sisters of Notre Dame de Namur*, Westminster, MD: Newman Press, 1964; Hughes, Catherine, N.D., "St. Julie: A Happy Saint," *The Month*, Sept./Oct. 1994, 400–405. **Web sites:** Sisters of Notre Dame de Namur include a streaming video about Julie's life. *http://www.sndden.org/*; Sisters of Notre Dame, Ohio Province: *http://www.sndohio.org/*; Sisters of Notre Dame, Chardon, Ohio, have links to other SND sites: *http://www.snd1.org/*.

Kateri Tekakwitha. Beatified 1980. **Sources:** Bechard, Henri, S.J., "Blessed Kateri Tekakwitha," *Canadian Catholic Review*, Jan. 1986, 24–27; Dunbar, *Saintly*

Women, 165–66; Greer, Allan, *Mohawk Saint: Catherine Tekakwitha and the Jesuits*, London: Oxford Univ. Press, 2004. **Web sites:** American Indian Cultural Resource Center, Marvin, SD: *http://www.bluecloud.org/dakota.html*; Site dedicated to Kateri with many useful links: *http://www.kateritekakwitha.org/kateri/*; Site maintained by the Mohawks of Kahnawake, Quebec, with information about her shrine: *http://www.lily-of-the-mohawks.com/*; National Shrine of Kateri Tekakwitha: *http://www.katerishrine.com/*; National Shrine of the North American Martyrs, Auresville, NY: *http://www.martyrshrine.org*.

Laura Evangelista. Beatified 1995. **Source:** Marcano, Dilia Barrios, A.R.C.J., *La Niña de Cristo*, read online at the order's website. **Web site:** Augustinian Recollects of the Heart of Jesus: *http://www.agustinasrecoletas.com/*.

Lydwina of Schiedam. Canonized 1890. **Sources:** Baring-Gould, *Lives of the Saints*, 4:189–98; Dunbar, *Saintly Women*, 1:460–61; Huysmans, J. K., *Saint Lydwine of Schieda*, trans. from French by Agnes Hastings, New York: Dutton, 1923; Thurston, *Physical Phenomena of Mysticism*, throughout. **Web sites:** Church dedicated to her in the Netherlands: *www.lidwina.nl*; Multiple Sclerosis Society of Ireland makes a case that Lydwina was one of the earliest cases of that disease: *http://www.ms-society.ie/history/hist_sls.html*.

Margaret of Castello. Beatified 1609. **Sources:** Anonymous, *Blessed Margaret of Castello, 1287–1320*, pamphlet from U.S. shrine website, read online at *www.avemaria.org/*; Bonniwell, Father William R., O.P., *The Life of Blessed Margaret of Castello, 1287–1320*, Rockford, IL: Tan Books, 1983. **Web sites:** This tourist site for the Umbria region has much information about Margaret under "Itinerari Religiosi": *http://www.itinerari.umbria2000.it/*; St Louis Bertrand Church in Lexington, KY, includes a lot of information and photographs of her incorrupt body, which is venerated in Città di Castello: *http://www.avemaria.org/*.

Maria Gabriella Sagheddu. Beatified 1983, at the end of Church Unity Week. **Sources:** Cusack, Pearse, O.C.S.O., *Blessed Gabriella of Unity: A Patron for the Ecumenical Movement*, Ros Cré, Ireland: Cistercian Press, 1995; Driscoll, Martha, O.C.S.O., *A Silent Herald of Unity: The Life of Maria Gariella Sagheddu*, Kalamazoo, MI: Cistercian Publications, 1990. **Web sites:** Virtual shrine: *http://www.mariagabriella.org/*; Her former monastery: *http://www.vitorchiano. org/*; Pontifical Council for Promoting Christian Unity: *http://www.vatican. va/roman_curia/pontifical_councils/chrstuni/*.

Marie Anne Blondin. Beatified April 29, 2001. **Sources:** Material provided by Jeannine Serres, S.S.A., Directress of the Marie Anne Blondin Centre, and by Madeleine Lanoue, S.S.A., Rita Larivée, S.S.A., and Miss Diane Gagnon, including a pamphlet by Odette Saint-Pierre, S.S.A. **Web sites:** Sisters of St Anne in Marlborough, MA: *http://www.sistersofsaintanne.org/*; Sisters of St Anne Motherhouse in Quebec: *http://www.soeursdesainte-anne.qc.ca/*.

Marie of the Incarnation Guyart. Some contemporary scholars spell her name Guyard, and even the Library of Congress gives both spellings. I have chosen Guyart because that is used by Watkins. Beatified 1980. **Sources:** Marie de l'Incarnation, Mere, *The Autobiography of Venerable Marie of the Incarnation, OSU, Mystic and Missionary*, trans. John J. Sullivan, S.J., Chicago: Loyola Univ. Press, 1964; Repplier, Agnes, *Mere Marie of the Ursulines*, New York: Literary Guild of America, 1931. **Web site:** Devotional site created by Hermann Giguère of Quebec: *http://www.geocities.com/hgig.geo/minc/*.

Mary Clopas. Sources: Baring-Gould, *Lives of the Saints*, 4:124–30; Dunbar, *Saintly Women*, 2:45–46; Wong, Christopher Y., "Mary of Cleophas," read online at *ewtn.com*; John 19:25; Matthew 28:1; Mark 16:1–2.

Mary of Egypt. Sources: Baring-Gould, *Lives of the Saints*, 4:15–24; Dunbar, *Saintly Women*, 2:48; Poppe, Erich, and Bianca Ross, *The Legend of Mary of Egypt in Medieval Insular Hagiography*, Portland, OR: Four Courts Press, 1996.

Mary Elisabeth Hesselblad. Beatified 2000. **Sources:** Marie, Dom Antoine, "Saint Bridget of Sweden," Abbaye Saint-Joseph de Clairval, France, Newsletter, July 23, 2001, read online at *www.catholicspot.com/abbayestjoseph/july.htm*; Tjader, Marguerite, *Mother Elisabeth: The Resurgence of the Order of Saint Birgitta*, New York: Herder & Herder, 1972. **Web sites:** Devotional site created by Maria di Lorenzo: *http://www.mariadilorenzo.net/*; Order of the Most Holy Savior of St Bridget: *http://www.brigidine.org/*; Order in Sweden, explains the four branches: *http://www.birgittaskloster.se/*.

Mary Euphrasia Pelletier. Beatified 1933; canonized 1940. Her name appears as Marie-Euphrasia in the Library of Congress, but English-speaking orders call her Mary. **Sources:** Anonymous, *Mirror of the Virtues of Mother Mary of St Euphrasia Pelletier: Foundress of the Congregation of Our Lady of Charity of the Good Shepherd of Angers*, London: Burns & Oates, 1888; Ball, Ann, *Modern Saints: Their Lives and Faces, Book Two*, Rockford, IL: Tan Books, 1990, 101–9; McVeigh, Jane T., *Rose Virginie Pelletier: The Woman and Her Legacy*, Lanham, MD: Univ. Press of America, 1997; Study Commission of Good Shepherd Sisters, *The Spirituality of Saint Mary Euphrasia*, New York, 1980. **Web sites:** Good Shepherd Sisters in North America: *http://www.goodshepherdsistersna.com/*; Congregation of Our Lady of Charity of the Good Shepherd (Good Shepherd Sisters) Generalate, Rome, Italy: *http://www.buonpastoreint.org/*.

Pauline von Mallinckrodt. Beatified 1985. **Sources:** Material provided by Anastasia Sanford, S.C.C., of the Sisters of Christian Charity Archives Center; Ball, *Modern Saints: Book Two*, 185–92; Lechner, Cecile, S.C.C., *At the Right Time She Came: Pauline von Mallinckrodt, Pioneer Social Worker*, Mendham, NJ: Sisters of Christian Charity, 1957; Wedmore, Delphine, S.C.C., *The Woman Who Couldn't Be Stopped*, [United States:] Sisters of Christian Charity, 1986; **Web sites:** Mallinckrodt Convent, Mendham, NJ: *http://www.scceast.org/index.htm*; Western Province, Wilmette, IL: *http://home.mindspring.com/~mjg2/sisters.html*; Companions of Pauline, a lay organization: *http://www.companionsofpauline.org/*.

Teresa Manetti. Beatified 1986. **Source:** *L'Osservatore Romano*. **Web site:** Commune of Campo Bisenzio has a page dedicated to the convent: *http://www .comune.campi-bisenzio.fi.it/citta/virtuale/info/list_mon.htm*.

Zita of Lucca. Canonized 1696. **Sources:** Baring-Gould, *Lives of the Saints*, 4:254–57; Dunbar, *Saintly Women*, 2:309–10; Natale, Sante, *Zita di Lucca: La Vergine dei Fiori e Della Carita*, Lucca: M. Pacini Fazzi, 1998. **Web site:** This tourist site has details about Lucca's annual festival in Zita's honor: *http://www.welcome-tuscany.it/tuscany/lucca/santa_zita_lucca.htm*.

Annotated Sources and Web Sites for May

Anna Rosa Gattorno. Beatified 2000. **Source:** Scaraffia, Lucetta, "Christianity Has Liberated Her and Placed Her Alongside Man in the Family," in *Women and Faith*, ed. Scaraffia and Zarri, 249–80. **Web site:** Sisters of St Anne: *http://www.cimefsa.org/*.

Battista Varano. Beatified 1843. **Sources:** Dunbar, *Saintly Women*, 1:98–99; London Oratory, *The Lives of S. Veronica Giuliani, Capuchin Nun, and of the Blessed Battista Varani, of the Order of S. Clare*, London: R. Washbourne, 1874; Varani, Battista, *My Spiritual Life*, trans. Joseph R. Berrigan, Toronto: Peregrina, 1989.

Blandine Merten. Beatified 1987 (the first woman beatified in the diocese of Trier since Hildegard of Bingen). **Sources:** Material provided by Sister Andrea Kohler,

Blandinen-Archives, Calvarienberg; Holböck, *New Saints, Volume 2, 259–62*; Visarius, M. Hermengildis, O.S.U., *A Hidden Spouse of Our Lord: The Life of Sister Blandine Merten, Ursuline*, New York: Benziger Bros., 1938. **Web sites:** Ursulines of Mount Calvary: *http://www.ursulinen-calvarienberg.de/*; Her birthplace: *http://www.dueppenweiler.de*.

Bona of Pisa. Although Bona was never formally canonized, in 1962 Pope John Paul XXIII designated her the patron saint of flight attendants. **Sources:** Dunbar, *Saintly Women*, 1:128; Thompson, *Cities of God*, 248 and throughout; Weinstein, Donald, and Rudolph M. Bell, *Saints and Society, 1000–1700*, Chicago: Univ. of Chicago Press, 1982, 31–34. **Web site:** Italian Association for the Study of Sanctity, Cults, and Hagiography has posted the biography by Gabriele Zaccagnini: *http://www.aissca.it/aissca/regioni/toscana/bibliografie/bibliografie_pisa_bona.html*.

Catherine of Bologna. Beatified 1592; canonized 1724. **Sources:** Grassetti, Giacomo, *The Life of St Catherine of Bologna*, see: Languet de la Villeneuve de Gergy, 279–507; Jameson, Mrs., *Legends of the Monastic Orders as Represented in the Fine Arts*, Boston: Houghton Mifflin, 1885, 392; Martinelli, Serena Spano, *Il Processo di Canonizzazione di Caterina Vigri (1586–1712)*, Florence: Sismel Edizioni del Galluzzo, 2003; Thurston, *Physical Phenomena of Mysticism*, 233, 285–86. **Web site:** Excerpt from *Seven Spiritual Weapons* posted by Harold Garrett-Goodyear: *http://www.mtholyoke.edu/courses/hgarrett/documents/cbologna.html*.

Catherine of Parc-aux-Dames. Apparently never formally canonized, but listed as Blessed in Watkins and Delaney, among others. **Sources:** Dunbar, *Saintly Women*, 1:150–51; Kleinberg, Aviad M., "A Thirteenth-Century Struggle Over Custody: The Case of Catherine of Parc-aux-Dames," *Bulletin of Medieval Canon Law*, vol. 20, 1990, 51. **Web site:** Photographs of the ruins of the abbey: *http://perso.wanadoo.fr/les35clochers/parcauxdam.html*.

Catherine Simon de Longpré. Beatified 1989. **Source:** Ponet-Bordeaux, Marthe (Jeanne Danemarie), *Catherine de Longpré, Mere Catherine de Saint Augustine; au Canada avec Une Heroique Missionaire de Seize Ans, 1632–1668*, Paris: B. Grasset, 1957. **Web sites:** Augustinians of the Mercy of Jesus: *http://www.augustines.org/index.htm*; Augustinians of the Midwest: *http://www.midwestaugustinians.org/*; Diocese of Quebec: *http://www.diocesequebec.qc.ca/histoire/catherine_st_augustin/index.htm*.

Catherine Troiani. Beatified 1985. **Sources:** Antoine Marie, Dom, O.S.B., *Letter of Saint Joseph Abbey*, Nov. 17, 1998, read online at *www.clairval.com/lettres/en/98/w181198290798.htm*; Falchi, M. Antonina, *Mamma Bianca in Terra d'Africa: La Serva di Dio Madre Maria Caterina Troiani di S. Rosa da Viterbo, Fondatrice delle Francescane Missionarie del Cuore Immacolato di Maria, 1813–1887*, Rome: Curia Generalizia, 1960; Holböck, *New Saints, Volume 2*, 58–61. **Web sites:** Franciscan Missionary Sisters of the Immaculate Heart of Mary: *http://www.fmihm.catholicweb.com/*; Franciscan Missionaries of the Immaculate Heart of Mary: *http://www.francescane.net/*; Franciscan Missionary Sisters of Coração: *http://www.irmasfranciscanas.org.br/*.

Colomba of Rieti. Beatified 1627. **Sources:** Bynum, Caroline Walker, *Holy Feast and Holy Fast: The Religious Significance of Food to Medieval Women*, Berkeley: Univ. of California Press, 1987, throughout; Dunbar, *Saintly Women*, 1:199–200; Faber, F. W., ed., *The Lives of St Rose of Lima, the Blessed Colomba of Rieti, and of St Juliana Falconieri*, New York: Edward Dunigan, 1847 (Saints and Servants of God Series), 199–350; Lehmijoki-Gardner, *Dominican Penitent Women*, throughout. **Web site:** Umbrian tourist site: *http://www.itinerari.umbria2000.it/*.

Dymphna of Gheel. Sources: Daughters of St Paul, *Devotions to St Dymphna*, Boston: Pauline Books & Media, 1977; Goldstein, Jackie L., and Marc M.L. Godemont,

"The Legend and Lessons of Geel [sic], Belgium: A 1500-Year-Old Legend, a Twenty-first Century Model," *Community Mental Health Journal*, vol. 39, Oct. 2003, 441–58. **Web sites:** Franciscan Mission Associates offer a pamphlet and devotions to Dymphna: *http://www.franciscanmissionassoc.org/*; National shrine in Massillon, OH (on the grounds of the state mental hospital): *http://www. natlshrinestdymphna.org*; Psychiatric Center at Gheel: *http://www.opzgeel.be/en/ home/htm/intro.asp*; Official site for annual Dymphna Days: *http://www.dimpnad-agen.be/dimpnadagen/*.

Imelda Lambertini. Beatified 1826. **Sources:** Daughters of St Paul, *Her Dream Came True: The Life of Blessed Imelda Lambertini*, Boston: Daughters of St Paul, 1967; Dorcy, *Saint Dominic's Family*, 144–46; Windeatt, Mary Fabyan, *Patron Saint of First Communicants: The Story of Blessed Imelda Lambertini*, Rockford, IL: Tan Books, 1991. **Web site:** Dominican Sisters of Blessed Imelda: *http://www.domeni-caneimeldine.it/home/*.

Joan of Arc. Beatified 1909; canonized 1920. **Sources:** Dunbar, *Saintly Women*, 1:431–32; Pernoud, Régine, and Marie-Véronique Clin, *Joan of Arc: Her Story*, trans. and revised by Jeremy du Quesnay Adams, New York: St Martin's Press, 1999. **Web sites:** Joan of Arc Museum, Rouen, France: *http://perso.wanadoo.fr/ musee.jeannedarc/*; St Joan of Arc Center, Albuquerque, NM, maintained by Virginia Froelick: *http://www.stjoan-center.com/*; Birthplace, now known as Domremy-la-Pucelle: *http://www.domremy.org/*.

Julian of Norwich. Although usually called Blessed, Julian was never formally beatified. **Sources:** Juliana of Norwich, *Revelations of Divine Love*, trans. with an Introduction by M. L. del Mastro, Garden City, NY: Doubleday, 1977; Julian of Norwich, *Showings*, trans. with an Introduction by Edmund Colledge, O.S.A., and James Walsh, S.J., New York: Paulist Press, 1978 (Classics of Western Spirituality Series); Obbard, *Medieval Women Mystics*, 119–56; Rist, Anna, "In His Image," *Canadian Catholic Review*, Dec. 1985, 21/421–24/424. **Web sites:** Order of Blessed Julian, a Contemplative Order of the Episcopalian Church: *http:// orderofjulian.org/home.html*; Internet shrine in Norwich, England, attached to the Anglican church of St Julian's: *http://www.julianofnorwich.org*.

Jutta of Prussia. Although the date of her beatification is vague, she is referred to as Blessed in the *Franciscan Book of Saints* and Holböck's *Married Saints and Blesseds*, among others. **Sources:** Dunbar, *Saintly Women*, 1:448–49; Holböck, *Married Saints and Blesseds*, 192; Mechthild of Magdeburg, *The Flaming Light of the Godhead*, trans. with an Introduction by Frank Tobin, New York: Paulist Press, 1998 (Classics of Western Spirituality Series), 216.

Magdalene of Canossa. Beatified 1941; canonized 1988. **Sources:** Ball, *Modern Saints: Book Two*, 20–26; Farina, Marcella, *Maddalena di Canossa*, Torino: Società Editrice Internazionale, 1995; Giordani, Igino, *Maddalena di Canossa*, Rome: Città Nuova, 1963; Kempf, *Holiness of the Church*, 201–3.

Margaret of Cortona. Canonized 1728. **Sources:** Cannon, Joanna, *Margharetta of Cortona and the Lorenzetti: Sienese Art and the Culture of a Holy Woman in Medieval Tuscany*, University Park: Pennsylvania State Univ. Press, 1999; Mauriac, François, *Saint Margaret of Cortona*, trans. Bernard Frechtman, New York: Philosophical Library, 1948; address of John Paul II at the shrine of Margaret of Cortona, May 23, 1993, *L'Osservatore Romano*, Spanish ed., June 4, 1993. **Web site:** Commune of Cortona: *http://www.cortonaweb.net/index.php#*.

Margaret Pole. Beatified 1886, the only woman among a group of fifty-four British martyrs of the religious wars. **Sources:** Dunbar, *Saintly Women*, 2:26–28; Pierce, Hazel, *Margaret Pole, Countess of Salisbury, 1473–1541: Loyalty, Lineage and Leadership*, Cardiff: Univ. of Wales, 2003. **Web site:** Tudor Place, maintained by

Jorge Castillo, has many details (click on Who's Who in Tudor History): *http://www.tudorplace.com.ar/*.

Maria Maddalena de' Pazzi. Beatified 1626; canonized 1669. **Sources:** Baring-Gould, *Lives of the Saints*, 5:381–82; Dunbar, *Saintly Women*, 60; *Maria Maddalena de'Pazzi: Selected Revelations*, trans. and with an Introduction by Armando Maggi, New York: Paulist Press, 2000; Thurston, *Physical Phenomena of Mysticism*, throughout. **Web site:** Carmelite Order (click on Great Figures): *http://www.ocarm.org/*.

Mariana de Paredes. Beatified 1853; canonized July 9, 1950. **Sources:** Baring-Gould, *Lives of the Saints*, 392–93; Boero, Joseph, S.J., *The Life of the Blessed Mary Ann of Jesus de Paredes y Flores, an American Virgin Called the Lily of Quito*, Philadelphia: Peter F. Cunningham, 1855; Dunbar, *Saintly Women*, 2:30; Keyes, Frances Parkinson, *The Rose and the Lily: The Lives and Times of Two South American Saints*, New York, Hawthorn Books, 1961. **Web sites:** St Mariana de Paredes Church, Pico Rivera, CA: *http://www.stmariana.org/*; Devotional site in Ecuador: *http://www.oremosjuntos.com/Santoral/Mariana.html*; Another devotional site: *http://members.aol.com/cecill757/Mariana.html*.

Marie Louise Trichet. Beatified 1993. **Sources:** Material provided by Chris Koellhoffer, I.H.M., Director of Communications, Daughters of Wisdom; Martindale, C. C., S.J., *The Queen's Daughters: A Study of Women Saints*, New York: Sheed & Ward, 1951, 145–46; *Jesus Living in Mary: Handbook of the Spirituality of St Louis de Montfort*, Daughters of Wisdom, read online at *ewtn.com/library/Montfort/Handbook/Daughtrs.htm*. **Web sites:** Montfortian Religious Family, consisting of the three religious companies, including the Daughters of Wisdom: *http://www.montfort.org/*; Daughters of Wisdom United States province: *http://www.daughtersofwisdom.org/*; Canadian Daughters of Wisdom, Ottawa, Ontario: *http://www.sagesse.ca/en/home/welcome.html*.

Mary Mazzarello. Beatified 1938; canonized 1951. **Sources:** Agasso, Domenico, *Saint Mary Mazzarello: The Spirit of Joy*, trans. Sr. Louise Passero, F.M.A., Boston: Pauline Books & Media, 1996; Ball, *Modern Saints: Book One*, 80–86; Hughes, Henry Louis, *Maria Mazzarello: Life and Times of the First Mother General of the Daughters of Our Lady Help of Christians*, St Louis: B. Herder, 1933. **Web sites:** Her hometown, Mornese: *http://www.mornese.pcn.net/*; Daughters of Mary Help of Christians (Salesian Sisters of Don Bosco): *http://www.cgfma-net.org*; Salesian Sisters of St John Bosco, Paterson, NJ: *http://www.salesiansisterseast.org*.

Maura. Sources: Baring-Gould, *Lives of the Saints*, 5:55–56; Dunbar, *Saintly Women*, 2:69–70; O'Malley, Vincent J., C.M., *Saints of Africa*, Huntington, IN: Our Sunday Visitor, 2001, 66–67. **Web site:** Maura inspired this epic poem by Charles Kingsley: *http://oldpoetry.com/oprintall/Charles%20Kingsley*.

Panacea. Beatified 1867 and never formally canonized, but her name is in the Roman Martyrology, and she is usually referred to as a saint, e.g., by Watkins. **Sources:** Dunbar, *Saintly Women*, 2:130–31; Givone, Pietro, *Eroina Valsesiana; Ossia, La Beata Panacea, Dramma Storico-Sacro in Quattro Atti*, Torino: Tipografia Libreria San Giuseppe degli Artigianelli, 1930. **Web sites:** *http://www.valsesiascuole.it/liceoborgosesia/multimediale/valsesia/arte/quarona.htm*; City of Quarona (click on the church of San Giovanni and you will eventually get to two vivid frescoes depicting the martyrdom of Panacea): *http://www.quaronasesia.it/*; Quarona's site for frescoes and photos of her festival: *http://www.webalice.it/quarona/BEATA/beatain.htm*.

Rita of Cascia. Beatified 1627; canonized 1900. **Sources:** "New Saints Canonized: Brilliant Scene in Rome at Ceremonies Where Pope Leo Officiated," *New York Times*, June 10, 1900, 18; "Canonization of La Salle," *New York Times*, May 25,

1900, 6; De Spens, Willy, *Saint Rita*, trans. Julie Kern, Garden City, NY: Double-day, 1962; Dunbar, *Saintly Women*, 2:189–90; Sicardo, Rev. Joseph, O.S.A., *Life of Sister St. Rita of Cascia of the Order of St Augustine, Advocate of the Impossible, Model of Maidens, Wives, Mothers, Widows and Nuns*, trans. from Spanish by Rev. Dan J. Murphy, O.S.A., Chicago: D. B. Hansen & Sons, 1916. **Web site:** Basilica of St Rita in Cascia, Italy, includes locations of shrines and convents dedicated to Rita all over the world: *http://www.santaritadacascia.org/*.

Rosa Venerini. Beatified 1952; canonized 2006. **Sources:** Material provided by Mary Rose Zaccari, M.P.V., of the Religious Venerini Sisters in Worcester, MA; Andreucci, A. G., S.J., *Rosa Venerini*, trans. Sr. Carmen Morzillo, M.P.V., 1999. **Web site:** Official site maintained by Anna Maria Tassi: *http://www.rosavenerini.org/*.

Theresa of Jesus Gerhardinger. Beatified 1985. **Sources:** Material provided by Sister Carolyn, S.S.N.D., Sister Kathy Jager, S.S.N.D, and Julie Gilberto-Brady, Communications Coordinator, of School Sisters of Notre Dame; Dympna, Sister, S.S.N.D., *Mother Caroline and the School Sisters of Notre Dame in North America*, St Louis: Woodward & Tiernan, 1928; Hindman, Jane F., *An Ordinary Saint: John Neumann*, New York: Arena Lettres, 1977, 82–86; Mast, Dolorita, *Through Caroline's Consent: Life of Mother Teresa of Jesus Gerhardinger, 1797–1879*, Baltimore: School Sisters of Notre Dame, 1958. **Web sites:** School Sisters of Notre Dame, North American Province: *http://www.ssnd.org/*; Sisters of Notre Dame Generalate: *http://www.gerhardinger.org/*; School Sisters of Notre Dame, Canadian Province: *http://www.ssndcanadian.org*; Dallas Province: *http://www.ssnddallas.org/*; St Louis Province: *http://www.ssnd-sl.org*.

Ubaldesca. The circumstances of Ubaldesca's canonization are obscure, but a church was dedicated to her in 1628, and Pope Sisto V (1585–1590) granted a plenary indulgence for those who prayed in her church in Malta on her feast day, May 28. **Sources:** Dunbar, *Saintly Women*, 2:276–77; Zaccagnini, Gabriele, *Ubaldesca, Una Santa Laica nella Pisa dei Secoli XII-XIII*, Pisa: Gisem-ETS, 1995. **Web sites:** Commune of Calcinaia: *http://www.comune.calcinaia.pi.it/manifestazioni.php*; Sovereign Military Order and Hospitaller Order of St John of Jerusalem, Rhodes, and Malta: *http://198.62.75.5/www1/gtl/smom/index.htm*.

Ulrika Nisch. Beatified 1987. **Sources:** Material provided by Doug Leonard, Director of Communications and Development, Holy Cross Sisters; Holböck, *New Saints, Volume 2*, 251–58. **Web sites:** Sisters of the Holy Cross, Helge: *http://www.klosterhegne.de/*; Diocese of Erzbistum-Freiburg: *http://www.erzbistum-freiburg.de/581.0.html*; Holy Cross Sisters, United States Province, Merrill, WI: *http://www.holycrosssisters.org/*; Friends of Ulrika, a lay group that meets annually at her former convent: *http://www.selige-ulrika.de/*.

Umiliana de'Cerchi. Beatified 1694. **Sources:** Dunbar, *Saintly Women*, 1:268–69; Schuchman, Anne M., "The Lives of Umiliana de'Cerchi: Representations of Female Sainthood in Thirteenth-Century Florence," in *Essays in Medieval Studies*, read online at *www.luc.edu/publications/medieval/vol14/14ch2.html*; Thompson, *Cities of God*, throughout.

Ursula Ledóchowska. Beatified 1983; canonized 2003. **Sources:** Ledóchowska, Countess Julie, *Poland Ravaged and Bereaved: A Lecture Delivered at Copenhagen on the 19th November 1915*, London: St Catherine Press, 1916; John Paul II, address to the Ursulines, *L'Osservatore Romano*, English ed., July 30, 1984; "Mother Ursula Ledochowska," *Times* [London], June 13, 1939, 18; "Poznan: Beatification of Ursula Ledochowska: Man's Bond with the Land Is the Basis for the Existence of Society," *L'Osservatore Romano*, English ed., July 4, 1983, 4–5. **Web sites:** Ursuline Sisters of the Agonizing Heart of Jesus: *http://www.*

orsolinescga.it/; City of Pniewy, Poland, has a page and monument dedicated to Ursula: *http://www.pniewy.bip.net.pl/*.

Wiborada of St Gall. Canonized 1047. **Sources:** Dunbar, *Saintly Women*, 2:174 (Rachild), 289–91 (Wiborada); Schulenburg, Jane Tibbetts, *Forgetful of Their Sex: Female Sanctity and Society ca. 500–1100*, Chicago: Univ. of Chicago Press, 1998, throughout. **Web sites:** Abbey Library of St Gallen: *http://www.stiftsbibliothek.ch/*; Mars Hill Graduate School Library, Bothell, WA (click on Library, scroll to the bottom and click on Wiborada's picture for more information): *http://www.mhgs.edu/library/*.

Annotated Sources and Web Sites for June

Aleydis of Le Cambre. Beatified 1702; canonized 1907. **Sources:** Dunbar, *Saintly Women*, 1:11–12 (Aleydis), 2:34 (Martha); Gelders-Michel, Marie-Therese, "Who Was Sainte-Alix?" article read online at *http://saintealix.free.fr/*; Raymond, Rev. M., O.C.S.O., *These Women Walked with God: The Saga of Citeaux Third Epoch*, Milwaukee: Bruce Publishing, 1956, 93–120. **Web sites:** New Melleray Abbey, Peosta, IA, has information about many Cistercian saints (click on Calendar): *http://newmelleray.org/*; This site, created by Lirie Zumbultas, describes the restoration of Le Cambre. It does not mention Aleydis but has illustrations of the abbey as it looked during her life: *http://www.paluche.org/nature/fr/tou436.htm*.

Anne Marie Taigi. Beatified 1920. **Sources:** Bessieres, Albert, S.J., *Wife, Mother and Mystic: Blessed Anna-Maria Taigi*, trans. from French by Rev. Stephen Rigby, ed. Douglas Newton, London: Sands & Col, 1952; Jones, *Women Saints*, 137–44. **Web site:** The Trinitarian Order has a page with pictures: *http://www.trinitari.org/*.

Anne of St Bartholomew. Beatified 1917. **Sources:** Anne of St Bartholomew, *Autobiografía*, Madrid: Espiritualidad, 1969; Dunbar, *Saintly Women*, 1:78. **Web sites:** Carmelite Generalate, Rome, Italy, has links to other sites: *http://www.ocd.pcn.net/*; Carmelite Sisters of Oklahoma City have a page dedicated to her: *http://www.oksister.com/*.

Audrey. Sexburga's daughters **Ermengilda** and **Ercongotha** became saints, as did her granddaughter **Werberga,** who was later an abbess at Ely. As for Audrey's other sisters, **Ethelburga of Barking** (October 11) cofounded the first religious house for women in England and **Withburga** (d. c. 743), the youngest, founded a monastery at Norfolk and is venerated on July 8. A half-sister, **Sethrida** (d. c. 660), born to their father's first wife, entered the abbey at Faremoutiers, succeeded the founder Fara (April 21) as abbess, and is venerated on January 20. **Sources:** Butler, *Lives of the Fathers, Martyrs and Other Principal Saints* (1845), 6:301–4; Cruz, *Incorruptibles*, 49–52; Dunbar, *Saintly Women*, 1:240, 281–84. **Web sites:** St Etheldreda's, the oldest Roman Catholic church in England, located in the heart of London: *http://www.stetheldreda.com/*; Ely Cathedral (Church of England): *http://www.cathedral.ely.anglican.org/*.

Blandina. Sources: Dunbar, *Saintly Women*, 1:125–27; Halsall, Paul, "The Letter of the Churches of Vienna and Lyons to the Churches of Asia and Phrygia Including the Story of the Blessed Blandina," read online at Medieval Sourcebook, Saints' Lives: *http://www.fordham.edu/halsall/source/177-lyonsmartyrs.html*. **Web site:** City of Lyons has details and photographs of the arena: *http://lyonsfr.ags.myareaguide.com/*.

Clotilda, Queen of France. Sources: Baring-Gould, *Lives of the Saints*, 4:23–27; Dunbar, *Saintly Women*, 1:191–93; Kurth, Godefroi, *Saint Clotilda*, trans. V. M. Crawford, New York: Benziger Bros., 1898.

Diana, Cecilia, and Amata. Diana was beatified in 1888, Cecilia and Amata in 1891. **Sources:** Drane, Augusta Theodosia, *The History of St. Dominic, Founder of the Friars Preachers*, London: Longmans, Green, 1891; Dunbar, *Saintly Women*, 1:49–50 (Amata), 168–69 (Cecilia), 229–30 (Diana); Vicaire, M. H., *Saint Dominic*, trans. Kathleen Pond, New York: McGraw-Hill, 1964. **Web sites:** Dominican Province of Albert the Great in Chicago, IL, has much more information, including some of the correspondence between Diana and Jordan of Saxony, under "Tradition": *http://www.op.org/domcentral/default.htm;* Dominican Province of San Tommaso d'Aquino has more about the Blesseds and pictures of Diana and Cecilia, under "La Santità nell'Ordine dei Predicatori": *http://www.domenicani.net/.*

Elisabeth of Schönau. Never formally canonized, but her name was entered in the Roman Martyrology in 1584. **Sources:** Brown, Raphael, comp., *The Life of Mary as Seen by the Mystics: From the Revelations of St Elizabeth of Schoenau, St Bridget of Sweden, Ven. Mother Mary of Agreda and Sister Anne Catherine Emmerich*, Rockford, IL: Tan Books, 1951, throughout; Dunbar, *Saintly Women*, 1:258–59, including Elisabeth's Ursula vision; Newman, Barbara, *Voice of the Living Light: Hildegard of Bingen and Her World*, Berkeley: Univ. of California Press, 1998, 104; Schönau, Elisabeth, *Complete Works*, trans. and ed. Anne L. Clark, New York: Paulist Press, 2000 (Clasics of Western Spirituality Series). **Web site:** Epistolae has posted 23 of her letters, translated from Latin by Schönau scholars: *http://db.ccnmtl.columbia.edu/ferrante/.*

Emilie de Vialar. Beatified 1939; canonized 1951. **Source:** Carroll, Malachy Gerard, *The Seal of the Cross: Saint Emilie de Vialar and the Institute of Saint Joseph of the Apparition*, Cork, Ireland: Mercier Press, 1955. **Web sites:** Sisters of St Joseph of the Apparition, India: *http://www.sjaindia.com;* Sisters of St Joseph of the Apparition, Malta: *http://www.stjoseph-apparition.org;* Friends of East Jerusalem Hospitals has information about the role the order has played in the Holy Land (click on St. Joseph): *http://www.fejh.org/.*

Florida Cevoli. Beatified 1993. **Sources:** Iriarte, Lazarao, O.F.M., *Beata Florida Cevoli: Discepola di Santa Veronica Giuliani (1685–1767)*, Siena: Cantagalli, 1993; London Oratory, *The Lives of S. Veronica Giuliani, Capuchin Nun, and of the Blessed Battista Varani, of the Order of S. Clare.* **Web sites:** Commune of Città di Castello: *http://www.cdcnet.net/en/;* Our Lady of Light Capuchin Poor Clares Monastery, Denver, has details about their way of life but no information about Florida: *http://www.midamcaps.org/sisters.asp.*

Germaine Cousin. Beatified 1854; canonized 1867. **Sources:** Baring-Gould, *Lives of the Saints*, 6:216–19; Cruz, *Incorruptibles*, 213–15; Dunbar, *Saintly Women*, 1:340; Thurston, *Physical Phenomena of Mysticism*, 389–91; biography compiled from official documents, provided by Jean-Pierre Jouffreau of the Association Pelerinage Sainte Germaine. **Web sites:** City of Pibrac has many details: *http://www.pibrac.com/;* Society of St Germaine of Pibrac has wonderful pictures and information about the pilgrimage: *http://perso.wanadoo.fr/saintegermaine/.*

Juliana Falconieri. Beatified 1698 (Levillain gives 1678); canonized 1729. **Sources:** Baring-Gould, *Lives of the Saints*, 6:267–68; Dunbar, *Saintly Women*, 1:442–43; Faber, *Lives*, 353–416; Lewis, D. B. Wyndham, *A Florentine Portrait: Saint Philip Benizi (1233–1285)*, New York: Sheed & Ward, 1959; Thurston, *Physical Phenomena of Mysticism*, 156–61. **Web sites:** Servite Sisters (Servants of Mary) in Omaha, NE: *http://osms.org/;* Friar Servants of Mary, United States Province, has a small pop-up biography of St Juliana and information about the Secular Order: *http://www.servite.org/;* St Juliana Falconieri Church in Chicago has pictures and links to more information about its patron: *http://stjuliana.org/stjuliana.php.*

Lutgard of Aywières. According to Thomas Merton, "Her title to sanctity was officially recognized by Rome without judicial process in 1584." **Sources:** Merton, Thomas, *What Are These Wounds? The Life of a Cistercian Mystic, Saint Lutgarde of Aywieres*, Milwaukee: Bruce Publishing, 1950; Merton, Thomas, and Patrick Hart, "Saint Lutgarde: Nun of Aywieres, Belgium," *Cistercian Studies Quarterly*, Sonoita, 2000, 217–30; Raymond, *Women Walked with God*, 3–49. **Web site:** New Melleray (Trappist) Abbey, Peosta, IA, has information about many Cistercian saints (click on Calendar): *http://newmelleray.org/*.

Mafalda, Queen of Castile. *See* Portuguese Princesses.

Margaret Bermingham Ball. Beatified 1992, with Dermot O'Hurley and sixteen Companion Martyrs of Ireland, the only woman in the group. **Sources:** Black, Annette, "Blessed Margaret Ball," biography posted at *www.whitehall.dublindiocese.ie* and read online; Brady, Ciaran, "The Beatified Martyrs of Ireland," *Irish Theological Quarterly*, Winter 1999, 379. **Web site:** Bl Margaret Ball chapel in Santry, Ireland, has a page dedicated to its patron (click on her portrait for more): *http://www.whitehall.dublindiocese.ie/StoryParish.htm*.

Margaret Ebner. Beatified 1979 (first person beatified by John Paul II). **Henry of Nordlingen** (d. c. 1352). Historian Valerie M. Lagorio writes that "Henry's correspondence with Margaret and her contemporary mystics represents the first collection of letters in the German language, and affords illuminating insights into the historical and religious events of the age." **Sources:** Dorcy, *Saint Dominic's Family*, 157–59; Ebner, Margaret, *Major Works*, trans. and ed. Leonard P. Hindsley, New York: Paulist Press, 1993 (Western Spirituality Series); Lagorio, Valerie M., "The Medieval Continental Women Mystics: An Introduction," in *An Introduction to the Medieval Mystics of Europe*, ed. Paul E. Szarmach, Albany: State Univ. of New York Press, 1984, 173; Underhill, Evelyn, *Mysticism: A Study in the Nature and Development of Man's Spiritual Consciousness*, New York: Noonday Press, 1955, 269, 465. **Web site:** Her former convent is now a Franciscan retreat center: *http://www.dillinger-franziskanerinnen-provinz-maria-medingen.de/*.

Marguerite Bays. Beatified 1995. **Source:** *L' Osservatore Romano*. **Web sites:** Foundation Marguerite Bays: *http://www.marguerite-bays.ch/*; Pilgrim site for St Jacques de Compostello includes details about Marguerite (click on Cheminement): *http://www.inforomont.ch/*.

Maria Droste zu Vischering. Beatified 1975. **Sources:** Ball, *Modern Saints: Book One*, 141–45; Chasle, Louis, *Sister Mary of the Divine Heart Droste zu Vischering: Religious of the Congregation of the Good Shepherd, 1863–1899*, trans. from the 2d French ed. by a Religious of the Congregation, New York: Benziger Bros., 1907; Kempf, *Holiness of the Church*, 245–49. **Web sites:** Good Shepherd Sisters in the Philippines: *Http://Www.Goodshepherdsisters.Org.Ph/Main0.Htm#Top*; Her convent in Portugal: *http://www.ex-maria-droste.rcts.pt/*.

Mariam Thresia Chiramel Mankidiyan. Beatified 2000. **Sources:** Chacko, K.C., *Mother Mariam Thresia*, Trichur: Holy Family Generalate, 1992; Clark, *Asian Saints*, 80; Mariam Thresia, Mother, *Selections: Writings of Mother Mariam Thresia*, ed. A. Mathias Mondadan (chief) and Ruby Therese Pavana (associate), Trichur: Holy Family Generalate 1991. **Web sites:** Her official website: *http://www.blessedmariamthresia.org/*; Blessed Alphonsa Mission, Chatsworth, CA, has a page dedicated to her: *http://shajimg.brinkster.net/syro/units/mt/*.

Maria Raffaella Cimatti. Beatified 1996. **Source:** *L'Osservatore Romano*. **Web site:** Hospitallers Sisters of Mercy: *http://www.consom.it/*.

Maria Theresa Scherer. Beatified 1995. **Sources:** Material provided by Doug Leonard, Director of Communications and Development, Holy Cross Sisters; Mee, Lucy, S.C.S.C., *The Servant of God: Mother Mary Theresa Scherer*, Merrill, WI:

Sisters of Mercy of the Holy Cross, 1988; Schnitzer, Constance, *A Case of Commitment*, Merrill, WI: Holy Cross/Franciscan Publishers, 1967. **Web sites:** Holy Cross Sisters, United States Province, Merrill, WI: *http://www.holycrosssisters.org/*; Holy Cross Sisters Motherhouse, Ingenbohl, Switzerland: *http://www .kloster-ingenbohl.ch/default.htm.*

Martyrs of Wangla. Beatified 1955; canonized 2000. Lucy Weng Chang's name appears in various spellings. **Source:** Clark, *Asian Saints,* 46. **Web sites:** Chinese Martyrs Church, Ontario Canada (click on Fourth Introduction and Weng Cheng): *http://www.chinesemartyrs.org/*; Cardinal Kung Foundation has information about today's Underground Church in China: *http://www.cardinalkungfoundation.org/.*

Mary of Oignies. Watkins lists her cult as unconfirmed, but she is listed as Saint in Butler, *Lives of the Fathers Martyrs and Other Principal Saints* (1845) and *The Catholic Encyclopedia* (1911). She is listed as Blessed in later editions of Butler and in Holböck. **Sources:** Baring-Gould, *Lives of the Saints,* 6:319–22; Bynum, *Holy Feast and Holy Fast,* 115; Dunbar, *Saintly Women,* 2:54–55; Holböck, *Married Saints and Blesseds,* 186–87; Vitry, Jacques de, and Thomas de Cantimpre, *Two Lives of Marie d'Oignies,* trans. Margot H. King and Hugh Feiss, O.S.B., Toronto: Peregrina, 2000. **Web site:** Photos of church containing some of her relics: *http://belgium.rootsweb.com/bel/0wl/jose/aiseau-presles/aiseau.htm.*

Melania the Elder. Sources: Clark, Elizabeth A., *Women in the Early Church,* Collegeville, MN: Liturgical Press, 1983, 213–23 (Message of the Fathers of the Church, Vol. 13); Dunbar, *Saintly Women,* 2:83–85.

Mercedes de Jesús. Beatified 1985. **Source:** Holböck, *New Saints, Volume 2,* 50–54. **Web sites:** Virtual shrine: *http://members.aol.com/navarro757/Mercedes.html*; Marianitas' home page: *http://marianitas.ec.*

Michelina of Pesaro. Beatified 1737. **Sources:** Dunbar, *Saintly Women,* 2:89–90; Habig, *Franciscan Book of Saints,* 661–64; Hallack and Anson, *These Made Peace,* 137–42. **Web site:** Museum of Pesaro website features a photograph of an altarpiece showing Michelina with six male saints that once hung in her chapel at St Francis in Pesaro: *http://www.museicivicipesaro.it/sezioni_pin_sala2_3.asp.*

Osanna of Mantua. Beatified 1694. **Sources:** Cruz, *Incorruptibles,* 156–57; Lehmijoki-Gardner, *Dominican Penitent Women,* throughout; Watkin, E. I., *Neglected Saints,* New York: Sheed & Ward, 1955, 141–64. **Web site:** Her former home is now a museum (click on Musei e Monumenti, then Musei della Città [Italian only]): *http://www.mumm.mantova.it/.*

Paula Frassinetti. Beatified 1930; canonized 1984. **Sources:** Ball, *Modern Saints: Book Two,* 194–201; Umfreville, Joyce, *A Foundress in Nineteenth Century Italy (Blessed Paola Frassinetti and the Congregation of the Sisters of St Dorothy),* Staten Island, NY: Edward O'Toole, 1939. **Web sites:** Parish of St Paola Frassinetti in Rufina, Italy: *http://www.parsantapaola.it/index.htm*; Sisters of St Dorothy in Brazil (Portuguese only): *http://www.ffsd-nf.edu.br/index.php.*

Portuguese Princesses. Canonized 1705 (Teresa and Sancha) and 1792 (Mafalda). **Sources:** Dunbar, *Saintly Women,* 2:3–4 (Mafalda), 214–15 (Sancha), 262–63 (Teresa); Raymond, *These Women Walked with God.* (143-78); **Web sites:** Portuguese tourist site has photos of tombs of Teresa and Sancha: *http://www.turismo-centro.pt/english/region/counties/penacova/impressao/monumentos.htm*; Portuguese Ministry of Culture has pages dedicated to Mafalda's monastery at Arouca and Teresa's monastery at Lorvão: *http://www.ippar.pt/monumentos/conjunto_arouca. html*; Mafalda's monastery at Arouca is now a museum: *http://museu-de-arouca. pt.vu/.*

Sancha. *See* Portuguese Princesses.

Tarsykia Olha Matskiv. Beatified 2001. **Source:** Material provided by Mother Frances Byblow, Superior General, S.S.M.I. **Web sites:** Sisters Servants of Mary Immaculate, Provincial House, Toronto, Ontario, Canada: *http://www.ssmi.org/*; Pelikan Performance is a multimedia show about contemporary saints, including Tarsykia (click on Martyrs): *http://www.pelikanperformance.com/*.

Teresa, Queen of Leon. *See* Portuguese Princesses.

Vincenza Gerosa. Beatified 1933; canonized 1950 (with Bartolomea Capitanio). **Source:** Kempf, *Holiness of the Church*, 206–7. **Web site:** Sisters of Charity of SS Bartolomea Capitanio and Vincenza Gerosa: *http://www.suoredimariabambina.org/*.

Annotated Sources and Web Sites for July

Alphonsa of India. Beatified 1986, first Indian woman beatified. **Sources:** Ball, *Modern Saints: Book One*, 388–95; Dempsey, Corinne G., *Kerala Christian Sainthood: Collisions of Culture and Worldview in South India*, New York: Oxford Univ. Press, 2001. **Web sites:** Official shrine: *http://www.alphonsa.net/*; St Mary's Church, site of her relics: *http://www.stmarybharananganam.com/*.

Amalberga of Ghent. Source: Dunbar, *Saintly Women*, 1:50–51. **Web sites:** St Amalberga Church, Mater, Belgium: *http://users.belgacom.net/bruyneel.dries/*; St Amelia Church, Tonowanda, NY: *http://www.stamelia.com/*.

Angelina of Montegiove. Beatified 1825. **Sources:** Dunbar, *Saintly Women*, 1:61–63 (Angelina), 2:137 (Paula of Foligno), 2:24 (Margaret Dominici); Hallack and Anson, *These Made Peace*, 162–68; McKelvie, Roberta A., *Retrieving a Living Tradition: The Recovery of the Historical Significance of Angelina of Montegiove as Franciscan Tertiary, Italian Beguine, and Leader of Women*, St Bonaventure, NY: Franciscan Institute, 1997. **Web sites:** Bernardine Franciscan Sisters consider her a founder: *http://www.bfranciscan.org/*; Umbria 2000 tourist site (click on Itineraries and Trips, then Religious Itineraries; be sure to go to bottom of page for more links): *http://www.english.umbria2000.it/*; Official site of the Basilica of St Francis of Assisi: *http://www.sanfrancescoassisi.org/*.

Anne. Sources: Anonymous, *Good St. Anne: Her Power and Dignity, Patroness of Christian Mothers*, Rockford, IL: Tan Books, 1998 (orig. pub. 1958 and 1963 by Benedictine Convent of Perpetual Adoration, Clyde, MO); Dunbar, *Saintly Women*, 1:65–68; Grace, Father Petr, C.P., "The Life of Saint Ann," *St Ann's Media*, read online at *www.themass.org*. **Web sites:** The Mary Page at the University of Dayton: *http://www.udayton.edu/mary/*; Shrine of Sainte-Anne-de-Beaupré, the oldest shrine in North America, has been associated with many miraculous healings and cures: *http://www.ssadb.qc.ca/*; Cathedral at Apt, France: *http://www.apt-cathedrale.com/*; St Ann's Media and National Shrine, Scranton, PA: *http://www.themass.org/*.

Anne-Marie Javouhey. Beatified 1950. **Sources:** Jones, *Women Saints*, 230–32, 234–33; Kempf, *Holiness of the Church*, 215–17 (Napoleon quote); Kittler, Glenn D., *The Woman God Loved*, Garden City, NY: Hanover House, 1959 (Teresa of Avila vision). **Web sites:** Sisters of St Joseph of Cluny in the Caribbean: *http://www.clunycarib.org/*; Sisters of St Joseph of Cluny in Dublin, Ireland, has links to other Cluny communities from Tanzania to Poland: *http://www.sjc.ie/*.

Bartolomea Capitanio. Canonized 1950 with Vincenza. **Sources:** Material provided by her order; Hallack and Anson, *These Made Peace*, 235. **Web site:** Sisters of Charity of St Bartolomea Capitanio and St Vincenza Gerosa: *http://www.suoredimariabambina.org/*.

Bridget of Sweden. Canonized 1391. **Sources:** Dunbar, *Saintly Women*, 1:137–39; Obbard, *Medieval Women Mystics*, 87–118; Redpath, Helen, *God's Ambassadress:*

St Bridget of Sweden, Milwaukee: Bruce Publishing, 1947; Tjader Harris, *Birgitta of Sweden*, throughout. **Web sites:** City of Vadstena's official Birgitta pages: *http://birgitta.vadstena.se/*; St Birgitta Foundation (Lutheran), Vadstena, Sweden: *http://www.birgittastiftelsen.se/*; Order of Our Most Holy Savior of St Bridget, Generalate, Rome (estab. by Mary Elisabeth Hesselblad): *http://www.brigidine.org/*; Brigittine Monks, Amity, OR: *http://www.brigittine.org/*; St Birgitta's Abbey, Vadstena, Sweden: *http://www.birgittaskloster.se/*.

Carmelite Martyrs of Compiègne. Beatified 1906. Of the sixteen martyrs, the four cited here were: Anne Marie Madeleine Françoise Thouret (Sister Charlotte of the Resurrection); Marie Ann Piedcourt (Sister Jesus Crucified); Anne Pelras (Sister Marie Henriette of Providence); and Marie-Geneviève Meunier (Sister Constance of Jesus). **Sources:** Bush, William S., *To Quell the Terror: The Mystery of the Vocation of the Sixteen Carmelites of Compiègne Guillotined July 17, 1794*, Washington, DC: Institute of Carmelite Studies, 1999; Loomis, Stanley, *Paris in the Terror: June 1793–July 1794*, Philadelphia: Lippincott, 1964, 401–3; Newkirk, Terrye, O.C.D.S., "The Mantle of Elijah: The Martyrs of Compiègne as Prophets of Modern Age," Washington, DC: Institute of Carmelite Studies, 1994, read online at *www.icspublications.org/archives/others/newkir.html*; Whitehead, Kenneth D., "Following the Lamb," *First Things*, May 2000, 9–10. **Web sites:** City of Compiègne has two pages dedicated to the Carmelites, under History: *http://www.compiegne.fr/index.php*; Carmel in France (click on Visages): *http://www.carmel.asso.fr/*; Carmelites of Quebec, Canada (click on Figures du Carmel): *http://www.lecarmel.org/*; Diocese of L'Oise has pages dedicated to its native daughter Anne Thouret: *http://catho60.cef.fr/histoire/temoins/Sr_Charlotte/Sr-Charlotte.htm*.

Carmelite Martyrs of Guadalajara. Beatified 1987. **Sources:** Ball, *Faces of Holiness*, 43–50; Holböck, *New Saints, Volume 2*, 153–62; Royal, *Catholic Martyrs*, 118–19. **Web site:** Discalced Carmelites of Ireland, Scotland, and Nigeria have the details for their Memorial Mass and Divine Office (click on Carmelite Feast Days): *http://www.ocd.ie/default.asp*.

Catherine Jarrige. Beatified 1996. **Sources:** Dupuy, Philippe, *Bienheureuse Catinon Menette, 1754–1836*, read online at *http://catholique-saint-flour.cef.fr/bienheureuse-catherinejarrige.htm*; *Courrier de l'Amitie Dominicaine*, Dec. 1996, read online at *http://province.dominicains.com/amdom/dec96.htm#jarrige*. **Web site:** Diocese of Saint Flour has information on local saints, including Catherine Jarrige (click on Liturgie Prière Sacraments, then l'Hagiographie): *http://catholique-saint-flour.cef.fr/index.htm*.

Christina the Astonishing. Never officially beatified, but listed as Blessed in Watkins and as Saint in Butler (1991). **Sources:** Cantimpré, Thomas de, *The Life of Christina the Astonishing*, Toronto: Peregrina, 1999; Dunbar, *Saintly Women*, 1:176–78; Thurston, *Surprising Mystics*, 147–55. **Web site:** A blogger in Nova Scotia offers much more information and links: *http://www.mirabilis.ca/*.

Clelia Barbieri. Beatified 1968; canonized 1989. **Sources:** Ball, *Faces of Holiness*, 51–58; Cruz, Joan Carroll, *Relics: The Shroud of Turin, the True Cross, the Blood of Januarius . . . History, Mysticism, and the Catholic Church*, Huntington, IN: Our Sunday Visitor, 1984, 232–33; Zappulli, Cesare, *The Power of Goodness: The Life of Blessed Clelia Barbieri*, trans. David Giddings, Boston: Daughters of St Paul, 1980. **Web site:** Her shrine in Le Budrie: *http://www.santuarioclelia.it/set_home.htm*.

Elizabeth, Queen of Portugal. Canonized 1625. **Sources:** Dunbar, *Saintly Women*, 1:115–16; McNabb, Vincent, O.P., *St. Elizabeth of Portugal*, New York: Sheed &Ward, 1938; Cirugiao, Maria J., and Michael D. Hull, "Elizabeth of Portugal: 'For, in Her Is a Spirit Intelligent, Holy, Unique,'" *The Wanderer*, July 4, 1996, read online at *www.ewtn.com/library/MARY/ELIZPORT.htm*. **Web sites:** Confraternity of St James, in London, England, is dedicated to the pilgrimage to Compostello and shows Elizabeth's route to the shrine (click on Routes, then Individual Routes): *http://www.csj.org.uk/index.htm;* Portugal's official tourist site (click on Tourism): *http://www.portugalvirtual.pt/.*

Kinga, Queen of Poland. Beatified 1690; canonized 1999. **Sources:** Dunbar, *Saintly Women,* 1:211–12 (Kinga), 436 (Jolanta/Yolanda); Holböck, *Married Saints and Blesseds,* 215–16. **Web sites:** Joachen Duckeck, creator of this site dedicated to caves, includes many details about Kinga's rock salt shrine in Wieliczka (click on Poland): *http://www.showcaves.com/;* Salt Works Museum: *http://www.muzeum. wieliczka.pl/;* Official site of the shrine: *http://www.kopalnia.pl/;* Staropolska: Old Polish Literature reprints some legends (click on Translations, then Middle Ages, and Religious Prose): *http://www.staropolska.gimnazjum.com.pl/.*

Lillian and Natalie of Córdoba. Sources: Colbert, Edward P., *The Martyrs of Cordoba (850–859): A Study of the Sources,* Washington, DC: Catholic Univ. of America Press, 1962, 235–46; Dunbar, *Saintly Women,* 2:102; Wolf, Kenneth Baxter, *Christian Martyrs in Muslim Spain,* read online at LIBRO: The Library of Iberian Resources Online: *http://libro.uca.edu/martyrs/,* 26–31. **Web site:** The Russian Orthodox Church in England has a detailed page about all the Martyrs of Córdoba: *http://www.orthodoxengland.btinternet.co.uk/oecordob.htm.*

Margaret of Antioch. Sources: Dunbar, *Saintly Women,* 2:11–12; Voragine, Jacobus de, *The Golden Legend,* vol. 4, read online at Medieval Sourcebook: *http://www .fordham.edu/halsall/basis/goldenlegend/index.htm.* **Web sites:** Church of St Margaret of Antioch (Church of England) includes a detailed biography: *http://www.lowerhalstow.org.uk/index.asp;* Commune of Mottola, Italy, has interesting frescoes showing her martyrdom: *http://www.comune.mottola.ta.it/english/ grotte14.php.*

Maria Goretti. Beatified 1947; canonized 1950. **Sources:** Ball, *Modern Saints: Book One,* 163–73; Ball, Ann, *Young Faces of Holiness: Modern Saints in Photos and Worlds,* Huntington, IN: Our Sunday Visitor, 2004, 113–23; Buehrle, Maria Cecilia, *Saint Maria Goretti,* Milwaukee: Bruce Publishing, 1950; DiDonato, Pietro, *The Penitent,* New York: Hawthorn Books, 1962. **Web sites:** Official shrine in Nettuno: *http://www.santuarionettuno.it/;* Maria's birthplace, Corinaldo: *http://www.santamariagoretti.it/;* her shrine in Haverstraw, NY: *http:// www.mariagoretti.org/index.htm.*

María de Jesús Sacramentado. Beatified 1992; canonized 2000. **Sources:** *L'Osservatore Romano;* Ball, Ann, "Vivo Cristo Rey!: 25 Mexican Martyr Saints," in *Saints of the Jubilee,* ed. Tim Drake, 13–28. **Web sites:** Saints of Mexico: *http://santosmexico.tripod.com.mx/santosmexico.htm;* City of Guadalajara, Mexico (click on Hospitales): *http://www.guadalajara.net/.*

Maria Teresa Kowalska. Beatified 1999 with Capuchin Martyrs of the Nazi Prison Camps, who were in turn part of the 108 Polish Martyrs venerated on June 12. **Source:** Capuchin Order. **Web sites:** Capuchin Franciscans: *http://www.capuchin.com/Charism/PolishMartyrs/five_capuchin_martyrs_of_poland.htm;* Capuchin Poor Clares, in the United States: *http://www.midamcaps.org/.*

Maria Theresa Ledóchowska. Beatified 1975. **Source:** Bielak, Valeria, *The Servant of God, Mary Theresa Countess Ledochowska, Foundress of the Sodality of Saint Peter Claver,* St Paul, MN: Sodality of St Peter Claver, 1944. **Web sites:** Claverian Sisters, Bellshill, Scotland: *http://www.claveriansisters.org.uk/;* Sisters of St Peter Claver, St Freiborg, Switzerland: *http://www.pierre-claver.ch/.*

Marie Madeleine Postel. Beatified 1908; canonized 1925. **Sources:** Blanchelande, Jean, *L'Abbaye de St-Sauveur-le-Vicomte,* Coutances, France: Arnaud Bellée,

1976; Habig, *Franciscan Book of Saints*, 505–7. **Web site:** Sisters of Marie-Madeleine Postel: *http://www.mmpostel.com/*.

Marija Petkovic. Beatified 2003. **Source:** Press Office of the Croatian Conference of Bishops. **Web sites:** A virtual shrine in English, Spanish, Italian, and Croatian: *http://marijapropetog.hr/*; Marija's hometown in Croatia also has pages devoted to her: *http://www.blato.hr/*.

Martha of Bethany. Sources: Dunbar, *Saintly Women*, 2:33; Voragine, *The Golden Legend*, vol. 4, read online at Medieval Sourcebook: *http://www.fordham.edu/halsall/basis/goldenlegend/index.htm*. **Web sites:** The city of Tarascon has details about the monster (click on History and Legends) and the Collegiate Church of St Martha, which contains her tomb and relics (click on Legacy of History): *http://www.tarascon.org/fr/index.php*; the Sisters of St Martha of Antigonish, Nova Scotia, Canada (the Marthas): *http://www.themarthas.com/*; Villajoyosa, Spain, has an annual festival honoring Martha as patron saint: *http://www.gva.es/festa/pagina1.htm*.

Martyrs of Orange. Beatified 1925. **Sources:** Loomis, Stanley, *Paris in the Terror*, throughout; Santogrossi, Br. Ansgar, O.S.B., "The Tradition of Holiness: Blessed Marie-Rose De Loye, Benedictine Nun and Martyr," *Mount Angel Letter*, June 2002, read online at *www.mtangel.edu*; Vilate, Joachim, *Causes Secrètes de la Révolution du 9 au 10 Thermidor: 1768–1795*, Paris: l'an III de la République, 1795. **Web site:** Diocese of Avignon has a beautiful virtual shrine: *http://catholique-avignon.cef.fr/saint-bien/rel-mart-or.htm*.

Martyrs of Shanxi. Beatified 1946, with Gregory Grassi and Companions; canonized 2000, with 120 Martyrs of China. Marie-Hermine de Jesus (Irma Grivot), b. April 28, 1866, Beaune, France; Maria Chiara (Clelia Nanetti), b. January 9, 1872, Rovigo, Italy; Marie della Pace (Marianna Giuliani), b. December 13, 1875, Aquila, Italy; Marie de Sainte Nathalie (Jeanne-Marie Kerguin), b. May 5, 1864, Brittany, France; Marie de Saint Just (Anne Moreau), b. April 9, 1866, La Faye, Atlantic-Loire, France; Marie Adolphine (Anna Dierkx), b. March 8, 1866, Ossendrecht, Holland; Maria Amandina (Pauline Jeuris), b. December 28, 1872, Herk-la-Ville, Belgium. **Sources:** Maleissye, Marie-Therese de, *A Short Life of Mary of the Passion (Helen de Chappotin), Foundress of the Franciscan Missionaries of Mary*, Bandra, Mumbai: St Pauls, 1997; Marie, Dom Antoine, O.S.B., "Blessed Hermine of Jesus," Abbey of St Joseph de Clairval, Flavigny-sur-Ozerain, France, Newsletter, Oct. 24, 2004, read online at *http://www.clairval.com/*. **Web sites:** Franciscan Missionaries of Mary (click on Our History): *http://www.fmm.org/index.htm*; Chinese Martyrs Church, Ontario, Canada (click on Fifth Introduction): *http://chinesemartyrs.org/*.

Mary Magdalene. Sources: Calef, Susan A., "The *Real* Mary Magdalene," *Liguorian*, Oct. 2004, 23–24; Dunbar, *Saintly Women*, 2:44–45. **Web sites:** Catholic Enquiry Office, supported by the Catholic Trust for England and Wales, has some very interesting pages, including links to articles about *The Da Vinci Code* and a recipe for madeleines: *http://www.life4seekers.co.uk/*; Shrine at Sainte Baume, France: *http://saintebaume.dominicains.com/*; virtual shrine maintained by a Frenchwoman who uses the pseudonym Victor Mortis: *http://www.marie-madeleine.com/sommaire.html*.

Sunniva of Bergen. Sources: Dunbar, *Saintly Women*, 2:233; Undset, Sigrid, *Saga of Saints*, trans. E. C. Ramsden, New York: Longmans, Green, 1934; Wolf, Rev. Hugh K., *St Ansgar's Bulletin*, Supplement, 1990. **Web sites:** In Selje, a church site with interesting photos of landmarks associated with her story (click on Sunniva): *http://www.seljekloster.no/*; St Sunniva School has a photo of a statue of the saint: *http://www.sunniva-studenthjem.no/sunniva.html*; Kinn commemorates Sunniva's journey in an annual pageant: *http://www.kinnaspelet.no/*.

Teresa of the Andes. Beatified 1987; canonized 1993. **Sources:** Ball, *Faces of Holiness*, 243–48; Ball, *Young Faces of Holiness*, 154. **Web sites:** Official Sanctuary of St Teresa of the Andes, Auco, Chile: *http://www.santuarioteresadelosandes.cl/*; A virtual shrine created by an anonymous brother of the Community of St John in Chile: *http://www.teresadelosandes.org/*.

Theneva of Glasgow. Source: Dunbar, *Saintly Women*, 2:249–50. **Web site:** St Enoch's Church in Glasgow (Church of Scotland): *http://www.st-enoch.org.uk/*.

Veronica Giuliani. Beatified 1804; canonized 1839. **Sources:** Courbat, Monique, "Veronica Giuliani: Writing and Rewriting," *Greyfriars Review*, vol. 13, no. 3, 297–320, trans. Edward Hagman, O.F.M., Cap. (orig. pub. in *Annali d'Italianistica: Women Mystic Writers* 13, 1995), read online at *http://web.sbu.edu/ friedsam/greyfriars/greyfriars_13_3_article4.pdf*; Dunbar, *Saintly Women*, 2:288; Salvatori, Abate Filippo Maria, *The Lives of S. Veronica Giuliani, Capuchin Nun, and of the Blessed Battista Varani, (1-286)*; Thurston, *Physical Phenomena of Mysticism*, throughout. **Web site:** Umbria 2000 tourist site (click on Itineraries and Trips, then Religious Itineraries, scroll to bottom): *http://www.english. umbria2000.it/*.

Zdenka Schelingova. Beatified 2003. **Sources:** Material provided by Douglas Leonard, Director of Communications and Development, Holy Cross Sisters, Merrill, WI; Royal, *Catholic Martyrs*, 225. **Web site:** Holy Cross Sisters: *http://www.holycrosssisters.org/beat.html*.

Annotated Sources and Web Sites for August

Assumption of Mary. Declared a dogma of the Catholic Church in 1950. **Sources:** Carroll, Donald, "Mary's Life After Jesus Died," *Catholic Digest*, Sept. 2003, 44–53; Cunneen, Sally, *In Search of Mary: The Woman and the Symbol*, New York: Ballantine Books, 1996; Schineller, Peter, S.J., *Why We Honor Mary*, St Louis, MO: Liguori, 1989. **Web sites:** Eternal Word Television Network Documents Library: *http://www.ewtn.com/index*; Mary page of the University of Dayton, OH: *http://www.udayton.edu/mary/*.

Bronislava of Poland. Beatified 1839. Although churches are dedicated to St Bronislava in Illinois and Wisconsin, she has never been formally canonized. **Sources:** Gonet, Rev. Anthony, ed., *Blessed Bronislava: Patroness of All Needs*, McKeesport, PA, 1945 (pamphlet); Schmadel, Lutz D., *Dictionary of Minor Planet Names*, 5th ed., New York: Springer-Verlag, 108. **Web sites:** International Site of the Canons Regular of Prémontré (Premonstratensians) (click on Famous for Bronislava and other saints): *http://www.premontre.org/*; Krakow Info has a page about St Norbert's Convent (click on Landmarks): *http://www.krakow-info.com/*; St Bronislava Catholic Church, Plover, WI (click on About Our Church): *http:// stbrons.com/*.

Clare of Assisi. Canonized 1255. **Sources:** Francis of Assisi, *Francis and Clare: The Complete Works*, trans. with an Introduction by Regis J. Armstrong, O.F.M., Cap., and Ignatius C. Brady, O.F.M., New York: Paulist Press, 1982; Mueller, *Clare of Assisi*, throughout. **Web sites:** Franciscan Cyberspot has much information about Francis and Clare (click on Francis): *http://198.62.75.1/www1/ofm/ melita.html*; Poor Clares of Eindhoven, The Netherlands: *http://web.inter.nl.net/ users/clarissenklooster/*; Poor Clares of Galway, Ireland: *http://www.poorclares.ie/*.

Clare of Montefalco. Beatified 1737; canonized 1881. **Sources:** Cruz, *Incorruptibles*, 103–5; Foran, Edward A., *The Life of St. Clare of the Cross*, London: Burns Oates

& Washbourne, 1935; Park, Katharine, "Relics of a Fertile Heart: The 'Autopsy' of Clare of Montefalco," in *The Material Culture of Sex, Procreation, and Marriage in Premodern Europe*, ed. Anne L. McClanan and Karen Rosoff Encarnación, Hampshire, England: Palgrave, 2002. **Web sites:** Commune of Montefalco (click on Arte for the links): *http://www.montefalco.it/*; Clare's shrine and monastery in Montefalco: *http://www.chiesainrete.it/chiaradamontefalco/*.

Edith Stein. Beatified 1987; canonized 1998. **Sources:** Oben, Freda Mary, *The Life and Thought of St. Edith Stein*, Staten Island, NY: Alba House, 2001; Slavin, Tim, "A Servant of the Cross," *New Covenant Magazine*, Oct. 1984, 20–22; Stein, Edith, *Self-Portrait in Letters: 1916–1942*, trans. Josephine Koeppel, O.C.D., Washington, DC: Institute of Carmelite Studies, 1993 (vol. 5 of *The Collected Works of Edith Stein*). **Web sites:** Discalced Carmelite Generalate, Rome, Italy: *http://www.ocd.pcn.net/*; Carmelites in Austria: *http://www.karmel.at/edith/*.

Elisabetta Renzi. Beatified 1989. **Source:** Bunson, Matthew, Margaret Bunson, and Stephen Bunson, *John Paul II's Book of Saints*, Huntington, IN: Our Sunday Visitor, 1999, 142 (her surname is misspelled Rienzi). **Web sites:** Sisters of Our Lady of Sorrows in New Orleans and Africa: *http://www.ols.org/*; Elisabetta Renzi Museum, Rimini, Italy: *http://www.museionline.it/eng/cerca/museo.asp?id=8640*; Coriano also has pages about the museum (click on Musei e Castelli, then Museo Elisabettano): *http://www.prolococoriano.it/*.

Elvira Moragas Cantarero. Beatified 1998. **Source:** Muñoyerro, Luis Alonso, "Elvira Moragas, Farmacéutica, Religiosa y Mártir," paper delivered at the Royal National Academy of Pharmacy, Madrid, 1961–62, read online at *http://www.ranf.com/pdf/inauguracion/1962.pdf*. **Web sites:** Discalced Carmelites of Ireland, Scotland, and Nigeria have a page dedicated to Maria Sagrario: *http://www.ocd.ie/*; Catholic devotional site: *http://www.devocionario.com/*.

Emily Bicchieri. Beatified 1769. **Sources:** Dorcy, *Saint Dominic's Family*, 123–26; Dunbar, *Saintly Women*, 1:268. **Web site:** Photograph of the exterior of the cathedral where Emily's relics are venerated (click on Itineraries and choose Vercelli): *http://www.piemonteonline.it/*.

Francesca Rubatto. Beatified 1993. **Source:** *L'Osservatore Romano*. **Web site:** Capuchin Sisters of Mother Rubatto, Rome, Italy: *http://www.scmrubatto.org/*.

Helen, Empress of Rome. **Sources:** Dunbar, *Saintly Women*, 1:369–72; Waugh, Evelyn, "St. Helena, Empress," *Saints for Now*, ed. Clare Boothe Luce, San Francisco: Ignatius Press, 1993 (orig. pub. 1952 by Sheed & Ward, New York), 96–112. **Web site:** St Helen's Greek Orthodox Church, Colchester, England: *http://homepage.ntlworld.com/orthodox.colchester/*.

Jane Frances de Chantal. Beatified 1751; canonized 1767. **Sources:** *Francis de Sales, Jane de Chantal: Letters of Spiritual Direction*, trans. Péronne Marie Thibert, V.H.M., selected and introduced by Wendy M. Wright and Joseph F. Power, O.S.F.S., New York: Paulist Press, 1988 (Western Spirituality Series); Jones, *Women Saints*, 194, 201–7. **Web sites:** Monastery of the Visitation, St Louis, MO: *http://www.visitationmonastery.org/*; Visitation Abbey in Tyringham, England: *http://www.vistyr.org/*.

Jeanne Delanoue. Beatified 1947; canonized 1982. **Sources:** Holböck, *New Saints and Blesseds of the Catholic Church: Blesseds and Saints Canonized by Pope John Paul II During the Years 1979–1983, Volume 1*, trans. Michael J. Miller, San Francisco: Ignatius Press, 2000, 216–20; McGinley, Phyllis, *Saint-Watching*, 50–51. **Web sites:** Diocese of Angers (French): *http://catholique-angers.cef.fr/*; Diocese of D'Evry Corbeil-Essonnes (French): *http://catholique-evry.cef.fr/*.

Jeanne Elisabeth Bichier. Beatified 1934; canonized 1947. **Source:** Butler, *Lives of* *the Saints* (1995), 264–65. **Web site:** Sisters of the Cross of St Andrew: *http://www3.planalfa.es/fillesdelacroix/*.

Jeanne Jugan. Beatified 1982. **Sources:** LeClerc, Eloi, *The Desert and the Rose: The Spirituality of Jeanne Jugan*, trans. from French by Claire Troche, London: Darton Longman & Todd, 2002; Trochu, Francis, *Jeanne Jugan: Sister Marie of the Cross, Foundress of the Institute of the Little Sisters of the Poor, 1792–1879*, trans. Hugh Montgomery, Westminster, MD: Newman Press, 1950; *Serenity*, published quarterly by the Little Sisters of the Poor in Baltimore, MD. **Web sites:** Little Sisters of the Poor, Totowa, NJ: *http://www.littlesistersofthepoor.org/*; Relatives of Jeanne Jugan include pages about her on their genealogy site: *http://cancagen.free.fr/Documents/Jeanne-Jugan.htm*; Little Sisters of the Poor, Greenock, Scotland: *http://www.littlesistersgreenock.org/*; Little Sisters of the Poor in Bangalore, India: *http://www.children-of-bangalore.com/*.

Jane of Aza. Beatified 1828. **Sources:** Dorcy, *Saint Dominic's Family*, 3–7; Dunbar, *Saintly Women*, 1:416. **Web site:** Province of Caleruega has information about Joan and Dominic (click on Monumentos): *http://perso.wanadoo.es/cm_romon/caleruega/pag0.html*.

Lydia Purpuraria. Sources: Philippians 4:3; Acts 16:6–10, 14–15; Baring-Gould, *Lives of the Saints*, 8:24.

Margaret Clitherow. Beatified 1929; canonized 1970, with the Forty Martyrs of England and Wales. **Sources:** Kennedy, Leonard A., C.S.B., "St. Margaret Clitherow, Martyr," *Christ to the World*, English ed., vol. 44, 1999, 422–25; Molinari, Paolo, S.J., "Canonization of 40 English and Welsh Martyrs," *L'Osservatore Romano*, English ed., Oct. 29, 1970; Monro, Margaret T., *St. Margaret Clitherow, the Pearl of York: Wife, Mother, Martyr for the Catholic Faith Under Queen Elizabeth I*, Rockford, IL: Tan Books, 2003. **Web sites:** St Wilfrid's Catholic Church, York: *http://www.stwilfridsyork.org.uk/*; York's tourism site (click on Themed Fact Sheets for the Saints and Sinners Tour): *http://www.york-tourism.co.uk/*.

María Encarnación Rosal. Beatified 1997. **Sources:** *L'Osservatore Romano*; O'Malley, Vincent J., C.M., *Saints of North America*, Huntington, IN: Our Sunday Visitor, 2004, 423–25. **Web sites:** A virtual shrine: *http://www.oremosjuntos.com/*; The monastery of Santa Catalina is now a luxury hotel: *http://www.convento.com/*.

Mariam Baouardy. Beatified 1983. **Sources:** Ball, *Modern Saints: Book Two*, 144–48; Neger, Doris C., "The Little Arab," *Sophia*, vol. 31, Jan.-Feb. 2001, read online at *www.melkite.org/sa33.htm*; Thurston, *Physical Phenomena of Mysticism*, 29. **Web sites:** Carmelite Province of the Most Pure Heart of Mary, Darien, IL, has more information and an ikon of Mariam: *http://carmelnet.org/chas/saints/maria3.htm*; Bethlehem Carmel has a slide show: *http://www.carmelholyland.org/*.

María Micaela Desmaisières. Beatified 1925; canonized 1934. **Source:** Kempf, *Holiness of the Church*, 199–201.

María Pilar Izquierdo Albero. Beatified 2001. **Source:** *L'Osservatore Romano*.

María del Tránsito Cabanillas de Jesús Sacramentado. Beatified 2002. **Source:** *L'Osservatore Romano*. **Web site:** A site dedicated to Madre Tránsito has details about her beatification miracle and many photographs of memorabilia and artifacts: *http://www.mariadeltransito.com.ar/*.

Mary Ellen MacKillop. Beatified 1995. McBrien incorrectly lists her as canonized and many others pick up this error. **Sources:** Gardener, Father Paul, S.J. (her postulator), beatification biography, read on line at *http://www.ewtn.com/library/MARY/bios95.htm#mackillop*; Jones, *Women Saints*, 231–32, 250–58; McClory, Robert, *Faithful Dissenters: Stories of Men and Women Who Changed the Church*, Maryknoll, NY: Orbis Books, 2000; Modystack, William, *Blessed Mary MacKillop: A Woman*

Before Her Time, Sydney: Lansdowne, 1982. **Web sites:** Sisters of St Joseph of the Sacred Heart: *http://www.sosj.org.au/*; Mary MacKillop Place, North Sydney, has many photographs from the museum: *http://www.marymackillopplace.org.au/*; Mary MacKillop Centre, Penola, also has many photographs: *http://www.mack-illop-penola.com/*.

Monica. Sources: Baring-Gould, *Lives of the Saints,* 5:67–73; Dunbar, *Saintly Women,* 2:96–98. **Web sites:** St Monica Sodality, an international organization that prays for souls to return to the faith, has a chapter in Chicago, IL: *http://www.assumptiongrotto.com/monica.htm*; Mai DeDeus Church, Puttar, India, also has a chapter (click on Church Association): *http://www.maidedeuschurchputtur.com/*.

Narcisa de Jesús. Beatified 1992. **Source:** Catholic Church in Ecuador, read online at *http://iglesia.interdecweb.net/EpiscopadoEcuatoriano/santos.htm.* **Web site:** Catholic Church of Ecuador (click on La Iglesia for Santos del Ecaudor): *http://iglesiaecaudor.org.ec/*.

Philomena. Canonized 1837. **Sources:** Dunbar, *Saintly Women,* 2:149–50; O'Sullivan, Paul, O.P., E.D.M., *Saint Philomena, the Wonder Worker,* Rockford, IL: Tan Books, 1993 (orig. pub. 1927 by Catholic Printing Press, Lisbon). **Web sites:** Universal Living Rosary Association of St Philomena, founded by Pauline Jaricot: *http://www.philomena.org/*; Sanctuary of St Philomena, in Mugnano del Cardinale: *http://www.philomena.it/*; Shrine of St Philomena, Miami, FL: *http://shrineofsaintphilomena.com/*.

Radegund, Queen of France. Sources: Allen, Charlotte, "The Holy Feminine," *First Things,* Dec. 1999, 37–44; Thiébaux, Marcelle, ed. and trans., *The Writings of Medieval Women,* vol. 14, series B, New York: Garland, 1987; Watkin, E. I., "St Radegund (518–587)," in *Saints for Now,* ed. Clare Boothe Luce, 46–52. **Web sites:** Poitiers Office of Tourism has some of the legends about Radegund: *http://www.ot-poitiers.fr/*; Diocese of Poitiers: *http://www.diocese-poitiers.com.fr/*.

Rose of Lima. Beatified 1668; canonized 1671. **Sources:** Dunbar, *Saintly Women,* 2:196–98; Keyes, *The Rose and the Lily,* throughout; Myers, Kathleen Ann, *Neither Saints nor Sinners: Writing the Lives of Women in Spanish America,* New York: Oxford Univ. Press, 2003, 23–43. **Web site:** Archdiocese of Lima: *http://www.arzobispadodelima.org/starosa/index.html.*

Sancja Janina Szymkowiak. Beatified 2002. **Source:** *L'Osservatore Romano.* **Web site:** Sisters of Our Lady of Sorrows (click on Servante de Dieu): *http://serafic.free.fr/*.

Teresa Jornet y Ibars. Beatified 1958; canonized 1974. **Sources:** *L'Osservatore Romano; Biblioteca Católica Digital,* read online at *www.mercaba.org.* **Web site:** Biblioteca Católica Digital has a lot of information: *http://www.mercaba.org/santos/santoral–08.htm*

Victoria Diez. Beatified 1993. **Source:** *L'Osservatore Romano.* **Web site:** Teresian Association: *http://www.institucionteresiana.org/*.

Annotated Sources and Web Sites for September

Agnes and Columba Kim. Beatified 1984. **Sources:** Dunbar, *Saintly Women,* 1:200–201; Kempf, *Holiness of the Church,* 345–60; Kim, Chang-mun, Father Joseph, editor, *Catholic Korea Yesterday and Today,* compiled and edited by Father Joseph Chang-mun Kim and John Jae-sun Chung, Seoul: Catholic Korea Publishing Co., 1964, 158–59; Kim, Chang-seok Thaddeus, *Lives of 103 Martyr Saints of Korea,* Seoul: Catholic Korea Publishing Co.64, 86–87; Neligan, *Saintly Characters,* 322; Pratt, Keith, and Richard Rutt, eds., *Korea: A Historical and Cultural Dictionary,* Surrey, England: Curzon Press, 1999, 280. **Web sites:** Catholic Bishops Conference of Korea has more information about the 103 Martyrs: *http:// www.cbck.or.kr/*; Korea National Tourism Organization site has information and photos about the shrines of the martyrs (click on Culture): *http://english.tour-2korea.com/index.asp.*

Amparo Carbonell and Carmen Moreno. Beatified 2001. **Sources:** Ball, *Modern Saints: Book One*, 332–35; Anonymous, "Carmen Moreno Benítez and Amparo Carbonell Muñoz: The Costly Price of Christian Love," *Hagiography Circle*, read online at *www.newsaints.faithweb.com/biographies/Salesianas.htm*; Salesians of Don Bosco, Eastern Province in the United States, article, "Salesian Holiness: Sisters Martyred in Spain," in *Salesiana*, and online at *http://www.salesians.org/ dba/842c.htm.***Web site:** http://www.salesians.org.

Anna Eugenia Picco. Beatified 2001. **Source:** *L'Osservatore Romano.* **Web site:** Little Daughters of the Sacred Hearts of Jesus and Mary: *http://www.pfiglie.org/.*

Anna Wang. Beatified 1955; canonized 2000. **Sources:** Royal, *Catholic Martyrs*, 317–18; Prayer card for Anna Wang, published by Mission to China Evangelization Project, Corpus Christi, TX. **Web site:** Chinese Martyrs Catholic Church, Ontario, Canada: *http://chinesemartyrs.org/.*

Beatrice de Silva. Beatified 1926; canonized 1976. **Sources:** Dehey, Elinor Tong, *Religious Orders of Women in the United States*, Hammond, IN: W. B. Conkey, 1930, 492–96; Dunbar, *Saintly Women*, 1:109–10. **Web sites:** Isabel of Spain: *http://www.queenisabel.com/*; Conceptionist Motherhouse, Toledo, Spain: *http:// www.concepcionistas.info.org/.*

Bernardina Maria Jablonska. Beatified June 6, 1997. **Sources:** Bunson, Bunson, and Bunson, *John Paul II's Book of Saints*, 245–46; Holböck, *New Saints, Volume 1*, 162–67; Kurek, Ewa, *Your Life Is Worth Mine: How Polish Nuns Saved Hundreds of Jewish Children in German-Occupied Poland, 1939–1945*, New York: Hippocrene Books, 1997, 145–57. **Web sites:** A virtual saints tour of Krakow, Poland: *http:// www.krakow.pl/en/*; Albertine generalate in Krakow: *http://www.albertynki.pl/.*

Brigida Morello. Beatified 1998. **Source:** *L'Osservatore Romano.*

Catherine of Genoa. Beatified 1675; canonized 1733. **Sources:** *Catherine of Genoa: Purgation and Purgatory, The Spiritual Dialogue*, trans. and with notes by Serge Hughes, New York: Paulist Press, 1979 (Western Spirituality Series); Cruz, *Incorruptibles*, 159–61; Dunbar, *Saintly Women*, 1:161–62; Holböck, *Married Saints and Blesseds*, 301–7. **Web site:** Philadelphia Art Museum reproduces Marco Benefial's painting *Christ Appearing to Saint Catherine*: *http://www.philamuseum.org/rome/a6.html.*

Catherine of Racconigi. Beatified 1808. **Sources:** Ashley, Benedict M., O.P., *Blessed Osanna d'Andreasi and Other Renaissance Italian Dominican Women Mystics*, read online at *www.op.org/domcentral/study/ashley/osanna.htm*; Bell, *Holy Anorexia*, 159–61; Dunbar, *Saintly Women*, 1:162–63; Dorcy, *Saint Dominic's Family*, 272–73; Zarri, "Living Saints," 219–304.

Dina Bélanger. Beatified 1993. **Sources:** Ball, Ann, *Faces of Holiness II: Modern Saints in Photos and Words*, Huntington, IN: Our Sunday Visitor, 2001, 116–22; Marie Sainte Cecile de Rome (Dina Belanger), *Canticle of Love*, trans. from French and abridged by Sister Mary St Stephen, Sillery, Quebec: Convent, 1938. **Web site:** Religious of Jesus-Marie in Canada: *http://www.jesus-marie.ca/.*

Douceline of Marseilles. Listed as Saint in Watkins. **Sources:** Dunbar, *Saintly Women*, 1:245; Kleinberg, Aviad M., *Prophets in Their Own Country: Living Saints and the Making of Sainthood in the Later Middle Ages*, Chicago: Univ. of Chicago Press, 1992, 121–23; Underhill, *Mysticism*, 216.

Edith of Wilton. **Sources:** Butler, *Lives of the Fathers* (1845), 9:205–6 (Edith), 140–43 (Wilfreda); Dunbar, *Saintly Women*, 1:252–53; Millinger, Susan, "Humility and

Power: Anglo-Saxon Nuns in Anglo-Norman Hagiography," in *Distant Echoes*, ed. John A. Nichols and Lillian Thomas Shank, vol. 1 of *Medieval Religious Women*, 115–29.

Emilie Gamelin. Beatified 2001. **Sources:** Code, Joseph B., *Great American Foundresses*, New York: Macmillan, 1929, 329–57; Gandia, Renato, "Foundress to Be Beatified," *Western Catholic Reporter*, Alberta, Canada, week of Sept. 24, 2001, read online at *www.wcr.ab.ca/news/2001/0924/mothergamelin092401.shtml*; Gandia, Renato, "Sisters Mark Commitment to Deaf," *Western Catholic Reporter*, week of Sept. 17, 2001, read online at *www.wcr.ab.ca/news/2001/0917/providencesisters091701.shtml*; Winzer, Margaret A., "Exclusion and Integration: The Case of the Sisters of Providence of Quebec," in *Deaf History Unveiled: Interpretations for the New Scholarship*, ed. John Vickrey Van Cleeve, Washington, DC: Gallaudet Univ. Press, 146–51. **Web sites:** Sisters of Providence, Montreal, Canada: *http://www.providenceintl.org/*; Emilie Gamelin Center, Montreal, Canada: *http://www.providenceintl.org/*.

Emilie de Rodat. Beatified 1940; canonized 1950. **Sources:** Giraud, Sylvain Marie, *The Spirit of Sacrifice and the Life of Sacrifice in the Religious State*, revised by Rev. Herbert Thurston, Cincinnati: Benziger Bros., 1905, 37; McNamara, Robert F., "St Emily," *Saints Alive*, read online at *http://www.stthomasirondequoit.com/SaintsAlive/id495.htm*; Staley, Tony, "Like a Persistent Spider, St. Emily de Rodat Never Gave Up," *The Compass*, Green Bay, WI: Catholic Diocese of Green Bay, Sept. 15, 2000, read online at *www.thecompassnews.org/compass/2000–09–15/00cn091512.htm*. **Web site:** St Emily Parish, Mount Prospect, IL: *http://www.stemily.org/*.

Helen of Bologna. Beatified 1828. **Sources:** Dunbar, *Saintly Women*, 2:1, 375–76; Holböck, *Married Saints and Blesseds*, 315–16. **Web sites:** St Cecilia in Ecstasy: *http://www.artonline.it/eng/opera.asp?IDOpera=136*; Opera Pia dei Vergognosi: *http://www.oppvbologna.it/*.

Hildegard of Bingen. Beatified 1324. **Sources:** Flanigan, Sabina, *Hildegard of Bingen, 1098–1179: A Visionary Life*, New York: Routledge, 1989; *Hildegard of Bingen: Selected Writings*, trans. with an Introduction and notes by Mark Atherton, London: Penguin, 2001; Jones, *Women Saints*, 2–3, 5–10; King, Ursula, *Christian Mystics: Their Lives and Legacies Throughout the Ages*, New York: Simon & Schuster, 1998, 80–83. **Web sites:** Portal dedicated to Hildegard: *http://www.hildegard.org/*; Hildegard of Bingen historical sites: *http://www.staff.uni-mainz.de/horst/hildegard/wirk/ewirk.html*.

Lioba of Bischoffsheim. **Sources:** Baring-Gould, *Lives of the Saints*, 9:417–21; Dunbar, *Saintly Women*, 1:461–63; Rudolf, "The Life of Saint Leoba," trans. C. H. Talbot, in *Soldiers of Christ: Saints and Saints' Lives from Late Antiquity and the Early Middle Ages*, ed. Thomas F. X. Noble and Thomas Head, University Park: Pennsylvania State Univ. Press, 1995, 255–77. **Web sites:** Benedictines of St Lioba (founded in Germany 1920, motherhouse in Denmark since 1935): *http://www.sankt-lioba-kloster.dk/*; Town of Creditor, England, has much information about native son Boniface and his mission to Germany: *http://www.crediton.co.uk/*.

Lucy de Freitas. Beatified 1867, with 204 Martyrs of Japan. **Sources:** Dunbar, *Saintly Women*, 1:473–75; Fujita, Neil S., *Japan's Encounter with Christianity: The Catholic Mission in Pre-Modern Japan*, New York: Paulist Press, 1991, 174–75; Hallack and Anson, *These Made Peace*, 195–200; Pedrosa, Cerefino Puebla, O.P., ed., *Witnesses of the Faith in the Orient: Dominican Martyrs of Japan, China and Vietnam*, trans. from Spanish by Sister Maria Maez, O.P., Manila: Life Today, 1989, 140–41.

María de la Cabeza. Beatified 1697; canonized 1752. **Sources:** Baring-Gould, *Lives of the Saints*, 5:146–48; Dunbar, *Saintly Women*, 2:53–54; Guiley, Rosemary

Ellen, *The Encylopedia of Saints*, New York: Facts on File, 2001, 157–58; Holböck, *Married Saints and Blesseds*, 159–61; Sánchez Molledo, José María, *Recorrido por el Madrid de San Isidro*, Madrid: Congregación de San Isidro de Naturales de Madrid, 2005, read online at *http://www.congregacionsanisidro.org/recorrido. htm*. **Web sites:** Shrine of San Isidro, patron of Madrid, Spain, has a page about his wife, María de la Cabeza: *http://www.congregacionsanisidro.org/*; St Isidore Church, Stow, MA: *http://www.stisidorestow.org/*; Recorrido por el Madrid de San Isidro: *http://www.congregacionsanisidro.org/recorrido.htm*.

Maria Euthymia Üffing. Beatified 2001. **Source:** *L'Osservatore Romano*. **Web sites:** Sisters of Mercy of Münster, Euthymia site (German): *http://www.euthymia.de/*; Diocese of Münster (click on Bistum Münster): *http://www.dioezesanbibliothek-muenster.de/*.

Marina of Omura. Beatified 1981; canonized 1987. **Sources:** Dorcy, *Saint Dominic's Family*, 389–90; Pedrosa, *Witnesses of the Faith*, 92–93, 128. **Web site:** Catholic churches and pilgrimage sites in Nagasaki, Japan: *http://www.tca-japan.com/*.

Martyrs of Nowogródek. Beatified 2000. The eleven include: Sister Maria Boromea (Veronika Narmontowicz), b. December 18, 1916; Mother Maria Stella of the Most Blessed Sacrament (Adelaide Mardosiewicz), b. December 14, 1888. **Sources:** Farrell, Michael J., "When It Comes to Saints, How Do You Spot the Right Stuff?" *National Catholic Reporter*, Feb. 25, 2000, read online at Proquest; Lapomarda, Rev. Vincent A., S.J., "The Eleven Nuns of Nowogrodek," Hiatt Holocaust Collection, College of the Holy Cross , Worcester, MA, read online at *http://www. holycross.edu/departments/history/vlapomar/hiatt/nuns11.htm*; Lively, Kathryn, "A Saintly Sacrifice: The Martyrs of Nowogródek," in *Saints of the Jubilee*, ed. Tim Drake, 3–8; Piotrowski, Tadeusz, *Poland's Holocaust: Ethnic Strife, Collaboration with Occupying Forces and Genocide in the Second Republic, 1918–1947*, Jefferson, NC: McFarland, 1998. Royal, *Catholic Martyrs*, 212–15. **Web sites:** Sisters of the Holy Family of Nazareth, Philadelphia, PA: *http://www.phila-csfn.org/sister.htm*; Sisters of the Holy Family, Monroe, CT: *http://www.ct-csfn.org/*; Site dedicated to Nowogródik (click on Navahrudak, then Maps, then Central Part of Navahrudak, then icon of Farney R. C. Church): *http://www.navahrudak.newmail.ru/*.

Notburga of Eben. Canonized 1862. **Source:** Dunbar, *Saintly Women*, 2:111–12. **Web sites:** Notburga Museum in Eben am Achensee (German only): *http:// www.notburga-museum.at/*; Achensee has details about the museum in English: *http://www.achensee.com/*.

Pulcheria Augusta. Sources: Baring-Gould, *Lives of the Saints*, 9:148–57; Butler, *Lives of the Fathers* (1845), 9:94–100; Dunbar, *Saintly Women*, 2:160–71; Gibbon, Edward, *The Decline and Fall of the Roman Empire*, London: Penguin, 1994, 2:263–383.

Richardis. Canonized 1049. **Sources:** Dunbar, *Saintly Women*, 2:186–87; Englebert, Omer, *Lives of the Saints*, trans. Christopher and Anne Fremantle, New York: Barnes & Noble, 1994, 356; Schulenburg, *Forgetful of Their Sex*, 70–71, 225. **Web site:** Eileen and Ralph Hayes created an informative site about Andlau Abbey: *http://www.andlau.com/*.

Rosalie of Palermo. Canonized 1630. **Sources:** Baring-Gould, *Lives of the Saints*, 10:53–57; Civello, Castrense, *Santa Rosalia*, Rome: Corso, 1967; Gerbino, Aldo, *La Rosa dell'Erota, 1196–1991*, Palermo: Dorica, 1991; Petrarca, Valerio, *Di Santa Rosalia, Vergine Palermitana*, Palermo: Sellerio, 1988. **Web sites:** Virtual shrine, created and maintained by Kenneth C. Ferlita: *http://www.ferlita.com/*; Palermo has a Rosalie web: *http://www.palermoweb.com/*.

Rose of Viterbo. Canonized 1457. **Sources:** Baring-Gould, *Lives of the Saints*, 9:57–65; Butler, *Lives of the Fathers* (1845), 3:80; Dunbar, *Saintly Women*, 2:195–96.

Web sites: City of Viterbo has information about the annual September procession in her honor (click on Events): *http://www.comune.viterbo.it/*.

Seraphina Sforza. Beatified 1754. **Sources:** Dunbar, *Saintly Women*, 2:220–21; Englebert, *Lives of the Saints*, 343–44; Holböck, *Married Saints and Blesseds*, 298–300.

Teresa of Calcutta. Beatified 2003. **Sources:** Guntzelman, Joan, "The Life of a Saint," *St Anthony Messenger*, Oct. 2003, 31–35; Zaleski, Carol, "The Dark Night of Mother Teresa," *First Things*, May 2003, 24–27. **Web sites:** Official site for the cause of canonization, San Diego, CA: *http://www.motherteresacause.info/*; Mother Teresa Center: *http://www.motherteresa.org/*.

Thérèse Couderc. Beatified 1951; canonized 1970. **Sources:** Ball, *Modern Saints: Book Two*, 202–9; Perroy, Henry, *A Great and Humble Soul: Mother Thérèse Couderc, Foundress of the Congregation of Our Lady of the Retreat in the Cenacle (1805–1885)*, trans. from French by John J. Burke, Westminster, MD: Newman Press, 1960; Surles, Eileen, *Surrender to the Spirit: The Life of Mother Thérèse Couderc, Foundress of the Society of Our Lady of the Retreat in the Cenacle, 1805–1885*, New York: P. J. Kenedy, 1951. **Web sites:** Sisters of the Cenacle, North American Province: *http://www.cenaclesisters.org/*; Jesuits of France: *http://www.jesuites.com/spiritualite/couderc/livrer.htm*.

Annotated Sources and Web Sites for October

Agnes de Jesus Galand. Beatified 1994. **Sources:** Dunbar, *Saintly Women*, 1:38; Dorcy, *Saint Dominic's Family*, 386–87; Thurston, *Physical Phenomena of Mysticism*, 144–45, 219, 231, 237–38, 347. **Web sites:** Diocese du Puy en Velay has pages for Agnes and the shrine of Our Lady of Puy: *http://catholique-lepuy.cef.fr/*; Dominican monastery of Langeac: *http://langeac.op.org/*.

Alexandrina Maria da Costa. Beatified 2004. **Sources:** Johnston, Francis, *Alexandrina: The Agony and the Glory*, trans. assistance by Anne Croshaw, Rockford, IL: Tan Books, 1982 (orig. pub. 1979 by Veritas, Dublin, Ireland); Woodward, *Making Saints*, 171–78. **Web sites:** Official shrine: *http://alexandrinabalasar.home.sapo.pt/*; Devotional site created by Alphonse Rocha: *http://alexandrina.balasar.free.fr/*; Salesians Order: *http://www.salesians.org/*.

Angadresima de Renty. Canonized 1321. **Source:** Dunbar, *Saintly Women*, 1:56. **Web site:** Diocese of L'Oise, France: *http://catho60.cef.fr/histoire/temoins/Ste_Angadreme/Ste_Angadreme.htm*.

Anna Schäffer. Beatified 1999. **Source:** Antoine Marie, Dom, O.S.B., "Anna Schäffer," Newsletter of Abbaye Saint-Joseph de Clairval, France, Feb. 2, 2003, read online at *www.catholicspot.com/abbayestjoseph/February–2003.htm*. **Web site:** Virtual shrine: *http://www.altmuehlnet.de/gemeinden/mindelstetten/anna/annastart.html*.

Benvenuta Bojani. Beatified 1765. **Sources:** Bell, *Holy Anorexia*, 127–30; Dorcy, *Saint Dominic's Family*, 102–4; Dunbar, *Saintly Women*, 1:115–16; Pazzi, Maria Maddalena de', *Maria Maddalena de' Pazzi*, trans. with an Introduction by Armando Maggi, Preface by E. Ann Matter, New York: Paulist Press, 2000, 23; Thompson, *Cities of God*, 358.

Bertilla Boscardin. Beatified 1952; canonized 1961. **Sources:** Andreoli, Vittorino, "Suor Bertilla, la Santa 'Testona' L'umiltà Assoluta," read online at *http://www.entraevedi.org/S.Maria%20Bertilla.htm*; Seabeck, Raymond, and Lauretta Seabeck, *Smiling Pope: The Life and Teaching of John Paul I*, Huntington, IN: Our Sunday Visitor, 2004, 18–19; Sicari, Antonio, *Ritratti di Santi*, read online at *http://users.libero.it/luigi.scrosoppi/santi/bertilla.htm*. **Web sites:** Sisters of

St Dorothy Daughters of the Sacred Heart: *http://www.suoredoroteevicenza.org/*; site inspired by *Solo de Amore*, a biography by Gino Alberto Faccioli: *http://digilander.libero.it/santabertilla/*.

Catherine, Queen of Bosnia. Listed as Blessed by the Croatian Conference of Bishops. **Sources:** Babinger, Franz, *Mehmed the Conquerer and His Time*, Princeton: Princeton Univ. Press, 1978, bk. 4, 222–25; Jones, William, *Crowns and Coronations: A History of Regalia*, London: Chatto & Windus, 1968, 76; Lambert, Malcolm, *The Cathars*, Oxford: Blackwell, 1998, 310–12. **Web sites:** Site devoted to Croatia, created by Darko Zubrinic, Zagreb, has much information about Queen Katarina: *http://www.hr/darko/etf/et02.html*; Croatian Conference of Bishops site commemorating John Paul II's 2003 visit to Croatia (click on Catholic Church Among the Croats): *http://www.pope.hr/*.

Ethelburga of Barking. Sources: Butler, *Lives of the Fathers* (1845), Vol. 10, 229–31; Dunbar, *Saintly Women*, 1:280; Schulenburg, Jane Tibbetts, "Female Sanctity: Public and Private Roles ca. 500–100," in *Women and Power in the Middle Ages*, ed. Mary Erler and Maryanne Kowelski, Athens, GA: Univ. of Georgia Press, 1988, 102–26. **Web sites:** London Borough of Barking and Degenham has much information about Barking Abbey, now an important archaeological site (click on Museums and Heritage Sites): *http://www.barking-dagenham.gov.uk/*; St Ethelburga's Centre for Peace and Reconciliation, London: *http://www.stethelburgas.org/*.

Faustina Kowalska. Beatified 1993: canonized 2000. **Sources:** Egan, Harvey D., *An Anthology of Christian Mysticism*, Collegeville, MN: Liturgical Press, 1991, 562–91; Odell, Catherine M., *Faustina: Apostle of Divine Mercy*, Huntington, IN: Our Sunday Visitor, 1998; Treece, *Apparitions*, 126–28. **Web sites:** Shrine of Divine Mercy, Poland: *http://www.sanktuarium.krakow.pl/*; National Shrine of Divine Mercy, Stockbridge, MA: *http://www.catholicshrines.net/states/ma9.htm*; Sisters of Our Lady of Divine Mercy, Dorchester, MA: *http://www.sisterfaustina.org/*.

Flora of Beaulieu. Beatified 1746; canonized 1852. **Sources:** Chanut, Abbot Christian-Philippe, "Sainte Flore, Religieuse Hospitalière de Saint-Jean," *Missel*, read online at *http://missel.free.fr/Sanctoral/10/21.php*; Dunbar, *Saintly Women*, 1:319–20; Guerin, Paul, *Les Petit Bollandists: Vie des Saints*, Paris: Bloud et Barral, 1876, 76–86. **Web site:** Hospitaller Order of St John of Jerusalem of Rhodes and Malta has a page devoted to Flora, with many illustrations: *http://www.smom-za.org/smom/*.

Frideswide of Oxford. Sources: Baring-Gould, *Lives of the Saints*, 11:484–87; Butler, *Lives of the Fathers* (1845), 10:416–17; Dunbar, *Saintly Women*, 1:327–28. **Web sites:** Historical Society of Haut-Pays, France: *http://www.histoirehautpays.com/*; Christ Church, Oxford: *http://www.chch.ox.ac.uk/*.

Keyne of Wales. Sources: Baring-Gould, *Lives of the Saints*, 10:178–80; Baring-Gould and Fisher, *Lives of the British Saints*, 2:52–54; Dunbar, *Saintly Women*, 1:451. **Web sites:** Keynsham, on the site of her woods, has a page about Keyne: *http://www.keynsham.co.uk/*; St Michael's Mount: *http://www.stmichaelsmount.co.uk/*; Well House, a hotel built on property that includes the site of Keyne's well: *http://www.wellhouse.co.uk/*.

Maddalena Panattieri. Beatified 1827. **Sources:** Dorcy, *Saint Dominic's Family*, 237–88; Dunbar, *Saintly Women*, 2:5; Lehmijoki-Gardner, *Dominican Penitent Women*, 249–50; Watkin, *Neglected Saints*, 151.

Magdalene of Nagasaki. Beatified 1981, with Lawrence Ruiz and Fifteen Companions, also known as the Sixteen Martyrs of Nagasaki; canonized October 18, 1987, with the same group. **Sources:** Dorcy, *Saint Dominic's Family*, 387–89; Williams, Frederick Vincent, *Martyrs of Nagasaki*, Fresno, CA: Academy Library Guild, 1956. **Web sites:** Catholic churches and pilgrimage sites in Nagasaki,

Japan; *http://www.tca-japan.com/*; Augnet, International Augustinian School site has much information under history, click on "Japan: Martyrs": *http://www .augnet.org/*; Augustinian Recollects consider Magdalene their patron saint: *http://www.augustinianrecollects.org/*.

Margaret Mary Alacoque. Beatified 1864; canonized 1920. **Sources:** *The Autobiography of Saint Margaret Mary*, trans. Sisters of the Visitation, Rockford, IL: Tan Books, 1986 (orig. pub. Sisters of the Visitation, Kent, England, 1930); Dunbar, *Saintly Women*, 1:29–30; *Letters of St Margaret Mary Alacoque*, trans. Fr. Clarence A. Herbst, S.J., Rockford, IL: Tan Books, 1997 (orig. pub. 1954 by Henry Regnery, Chicago). **Web sites:** Official site of Paray-le-Monial and its shrines: http:// www.sanctuaires-paray.com; Jesuit site: *http://www.jesuites.com/missions/spiritualite/paray.htm*.

Marguerite d'Youville. Beatified 1959; canonized 1990. **Sources:** Material provided by Sister Suzanne Forget, S.G.M.; Ferland-Angers, Albertine, *Mother d'Youville: First Canadian Foundress*, trans. Richard R. Cooper, Montreal: Sisters of Charity of Montreal, 2000; Fitts, Sister Mary Pauline, G.N.S.H., *Hands to the Needy: Blessed Marguerite d'Youville, Apostle to the Poor*, Garden City, NY: Doubleday, 1958 (reissued in 2000 in commemoration of the 250th anniversary of the foundation of the Grey Nuns as a religious organization); Jones, *Women Saints*, 208–14; Lefevre, Marie Cecilia, S.G.M., and Rose Alma Lemire, S.G.M., *A Journey of Love*, Lexington, MA: Sisters of Charity of Montreal (pamphlet). **Web site:** Sisters of Charity of Montreal: *http://www.sgm.qc.ca/*.

Maria Angela Truszkowska. Beatified 1993. **Source:** Tkacz, Mary Casimir, C.S.S.F., *Mother Angela: A Pictorial Life of the Servant of God Mother Mary Angela*, Rome: Edizione Paoline, 1967. **Web sites:** Felician Sisters Generalate, Rome, Italy: *http:// www.feliciansisters.org/*; Felician Sisters, Chicago, IL, U.S. Motherhouse: *http:// www.felicianschicago.org/*; Museum and Archives of Mary Angela Truszkowska, Krakow, Poland: *http://www.muzeum-mat.cssf.opoka.org.pl*.

María Soledad Torres Acosta. María Soledad (= Solitude) refers to Mary alone after the Crucifixion. Beatified 1950; canonized 1970. **Sources:** Ball, *Modern Saints: Book One*, 96–101; Martindale, *The Queen's Daughters*, 155–56; McNamara, Father Robert F., "St Mary Soledad," *Saints Alive*, read online at *www.stthomasirondequoit.com/SaintsAlive/id596.htm*. **Web sites:** Servants of Mary, Ministers to the Sick, Kansas City, KS: *http://www.sisterservantsofmary.com/*; Archdiocese of Madrid: *http://www.archimadrid.es/siervasdemaria/*.

Marie Poussepin. Beatified 1994. **Sources:** Dorcy, *Saint Dominic's Family*, 482–84; Johannès, Franck, "Marie Poussepin Blessed and Beatified ... from Dourdan to the Vatican," *Métro de Libération*, Oct. 19, 1994, p. M4, read online at *http:// catholique-evry.cef.fr/prier/saints/saints002.php*; Magli, Ida, *Women and Self-Sacrifice in the Christian Church: A Cultural History from the First to the Nineteenth Century*, trans. Janet Sethre, Jefferson, NC: McFarland, 2003, 245; Preteseille, Bernard, *Marie Poussepin, ou, L'exercice de la Charité*, Chambray-le-Tours: C.L.D., 1989. **Web sites:** Dominican Sisters of the Presentation of Mary, United States Province, Dighton, MA: *http://www.dominicansistersofthepresentation.org/*; Dominican Sisters of the Presentation of Mary, Bogotá, Colombia: *http://www.presentacionprovinciasantafe.com/*.

Marie-Rose Durocher. Beatified 1982. **Sources:** Fink, John F., *American Saints: Five Centuries of Heroic Sanctity on the American Continents*, Staten Island, NY: Alba House, 2001, 67–73; Lacroix, Marthe, S.N.J.M., "In His Image: Blessed Eulalie Durocher—Mother Marie-Rose (1811–1849), Foundress of the Sisters of the Holy Name of Jesus and Mary," *Canadian Catholic Review*, Feb. 1986, 24–27; O'Malley, *Saints of North America*, 383–86. **Web sites:** Sisters of the Holy

Names of Jesus and Mary, International Home Page: *http://www.snjm.org/*;
Saint-Antoine-sur-Richelieu, Quebec: *http://www.saint-antoine-sur-richelieu.ca/*.

Marie-Thérèse Soubiran. Beatified 1946. **Sources:** Martindale, *The Queen's Daughters*, 184–88; Trochu, *Jeanne Jugan*, 123. **Web site:** Sisters of Marie Auxiliatrice, International: *http://www.marieaux.org/*.

Mary Frances of the Five Wounds. Beatified 1843; canonized 1867. **Sources:** Caffiero, Marina, "From the Late Baroque Mystical Explosion to the Social Apostolate, 1650–1850," in *Women and Faith*, ed. Scaraffia and Zarri, 195–98; Dunbar, *Saintly Women*, 2:66–67; Thurston, *Physical Phenomena of Mysticism*, 55–56 (stigmata), 153 (Eucharistic miracles), 230 (odor of sanctity). **Web sites:** City of Naples has a "Santi" section for saints: *http://www.dentronapoli.it/*; Firpo Net links to her house, now a shrine: *http://www.firponet. com/Francesco/Servants/MFrancesca/casa_di_MF.htm*.

Mechthild of Magdeburg. Never formally canonized, but often listed as a saint (e.g., in Dunbar) and as a blessed in *The Book of Saints*, 4th ed. **Sources:** Howard, John, "The German Mystic: Mechthild of Magdeburg," in *Medieval Women Writers*, ed. Katharina M. Wilson, Athens: Univ. of Georgia Press, 1984, 153–85; Mechthild of Magdeburg, *The Flowing Light of the Godhead*, trans. with an Introduction by Frank Tobin, Mahwah, NJ: Paulist Press, 1997 (Classics of Western Spirituality Series); Petroff, Elizabeth A., ed., *Medieval Women's Visionary Literature*, New York: Oxford Univ. Press, 1986, 207–12; Ranft, Patricia, *Women and the Religious Life in Premodern Europe*, New York: St Martin's, 74–76. **Web site:** St Mary's monastery at Helfta, once known as the Crown of German Convents, is being restored to honor the mystics: *http://www.kloster-helfta.de/*.

Our Lady of the Rosary. Sources: Bicheno, Hugh, *Crescent and Cross: The Battle of Lepanto, 1571*, London: Orion Books, 2003; Lewis, D. B. Wyndham, "St. Pius V, Pope (1504–1572)," in *Saints for Now*, ed. Clare Boothe Luce, 230–45; Novak, Michael, *The Universal Hunger for Liberty: Why the Clash of Civilizations Is Not Inevitable*, New York: Basic Books, 2004, 193; Stevens, Clifford, *The One Year Book of Saints*, Huntington, IN: Our Sunday Visitor, 1989, 304; Sullivan, Most Rev. James S., Bishop of Fargo, "The Transforming Power of Fatima," *Christ to the World*, Nov. 1999, 169–73. **Web sites:** Eternal Word Television Network has many pages about the Rosary and how to pray it: *http://www.ewtn.com/*; World Apostolate of Fatima: *http://www.mostholyrosary.org/*; Confraternity of the Rosary, Portland, OR: *http://www.rosary-center.org/*; Confraternity of the Holy Rosary: *http://www.santorosario.net/*.

Pelagia the Penitent. Sources: Baring-Gould, *Lives of the Saints*, 10:169–80; Blunt, *Great Magdalens*, 17–20; Dunbar, *Saintly Women*, 2:140–43; James, Deacon of the Church of Heliopolis, "The Life of Our Holy Mother Pelagia the Nun, Who Was Once a Harlot," Chrysostom Press, read online at: *http://www.chrysostompress.org/collection/1008_pelagia*.

Restituta Kafka. Beatified 1998. **Sources:** Knight, Hans, "The Nun and the Nazis," *Catholic Digest*, Feb. 1992, 14–17; McNamara, Father Robert F., "Blessed Restituta Kafka," *Saints Alive*, read online at *http://www.stthomasirondequoit.com/SaintsAlive/id241.htm*; Royal, *Catholic Martyrs*, 135. **Web sites:** Franciscan Sisters of Christian Charity, Vienna, Austria: *http://restituta.net/*; Franciscan Sisters of Christian Charity, Argentina: *http://www.geocities.com/franciscanasviena/Entradas.htm*; Catholic Heritage Curricula has pages dedicated to Catholic Heroes of the Holocaust in its Free Curricula section: *http://www.catholichomeschooling.com/*; Simon Wiesenthal Center Museum of Tolerance Online Multimedia Learning Center has a page dedicated to Restituta: *http://motlc.learningcenter.wiesenthal.org/gallery/pg30/pg6/pg30679.html*.

Tabitha of Joppa. Sources: Dunbar, *Saintly Women*, 2:238; Acts of the Apostles 9:36–43.

Teresa of Avila. Beatified 1614; canonized 1622. **Sources:** *Collected Works of St. Teresa of Avila*, vols. 1 and 2, trans. Kieran Kavanaugh and Otilio Rodriguez, Washington, DC: Institute of Carmelite Studies, 1976 and 1980; Culligan, Kevin, O.C.D., "Teresa of Jesus: A Personality Profile," *Spiritual Life*, Fall 1983, 131–62; Dunbar, *Saintly Women*, 2:263–68; Felicia, Sister, O.S.A., *Seven Spanish Mystics*, Cambridge, MA: Society of St John the Evangelist, 1947; Walsh, William Thomas, *Saint Teresa of Avila: A Biography*, Milwaukee: Bruce Publishing, 1943. **Web sites:** Teresian Carmel, Austria: *http://www.karmel.at/eng/ocd.htm*; International Carmelite website: *http://www.ocarm.org/*; Discalced Carmelites, Australia: *http://www.carmelite.com/*; Corazones, a portal maintained by Las Siervas de los Corazones Traspasados de Jesús y María: *http://www.corazones.org/*.

Theodore Guérin. Beatified 1998; canonized 2006. **Sources:** Day, *Dictionary of Religious Orders*, 346–47; Fink, *American Saints*, 83–90; Guerin, Theodore, *Journals and Letters of Mother Theodore Guerin, Foundress of the Sisters of Providence of Saint Mary-of-the-Woods, Indiana*, ed. Sister Mary Theodosia Mug, St Mary-of-the-Woods, IN: Providence Press, 1937; Tucker, Ruth A., and Waler L. Liefeld, *Daughters of the Church: Women and Ministry from New Testament Times to the Present*, Grand Rapids, MI: Zondervan, 1987, 278; Mitchell, Penny Blaker, "Blessed Theodore Anne-Therese Guerin," *Biographies of the Blesseds 1998*, read online at *http://www.ewtn.com/library/MARY/bios98.htm#THEODORE*. **Web sites:** Sisters of Providence, St Mary-of-the-Woods, IN: *http://www.spsmw.org/*; Archdiocese of Indianapolis's *Criterion* has a page with links to many articles about Theodore Guérin: *http://www.archindy.org/criterion/local/causes/*.

Thérèse of Lisieux. Beatified 1923; canonized 1925. **Sources:** Lisieux, St Thérèse, *The Autobiography of St Thérèse of Lisieux: The Story of a Soul*, trans. with an Introduction by John Beevers, Garden City, NY: Image Books, 1957; Milord, James E., "Saint for a Violent Society," *Spiritual Life*, Sept. 1985, 131–39. **Web sites:** Society of the Little Flower, Chicago, IL: *http://www.littleflower.org/*; National Shrine of St Thérèse, Darien, IL: *http://www.saint-Thérèse.org/*; Canadian Shrine of St Thérèse, Niagra Falls, Ontario: *http://www.saint-Thérèse.org/shrine.nsf/*; Shrine at Lisieux, France: *http://Thérèse-de-lisieux.cef.fr/*.

Ursula and Companions. It will come as little surprise that although Ursula was one of the most beloved saints in Church history, she was removed from the Roman Calendar in 1969 because of a lack of historical evidence. She remains in the Roman Martyrology, however. **Sources:** Baring-Gould, *Lives of the Saints*, 13:535; Dunbar, *Saintly Women*, 1:258 (Ursula revelation), 2:278–80 (Ursula and Companions); Fleming, William Canon, *A Complete History of the British Martyrs from the Roman Occupation to Elizabeth's Reign*, New York: Benziger Bros., 1904, 16–17. **Web sites:** Sisters of the Irish Ursuline Union: *http://www.ursulines.ie/*; Ursuline Sisters of Youngstown, OH: *http://www.theursulines.org/*; Shrine of St Ursula, Cologne: *http://www.heilige-ursula.de/*.

Annotated Sources and Web Sites for November

Agnes of Assisi. Canonized 1753 . **Sources:** Armstrong and Brady, *Francis and Clare: The Complete Works*, 170-71, 203; Raiola, Chiara Mariana, O.S.C., "Saint Agnes of Assisi," read online at *www.poor-clares.org/eindhovn/script/agns-assi.html*. **Web site:** Poor Clares of Spokane, WA: *http://www.poorclare.org/*.

Agostina Pietrantoni. Beatified 1972; canonized 1999. **Sources:** Ball, *Modern Saints: Book One*, 126–31; *L'Osservatore Romano*. **Web sites:** Sisters of Charity of St Jeanne Antide Thouret: *http://www.suoredellacarita.org/*; Home page of Pozzaglia Sabina has much information: *http://www.sabina.it/comuni/pozzaglia.html*; Sisters of Charity of St Joan Antide (United States): *http://www.scsja.org/*.

Alice Kotowska. Beatified 1999, among the 108 Polish Martyrs. **Sources:** Material supplied by Sister Christine Marie, C.R.; Florczak, Sister Teresa Matea, C.R., *Like a Drop of Water in the Ocean: The Life and Martyrdom of Blessed Sister Alice Kotowska*, trans. from Polish by Sister Mary Hermina Widlarz, C.R., ed. Sister Alexandra Jazwinski, C.R., Poznan: Congregation of the Sisters of the Resurrection, 1999; McNamara, Bill, "New Bedford Nuns Eager to See Beatified Member of Their Order Canonized," *News-Standard* (New Bedford, MA), June 6, 1999, read online at *http://www.s-t.com/daily/06–99/06–14–99/c01li076.htm*; McNamara, Robert F., "St. Alice Kotowska, C.R.," *Saints Alive*, read online at *http://www.stthomasirondequoit.com/SaintsAlive/id289.htm*. **Web site:** Sisters of the Resurrection, Castleton, NY: *http://www.resurrectionsisters.org/*.

All Saints. In 731 Pope Gregory III consecrated a chapel in St Peter's Basilica in honor of all the saints and appointed the feast of All Saints to be observed henceforth on November 1. **Sources:** Baring-Gould, *Lives of the Saints*, 13:1–10; Butler, *Lives of the Fathers* (1845), 11:1–24; Marie des Douleurs, Mother, "All Saints," *Magnificat*, Nov. 2004, 41–43; Thomas Aquinas, "The Communion of Saints," *Magnificat*, Nov. 1999, 35–36. **Web sites:** Theology Library at Spring Hill College (third oldest Jesuit college in the United States), Mobile, AL, has extensive information about saints: *http://www.shc.edu/theolibrary/saints.htm*; Congregation for the Causes of Saints, official Vatican site: *http://www.vatican.va/roman_curia/congregations/csaints/index.htm*.

Alpaïs of Cudot. Beatified 1874. **Sources:** Buber, Martin, *Ecstatic Confessions: Collected and Introduced by Martin Buber*, ed. Paul Mendes-Flohr, trans. Esther Cameron, New York: Harper & Row, 1985, 45–47; Bynum, *Holy Feast and Holy Fast*, throughout; Dunbar, *Saintly Women*, 1:48. **Web site:** Local parishes sponsor an annual pilgrimage: *http://paroisses89.cef.fr/aillant/article.php3?id_article=119*.

Bertilla of Chelles. Sources: Baring-Gould, *Lives of the Saints*, 13:156–57; Butler, *Lives of the Fathers* (1845),Vol.11, 125–28; Dunbar, *Saintly Women*, 1:121; Power, Eileen Edna, *Medieval English Nunneries, c. 1275 to 1535*, Cambridge: Cambridge Univ. Press, 1922, 95–97; Schulenburg, *Forgetful of Their Sex*, 97–98, 394–95. **Web site:** Abbey of Notre Dame de Jouarre: *http://perso.wanadoo.fr/abbayejouarre/*.

Catherine of Alexandria. Sources: Baring-Gould, *Lives of the Saints*, 14:540–42; Dunbar, *Saintly Women*, 1:149–50; Giorgi, Rosa, *Saints in Art*, trans. Thomas Michael Hartmann, Los Angeles: Getty Museum, 2003, 76–79; Voragine, *The Golden Legend*, vol. 7, read online at *http://www.fordham.edu/halsall/basis/gold-enlegend/GoldenLegend-Volume7.htm#Katherine*. **Web site:** Kappa Gamma Pi, the national Catholic college graduate honor society, gives an annual Catherine Award in honor of its patron: *http://www.kappagammapi.org/*.

Catherine Labouré. Beatified 1933; canonized 1947. **Sources:** Ball, *Modern Saints: Book Two*, 132–43; Dirvin, Father Joseph I., C.M., *Saint Catherine Laboure of the Miraculous Medal*, Rockford, IL: Tan Books, 1984 (orig. pub. 1958 by Farrar, Straus & Cudahy). **Web sites:** Daughters of St Vincent de Paul: *http://www.filles-de-la-charite.org/en/catherine_Labouré.html*; Central Association of the Miraculous Medal, Philadelphia, PA: *http://www.cammonline.org/*; Association of the Miraculous Medal, Perryville, MO, Congregation of the Mission, Midwest Province (Vincentians): *http://www.amm.org/*; Chapel of the Apparitions, Paris, France: *http://www.chapellenotredamedelamedaillemiraculeuse.com/EN/a.asp*.

Cecilia of Rome. Sources: Baring-Gould, *Lives of the Saints*, 14:503–5; Cruz, *Incorruptibles*, 43–46; Dunbar, *Saintly Women*, 1:167–68. **Web sites:** Irina Popov, a musician, has created a virtual shrine: *http://www.geocities.com/Paris/Parc/4974/pipe_organ/*; Dominican Sisters of St Cecilia, Nashville, TN: *http://nashvilledominican.org/Main.htm.*

Delphine de Signe. Beatified 1694. **Sources:** Dunbar, *Saintly Women*, 1:200, 222–27; D'Oppéde, De Forbin, *La Bienheureuse Delphine de Sabran et les Saints de Provence au XIV Siècle*, Paris: Librairie Plon, 1883. **Web site:** Diocese of Avignon (click on Le Diocése): *http://catholique-avignon.cef.fr/.*

Elizabeth. A tradition of the second and third centuries identifies her husband, Zechariah, as the same priest whose martyrdom in the temple is mentioned by Christ (Matt. 23:35). **Sources:** Luke 1:5–25, 39–80; Baring-Gould, *Lives of the Saints*, 13:147–49; Dunbar, *Saintly Women*, Vol. 1,256–57; Ketter, Peter, *Christ and Womankind*, trans. and ed. Isabel McHugh, Westminster, MD: Newman Press, 1952. **Web site:** Mary page, University of Dayton, OH, has much information about the Visitation: *http://www.udayton.edu/mary/marypage21.html.*

Elizabeth the Good. Beatified 1766. **Sources:** Dunbar, *Saintly Women*, 1:266; Forster, Marc R., *Catholic Revival in the Age of the Baroque: Religious Identity in Southwest Germany, 1550–1750*, Cambridge: Cambridge Univ. Press, 2001, 89–90; Habig, *Franciscan Book of Saints*, 826–28; Hallack and Anson, *These Made Peace*, 122–25; Thurston, *Physical Phenomena of Mysticism*, 148–49, 341. **Web site:** Franciscan convent, Reute (click on Wir über uns, scroll to Die Gute Beth): *http://www.kloster-reute.de./.*

Elizabeth of Hungary. Canonized 1235. **Sources:** Baring-Gould, *Lives of the Saints*, 14:415–57; Dunbar, *Saintly Women*, 1:259–64; Elliott, Dyan, *Proving Woman: Female Spirituality and Inquisitional Culture in the Later Middle Ages*, Princeton: Princeton Univ. Press, 85–116; Mechthild of Magdeburg, *Flowing Light of the Godhead*, 215–16. **Web site:** Elisabeth church, Marburg, Germany, includes a virtual tour: *http://www.elisabethkirche.de/.*

Elizabeth of the Trinity. Beatified 1984. **Sources:** Catez, Elizabeth, "Prayer to the Trinity," *Spiritual Life: A Quarterly of Contemporary Spirituality*, published by the Washington Province of Discalced Carmelites, Winter 1984; Dorgan, Margaret, D.C.M., "The Message of Blessed Elizabeth of the Trinity," *Spiritual Life*, Summer 1985, 67–70; Goldman, Rita E., "Inner Vocation," *Spiritual Life*, Summer 1982, 87–91; Holböck, *New Saints, Volume 2*, 36–40; Humphreys, Carolyn, O.C.D.S., *Elizabeth of the Trinity*, San Francisco: Ignatius Press, 2003; LaCugna, Catherine M., "Elizabeth of the Trinity," *Spiritual Life*, Spring 1985, 3–6. **Web sites:** Carmel, Dijon, France: *http://www.carmel.asso.fr/*; Carmelite Monastery of New Orleans, Covington, LA: *http://ettinger.net/carmelcov/*; Discalced Carmelites of St Louis, MO: *http://www.ourgardenofcarmel.org/*; Devotional site: *http://ettinger.net/carmelcov/elizabeth.html*; Discalced Carmelite Order Home Page: *http://www.ocd.pcn.net/.*

Flora and Mary. Sources: Colbert, *Martyrs of Cordoba*, 224–35; Coope, Jessica A., *The Martyrs of Cordoba: Community and Family Conflict in an Age of Mass Conversion*, Lincoln: Univ. of Nebraska Press, 1995, 24–78; Dunbar, *Saintly Women*, 1:319 (Flora), 2:53 (Mary); Florian, Jean Pierre Claris de, *The Moors in Spain*, n.p.: Werner Co., 1910; Lane-Poole, Stanley, *The Moors in Spain*, New York: Putnam, 1886, 78–95; Wolf, Kenneth, *Christian Martyrs in Muslim Spain*, chaps. 2 and 4.

Frances Xavier Cabrini. Beatified 1938; canonized 1946. Her motto is printed as it appears in *To the Ends of the Earth*; the wording differs slightly from the New American Bible. **Sources:** Benedictine of Stanbrook Abbey, *Frances Xavier Cabrini: The Saint of the Emigrants*, London: Burns Oates & Washbourne, 1944;

Cabrini, Frances X., *To the Ends of the Earth: The Missionary Travels of Frances X. Cabrini*, trans. Philippa Provenzano, M.S.C., New York: Center for Migration Studies, 2001; Jones, *Women Saints*, 231, 259–67; Keyes, Frances Parkinson, *Mother Cabrini: Missionary to the World*, New York: Farrar, Straus & Cudahy, 1959; Maynard, Theodore, *Too Small a World: The Life of Mother Cabrini*, Milwaukee: Bruce Publishing, 1945; Sullivan, Mary Louise, M.S.C., *Mother Cabrini: "Italian Immigrant of the Century,"* New York: Center for Migration Studies, 1992. **Web sites:** Missionary Sisters of the Sacred Heart of Jesus: *http://www.mothercabrini.com/*; St Francis Cabrini Shrine, New York, NY: *http://www.cabrinishrineny.org/*; Mother Cabrini Shrine, Golden, CO: *http://www.den-cabrini-shrine.org/*; Cabrini Mission Corps, Radnor, PA (a lay mission): *http://www.cabrini-missioncorps.org/*; Cabrini Mission Foundation, New York, NY: *http://www.cabrinifoundation.org/*; Casa Natale (her birthplace): *http://www.casanatalecabrini.com/*.

Gaetana Sterni. Beatified 2001. **Sources:** *L'Osservatore Romano; Magnificat,* Nov. 2003, 355. **Web site:** Sisters of the Divine Will: *www.suoredivinavolonta.it/*.

Gertrude the Great. Canonized 1677. **Sources:** Gertrude of Helfta, *The Herald of Divine Love,* trans. and ed. Margaret Winkworth, New York: Paulist Press, 1993 (Classics of Western Spirituality Series); Gertrude the Great, St, *The Herald of Divine Love,* Rockford, IL: Tan Books, 1983 (orig. pub. by the Benedictine Convent of Perpetual Adoration, Clyde, MO). **Web site:** The historic monastery at Helfta is being restored: *http://www.kloster-helfta.de/*.

Hilda of Whitby. Sources: Dunbar, *Saintly Women,* 1:381–83; Jones, *Women Saints,* 194, 196–200; Madeleva, Sister M., "St. Hilda of Whitby (617–680)," in *Saints for Now,* ed. Clare Boothe Luce, 113–27; Parbury, Kathleen, *Women of Grace: A Biographical Dictionary of British Women Saints, Martyrs and Reformers,* Boston: Oriel Press, 1985, 186–88; **Web sites:** Order of the Holy Paraclete, a community of Anglican women founded in 1915, has much information: *http://www.ohp-whitby.org/*; Town of Whitby has pages dedicated to Hilda and the Abbey: *http://www.whitby-uk.com/*.

Ilona of Hungary. Never formally recognized, but according to Dorcy she "has long been called 'blessed' in popular terminology. She enjoys a local cult, and her cause is one which may be advanced in the next few years." Watkins lists her as Blessed; Farges calls her Saint. **Sources:** Dorcy, *Saint Dominic's Family,* 72–74; Drane, *Spirit of the Dominican Order,* 180; Dunbar, *Saintly Women,* 1:374–75; Farges, Msgr. Albert, *Mystical Phenomena Compared with Their Human and Diabolical Counterparts,* trans. from French by S. P. Jacques, London: Burns Oates & Washbourne, 1926, 556; Catherine, Sister Mary, O.P., *Margaret, Princess of Hungary,* 24–29, 35, 63; Summers, Montague, *Physical Phenomena of Mysticism,* London: Ryder & Co., 1950, 157–58, 177.

Jane of Signa. Beatified 1798. **Sources:** Benelli, Moreno, and Remo Vannini, *Vita e Miracoli della Beata Giovanna da Signa: Memorie di una Comunità,* Signa: Masso delle Fete, 1995; Cohn, Sam K., *The Black Death Transformed: Disease and Culture in Early Renaissance Europe,* New York: Oxford Univ. Press, 2002, 75–76; Dunbar, *Saintly Women,* 1:423–24; Goodich, Michael E., *Violence and Miracle in the Fourteenth Century: Private Grief and Public Salvation,* Chicago: Univ. of Chicago Press, 1995, 106, 122; Habig, *Franciscan Book of Saints,* 819–20; Hallack and Anson, *These Made Peace,* 34–37. **Web site:** Commune of Signa (click on Storia): *http://www.comune.signa.fi.it/*.

Josaphata Michaelina Hordashevska. Beatified 2001, in Lviv, with Mykolai Charnetsky and Companions. **Sources:** Material provided by Sister Frances Byblow, S.S.M.I.; Slawuta, Sister Dominica G., S.S.M.I., *Prayer and Service: A Biography of the Servant of God Josaphata Hordashevska,* Toronto: S.S.M.I., 1996;

Slawuta, Sister Dominica G., and Sister Victoria Hunchak, S.S.M.I., eds., *Glory to You, O Lord: Sisters Servants of Mary Immaculate, the First Hundred Years*, Rome: S.S.M.I., 1992. **Web site:** Sister Servants of Mary Immaculate, Toronto, Canada: *http://www.ssmi.org/*.

Lucy of Narni. Listed in the Roman Martyrology on November 15; venerated at Narni on November 16 and by the Dominican Order on November 14. Beatified 1710. (Some sources give 1720, but this is incorrect.) **Sources:** Cruz, *Incorruptibles*, 166–67; Dorcy, *Saint Dominic's Family*, 267–70; Dunbar, *Saintly Women*, 1:473; Fullerton, *Life of St. Frances of Rome*, 139–58; Lehmijoki-Gardner, *Dominican Penitent Women*, throughout; Matter, E. Ann, "Prophetic Patronage as Repression: Lucia Brocadelli da Narni and Ercole d'Este," in *Christendom and Its Discontents*, ed. Scott L.Waugh and Peter D. Diehl, New York: Cambridge Univ. Press, 1996, 168–76. **Web site:** City of Narni's Home Page, Notizie Utile section (click on Cultura, then Santi e Beati): *http://www.comune.narni.tr.it/*.

Lucy of Settefonti. Beatified 1779. **Sources:** Dunbar, *Saintly Women*, 1:471–72; Monson, Craig A., *Disembodied Voices: Music and Culture in an Early Modern Italian Convent*, Berkeley: Univ. of California Press, 1995, 25–26; Vigilucci, *Camaldoli*, 111–14. **Web sites:** Camaldolese Oblates, Berkeley, CA, offer information about Order history and the Rule: *http://www.camaldolese.com/*; Parco dei Gessi Bolognese e'Calanchi dell'Abadessa: *http://www.parks.it/parco.gessi. bolognesi/Eindex.html*.

Margaret of Scotland. Officially recognized in 1250, although venerated as a saint from the time of her death. **Sources:** Baring-Gould, *Lives of the Saints*, 6:136–38; Bartlett, Robert, ed., *The Miracles of St Aebba of Coldingham and St Margaret of Scotland*, New York: Oxford Univ. Press, 2003; Brooke, Christopher, *The Saxon and Norman Kings*, Oxford: Blackwell, 2001, 69–71; Dunbar, *Saintly Women*, 2:13–17. **Web sites:** Queen Margaret of Scotland Girls' Schools Association has much information about its patron saint: *http://www.qmssa.org/*; St Margaret's Parish, Dunfermline: *http://www.armour.telinco.co.uk/*; Dunfermline Abbey (Church of Scotland): *http://www.dunfermlineabbey.co.uk/*; Margaret Queen of Scotland Guild: *http://www.stmargaretschapelguild.com/*.

Maria Corsini. Beatified 2001 (with Luigi Beltrame Quattrocchi). **Sources:** Knowles, *Modern Heroes of the Church*, 173–76; *L'Osservatore Romano*. **Web sites:** International Catholic Action: *http://www.azionecattolica.it/*; Luigi and Maria Beltrame Quattrocchi Foundation: *http://www.fondazionebq.it/*.

Maria Fortunata Viti. Beatified 1967. **Sources:** Material provided by Suzanne McKenzie, Mount Angel Library, St Benedict, OR, and by Monastero Benedettine, Veroli, Italy; Locher, Gabriel, O.S.B., *A Brief Biography of Sister Mary Fortunata Viti of Santa Maria dei Franconi, Veroli, Italy; Lay Sister in the Benedictine Convent, 1827–1922; A Hidden Life of Sanctity Brought from Obscurity to Light*, trans. from German by Stephen Radtke, O.S.B., Clyde, MO: Benedictine Convent of Perpetual Adoration, 1940; Sarra, Andrea, *The Blessed Mary Fortunata Viti: Oh, the Power and the Love of God!*, trans. and adapted from the original Italian, St Benedict, OR: Benedictine Press, 1972; Sarra, Andrea, *Felicetta: Una Vita Contemplando la Potenza e Carità di Dio*, Veroli: Benedettine, 2004.

Mary of the Passion. Beatified 2002. **Sources:** Cullen, Thomas F., *The Very Reverend Mother Mary of the Passion and Her Institute*, Providence, RI: Franciscan Missionaries of Mary, 1929; *Magnificat*, Nov. 2003, 195; Maleissye, Marie-Therese de, *A Short Life of Mary of the Passion (Helen de Chappotin): Foundress of the Franciscan Missionaries of Mary*, Bandra, Mumbai: St Pauls, 2002 (source for quote); Motte, Mary, F.M.M., "Helene de Chappotin de Neuville (Marie de la Passion)," in *Biographical Dictionary of Christian Missions*, ed. Gerald H. Anderson, Grand Rapids, MI: Eerdmans, 1998, 127–27; Salotti, Rev. Charles, D.D., *Sister Mary Assunta: The Seraphic Flower of the Franciscan Missionaries of Mary*, trans. Rev. Thomas F. Cullen, Whitefish, MT: Kessinger, 2003 (orig. pub. 1931 by the Franciscan Missionaries of Mary, North Providence, RI). **Web sites:** Franciscan Missionaries of Mary in the World: *http://www.fmmusa.org/*; Franciscan Missionaries of Mary, United States: *http://www.fmmusa.org/*; Franciscan Missionaries of Mary, United Kingdom: *http://www.fmmuk.org/index.htm*.

Maxellendis. Canonized 673. **Sources:** Dunbar, *Saintly Women*, 2:80; Le Jan, Regine, and Laurent Morelle, "Merovingian Women as Mirror of Carolingian Hagiography: Engagement, Death and Sanctity in the Holy Life of Maxellendis," Paris: Univ. of Paris, Pantheon-Sorbonne, Laboratoire de Medievistique Occidentale de Paris, 17–19, read online at *http://lamop.univ-paris1.fr/W3/morelle. pdf*; Spijker, Ineke van 't, "Family Ties: Mothers and Virgins in the Ninth Century," in *Sanctity and Motherhood: Essays on Holy Mothers in the Middle Ages*, ed. Anneke B. Mulder-Bakker, New York: Garland Science (Garland Medieval Casebooks Vol. 14), 165–90. **Web sites:** Diocese of Cambrai has a week-long celebration honoring her as the patron of Caudry: *http://www.cathocambrai.com/*; Basilica of Caudry, dedicated to Maxellendis: *http://www.mairie-caudry.fr/*.

Rose Philippine Duchesne. Beatified 1940; canonized 1988. **Sources:** Material provided by Sister Frances Gimber, R.S.C.J., Archivist, U.S. Province, who confirmed that feast day is November 18; Callan, Louise, *Philippine Duchesne: A Frontier Missionary of the Sacred Heart*, Westminster, MD: Newman Press, 1957; Emery, S. L., "Mother Duchesne, R.S.H., an Uncanonized American Saint," *Catholic World*, vol. 65, no. 389, 687–88; Callan, *American Saints*, 75–81; Kilroy, Phil, *Madeleine Sophie Barat: A Life*, Mahwah, NJ: Paulist Press, 2000, 40–42, 127–29. **Web sites:** Shrine in St Charles, MO: *http://www.ash1818.org/shrine. htm*; Shrine in Mound City, KS: *http://www.catholicshrines.net/states/ks1.htm*; Society of the Sacred Heart International home page: *http://www.rscjinternational.org/*; Religious of the Sacred Heart, U.S. Province: *http://www.rscj.org/*; Potawatomi Nation's Shrine of Our Lady of Snows, Mayeta, KS: *http://www. pbpindiantribe.com/snow/*.

Annotated Sources and Web Sites for December

Adelaide, Empress. Canonized 1097. **Sources:** Baronc, Giulia, "Society and Women's Religiosity, 750–1450," in *Women and Faith*, ed. Scaraffia and Zarri, 48–49, 50; Dunbar, *Saintly Women*, 1:5–9; Holböck, *Married Saints and Blesseds*, 126–30. **Web site:** City of Seltz in Alsace, France, has information about abbeys founded by Adelaide: *http://ville-seltz.fr/*.

Agnes Phila and the Martyrs of Thailand. Beatified 1989. **Sources:** Clark, *Asian Saints*, 66–68; Coday, Dennis, "Shrine Honors Mekong Martyrs," *National Catholic Reporter*, April 16, 2004; Ball, *Young Faces of Holiness*, 201–6. **Web site:** Pelikan Performance, a theater company, has created a multimedia performance piece about Agnes and Lucy: *http://www.pelikanperformance.com/*.

Anastasia of Sirmium. Sources: Baring-Gould, *Lives of the Saints*, 12:278–79; Dunbar, *Saintly Women*, 1:53–54.

Anuarite Nengapeta. Beatified 1985. **Sources:** Ball, *Faces of Holiness*, 169–74; Jones, *Women Saints*, 42, 65–68. **Web sites:** *Afriquespoir*, a Catholic magazine, has several articles about Anuarite and other contemporary African martyrs, use the search function: *http://www.afriquespoir.com/*; National Black Sisters' Conference, Washington, DC: *http://nbsc68.tripod.com/*.

Barbara of Nicomedia. Source: Dunbar, *Saintly Women*, 1:99–100. **Web sites:** St Barbara's Church in Woburn, MA: *http://www.rc.net/boston/st_barbara/ homepg.htm*; St Barbara's Greek Orthodox Church, New Haven, CT: *http:// www.saintbarbara.org/*.

Bibiana. Sources: Baring-Gould, *Lives of the Saints*, 15:10–11; Dunbar, *Saintly Women*, 1:122 (Bibiana), 217 (Dafrosa), 227 (Demetria). **Web site:** St Vivian's Church, Cincinnati, OH, has photographs of her shrine in Rome: *http://www .stvivian.org/patron.html*.

Christina of Markyate. Her marriage was finally annulled by the archbishop Thurstan of York in about 1122. **Sources:** Amt, Emilie, ed., *Women's Lives in Medieval Europe: A Sourcebook*, New York: Routledge, 1993; Talbot, C. H., ed. and trans., *The Life of Christina of Markyate: A Twelfth Century Recluse*, Oxford: Clarendon Press, 1959. **Web site:** University of Aberdeen, Scotland, has posted the complete Psalter created for her by Geoffrey of Gorham: *http://www.abdn .ac.uk/stalbanspsalter/english/essays/introduction.shtml*.

Crispina of Thagura. Sources: Baring-Gould, *Lives of the Saints*, 12:50–52; Dunbar, *Saintly Women*, 1:242; O'Malley, *Saints of Africa*, 166–67.

Elena Guerra. Beatified 1959. **Sources:** Bell and Mazzoni, *Voices of Gemma Galgani*, 11, 176; Mansfield, Patti, "Perpetual Pentecost: Did a Nineteenth Century Italian Nun Foresee the Charismatic Renewal?" *New Convenant*, May 1989, 9; Synan, Vinson, *The Holiness-Pentecostal Tradition: Charismatic Movements in the Twentieth Century*, Grand Rapids, MI: Eerdmans, 1997, 237–38. **Web sites:** Devotional site created by Gianmarco De Vincentis: *http://www.radicchio.it/beataelenaguerra/congregazione.htm*; Oblate Sisters of the Holy Spirit: *http://web.tiscali. it/oss/*; International Catholic Charismatic Renewal: *http://www.iccrs.org/*.

Eulalia of Mérida. Canonized 1644. **Sources:** Baring-Gould, *Lives of the Saints*, 15:124–25; Butler, *Lives of the Fathers* (1845), 12:174–79. **Web sites:** City of Mérida: *http://www.merida.es/semanasanta05.asp*; Totana, Murcia, Spain, site dedicated to 2004 jubilee celebrations has information about her shrine: *http:// www.totana.es/jubilar/*; Totana's web portal also has pages about Eulalia: *http:// www.totana.net/*.

Fabiola of Rome. Sources: Dietz, Maribel, *Wandering Monks, Virgins and Pilgrims: Ascetic Travel in the Mediterranean World, 300–800*, University Park: Penn State Univ. Press, 2005, 1, 130; Dunbar, *Saintly Women*, 1:304–5.

Frances Schervier. Beatified 1974. **Sources:** Fietzek, Petra, *The Life of Frances Schervier: Words Are Not Enough*, trans. from German by Eileen A. Opiolka, Brooklyn, NY: Franciscan Sisters of the Poor, 2002; Kempf, *Holiness of the Church*, 243–44. **Web sites:** American Province of the Franciscan Sisters of the Poor has been independent since 1959; the motherhouse is in Brooklyn, NY: *http://www.franciscansisters.org/*; Sisters of the Poor of St Francis, Aachen, Germany: *http://www.schervier-orden.de*.

Holy Family of Nazareth. Sources: Burke, Cormac, "The Family: The School of Love," *Magnificat*, Dec. 1998, 378–79, reprinted from *Our Sunday Visitor's Encyclopedia of Catholic Doctrine*; John Paul II, "The Holy Family," *Magnificat*, Dec. 2003, 134–35, reprinted from *L'Osservatore Romano*. **Web sites:** Holy Family Cathedral, Kuwait: *http://www.catholic-church.org/kuwait/*; Ukranian Catholic National Shrine of the Holy Family, Washington, DC: *http://www.ucns-holyfamily.org/*.

Holy Innocents. Sources: Giorgi, *Saints in Art*, 167–68; Voragine, Jacobus de, *The Golden Legend: Readings on the Saints*, vol. 1, trans. William Granger Ryan, Princeton: Princeton Univ. Press, 1993, 56–59; Zuffi, Stefano, *Gospel Figures in Art*, Translated by Thomas Michael Hartman, Los Angeles: The J. Paul Getty

Museum, 114–15. **Web sites:** Church of the Holy Innocents, New York, NY: *http://www.innocents.com/*; Rachel's Vineyard is an organization providing support for women, men, and couples who have experienced abortion: *http://www .rachelsvineyard.org/*; Sisters of Life is a religious order dedicated to protecting the sacredness of human life: *http://sistersoflife.org/*.

Immaculate Conception. Declared dogma by Pope IX in 1854 and Patroness of the United States in 1857. **Sources:** Amorth, Father Gabriele, "Immaculate Instrument," *Magnificat*, Dec. 2001, 130–31; Baring-Gould, *Lives of the Saints*, 15:108–9; Cameron, Peter John, O.P., *Magnificat*, Dec. 2003, 2–5; Cunneen, Sally, *In Search of Mary: The Woman and the Symbol*, New York: Ballantine Books, 1996; Dunbar, *Saintly Women*, 2:43. **Web site:** Basilica of the National Shrine, Washington, DC: *http://www.nationalshrine.com/*.

Liduina Meneguzzi. Beatified 2002. **Source:** *L'Osservatore Romano*.

Lucy of Syracuse. Sources: Baring-Gould, *Lives of the Saints*, 12:168–70; Dunbar, *Saintly Women*, 1:469–70; Giorgi, *Saints in Art*, 230–33. **Web sites:** Church of St Lucy, Newark, NJ: *http://www.saintlucy.net/saintlucy.htm*; Devotional: *http:// www.carasantalucia.it/*; Shrine of St Lucy: *http://www.basilicasantalucia.it/*.

María Angela Astorch. Beatified 1982. **Sources:** Dunbar, *Saintly Women*, 1:60; Haliczer, *Between Exaltation and Infamy*, throughout. **Web site:** Devotional site: *http://usuarios.lycos.es/fegarma/sor_angela1.htm*.

Maria Crocifissa di Rosa. Beatified 1940; canonized 1954. **Sources:** Agasso, Domenico, "Santa Maria Crocifissa (Paola) di Rosa," read online at *www.Santi-Beati.it*; McNamara, Rev. Robert, "St Mary di Rosa," read online at *www.stthomasirondequoit.com*; *Magnificat*, Dec. 2004, 202. **Web site:** Sisters of Charity of Santa Maria Crocifissa di Rosa: *http://www.ancelle.org/*.

Maria Josepha Rossello. Beatified 1938; canonized 1949. **Sources:** Ball, *Modern Saints: Book Two*, 175–81; Menezes, Wade, C.P.M., "An Answer to a Crisis of Faith: Adoring the Lord in the Year of the Eucharist," *Lay Witness*, March/April 2005, 4, read online at *http://www.cuf.org/Laywitness/Articles/Archive/MA05/ MA05Menezes.pdf#search='Mary%20Joseph%20Rossello*. **Web sites:** Unofficial home page for the order: *http://digilander.libero.it/cubiculum/itmgr_frm.htm*; Official home page: *http://www.fdmnet.org/*; Basilica of Our Lady of Mercy, Savona: *http://www.santuariosavona.it/*.

María Maravillas de Jesús. Beatified 1998; canonized 2003. **Sources:** *L'Osservatore Romano*; Anonymous, "Sr. Maravillas of Jesus, OCD, 1891–1974," *Carmel Clarion*, read online at *http://www.helpfellowship.org/OCDS%20Lessons/Lesson%2021. htm*; Antoine Marie, Dom, O.S.B., "Blessed Mother Maravillas of Jesus," *Saint Joseph Abbey Letter*, read online at *http://www.clairval.com/lettres/lettre_ 1.php?id=2181000*. **Web sites:** Diocese of Getafe, Spain (click on Santas and on Santuarios): *http://www.diocesisgetafe.es/*; Marian Information Center, Las Vegas, NV: *http://www.lasvegasmariancenter.com/madre.htm*; Discalced Carmelite Nuns of Arlington, TX, have a page dedicated to the St Teresa Association: *http:// www.carmelnuns.com/*.

Mary of the Angels. Beatified 1865. **Sources:** Dunbar, *Saintly Women*, 2:63–64; Thurston, *Surprising Mystics*, 231. **Web site:** Carmelite Sisters of St Therese of the Infant Jesus, Oklahoma City, OK: *http://www.oksister.com/*.

Matilde Téllez Robles. Beatified 2004. **Source:** *Catholic Online*, "Matilde Téllez Robles: A Unifier of Prayer and Action," unsigned interview with Father Sáez de Albéniz, her postulator, March 16, 2004, read online at *http://www.catholic. org/featured/headline.php?ID=785*. **Web sites:** Daughters of Maria Mother of the Church maintain a site dedicated to Madre Matilde: *http://www.madrematilde.*

com/; Home page of the Daughters of Maria Mother of the Church: *http://www3. planalfa.es/madrematilde/DEFAULT.htm.*

Mattia dei Nazarei. Beatified 1765. **Sources:** Cruz, *Incorruptibles,* 109–10; Dunbar, *Saintly Women,* 2:78. **Web sites:** "Photo album" of her convent and artifacts: *http://www.firponet.com/Francesco/Servants/BeataMattia/Album_di_Mattia.htm;* Illustrated biography: *http://www.firponet.com/Francesco/Servants/MFrancesca/ Fran_serv_MFlife.htm;* Franciscan Marian Association (click on the mouse, then on Servants of God): *http://www.firponet.com/francesco/Fran_home.htm;* City of Matelica has a photograph of the exterior of the church where she is venerated (click on Tourism): *http://www.comune.matelica.mc.it/asp/home.asp.*

Nativity, Saints at the. Sources: Tjader Harris, *Birgitta of Sweden,* 9, 159–60, 202– 6; Trexler, Richard C., *Journey of the Magi: Meanings in History of a Christian Story,* Princeton: Princeton Univ. Press, 1997, 100–101; Zuffi, *Gospel Figures,* 75.

Nino of Georgia. Sources: Baring-Gould, *Lives of the Saints,* 15:189–91; Dunbar, *Saintly Women,* 1:174, 2:107–8. **Web sites:** Sisters of St Chretienne (the Christian) take their name from Nino and consider her their patron saint. Their U.S. Province is in Wrentham, MA: *http://www.sistersofstchretienne.org/;* Georgia Tourist Information has photos of her landmarks: *http://www.visitgeorgia.ge/ index.htm;* Parliament of Georgia includes a photograph of her icon: *http://www .parliament.ge/GENERAL/mtskheta/mtskheta.html.*

Odilia of Alsace. Canonized 1807. **Sources:** Baring-Gould, *Lives of the Saints,* 15:174–75; Dunbar, *Saintly Women,* 2:114–16. **Web site:** Shrine at Mount Sainte-Odile: *http://www.mont-sainte-odile.com/.*

Olympias of Constantinople. Sources: Baring-Gould, *Lives of the Saints,* 12:206–7; Dunbar, *Saintly Women,* 1:121–22. **Web site:** Eulogos, a Catholic site based in Rome, has the text of all twelve letters of John Chrysostom to Olympias: *http:// www.eulogos.net/.*

Our Lady of Guadalupe. Sources: Elizondo, Virgilio P., "Our Lady of Guadalupe: A Guide for the New Millennium," *St. Anthony Messenger,* Dec. 1999, read online at *http://www.americancatholic.org/Messenger/Dec1999/feature2.asp;* Spretnak, Charlene, *Missing Mary: The Queen of Heaven and Her Re-emergence in the Modern Church,* New York: Palgrave Macmillan, 2004, 189–91; Wintz, Jack, O.F.M., "The Story of Our Lady of Guadalupe," *St. Anthony Messenger,* Dec. 1999 (excerpted from "Why Everyone Comes to Guadalupe," Dec. 1984), read online at *http:// www.americancatholic.org/Messenger/Dec1999/feature2.asp.* **Web sites:** Basilica of Santa María de Guadalupe, Mexico: *http://www.virgendeguadalupe.org.mx/;* Our Lady of Guadalupe, Patroness of the Americas, devotional site: *http://www.sancta. org/;* University of Dayton Mary page: *http://www.udayton.edu/mary/meditations/ guadalupe.html.*

Paola Elisabetta Cerioli. Beatified 1950; canonized 2004. **Source:** *L'Osservatore Romano.* **Web site:** Institute of the Holy Family official site: *http://www.istituto-sacrafamigliabg.it/index1.html#.*

Virginia Centurione Bracelli. Beatified 1985; canonized 2003. **Source:** Magaglio, Riccardo, *Una Patrizia Genovese Antesignana della Moderna Assistenza Sociale,* Genoa: A.G.I.S., 1972. **Web sites:** Congregation of Daughters of Our Lady of Mount Calvary in Rome: *http://web.tiscali.it/fnsmc/virginia.html;* Sisters of Our Lady of Refuge at Mount Calvary, in Genoa: *http://www.arcidiocesi.trento.it/vita-consacrata/religiose/vc_irf_brignoline.htm.*

BIBLIOGRAPHY

Titles that were used for only one particular saint are mentioned in Annotated Sources and Web Sites.

Butler's Lives of the Saints

Butler, Alban. *The Lives of the Fathers, Martyrs and Other Principal Saints: Compiled from Original Monuments and Authentic Records*. 12 vols. Dublin: James Duffy, 1845.

Butler, Alban. *Butler's Lives of the Saints: New Full Edition*. 12 vols. Revised by Sarah Fawcett Thomas, Kathleen Jones et al. Collegeville, MN: Liturgical Press, 1995–2000.

Walsh, Michael, ed. *Butler's Lives of the Saints: New Concise Edition*. Burnes & Oates, 1991. A single volume, it omits all Blesseds.

General

Adels, Jill Haak. *The Wisdom of the Saints: An Anthology*. New York: Oxford Univ. Press, 1987.

Attwater, Donald. *Martyrs: From St. Stephen to John Tung*. New York: Sheed & Ward, 1957.

The Book of Saints: A Dictionary of Servants of God Canonized by the Catholic Church Extracted from the Roman and Other Martyrologies. 4th ed. Compiled by the Benedictine Monks of St Augustine's Abbey, Ramsgate. New York: Macmillan, 1947.

The Book of Saints: A Dictionary of the Servants of God. 6th ed., rev. Compiled by the Benedictine Monks of St Augustine's Abbey, Ramsgate. Wilton, CT: Morehouse, 1989.

Bibliotheca Sanctorum. Rome: Istituto Giovanni XXIII della Pontificia Università Lateranense, 1964.

Ball, Ann. *Modern Saints: Their Lives and Faces, Book One*. Rockford, IL: Tan Books, 1983.

————. *Modern Saints: Their Lives and Faces, Book Two*. Rockford, IL: Tan Books, 1990.

Baring-Gould, Rev. Sabine. *The Lives of the Saints: With Introduction and Additional Lives of English Martyrs, Cornish, Scottish, and Welsh Saints, and a Full Index to the Entire Work*. Edinburgh: John Grant, 1914.

Baring-Gould, Sabine, and John Fisher. *The Lives of the British Saints: the Saints of Wales and Cornwall and Such Irish Saints as Have Dedications in Britain*. London: C. J. Clark, 1907. Vols 1–4.

Bell, Rudolph M. *Holy Anorexia*. Chicago: Univ. of Chicago Press, 1985.

Blunt, Hugh Francis. *The Great Magdalens*. New York: Macmillan, 1928.

Bokenkotter, Thomas. *A Concise History of the Catholic Church*. Revised and Expanded Edition. New York: Doubleday Image Books, 1990.

Bornstein, Daniel, and Roberto Rusconi, eds. *Women and Religion in Medieval and Renaissance Italy*. Translated by Margery J. Schneider. Chicago: Univ. of Chicago Press, 1996.

Code, Joseph B. *Great American Foundresses*. New York: Macmillan, 1929.

Currier, Rev. Charles Warren. *History of Religious Orders: A Compendious and Popular Sketch of the Rise and Progress of the Principal Monastic, Canonical, Military, Mendicant, and Clerical Orders and Congregations of the Eastern and Western Churches.* New York: Murphy & McCarthy, 1896.

Day, Peter. *A Dictionary of Religious Orders.* London: Burns & Oates, 2001.

Dehey, Elinor Tong. *Religious Orders of Women in the United States: Accounts of Their Origins, Works, and Most Important Institutions Interwoven with Histories of Many Famous Foundresses.* Revised from 1913 edition. Hammond, IN: W. B. Conkey, 1930.

Delaney, John J. *Dictionary of Saints.* 2d ed. New York: Doubleday, 2003.

Dunbar, Agnes B. C. *A Dictionary of Saintly Women.* Vols. 1 and 2. London: George Bell & Sons, 1905.

Englebert, Omer. *Lives of the Saints.* Translated by Christopher and Anne Fremantle. New York: Barnes & Noble, 1994.

Faber, F. W., ed. *The Lives of St Rose of Lima, the Blessed Colomba of Rieti, and of St Juliana Falconieri.* Saints and Servants of God Series. New York: Edward Dunigan, 1847.

Giorgi, Rosa. *Saints in Art.* Translated by Thomas Michael Hartmann. Los Angeles: Getty Museum, 2003.

Groeschel, Benedict J. Groeschel, C.F.R. *A Still, Small Voice: A Practical Guide on Reported Revelations.* San Francisco: Ignatius Press, 1993.

Guiley, Rosemary Ellen. *The Encylopedia of Saints.* New York: Facts on File, 2001.

Holböck, Ferdinand. *Married Saints and Blesseds Through the Centuries.* Translated by Michael J. Miller. San Francisco: Ignatius Press, 2001.

———. *New Saints and Blesseds of the Catholic Church: Blesseds and Saints Canonized by Pope John Paul II During the Years 1979–1983, Volume 1.* Translated by Michael J. Miller. San Francisco: Ignatius Press, 2000.

———. *New Saints and Blesseds of the Catholic Church: Blesseds and Saints Canonized by Pope John Paul II During the Years 1984 to 1987, Volume 2.* Translated by Michael J. Miller. San Francisco: Ignatius Press, 2003.

Holweck, Rt. Rev. F.G. *A Biographical Dictionary of the Saints with a General Introduction on Hagiology.* St Louis: B. Herder Book Co., 1924. Republished by Gale Research, 1969.

King, Ursula. *Christian Mystics: Their Lives and Legacies Throughout the Ages.* New York: Simon & Schuster, 1998.

Knowles, Leo. *Modern Heroes of the Church.* Huntington, IN: Our Sunday Visitor, 2003.

Koneberg, Hermann, O.S.B. *Blessed Ones of 1888.* Translated from the German by Eliza A. Donnelly. New York: Benziger Bros., 1888.

Languet de la Villeneuve de Gergy, Jean Joseph. *The Life of the Venerable Mother Margaret Mary Alacoque, Religious of the Order of the Visitation and of Catherine of Bologna.* Saints and Servants of God Series, vol. II. London: Thomas Richardson & Son, 1850.

Lanzi, Fernando, and Gioia Lanzi. *Saints and Their Symbols: Recognizing Saints in Art and in Popular Images.* Translated by Matthew J. O'Connell. Collegeville, MN: Liturgical Press, 2004.

Levillain, Philippe. *The Papacy: An Encyclopedia.* New York: Routledge, 2002.

Luce, Clare Boothe, ed. *Saints for Now.* San Francisco: Ignatius Press, 1993. Reprint; originally published New York: Sheed & Ward, 1952.

Magnificat. These monthly missals feature brief biographies of saints and are a great starting place, but not always accurate. (For example, they suggest that Flora and

Mary were sisters whereas all other sources say that Flora met Mary while she was in hiding.)

Martindale, C.C., S. J. *The Queen's Daughters: A Study of Women Saints*. New York: Sheed & Ward, 1951.

Mazzoni, Cristina. *Saint Hysteria: Neurosis, Mysticism, and Gender in European Culture*. Ithica, NY: Cornell Univ. Press, 1996.

McBrien, Richard P. *Lives of the Saints from Mary and St. Francis of Assisi to John XXIII and Mother Teresa*. San Francisco: HarperSanFrancisco, 2001.

McGinley, Phyllis. *Saint-Watching*. New York: Viking, 1969.

Monro, Margaret. *A Book of Unlikely Saints*. New York: Longmans, Green, 1943.

Moynahan, Brian. *The Faith: A History of Christianity*. New York: Doubleday, 2002.

Neligan, Rev. William H. *Saintly Characters Recently Presented for Canonization*. New York: Edward Dunigan & Bro., 1859.

O'Malley, Vincent J., C.M. *Saints of Africa*. Huntington, IN: Our Sunday Visitor, 2001.

L'Osservatore Romano. The Vatican's official newspaper of record.

Parbury, Kathleen. *Women of Grace. A Biographical Dictionary of British Women Saints, Martyrs and Reformers*. Boston: Oriel Press, 1985.

Sharp, Mary. *A Traveller's Guide to Saints in Europe*. London: Hugh Evelyn, 1964.

Watkin, E. I. *Neglected Saints*. San Francisco: Ignatius Press, 1994. Originally published New York: Sheed & Ward, 1955.

Weninger, F. X., D.D., S.J. *Appendix to Lives of the Saints Containing Lives of Modern Saints and Beatified Servants of God*. Vol. 3. New York: P. O'Shea, 1882.

Wood, Diana, ed. *Martyrs and Martyrologies: Papers Read at the 1992 Summer Meeting and the 1993 Winter Meeting of the Ecclesiastical History Society*. London: Blackwell, 1993.

Zuffi, Stefano. *Gospel Figures in Art*. Translated by Thomas Michael Hartmann. Los Angeles: Getty Museum, 2003.

Patron Saints

Chiffolo, Anthony F. *Be Mindful of Us: Prayers to the Saints*. Liguori, MO: Liguori, 2000.

Roeder, Helen. *Saints and Their Attributes with a Guide to Localities and Patronage*. Chicago: Henry Regnery, 1956.

First Century Through Middle Ages

Berman, Constance H. *Women and Monasticism in Medieval Europe: Sisters and Patrons of the Cistercian Reform*. Kalamazoo, MI: Consortium for the Teaching of the Middle Ages, Medieval Institute Publications, 2002.

Bond, Francis. *Dedications and Patron Saints of English Churches; Ecclesiastical Symbolism, Saints and Their Emblems*. New York: Oxford Univ. Press, 1914.

Boyd, Catherine E. *A Cistercian Nunnery in Mediaeval Italy: The Story of Rifreddo in Saluzzo, 1220–1300*. Cambridge, MA: Harvard Univ. Press, 1943.

Brown, Raphael, comp. *The Life of Mary as Seen by the Mystics: From the Revelations of St Elizabeth of Schoenau, St Bridget of Sweden, Ven. Mother Mary of Agreda and Sister Anne Catherine Emmerich*. Rockford, IL: Tan Books, 1951.

Bynum, Caroline Walker. *Holy Feast and Holy Fast: The Religious Significance of Food to Medieval Women*. Berkeley: Univ. of California Press, 1987.

Clark, Elizabeth A. *Women in the Early Church*. Collegeville, MN: Liturgical Press, 1983. Message of the Fathers of the Church Series, Vol. 13.

Drane, Augusta Theodosia. *History of St. Catherine of Siena and Her Companions.* London: Burns & Oates, 1887.

Fullerton, Lady Georgiana. *The Life of St. Frances of Rome, of Blessed Lucy of Narni, of Dominica of Paradiso and of Anne de Montmorency.* New York: D. & J. Sadlier, 1885.

Head, Thomas, ed. *Medieval Hagiography: An Anthology.* New York: Routledge, 2001.

Jameson, Mrs. *Legends of the Monastic Orders as Represented in the Fine Arts.* Boston: Houghton Mifflin, 1885.

Jansen, Katherine Ludwig. *The Making of the Magdalen: Preaching and Popular Devotion in the Late Middle Ages.* Princeton: Princeton Univ. Press, 2000.

Keyes, Frances Parkinson. *Three Ways of Love.* New York: Hawthorn Books, 1963.

Kleinberg, Aviad M. *Prophets in Their Own Country: Living Saints and the Making of Sainthood in the Later Middle Ages.* Chicago: Univ. of Chicago Press, 1992.

McNamara, Jo Ann, and John E. Halborg, eds. and trans., with E. Gordon Whatley. *Sainted Women of the Dark Ages.* Durham, NC: Duke Univ. Press, 1992.

Mooney, Catherine M., ed. *Gendered Voices: Medieval Saints and Their Interpreters.* Philadelphia: Univ. of Pennsylvania Press, 1999.

Mulder-Bakker, Anneke B. *Lives of the Anchoresses: The Rise of the Urban Recluse in Medieval Europe.* Translated by Myra Heerspink Scholz. Philadelphia: Univ. of Pennsylvania Press, 2005.

Newman, Barbara. *Voice of the Living Light: Hildegard of Bingen and Her World.* Berkeley: Univ. of California Press, 1998.

Nichols, John A., and Lillian Thomas Shank, eds. *Distant Echoes.* Vol. 1 of *Medieval Religious Women.* Kalamazoo, MI: Cistercian Publications, 1984.

Obbard, Elizabeth Ruth. *Medieval Women Mystics Gertrude the Great, Angela of Foligno, Brigitta of Sweden, Selected Spiritual Writings.* Hyde Park, NY: New City Press, 2002.

Perrotta, Louise Bourassa. *Saint Joseph: His Life and His Role in the Church Today.* Huntington, IN: Our Sunday Visitor, 2000.

Petroff, Elizabeth Alvida. *Body and Soul: Essays on Medieval Women and Mysticism.* New York: Oxford Univ. Press, 1994.

Power, Eileen Edna. *Medieval English Nunneries: c. 1275 to 1535.* Cambridge: Cambridge Univ. Press, 1922.

Raymond, Rev. M., O.C.S.O. *These Women Walked with God: The Saga of Citeaux Third Epoch.* Milwaukee: Bruce Publishing, 1956.

Riche, Pierre. *The Carolingians: A Family That Forged Europe.* Translated from the French by Michael Idomir Allen. Philadelphia: Univ. of Pennsylvania Press, 1993.

Schulenburg, Jane Tibbetts. *Forgetful of Their Sex: Female Sanctity and Society ca. 500–1100.* Chicago: Univ. of Chicago Press, 1998.

Thompson, Augustine, O.P. *Cities of God: The Religions of the Italian Communes, 1125–1325.* University Park: Penn State Univ. Press, 2005.

Vauchez, Andre. *Sainthood in the Late Middle Ages.* New York: Cambridge Univ. Press, 1997.

Voragine, Jacobus de. The Golden Legend or Lives of the Saints. Compiled by Jacobus de Voragine, Archbishop of Genoa, 1275. First edition published 1470. English edition by William Caxton, first edition 1483, edited by F. S. Ellis, Temple Classics, 1900 (reprinted 1922, 1931). Read online at Internet Medieval Sourcebook, edited by Paul Halsall: *http://www.fordham.edu/halsall/sbook.html.*

Waugh, Scott, L., and Diehl, Peter D. *Christendom and Its Discontents: Exclusion, Persecution, and Rebellion, 1000–1500.* New York: Cambridge Univ. Press, 1996.

Weinstein, Donald, and Rudolph M. Bell. *Saints and Society, 1000–1700.* Chicago: Univ. of Chicago Press, 1982.

Sixteenth Century (Counter-Reformation)

Drane, Augusta Theodosia. *Christian Schools and Scholars or, Sketches of Education from the Christian Era to the Council of Trent.* New ed., edited by Walter Gumbley, O.P., London: Burns Oates & Washbourne, 1924.

Haliczer, Stephen. *Between Exaltation and Infamy: Female Mystics in the Golden Age of Spain.* New York: Oxford Univ. Press, 2002.

Nineteenth Century

Bury, J. B. *History of the Papacy in the Nineteenth Century (1864–1878).* Edited, with a memoir, by the Rev. R. H. Murray. London: Macmillan, 1930.

Mazzucchi, Leonardo, S.C. *The Life, the Spirit and the Works of Father Louise Guanella.* Translated from the Italian and edited by Peter DiTullio, S.C. Springfield, PA, 1980.

Twentieth Century

Kurek, Ewa. *Your Life Is Worth Mine: How Polish Nuns Saved Hundreds of Jewish Children in German-Occupied Poland, 1939–1945.* New York: Hippocrene Books, 1997.

Lelièvre, Abbé Thierry. *100 Nouveaux Saints et Bienheureux de 1963 à 1984, leur vie et leur Message.* Paris: Téqui, 1985.

Royal, Robert. *The Catholic Martyrs of the Twentieth Century: A Comprehensive World History.* New York: Crossroad, 2000.

Americas

Fink, John F. *American Saints: Five Centuries of Heroic Sanctity on the American Continents.* Staten Island, NY: Alba House, 2001.

Habig, Marion A., O.F.M. *Heroes of the Cross: An American Martyrology.* 3d ed. Paterson, NJ: St Anthony Guild Press, 1947.

O'Malley, Vincent J. *Saints of North America.* Huntington, IN: Our Sunday Visitor, 2004.

Tylenda, Joseph N., S.J., ed. *Portraits in American Sanctity.* Chicago: Franciscan Herald Press, 1982.

Asia

Cardinal Kung Foundation, Stamford, CT: *http://www.kungpinmei.org/.*

Clark, Francis X., S.J. *Asian Saints: The 486 Catholic Canonized Saints and Blessed of Asia.* 2d ed., rev. Quezon City, The Philippines: Claretian Publications, 2000.

Fujita, Neil S. *Japan's Encounter with Christianity: The Catholic Mission in Pre-Modern Japan.* New York: Paulist Press, 1991.

Kim, Chang-mun, Father Joseph, ed. *Catholic Korea: Yesterday and Today.* Compiled and edited by Father Joseph Chang-mun Kim and John Jae-sun Chung. Seoul: Catholic Korea Publishing Co., 1964.

Kim, Chang-seok Thaddeus. *Lives of 103 Martyr Saints of Korea.* Seoul: Catholic Publishing House, 1984.

Pedrosa, Cerefino Puebla, O.P., ed. *Witnesses of the Faith in the Orient: Dominican Martyrs of Japan, China and Vietnam.* Translated from the Spanish by Sister Maria Maez, O.P. Manila: Life Today, 1989.

The Chinese Martyrs Catholic Church, Markham, Ontario, maintains a site with biographies of many of the martyrs: *http://chinesemartyrs.org/.*

Augustinians

Rotelle, John E., O.S.A., ed. *Book of Augustinian Saints*. Villanova, PA: Augustinian Press, 2000.

Beguines

Geybels, Hans. *Vulgariter Beghinae: Eight Centuries of Beguine History in the Low Countries*. Turnhout, Belgium: Brepols, 2004.

Simons, Walter. *Cities of Ladies: Beguine Communities in the Medieval Low Countries, 1200–1565*. Philadelphia: Univ. of Pennsylvania Press, 2001.

Camaldolese

Vigilucci, Lino. *Camaldoli: A Journey into Its History and Spirituality*. Translated by Peter Damian Belisle. Trabuco Canyon, CA: Source Books, 1995.

Celts

Meehan, Bridget Mary, and Regina Madonna Oliver. *Praying with Celtic Holy Women*. Liguori, MO: Liguori, 2003.

O'Hanlon, John. *Lives of the Irish Saints*. Dublin: James Duffy & Sons, 1875.

Pennick, Nigel. *The Celtic Saints: An Illustrated and Authoritative Guide to These Extraordinary Men and Women*. New York: Sterling Publishing Co., 1997.

Sellner, Edward C. *Wisdom of the Celtic Saints*. Notre Dame, IN: Ave Maria Press, 1993.

Tregarneth, Anita. *Founders of the Faith in Wales*. Liverpool: Brythen Press, 1947.

Dominicans

Ashley, Benedict M., O.P. "Blessed Osanna d'Andreasi and Other Renaissance Italian Dominican Women Mystics." Read online at Dominican Central: *www. op.org/domcentral/study/ashley/osanna.htm*.

Bonniwell, William R., O.P. *A History of the Dominican Liturgy, 1215–1945*. 2d ed., rev. New York: Joseph F. Wagner, 1945.

Conway, Placid, O.P., trans. *Lives of the Brethren of the Order of Preachers, 1206–1259*. New York: Benziger Bros., 1924.

Dominican Novices. *Dominican Saints*. Rockford, IL: Tan Books, 1995. Reprint; originally published Washington, DC: Rosary Press, Dominicana Publications, 1921.

Dorcy, Sister Mary Jean, O.P. *Saint Dominic's Family: The Lives of Over 300 Famous Dominicans*. Rockford, IL: Tan Books, 1983. Originally published by the Priory Press, 1964.

Drane, Augusta Theodosia (Mother Francis Raphael, O.S.D.). *The Spirit of the Dominican Order: Illustrated from the Lives of Its Saints*. New York: Benziger Bros., 1896.

Hinnebusch, William A. *The History of the Dominican Order*. Staten Island, NY: Alba House, 1966.

Lehmijoki-Gardner, Maiju, ed. and trans. *Dominican Penitent Women*. New York: Paulist Press, 2005. Classics of Western Spirituality Series.

France

Loomis, Stanley. *Paris in the Terror: June 1793–July 1794*. Philadelphia: Lippincott, 1964.

Franciscans and Poor Clares

Anonymous. *St. Clare and Her Order: A Story of Seven Centuries.* Edited by the author of *The Enclosed Nun.* London: Mills & Boon, 1912.

Goad, Harold Elsdale. *Franciscan Italy.* London: Methuen, 1926.

Habig, Marion A., O.F.M. *The Franciscan Book of Saints.* Chicago: Franciscan Herald Press, 1959. This is a revised and greatly augmented version of a book first published as *The Poverello's Round Table*, by Sister M. Aquina Barth, O.S.F.)

Hallack, Cecily, and Anson, Peter F. *These Made Peace: Studies in the Lives of the Beatified and Canonized Members of the Third Order of St Francis of Assisi.* Revised and edited by Marin A. Habig, O.F.M. Paterson, NJ: St Anthony Guild Press, 1957.

Protestant Reformation

Molinari, Paul, S.J. *The Canonization of the Forty English and Welsh Martyrs: a Commemoration Presented by the Postulators of the Cause.* London: Office of the Vice-Postulator, n.d. His introduction contains a particularly lucid history and explanation of the canonization process. (See also his article in *L'Osservatore Romano*, English ed., Oct. 29, 1970.)

Walsh, James, S.J. *Forty Martyrs of England and Wales: Canonized by His Holiness Pope Paul VI on 25 October 1970.* Pamphlet.

Scandinavia

St. Ansgar's Bulletin. St Ansgar's Scandinavian Catholic League, New York, NY.

Spain

Colbert, Edward P. *The Martyrs of Córdoba (850–859): A Study of the Sources.* Washington, DC: Catholic Univ. of America Press, 1962.

Florian, Jean Pierre Claris de. *The Moors in Spain.* N.p.: Werner Co., 1910.

Lane-Poole, Stanley. *The Story of the Moors in Spain.* New York: Putnam, 1886.

Pérez de Urbel, Fray Justo. *Catholic Martyrs of the Spanish Civil War, 1936–1939.* Translated by Michael F. Ingrams. Kansas City, MO, 1998.

Wolf, Kenneth Baxter. *Christian Martyrs in Muslim Spain.* Read online at LIBRO: The Library of Iberian Resources Online: *http://libro.uca.edu/martyrs/*.

Other Books Consulted

Ball, Ann. *Faces of Holiness: Modern Saints in Photos and Words.* Huntington, IN: Our Sunday Visitor, 1998.

———. *Faces of Holiness II: Modern Saints in Photos and Words.* Huntington, IN: Our Sunday Visitor, 2001.

———. *Young Faces of Holiness: Modern Saints in Photos and Worlds.* Huntington, IN, Our Sunday Visitor, 2004.

Cruz, Joan Carroll. *Angels and Devils.* Rockford, IL: Tan Books, 1998.

———. *The Incorruptibles: A Study of the Incorruption of the Bodies of Various Catholic Saints and Beati.* Rockford, IL: Tan Books, 1977.

———. *Relics: The Shroud of Turin, the True Cross, the Blood of Januarius . . . History, Mysticism, and the Catholic Church.* Huntington, IN: Our Sunday Visitor, 1984.

———. *Secular Saints: 250 Canonized and Beatified Lay Men, Women and Children.* Rockford, IL: Tan Books, 1989.

De Caussade, Jean-Pierre. *Abandonment to Divine Providence.* Translated with an Introduction by John Beevers. New York: Doubleday, 1975.

Drake, Tim, ed. *Saints of the Jubilee*. Bloomington, IN: 1st Books, 2002.

Farges, Msgr. Albert. *Mystical Phenomena Compared with Their Human and Diabolical Counterfeits: A Treatise on Mystical Theology in Agreement with the Principles of St Teresa Set Forth by the Carmelite Congress of 1923 in Madrid*. Translated from the French by S. P. Jacques. London: Burns Oates & Washbourne, 1926.

Jones, Kathleen. *Women Saints: Lives of Faith and Courage*. Maryknoll, NY: Orbis Books, 1999.

Kempf, Rev. Constantine, S.J. *The Holiness of the Church in the Nineteenth Century: Saintly Men and Women of Our Own Times*. Translated from the German by Rev. Francis Breymann, S.J. New York: Benziger Bros., 1916.

Molinari, Paul, S.J. *Saints: Their Place in the Church*. Translated from the Italian by Dominic Maruca, S.J. New York: Sheed & Ward, 1965.

Scaraffia, Lucetta, and Zarri, Gabriella, eds. *Women and Faith: Catholic Religious Life in Italy from Late Antiquity to the Present*. Cambridge: Harvard Univ. Press, 1999.

Thurston, Herbert, S.J. *The Physical Phenomena of Mysticism*. Edited by J. H. Crehan, S.J. Chicago: Henry Regnery, 1952.

———. *Surprising Mystics*. Edited by J. H. Crehan, S.J. Chicago: Henry Regnery, 1955.

Treece, Patricia. *Apparitions of Modern Saints: Appearances of Therese of Lisieux, Padre Pio, Don Bosco, and Others, Messages from God to His People on Earth*. Ann Arbor: Servant Publications, 2001. Abridged and updated version of the book formerly entitled *Messengers*.

Underhill, Evelyn. *Mysticism: A Study in the Nature and Development of Man's Spiritual Consciousness*. New York: Noonday Press, 1955.

Wilson, Ian. *Stigmata: An Investigation into the Mysterious Appearance of Christ's Wounds in Hundreds of People from Medieval Italy to Modern America*. New York: Harper & Row, 1989.

Internet Sites

Agencia Católica de Informaciones en América Latina: *www.aciprensa.com*.

Carmelite Sisters of Baltimore: *http://www.baltimorecarmel.org/*.

Catholic Community Forum, sponsored by Liturgical Publications of St Louis, MO, includes a Patron Saints Index: *http://www.catholic-forum.com/*.

Epistolae: Letters to and from women in the Middle Ages, originally collected and translated by Professor Joan Ferrante of Columbia University, and since expanded with contributions from other scholars: *http://db.ccnmtl.columbia.edu/ferrante/*.

Eternal Word Television Network (EWTN): *http://www.ewtn.com/*.

Hagiography Circle: *http://newsaints.faithweb.com/*.

The Holy See, official site: *http://www.vatican.va/*.

Internet Medieval Sourcebook, part of the Online Reference Book for Medieval Studies, Paul Halsall, sources editor, Fordham University: *http://www.fordham.edu/halsall/sbook.html*.

Miriam and Aaron: The Bible and Women, created by Julia Bolton Holloway: *http://www.umilta.net/bible.html*.

Monastic Matrix: A Scholarly Resource for the Study of Women's Communities from 400 to 1600 C.E. (University of Southern California): *http://monasticmatrix.usc.edu/*.

Nominis: *http://nominis.cef.fr/*.

Other Women's Voices: Translations of Women's Writings Before 1700, maintained by Dorothy Disse: *http://home.infionline.net/~ddisse/index.html*.

Saints Alive: Father Robert F. McNamara of St Thomas the Apostle Church, Rochester, NY, posts a series of articles on the saints: *www.stthomasirondequoit.com*.

Santi Beati e Testimoni: *http://www.santiebeati.it/index.html*.

St Wilfrid's Catholic Church, Yorkshire, England: *http://www.stwilfridsyork.org.uk/*.

Index of Entries

These are dates on which the Saints and Blesseds appear in the book and not necessarily their official feast days. For reasons of space, this index does not include saintly associates mentioned in passing. Information about many of them may be found in the Notes, Annotated Sources and Web Sites, and Bibliography.

Adelaide, Empress, St, December 16
Agatha of Catania, St, February 5
Agnes de Jesus Galand, Bl, October 19
Agnes Kim Hyo-ju, St, September 20
Agnes Kou Ying Tsao, St, March 13
Agnes of Assisi, St, November 19
Agnes of Montepulciano, St, April 20
Agnes of Prague, St, March 6
Agnes of Rome, St, January 21
Agnes Phila, Bl, December 18
Agostina Pietrantoni, St, November 12
Alexandrina Maria da Costa, Bl, October 14
Aleydis of Le Cambre, St, June 15
Alice Kotowska, Bl, November 11
Alix Le Clerc, Bl, January 9
All Saints, Feast of, November 1
Alpaïs of Cudot, Bl, November 3
Alphonsa of India, Bl, July 21
Amalberga of Ghent, St, July 10
Amata of San Sisto, Bl, June 9
Amparo Carbonell, Bl, September 22
Ana de los Angeles Monteagudo, January 19
Anastasia of Sirmium, St, December 26
Angadresima de Renty, St, October 24
Angela de la Cruz, St, March 2
Angela Merici, St, January 27
Angela of Foligno, Bl, January 11
Angela Salawa, Bl, March 27
Angelina of Montegiove, Bl, July 15
Anna Eugenia Picco, Bl, September 7
Anna Katharina Emmerich, Bl, February 15
Anna Rosa Gattorno, Bl, May 6
Anna Schäffer, Bl, October 4
Anna the Prophetess, St, February 2
Anna Wang, St, September 29
Anne Line, St, February 27
Anne Marie Taigi, Bl, June 10
Anne of St Bartholomew, Bl, June 7
Anne, Mother of Mary, St, July 26
Anne-Marie Javouhey, Bl, July 14

Annunciata Cocchetti, Bl, March 19
Antonia of Florence, Bl, February 29
Anuarite Nengapeta, Bl, December 1
Apollonia of Alexandria, St, February 9
Assumption, Feast of, August 15
Audrey, St, June 23

Barbara of Nicomedia, St, December 4
Barbe Acarie, Bl, April 7
Bartolomea Capitanio, St, July 11
Bathildis, Queen of France, St, January 29
Battista Varano, Bl, May 31
Beatrice de Silva Meneses, St, September 2
Benedetta C. Frassinello, St, March 21
Benvenuta Bojani, Bl, October 30
Bernadette Soubirous, St, April 16
Bernardina Maria Jablonska, Bl, September 25
Bertilla Boscardin, St, October 22
Bertilla of Chelles, St, November 6
Bibiana of Rome, St, December 2
Blandina of Lyons, St, June 2
Blandine Merten, Bl, May 18
Boleslawa Lament, Bl, January 22
Bona of Pisa, St, May 29
Bridget of Sweden, St, July 23
Brigid of Ireland, St, February 1
Brigida Morello, Bl, September 12
Bronislava of Poland, Bl, August 28

Carmelite Martyrs of Compiègne, BB, July 17
Carmelite Martyrs of Guadalajara, BB, July 19
Carmen Moreno, Bl, September 22
Casilda of Toledo, St, April 19
Catalina Tomás, St, April 1
Catherine dei Ricci, St, February 22
Catherine Jarrige, Bl, July 3
Catherine of Alexandria, St, November 25

Catherine of Bologna, St, May 9
Catherine of Genoa, St, September 15
Catherine of Pallanza, Bl, April 26
Catherine of Parc-aux-Dames, Bl, May 4
Catherine of Racconigi, Bl,
  September 11
Catherine of Siena, St, April 29
Catherine of Sweden, St, March 24
Catherine Simon de Longpré, Bl, May 23
Catherine Zoe Labouré, St,
  November 28
Catherine, Queen of Bosnia, Bl,
  October 23
Cecilia Caesarini, Bl, June 9
Cecilia of Rome, St, November 22
Christina of Markyate, St, December 29
Christina the Astonishing, Bl, July 25
Clare Gambacorta, Bl, April 4
Clare of Assisi, St, August 11
Clare of Montefalco, St, August 17
Clare of Rimini, Bl, February 14
Claudine Thévenet, St, February 3
Clelia Barbieri, St, July 12
Clotilda, Queen of France, St, June 3
Colette of Corbie, St, February 7
Colomba of Rieti, Bl, May 20
Columba Kim Hyo-im, St, September 20
Crescentia Höss, St, April 5
Crispina of Thagura, St, December 5
Cunegunda the Empress, St, March 8

Delphine de Signe, Bl, November 29
Diana Andalò, Bl, June 9
Dina Bélanger, Bl, September 8
Dorothy, St, February 6
Douceline of Marseilles, St, September 1
Dwynwen, St, January 25
Dymphna of Gheel, St, May 15

Edith of Wilton, St, September 16
Edith Stein, St, August 9
Ela Fitzpatrick, Bl, February 24
Elena Guerra, Bl, December 23
Elfleda of Whitby, St, February 18
Elisabeth of Schönau, St, June 18
Elisabetta Renzi, Bl, August 14
Elizabeth Ann Seton, St, January 4
Elizabeth Canori Mora, Bl, February 19
Elizabeth of Hungary, St, November 17
Elizabeth of the Trinity, Bl, November 8
Elizabeth the Good, Bl, November 23
Elizabeth, Queen of Portugal, St, July 4

Elizabeth, St, November 5
Elvira Moragas Cantarero, Bl,
  August 12
Emilie de Rodat, St, September 19
Emilie de Vialar, St, June 24
Emilie Tavernier Gamelin, Bl,
  September 24
Emily Bicchieri, Bl, August 19
Ethelburga of Barking, St, October 11
Eugénie Milleret de Brou, Bl, March 10
Eulalia of Mérida, St, December 10
Eusebia of Hamay, St, March 16
Eusebia Palomino, Bl, February 17
Eustochia Calafato, St, January 20
Eustochia of Padua, Bl, February 13

Fabiola of Rome, St, December 31
Fara of Faremoutiers, St, April 21
Faustina Kowalska, St, October 5
Felicity and Perpetua, SS, March 7
Filippa Mareri, Bl, February 16
Fina Ciardi, St, March 12
Flora of Beaulieu, St, October 2
Flora of Córdoba, St, November 24
Florida Cevoli, Bl, June 12
Frances of Rome, St, March 9
Frances Schervier, Bl, December 14
Frances Xavier Cabrini, St, November 13
Francesca Rubatto, Bl, August 6
Frideswide of Oxford, St, October 27

Gaetana Sterni, Bl, November 26
Gemma Galgani, St, April 11
Geneviève of Paris, St, January 3
Genoveva Torres Morales, St, January 5
Germaine Cousin, St, June 13
Gertrude of Delft, Bl, January 16
Gertrude of Nivelles, St, March 17
Gertrude the Great, St, November 15
Gianna Beretta Molla, St, April 28
Giovanna Maria Bonomo, Bl, March 1
Gladys of Wales, St, March 29

Helen of Bologna, Bl, September 23
Helen, Empress of Rome, St,
  August 18
Hilda of Whitby, St, November 4
Hildegard of Bingen, Bl, September 17
Holy Family of Nazareth, Feast of,
  December 27
Holy Innocents, Feast of, December 28
Hosanna of Kotor, Bl, April 15

Humbeline, Bl, February 12
Hyacintha Mariscotti, St, January 30

Ilona of Hungary, Bl, November 9
Imelda Lambertini, Bl, May 12
Immaculate Conception, December 8
Ita of Limerick, St, January 15

Jacinta Marto, Bl, February 11
Jane Frances de Chantal, St, August 5
Jane of Aza, Bl, August 8
Jane of Signa, Bl, November 10
Jeanne de Valois, Queen, St, February 20
Jeanne Delanoue, St, August 16
Jeanne Elisabeth Bichier des Ages, St,
    August 1
Jeanne Jugan, Bl, August 29
Jeanne-Marie de Maillé, Bl, March 28
Joan of Arc, St, May 30
Josaphata M. Hordashevska, Bl,
    November 21
Josefa Maria of Beniganim, Bl,
    January 24
Josephine Bakhita, St, February 8
Julian of Norwich, Bl, May 13
Juliana Falconieri, St, June 19
Juliana of Busto-Verghera, Bl, April 26
Juliana of Mont-Cornillon, Bl, April 6
Julie Billiart, St, April 8
Jutta of Prussia, Bl, May 5

Kateri Tekakwitha, Bl, April 17
Katherine Celestyna Faron, Bl, April 3
Katharine Mary Drexel, St, March 3
Keyne of Wales, St, October 9
Kinga, Queen of Poland, St, July 24

Laura Evangelista, Bl, April 2
Léonie Aviat, St, January 10
Liduina Meneguzzi, Bl, December 3
Lillian of Córdoba, St, July 27
Lioba of Bischoffsheim, St, September 28
Louise de Marillac, St, March 15
Lucy de Freitas, Bl, September 21
Lucy Filippini, St, March 25
Lucy of Narni, Bl, November 14
Lucy of Settefonti, Bl, November 7
Lucy of Syracuse, St, December 13
Lucy Wang Cheng, St, June 28
Lutgard of Aywières, St, June 16
Lydia Purpuraria, St, August 3
Lydwina of Schiedam, St, April 14

Maddalena Panattieri, Bl, October 13
Mafalda, Queen of Castile, St, June 17
Magdaléne of Canossa, St, May 8
Magdalene of Nagasaki, St, October 20
Marcella of Rome, St, January 31
Margaret Bermingham Ball, Bl, June 21
Margaret Clitherow, St, August 30
Margaret Ebner, Bl, June 1
Margaret Mary Alacoque, St, October 16
Margaret of Antioch, St, July 20
Margaret of Città di Castello, Bl,
    April 13
Margaret of Cortona, St, May 16
Margaret of Hungary, St, January 18
Margaret of Scotland, St, November 16
Margaret Pole, Bl, May 24
Marguerite Bays, Bl, June 26
Marguerite Bourgeoys, St, January 12
Marguerite d'Youville, St, October 17
María Angela Astorch, Bl, December 6
María Angela of St Joseph, Bl, July 19
Maria Angela Truszkowska, Bl,
    October 10
Maria Catherine of St Rose of Viterbo,
    Bl, May 11
Maria Corsini, Bl, November 27
Maria Crocifissa di Rosa, St,
    December 21
María de Jesús Sacramentado, Bl, July 31
María de la Cabeza, Bl, September 27
Maria de Mattias, St, February 4
María del Tránsito Cabanillas, Bl,
    August 25
Maria Droste zu Vischering, Bl, June 5
María Encarnación Rosal, Bl, August 2
Maria Euthymia Üffing, Bl,
    September 13
Maria Fortunata Viti, Bl, November 20
Maria Gabriella Sagheddu, Bl, April 22
Maria Goretti, St, July 6
María Josefa Sancho de Guerra, Bl,
    March 20
Maria Josepha Rossello, St, December 7
Maria Karlowska, Bl, March 30
Maria Maddalena de' Pazzi, St, May 25
María Maravillas de Jesús, St,
    December 11
María Micaela Desmaisières, August 24
María Pilar Izquierdo Albero, Bl,
    August 22
Maria Pilar of St Francis Borgia, Bl,
    July 19

Maria Raffaella Cimatti, Bl, June 30

María Soledad Torres Acosta, St, October 12

Maria Teresa Kowalska, Bl, July 28

Maria Theresa Ledóchowska, Bl, July 5

Maria Theresa Scherer, Bl, June 14

Mariam Baouardy, Bl, August 21

Mariam Thresia Chiramel Mankidiyan, June 6

Mariana de Parades, St, May 26

Marianne of Molokai, Bl, January 23

Marie Anne Blondin, Bl, April 18

Marie Louise Trichet, Bl, May 21

Marie Madeleine Postel, St, July 16

Marie of the Incarnation, Bl, April 30

Marie Poussepin, Bl, October 28

Marie Rivier, Bl, February 21

Marie-Rose Durocher, Bl, October 18

Marie-Thérèse Haze, Bl, January 7

Marie-Thérèse Soubiran, Bl, October 26

Marija Petkovic, Bl, July 2

Marina of Omura, St, September 30

Martha of Bethany, St, July 29

Marthe Le Bouteiller, Bl, March 18

Martillo Morán, Bl, August 31

Martyrs of China: See Agnes Kou Ying Tsao; Anna Wang; Martyrs of Wangla; Martyrs of Shanxhi

Martyrs of England and Wales: See Anne Line; Margaret Clitherow

Martyrs of the French Revolution: See Carmelite Martyrs of Compiègne; Martyrs of Laval; Martyrs of Orange

Martyrs of Japan. See Lucy de Freitas, Martyrs of Nagasaki

Martyrs of Korea. See Agnes Kim Hyo-ju, Columba Kim Hyo-im,

Martyrs of Laval. BB, March 5

Martyrs of Nagasaki. See Marina of Omura, Magdalene of Nagasaki,

Martyrs of Nowogródek, BB, September 6

Martyrs of Orange, 32, BB, July 1

Martyrs of Shanxi (Shangsi), BB, July 7

Martyrs of Thailand, BB, December 18

Martyrs of the Spanish Civil War. See Amparo Carbanell; Carmelite Martyrs of Guadalajara; Carmen Moreno; Elvira Moragas Cantarero; Victoria Diez

Martyrs of Ukraine. See Tarsykia Olha Matskiv; Olympia Bida

Martyrs of Wangla, SS, June 28

Martyrs of World War II: see Alice Kotowska; Katharine Celestyna Faron; Maria Teresa Kowalska; Martyrs of Nowogródck; Natalie Tulasiewicz, Restituta Kafka, Edith Stein

Mary Clopas, St, April 9

Mary Elisabeth Hesselblad, Bl, April 12

Mary Ellen MacKillop, Bl, August 7

Mary Euphrasia Pelletier, St, April 24

Mary Fan Kun, St, June 28

Mary Frances of the Five Wounds, St, October 6

Mary Magdalene, St, July 22

Mary Mazzarello, St, May 14

Mary of Córdoba, St, November 24

Mary of Egypt, St, April 10

Mary of Oignies, Bl, June 25

Mary of the Angels, Bl, December 19

Mary of the Passion, Bl, November 2

Mary Qi Yu, St, June 28

Mary Xheng Xu, St, June 28

Mary, Mother of God, January 1

Mary: see also: Assumption; Our Lady of the Rosary; Immaculate Conception; Our Lady of Guadalupe

Matilda of Saxony, Queen, St, March 14

Matilde Téllez Robles, Bl, December 22

Mattia dei Nazarei, Bl, December 30

Maura, St, May 3

Maxellendis, St, November 30

Mechthild of Magdeburg, Bl, October 31

Melania the Elder, St, June 8

Mercedes de Jesús Molina, Bl, June 4

Michelina of Pesaro, Bl, June 22

Monica of Carthage, St, August 27

Narcisa de Jesús Martillo Morán, Bl, August 31

Natalie of Córdoba, St, July 27

Natalie Tulasiewicz, Bl, March 31

Nativity, Saints at the, December 25

Nino of Georgia, St, December 15

Notburga of Eben, St, September 14

Odilia of Alsace, St, December 9

Olympia Bida, Bl, January 28

Olympias of Constantinople, St, December 17

Osanna of Mantua, Bl, June 20

Our Lady of Guadalupe, December 12

Our Lady of the Rosary, October 7

Panacea de Muzzi, St, May 1
Paola Elisabetta Cerioli, St,
    December 24
Paula Frassinetti, St, June 11
Paula Montal Fornés, St, February 26
Paula of Tuscany, Bl, January 14
Pauline von Mallinckrodt, Bl, April 25
Pelagia the Penitent, St, October 8
Philomena of Mugnano, St, August 10
Placide Viel, Bl, March 26
Portuguese Princesses, Three, SS,
    June 17
Pulcheria Augusta, Empress, St,
    September 10

Radegund, Queen of France, St,
    August 13
Rafqa of Lebanon, St, March 23
Raphaela María Porras, St, January 6
Restituta Kafka, Bl, October 29
Richardis, Empress, St, September 18
Rita of Cascia, St, May 22
Rosa Venerini, St, May 7
Rosalie of Palermo, St, September 4
Rose of Lima, St, August 23
Rose of Viterbo, St, September 3
Rose Philippine Duchesne, St,
    November 18
Roseline Villeneuve, St, January 17

Sancha, Princess of Portugal, St, June 17
Sancja Janina Szymkowiak, Bl, August 4
Scholastica, St, February 10
Seraphina Sforza, Bl, September 9
Stephanie Quinzani, Bl, January 2
Sunniva of Bergen, St, July 8
Sybillina Biscossi, Bl, March 22

Tabitha of Joppa, St, October 25
Tarsykia Olha Matskiv, Bl, June 27

Teresa Eustochio Verzeri, St, March 4
Teresa Grillo Michel, Bl, January 26
Teresa Jornet y Ibars, St, August 26
Teresa Margaret Redi, St, March 11
Teresa Maria of the Cross Manetti, Bl,
    April 23
Teresa of Avila, St, October 15
Teresa of Calcutta, Bl, September 5
Teresa of the Andes, St, July 13
Teresa of the Child Jesus and St John of
    the Cross, Bl, July 19
Teresa, Queen of León, St, June 17
Theneva of Glasgow, St, July 18
Theodore Guérin, St, October 3
Theresa of Jesus Gerhardinger, Bl,
    May 10
Thérèse Couderc, St, September 26
Thérèse of Lisieux, St, October 1

Ubaldesca Taccini, St, May 28
Ulrika Nisch, Bl, May 17
Umiliana de'Cerchi, Bl, May 19
Ursula and Companions, SS, October 21
Ursula Ledóchowska, St, May 27

Verdiana, St, February 23
Veronica Giuliani, St, July 9
Veronica of Binasco, Bl, January 13
Victoria Diez, Bl, August 20
Villana de Botti, Bl, February 28
Vincenza Gerosa, St, June 29
Virginia Centurione Bracelli, St,
    December 20

Walburga, St, February 25
Wiborada of St Gall, St, May 2

Zdenka Schelingova, Bl, July 30
Zdislava of Lemberk, St, January 8
Zita of Lucca, St, April 27